CANADIAN
INTERNET
HANDBOOK

1995 EDITION

Jim Carroll
Rick Broadhead

Prentice Hall Canada Inc.
Scarborough, Ontario

Canadian Cataloguing in Publication Data

Carroll, Jim, 1959—   .
        Canadian Internet handbook

1995 ed.
Includes index.
ISBN 0-13-329350-5

1.   Internet (Computer network) - Handbooks, manuals, etc. I. Broadhead,
     Rick. II. Title.

TK5105.875.IS7C37 1994 004.6'7 C94-932283-0

Prentice-Hall, Inc., Englewood Cliffs, New Jersey
Prentice-Hall International (UK) Limited, London
Prentice-Hall of Australia, Pty. Limited, Sydney
Prentice-Hall Hispanoamericana, S.A., Mexico City
Prentice-Hall of India Private Limited, New Delhi
Prentice-Hall of Japan, Inc., Tokyo
Simon & Schuster Asia Private Limited, Singapore
Editora Prentice-Hall do Brasil, Ltda., Rio de Janeiro

ISBN 0-13-329350-5

Production Editor: Kelly Dickson
Production Coordinator: Anita Boyle-Evans
Cover and Interior Design: Alex Li
Cover Image: Imtek Imagineering/ Masterfile
Page Layout: VISU*TronX* / Dawn Girard
        4 5 W 98 97 96 95

Printed and bound in Canada.

Every reasonable effort has been made to obtain permissions for all articles and
data used in this edition. If errors or omissions have occurred, they will be
corrected in future editions provided written notification has been received by the
publisher.

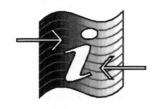

CONTENTS

· ·

Chapter 3   43
The Internet in Canada

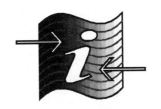

FOREWORD

· ·

Awareness of the information highway has increased dramatically in New Brunswick since the creation of Canada's first Information Highway Secretariat in January 1994. The commitment to the glass highway came after the realization that it is central to the generation of wealth and our job creation efforts. But it has been and still remains a difficult road to travel, in part because of the relatively low level of computer literacy in the over-40 generation. I can speak about this from personal experience.

To celebrate the launching of the New Brunswick task force on the information highway, I was asked to send an e-mail message over the Internet to federal Industry Minister John Manley. I learned to type in high school, but was quite unfamiliar with the functioning of electronic mail, or for that matter with many of the other features of the info-highway. It was, however, clear in my mind that to increase the use of info-highway technology in business and government I had to send a strong message.

I had to show New Brunswickers that I was personally committed to taming the new technology. The event went extremely well and my message was successfully sent to Mr. Manley. And the gamble is still paying dividends.

The New Brunswick government is changing itself and, in the process, acting as the catalyst for business growth. We're on several highway systems. We communicate via Talk-Mail, Internet E-mail as well as by local and wide area networks. We promote New Brunswick tourism and our economic investment potential via World Wide Web, track our time through electronic calendaring, hold meetings via video-conferencing, and manage information flow electronically.

Communications networks are springing up between our hospitals, schools and libraries. Our distance education network is providing college and university courses to over 50 communities province-wide. Multimedia information kiosks in malls and other public areas are bringing government information and services directly to our clients 24 hours a day. New Brunswickers can even sign up for the moose draw using the latest in computerized telephone technology.

New Brunswick is connected. This has generated a host of parallel activities in the private sector.

We have new companies emerging every day developing Internet interface tools, training packages to be offered on the highway, establishing New Brunswick's own electronic mall, and developing innovative software applications.

All these applications developed and test-run in New Brunswick, are done so with a keen eye to their export potential.

As I talk with businesspeople across the province, I am continually amazed with how many are already using the highway, and have been for years. The research and information they have been able to tap into has helped them maintain their competitive edge, whether they are producing heat sensors or lottery machines.

The information highway is an enormous opportunity. We can play wait and see, or we can take the bull by the horns and use it to our advantage. Obviously, we have chosen the latter.

While other jurisdictions are only now planning their investment in infrastructure, New Brunswick is miles ahead. Thanks to NBTel, New Brunswick is the only jurisdiction in North America with a universally employed, fully-digital fibre-optic communications system.

NBTel's investment in the Beacon initiative, announced in April 1994 by the Stentor alliance of telecommunications providers, will lead to the deployment of a broadband network by mid-1995. It will allow business and residential customers to access such services as video on demand, games on demand, home shopping, home banking, as well as an array of health, educational, business and information services.

NBTel expects to provide this access to 20,000 homes and businesses in Saint John by the end of 1995 and to 60 per cent of all New Brunswick homes and businesses by December 1998.

The recent decision by the Canadian Radio-television and Telecommunications Commission to free local telephone service from monopoly control by telephone companies will make us even more competitive and will further enhance our research and development capabilities.

Fundy Cable Ltd., for instance, is already offering both cable and telephone service to subscribers in Leicester, England in co-operation with two other companies, one Canadian and the other British. Fundy Cable serves 74 per cent of all cable subscribers in New Brunswick. Cable companies have broadband cable systems in place capable of carrying hundreds of television signals and an almost limitless number of telephone circuits.

New Brunswick is using its leading edge in communications technology to successfully attract new investment and jobs to the province. Government's role as a model user is central to this initiative.

Our commitment to the info-highway is changing the way we do business, the way we work and the way we play. It is helping us take our place as equal partners in the Canadian confederation. It is therefore natural that we continue to pursue our work with private and public sector stakeholders to protect and, indeed, increase our lead.

In conclusion, I would like to congratulate the authors of the second edition of this handbook, Jim Carroll and Rick Broadhead, for putting the Internet in its Canadian perspective in a very clear and informative manner.

Frank McKenna
Premier of New Brunswick

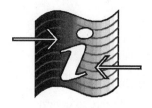

ACKNOWLEDGEMENTS

· ·

A number of people deserve special mention for their help with this book. Eric Jones and the staff at Prentice Hall Canada provided guidance and support when we needed it. Kelly Dickson and her editorial staff deserve particular recognition for coordinating a tight production deadline. Heather Dhanasar, Andrea Aris and the entire marketing team gave us superb promotional support. Judy Bunting in the Professional, Trade and Reference Division has been particularly helpful.

This book would not be as complete if it were not for the thorough technical review of the manuscript by both Eric Carroll of the University of Toronto, and, for the second year in a row, Mike Martineau of NSTN Inc. We appreciate their efforts in dealing with our tight deadlines.

Additional thanks go to Bruce Becker for giving us permission to reprint his comprehensive listing of Canadian USENET newsgroups; John Demco, the CA Domain Registrar, for permission to reproduce his CA Domain documents, including the list of organizations registered in the CA Domain; and to James Milles of the Saint Louis University Law Library (and owner of NETTRAIN discussion list) for permission to reproduce his reference document on mailing list commands.

A separate and special thanks goes to InfoRamp Inc., in particular Osama Arafat and Stuart Lombard, for providing us with Internet accounts and copies of their award-winning "Pipeline" software. InfoRamp is also the supplier of our mail robots.

We would like to express our gratitude to Premier Frank McKenna of New Brunswick for contributing the foreword to this edition. As we began preparing the 1995 edition, we unanimously agreed that Premier McKenna is the only major government leader in Canada who has indicated a clear understanding of the strategic significance of the Internet. Through his efforts in New Brunswick, Premier McKenna has demonstrated that even as discussion about the much-hyped information highway continues, there are a lot of real and practical capabilities that exist with the Internet as it exists today. Premier McKenna deserves the praise of all Canadians, for he is one of our few public leaders who has clearly demonstrated that he clearly understands the significance of the world's largest *global knowledge network* to the citizens, companies and organizations in New Brunswick and Canada.

We would like to thank all the Internet service providers, Gopher administrators, IRC administrators, Web Masters, and librarians who patiently answered our questions and put up with our constant deadlines and requests for clarification.

The Canadian Internet Timeline is the result of our efforts to chronologically piece together the history of the Canadian Internet. We'd like to thank the many Canadian Internet experts who contributed to the project, including Eric Carroll, John Demco, Alan Emtage, Ken Fockler, Berni Gardiner, Jim Hancock, Richard Lawrence, Jack Leigh, David Macneil, Michael Martineau, Rory O'Brien, Tim Symchych, Roger Taylor, Vincent Taylor, Mario Vachon, and Roger Watt.

Infomart/Dialog Canada Inc. provided on-line research services through their Infomart on-line service. With all the excitement about the Internet in Canada, many people often miss the fact that a thriving commercial on-line database industry exists in Canada. Many of the newspaper and newswire quotes throughout this book were obtained through searches performed on the Infomart service, a service which is truly invaluable in the ongoing quest for information. Huw Morgan, President of Infomart/Dialog Canada Inc., deserves a special word of thanks for his patience in dealing with the over-exuberant use of the account provided to the authors.

We are especially grateful to Roger Taylor, of the U.S. National Science Foundation. for giving us permission to print his paper on the history of the CA*net. You'll find it in Appendix B.

Cybersmith Inc. of New Brunswick, in particular, Dale Edgar and Tim Smith, are the Internet whizzes behind our World Wide Web site **<http://www.csi.nb.ca/handbook/handbook.html>.** We'd like to thank them for their ongoing support for the book.

This section would not be complete without a special thank you to our families for their emotional support. Jim would like to thank his wife, Christa, for her efforts in 'surfing' the Internet, often on short notice, to verify addresses, information and other tidbits, and his son, William Carroll, who would often miss his Daddy while the book was being written. That Christa can put up with such a disorganized husband is testimony to her patience. Rick would like to thank his parents, Rick and Violet Broadhead, and his sister, Kristin, for their support and encouragement while the book was in progress. They endured Rick's countless hours of typing, often into the early hours of the morning. Finally, Jim would like to thank Oma and Opa for use of their basement during a time when a quiet place was much needed in order to write!

Finally, the authors would like to acknowledge the support of all the Canadian Internet users who have cheered us on and sent us suggestions, comments, and contributions. We appreciate your ongoing support and enthusiasm.

Jim Carroll
Rick Broadhead

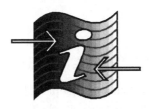

ABOUT THE AUTHORS

· ·

Jim Carroll, C.A. is principal owner of J.A. Carroll Consulting, a Mississauga-based firm which assists organizations with the strategic use of telecommunications technology. Through J.A. Carroll Consulting, Mr. Carroll has assisted a number of organizations with the strategic use of the Internet to support global marketing, support or customer-based activities. Mr. Carroll is a prolific writer and a regular monthly columnist on electronic mail in *Computing Canada* as well as in a number of other publications. Mr. Carroll is a popular speaker and seminar leader with respect to the Internet, and is in particular demand by companies and organizations seeking advice and strategies dealing with the global information highways and the Internet. Mr. Carroll is represented nationally and internationally by the National Speakers Bureau of Vancouver, B.C., which can be reached at 1-800-661-4110 or 1-604-224-2384, or by sending a message to **seminar@jacc.com**.

Rick Broadhead, B.B.A., is the principal owner of Intervex Consulting, a Toronto-based consulting firm. He speaks regularly to business, professional, and government audiences on the subject of the Internet, and is adept at speaking about the Internet in non-technical language. Mr. Broadhead was active in efforts to launch the Toronto Free-Net, a Toronto-based computer network. Mr. Broadhead is also currently pursuing his MBA at York University in Toronto. He can be reached on the Internet at **rickb@hookup.net**.

CONTACTING US

Clearly, the awesome success of the 1994 edition of the *Canadian Internet Handbook* took us by surprise. The book hit bestseller lists across Canada, reaching #1 in the *Toronto Star*, *Ottawa Citizen*, *Financial Post* and several other regional newspapers. Clearly, the Internet has caught the imagination of Canadians.

As Internet authors, our work is never done, since the Internet is constantly changing. We are already planning the 1996 edition of the *Canadian Internet*

Handbook, and we welcome your comments, criticisms, observations, and suggestions.

If your favourite Canadian Internet resource (mailing list, World Wide Web site, Gopher site, etc.) doesn't appear in this book, we invite you to forward the relevant information to us (description of resource, location, etc.), and we'll consider it for inclusion in the next edition.

If you're a new commercial Internet provider in Canada, or a Canadian organization that is using the Internet in an innovative way, we'd love to hear from you!

Here's how to contact us on the Internet:

handbook@uunet.ca   To reach both Rick Broadhead and Jim Carroll
rickb@hookup. net   To reach Rick Broadhead
jcarroll@jacc.com   To reach Jim Carroll

OUR MAIL ROBOT

We have established an automated mail response system (or 'mail robot') which provides information on the Canadian Internet Handbook by e-mail. To obtain current information about the book, the status of the 1996 edition, or to find out other information in general, send a message to **info@handbook.com**. This is a computer, not a human, and you will receive an automatic reply that will provide information on how you can find out more about the Canadian Internet Handbook, including our on-line resources, ordering instructions, and other relevant information.

OUR WORLD WIDE WEB SITE

Sackville, New Brunswick is home to the Canadian Internet Handbook's World Wide Web site. You can access our home page by pointing your browser to: **http://www.csi.nb.ca/handbook/handbook.html**.

....

INFORMATION HIGHWAYS AND THE INTERNET

....the world will see larger numbers of small computers produce the largest organization in history, the synergistic network. A billion computers, when linked together, will have, through the power of synergy, the dynamic to become stronger than 10 billion individual unlinked computers. The desert wasteland of TV will disappear as the lush jungle of diversity and communication flowers, flourishes, and completely rides over television and the telephone.

The Network: Say good night to television, by Frank Ogden,
from The Daily News (Halifax), Sun 12 Jun 94

David Letterman jokes that his show is an information highway "without the information."

Associated Press, Wed 02 Feb 94

The phrase of the year seems to have been *"information highway"* — and its close cousin *information superhighway*, the trendy *infobahn*, and the ultra-modern *i-way*.

You can't go anywhere today without hearing the phrase. It has entered our popular vocabulary.

Politicians regularly litter their policy pronouncements with the phrase, telecommunications companies speak of it with reverence and entertainment companies view it with excitement. Newspapers and magazines use it with abandon in their "how wonderful the future will be" articles.

The phrase has become a catch-all for a grand vision of a system that will create employment, offer hope to our beleaguered economy, make companies billions of dollars in new revenue, and perhaps, one could wonder, cure the common cold.

With all the talk about it, the public still looks at it with perhaps even a greater degree of confusion than a year ago.

In January 1993, the phrase "information highway" or variations of it appeared just 57 times in articles stored in the Nexis database from hundreds of newspapers, magazines and other sources. Last month, it was used 1,480 times. Business Week used it 14 times in one article last November.

Associated Press, Wed 02 Feb 94

The phrase has quickly become universally disliked, and those who use it are viewed in the Internet community as being naive about the real state of the globally networked world. You see, as we will explain, the information highway is already here in the form of the Internet.

The information highway — it's perhaps the most overused phrase of the 1990's. And we aren't even halfway through the decade!

WE ARE ALL CONFUSED!

If anything became apparent during 1994, it is that no one can seem to agree on what the information highway is.

You see, when it comes to a definition of what the information highway is, it depends on which particular organization you happen to be talking to, since everyone has their own idea of what it consists of.

While theories abound, there's no universally agreed definition of what the information highway will be or what will travel on it.

The most common vision is of a high-speed communications network that will use new transmission technologies to carry computer data, television and telephone services on a single line.

But the agreement stops there. Some plans are based on costly networks of fibre optic cables which have vastly higher capacity than traditional copper wires. Other network schemes plan to use radio waves. And still others suggest that powerful new satellite networks transmitting directly to homes are the way of the future.

Nobody fully agrees on what the information highway will be,
Southam News, Tue 18 Jan 94

HIGHWAY HYPE

The best way to put into perspective the *reality* of the Internet is to first understand the *hype* of the information highway.

1994 saw a dizzying number of announcements about the highway, not only in Canada, but around the world. To many, it seemed that there was unbelievable excitement in the media, the press, in industry and in government.

A tour down the news wires through the last year offers a fascinating glimpse into the hype that surrounds the Canadian portion of the global information highway.

Governments across Canada promise us that the highway will cure economic ills, and have established information highway committees to examine how it can be used to rebuild the economy and create jobs:

- A special council has been formed to help the Nova Scotia government get on the information highway. The formation of the Premier's Council on the Electronic Marketplace is one of the recommendations of the recently completed electronic highway study.

  Standard Broadcast News, Tue 22 Mar 94

- Jobs, universal access and maintaining Canadian culture and sovereignty are at the core of the federal government's objectives for an information super-highway, the minister in charge said today. "We want to put Canada in cyberspace," Jon Gerrard, secretary of state for science, told a conference on the electronic highway.

  New info highway, old preoccupations for Ottawa
  Business Information Wire, Wed 02 Feb 94

In Canada, much of the discussion about the highway has centered around who will control access to the television of the future, a huge, 500-channel universe in which we can channel-click to our hearts delight.

Certain themes seem to run through the press releases and statements of intent by Canada's major organizations. It's a home video system of such sophistication that we will never have to go outside again! It's a system in which we as consumers will be able to press a button on our remote control, and presto!, a pizza is delivered directly to our door. You can even buy fried chicken!

- Some Videotron customers can already call up movies, order fried chicken and send electronic mail using a TV set and special remote control.

  Infobahn "still 3-7 years down the road": Spicer
  Business Information Wire, Mon 16 May 94

The information highway — it's the ultimate couch potato system!

There is a surprising commonality in what is said about the highway in Canada by our leading telephone and cable firms. There isn't a press release or news article about the highway that somehow doesn't mention home banking, home shopping, or video on demand.

- Under the Stentor proposal, called the Beacon Initiative, the phone companies will upgrade their networks to provide two-way transmission of voice, video and data messages. That opens the door for a host of interactive services such as home shopping and banking.

Static over Stentor $8.5b upgrade plan
Business Information Wire, Tue 05 Apr 94

- Canada's major phone companies will spend up to $12 billion over the next decade to bring video phones, home shopping, on-demand movies and other interactive services into most Canadian homes, says a Toronto newspaper.

Phone companies plan info highway investment
Business Information Wire, Tue 05 Apr 94

- Cable TV companies are spending billions of dollars on improvements that they say will pave the way for hundreds of channels, plus video services like home banking and shopping.

Infobahn "still 3-7 years down the road:" Spicer
Business Information Wire, Mon 16 May 94

There is one other interesting fact about the debate on the information highway in Canada.

Canada's telephone and cable companies are arguing about the information highway — not about the information that should be on the highway, but about who should own it.

- "The federal government should stop talking and decide who gets to own what in the dawning era of the information highway," says the head of telecommunications giant BCE Incorporated.

Standard Broadcast News, Wed 27 Apr 94

We wonder why there isn't more talk about content?

INFORMATION HIGHWAY REALITY

With all the hype about the information highway, there is a growing realization across the country that perhaps our telecommunications mavens, government policy makers and news media have become absolutely too giddy in their excitement over something that is still, many years away.

The richest man in North America has cut through the hype and has called the bluff of the participants in the information highway discussion.

- Bill Gates, the head of Microsoft Corp., told media executives Wednesday that a full-fledged information highway will not be in place until the next century.

Gates: Info highway at least six years away
Business Information Wire, Thu 14 Jul 94

The head of the CRTC, the regulatory authority that oversees telecommunication direction in this country, agrees:

- Despite all the hype, most people won't be able to cruise the information superhighway for years, says the federal communications commissioner. It's a bit soon to expect hundreds of television channels and vast electronic networks piping scores of movies and games into homes, Keith Spicer told the Canadian Cable Television Association's annual conference today.

Infobahn "still 3-7 years down the road": Spicer
Business Information Wire, Mon 16 May 94

The level of hype often reaches ridiculous proportions for a system that is many years away.

The skeptics are beginning to have their say:

- Last month, *PC Week* columnist Jim Louderback, noting "information highway" evolved to "information superhighway" in 1993, predicted that by 1997 it will be the "Super-duper tubular mega-wow I can't believe it's not butter highway."

Associated Press, Wed 02 Feb 94

As Canadians, we should all stand up and say, no more. Ban the phrase! Art Buchwald, the Washington-based humor columnist, said it best:

- I am also starting a campaign to stop people from using the phrase 'information highway' as a means of describing a new method of communicating with another electronic system. I am recommending a five-day jail term for anyone who uses the term.

WHAT IS THE HIGHWAY, TAKE 2

It should be clear by now that nobody can seem to agree what the information highway is, and that it is a system that is still many, many years away.

Cutting through the press releases and policy statements and vision papers, it is clear that the information highway in Canada, as talked about by many major organizations, does not yet exist.

It is also clear that there will be two types of information highways in Canada, and indeed, around the world. One you will access through your television, and one you will access through your computer.

In order to help simplify each type of highway, we refer to the television-based version as the "couch-potato highway," and refer to the other as the "cerebral highway."

If you listen carefully to the discussion by the major organizations involved in the couch potato highway, you will find that much of the discussion centers around the invention of a device to fit on top of your television. The device would let you run your credit card through it to purchase a product — the whole idea is to give you a device that will let you buy stuff. While they do talk of other applications, the focus of the TV-based information highway seems to be on how to get the consumer to buy things.

Watch TV, run your credit card through the reader, click on your remote. Presto! The Canadian Home Shopping Information SuperHighway!

This, in face of a survey which showed that only 21% of Candians were interested in an information highway that allowed home shopping.

THE HYPE COMES HOME

The *Canadian Internet Handbook* doesn't want to spoil the party, but there is an increasing recognition that the hype of the highway is outstripping the reality of what the consumer is willing to buy.

There is also a growing belief in Canada and worldwide that perhaps we shouldn't concentrate our efforts on building a highway in Canada that lets us order fried chicken through our television.

Instead, we should concentrate on building a highway that lets us compete in the world economy, enhance our knowledge, and improve our skills.

That highway is the Internet.

THEY'VE GOT IT ALL WRONG

> *"The big sumo-wrestler corporations that are stumbling around trying to dictate the information superhighway have entirely missed the point," says Wired's publisher. "It's not about content, it's about connectivity."*
>
> New York Times, Sun 29 May 94

Many people, across Canada and around the world, have come to realize that the information highway is what you get when you plug the computers of the world together.

The Internet has emerged as the core and foundation of this "cerebral" information highway.

It's a completely different type of system than what the major corporations are talking about. Out on the Internet, you don't run your credit card through a reader. You don't order fried chicken with your TV remote control. You don't have limited access to the highway through some small device on top of your television that wants your credit card.

Instead, you do what you do best with your computer — you use your keyboard to write, communicate and debate with other people around the world, and to look and search for information on a global basis.

You interact. You communicate. You become part of a system that is no less than a worldwide revolution, and a system that promises to change man forever.

THE REALITY OF THE INTERNET

> *The information superhighway is already a stale cliché. It will not evolve under the auspices of Wall Street control or megacorporations. It is growing from the personal computer grassroots, thanks to the burgeoning, democratic Internet.*
>
> The information future: out of control – (and it's a good thing, too), New York Times Magazine, Sun 01 May 94

The Internet, stripped down to its fundamentals, is simply the world's largest computer network.

Linking together some 30, 40 or 50 million people, depending on who you talk to, the Internet has become the information highway for many people.

It is a highway that people are discovering leads to personal enrichment, one that leads to new business opportunities, and one that leads to new friendships that are global in nature.

The Internet happens to be many things to many people:

- it's the world's largest computer network

One of the most difficult things about the network called the Internet is that no one really knows how big it is. Its nature means that it is impossible to measure accurately — the best anyone can hope to do is to estimate its size.

Estimates have ranged from a low of 3 million people to perhaps 60 or 70 million people. The real number is probably somewhere in between — with the best estimates now indicating some 40 million people are participating worldwide.

- it's a unique global revolution

The Internet is shaping Canadian and global history.

In Canada, the technology of the Internet along with fax machines and cellular phones has shown how difficult it can be to prevent the free flow of information. The Internet has had an effect on the evolution of democracy in the former Soviet Union. It has become a global force that is affecting the world much the way that CNN has.

- it's the world's largest pen pal system

Daily, the Internet is used around the world by people who have indicated that they enjoy simple interaction with other citizens around the globe through computer networks.

Using electronic mail and other tools, people are reaching out so that someone in Moose Jaw is as close electronically as someone in Hong Kong. Through the Internet, it is as easy to communicate with someone in Estonia as it is metro Toronto.

The Internet is bringing cultures together around the world, and is probably doing more to provide a greater understanding between different peoples than any other invention by man.

- it's a massive global information service

The Internet is chock full of information — some of it useful, some of it useless, and some of it of questionable taste. Governments worldwide are making available public information, so that it is available to everyone. The United Nations views the Internet as a powerful tool to "free" information. Corporations have realized the Internet is a powerful corporate public relations tool. Individuals have realized that the Internet is a new opportunity to become editors of newly established "electronic newsletters."

Quite simply, the Internet is rapidly becoming the storehouse of all of human knowledge.

- it's a technology platform, a common method to link networks between companies

Internet has, in many ways, become the standard for inter-enterprise computing. A computer networking protocol known as TCP/IP has become the de facto standard method by which you would link a computer from your company to that of another company.

The Internet offers an unprecedented degree of connectivity from one business to another, from one organization to another, from customers to business and from business to customers. Its massive growth means that a link into it offers an organization a unique opportunity to participate in global commerce, a way of business that has not previously been seen on our planet.

Organizations which learn how to internetwork — that is, support communications and activities between themselves, their customers, their suppliers, their business associates and others — will be the ones to survive and prosper in the future.

- it's a set of standards for data communications, based on TCP/IP, that allows companies to develop software without having to worry about how to develop links to other types of computers

Michael Martineau, President of NSTN Inc., an Internet service provider, states that "I think this particular point is highly undervalued. For the first time, we have the ability to develop applications for a common communications standard — TCP/IP. With the Internet, it is now possible for developers to focus on bringing new applications to market without having to be concerned with all the problems of developing a common communications method."

Michael goes on to point out a number of recently released Internet applications which support video, "electronic whiteboards," and even games such as backgammon through the Internet, all of which have been made available on the Internet for multiple different computer systems, due to the common technology involved.

- it's a marketplace without boundaries

Ironically, the Internet is emerging as a place where people are shopping — albeit in a completely different method than proposed for the television-based information highway.

There can be no doubt that we are entering an era in which business will be conducted on a regular basis, between companies and customers through computer networks. As the world's largest computer network, the Internet represents a substantial global marketplace with significant new business opportunities. An interesting point is that only those people and organizations that take time to learn the unique Internet culture are learning how to prosper on the network.

- it's the next logical step in the evolution of computer systems

First we had individual personal computers, which freed computing power from the sacred and controlled mainframe. Organizations then wired themselves with local area networks, or LANs, which permitted the sharing of computer resources within one location. This was followed by WANs, or wide area networks, which extended the reach of LANs throughout an organization across large geographical distances.

The Internet takes us to the next logical step, by giving us a GAN, or *global area network,* by interconnecting millions of computers, individuals, companies and organizations from around the world.

Need a simple explanation? It's a big network of computers.

The biggest.

WHY ARE CANADIANS USING THE INTERNET?

All across the country, Canadians have discovered the resources offered by the Internet.

In this book, we will introduce you to terms like Telnet, FTP, USENET, mailing lists, Gopher, Archie, WAIS and World Wide Web. In subsequent chapters, we will take a look at each of these technologies in greater depth. Understanding the technology is an important part of understanding how you can use the Internet.

The Internet is full of technology and full of tools, all of which help you to send and receive electronic mail, participate in discussions about topics, and access information resources.

The best way to understand the Internet is to hear from Canadians just what they do with the network on a daily basis. To help put it into perspective, we put out a call on the network and asked people to tell us what they did on the Internet on a typical day.

The answers are illuminating:

- Andrew Clarke (**aclarke@dynatek.ca**) notes that he is the "media relations guy at DynaTek Automation Systems in Halifax. I use the Internet daily to correspond with journalists around the world. I have recently joined a service called MediaNet which takes journalists' requests for info sources and then sends these requests to people like me if the topic is something on which our company can provide info. It is all done via the Internet. This helps me do my job because I can reach editors and writers around the world, meaning with a limited staff I can cover way more turf. Our company ships product worldwide, which means we need PR worldwide, and if a company wants to be frugal, they hire one guy like me and I cover the world."

Use of the Internet isn't restricted to business activities. "I also use the Internet to keep in touch with friends around the country. And mailing lists make for good morning reading, on topics like fly fishing and running, with a strong cup of coffee."

- Debbie Compeau (**dcompeau@ccs.carleton.ca**), a professor of MIS at Carleton University, indicates that she uses the Internet "to support both my professional activities, as well as some personal interests. On the professional side, I use e-mail to keep in touch with my students (in addition to regular office hours etc.). I also use e-mail to exchange assignments and course outlines with colleagues at other institutions. Recently, a colleague at University of Calgary and I have decided to give our MIS students a joint assignment, where they have to exchange mail with a student at the other university to find out about news stories in the local paper on a particular day.

"I also use Internet e-mail to work with research colleagues — both exchanging ideas and papers to work on.

"On the personal side, I subscribe to newsgroups on quilting and textiles. Since I've been actively reading this newsgroup, I've started a couple of new projects, and generally become much more interested in my textile activities.

"Lastly, I recently found one of my cousins is an Internet e-mail user — I now keep in touch with her (and other family members who are on the net) much more than I would otherwise."

- Duncan MacDonnell (**Duncan_MacDonnell@mindlink. bc.ca**) says that "Today, when I arose I checked my on-line mailboxes to see if there was any interesting direct correspondence or indirect e-mail from any of the on-line mailing lists to which I belong.

"Later, I composed and sent an e-note to a local MLA, who I had met on-line, thanking him for attending a meeting I had organized on sustainable communities where we discussed creating an on-line site and other issues. I also composed and sent follow-up e-notes to a couple of other people who had attended the same session. As well, I replied to an invitation to a Walt Disney movie night from a Vancouver Freenet sysop, whom I also met through on-line interactions. And now I am composing this note before going for a bike ride in nearby Stanley Park.

"The Internet helps me connect with people I might not otherwise. It allows me to efficiently peruse areas of interest that may not be covered by the mass media or who do so poorly. It allows me the opportunity to debate and comment on-line on issues that are of interest as well as directly e-commenting to media who are on-line and solicit feedback — particularly CBC-Radio. And it allows me to stay in regular contact with friends who I could not economically contact otherwise."

- Gary Black (**garybl@gov.nt.ca**) says "I read a ton of e-mail, though not nearly as many as the 401 I had to plough through when I came back from a trip on Tuesday! I answered all of the mail requiring a reply.

"I searched (successfully) for recipes for the swordfish I plan to serve for supper. Then I ordered a free set of Esperanto lessons. I subscribed to a family math news letter, an on-line graphics magazine and a mailing list on Talented and Gifted kids. I received advice on how to set up an address list in my e-mail program as a result of a question I posted in **newusers.questions**. I offered assistance to newusers who had posted questions. I volunteered to help kids with homework questions. I added to discussions on education, Canadian bilingualism and Australian cuisine. I responded to a couple of people in search of pen pals. Finally, I downloaded a couple of software programs from an FTP site and some graphics from another."

- Gerry O'Brien (**gerryobr@nbnet.nb.ca**) indicates that "Mosaic has turned out to be my main time taker. I use it to browse the Internet and see what interests me. I spend mega time as well reading newsgroups. Lots of info on a wide range of topics as well. I have been able to respond to home repair questions concerning my trade of HVAC/R. The Internet has provided me with many hours of entertainment as well as access to software and problem solutions I never dreamed possible."

- Glen Reesor (**glenr@cu74.crl.aecl.ca**) notes, among other things, that "I received e-mail from my parents in Alberta, telling me they're just leaving for Ontario, and letting me know when they expect to arrive."

- John Kajfes (**jkajfes@io.org**) states that "I live in Pickering, Ontario, but spend a great deal of time commuting to Toronto for business.

"I've been around computers for some twenty years now and as yourself have seen many, many changes. Some good and some not so good. After reading several articles on the Internet and going through your handbook, I made the decision to get whatever hardware/software combination it was necessary to gain access to the Internet. My reason for doing so was to extend my ability to reach out globally.

"Access to the Internet became a sudden priority. The single most important aspect being global access. 'To go where no man has gone before,' comes to mind, because that's what I felt when I started surfing the net. I couldn't believe the amount of data that was available and accessible!"

- Melvin Klassen (**klassen@sol.uvic.ca**) says he "received a message from my father this week, currently on sabbatical from UNB in Adelaide Australia.

(At Flinders College). In this message, he told me his phone number and address. They arrived mid-July, and didn't get a telephone installed until last week. He had an e-mail address within two or three days of arriving, though. We had been carrying out a 'father-son' talk, after recent events in my life.

"I went to lunch with someone on Thursday where I was offered a job. This contact and the actual details for when/where to have lunch occurred because of a professional peer-relationship established over the network."

- Ken Campbell (**eye@io.org**) of Toronto's *Eye* magazine indicates that "We now regularly upload the entire text of the issue to USENET (widely spread about, along with a local group io.eye); we maintain a gopher site from which I've received lots of mail from ex-patriate Torontonians (in Halifax, Singapore, South Africa, Germany, to name a few) who have expressed thanks for being able to keep up on Toronto from afar; we have a mailing list, which goes out to the likes of the *Globe and Mail* and Ryerson journalism school, along with several dozen others, including other BBS's, like CRS and Magic, which then offer all this to their own users; and we have a web page, currently under construction, which includes a database form of movie listings, among lots of other things, such as a selection of local non-label bands (more to come). We hope to soon start storing poetry reading samples from local writers, etc. And this has all led to me being able to convince management of *eye magazine* that a regular weekly column on _net culture_ (not just nuts and bolts) is the way to go."

Clearly, the diversity and the range of information on the Internet have permitted Canadians to move beyond their own local boundaries and communicate and access information from around the world.

WHAT DO PEOPLE USE IT FOR?

Everything and anything. The Internet is many things to many people. Take a look around, and you will find that people use it for:

- sending and receiving global e-mail

Across Canada, people are using Internet in order to send and receive Internet electronic mail. E-mail, as it is known, is fast, effective, and quickly becoming a common method of communicating across Canada and around the world.

E-mail is being used within business to support communications between companies. Students are learning to communicate with other students around the world via e-mail in order to find information for class projects. Researchers located in different parts of the world collaborate on projects through e-mail. E-mail is a technology that is reshaping the way people interact, and is making the world a smaller place.

Not only that, but as more and more people join the Internet, people discover that they can use it for personal communications as well. Rose Mulvale (**rmulvale@fox.nstn.ns.ca**) says that "Last evening, my brother brought to my attention the fact that he and I have 'communicated' more often via Internet in the past three months than we did in some 30 years of phone/'snail mail'....!" Snail mail is a term often used to describe regular paper mail, and is a comment on the fact that Internet e-mail is often instantaneous in delivery.

- discussing topics, sharing information with their peers, and seeking support

Through areas of the Internet known as USENET and through what are known as electronic mailing lists, people are participating in discussions on tens of thousands of topics.

Do you want to talk to others about the evolution of the information highway in Canada? Join the USENET newsgroup **can.infohighway,** where a number of people are trading messages on-line. Have a question about investing in Canada? Try posting your question to the USENET newsgroup **misc.invest. canada**. Interested in the Society for Creative Anachronism? Check out **alt.heraldry.sca**. Roller coasters? **rec.roller.coaster**. Want to get involved in a discussion between chemistry students and teachers? Join the "Chemistry Telementoring" mailing list by sending an e-mail message to **chemistrytm-request@dhvx20.csudh.edu**.

The list goes on and on, with more topics than you can even begin to dream about.

Through USENET newsgroups, people post questions to others from around the world who share an interest in a topic. The unique spirit and cooperative nature of the Internet means that complete strangers often spend a few minutes to type out an answer to your question.

People are gaining a brand new capability by learning to use the Internet to globally "knowledge network" in this way, and by doing so are generally improving their skills, an important fact as we continue to wake up to the reality of global competition.

- accessing files and data, including sound, image, data, text and searching for information

Some have said that the Internet is the world's largest library, an on-line database of such scope and reach that it contains the ability to access more information than the human race has ever had at its disposal.

Everything from Vatican artworks to Tibetan monk chants to CBC radio shows and instructions for how to make good home-made beer can be found on the Internet. The information that is available is diverse, bizarre, and astonishing all at the same time.

Through the use of software known as Mosaic, you can access a World Wide Web server that contains the actual sound of last week's CBC shows, including *As It Happens* and *Quirks and Quarks*. Or, using Gopher, you can access a Gopher server to view the popular Dilbert comic strip. Using programs known as FTP and Telnet, you can travel to and retrieve files from computer systems around the world, including documents on free trade, government budget releases, policy papers or a listing of the worst 100 songs of all time. (They're gross!)

The Internet is an absolutely massive source of information!

• "surfing"

Exploring the Internet has become a leisure-time activity for many.

Traveling from location to location and from country to country by modem, you might find yourself reviewing subway maps of Toronto on a computer in Paris at one moment, and the next moment find yourself looking at an NBA basketball schedule.

The World Wide Web, an enormous system of interlinked computer systems, provides an addictive system of information that includes sound, graphics and images, and that permits you, when you use the closely related Mosaic software, to travel from site to site merely by clicking your mouse.

• putting out newsletters and establishing Internet resources

Anyone can be a publisher on the Internet! Anyone can contribute! Do you think there should be a site which provides information about the Canadian dairy industry? Establish one! Do you think we need a site that includes information about Canadian attitudes on wine? Put one up! Do we need a newsletter about the Toronto Raptors NBA team? Write one, and make it available to anyone on the Internet who chooses to subscribe to it.

Professor Derek de Kerckhove, the current director of the McLuhan Centre at the University of Toronto, has made clear that he believes the Internet is an extension of human knowledge. "He prefers to describe the electronic information network that covers the globe with the image of the external brain, a typical McLuhan metaphor, which emphasizes how every kind of technology is an extension of the human body. The real future, de Kerckhove suggests, is not taking place in boardrooms, but on the Internet, the global system of computer networks that is already being used by millions of people. There are perhaps 10 million people, and 20 million in the next two years, already exchanging information around the world, evolving new economies, and new customs." (*Globe and Mail*, May 25, 1994)

THE INTERNET IN CANADA

The Internet continues to gain momentum in Canada. Its role in government, education, commerce and the arts is being increasingly recognized throughout the country.

Turn to any activity, and you might see some type of Internet initiatives. Examples from throughout 1994 demonstrate the diversity and reach of the network:

- on August 22, 1994, Anne Swarbrick, Minister of Culture, Tourism and Recreation for the Province of Ontario, indicated that a planned central reservations system in development for the tourism industry should be linked to the Internet, stating that it would permit potential tourists from around the world to gain information about traveling to Ontario;

- on June 24, 1994, the Canadian Conference on the Arts being held in Victoria, BC, previewed "Culturenet," a network that received $200,000 of funding in order to determine how Canadian arts organizations can best participate in the global Internet. Plans are to include the ability for Canadian artists to post sound, images, text, and one day, real time video to the Internet, and to use the service to promote Canadian artists and arts organizations worldwide;

- in February, Premier Frank McKenna publicized his Internet address to a Toronto conference (**premier@gov.nb.ca**); followed shortly thereafter by federal Industry Minister John Manley (**manleyj@istc.ca**) and Secretary of State for Science Jon Gerrard (**gerrard@istc.ca**). New Brunswick began an aggressive campaign to place public information on the Internet. In BC, a provincial member of the legislature put forth a private member's bill which would require much of BC's public information concerning bills, committees and other government activities to be made available on the Internet;

- throughout the year, the Internet was mentioned over and over again as being the location where much of the banned information on the Karla Homolka trial in Ontario was available. Most certainly this is true — in fact, it is possible to visit a location in Indiana which contains the full transcript of every TV show and newspaper article from around the world which has mentioned banned details. Entire squadrons of cyber-people took it upon themselves to demonstrate to the rest of the world the futility of the ban in light of the overwhelming presence and technology of the network;

- in June, an initiative was announced in Ontario to link every school to the Internet. A similar announcement had been made in New Brunswick some time before. Across the country, educators were waking up to the opportunities presented by providing students access to global knowledge;

- the Internet was extended to the Yukon and Northwest Territories in 1994:

  NTNet, an initiative for the Northwest Territories, was established to "act as the Northwest Territories representative to CA*net; to promote the free exchange of information in the Northwest Territories using computer technology; to provide, promote and manage a wide area network connection for all the communities in the Northwest Territories together and to points in the South via the Internet; to provide free or low-cost access to the network by the public and educational institutions throughout the Northwest Territories; to provide commercial access to the network at a reasonable cost; to provide and encourage others to provide information on the network which is relevant to the Northwest Territories in general, and to communities in particular."[1] Thus, NTNet plans to be all things to all people in the Northwest Territories.

Quite simply, the Internet is a network that is reshaping the country, and for many people, it is the information highway:

The Canadian arm of the Internet has grown dramatically to the point where it now services over one million people in education, business, government and individual public arenas. It has evolved from an academic, research and development model to an open and accessible multi-purpose infrastructure, the prototype for the information highway.

CA*net Annual Report, 1994

IN THIS BOOK

This book is sprinkled with the names of particular Internet applications, including e-mail, FTP, Telnet, Gopher, World Wide Web (or WWW), Mosaic, Archie and IRC.

Each of these applications are described in some depth in Chapters 5 to 8. Until you get to those chapters, the following short reference might be useful before you start to take a look at case studies in Chapter 2, the Internet in Canada in Chapter 3 and Internet Fundamentals in Chapter 4.

E-mail	The ability to send a message from your system to someone else on the Internet.
Mailing lists	Systems which combine the e-mail addresses of 2 to several thousand Internet users. These are often used to discuss and debate topics, to publish newsletters, or for any other purpose imaginable. A message sent to a mailing list reaches every individual that belongs to that mailing list. There are mailing lists on thousands and thousands of topics.
USENET	An area of the Internet that is organized into several thousand topics. Similar to mailing lists, but usually accessed with different software.
Telnet	The ability to use the Internet to reach a computer located somewhere else on the Internet, in order to run a program on that computer.

FTP	File Transfer Protocol, the ability to retrieve files from computers located on the Internet. This is often used to retrieve documents or computer programs made available by individuals or companies from throughout the Internet.
Archie	A program used to locate other programs or files located on the Internet.
Gopher	Gopher is both a database of information as well as a program used to access that information. There are several thousand Gopher databases available from around the world.
World Wide Web	A database or "server" application that contains information that can be accessed with special "browser" software. A WWW server can include text, sound, image, voice and even moving pictures.
Mosaic	The software most often used to access WWW servers.
IRC	An interactive 'chat' program used through Internet.

INFORMATION POINTERS

Throughout this book, we provide pointers to documents, files or programs that might be useful to you, or on how to access particular information sources on the Internet.

For example, in the following chart we provide information on how to access a database to search for users on the Internet.

TO ACCESS WHOIS AT THE INTERNIC

Using Gopher	
Site:	ds.internic.net
Path:	Select: InterNIC Directory and Database Services (AT&T) InterNIC Directory Services ("White Pages") The DS WHOIS Database
Instructions:	Enter name of person you wish to do search on.

These instructions can be found for methods to retrieve files through electronic mail (or e-mail), through FTP or through Gopher. Until you become comfortable with the use of these applications, you might have to refer to the particular chapter where examples of the use of these applications are presented.

Keep in mind that the Internet is in a state of flux. All of these locations were verified at the time of printing of this book, but inevitably some locations will change, move or disappear forever. This book cannot guarantee that the listings as provided in this book will stay consistent.

BOLDED CASE

Locations that you might access on the Internet are usually expressed in **bolded letters**, as are user ID's, mailing lists, USENET newsgroups, FTP archives, Gopher locations, World Wide Web servers, Telnet sites and other resources.

---

1. From "NTNet Society, Public Acces Networking in the Northwest Territories, A Business Plan," dated June 1994.

CHAPTER 2

USING THE INTERNET IN CANADA

The Internet is the largest functioning anarchy in the world. Every day hundreds of millions of messages are passed without the benefit of a central authority. Every day millions of words are added and build an immense distributed document, one that is under eternal construction, constant flux.

Originally from The Guardian, and reprinted in The Ottawa Citizen, Sun 26 Jun 94

Across Canada, organizations of every type are learning to use the Internet to their own advantage.

The following case studies present but a small picture of the diversity of use of the network throughout Canada.

COTT CORPORATION

Cott Corporation, based in Toronto, is a company in the forefront of a revolution in global retailing — the move to private, store-labeled product. As the provider of private label cola and other pop to companies such as Loblaws, Shoppers Drug Mart and other major retail chains, the company is experiencing astonishing growth rates.

As a result of the growing volume of overseas business, it also has a need to communicate throughout the world with major organizations — both suppliers and customers. Jeremy Rasmussen, in charge of IT for the organization, saw the Internet as a simple method of providing such communications. "We wanted a simple, straightforward method of communicating. We didn't want to have to do a bunch of different links to different suppliers. We saw Internet e-mail as a far-reaching, powerful method to reach customers all over the world."

Through the last several months, the company has been running a test of a link from the corporate e-mail system at Cott to the Internet. "At this time, we haven't done a big announcement to all staff about our Internet link," he notes. "It started out as a pilot, but as we see it being used, we realized that it is quickly gaining ground and interest." Cott has linked its internal Banyan Vines Intelligent Messaging backbone system to the Internet through UUNet Canada. Staff, using the Windows-based BeyondMail system which links to the Banyan system, merely have to choose one address in the directory in order to be able to send out to the Internet. "Staff anywhere in the world on the Cott corporate-wide area network can send a message to the Internet, which is routed back out through our gateway in Toronto."

The pilot has involved Internet e-mail to five different customers and three suppliers, including some as far away as South America and Spain. "We plan on putting out a formal announcement sometime soon," notes Jeremy. He might have to do it sooner rather than later, since the reaction to the trial has been remarkable. "I've had people coming to me saying that they've got to have access to the Internet, including Internet e-mail."

For Jeremy and Cott Corporation, Internet e-mail is a strategic business application. "We have to make it easy for our customers and suppliers to do business with us," indicates Jeremy. "We want to be as easy to deal with as we can. This includes making it easy for outside organizations to deal with us. I would say that we will bend over backwards to support an electronic business relationship."

Internet e-mail is perhaps but a first step for Cott Corporation. "I really believe that this is something that will support a lot more of our activities in the future, but I'm not quite sure what it is," says Jeremy. "We are really watching the water to see the way that we should jump in the future. It's important to note that we don't market to end customers —instead, we sell directly to other corporations. As a result, we wouldn't want to try to use the Internet to market to customers."

Internet e-mail will prove to be a major benefit for Cott Corporation. "I'm convinced that it is about to explode, and that the critical mass for intercompany communications is forming on the Internet. We at Cott have to be there. The biggest application will be simple e-mail and a lot of data between us and our clients."

The Internet has also been a great benefit to the IT department at Cott Corporation. "We use the Banyan Vines networking system in our organization," reports Jeremy, "and so we make a lot of use of Banyan lists and USENET newsgroups. It's become critical to us in our support activities."

Jeremy can be reached on the Internet by sending a message to **jrasmuss@cott.com.**

MICROPLEX SYSTEMS LTD.

We put out a call to the Internet when preparing the 1995 edition looking for a company which was enjoying substantial business success as a result of its presence on the Internet. We got this message back from Steve Balaban, Marketing

Manager for Microplex. We thought it was so good that we are reprinting his message here in entirety.

Talk to any politician, and you will hear that Canada has to focus on developing a successful, healthy high-tech sector to promote future job growth in the country. Microplex Systems has to be a model that all other Canadian companies should look to in determining why they should be on the Internet.

```
Microplex Systems Ltd. is a Burnaby-based manufacturer of
LAN and WAN products.  Our primary product line consists
of multi-protocol Ethernet and Token Ring print servers
which support TCP/IP, IPX/SPX, AppleTalk, and  NetBios
over TCP/IP.  We export approximately 95% of all our prod-
ucts primarily to the US, Europe, and PacRim countries.
Although we do some exporting to the Middle East, Eastern
Europe, Mexico, and South America.
We have been Internet users and champions for several
years, and have benefited from this network in many ways.
Our initial purpose for Internet access was for email and
Internet surfing.
As we developed print servers based on TCP/IP protocols,
we realized that many of the customers we would sell to
would likely have Internet access. To help facilitate cus-
tomer support, we included our email support address
(support@ microplex.com) and found that many customers be-
gan to contact us via the Internet regarding support is-
sues.  We were able to look at screen dumps from their
print servers which relayed specific information necessary
to quickly troubleshoot any problems or bugs relating to
these devices.
We are also able to access the actual print servers in-
stalled at customers' sites via the Internet to assist
them in reconfiguring or obtaining status when they grant
us password access to their systems.  This doesn't happen
too often for obvious reasons! :-)
As momentum grew for Internet access, more and more people
began to use it to communicate with our company.  We added
our email address  (info@microplex.com) to all promotional
materials and ads, and found that a good percentage of our
sales leads come to us via email.
We also set up an ftp site to provide access to the latest
firmware, host software, bug fixes, release notes, techni-
cal documents, product history, and all other relevant in-
formation.
To help announce new products and other PR-related infor-
mation regarding our print servers, we post email to a
specific newsgroup called comp.newprod.  This is a moder-
ated group and requires careful editing of press releases
so that only the essential facts are presented.
(Absolutely no fluff is tolerated!)  As you are aware,
there is a thing called netiquette when using the Inter-
net, and violating the guide lines associated with its use
can produce severe negative repercussions.  We are also a
Sun Catalyst 3rd party developer. As such we are entitled
to and have used Sun's SunFlash to broadcast our product
```

```
news to all of Sun's worldwide customer base.
In the last 6 months we began advertising on the World
Wide Web via GNN (the Global Network Navigator) which pro-
vides a pointer to our Web Server.
Our URL address is http://microplex.com and is also in-
cluded in our ads to help simplify access to product in-
formation any time of day.  (Have a look at it and you'll
find out all you want about our company and products.)
Using this means of advertising on the Internet is more
efficient and much less expensive than having automatic
fax back service or traditional magazine advertising.
Potential and existing customers using Mosaic can obtain
all product promotional materials, company profile, view
pictures of each employee at Microplex, obtain software
and firmware upgrades, and all other relevant information.
Although it costs us to use GNN for promoting our prod-
ucts, we are very pleased with the volume of users access-
ing our Web Server.  We have noticed, by reviewing the
weekly and monthly log reports produced by our Web Server,
that a significant amount of hosts are accessing it, even
at this early stage of Mosaic proliferation.  We have also
noticed a lot of interest from international sites, as we
typically see in excess of 50 countries on our log
reports.
We have also been able to utilize the Internet in licens-
ing and joint development with companies in France, the
UK, Australia, the US, even Iceland.
The exchange of technical/engineering information via the
Internet has helped to expedite product design, develop-
ment, testing, and deployment in these partnering arrange-
ments.
```

Talk about learning to use the Internet to support global business activities. The experience of Microplex certainly puts into perspective the profound impact the Internet can have on business in the high-tech sector!

Steve Balaban of Microplex Systems Ltd. can be reached at **sjb@microplex.com**. In addition, you can check out the FTP site: **ftp.microplex.com**, and the World Wide Web/Mosaic site at **http://www.microplex.com**. To give you an idea of what's on-line, here's some pictures of their World Wide Web server:

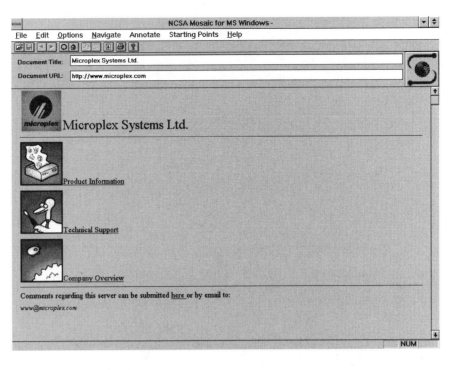

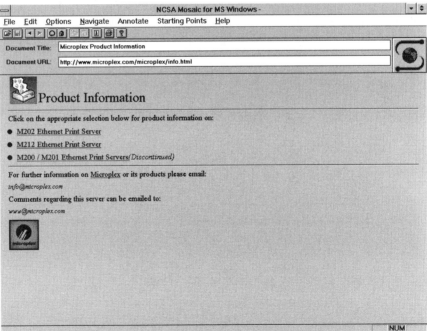

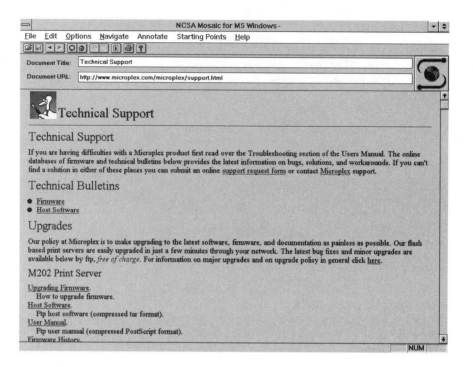

DATARADIO INC.

Microplex is not an anomaly when it comes to Canadian companies learning to do business in Cyberspace.

Dataradio Inc. in Montreal, Quebec, designs and manufactures radio-based modem equipment for use in private radio networks, including banking terminals and inquiry/dispatch systems for public safety (police, fire, ambulance) and utility (hydro, gas) networks.

Dataradio products have also been used on subway pixelboards for information & advertising, and in Environment Canada's own WeatherCopy service.

From a simple dial-up UUCP link to an Internet Service Provider that provided e-mail access to Dataradio and its Atlanta sales and support office, their connection has grown to a dedicated Internet link serving 30 in-house users, 3 dial-up ports for full Internet access via SLIP, and UUCP e-mail services for almost 25 remote sites, including traveling salespeople and technicians.

"The Internet is important to us in three ways," says Andrew Morrow, Director of Software Development. "First, we get technical support for the programs and equipment that we use from suppliers who are also on the Internet. Second, we provide support via the Internet — customers report problems by e-mail and we can use the FTP file transfer protocol to send software updates at a fraction of the time and cost it takes to mail diskettes or EPROM chips. Third, our radio-modems can be used by customers to implement their own inter-networks, so as the Internet grows so does the utility of our products!"

Dataradio also uses the Internet to receive sales requests, and to distribute and collect marketing surveys to guide their research and development efforts.

"Internet mail is a vast improvement over the fax machine when contacting customers in places like the Far East," Andrew notes. "Where faxes often arrive anywhere from slightly garbled to completely illegible, Internet e-mail never misses a character."

Andrew Morrow can be reached at **amorrow@dataradio.com**. For a Montreal weather report captured by one of Dataradio's WeatherCopy receivers, send an e-mail message to **weather@dataradio.com**.

ADDICTION RESEARCH FOUNDATION

The Addiction Research Foundation is a research organization that specializes in examining the harmful effects of addiction. It takes on a public role of helping society to deal with difficult addiction issues.

Scientists in the foundation have a need to communicate with others in their field from around the world, in order to perform basic and advanced research. In addition, there is a high degree of collaboration in the field globally, and the Internet supports these activities. Finally, the Addiction Research Foundation has a need to communicate with many global organizations, and is already doing so with the World Health Organization.

The Foundation has implemented a 56 kbps direct link into the Internet. There is a direct link from their local area network-based WordPerfect Office software, so that individuals only had to learn one e-mail system. "We really want to have only one e-mail system," notes Ron Service, head of the IT department at the Foundation.

"There are all kinds of information on listservs and USENET that the staff can participate in. There are a number of groups talking about addiction topics, so it is an important resource for the organization."

In addition to e-mail and discussion groups, the Foundation also plans to be an information provider. "Already, the Foundation has a BBS (computer-based bulletin board system), with two key applications, the Substance Abuse Network of Ontario and the Ontario Tobacco Research Unit," says Ron. "While the BBS is accessible to health care professionals via dialup and the Internet, plans are to make it available to the public in the very near future."

To establish the link to the Internet, the Foundation put in place a SCO Unix server, router and, of course, an appropriate firewall to restrict inbound access. By having their own Unix server, the organization can provide other services in the near future. "We have the software, and it is only a matter of a little effort to get it in place," says Ron.

"We had a group of about five people here behind the Internet project," notes Ron, "including some of the scientists who had heard about the Internet and wanted to join. The subject of Internet use at the foundation surfaced last October and it was part of our strategic plan, so by March/94 we were connected with over 80 E-mail users. Since then, we have a network roll-out schedule that is now in progress, and we expect to have over 170 trained users with Internet access by year-end."

Ron Service can be reached by sending a message to **rservice@arf.org.**

ABLELINK

Dr. Arlette Lefebvre is staff psychiatrist at Toronto's Hospital for Sick Children. She should also be considered a revolutionary in the application of on-line technology to therapeutic medicine.

"When I first got a modem several years ago, I communicated with a young blind fellow on-line. It occurred to me at the time that with on-line it doesn't matter who you are or what you are — it's what you say that counts."

Dr. Lefebvre became interested in the opportunity that on-line communications might offer in her role of counseling children with severe burns, disfigurement and other disabilities. "It's important to change any stigma that they might have as a result of their condition."

She tried to start up an on-line discussion group on a major Canadian bulletin board system for some of her hospital patients to participate, but it wasn't really successful. "The kids found it too scary on a general BBS system. That's when I met Brian, on-line," says Arlette.

She had mentioned her ideas on-line of a special BBS that kids in hospitals could belong to. She was introduced to Brian Hillis, who was also a user of that particular BBS.

Brian had been a fireman with the Toronto Fire Department for twenty-five years, and had gained an interest in computers during his last seven years with the department. As a fireman, he was intimately familiar with the severe emotional impact of severe burns and other medical tragedies on children. He and Arlette developed a rapport on-line, Arlette sharing her dream and Brian sharing his expertise.

The idea for Ability Online, an environment that would cater to the unique information and discussion needs of "her kids," was born.

The name, Ability Online, describes their goal perfectly. The idea was that there should be a place in which kids in the hospital could interact with children in schools. That there should be no distinction between who was disabled and who was not. That the system would be a vehicle to encourage the children at the hospital to rejoin the world. That this would occur by getting such an interaction going between the hospital world and the outside world.

It started as a small bulletin board system with one individual in a hospital and six children outside. "Within a year, we were at a point where we thought we would be five years hence," notes Brian.

"I've worked with kids who have been in a hospital for ten years, and they have been terrified of getting out into the real world. Through Ability Online, we've been able to put them in touch with people like Barbara Turnbull, who was paralyzed in a robbery in Toronto ten years ago. It provides them with a degree of encouragement that is unmatched."

"We have several goals," notes Arlette in talking about the network. "First, we use the network so that kids in the hospital, in bed, can communicate with others outside who have been through the same thing." Arlette tells the story of a young skater, who recently came down with meningitis and lost both legs. "We put her in touch on-line with Carlos Costas, the young chap who had lost both legs, who recently swam across Lake Ontario, and she came around. No psychiatrist or health professional could do that.

"Our second goal is that we use the network to integrate the disabled and non-disabled. It's important to get regular teens and sick kids on-line together. We have an attitude that we are all friends, and it's amazing to see some of the friendships that are established on-line."

Today, Ability Online is a Canadian charitable organization using a typical BBS platform to put children and adolescents with disabilities in touch with the world electronically. "We handle over 25,000 calls a month into this system, which uses a software gateway to connect to our Internet service provider. We provide access to Internet e-mail and news to allow many of these kids to exchange messages with new pen pals all around the world."

The impact of the Internet link has been significant. Once members of Ability Online are comfortable with on-line communications, they can venture out into the larger Internet world via e-mail and discussion groups. Simple Internet e-mail is a powerful capability for the system — in June 1994, some 60,000 messages were sent to and from the Internet by members of Ability Online.

"With over 4,000 users on-line, we provide a totally free environment for kids and young adults to communicate with disabled and non-disabled peers, as well as adult mentors," notes Brian. He relates the story of a woman who joined Ability Online so that she could get Internet e-mail to contact her son in Asia. "She now is the hostess for our welcome conference, and spends a lot of volunteer time answering questions. She has become an invaluable addition to our system."

Brian spends much of his working day supporting the system, answering questions, and helping kids discover the world of communications. Talking with Brian, you can't help but catch the passion and enthusiasm that he brings to the task. "We never imagined in our wildest dreams what Ability Online could do," says Brian.

For Dr. Lefebvre, the on-line world is a passion, particularly given the positive impact it has on her patients. She indicates that she spends 5½ hours each night on her personal e-mail, reviewing medical research lists and participating in other discussion areas.

"Ability Online works," she says, "because it links the children to others who have been through the same experience." She tells us about the figure skater who most recently learned to dance once again. "The only thing that worked is that she 'talked' on-line to someone who has been there."

Indeed. With people like Dr. Lefebvre and Brian Hillis, cyberspace and the Internet are establishing a whole new level of therapeutic medicine. Perhaps there couldn't be a better role for networking technology in Canada.

Brian Hillis can be reached by sending a message to **brian.hillis@ablelink.org**. Dr. Lefebvre can be reached by sending a message to **arlette.lefebvre@ablelink.org**.

RCMP/GRC, COMPUTER CRIME DIVISION

Corporal Craig Hannaford is the non-commissioned officer (NCO) in charge of the Technological Crime Section for the Royal Canadian Mounted Police in Ottawa. He has been a user of the Internet for a little over a year.

"We aren't on the Internet for investigative purposes," is the first point that Craig makes. "We are actually using it to support communications among a network of computer crime investigative authorities around the world." Craig, a Certified General Accountant by background, goes on to explain that he is a member of an international committee struck several years ago to share information with respect to common computer crime problems. "The Internet was identified as a tool to keep the group in touch," he indicates, "and to permit us to communicate quickly."

"We can't send classified stuff through the Internet," says Craig, "related to a particular case, given the security risk perceived with the network. However, we do use it to seek technical assistance, or to get ideas on how to deal with a particular case. I might put a message out to the group, for example, to ask 'how might I deal with this situation?'"

The network includes, at this time, individuals from the FBI, the RCMP, most major European countries and Australia. He hopes to see more countries coming on board soon from Eastern Europe and the Far East. "Each country has a few experts in computer crime, and we would like to see them participating." Craig notes that any law enforcement agency with computer crime expertise can join.

"The network is evolving informally, rather than by any formal plan," he indicates. He explains a recent situation in which he needed information from someone in Australia. "I was able to obtain it much quicker than by using fax or other methods. With my counterparts reachable directly on the Internet, I don't have to go through the hierarchies that exist. It's more personal, and more direct."

Craig has many plans with respect to what the network could be used for in the future. "A big issue is standard computer crime investigation methods. Computer crime has no borders, and we have to learn how to deal with different jurisdictions, and have to ensure that we are investigating in the same manner around the world." Craig believes that having everyone in close touch through the Internet will help them to develop a standard method much quicker.

Craig also believes that they will have to play a role as networking technology continues to become a part of everyone's working lives. "There hasn't been a tremendous problem with computer crime on the Internet to date. But we want to be pretty proactive and will want to become involved as the whole information highway evolves."

Craig understands that the Internet is a unique development. "We want to build a rapport with the network. If there are people out there who need to reach us or get a hold of us, we want them to know that they can. We think that our presence on the Internet can be like a police community relations vehicle."

Craig also notes that, although it is not the main objective, the Internet will become just another investigative tool. "There's a lot of intelligence out there that would be useful, and we have to understand it." No doubt the continuing emergence of technology such as the Internet will pose many difficult questions for Canadians in years to come. The RCMP, like all of us working in cyberspace, realize that we are at a very early stage with the evolution of networked technology, and need to prepare for the new way in which our society will function in the future.

"We are at a learning stage," Craig is quick to point out. "Telecommunications is coming into play, and we intend to be there as it is."

Corporal Hannaford can be reached by sending a message to **channaf@hookup.net.**

CANADIAN MUSICAL ARTISTS

Various Canadian musical artists from folk and traditional music to popular rock bands to heavy metal bands are discovering that the Internet is a useful method of keeping in touch with their fans.

Malibu Stacey is an alternative band, currently quite popular on the college circuit. Given the heavy presence of the Internet throughout universities across Canada, use of the Internet by the band was a natural step. "We have been running an e-mail newsletter which concerns independent music generally, with some Malibu Stacey propaganda snuck in" notes Tophe, a member of the band and the Internet spokesperson for the band. "If you would like to be included on our mailing list, or would like more info concerning our band, drop me a line at **cdelias@systems.watstar. uwaterloo.ca."**

Walsyngham Way is an early/traditional music group based in Winnipeg. "As a member of the group, I serve as its 'net presence,'" says Linda Lassman. Linda indicates that her plans are to use the Internet to make it easier to distribute their CD. "Anyone interested can contact us via my e-mail address for information about either the CD specifically or the group in general at **lassman@bldgdafoe.lan1.umanitoba.ca.**"

Mark Jeftovic (**markjr@io.org**) is a computer programmer by trade, and is also the guitarist in a heavy-rock band called LANDSLIDE. "My latest endeavor is to create a music-industry-specific resource on the net. So far this has taken the modest form of a World Wide Web site called the Online Shmooze. At present it has bios, contact info, tour dates for a few independent bands and indie labels, as well as ezines, other links, and forums for print-based alternative music mags." To access the site with Mosaic, travel to **http://www.inforamp.net/pwcasual/ index.html**. Mark indicates that he has grandiose plans for the system, including a plan to have sound-bites from bands on the server.

"We are providing fan support and a newsletter through e-mail," notes Donald Quan of the legendary Canadian band Lighthouse. "Future plans include an official mailing, possibly a full-time newsgroup." "Lighthouse" can be reached via Internet e-mail at **lh@qmusic.com.**

The Tragically Hip, a Canadian band gaining significant international attention, responded from their Internet mailbox (**thehip@hookup.net**) that the reason they joined the Internet was to "keep in touch with the music fans and get information (out & in) in a timely manner." They soon learned that e-mail is used a lot once someone famous joins the Internet. "We are somewhat overwhelmed by the response at this point."

It's not just artists discovering the network — inevitably, the more astute record companies learn about the power of the Internet. Nettwerk is a Canadian label that specializes in new acts, and represents the very popular Sarah Mclachlan and other leading talent.

Currently, Nettwerk offers a computer bulletin board system filled with sound samples, cover art, discographies, and other information — with much of the information accessible through the Internet. They also run an Internet "mailing list server" that returns information on various topics, usually within a day or two. A good place to start out to get information about Nettwerk Internet resources is to send a message to **info@nettwerk.wimsey.com.**

Nettwerk sends out the Nettwerk Internet Newsletter on a quarterly basis. The electronic publication details information concerning concert dates, release dates and other information. To join the list, send a message to **nettwerk@Mindlink.bc.ca.**

Nettwerk has plans to get more involved with the Internet. "By the end of the year, we hope to be a site and provide listserv functions, Gopher, FTP, Telnet and World Wide Web," notes Cathy Barrett, in charge of information systems for Nettwerk Productions.

Clearly, the Internet in Canada offers a significant opportunity for the arts and entertainment communities to discover new methods of reaching their audiences. We can only expect the Internet to become much richer in terms of cultural content in the years to come.

DISTANCE EDUCATION ACROSS CANADA

Much of the talk about the information highway in Canada has focused on its potential benefits to our education sector. In particular, there has been discussion of how the highway could be used to link classrooms, research experts and educators across the country.

Yet, it's already happening; the Internet has been supporting such activities for some time. Prof. P.D. Guild is the Chair of Management of Technological Change at the Faculty of Engineering in the University of Waterloo and in the School of Communication in Simon Fraser University.

Since 1991, he has been involved in a unique "distance learning project" utilizing CA*net, one of the major Internet networks in Canada.

The concept of remote distance education, or the ability to provide "virtual classrooms" across Canada via the Internet, is gaining increasing attention. This project has provided such capability for more than three years. "Since January

1991, graduate courses in management of technological change have been conducted using a distance education link between University of Waterloo in Ontario and Simon Fraser University in British Columbia," indicates Professor Guild. "It's an interactive multimedia (audio/video/graphic) link, supporting audio, video and graphics, and we do it through the current Internet."

Most recently, the project has been supported by Apple Macintosh computers, a long distance call through a speakerphone, and video conferencing through the Internet using software known as CU-SeeMe, made available by Cornell University on the Internet. This provides compressed motion video between the classrooms through the Internet network. During 1992, a third node in the link was added, with the participation of the University College of Cape Breton in Nova Scotia.

Even though the course now spans four time zones and 5,000 kilometers, the linkup works close to real-time, with only several seconds delay in data transmission over the Internet. Professor Paul Guild and his counterpart, Richard Smith, at Simon Fraser University plan to add other nodes at other academic sites and possibly some industrial sites as well in the future.

"We refer to our Mac-based distance education system as "the enormous room" which comes from a book title by e.e. cummings. And that's about how it feels," says Guild. "We never totally forget that some students can see the Atlantic while others can see the Pacific."

Sometimes this leads to interesting results. "The first five to ten minutes of class connect time is entirely social," says Guild. "One day last February, the SFU folks were describing spring flowers poking through the ground, while those at UCCB and UW described their backaches from shoveling snow!"

"Though the technology is impressive," Smith says, "to us it's just like a blackboard. What we're really interested in is discussing management of technological change on this electronic blackboard." A telephone conference call is initiated in Vancouver just before 8:00 am to connect the three groups at the lowest possible billing rate. Little video cameras sit atop the monitors so black and white video images of participants appear on all the computer screens, too.

Three courses have now been delivered using this technology: managing new product and service introduction; merging technology strategy with business strategy; and case study research methods for technology management. Class sizes have ranged from ten to twenty learners, which is typical for this form of graduate class. The graduate students participating have rated the course very highly.

"Another course is now in the planning phase and will involve course content from scholarly publications in the field of management science and from top quality material published electronically on World Wide Web (WWW) servers," says Guild in talking of his future plans. "All course materials will be organized in a systematic fashion and distributed by way of Web servers on the Internet."

Professor Guild can be reached via the Internet at **guild@sail.uwaterloo.ca**. The course material Web site, under construction, can be reached using Mosaic, at the URL: **http://edie.cprost.sfu.ca/motc/motc-research. html**.

CANADIAN AIRLINES

"We are still defining what it is we want to do on the Internet," notes Grant Fengstad. "We are still trying to finalize what it can do for us." Yet, Canadian Airlines has already established an impressive World Wide Web server on the network.

"Our connection to the Internet began four years ago using simple dial-up access in order to provide support to our information technology group," says Grant. "Today, we've got a 128kbps line to BCNet, and might bump it up to T1 if conditions warrant."

Through the link, Canadian has provided a path from its two internal e-mail systems to the Internet. "One of our first objectives was to provide external e-mail capability, and so we wrote our own gateway to do this." Although the e-mail link hasn't been widely broadcast throughout Canadian, it has attracted a lot of use. "Today, we've got about 1,000 people from throughout the organization sending and receiving Internet e-mail. This includes not only computer techies, but people from the flight ops department, maintenance and engineering, and some people from the pilot groups."

Grant notes that every employee with an e-mail box at Canadian could send and receive Internet messages if they wanted to. "We have not tried to restrict its use in any way. A few people are now starting to list their Internet address on their business cards."

In another significant initiative, Canadian established a World Wide Web server in the summer of 1994. "We just finished a presentation to our Vice President of Sales and Marketing outlining what the Web could do for our marketing efforts. In my mind, we could offer all kinds of airline services on-line." Currently, the Web server includes a bit of detail about services of the airline, and the ability to look up flight schedules.

Grant is quick to point out that he is very cognizant of Internet culture when it comes to providing services through the Internet. "I've been on the network for nine years, and I am very sensitive to the culture. It's important to respect it in whatever we do." The design of the Canadian Web server shows that sensitivity — one of the first things that Grant did in bringing it on-line was to include a suggestion area. "A feedback process with the Internet community is important. Already, we have had a number of useful suggestions from people visiting our site. We want our Internet site to be customer-driven, and we want to be able to define and modify our services according to what people want."

"The business case for the Internet is important," he notes, in talking about the future use of the Internet by the airline. "What we would want to do is use it as a tool to build a rapport with the customer. We can do that with such things as our Canadian Plus program, or some of our other programs, by putting them on the Internet."

Grant can be reached by sending a message to **g.fengstad@cdnair.ca**. The Canadian Airlines World Web server can be accessed using Mosaic software at **http://www.cdnair.ca**.

TOSHIBA CANADA LIMITED

The sales force in the Information Systems Group of Toshiba Canada has begun to discover the value of an Internet e-mail link through the last year.

"We use the Internet to communicate with our P.R. agency, Fortune 500 accounts, and for product marketing and sales functions," notes Stephen Feldman, a Product Marketing Specialist in Markham. Toshiba has linked an internal Lotus cc:Mail system to the Internet, and over forty salesmen in the group now use it regularly. "We can get information out to Fortune 500 accounts about new products as quickly as possible," he indicates. "We also use it to communicate with Toshiba in Germany and Australia, although we have a direct cc:Mail link to the US."

Although business cards don't yet list Internet addresses, most people do know their addresses. "We've been finding an increasing number of our accounts requesting the ability to communicate with us via the Internet," states Stephen.

Stephen himself participates in dozens of USENET newsgroups. "It's useful for our engineering and service groups as a means of keeping on top of PC technology." He hopes that the organization can soon begin to take some additional steps. "We're hoping to launch an FTP site at our Markham headquarters. We can support customers through our bulletin board and through CompuServe, but we are finding more accounts are requesting the ability to get files from us through the Internet."

Establishing the business case for such a link is critical, notes Stephen. "A lot more customers are on the Internet, and being there is becoming more important for us."

Stephen can be reached on the Internet by sending a message to **stephen_feldman@tcl.com**.

HAIBECK COMMUNICATIONS

"We view the Internet as a marketing tool for our clientele. It's just one tool of many tools that can be used in an effective marketing campaign," states Tod Maffin, an account executive for this Vancouver-based public relations firm.

Haibeck specializes in public relations campaigns involving print, television, radio and the Internet. Services offered include strategic planning, advertising placement, media relations, and other services. Although small, the company boasts an impressive list of clientele.

Think about it — the standard list of public relations vehicles for this company *includes the Internet*. In other words, Haibeck helps organizations to use the Internet as a public relations tool.

Tod Maffin is very cautious when it comes to talking about use of the Internet in this way. This comes from a background of having worked with on-line services. "I've always been interested in modems, since I was 14," he indicates. Like most successful businessmen who have learned about the Internet, he has also learned to respect its culture and to work within that culture in order to be successful.

"When thinking about using the Internet, there are a couple of things you need to be careful with. First, know your audience, and second, be subtle."

When it comes to knowing your audience, you've got to consider if the potential target market is on the Internet. "If we were to do some work for Digital Equipment locally, we would know that their audience is on the Internet. Yet, the Internet probably isn't going to be relevant to a local credit union," says Tod.

"You must also respect that people don't want junk mail" when it comes to an Internet public relations campaign, he indicates. Tod mentions a local bottled water company. "We are helping them to establish and sponsor a water information center on the Internet. They've got a lot of information that they could contribute, including research information, water quality test results, stuff like that." Haibeck is helping the company to be, in effect, a good on-line citizen. The site will also include the logo of the company as well as information on the products it sells. It is clear that Haibeck understands that you don't advertise on the Internet, you market, and that there is a subtle difference between the two. The key is to market in an unobtrusive manner.

Interestingly enough, Haibeck hasn't started to exploit the capabilities of Internet e-mail to the full degree. "We are a small firm of four individuals but have a large network of suppliers and writers, perhaps thirty people," notes Todd. "But a lot of our communications aren't yet via e-mail." Tod thinks this could rapidly change as more people join the network.

Certainly, he sees interest in the local clients in the Internet. "There is a demand by people — they've heard about it, but they don't know what is possible."

Finally, Haibeck markets itself on the Internet in an unobtrusive fashion. Their World Wide Web server (at **http://infomatch.com/0h/docs/users/haibeck**) provides detailed information about the company and is a very effective on-line public relations vehicle:

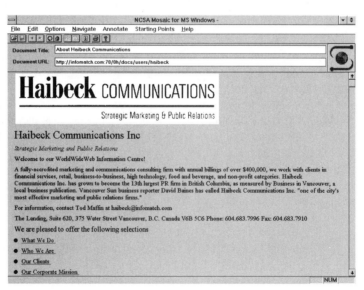

Todd Maffin can be reached via Internet e-mail at **haibeck@infomatch.com**.

INTERNATIONAL TELETIMES

"Ian . . . . . . again."

The tiny voice at the other end of the telephone was calling to his brother, Ian Wojtowicz, the editor of *International Teletimes*, an "on-line magazine" available on the Internet.

Ian, just your typical 17-year-old, receiving yet another phone call at home from someone who wanted to talk about his internationally recognized and award-winning publication *International Teletimes.*

"Sure, I get quite a few calls," he admits.

Ian certainly isn't your average 17-year-old — he is a veteran of cyberspace publishing, and probably has more insight into the issues and methods related to global computer-based journalism than many veterans of the print publication industry.

The publication has recently received not only significant attention in the Internet community, it has gained the interest of others outside it. It's been the subject of a CBC story, and has been covered in the local and even international computer press:

> Wojtowicz, a Vancouver resident, has become an Internet celebrity with his weekly online magazine, International Teletimes. Voted one of the 12 best points-of-interest on the entire 'net earlier this month by GNN (the California information service-cum-magazine that focusses on 'net developments). International Teletimes is a case study in what can be accomplished when a good idea meets personal drive.

> *A good idea meets personal drive*
> *Vancouver Sun, Sat 02 Jul 94*

International Teletimes is truly international. "We've got a fairly large staff and a lot of contributors. I've got a copy editor in Tokyo who does the physical editing. I've also got people in the UK and the United States." Ian has been trying to figure out with his editorial team how they can use the Internet to plan future issues on-line, in real time. He's examined the use of the live, real time "chat" facility on the Internet (known as IRC, or Internet Relay Chat — see Chapter 8) for their production meetings.

The publication has certainly enjoyed success. Ian figures that perhaps about 5,000 people read it regularly around the globe, but admits that he has no way of being sure.

Like many people learning the advantages of the Internet, Ian got his start through computer bulletin boards. *"International Teletimes* started as a publication distributed on bulletin boards — nothing more than that. One thing led to another, and it started to spread around the world. I never imagined that it would grow the way it did."

Talking with Ian, you could swear that you are talking to a veteran of the publishing industry. "We didn't have an editorial focus until May of 1993. It's now a monthly international publication that focuses on cultural topics that are global in nature."

Today, the publication is free to anyone on the Internet. "At the moment it is," says Ian. "We are looking at ways to turn it commercial, and are trying to figure out how to do that."

Why does he do it? "I enjoy it. I get a kick out of producing a publication, and getting responses from readers." Will he ever do a paper version? "I can never imagine doing that," he says.

And finally, what does the future hold for Ian? "I imagine I might do something related to this. I think about it a lot." Yet, you can't help but feel that Ian is getting a little tired of people asking him what he plans on doing in the future, when he is enjoying so much of what he is doing today.

Here's one of the introductory screens for the publication:

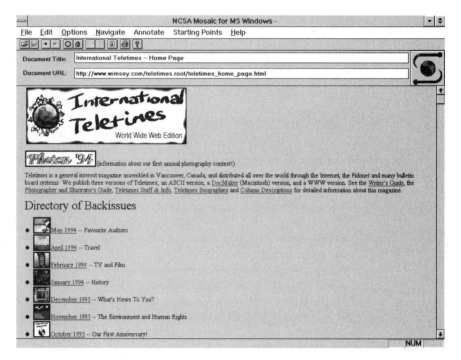

Ian can be reached by sending a message to **editor@teletimes.com.** The magazine can be visited on-line through your World Wide Web browser, at **http://www.wimsey.com/teletimes/teletimes_home_page.html.**

ADAM WALKER

Adam Walker is another young person who has learned how to use the Internet. He's a bit younger than Ian Wojtowicz.

Shortly after publishing the 1994 *Canadian Internet Handbook*, we received the following message:

```
From:    awalker@wbb.com (MajorBBS: Awtw)
Message-Id: <9405312002.D04230M@wbb.com>
X-Mailer: UUPlus Mail 1.42
To: handbook@uunet.ca
Subject:   hi!
Date:      Tue, 31 May 1994 16:02:35 -0400

Hello Jim & Rick!
I have your book even though I'm 10!
I have a great interest in The Internet and BBSing!
Please in your new HandBook please list other endings for
listing!
(I mean like .net, .com, .mil and .us)
Thanks!
Adam Walker
Awalker@WBB.Com!
bye!
```

Intrigued, we decided to call Adam to find out what he uses the Internet for.

"I'm interested in BBS's," he indicated when we contacted him during his summer break. "I signed on to the World's Biggest Bookstore, and it had Internet e-mail and USENET listed. I thought it would be cool." Adam uses a personal computer at home, with a high speed modem.

So far, Adam has been using Internet e-mail and USENET, and has worked with finger and Telnet. "I send e-mail to my dad at work, and to one of his colleagues in Boston," notes Alan, "as well as to you and Rick. I'm interested in BBS's so I've posted a few messages on USENET to **alt.bbs**, and have looked at some of the humor groups."

"No one knows that I am 10," he indicates. "On the World's Biggest Bookstore system, I communicate with some 15- and 16-year-olds, and they don't really care that I am 10."

"I've used Telnet to get to a BBS location in Minnesota, and have gone to the Free-Nets in Ottawa and Victoria. However, I don't have an ID there so I am just starting to explore." Next on his list to learn? "FTP," says Adam. "I want to be able to get into file archives and stuff like that."

Why does Adam find the Internet, and BBS, interesting? "I can go to different places. You can read stuff, look at different things, and read news," states Adam. Asked what his mother thinks about his on-line explorations, he says "she thinks its kind of cool."

Some of Adam's friends also have Internet addresses, but the school that he attends does not. At the time we spoke, he wasn't aware of plans announced by the Ontario government to bring Internet access to every school in the province, but thought it was a good idea. "I would try to do other things," he says. "It is helping me, because you learn how to communicate and use computers."

Adam's parents, Deborah and Peter, think it's a good idea for their son to learn to explore cyberspace, and aren't worried too much about the negative aspect of the Internet. "We've discussed with him the various things to look out for in e-mail and newsgroup postings, mainly warning him not to give out any personal information, such as passwords, telephone numbers, addresses and other information which someone could use to make themselves sound as if they were familiar or friendly to him. We have given him very strict instructions to never engage in any 'conversation' of a personal nature with anyone, electronically or otherwise. He knows what to do, for example, if someone on the BBS or through the Internet was to ask him to meet them. It's every parent's responsibility to try their best to make sure their children know the facts, and how to handle situations that may arise." Adam is being streetproofed for the information highway.

Adam is a lucky kid — he's growing up learning that knowledge comes not only from the library, but also from computer networks such as the Internet. The skills that he is learning now will probably play a major role in what he can do in a career in the future. It's kids like Adam, with their enthusiasm to learn about the on-line world, that bode well for the future role of the Internet in our society.

Adam can be reached by sending a message to **awalker@wbb.com**. His father, Peter, can be reached by sending a message to **CA326526@ibmmail.com.**

CARE CANADA

As a charitable organization which gets directly involved in the frontlines of world-wide famine relief, CARE Canada certainly has its share of global communications. Through the last year, it has begun to discover that the Internet can play a major role in these efforts.

"We've been using e-mail for almost a year. About 25% of our staff have been regular users" says Phil van Mossell, CARE's head of information technology. Yet, use was limited because the e-mail system that CARE used internally was different than the one used for the Internet.

"The learning curve was too high with two different systems," he notes. "We decided we had to integrate e-mail into our in-house system, and are just now finishing that off." When complete, anyone using the cc:Mail system used by the organization in Canada will also be able to use cc:Mail to send a message to the Internet.

Even though they've had a few teething problems, the Internet is displaying its worth to the organization, particularly when it comes to remote communications. "We've got a field worker in Zambia at a local field office that we communicate with," notes Phil. "And I am just beginning to exchange test messages with another field worker in Angola." In both cases, the global reach of the Internet to other related e-mail systems has been the key to its use.

Both field offices in Africa have access to a global communications network system known as Fido. Their e-mail is relayed to London, England, and from there to the Internet.

Phil thinks that the Internet has a definite role in CARE and will continue to gain support. "People understand what they can do in a general sense," he says. "People have heard about it, and management certainly supports our efforts." Phil indicates that a direct Internet link is the next step, but that for now it is a matter of logistics in figuring out how to do this.

Phil can be reached on the Internet by sending a message to **phil@care.ca.**

IMAX CORPORATION

IMAX, based in Toronto, Ontario, is a globally recognized company involved in the production and distribution of large-screen films, including several award-winning movies about space exploration, the discovery of the Titanic, and even the Rolling Stones in concert.

"We got onto the Internet as the result of people joining IMAX from companies where the Internet had already been used," notes Hugh Murray, a member of the film technology division in IMAX. "I joined from Xerox and had been using the Internet for some time. Another fellow joined at the same time as me, and he was also very involved in the Internet community.

"We convinced management that we should have a link to the Internet, and they agreed," he goes on. Today, the Internet is used for e-mail and for USENET news within the film technology group, but is gaining attention elsewhere in the organization. "The use of it has spread, and its usefulness is generally acknowledged around the company."

Internet e-mail has proven to be a major benefit in providing quick access to many of the partners that IMAX might work with on a project. "We use it to communicate with people around the world, including filmmakers. We are slowly finding that a lot of those people are getting connected to the Internet. We are also communicating with the Jet Propulsion Laboratory with regard to one of our space films. We communicate with people involved in special effects and sound effects companies." Hugh lists an impressive list of partners that they reach through the Internet.

"Another example is that we are working with a computer graphics house located in Sweden, and are doing much of the project management through the Internet." Clearly, IMAX is learning to function in the global economy and is supporting many project partnerships through the efficiency of Internet e-mail.

So far, Hugh and the rest of the staff in the film technology department have been sending and receiving Internet e-mail on behalf of others in the company who don't have access. "We now have agreement that we need to link the internal e-mail system for the company, cc:Mail, to the Internet, so that anyone can send and receive messages directly."

In addition, Hugh and others in the company track various USENET discussion groups for topics in which IMAX has an interest. "Right now, for example, we are tracking the groups **comp.graphics, sci.optics, rec.arts.movie.production** and **rec.video.production**." Hugh notes that each of these newsgroups provides a regular source of information about technology, methods, ideas and suggestions.

They've also used the Internet to find new staff. "A recent position was filled as the result of a job posting that we put up on the Canadian USENET newsgroups, **can.jobs** and **ont.jobs**." Another individual in IMAX tracks a mailing list which includes announcements of all news patents and technology. "He's indicated that it has become fundamental to his job," as it helps IMAX guard against patent infringement, as well as keeping on top of new technologies.

"I think management does understand the importance of the Internet now," says Hugh. "Four years ago, it would have been an uphill battle, but recently it's all come together."

When asked if he can use the Internet to send e-mail to Mick Jagger concerning their full-length movie of the Rolling Stones in concert, he just chuckles.

Hugh can be reached by sending a message to **hugh@imax.com.**

WESTCOM TV/RADIO GROUP LTD.

Westcom is a division of Western International Communications, and is an umbrella organization for a collection of eight television and eleven radio broadcasting stations across Canada, including Superchannel, and a controlling interest in Cancom. Communication is a primary focus for the Westcom IT Group, located out of BCTV in Vancouver, BC.

The project originated from a need to provide a communication forum to bring together "knowledge groups" located in the various Westcom affiliates. At the time, Westcom was using CompuServe as a mail interface between a small group of users, but the cost and limited scope of a CompuServe forum sent Westcom looking for alternatives.

Chris Beckett, a software developer and systems engineer in the IT Group, was given the mandate of evaluating Westcom's intercommunication needs. "Above all we were looking for flexibility. In addition to our needs for a national Westcom forum, our station networks were growing, and demands internally for expanded e-mail capability between them were growing as well. Increasing competition in the marketplace also meant that we were looking for new ways to reach out and provide service to our viewers and customers alike."

Given a plethora of hardware at Westcom (including hardware from DEC, PC's, MacIntosh, Unix, AS400 and System36, running a variety of operating systems), there was a need to select an e-mail system which could link multiple different environments. "In all categories; cost, availability, services, connection to viewers, customers, and partners, the Internet won hands-down."

Current activities Westcom is implementing around the Internet are many and varied. First and foremost, Internet e-mail is today being utilized to link all stations throughout the Westcom group. Some of the larger stations including BCTV and CHCH in Hamilton are linking the Internet directly into their own local mail systems like MS Mail and VMS Mail. Others are using Internet e-mail more directly.

Use isn't restricted to e-mail. "We are hoping to utilize the Internet for accepting news tips, and for accessing the vast information resources for researching news stories," notes Chris when asked about use of the Internet as a knowledge tool. Knowledge access through the Internet today is limited to technical staff involved in a "Computer Future Group," a group of people who are using an internal USENET discussion group to discuss and plan issues related to information technology in the organization. In addition, the IT Group at Westcom uses the Internet to find new software development tools, and in order to share software development techniques with developers from around the world.

The opportunities for use of the Internet as a promotional tool related to their TV shows has not escaped Westcom. "The BCTV Sales Department is utilizing the Internet in cooperation with Mindlink, a local BBS and Internet provider, in order to do an electronic promotion for the popular TV series *Babylon 5*. The promotion involves giving away free introductory memberships and interface software for an interactive *Babylon 5* program serviced by the Internet," says Chris.

Radio stations are discovering that the Internet allows a new level of feedback with their listeners. AM640/Q107, popular rock stations in Toronto, have begun to accept user comments electronically with regard to some of their feature talk shows like *Toronto Talks* and *Touchtone*. These programs can be reached at **toronto_talks@am640.wic.ca** and **touchtone@am640.wic.ca** respectively. "Future plans include listing an Internet address for news programs like the popular BCTV *News Hour*. We are also evaluating the use of Mosaic so that Westcom stations can establish home pages that list special broadcasting events, and other points of interest in broadcasting."

Broadcasting stations in Canada are required to submit monthly logs to the CRTC. Westcom stations will be particpating in a test project established by the CRTC to accept these logs electronically using Internet mail.

On the subject of putting together their Internet project, Chris notes that "while interest is very high, and service possibilities are high, the going has been slow. The only ones really utilizing the Internet currently are our technical users. The wide variety of tools and jargon make dropping it on the average end-user's desktop unrealistic. Administration chores related to coordinating with the remote stations has been difficult as well. Several things, however, are helping to make Internet integration easier for corporations. New GUI tools and the wide availability of training materials are allowing us to develop end-user packages to help bring non-technical users up to speed fast. As well, the increasing level of commercial services available are making the Internet an easy sell to users who are looking to make their jobs and lives easier.

"I can see the Internet as a research tool for our news people being a really big feature once we can get some training organized. And e-mail! E-mail is what really drew us to the Internet in the first place and would probably justify the cost and effort alone, without the other services. I think the Internet is great. In the IT business, everyone seems to have varying opinions on any popular technology for and against. I haven't met anyone that didn't consider the Internet a plus. That really says something!"

Chris Beckett can be reached by sending a message to **cbeckett@wic.ca.**

YUKONNET OPERATING SOCIETY

On February 5, 1994, Richard Lawrence of Whitehorse, Yukon, sent a message to us describing how he used the Internet from the North.

```
The service I administer was set up a year ago to provide
users of NEXTSTEP software in the Yukon a link to Internet
e-mail. The University of Alberta kindly supplied a feed
that allowed my machine to poll for e-mail (via a long-
distance phone call to Edmonton) whenever I wished. At
present, only about 10 people have made use of this feed
```

```
(most of whom are members of the local NeXT User Group).
But we haven't advertised the service, nor do we provide
full Internet access because of the extremely high long
distance charges in the North. The hope is that some day
either the government (Yukon or federal) or a coalition of
people or agencies will pay for a direct line or satellite
link to provide full Internet service to the Yukon. To
date, this has been a pipe dream, so a few of us using
NeXT (ie. UNIX) machines have set up SLIP connections to
the Univ. of >British Columbia through its high speed dial
up service and use it sparingly (again, because of long
distance charges).
```

A lot has changed since that date. Richard reports that "six months later, I am pleased to tell you that a small group of us have gone on to form the YukonNet Operating Society, a non-profit organization that has made formal application to CA*net to become the Internet regional service provider for the Yukon."

The initiative has gained a lot of attention. "We now have over fifty members and have made a great deal of progress in our talks with CA*net and North-wesTel, the telephone company for much of northern Canada. If all works out as we hope, we'll be up and running in the fall with enough customers in government, business and from home to give us a good financial start."

It's not just getting the service up and running that they are thinking about. "We also plan to offer value-added services, such as setting up a pilot World Wide Web server for Yukon Tourism. So this is all rather exciting, to say the least."

Already, the limited access that the group has available has shown its benefits. "Initially, e-mail was a way for our members to get fast access to computer information from 'outside.' But by burrowing an electronic hole to the world, the outside has also come to us in a bigger way than we imagined. Researchers across the country write to find out how to get access to researchers in the Yukon, friends write to learn how to get in touch with friends and so on. Our little straw, borne of one small need, has felt the effects of attaching to a fire hose. More people want an electronic path out and an increasing number want a path in. That's no doubt why YukonNet was created.

"YukonNet's goal is to link Yukon to the world and the world to Yukon. An electronic Alaska Highway, if you will. Though this all sounds corny and cliché-ridden, the truth of the matter is that this technology helps build its own future, much of which we can't clearly see today."

As things currently stand, the startup of YukonNet will involve the collaborative funding and administrative effort of the Government of Yukon, NorthwesTel, and CA*net. YukonNet will be administered by a board consisting of three members from NorthwesTel and three members from the YukonNet Operating Society (a registered non-profit). It plans to offer SLIP/PPP, dedicated connections, and perhaps shell acess.

Richard is now the project manager for YukonNet, and can be reached by sending a message to **richard@north.nugyt.yk.ca**.

C H A P T E R   3

····································

THE INTERNET IN CANADA

The Canadian Internet is one of the most important developments in Canadian history, as important as the development of the trans-Canada highway system, the St. Lawrence Seaway and the CPR.

It will be used for civic discourse, commerce and delivery of government services, becoming a key component of Canadian society.

CA*net, 1994 Annual Report

In this chapter, we will examine the Internet in Canada in order to understand how it can be used by individuals or organizations. This chapter explores the organizations that make up the Internet in Canada. By the end of this chapter, you will have an understanding of:

• the major players involved in the Internet community in Canada

• acceptable use policies and commercial use of the network

• future trends with the Internet in Canada.

THE HISTORY OF THE INTERNET

The history of the Internet has been told countless times, in many magazine articles and books, so we don't want to repeat it here in detail.

The basic facts are that the Internet began as an initiative in 1969 by the U.S. Department of Defense to establish a reliable communications network. The result was an effort to link the military establishment, universities and defense contractors by computer into a network known as the ARPANET.

The ARPANET was based on a common set of communication protocols known as TCP/IP.

In the mid-1980's, the National Science Foundation began to provide funding for the establishment of research and academic networks throughout the U.S., and began to link those networks into a high-speed network known as the NSFNet, which eventually replaced the ARPANET and which was built using the same TCP/IP protocols as originally established in ARPANET.

As the NSFNet evolved in the United States, the national research and academic networks NetNorth and CDNNet emerged in Canada. Although not based on Internet protocols, these two networks provided a starting point for the establishment of a Canadian Internet network, which eventually emerged in CA*net in 1989. CA*net linked itself to NSFNet as a first, important step, replacing the more direct link that some Canadian networks had already put in place.

Elsewhere around the world, a similar pattern of smaller networks linked into country networks occurred. Eventually, networks from each country were linked to each other, primarily through the NSFNet.

The arrival of commercial Internet providers in Canada and elsewhere resulted in an explosion of Internet traffic from the early 90's, and a rapid shift in the type of traffic on the global Internet.

Commercial networks were linked to academic networks such as NSFNet and CA*net, often in round-about ways, further expanding the range and scope of the network.

In this way the Internet was created.

ACCESSING THE INTERNET IN CANADA

Up until about 1989 in Canada, you had to be with an academic or research institution in order to be able to join the Internet.

However, from about 1990, the arrival of a number of Canadian and U.S. commercial Internet providers has meant anyone with a PC, a modem and money to spend can join the Internet. In some locations, you don't even have to pay to join the network: for example, in Ottawa and Victoria, community initiatives known as Free-Nets provide free access to some (not all) Internet services. Municipal Area Internet Networks are also starting to appear in a number of communities, providing low-cost, at-cost Internet connectivity. As well, a number of local bulletin board systems[1] are providing Internet access as part of their service offerings.

The proximity of Canada to the U.S. results in additional Internet access methods. Major U.S. communication services such as Delphi and BIX offer full Internet capabilities, with access via a local telephone call in major Canadian cities.

In Appendix C, *The Directory of Canadian Internet Service Providers* details the various methods by which you can link into the Internet in Canada. This includes Canadian regional networks, and Canadian commercial Internet providers and U.S. providers.

Given the diversity of methods by which you can join the Internet in Canada, it is important to understand who the major players are in the Canadian Internet environment, and the type of service that each provides.

REGIONAL NETWORKS

If we start anywhere, we have to start with the regional networks.

Although they are referred to as the "regional networks," they are simply each province's and territory's own network. Added to ten existing regional networks in 1994 were regional networks in the Yukon and Northwest Territories, as well as the GTIS (Government Telecommunications Informatic System), a federal government network.

(Several of these networks are very new —YukonNet and NTNet were only created in 1994.)

REGIONAL NETWORKS IN CANADA

Alberta	ARnet
British Columbia	BCnet
Federal Government	GTIS (Government Telecommunications Informatic System)
Manitoba	MBnet
New Brunswick	NBNet
Newfoundland	NLnet
Northwest Territories	NTnet
Nova Scotia	NSTN (Nova Scotia Technology Network)
Ontario	ONet
Prince Edward Island	PEINet
Quebec	RISQ (Reseau Interordinateurs Scientifique Quebecois)
Saskatchewan	SASK#net
Yukon	YukonNet

Historically, the regional networks have been a hybrid — with some providing access only to the research and academic communities in their province on a cost recovery basis, while others provided both academic/research access as well as for-profit commercial Internet access to any individual or organization.

However, this is changing, as more of the regional networks drop restrictions on use of the Internet for only research/academic purposes.

The regional networks include:

- ONet, the largest regional network in Canada, which historically provided academic/research access throughout the Province of Ontario but is rapidly evolving to become a provider of Internet services to any organization.

The largest regional network in Canada, it provides access to "all of the province's 18 universities, 22 community colleges, 15 federal government departments and agencies, 12 major private sector corporations, three research centres, five provincial ministries and agencies, five medical and hospital research establishments."[2]

Originally, the mission of ONet was strictly an academic and research one, with the goal of faciliating "the exchange of information among researchers and educators throughout Ontario, and to provide Ontario-based researchers with access to Canadian and international sources of information."

However, ONet is like many regional networks in that it is in a period of transition from being an academic/research network to a network that will sell Internet access to any individual or organization that wants to buy it, operating on a cooperative as opposed to a profit-oriented basis. ONet has recently incorporated itself as the cooperative ONet Networking Inc., and plans to become more actively involved in the commercial Internet marketplace in Ontario.

Other regional providers, such as NBNet and PEINet, are for-profit organizations run by the telephone companies in the provinces of New Brunswick and Prince Edward Island respectively. Each network has recently undergone a transition to this type of status, having originally focused on the academic/research communities in their province.

- NSTN Inc., originally formed for the purpose of providing Internet access in Nova Scotia, now actively sells Internet access in the Toronto and Ottawa areas as well. It has never had a strict academic/research mandate, and has been in the business of selling Internet access to anyone since its inception.

Historically, then, some regional networks in Canada had a pure academic/research mandate with respect to their role in the Canadian Internet networking scene, while others have been particularly aggressive in providing networking services to the commercial sector since their inception.

Yet, this historical difference is rapidly blurring today as most of the regional networks with an academic/research focus abandon such a focus to become either a profit-oriented enterprise or a co-op with a focus on providing service on a cost-recovery basis.

CA*net

The regional networks are linked together across Canada through CA*net,[3] the major Internet system in Canada today.

CA*net was established in the late eighties in order to foster a cooperative environment for connectivity between Canada's regional networks. Even though CA*net is the national network, it really is just a coordinating body for the regional (or provincial and territorial) networks.

In the CA*net Strategic Plan released in June 1994, it was noted that "CA*net's mission is to make available a national network (what has become known as an information highway), to facilitate open, ubiquitous and affordable access to national and international information resources."

Originally, a few of the regional networks (primarily ONet, BCNet and RISQ) were the only way to get onto the Internet in Canada. Each had links to the U.S.-based NSFNet, and exchanged traffic amongst themselves via the U.S. CA*net was created in 1989 in order to encourage and support direct connectivity between these networks, with original funding by the National Research Council. (Currently, the Council, known as the NRC, is no longer involved in funding.)

Today, CA*net connects these twelve regional networks (and the one federal government network) through the organization CA*net Networking Inc. During 1994, it completed a project to upgrade inter-region network links to what is known as T1 speed, from a mixture of lower speed lines, thus providing a true high-speed networking backbone across the country.

CA*net is linked to the major American research network NSFNet (the National Science Foundation network) via high-speed links to NSFNet access points found at three U.S. universities (Cornell, Princeton and the University of Washington). Through these links, it provides the twelve regional Canadian networks and the federal network with access to the rest of the global Internet.

At this time, CA*net is funded by member fees paid by the twelve regional networks and the federal network, as well as through an operating grant from CANARIE. CA*net is also represented on the Board of Directors of CANARIE Inc., a new initiative with the mission "to support the development of a communications infrastructure for a knowledge-based Canada." CANARIE is discussed near the end of this chapter.

In return, CA*net is responsible for coordinating the provision of networking services to these regional networks — in effect, combining the purchasing power of the ten provinces and two territories to obtain lower cost network services.

CA*net also provides national network maintenance and administrative services over the CA*net network, through a joint venture of the University of Toronto and Integrated Network Services Inc.

An important aspect of CA*net is that it provides a Canadian presence in the international networking community. Although many of the regional networks could likely get cheaper Internet access by going directly to the U.S., by working together the regional networks can promote the Canadian networking environment and associated industries, as well as help build a national Canadian networking infrastructure.

> CA*net Goals, from the 1994 Strategic Plan
>
> - To provide network connectivity and associated services within Canada and to international networks.
> - To improve access to networks in all sectors of Canadian society and to all parts of Canada.
> - To promote co-operation and understanding in the Canadian networking community.
> - To promote the growth of networking in Canada.
> - To facilitate, promote and co-ordinate open networking standards in Canada.
> - To represent the Canadian Internet community to national and international networking organizations, agencies and initiatives.

COMMERCIAL NETWORKS IN CANADA

The Internet networking scene continues to quickly change as the result of continued growth in the number of commercial Internet providers across the country.

"Commercial Internet providers" is the phrase that is used to describe those for-profit companies which sell Internet access to the general public, organizations and corporations.

Under this definition, quite a few of the regional networks (such as NB*Net and NSTN Inc.) could also be classified as commercial Internet service providers. This begs questions of what makes a regional network and what makes a commercial network? There is no distinction in many cases, other than the fact that a regional network as discussed above is one that has agreed to pay a fee to CA*net for access to the national CA*net backbone.

Ignoring that bit of distinction, commercial Internet providers in Canada range from very small to very large organizations. Essentially, there are two types of providers in Canada:

- those in the corporate connectivity marketplace, by companies that specialize in selling high-speed "dedicated" access to corporate organizations that need to put in place a dedicated link to the Internet;

- those in the dial-up marketplace, by providers which specialize in providing individual and corporate access to the Internet through dial-up modem access.

Companies in the first category include:

- *fonorola*, a company involved in the resale of telephone services across Canada. Its primary revenue is derived from the sale of discounted long distance service, data transmission lines and other services to large corporate accounts.

  It is also a national Internet service provider and focuses on selling high-speed access to organizations seeking direct Internet connectivity.

In addition, *fonorola* sells Internet access to several other Internet service providers which focus on the consumer marketplace, such as Inforamp in Toronto, UUNorth in Toronto and Resudox in Ottawa.

- UUNet is a national provider based in Toronto. An affiliate of UUNet Communications Inc., one of the largest Internet providers in the U.S., it provides both dedicated corporate connectivity and dial-up connectivity to organizations.

  In addition, it is the provider of Internet services to several consumer-based Internet service providers such as NetAccess Systems in Hamilton and UUISIS in Nepean.

- Worldlinx, a subsidiary of Bell Canada, entered the Internet service provider business in June 1994, indicating that it planned to focus on providing dedicated Internet connectivity to major organizations.

Across Canada, there are an ever-increasing number of consumer based Internet service providers providing dial-up individual and corporate access. Part of the reason for an increase in the number of these vendors is due to the fact that anyone can start up such a company by purchasing high-speed access to the network from companies such as *fonorola* or UUNet. Examples include:

- InfoRamp in Toronto, which has licensed the innovative Pipeline software from The Pipeline Network Inc., a U.S.-based service provider. Pipeline for Windows provides a simple and effective front end to most Internet services, thus making InfoRamp one of the easiest to use Internet service providers around.

- Wimsey Information Services, based in British Columbia, which sells individual and corporate access in the Vancouver area. Wimsey buys its access from BCnet, the regional network for BC. Wimsey provides several types of dial-up access to the Internet, and includes with the account public domain software to make the Internet easier for users of Microsoft Windows and Macintosh computers.

  Wimsey provides a link from corporate MS-Mail systems to Internet e-mail. Corporate organizations joining the network can place information about their products and services in Wimsey's on-line corporate summary accessible via World Wide Web/Mosaic.

There are no hard and fast rules as to what providers sell what services — some companies straddle both the dial-up and corporate connectivity markets. Based in Ontario, HookUp Communications sells access to individuals and organizations seeking casual dial-up connectivity, as well as selling dedicated corporate access to the Internet.

All in all, across Canada we are seeing an ever-increasing number of commercial Internet service providers, with a lot of breadth and diversity in the services offered.

However, the reality is that like most things Canadian, there is a concentration of access in major metropolitan areas and less choice in small towns and cities and rural areas. This fact is closely related to a debate in the Canadian networking community concerning public subsidization of CA*net and some regional networks, as discussed in the section "public Internet funding" below.

The result of all of these organizations getting involved in the commercial Internet provider business is an increasing number of methods by which someone can join the Internet in Canada, as well as a wide variation in the cost to access and use of the Internet.

The *Directory of Canadian Internet Service Providers* in Appendix C includes a detailed overview of current commercial Internet providers in Canada.

U.S. COMMERCIAL NETWORKS

Even organizations without a physical office in Canada are selling Internet access to Canadians.

Delphi, a large-scale communication service based in the U.S., provides full Internet access to several hundred thousand subscribers around the globe. Since Delphi is accessible via a local phone call to a data network in most Canadian cities, it has effectively become an Internet provider in Canada.

We can expect to see many more services like Delphi offering Internet access. The giant CompuServe information service, with well over 1,000,000 subscribers around the globe, continues with its plans to provide its members with full Internet capability. As CompuServe indicated in a press release in early 1994, "CompuServe will introduce access to a variety of Internet resources, including the popular Internet USENET Newsgroups, remote log-in to Internet hosts and file transfer from Internet archive sites. Rates have yet to be determined, and CompuServe is developing an easy-to-use interface for CompuServe members who are not Internet experts."

As at September 1994, CompuServe could be used to send and receive Internet e-mail, and members could subscribe to USENET newsgroups. CompuServe is widely used across Canada and will become a major player in providing access to the Internet.

FREE-NETS

The purpose of a Free-Net is two-fold; first, to ensure that there are no barriers of access to the global Internet within a community, and second, to establish a community-based information resource that contains a wealth of local information.

Free-Nets usually provide limited access to the Internet by restricting their services to the use of Internet e-mail, Gopher, USENET and Telnet.

Free-Nets exist because of the hard work and dedication of volunteers throughout the community. Free-Nets, which are free to their users, are funded through government grants and by donations from corporate organizations.

There are several operating Free-Nets at this time, and several more are in the project planning phase. For example, they include:

- the Victoria Free-Net, "a community-based computer network available at no cost to residents and visitors of the Greater Victoria region" (as it notes in its on-line Gopher server).

Corporate and other organizations contributing funding or services to the Victoria Free-Net have included Sun Microsystems Canada, the British Columbia Telephone Company, Telebit Corporation, Camosun College, the Greater Victoria Public Library, the Vancouver Island Advanced Technology Centre, the Pacific Region Association for Telematics (PRAT), British Columbia Energy Council, Softwords Research International, Inc., ZED Data Systems Corporation and Island Publishers Ltd. As you can see, Free-Nets have been successful at obtaining significant corporate support.

In its on-line material, the Victoria Free-Net summarizes its mandate:

Goals of the Victoria Free-Net

- computer-mediated communications among VICTORIA FREE-NET users and community members;
- easy access to information posted by community organizations;
- individuals, businesses, and government;
- community events information;
- worldwide electronic mail;
- access to selected online public access resources throughout the world; and
- alternative news services.

- The Toronto Free-Net (TFN), an initiative that started in August 1993, was not yet operational as of September 1994, but planned to be on-line soon.

Funded with a $400,000 grant from Rogers Communications Inc., with operating support from Ryerson Polytechnic University, equipment donations from Sun Microsystems Canada, and a matching grant from the Ontario Network Infrastructure Program, the TFN plans on opening up to the community with up to 100 dial-in phone lines.

The Directory of Community Networking Organizations in Canada in Appendix O includes a listing of most operating Free-Nets in Canada, as well as contacts for the organizing committees for other Free-Nets.

OTHER ORGANIZATIONS AFFECTING THE INTERNET IN CANADA

In Canada, there are a number of other organizations and initiatives which will have a major influence on how the Internet will evolve in Canada. These include CANARIE and the Federal Information Highway committee.

In addition, there are several other organizations or committees in Canada which help to make the Internet "work." Two of these are the CA Domain Registrar and CA*net IP Registry, two groups which are involved in the ongoing administration of the network in Canada.

CANARIE

CANARIE is also an important component of the Canadian Internet scene, even though it is not an Internet service provider.

CANARIE (Canadian Network for the Advancement of Research, Industry and Education), an initiative funded by industry and government, was established in order to further networking in Canada. Funded with some $26 million from the federal government and some $100 million in total, including funds from the private sector, CANARIE includes representatives of CA*net, the federal government and other organizations.

CANARIE's mission is "to support the development of the communications infrastructure for a knowledge-based Canada, and thereby contribute to Canadian competitiveness in all sectors of the economy, to prosperity, to job creation and to our quality of life." CANARIE will play a major role in determining what the Internet is to become in Canada.

CANARIE plans to focus on three areas:

- expanding and upgrading CA*net.

   This goal was largely achieved through 1994, with the implementation of high-speed T1 access on the CA*net network to all regional networks, with the exception of the Yukon and North West Territories. This provides a CA*net network that has approximately 27 times the data capacity of the previous network, based mostly on 56kb lines.

- establishing high-speed experimental test networks.

   This was done in 1994 through the sponsorship of grants of $250,000 each to OCRInet (the Ottawa Carleton Research Network) and Rnet in British Columbia.) These initiatives are networks based on what is known as ATM (Asynchronous Transfer Mode) technology — a blazingly fast networking technology for future local area and wide area networks such as the Internet. While today's local area networks are rated at capacities of 4, 10 or 16 megabites per second (mbs), ATM starts at 155mbs per second and goes all the way to 2,500mbs: an improvement of anywhere from 25 to 625 in the capacity of today's networks. Research into high-speed networking issues in

Canada as funded by CANARIE will help Canadian high-tech companies learn about the many issues associated with such a dramatic change.

- stimulate investment in high-tech networking technologies in Canada.

In 1994, CANARIE awarded funding of $7 million toward some 15 projects, some related to the Internet and others related to high-speed networking as described above.

From a press release issued on February 21, 1994, it was noted that "the $7 million will result in a total investment in the fifteen projects of close to $25 million, with over fifty participating organizations, including universities and research institutions. The CANARIE program provides funding on a 50:50 cost-shared basis to projects which support development of new networking products and applications."

These projects included funding for an effort to develop a method of providing wireless access to Internet news, mail and data transfer services, based on the "Internet Anywhere" product available from Mortice Kern Systems Inc. (MKS), Kitchener, Ontario. More information about this product can be found in Chapter 9. Another grant was provided to Bunyip Information Systems Inc., the developers of the popular Archie program, for the development of a program to be used for accessing and managing information on the Internet.

Other funding was provided for research into high-speed networking issues, including management, development of hardware and software, research and other matters related to upgrading Canada's information infrastructure.

THE INFORMATION HIGHWAY COMMITTEE

On March 16, 1994, Federal Industry Minister John Manley announced the formation of the National Advisory Council on the Information Highway. The group was charged with the responsibility of providing "advice and guidance to the government on how to accelerate the development and implementation of the information highway consistent with the Government's policy objectives and principles."

The committee has a nationally high profile, and has obviously been examining many of the issues related to the information highway in Canada. However, it seems to be focused on issues of who should "own" the highway, and has concentrated much of its efforts on the television-based information highway. Certainly one of its foremost responsibilities has been to discuss and debate the issue of telephone vs. cable company competition in Canada.

The committee will most certainly influence what happens with the Internet in Canada. However, since the first thirty appointees to the committee were primarily senior representatives from Canada's telecommunications, cable, television and telephone industries, the sad reality is that probably few of the Information Highway Committee participants would even know the Internet if they fell over it.

(An informal estimate indicated that certainly fewer than half even had access to Internet e-mail.)

Fortunately, the committee does include at this time the participation of a few Internet representatives, most notably Dave Sutherland from National Capital FreeNet. To his credit and to the credit of other participants like him, Dave has been ensuring that the committee continues to be aware of the significance of the global Internet to the overall development of an "information highway" in Canada. In addition, Industry & Science Canada has been instrumental in seeing that the Internet is used as a vehicle in which information from the committee is made available to average Canadians.

Hopefully, over time, the committee will begin to insure that its plans include a focus on Internet initiatives and less on a highway in which Canadians can order fried chicken with their TV remote control.

CA DOMAIN REGISTRAR

In Chapter 4, we take a look at the "domain name" system, which allows organizations to establish unique addresses on the network (such as **jacc.com** or **yorku.ca,** the domains the two authors of the book can be found in.)

The CA Domain Registrar (currently, John Demco in the Department of Computer Science at the University of British Columbia) is responsible for overseeing all applications for Canadian domain names and for maintaining a database of these registrations. A Domain Registrar committee, which includes representatives from all regional networks and several major commercial Internet providers in Canada, actually approves all new applications for domain names in Canada.

CA*net IP REGISTRY

This organization oversees the allocation of what are known as Class C IP addresses in Canada. This topic is discussed in greater depth in Chapter 4.

U.S. AND INTERNATIONAL INTERNET ORGANIZATIONS

Outside of Canada, there are many other organizations involved in the Internet.

As we have indicated, no one runs or owns the Internet — it is a global network supported by many thousands of participating networks.

However, any cooperative effort of this scope requires a high degree of coordination, standardization and registration. There are a number of organizations responsible for these activities, including the following:

- Internet Society — an organization dedicated to promote the growth of the Internet. The key mission of the Society is "to provide assistance and support to groups involved in the use, operation and evolution of the Internet."

   Anyone can join the Internet Society. For a small fee, you will receive a quarterly newsletter reporting on Internet issues, and can participate in an on-line mailing list to which Internet news and developments are posted.

- Internet Architecture Board — an organization which coordinates research and development into Internet-related issues, and standard setting for Internet activities. The IAB, as it is known, is responsible for the technical evolution of the network.

- Internet Engineering Task Force — A component of the IAB, it develops Internet standards for review by the IAB.

- InterNIC — The Internet Network Information Centre (InterNIC) run by AT&T, General Atomics and Network Solutions, Inc. InterNIC serves as a registrar for Internet domain names and network numbers (as described in the next section), and provides information and directory services concerning the Internet. If you want to register a domain name outside of the Canadian domain (as described in Chapter 4), you can do so through the InterNIC. The InterNIC has established a number of extremely useful Internet services, including several which provide pointers to useful Internet resources from around the world.

- Commercial Internet Exchange (CIX) — CIX is responsible for exchanging Internet traffic directly between commercial Internet providers, thus avoiding any restrictive acceptable use policies. CIX also gets involved in issues having to do with the ongoing commercialization of the Internet.

FINALLY, THOUSANDS OF INDIVIDUALS . . .

As a fellow named Ed Levinson (**levinson@sfu.ca**) pointed out to us after the release of the 1994 edition of this book, "the Internet was created through a spirit of cooperation."

This is most certainly true, and it is important to note that, overall, the Canadian and global Internet exists and functions because of a massive national and worldwide cooperative effort involving the participation of many organizations and many individuals.

In Canada, aside from the many organizations listed above, there is an army of individuals who work with the Canadian Internet infrastructure on a tireless basis, often on a voluntary basis or in addition to their regular job responsibilities, in order to ensure that Canada has a reliable, stable, evolving Internet infrastructure.

As Peter Deutsch, the developer of the program Archie, noted in a column in *Internet World* in March/April 1994, "what appears to tie together this disparate group of connectivity providers, developers, operators, and users is the shared conviction that we're all working on something important."

COMMERCIAL USE OF THE INTERNET

If you are a user of the Internet already, or if you had heard about it previously, no doubt you have come across the term "Acceptable Use Policy" (or "AUP").

You might have heard that you cannot use certain parts of the Internet for commercial purposes. You might be quite confused, as many people are in Canada, as to the status of the Internet today when it comes to doing business on the network.

Certainly, the Internet in its early days was a network which permitted only certain types of use, and was often restricted to the academic and research communities. Today, the Internet remains a global cooperative network made up of the participation of many individual networks, some of which still have an AUP in place, but many of which do not.

In this section, we will help you understand what AUP's are and how they might or might not be relevant to you. We will also describe how AUP's have disappeared (or are in the process of disappearing) to be replaced by "terms and conditions," principles which will guide the evolution of the Internet in the years to come.

In Chapter 10, we discuss the issues of doing business on the Internet, and the importance of respecting the unique Internet "culture" if you plan on using it for business purposes.

ORIGIN OF ACCEPTABLE USE POLICIES

Many of the regional and national Internet networks around the world were originally created and funded by governmental agencies for the specific purpose of linking educational and research institutions. Their mandate was clear: networking should occur in order to enhance local, regional and national research and development (R&D).

As these Internet networks were created in the 1980's, they placed a restriction on what they could be used for — usually education, research or development activities. They specified that they could not be used to make money, nor could they be used to support profit-oriented activities. These restrictions came to be known as Acceptable Use Policies, or AUP's. It should be noted that not all regional networks had a formally spelled out AUP — for example, NSTN in Canada never had one.

Many of these networks put in place their policy in order to conform to a stringent AUP imposed on them through their connectivity to the U.S. NSFNet. As the primary U.S. national academic and research-oriented Internet network, the NSFNet had a very restrictive AUP that limited the type of information that could be transmitted across the network. For example, the NSFNet AUP specifically prohibited "use for for-profit activities (consulting for pay, sales or administration of campus stores, sales of tickets to sports events, and so on) or use by for-profit institutions...." and prohibits "extensive use for private or personal business."

Any network, including regional as well as commercial networks in Canada, had to agree to the terms of the NSFNet AUP if they sought to "plug into it" (which most of them did, since the NSFNet was the "heart" of the global Internet for many years.)

EVOLVING AUP'S

AUP's did not specifically prohibit use of the Internet by commercial organizations — they restricted use to specific purposes.

The result was that a number of commercial companies, primarily computer system vendors, began to use the Internet to provide technical support to organizations involved in research and development — which clearly was not a ban of the AUP. In addition, many defence contractors began to communicate using the NSFNet because they were doing work for the Department of Defense, providing further momentum to TCP/IP-based networks.

Yet, because of these two "loopholes" in the AUP, and because of abuse of the "educational" provisions of the AUP, network usage grew. By the late 1980's, use of the Internet was growing at exponential rates.

It was clear that there was potential for profit-oriented companies to provide Internet networking capabilities, and it was also clear that in many cases the NSFNet AUP was being abused or ignored.

This situation led to the arrival of a number of "commercial Internet providers" in the late 1980s — companies in the business of selling access to the Internet for a profit, to companies that wanted to use the Internet in their profit-directed activities.

As the number of commercial Internet providers grew, they established a Commercial Internet Exchange (or CIX). The creation of CIX permitted these commercial Internet providers to exchange Internet traffic among themselves without ever touching networks with Acceptable Use Policies — thus permitting broad use of the Internet for any purpose whatsoever.

WHAT'S THE STATUS TODAY?

Given the increasing number of methods by which you can access the Internet in Canada, an important question that needs to be asked is: can you use it for commercial purposes, or is it a restricted network?

According to Tony Rutkowski, President of the Internet Society, "it's a non-issue. It's already been commercialized."

The topic of commercialization of the Internet raises the ire of many people on the network. Yet, it really has become an academic question, of interest only to those who like to debate the issue *ad nauseam*. Plain and simply, the Internet is being used for business worldwide — to deny that is to deny reality.

While it is true that the Internet began as a network to support the exchange of information for academic and research purposes, today the Internet has evolved into a global network that is increasingly used by business for commercial purposes. In Canada, we are seeing an increasingly substantial number of corporate organizations obtaining their own Internet network addresses, as indicated in Figure 3.1.[4]

FIGURE 3.1: NETWORK REGISTRATIONS IN THE CANADIAN (.CA) DOMAIN

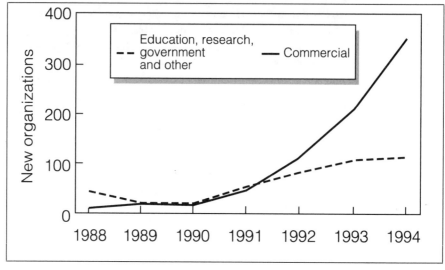

The number of corporate registrations is increasing for a variety of reasons. In some cases, registration has been the result of a conscious decision by an organization to make use of the Internet, while in other cases alert technical staff realize that they had better register the organization name and obtain sufficient networking addresses while there is still time.[5] Still other registrations are due to the ongoing use of the Internet for commercial purposes.

A full list of Canadian organizations with registered Internet domains is included in Appendix P, *Directory of Canadian Organizations with Registered Internet Domains.*

The Status of Commercialization

The result of the commercialization of what was once strictly an academic and research network is that AUP's are in a period of transition, rapidly disappearing as they are replaced by "terms and conditions."

In the U.S., the NSFNet is scheduled to be phased out through late 1994 and early 1995, to be replaced by several of the major commercial networks. NSFNet moneys will go directly to various regional U.S. networks, permitting them to purchase their Internet connectivity from a variety of suppliers, rather than being used to establish one high-speed academic research network. Coincident with the disappearance of NSFNet is the disappearance of its AUP.

In Canada, most regional networks have abandoned or are in the process of abandoning their AUP (if they ever had one in the first place.) As well, there is talk of privatizing CA*net.

The Arrival of Terms and Conditions

An AUP could be considered to be a restriction over network content, as it spells out what you can and cannot send through the network.

In many cases, "content"-based AUP's are being replaced by "terms and conditions," operating agreements or policies which guide your use of the network as a good neighbor to all other Internet participants.

The Internet is recognizing that as it becomes more commercialized it must learn to deal with activities that are not in the best interests of the overall network. Terms and conditions are being put in place so that your use of the Internet does not necessarily have a negative impact on the Internet by your neighbors, who might be customers of the same Internet service provider or users of other Internet services.

Terms and conditions are arising for a number of reasons, one of the primary ones being the fact that some individuals view the Internet as a prime target for "junk mail."

For many reasons, most of which are described in Chapter 10, junk mail on the Internet doesn't work. Flooding the net with junk mail certainly isn't in the interest of ensuring smooth, reliable network traffic on a global basis.

Yet, some *idiots* continue to think that junk mail on the Internet will be successful. Nowhere was this more apparent than in mid-1994 when an Arizona law firm flooded the Internet with a message about an immigration lottery. The Internet rebelled in terror by sending them several hundred thousand e-mail messages of protest, effectively shutting down their access to the network (and shutting down most other users of that particular Internet provider.)

"Terms and conditions" are being put in place to guard against such an abuse of network resources. Increasingly, subscribers to the Internet are being asked to agree to such terms and conditions. As well, several networks are beginning to spell them out in greater depth.

The CA*net AUP as it still exists begins to touch on the issue of "terms and conditions" in section 2 below, and is a good example of the direction that many networks and Internet participants will take over time.

CA*net Mandate, Acceptable Use Policy, and Statement of Regional Responsibility (November, 1990)

Mandate:

CA*net is a national data communications network which exists to support the research, education, and technology transfer missions of its member networks and their client corporations and institutions.

Acceptable Use:

1. All use must be consistent with the mandate of CA*net.

2. Use of the network must avoid:

– interfering with the work of other network users, and

– disrupting the nodes and services of CA*net or any of the connected networks.

3. Use of the network for any illegal purposes, or to achieve unauthorized access to systems, software, or data is prohibited.

Responsibilities of Regional Networks

It is the responsibility of regional networks connected to CA*net to ensure that their acceptable use policy encompasses the acceptable use policy of CA*net and that they ensure that their clients are aware of these policies and agree to abide by them. If a regional network learns that one of its clients is violating the CA*net acceptable use policy then it should take whatever action is necessary to ensure that such violation is halted.

Today, most commercial Internet providers do not have AUP's in place. Few of the regional providers have an AUP left in place. Most are putting in place "terms and conditions."

This brings us back to our original question: can you use the Internet for business purposes?

The answer is yes, if you are not on a network that has an AUP, but you must respect the unique culture of the Internet in doing so. If you do not understand and respect its culture, you will fail in your efforts, and will likely invite the wrath of the global Internet onto your shoulders.

The issue of how to do business on the Internet while respecting its culture is reviewed in greater depth in Chapter 10.

PUBLIC INTERNET FUNDING

In Canada, within the Internet community, there continues to be a debate over the role of government funding to certain of the major regional networks.

Perhaps the easiest way to understand the state of the Internet in Canada with respect to this issue is to understand how e-mail messages are routed between the two authors of this book. The routing is, to say the least, bizarre.

For example, a message between the two authors of this book traveled the route indicated in Figure 3.2.[6] This was still the case in 1994.

FIGURE 3.2: MESSAGE ROUTING

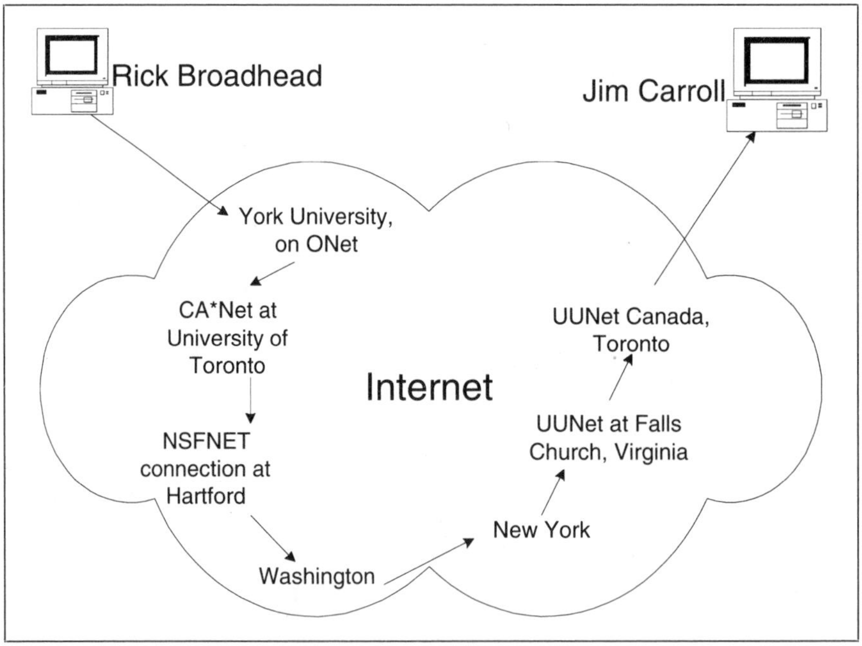

Although such routing does not result in any incremental cost for a message, it does result in additional network complexity, and over time, higher costs overall for organizations participating in the Internet in Canada. In addition, as use of the Internet grows, it has a profound performance impact, particularly when it involves the transfer of large files.

It is not just e-mail that is affected by this routing, but any Internet application.

WHY IS THIS SO?

The reason for this bizarre message routing is the fact that UUNet Canada and ONet, the ultimate providers of Internet services to the two authors of this book (one through his domain, **jacc.com** at UUNet, the other through an ID at York University, a participant in ONet) will not agree to an exchange of information directly between them. Instead, each routes traffic destined to the other through the network links that they have to organizations in the US.

There are no technical barriers to these two organizations agreeing to exchange Internet information directly — for example, *fonorola* and UUNet agreed early in 1994 to exchange information directly, thus bypassing a complex US path.

The barrier that is in the way is the Canadian debate over the role of public Internet funding in Canada, and the role of networks as social policy vs. profit-oriented enterprises.

The issue is a complex and difficult one and is not easily answered.

A PRACTICAL EXAMPLE — ONTARIO

UUNet Canada, *fonorola* and other commercial providers are in the business of selling access to the Internet on a for-profit basis. Organizations such as these find it difficult to understand why they should have to compete in the commercial marketplace against organizations such as ONet, which receive government funding.

If we take a look at Ottawa, for example, a number of government departments have established their Internet link through ONet. UUNet and *fonorola* have been effectively shut out of selling Internet access to the federal government in Ottawa as the result of the activities of ONet, which can offer lower cost access.

From the perspective of commercial providers, the situation becomes worse as ONet becomes a competitor in the commercial marketplace, operating as a cooperative that is funded to some extent with public money.

ONet receives some degree of government funding in support of its operations, in addition to support through member fees. For example, it is the recent recipient of a $5 million grant from the Ontario Network Infrastructure Program. To be provided over three years, $1.6 million of the moneys will be used for ongoing management of the network, $2 million will be spent to upgrade the network to higher speed "T1" lines throughout major areas of the province and $1.4 million will be spent to cover the additional costs associated with the upgrade to a higher speed CA*net network. It is important to note that ONet members, including educational institutions, government bodies and research organizations, will pay another $5 million in member contributions, thus resulting in a total $10 million budget over three years.

ONet takes the position that it is one of the few networking organizations in Canada to take on the role of providing Internet access to locations where commercial Internet providers have no plans to go because of the likelihood of little or no profit. Government policy through initiatives such as the Ontario Network Infrastructure Program (ONIP) encourages networking to remote and smaller communities, and organizations such as ONet have taken up the challenge.

It argues that public funding is necessary to cover its costs of providing Internet access to remote locations and small cities and towns, since it certainly won't earn back its investment through usage or membership fees. In effect, ONet is in a situation in which access to remote regions is subsidized through government grant and through membership fees, because of certain government policy objectives.

What's right and wrong in this case? Certainly the social objectives of ONet are commendable, as its argument about commercial providers ignoring remote regions and smaller locations is true — while major metropolitan centers such as Vancouver and Toronto have seen a wealth of Internet service providers arrive, it can be very difficult to find similar low cost access in Thunder Bay or in Flin Flon, Manitoba.

Quite simply, a high-speed Internet link to locations such as these might not exist for some period of time if left up to the commercial sector.

The question is really one of whether Canada should encourage networking to remote communities through social policy and government funding or leave it up to the commercial sector. There are no easy answers, and everyone will have a different opinion on this issue.

A Direct Link

There is virtually no technical reason preventing ONet and UUNet or ONet and *fonorola* from linking to each other directly. The only thing in the way is a debate about the cost that should be charged for doing so.

From the perspective of ONet and CA*net, moneys have been invested in developing a high-speed national infrastructure supporting networking right across Canada — an expensive undertaking. These organizations would want to charge the commercial providers a fee that represents a fair proportion of the investment that has been made.

From the perspective of organizations like *fonorola* and UUNet, some of this infrastructure has been funded with public moneys, and so it doesn't make sense to charge a fully proportionate fee. Obviously, they would like to establish a more direct link with networks such as ONet in order to avoid having to send messages, as seen in the example above, through their southbound U.S. connection. Yet, they won't do so if the proposed fee is far more than what they currently spend to route the traffic through the US.

To boil the issue down, it's a question of whether organizations such as UUNet and *fonorola* should be expected to share in the full cost of developing a national networking infrastructure that has social purposes, as found in CA*net and ONet, or whether they should pay only a partial cost.

What's right and what's wrong? Once again, its easy to understand both sides of the argument.

One practical result is that ONet refuses to permit UUNet to enjoy the benefits of its publicly funded infrastructure to reduce its own operating costs, and refuses to permit a direct connection unless a full fee is paid.

In the meantime, the debate goes on and bizarre message routing strategies continue.

It's a large and difficult problem, with no easy answers.

WHERE DOES THE MONEY GO?

Many people, when confronted with the complexity of the Internet, wonder where their money goes when they pay their Internet service provider.

When you buy access to the Internet, you buy access to connectivity. Organizations such as ONet, UUNet, Wimsey, NSTN and every other Internet provider, whether they are commercial or non-commercial in nature, sell connectivity.

If you pay your money to UUNet, you are paying for the connectivity that UUNet has established. UUNet and the technical wizards that run it (like the technical wizards at every Internet provider) have used Internet technology, as described in the next chapter, to provide a route from their location to every other location on the Internet.

Thus, you are paying your money for the purchase of connectivity to every other individual and computer that makes up the global Internet. The money doesn't go to some large Internet company somewhere — instead, it is used by your service provider to pay for the infrastructure necessary to supporting connectivity, and hopefully, to make a profit.

THE FUTURE FOR THE INTERNET IN CANADA?

The Internet in Canada is at a point of transformation and is faced with a number of significant issues. Three of the most significant are the arrival of major telecommunications companies into the business of Internet service provision, higher access speeds and continued growth of the network in Canada.

LARGER INTERNET PROVIDERS

Undoubtedly, larger telecommunications companies will get involved in the Internet service provider business.

Already, Bell Canada has signaled its intention to participate through its unregulated Bell Worldlinx subsidiary. In June of 1994, Worldlinx indicated that it planned to begin selling dedicated Internet access to corporations across Canada.

Rogers Communications Inc. began testing access to the Internet through its cable wires in the Toronto area, arranging for its services through UUNet Canada and *fonorola*. It also announced a joint venture with Intel, the world's largest manufacturer of computer processors, to develop a "cable modem," permitting access to on-line services through cable lines. Should it decide to roll out its Internet access service, it will allow the consumer or business to purchase very high speed Internet access through the home or office cable TV wire.

It will take some time for these major players to become comfortable with the Internet and to learn how to work with it. Both Rogers and Bell are organizations that have enjoyed success through the monopoly that they have held in their particular field. Operating in a monopoly marketplace is quite different from operating in a distributed anarchy like the Internet. As a result, organizations like Rogers and Bell have a lot of learning yet to do.

It will take some effort for organizations like this to gain the respect and admiration of the Internet community. The Internet is extremely sensitive about the participation of major telecommunication organizations like Bell and Rogers, and there is a lot of suspicion that their participation will lead to an unhappy change in the nature of the Internet. Charges that they will eventually come to manage content on the network are hurled by some, while others believe that these organizations will seek to position themselves with monopoly control over the network.

These concerns ignore the fact that the Internet is a massive global system with millions of participants. It is a system that is virtually uncontrollable by any one entity. Certainly the global Internet, with some thirty to forty million global participants, won't come to be controlled by relatively small Canadian organizations like Bell Canada and Rogers Communications.

FASTER INTERNET ACCESS

The participation of companies like Bell and Rogers will lead to a situation in which higher speed Internet access to the home and business will be available much sooner. In many cases, their participation will be limited to being providers of a high-speed link that other Internet service providers might provide.

Tests of cable Internet access in the Toronto area are already demonstrating that it is entirely possible to have an extremely fast Internet link directly into the home or office via cable line. Although pricing is yet to be worked out, this could be an extremely positive offering in the near future.

On the other hand, Bell Canada and other telephone companies across Canada are slowly discovering that a technology that they have talked about for ten years is gaining interest. ISDN (which stands for Integrated Services Digital Network) access will provide home or business access to the Internet at speeds some four to ten times faster than the currently fastest available dial-up modem in the marketplace. In the Toronto marketplace, HookUp Communications and UUNet Canada already sell ISDN-based access to the Internet.

MORE USAGE

Internet initiatives continue to gain momentum in Canada.

In the field of education, we have seen announcements and statements of intent by several provinces to see every elementary and high school linked to the network in the next several years. We have seen John Manley, the closest thing to a champion for the Internet in Ottawa, announce a plan to provide one-stop access to government information through the Internet. We continue to see a headlong rush into Internet connectivity by major organizations in Canada.

Quite clearly, in many ways, we are at a very early stage with the Internet in Canada. To paraphrase a popular song from Bachman Turner Overdrive, a popular rock band of the eighties, "you ain't seen nothin yet."

---

1. Bulletin board systems, or BBS, are computer networks accessible by modem. Usually established by hobbyists, they provide access to computer files, games, electronic mail, discussion groups and other services.

2. From "ONet — Designing for the Future," March 1993, a document submitted to the Ontario Government with respect to a grant application under the Ontario Network Infrastructure Program.

3. The proper title for the organization is CA*net Networking Inc. For purposes of brevity, CA*net is used throughout the book.

4. This chart is for those organizations in the Canadian domain, and is from information maintained by CA*net. In Chapter 4, we review the "domain naming" system in further depth. It should be noted that organizations registering in the Canadian (.ca) domain are not the only organizations in Canada using the Internet. This chart is current as of September 1994.

5. As previously mentioned, the Internet is based upon TCP/IP networking protocols. These protocols include the use of "IP addresses," which are addresses of four sets of numbers, separated by periods, i.e.; 121.2.11.5. IP addressing is discussed in greater depth in Chapter 4, including discussion of the fact that there is an upper limit on the number of available IP addresses.

6. A key reason for the success of the Internet is that information is easily re-routed through the network, thus making the Internet literally failure-proof. For example, if any system in the example were unavailable, an alternate route would be automatically found.

INTERNET FUNDAMENTALS

I don't think there is a realistic view of how to build a global communication network other than, pretty much at this point, the Internet. I think the Internet guys who are — maybe we're all suffering from delusions of grandeur — but we're at least thinking about what the whole system is going to look like as a system, and trying to design a sysem from the top down that has those capabilities.

Noel Chiappa, architect of the Proteon router, when asked about cable companies, telephone companies and the information highway.

*Excerpt from Geek of the Week, a weekly radio show distributed through the Internet.
Copyright 1994, Internet Multicasting Service.*

In this chapter, we examine the fundamental protocol of the Internet, TCP/IP, including an overview of the Internet Domain Name System. We also examine the "client/server" model of computing. Finally, we will bring these two pieces together by taking a look at the role of Internet Domain Name servers, to give you a bit of an idea of how the Internet "works."

The Internet Domain Name System will have an impact on every Internet tool that you might use, from Internet e-mail, to systems like Archie, Gopher and WAIS. As a result, it's important that you have an understanding of what makes up Internet domain names.

Understanding the client/server model as it affects the Internet will help you understand the reasons for some of the limitations that might exist on your use of the Internet.

Finally, understanding domain name servers might answer some of your curiosity about how the Internet knows to get you from your location to somewhere else out there.

TCP/IP BASICS

The Internet is based on a computer networking protocol known as TCP/IP (Transmission Control Protocol/Internet Protocol), developed as part of the original ARPANET initiative described in the previous chapter.

The TCP/IP protocol includes the use of numeric IP addresses and Domain Names. An example of a numeric IP address is **131.162.2.77**. An example of a name under the Domain Name system is **vm1.yorku.ca**.

The IP address and Domain Name system form the heart of the global Internet.

WHY IS THIS IMPORTANT?

As you travel the Internet, you will often see phrases such as **Telnet to 131.162.2.77** or **ftp to ftp.cdnnet.ca.** This means that you will use either the numeric IP address or domain name when you establish a link to another computer on the Internet. Specific Internet applications that you might use, including e-mail, FTP or Telnet, will use IP addresses and Domain Names. This requires that you have some understanding of the IP addressing and Domain Name scheme.

IP ADDRESSES

An IP address is a fundamental component of the TCP/IP networking protocol.

IP addresses consist of four sets of numbers separated by periods. For example, a particular computer at Acadia University in Nova Scotia has the IP address **131.162.2.77.** The address is unique throughout the Internet world, and will be used by individuals and by Internet applications to reach Acadia University.

Think of an IP address as being the Internet equivalent to a telephone number, since it refers to the address of a specific computer on the Internet. Originally, you had to use IP addresses with various Internet applications; however, the Internet domain name system described below is now used almost exclusively in that regard. Hence, in most circumstances, you are not expected to directly use IP addresses.

The current IP numbering scheme allows for what are known as Class A, B and C addresses. Class A addresses are allocated only to the largest organizations or networks. At the other end of the spectrum, Class C addresses are used by smaller or medium-sized organizations or networks.

In many cases, multiple Class C addresses are used by one organization. This is particularly true as the Internet continues to grow. Under the current IP address protocol, there is an upper limit on the number of potential A, B and C addresses.[1]

HOW DO I KNOW IF I NEED AN IP ADDRESS?

The question as to whether you need your own IP address will have to do with how you plan on accessing the Internet.

If you plan on linking the networks in your organization "directly" to the Internet at some time, you will need an IP address. An IP address is fundamental to establishing this direct link, as it provides a unique identity for your network in the global Internet.[2] Registered IP addresses in Canada are obtained from the CA*net IP Registry, as detailed below.

If you plan on accessing the Internet through what is known as a SLIP account, you will need an IP address. This will usually be assigned to you by your Internet service provider.

If you access the Internet in any other way (i.e., usually through a dial-up modem, through a bulletin board, through what is known as a "shell account," or through an "e-mail gateway,") you do not need an IP address. In this case, IP addresses will not be terribly important to you other than as a means of reaching certain Internet resources.

HOW DO I GET AN IP ADDRESS IF I NEED ONE?

Organizations in Canada desiring an IP address must obtain it from the CA*net IP Registry, which has been allocated a set of numbers by the InterNIC for use within Canada. At this time, only Class C addresses are available for use in Canada.

Appendix F contains the form *Canadian Internet Protocol Network Number Application for Class C Network Number(s)*, which should be used by Canadian organizations wishing to obtain an IP address.

OBTAINING THIS APPLICATION FORM BY FTP

Using Anonymous FTP	
FTP site:	ftp.canet.ca
Directory:	Select:
	canet
	templates
File:	ip-req.txt

OBTAINING IT BY E-MAIL

Using E-mail	
Send message to:	ipregist@canet.ca

Keep in mind that since there is an upper limit in the number of available IP addresses as mentioned above, and although solutions are in the works, the best advice is — if your organization does not yet have a registered IP address and you plan on linking your network directly to the Internet at some point in the future, plan ahead and get one now.

INTERNET DOMAIN NAMES

Since people often remember names better than they do numbers, the people involved in the Internet came up with the Domain Name System. This permits each computer (referred to as a "host") on the Internet to be reached by a simple name rather than just by IP addresses.

Internet applications such as Telnet, FTP and gopher can be used with either an IP address or a host name based on the Domain Name System to reach a particular computer.

You should always use the domain name in order to avoid any problems that might occur in case a particular Internet resource is moved from one computer to another.

THE DOMAIN NAME SYSTEM

Figures 4.1 and 4.2 give some examples of the registered names for several Canadian organizations.

As we can see in Figure 4.1, several Canadian organizations have registered in what is known as the Canadian domain, and have **.ca** at the end or their domain name. In Figure 4.2, we can see that a number of other Canadian organizations have registered in other domains known as **.com**, .org, .net, .edu and .gov.

FIGURE 4.1: ORGANIZATIONS IN THE "CANADIAN .CA DOMAIN"

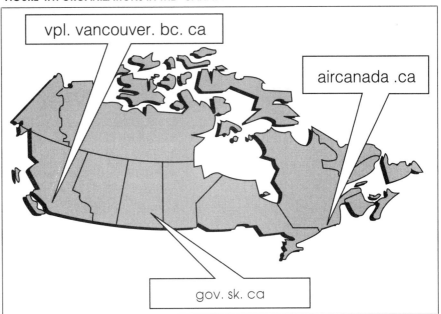

FIGURE 4.2: ORGANIZATIONS IN THE TOP-LEVEL "ZONE NAMES"

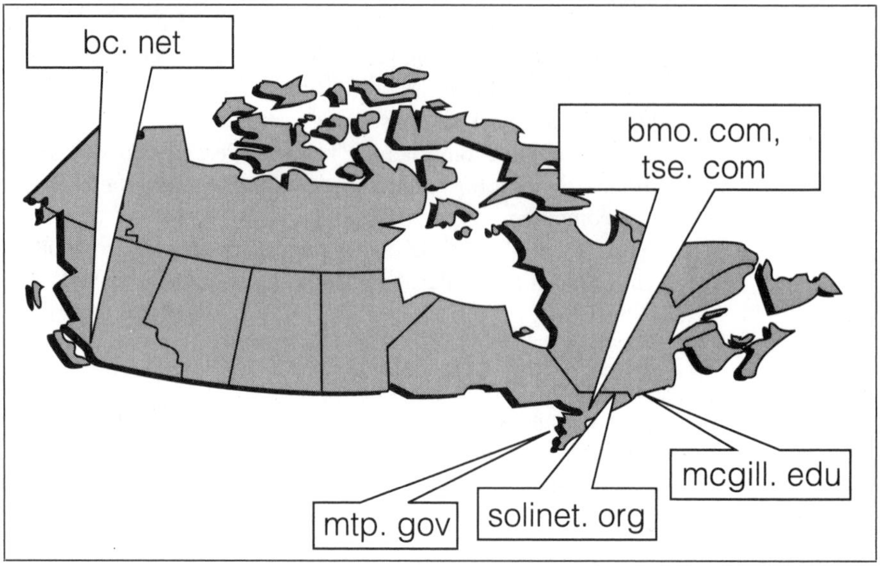

These organizations include:

Domain name	Organization
aircanada.ca	Air Canada
gov.sk.ca	Government of Saskatachewan
vpl.vancouver.bc.ca	Vancouver Public Library
bmo.com	Bank of Montreal
mtp.gov	Metropolitan Toronto Police
solinet.org	Canadian Union of Pubic Employees
mcgill.edu	McGill University, Montreal
tse.com	Toronto Stock Exchange

WHAT TYPE OF DOMAIN NAME WILL YOU HAVE?

If you purchase a dial-up Internet account that you will access by modem for your own use, often your account will be assigned to the existing domain of your Internet service provider. For example, if you get a dial-up Internet account from the B.C.-based provider Mindlink, you will be assigned to the domain **mindlink.bc.ca**. If you obtain an account from InfoRamp, you will be assigned to the domain **inforamp.net**. Using the examples above, your Internet e-mail ID would look like **YOUR-NAME@mindlink.bc.ca** or **YOUR**

NAME@inforamp.net, depending on the provider you were using. **YOUR-NAME** will, of course, be replaced by your personal account name.

YOUR OWN DOMAIN NAME

If you plan on linking your organization to the Internet, you can obtain an Internet domain name for your organization — usually for a small fee. This involves registering in either the Canadian domain or registering in one of the "descriptive zone names."

You might want to have your own Internet domain name, primarily as a means of establishing to your customers, trading partners, business associates or others that you are serious about the role you plan to have the Internet play in your organization.

The *Directory of Canadian Internet Providers* in Appendix C provides information on which providers offer domain name registration service and what fee applies, if any.

TOP-LEVEL DOMAINS

As can be seen in Figures 4.1 and 4.2, at the right-most portion of every Internet host name is a top-level domain, which is either:

- a country code

  Country codes are two-character codes, as defined by the International Standards Organization. The country code for Canada is **.ca.**

  or

- a descriptive zone name

  These descriptive zone names include the following categories:

.com	Commercial organizations
.edu	Educational institutions or sites
.gov	Government institutions or sites
.int	International organizations (i.e., NATO)
.mil	Military sites
.net	Network organizations; often used by organizations reselling Internet services
.org	Other organizations

CHOOSING WHERE TO REGISTER

The choice of whether your organization should register in the Canadian (.**ca**) domain or within one of the descriptive zone names as outlined above depends on several factors, mostly having to do with the image your organization wishes to create with respect to its Internet domain name.

If you want to create an international image, and don't necessarily want to create an image of being a strictly Canadian organization, you would choose to register in one of the descriptive zone names. If, on the other hand, you mostly do business in Canada, you might choose to register in the Canadian domain.

A few examples help illustrate this fact:

- Delrina Corporation is a Toronto-based software company known internationally for its award-winning products, including WinFax Pro. Because of the fact that it has an international image as opposed to a strictly Canadian image, it chose to register as **delrina.com**.

- Air Canada does business around the world, but it wants to create an image that is closely linked to its home base, Canada. As a result, it registered in the Canadian domain as **aircanada.ca**.

- BRK Brands Canada, which distributes the First Alert series of home safety products as well as other products, primarily does business in Canada. As a result, it chose to register in the Canadian domain as **brkbrands.ca**.

It isn't just an issue of national or international image when it comes to registration. Looking at Figure 4.2, we can see that some organizations have registered outside of the .**ca** domain, when we might think they should have registered in the Canadian domain (for example, McGill University, in the .**edu** domain).

Several Canadian organizations have chosen to register in the descriptive zone names for several reasons, including:

- Historical reasons. For example, several educational institutions registered in the .**edu** domain prior to the establishment of a Canadian (.**ca**) domain, and have kept that domain name.

- It indicates the organization type. Some choose to register in the .**org** or .**gov** descriptive zone names instead of the Canadian domain name as they believe it helps them indicate to the Internet community the type of organization they are. A commonly used zone name, .**net**, is used by many Internet service providers in Canada (i.e., **hookup.net**, **inforamp.net**.)

- They can't register the name they wanted in the .**ca** domain. Some organizations chose to register in the descriptive zones because their proposed name wasn't accepted by the Canadian authorities. For example, the Addiction Research Foundation registered as **arf.org**, because the Canadian Domain Committee did not believe **arf.ca** to be an acceptable name.

- Frustration with the current Canadian domain name system. In particular, smaller organizations which are required to use provincial and municipal subdomains as described below often do not like the complex names that might arise, for example, **prince-rupert.bc.ca.** As a result, some organizations turn to the InterNIC to register directly within a **.com** or **.org** domain.

Certainly, when it comes to registration of a domain name on the Internet, diversity is the watchword!

REGISTERING UNDER THE CANADIAN (.CA) DOMAIN

If your organization registers in the *Canadian domain*, your Domain Name might include *provincial* and *municipal* domains. A *company* or *organization* name is also included.

Figure 4.1 provides examples of several organizations which have registered in the Canadian (or **.ca**) domain. The names used by two of the organizations use *subdomains*.

In Canada, under the **.ca** domain, a geographically oriented *subdomain* hierarchy is used. This means the domain name that you can obtain will be determined by the scope or presence of your organization within Canada.

Subdomains, when used, include:

- a provincial code, i.e., **.sk** for Saskatchewan in the example in Figure 4.1.

- a city or municipality name, i.e., **vancouver** in the example in Figure 4.1.

The Canadian Domain Registrar provides the following rules of guidance to determine what type of subdomain name an organization can obtain in Canada:

- if the organization is national in scope, i.e., has presence in more than one province, or is incorporated or chartered nationally, the name of the company is used with the .ca domain name, i.e., **aircanada.ca.**

- if the organization is based in only one province, but has multiple locations in the province, the province name is included, i.e., **gov.sk.ca.**

- if the organization is small and based in only one jurisdiction, the municipality name is included in the subdomain name, i.e., **vpl.vancvouver.bc.ca.**

The following codes are used within Canadian subdomains for provinces and territories in Canada.

Code	For organizations registered in:
.ab	Alberta
.bc	British Columbia
.mb	Manitoba

.nb	New Brunswick
.nf	Newfoundland
.ns	Nova Scotia
.nt	North West Territories
.on	Ontario
.pe	Prince Edward Island
.qc	Quebec
.sk	Saskatchewan
.yk	Yukon

Registration under the Canadian (**.ca**) domain is coordinated by the CA Domain Registrar, currently John Demco at the Department of Computer Science at the University of British Columbia.

Appendix F includes the document *Internet Forms*, which provides full details for registering with the Canadian **.ca** domain. You can obtain this document by using FTP or e-mail.

Using Anonymous FTP	
FTP site:	ftp.cdnnet.ca
Directory:	ca-domain
File:	application-form

Using E-mail	
Send message to:	archive-server@relay.cdnnet.ca
In text of message, type:	send ca-domain application-form

Most Internet service providers in Canada offer domain name registration services, and will fill out and submit the form for you for a nominal fee. Filling out the form on your own can be difficult, particularly if you are not familiar with the nuances of the Internet.

Even if you retrieve this form and fill it out yourself, you should not send a registration application directly to the CA Domain Registrar. Instead, you should submit the form to your Internet service provider.

Once received, your application is reviewed by the CA Domain Committee and you are informed, usually within two weeks, as to whether your application has been accepted with the name you requested, or if changes are suggested.

You should keep in mind that you should usually seek guidance from your Internet service provider about the name you plan on choosing, as they will be best able to let you know whether the name you have selected will be acceptable to the committee.

REGISTRATIONS UNDER A DESCRIPTIVE ZONE NAME

You follow a different process if you choose to register within one of the descriptive zone names (i.e., **.com**, **.edu**, etc.)

In this case, you register directly with InterNIC Registration Services, a component of the Internet Network Information Centre. You would usually do this through your Internet service provider. Much more flexibility in your domain name is possible, since it can consist of a domain name of up to twenty-four characters, followed by the three-character descriptive zone name, i.e. **.com**, **.edu**, etc.

If you would like to understand how to register directly in one of these descriptive zone names, you can obtain the document **domain-template.txt,** by using FTP or Gopher.

Using Gopher	
Site:	rs.internic.net
Path:	Select:
	Internic Registration Services
	Internic Registrations Archives
	Templates
File:	domain-template.txt

FTP site:	rs.internic.net
Directory:	templates
File:	domain-template.txt

Completion of these forms requires some technical knowledge about the Internet. We recommend once again that you get your Internet service provider to complete and submit the forms on your behalf.

OTHER ISSUES RELATED TO DOMAIN NAMES

There are two other issues related to the Domain Name System.

- There are many organizations not yet directly on the Internet; i.e., they do not have a computer that directly connects to the Internet, and hence cannot be directly reached via the Internet.[3]

  Yet, these organizations might desire to link their internal e-mail system into the Internet using their own domain name. In order to do this, they must have a name registered on the Internet.

To get around this dilemma, the concept of an MX (Mail Exchange) record was introduced, which allows an organization to obtain and use a name for purposes of e-mail.

Accordingly, as we examine the domain name scheme, keep in mind that any organization, even if it is not directly linked to the Internet, can participate in the Internet Domain Name System.

- There is nothing to prevent an organization from registering within multiple domains. For example, the University of Toronto can be found with the subdomain names **utoronto.ca** and **toronto.edu.** The Internet service provider *f*onorola has both **fonorola.net** and **fonorola.ca.**

- The continued rapid growth of the Internet means that many domain names are being claimed very quickly. As a general rule, you should plan on reserving a name for your organization as quickly as possible, even if you do not have plans to link your organization to the Internet in the near future. This will help to prevent having some other organization with a similar name from reserving the name you might want.

You might even consider reserving the name with both the Canadian Domain Registrar and with the InterNIC so that both options are available to you in the future.

Appendix P, the *Directory of Canadian Organizations with Registered Internet Domains*, contains a complete listing of the domain names used by Canadian organizations.

CLIENT/SERVER COMPUTING AND THE INTERNET

In the chapters that follow, we'll take a look at major Internet applications:

- Chapter 5: Internet Electronic Mail (e-mail)

- Chapter 6: Knowledge Networking, using applications such as Internet mailing lists and USENET

- Chapter 7: Remote Access Applications, such as Telnet and FTP

- Chapter 8: Knowledge Retrieval Applications, such as Gopher, Hytelnet, Archie and World Wide Web

If you read computer magazines or work in the industry, you will be inundated with articles that mention client/server computing.

To understand how you might make use of the these applications in different software environments, it's important to understand the client/server model of computing.

A TECHNICAL DEFINITION OF CLIENT/SERVER COMPUTING

In the client/server computing model, a client computer runs a program that acts on behalf of a user to access data located on a server computer. It's really that straightforward.

FIGURE 4.3: CLIENT/SERVER MODEL

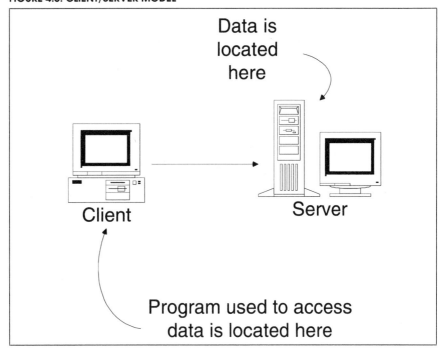

The client computer contains the program that formulates a query or runs a program, while the server contains the horsepower and capability to access the data it stores.

A client can be used to access any number of server applications, resulting in more flexible application design capabilities. Likewise, a single server can service a number of clients.

The client/server model is at the heart of the Internet, as:

- each participant in the Internet is a client;

- each resource on the Internet is located on a server somewhere in the world.

When you use various Internet applications, the location of the client that you use will often have a direct effect on:

- how an Internet application is used;

- how easy it is to use;

- what the application looks like as you use it;

- the speed with which the application runs.

Although it is not a hard and fast rule, it can be said that those who are considered to be directly connected to the Internet can use a far greater number of sophisticated Internet clients and hence will enjoy much easier use of the Internet, than those who are not directly connected to the Internet.

METHODS OF ACCESSING THE INTERNET

Only certain individuals on the Internet are considered to be "directly connected" to the network.

In Chapter 9, we take an in-depth look at the ways you can link yourself or your organization to the Internet. This will include examination of five basic methods of establishing Internet connectivity, as seen in the following diagram:

FIGURE 4.4: METHODS OF LINKING TO THE INTERNET

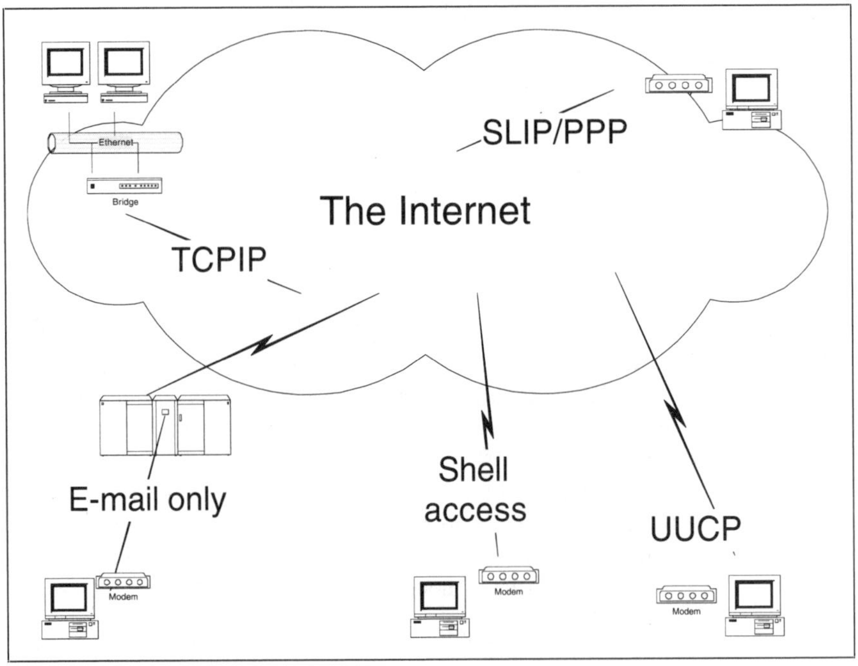

The type of connection impacts on the capabilities of the user:

- Those who only send and receive e-mail to the Internet are not "directly connected" to the Internet and can do little else besides sending and receiving e-mail.

- Users of UUCP are not "directly connected" to the Internet and can do no more than Internet e-mail and participate in USENET newsgroups.

- Individuals with a shell account are not "directly connected" to the Internet.

If you have such a connection, the "client" software that you will use is usually located on your Internet service provider, resulting in limitations in the sophistication of the programs that you can use. If your Internet service provider does not provide a client for a particular Internet application, you can use the Internet capability known as Telnet to link to a site that does have a client you can use, again limiting the sophistication and ease of use in what you can do.

- Individuals on networks that have a "hardwired" (i.e., permanent) TCP/IP network connection to the Internet are considered to be "directly" on the Internet. As well, individuals or networks with SLIP or PPP access via a dial-up modem are also considered to be "directly" on the Internet.

Individuals with such direct connectivity can use many of the more sophisticated and useful versions of client software when interacting with the Internet, and hence, will enjoy greater ease of use with the network. In particular, it is only these individuals who can use Mosaic, which is the client application certainly gaining the most attention on the Internet. Mosaic is detailed in Chapter 8.

If you have such a connection, you are running the "client" software directly on your own computer.

SHELL ACCOUNTS VS. SLIP/TCP/IP ACCOUNTS

Because the "communications software" used to dial into a shell account does not involve the use of TCP/IP, a shell account user will often find that the Internet is difficult to deal with and learn. Although most major Internet applications, including Gopher, FTP and Archie, can be used, they are accessed using a client located at the Internet service provider or elsewhere on the Internet. Since the client is not on the PC of the user, it is less sophisticated and more difficult to use.

On the other hand, individuals with dial-up SLIP access to the Internet or those who have a direct network link can run most clients directly on their own PC, since they are using TCP/IP. This means that they can use many of the easy to use Windows and Mac-based Internet applications, including Mosaic, making their use of the Internet much more straightforward.

The result of this is that when it comes to dial-up access to the Internet, SLIP accounts are in great demand, with a lessening of demand for shell account access.

Keep in mind that as a general rule you need a relatively powerful computer (in the DOS world, 80386 or better) to access a SLIP account, while any computer can be used to access a shell account. Hence, shell account access is still very important and very worthwhile.

HOW DOES THE INTERNET WORK?

The Internet works because IP addresses, the Domain Name System, and client/server computing come together in a method that permits your computer on the Internet to access any other computer on the Internet that has been made available as a resource.[4]

IP addresses and domain names are at the heart of the method the Internet uses to permit you to send an electronic mail message to someone else, or to give you the ability to link to another computer somewhere else on the Internet in order to access information.

Key to this is the use of a hardware (or sometimes software) device known as a router, and the use of a Domain Name Service (DNS), a specialized distributed database found throughout the Internet.

THE ROLE OF IP ADDRESSES

When you establish a "direct connection" from your network to the Internet, you put in place a hardware device known as a router. The router defines how information from your network (known as "packets") should be sent from your internal network to the outside, global Internet.

The router defines the physical devices that can be reached at your network, and establishes a link to your Internet provider.

Usually your router will define that any "packets" destined for IP addresses outside of your organization should be sent to your Internet service provider.

THE ROLE OF A DOMAIN NAME SERVER

A Domain Name Server (DNS) provides an IP address for a request that is made based on a domain name. By doing so, it helps route your request to the appropriate destination.

A DNS is like a phone book that interprets an address you type in (which might be an IP address or domain name), looks it up in a Domain Name Server (a database of Domain Names) and determines the IP address for the destination. The Domain Name Service in effect takes care of figuring out how to get from your location to the location (or server) that contains the information you want, based on what you requested with your software (or client).

All Internet service providers and most organizations with direct Internet connectivity establish a DNS in order to support their participation in the network.

A WORKING EXAMPLE

In this example, we look at how the router and DNS work for an individual who has a direct connection to the Internet.

The concepts are very similar for an individual with dial-up shell access to the network, except the client is usually located at the Internet service provider.

Let's say you want to use an application known as FTP to retrieve a file from a computer somewhere on the Internet. We'll take a look at this in a *greatly simplified example*.

The three PC's at the top of the following diagram, the UNIX server, the firewall and the router, are all components of your own local area network. The role of each of these components is discussed further in Chapter 9.

You usually use FTP by using your FTP client to type in the address of the FTP server you want to access; i.e. **ftp.cdnnet.ca**. (We review FTP in detail in Chapter 7.)

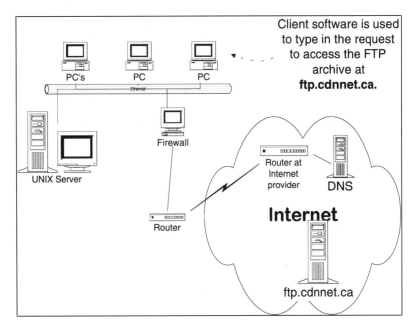

Your request is examined by your client software, which determines that this is not a request for a file from your local area network. The router at your location "routes" the request to your Internet service provider using the IP protocol.

The Domain Name Server at your Internet service provider is then queried to figure out how to establish a link to the resource **ftp.cdnnet.ca**. In effect, it looks up the IP address for that location.

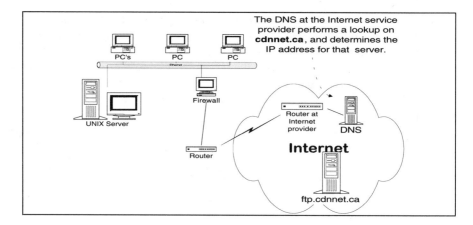

Having done so, it then opens a link to this location using the IP address of the **ftp.cdnnet.ca** location.

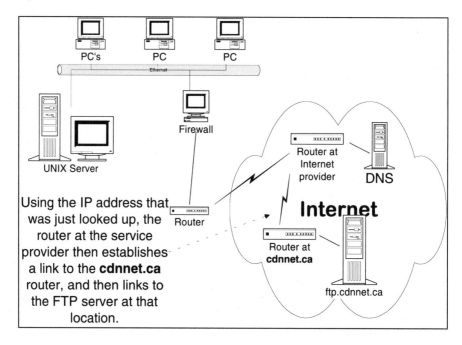

Your client software then retrieves the file and then closes the connection.

This router-to-router link uses TCP/IP networking to establish the link via any possible number of communication technologies.

What makes this work behind the scenes isn't really important to you as an Internet user — the magic of the Internet is that it does.

Routers, combined with the Domain Name Service, are really the components that make the Internet work. Routers provide the ability to "route" information through the global Internet, while DNS provides a common means of identifying the "route" that should be followed. Together, these two components provide no less than a global directory and a global "switchboard" that define how any computer on the Internet can be linked to any other computer on the Internet.

---

1. Although a solution to this problem does not yet exist, there are a number of alternatives being examined by the Internet community to solve the problem. Current thinking is that the Internet is not in any serious danger of completely running out of these addresses for some time.

2. Although an organization with a private TCP/IP network can use any set of IP numbers it wishes, those that participate in the global Internet must obtain a registered IP address in order to provide a unique identity to the rest of the Internet. There have been a number of organizations with private TCP/IP networks that encountered substantial difficulty when they tried to join the Internet, since they had not obtained registered IP addresses from the InterNIC or its predecessors. Keep in mind that you can also use a set of "hidden network numbers," specially reserved IP addresses any organizaton can use, as long as their internal network cannot be reached by the outside Internet.

3. Even so, these organizations might have obtained an IP address from InterNIC or the CA*net Domain Registry to prepare themselves for eventual direct connectivity to the Internet.

4. Most organizations that establish a "direct connection" to the Internet also establish a "firewall," which restricts access from the outside world to only certain servers. This i.s discussed in more depth in Chapter 9. The diagrams that follow are repeated in Chapter 9, with an explanation given to each component not explained here.

C H A P T E R   5

· ·

INTERNET ELECTRONIC MAIL

Probably by the turn of the century, E-mail is going to be as much a part of people's lives as answering machines and cable TV.

Mailbox runneth over? You must be using E-mail
Los Angeles Times, Mon 11 Apr 94

In an age of information highways, multimedia, CD-ROM and other exciting technologies, electronic mail or e-mail can seem decidedly dull.

Although it might be new to you, there are a lot of people in Canada and around the world who have used e-mail for several years to send messages within their company. Since it is a technology that has been with us for some fifteen years or more, many people just can't get excited about it.

Yet, establish a personal mailbox on the Internet and something magical happens — you discover that you can reach out to the world. Link a corporate e-mail network to the Internet, and an organization discovers that many of its business activities can be made more straightforward through the sheer efficiency of global Internet e-mail.

Internet e-mail has established a new method for people and organizations to communicate around the globe.

GROWTH OF INTERNET E-MAIL

In Feb 1993, 476 million messages were transmitted via the Internet, which was double the number sent in 1992. By Feb 1994, the number doubled again, rising to 837 million.

Mailbox runneth over? You must be using E-mail
Los Angeles Times, Mon 11 Apr 94

Many organizations have discovered that a link to Internet e-mail is the most useful application of all Internet capabilities.

The reason for this is that e-mail is the only application that extends well beyond the boundaries of the real Internet, and involves many other e-mail systems and many different technologies.

Read the press today, and you will likely see an Internet e-mail ID. Watch TV, and you might notice that popular TV shows are starting to list them. Get a business card from someone, and you might notice that an Internet address is listed.

With a simple Internet e-mail address, it is estimated that you can reach some 60 million people around the globe.

Internet e-mail is entering popular culture and has quickly become as essential for some business and personal relationships as the fax number was in the mid-80's.

The Internet has become the de facto method for the exchange of e-mail between people, between companies and between organizations around the world.

INTERNET E-MAIL IN CANADA

Canada is very much at the forefront in the massive adoption of Internet e-mail. In a survey in *Electronic Mail and Microsystems* (EMMS) on January 1, 1994, a publication which examines the global e-mail industry, Canada was listed in fifth place in terms of the number of e-mailboxes (1.7 million) and the estimate of how many of them had access to Internet e-mail (600,000).

There is an increasing trend for individuals and organizations to publicize their Internet e-mail address, or to link their organizational e-mail systems to the Internet. Examples are many in Canada; for example:

• popular columnist Gary Dunford of the *Toronto Sun* (**pagesix@aol.com**)

"As the guy who writes the *Toronto Sun's* daily page six column of politics, entertainment and opinion, it's handy to have a simple, easy-to-remember e-mail address where readers can contact the column," notes Gary. "Much of my daily e-mail is people seeking further info or contacts for items that appear in the column; many use it to supply info or leads; increasingly, many publicists and companies using media lists use it for publicity or news releases."

Gary is noticing that the trend to use the Internet is gaining momentum. "Increasingly, the people who normally would be most likely to supply material to the column have access to e-mail through the Internet, academic systems and commercial on-line services. It's also the most convenient way for me to organize quick, same-day responses."

- Over 6,000 users at George Westons, a major Canadian food, retail and resource conglomerate, can send and receive Internet e-mail. These individuals, located in some seventy offices across North America, and in Australia, the UK, Hong Kong and Bermuda, can use a newly implemented e-mail link to the Internet to reach the outside world.

Approximately 10% of those linked to the system are already using Internet e-mail to communicate for personal and business needs.

Pharid Jaffer (**pnj@weston.ca**), the Director of Information Systems in the corporate office of George Westons, notes that "Increasingly, we are using the Internet for e-mail communications with our customers and business partners. In addition, many of the senior personnel at George Weston Limited will have their Internet address displayed on their business cards!"

- In an amusing story about Internet e-mail, Michael Nekechuk, Manager of Electronic Commerce Strategy at Canada Post, (**ap915@freenet. carleton.ca**), reports that "While I was at work reviewing postings on the EDInet related to my work at Canada Post, I had a need to talk with my wife. After many unsuccessful attempts to get through by phone, always a busy signal, I began to suspect that my 10-year-old son Devon was logged on to the National Capital Free-Net reading the computer games SIG postings.

"Acting on my suspicions, I quickly composed an e-mail and sent it off to my Free-Net account requesting that Devon temporarily relinquish the only voice line to the household. Having only one phone line and a son who, like the rest of us loses track of time when interest is high, the Internet was my only connection to my family and it worked."

In December 1993, *The Matrix*, a newsletter which reviews Internet developments, estimated that anywhere from 34.5 million to 69.1 million people around the world were using e-mail systems somehow linked to the Internet.[1]

Even though many of these people would not be aware that they have such a link to the Internet, a lot of organizations are beginning to exploit the connectivity that they already have, as we saw in Chapter 2.[2]

The result is an ever-increasing use of Internet e-mail for all kinds of business, social, personal and organizational communications.

The practical impact of the rapid adoption of Internet e-mail is that those individuals without an Internet e-mail address are feeling a little left out — and feel compelled to get one.

WHAT IS INTERNET E-MAIL?

Internet e-mail addresses are based on the Internet Domain Name System described in Chapter 4, which provides for standard format addresses to be used throughout the network. It's easy to recognize an Internet e-mail address — it is usually of the form **someone@somewhere**; for example, **jcarroll@jacc.com.**

A strict definition of Internet e-mail is that it consists of e-mail sent and received from computers directly connected to the Internet.

However, that definition is unworkable today, given the number of other systems connecting to the Internet.

The simple fact of the matter is that Internet e-mail, because of its easily recognized address, is increasingly used for inter-organizational communications, and is rapidly emerging as the backbone of a globally linked e-mail network.

Many different types of e-mail technologies are now being linked to the Internet. These systems include:

- local area network, or LAN-based e-mail systems

Many organizations are actively implementing LAN-based e-mail systems, such as Microsoft MSMail, Lotus cc:Mail, Lotus Notes and WordPerfect Office, to support exchange of e-mail within the companies.

FIGURE 5.1: E-MAIL SYSTEMS CONNECTED TO THE INTERNET

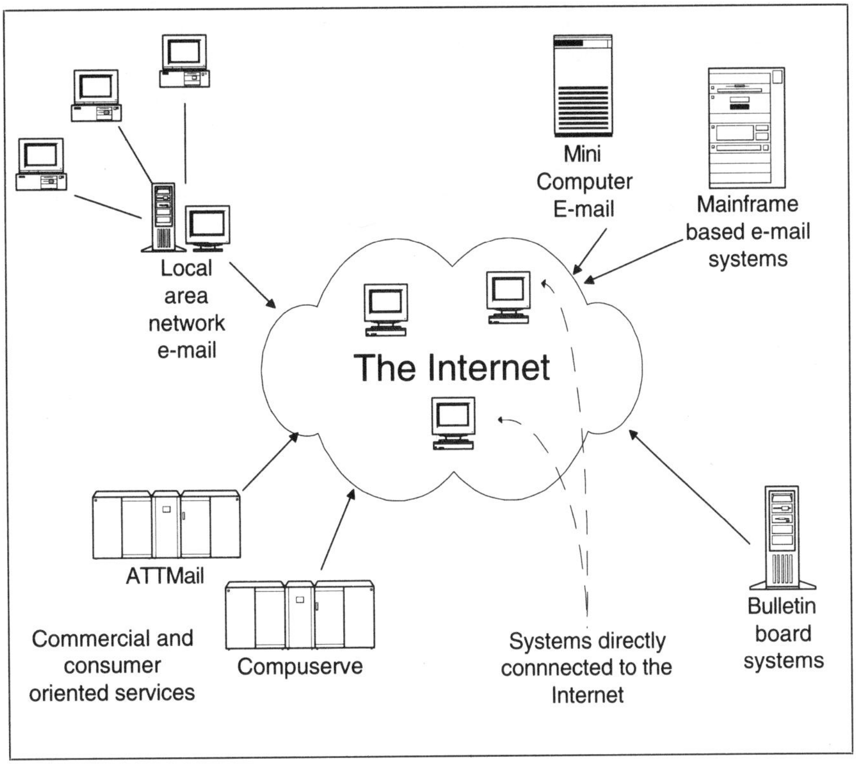

The number of LAN-based e-mail users in corporate organizations is expected to grow to some 40 million in North America by 1995, according to the publication *EMMS*.

Organizations with advanced LAN e-mail strategies involving these technologies are actively implementing software that permits people to send and receive messages from the Internet.

As a result, many people within organizations implementing cc:Mail, MSMail or other similar LAN e-mail systems are finding that they have the capability to reach individuals on the Internet.[3]

For example, BRK Brands Canada, the company we've already mentioned that wholesales the First Alert series of home safety products, has linked an internal Lotus cc:Mail network to Internet e-mail. Any of the twenty or so employees can send a message out to anyone on the Internet from within cc:Mail, and anyone can send a message to someone at BRK Brands by sending a message to an ID of the form

firstname_lastname@brkbrands.ca.

- in-house mainframe and minicomputer systems, such as IBM PROFS or Digital All-in-1

These systems, the predecessor to LAN-based e-mail, are still in wide use throughout many organizations, particularly *Fortune 1000* companies and major government bodies.

Companies are linking their mainframe and minicomputer e-mail systems to the Internet.

For example, the Ontario government, which uses a number of these systems as well as LAN-based e-mail systems, is linked to the Internet through the sub-domain, **epo.gov.on.ca**. Individuals on an e-mail system in the provincial government can choose to register a user code with the EPO ("Electronic Post Office"), and have an Internet e-mail ID of the form of **usercode@epo.gov.on.ca**. Any messages sent to that ID are automatically routed into the internal e-mail system.

The Ontario government is not alone — Alan Guilbault (**aguilbault@galaxy.gov.bc.ca**), in charge of e-mail strategy for the government of BC, notes that "we have a central electronic post office called 'GEMS' (Government Electronic Messaging Service) which currently delivers some 3 million notes a month between Government departments. GEMS handles all traffic to and from the Internet, routing messages to any of 40,000 Government staff using 12 different e-mail systems through the sub-domain **gems.gov.bc.ca**."

- bulletin board systems (BBS), which range in size from a couple of dozen people to thousands of subscribers

For example, Canada Remote Systems, historically Canada's largest BBS, has linked its e-mail system to Internet e-mail (as well as providing access to other Internet services), thus providing their customers with access to the world.

- commercial e-mail systems, such as AT&TMail and MCIMail, and in Canada, TheNet:Mail (formerly Envoy 100) and Immedia

Organizations which do not run e-mail on their own LAN's, minicomputers or mainframes often end up buying e-mail on commercial e-mail systems. In addition, some *Fortune* 500 companies have adopted commercial e-mail systems for their communications to external companies.

Yet, even as these systems encountered growth in the 1980's, they now find their business base under attack by the attractiveness and low cost of Internet e-mail. These systems have responded by providing direct links to Internet e-mail.

At the Information Technology Association of Canada (ITAC), an internal cc:Mail network is linked to Immedia, a commercial e-mail provider based in Montreal. Since Immedia is linked to the Internet, ITAC essentially has access to Internet e-mail — through the Internet domain, **immedia.ca**.

- consumer-based communication services which include e-mail capabilities

Systems such as CompuServe, BIX, Prodigy and GENIE have several million users scattered throughout the world. Subscribers use these services to participate in on-line conversations, access software and technical support, and perform other on-line activities.

These systems have been very aggressive in linking their e-mail to Internet e-mail, and have effectively become part of the global Internet e-mail system.

In addition to these many different e-mail systems with indirect connectivity to the Internet, there are many companies with a more direct connection to Internet e-mail.

These organizations use a variety of client e-mail software systems like Elm, Pine, Eudora, Pegasus and Z-Mail within UNIX, DOS or other operating platforms. Many of these systems provide an excellent, simple to use interface to e-mail.

When dealing with Internet e-mail, you must realize that everyone you deal with might read, send and work with Internet e-mail in a way that is completely different from the way that you work with it. With so many different systems linked to Internet e-mail, there is a wide variety of Internet e-mail software in use.

Some will find it easy to send and receive e-mail because they have access to simple, straightforward client software, while for others, e-mail will be difficult because the client software they use is less straightforward. According to Mike

Martineau of NSTN, Inc., "I think we need to remember that people's view of the Internet is significantly colored by the client software they use."

EXAMPLES OF INTERNET E-MAIL

As an example, consider two very different interfaces used to create an Internet e-mail message, both on a PC.

In this first screen, a Windows-based e-mail program known as Pegasus Mail is used to create the message:

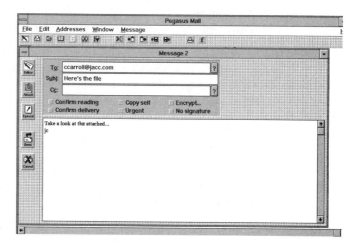

In this second case, the Lotus cc:Mail software has been linked to the Internet. In this case, the user selects "Internet" from a list of post offices, and then types or selects an address. The user can maintain their own list of Internet addresses:

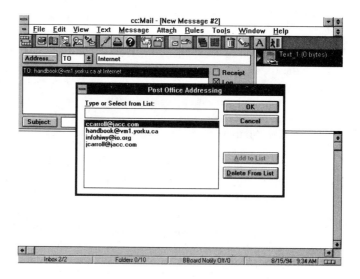

Given the wide number of possible methods by which people can access and use the Internet, it's not possible within this book to detail all the steps involved in dealing with your own Internet e-mail. For that, we suggest you refer to the manual of the particular client software you use, and discuss with your Internet service provider any special technical considerations.

THE STRUCTURE OF AN INTERNET E-MAIL MESSAGE

An Internet e-mail message has several distinct parts.

Although any particular message might be more or less complex, a sample Internet message looks like this in plain text: [4]

```
Date sent: Fri, 12 Aug 1994 21:45:44 -0400
To:  jcarroll@jacc.com
From: thehip@hookup.net (The Tragically Hip)
Subject: Re: Canadian Internet Handbook

>Here's a reminder; can we pursue this?
>jc

Yes.. go ahead & send the questions and we'll try to an-
swer them as best as we can...

-------------------------------------------

The Tragically Hip
thehip@hookup.net
P.O. Box 37, Station "C"
Toronto, Ontario
M6J 3M7 Canada

-------------------------------------------
```

Take a moment and examine the message. You will note that it includes the following components, or fields:

- Date sent:

  The date/time the message was created by the sender.

- To:

  The intended recipient of the message.

  In this case, the message is being sent to the Internet ID, **jcarroll@jacc.com.**

- From:

  The name of the sender, and the full Internet address of the sender. In this case, the sender is **thehip@hookup.net**. The software has also included the senders full name (The Tragically Hip).

- Subject:

  Details the subject line entered by the sender. In this case, the message shown is a response to an original message, and so the software has placed a Re: in front of the original subject.

Depending on the e-mail software you use, you might also see other fields, including:

- cc:

  Messages can also include a cc:, or carbon copy field. This indicates that the message has also been copied to other people. In addition, a bcc: (blind carbon copy) field might be found within some messages.

- In-Reply-to:

  A field used by many e-mail systems to cross reference messages.

- Message-Id:

  A unique message address, generated by the e-mail system of the sender.

- Mime-Version: and Content-Type

  Appears or is used if the sender of this message is working with the newest evolution of Internet e-mail, known as MIME (Multipurpose Internet Multimedia Extensions), which provides interesting new e-mail capabilities. MIME significantly extends the capabilities of simple Internet e-mail, and is discussed in greater depth later in this chapter.

- X-mailer:

  Internet messages also often include an X-mailer: field, which indicates the e-mail client software used to create the message.

Other fields might appear in the message, again depending on the particular software that is in use.

Finally, the message contains the text or body of the message. Note that the text includes the lines:

```
>Here's a reminder; can we pursue this?
>jc
```

The e-mail software used by the Tragically Hip has inserted this text of the original message and has highlighted it for reference purposes. This feature is discussed in greater depth below.

Finally, the e-mail message includes a signature or standard piece of information added to every message by the sender. In this case, the signature is simple and straightforward:

```
----------------------------------------------------------------

The Tragically Hip
thehip@hookup.net
P.O. Box 37, Station "C"
Toronto, Ontario
M6J 3M7 Canada


----------------------------------------------------------------
```

It should also be noted that much of the software for the Internet strips an Internet message down to its fundamentals, by showing only a To:, From: and Subject: field. For example, this message, when viewed with Pegasus Mail for Windows, appears as follows:

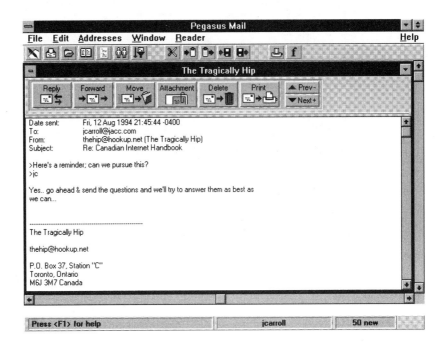

ANSWERING MESSAGES

Once you are on the Internet, you might find that you receive a lot of e-mail each and every day.

To help you remember what a particular message is about, many of the e-mail systems used with the Internet quote the original message text in the response. "Quoting" the original message is optional.

For example, if we reply to the message above, our e-mail software (in this case, Pegasus Mail for Windows) inserts a special marker in front of the original message text. This helps the recipient and sender to clearly outline which was the original message and which was the response.

In the sample message, a special marker has been placed by the software in front of the text of Jim Carroll's original message — using a > symbol. (Many different types of markers are used.)

This feature helps you to easily refer to the original message in your response, and is a courtesy that is much appreciated by the Internet community.

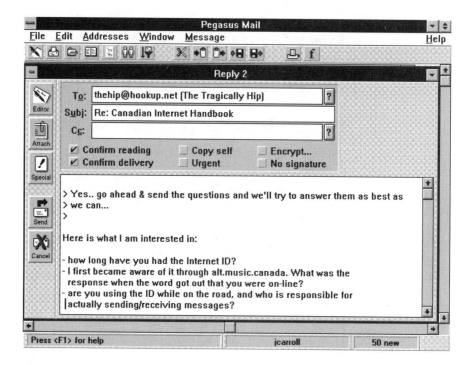

AN E-MAIL SIGNATURE

The sample message includes an e-mail signature which provides further information concerning the sender. In this case, the signature includes the name of the sender (The Tragically Hip), the e-mail address and a paper address.

Most e-mail signatures include the name of the author, the title, company address, and fax and telephone numbers, as well as the Internet e-mail address of the sender.

Most Internet e-mail systems automatically append "signatures" to the end of messages. Other systems connected to the Internet, such as CompuServe, don't; accordingly, you shouldn't always expect to see them in every Internet message.

In general, signatures should be concise, and should not be overdone. In a document released on USENET called "A Primer on How to Work With the USENET Community," by Chuq Von Rospac, guidance is given with respect to how to structure signatures. Although the document is specific to use of the USENET news system, the guidance is equally applicable to e-mail signatures.

> "Signatures are nice.... Don't overdo it. Signatures can tell the world something about you, but keep them short. A signature that is longer than the message itself is considered to be in bad taste. The main purpose of a signature is to help people locate you, not to tell your life story. Every signature should include at least your return address relative to a major, known site on the network and a proper domain-format address. Your system administrator can give this to you. Some news posters attempt to enforce a 4 line limit on signature files -- an amount that should be more than sufficient to provide a return address and attribution."

BINARY FILES AND ENCLOSURES

On occasion, you will receive a message that contains a "binary enclosure" or file. This means that someone has sent you an electronic mail message that contains a computer program, a computer document or some other type of file.

A computer file contains different information than the "plain text" that you see in a message, and hence is "attached" to the message. This permits you to save it to your own computer for your own use.

Due to the fact that computer programs and document files from computers contain special codes that can't be represented in "plain text," they have to be "encoded" in some way to be sent through the message. This makes it necessary in many cases for you to have to "extract" the file from your message, and sometimes "decode" it. It's confusing, but once you do it a few times, you'll get the hang of it.

The exact method that you will use to "extract" the file from the message, "decode" it and save it to your computer will vary depending on the e-mail software that you might be using. Some e-mail software automatically "decodes" enclosures, while with others you will need to save the mail message in a file and then use a separate program to decode the file.

On the Internet, binary files and enclosures are usually included in the message in one of three types, either "uuencoded," "binhex," or MIME.

If the file is "uuencoded," the binary file has been turned into rows and rows of text and included in the message, which looks like gibberish, i.e.:

```
begin 644 config.sys
M1$5624-%/4,,Z7$1/4UU3(24U%32Y365,-"D1%%5SE%#13U5#.EQ$%#.EQU
,S@VM+D5#12!.3T%
4PT*0E5D524STS,"PP!#0I&24%4STX,`T*1]3/550@T*
```

The gibberish is then "uudecoded" at the receiving end, to restore the program or file to its original form. If it was attached using "binhex" or MIME, it looks somewhat similar if your system doesn't support binhex or MIME.

MIME is a rapidly emerging Internet standard to permit a more straightforward exchange of binary files and enclosures, and is discussed in greater depth at the end of this chapter. MIME messages also look like "uuencoded" files if you receive them and do not have MIME-capable software. However, if you are using MIME, your software will automatically recognize the contents of the message as a file attachment.

E-MAIL ADDRESSES

Internet e-mail uses the domain-name style of addressing, based upon the Domain Name System.

An Internet e-mail address usually consists of a name or some identifier, followed by an @ symbol, followed by the Domain Name. For example, **jcarroll@jacc.com** contains the user name (**jcarroll**) and the domain name (**jacc.com**, which stands for J.A. Carroll Consulting, and which is listed in the commercial, or **.com**, domain).

As seen in Chapter 4, the Internet Domain Name System results in e-mail addresses in Canada that:

- Uses a **.ca** extension, if registered within the Canadian domain.

  The address might include a city/jurisdiction name and province, depending on the size of the organization, and the location of that organization within Canada.

  Within the Canadian domain, some Internet addresses in Canada would appear with names such as **Pete_Smith@mediumcorp.ab.ca** for an organization in Alberta, **Tjones@smallco.ns.ca** for a company in Nova Scotia, or **Al_Stevens@bigcompany.ca** if the company is national in scope.

- Other Internet addresses, within organizations that are not part of the Canadian domain but are registered directly with the Internet InterNIC, might have Internet addresses that end in **.com, .edu, .gov**, or other extensions.

  Such an address will usually include the name of the organization next to the extension, i.e., **TJones@Bigco.com**.

E-MAIL STYLES

It is important to note that the information that appears in front of the @ symbol in an e-mail address will vary depending on the particular e-mail system used, the Internet vendor and the way that names are used within the organizational e-mail system.

- Some addresses will use some combination of the first name and last name i.e., Pete_Smith or Psmith or pete.smith. Since spaces are not allowed, the first and last name are separated, usually by a _ character or dot.

- Other addresses might use alpha-numerical characters, i.e., 76467.3502 for someone on CompuServe, 384-9385 for an address on MCIMail or aa1234 for an address on a Free-Net.

- Other addresses might use nicknames or nonsense names.

In other words, there are no rules on what must be used in front of the @ symbol. Some sites will let you choose your own address.

The result is an incredible diversity of addresses throughout the Internet.

REACHING OTHER E-MAIL SYSTEMS

One reason for the explosion in the use of Internet e-mail is the fact that the domain method is, compared to the alternatives, easy to use and easy to understand.

As indicated, many other e-mail systems are linking to the Internet in order to provide their users with expanded e-mail connectivity.

The following section describes how to send messages to these other e-mail systems.

CONSUMER-ORIENTED SYSTEMS

A number of large, consumer-oriented on-line systems with close to 5 million users have linked themselves to the Internet. Using a few simple rules, you can reach people on the following systems:

Name of Service	Mail Extension	Addressing details
America Online	aol.com	userid@aol.com
BIX	bix.com	userid@bix.com
CompuServe	compuserve. com	user #@compuserve. com. CompuServe addresses consist of a nine-digit number, separated by a comma, i.e., 76467,3502. Remember to substitute a . for the , in the CompuServe address; i.e., 76467,3502, becomes 76467.3502@compuserve.com when sending e-mail to/from the Internet.
Delphi	delphi.com	userid@delphi.com
GEnie	genie.com	userid@genie.geis.com
Prodigy	prodigy.com	userid@prodigy.com. Recipient must be registered with Prodigy to receive mail.

Individuals of these networks can be reached by combining their on-line user address with the extension listed above. For example, to reach someone on CompuServe, send a message to their user ID, followed by @compuserve.com. To reach the CompuServe address of one of the authors, send a message to **76467.3502@compuserve.com**.

COMMERCIAL E-MAIL SYSTEMS

Individuals using commercial e-mail vendors are also reachable from the Internet, using the following syntax.

Name of System	Mail Extension	Addressing Details
AT&TMail	att.com	userid@attmail.com
The:Net Mail (Envoy 100, iNet 2000)	tc.resonet. com	/pn=jane.dove@ts.resonet. com [5]
GEIS (GE Quikcom)	ge.com	userid@org.geis.com. Only reachable if the organization has agreed to accept external e-mail from the Internet.
Immedia	immedia.ca	userid@immedia.ca
MCIMail	mcimail.com	user#@mcimail.com. User# is an eight digit number, separated by a dash.

Other alternatives are possible, depending on the e-mail system you are trying to reach.

HOW COMPLEX CAN INTERNET ADDRESSING GET?

E-mail addressing can get very complex, very quickly — particularly if you are trying to reach people on the e-mail system of an organization that is not directly connected to the Internet, but is connected through one of the commercial e-mail vendors such as AT&TMail or MCIMail.

For example, many organizations are linking their in-house e-mail systems to commercial e-mail vendors. Some of the vendors have done a good job in developing Internet gateways, others have not.

The particular blend of software in use at an organization will directly impact how easy it is to reach a particular person within a particular company.

For example, staff at Ernst & Young in Canada make use of MSMail on their in-house Macintosh-based local area network. Their MSMail system is also linked into the commercial service GE Quikcom, so staff at E&Y are reachable by sending to **username@ey.geis.com**. This is a relatively simple Internet address.

On the other hand, organizations which use The:Net mail service generate particularly ugly Internet addresses. Imagine receiving a message of the form **/PN=JAY.J.0MACARTHUR/DD.ID=JAY.MACARTHUR/ADMD=TELECO**

M.CANADA/C=CA/@resonet.com. Whew! (This ID mixes in what is known as X.400 — see below.)

One would hope that The:Net would invest in its gateway product to correct this deficiency, permitting an address that would be simpler and more straightforward, something like **userid@thenet.com**.[6]

REJECTED MESSAGES

On occasion, you will receive notification that a message sent to someone has been rejected, or a notification that the message has not been delivered.

A rejected message looks like this:

```
To: jacc.com!jcarroll@jacc.uucp
From: The Post Office <postmaster@uunet.ca>
Subject: Delivery problems with your mail
Date sent: Thu, 1 Sep 1994 16:39:08 -0400

A copy of your message is being returned to you due to
difficulties encountered while attempting to deliver your
mail.

This is an automatic message.

The following errors occurred during message delivery
processing:

<smtp schoolnet.carleton.ca ra-
chel.welch@schoolnet.carleton.ca 88>: 550
<rachel.welch@schoolnet.carleton.ca>... User unknown

---------- Original Message ----------
```

The message usually includes the original message you sent.

Rejection messages come in all kinds of flavors, and will often look different depending on where they originated.

If you get a rejected message, carefully check the e-mail address you sent the original message to. Quite often, a simple spelling mistake in the address will have been made. Other times, you should check with the person (by phone or otherwise, of course) to verify their address.

When you have a rejected message, you can usually forward it to the correct ID, but be sure to edit out all the details in the rejected message header.

A GLOBAL STANDARD FOR E-MAIL

Finally, when it comes to Internet e-mail, you should recognize that there is a global standard for e-mail. It's called X.400.

Fortunately, Internet e-mail has nothing to do with it.

X.400 is a standard adopted by an international standards body (CCITT) defining how e-mail should be exchanged among different e-mail systems.

X.400 works well at a technical level, but fails miserably as a simple, easy to use method of sending and receiving e-mail. It simply requires the user to know too much about X.400 to be able to use it.

For example, one of the authors of this book has had, at various points of time, the following X.400 addresses on three different commercial e-mail systems:

```
C=CA;A=TELECOM.CANADA;DD=ID=JA.CARROLL;F=JIM;S=CARROLL

C=US;A=MCIMAIL;DD=ID=JCARROLL;F=JIM;S=CARROLL

/C=CA/AD=ATTMAIL/O=JACC/PN=JIM.CARROLL
```

His Internet address is **jcarroll@jacc.com**.

Which would you prefer?

You will find a lot of business cards with Internet addresses appearing on them. You won't find many listing X.400 addresses. The world is quickly accepting the use of Internet e-mail addresses, because they are easy to understand and easy to use. It would appear that X.400 addresses are being rejected out of hand, because they are confusing, complex, and not easy to use or remember.

Yet, there are some users and people who believe that X.400 has a role to play. Alan Guilbault, the Director, Office Information Systems, of BC Systems Corporation, who is responsible for e-mail strategy of the BC Government (**aguilbault@galaxy.gov.bc. ca**), notes that "X.400 is important as a standard for the commercial networks that must guarantee reliable delivery and security for their customers." There is a ring of truth in this, as we will see in the final section of this chapter, Problems with Internet E-mail.

As a result, X.400 is being used in Canada, particularly as a system to support the exchange of formal business transaction documents between those companies participating in a form of commerce known as EDI (Electronic Data Interchange.) However, it would seem that its use is not extending beyond that population.

There are some people who are still convinced of the belief that X.400 is the right way to go when it comes to inter-organization e-mail. Yet, this group is dwindling in the face of overwhelming use of the Internet. Their arguments tend to dissolve once you get involved in pointing out the sheer incomprehensibility of X.400 e-mail addresses.

E-MAIL ETIQUETTE

When sending and receiving e-mail on the Internet, you should keep in mind this simple rule:

What you type and what you say in your e-mail messages could one day come back to haunt you. Be careful.

The use of Internet e-mail (or any e-mail system) requires an on-line etiquette, or a set of manners, that you should keep in mind.

E-MAIL IS DIFFERENT

There are several characteristics about e-mail that should make you cautious in the way you use it.

- E-mail is fast.

  In the "good old days," before the arrival of computer technology, people were careful with paper letters. A response took time to prepare, was well thought out and was probably reviewed a few times before being sent. There was no room for error on paper correspondence.

  That's not the case with e-mail. Within seconds of receiving a message, you can respond — often, without thinking about what you've typed.

  Do you really want people to receive messages that you haven't carefully thought about?

- E-mail is wide-reaching.

  Within seconds, you can create a message or response to a message that will reach one person, twenty people or thousands of people (particularly if you're responding to a mailing list posting. If the mailing list is linked to a USENET newsgroup, your message will reach an even larger audience.)

  If you write an e-mail message in anger, you might say something that you regret. Do you really want to send copies of your message to a lot of people?

- E-mail is easily saved.

  Computer technology permits people to easily store the e-mail messages they send or receive. [7]

  What this means is that any e-mail message you send to someone could end up in their personal data archive, or even in an organizational archive. If you are posting to an Internet mailing list, your message could end up in several archives around the world that are open to public viewing.

  If you write something controversial or stupid, do you want to risk having your words come back to haunt you?

- E-mail is easily forwarded.

  E-mail technology promotes the easy distribution of information. What you write and send to someone can be easily forwarded by them to someone else, or posted to a global mailing list or USENET newsgroup. They might not realize that you intended the message for limited distribution. Before you know it, your message could be sent all over the world.

  Do you really want a message that you intended for just one person to be forwarded to a number of people?

- E-mail is easily misinterpreted.

The person reading your e-mail message can't see your body language. They can't see if you're smiling, frowning or crying as you write. It is more difficult for them to interpret what you have written.

Often this leads to misinterpretation — what they think you mean is often not what you really mean.

Do you want to run the risk of having someone misunderstand your message?

FLAMING

The on-line world has come up with a term to describe what happens to people who ignore these risks, and who write an e-mail message while their emotions are not in check.

It's called flaming.

Flaming is the tendency for people to quickly type out an e-mail message in anger, without thinking the message through.

Remember this warning.

At some time, you will regret sending an e-mail message. You'll regret it a lot.

E-MAIL GUIDANCE

A few simple suggestions might make it easier for you to avoid problems sending e-mail messages.

- Don't use just capitals in your messages. This is called shouting. Imagine receiving a message that looks like this:

  GREG. WE NEED TO UNDERSTAND HOW TO REORGANIZE FOR THE JUNE 5TH MEETING. IT'S IMPORTANT THAT WE GET TOGETHER NOW. CALL ME SOON.

  Messages like this are difficult to read, and cause others frustration with the messages you send them. Always be careful to type in upper and lower case.

- Use a meaningful subject line. Remember that the person you're sending the message to might receive tens or hundreds of messages each day. To make it easier for them to deal with your message, provide a subject line that's meaningful and to the point.

- Take your time thinking about a response to a message especially if the message makes you mad. The best advice is to get up, go for a glass of water or have a cup of coffee. Or take a walk. Or go shopping, watch TV or read a book. Don't ever respond to a message when you are mad!

- Don't send a carbon copy of your message to the rest of the world, unless you have to. When sending an e-mail message, it's easy to send copies to a lot of people, including people who might have no interest in your message. Be judicious about the people who get a copy of the message.

- Summarize what you are responding to.

If you're lucky, you're using an Internet e-mail software package that quotes the original message text in your response, as we saw in the section "Answering Messages" above. Be sure to use this feature to make it easier for the recipient to remember what the message was about. Edit it down so that you're leaving in only the relevant text. *There's nothing worse than getting three pages of an original message with a few words in response at the end.*

- Use special characters to label your emotion. For example, to *highlight* a point, consider using >>>>>special<<<<<< characters to emphasize certain words or phrases. For example, rather than typing in a message that looks like this:

```
It is important that we meet as soon
as possible.
```

you might type

```
It is !!!!!!important!!!!!! that we meet as soon as
possible.
```

This will help get the urgency of the situation across.

As you use the Internet, you will discover that people use all kinds of neat tricks to help them emphasize points within their messages. Carefully observe, and in time, you will come up with your own distinctive Internet writing style.

SMILEYS

The e-mail world has come up with an ingenious way of expressing emotion within a message by the use of with special characters that some call *emoticons*. Others call them smileys.

A smiley is a set of symbols that, when turned on its side, represents some type of character. For example, a (-: is really a sideways smiley face; a (-; is a sideways smiley face winking, while)-: is a sad face with a frown.

A :-) is often used in a message to indicate that the preceding remark was made in jest. Smileys are important so that people don't misinterpret what you type.

These characters can be used within e-mail messages to add additional emphasis. For example.

```
Pete,
Your summary was interesting(-;.
```

```
    Have a good day.
    John
```

or another message

```
    Pete,
    I didn't get the report finished. )-:
    Call me.
    John
```

There are so many possible smileys that a book has been written about them.

As you use the Internet, you'll see a lot of smileys in use within messages. Begin to accumulate your own special list of them. If you are looking for more, you can find a number of sites on the Internet that keep lists of smileys.

HOW DO I LOCATE AN INTERNET E-MAIL ADDRESS?

At some point you'll want to determine how to obtain the e-mail address of a particular person or organization.

Invariably, as you use various parts of the Internet, you will come across a message from someone that reads as follows:

```
    I am looking for Bob Smith in Toronto. Does anyone know his
    Internet address?
```

The question is silly, since there is no easy answer. Most important, Bob Smith might not have an Internet address!

The Internet does not have any central storage location that lists all possible users of the network. Although there are a variety of services located throughout the Internet that let you find addresses of various people, these services are not comprehensive, and are not really a good solution to your dilemma.

Fortunately, many people are starting to list their Internet addresses on their business cards, and addresses are beginning to gain as much acceptance on business cards and correspondence as fax numbers did in the mid-80s.'

SIMPLE SOLUTIONS

The easiest way to find out the Internet address of people is probably simply to ask. Pick up the phone and call them. Maybe they know. If they know they are on the Internet, and know how to send a message, but don't know what their address is, ask them to send a message to your Internet address. You'll see what their address is, and can respond to them in the future.

WHOIS

If this doesn't work, and you must begin exploring the world of the Internet to try to locate an address, take a deep breath. There are a lot of resources on-line to look into.

Many of these resources are known as WHOIS servers, simple programs that let you query for the name of an organization or individual.

One of the most popular is the WHOIS database, located at the resource services department of the Internet Network Information Centre (InterNIC).

Although the database is not comprehensive, it is a useful starting point. To access the database, Telnet to **rs.internic.net,** and type **whois** at the InterNIC prompt, as seen on the following screen.

```
                                  E:94% VT100 ‡   00:03:16  4:12p
                                  CML 205-876-5618 (DSN)746
Carroll Auto Sales (NET-C105571)C105571                198.249.80.0
Carroll College (CARROLL)        CARROLL1.CC.EDU       140.104.1.1
Carroll College (NET-CARROLLNET)CARROLLNET             140.104.0.0
Carroll College (NETBLK-CRRLLCLG) NETBLK-CRRLLCLG   199.5.171.0 - 199.5.172.0
There are 16 more matches.  Show them? y
Carroll College (CC-DOM)                               CC.EDU
Carroll County General Hospital (NET-CCGH-1) CCGH-1    198.51.120.0
Carroll County General Hospital (NET-CCGH-2) CCGH-2    198.51.121.0
Carroll Pont./Bui/GMC (NET-C104612) C104612            192.224.208.0
Carroll, Eric M. (EC43)         eric@UTCS.UTORONTO.CA     (416) 978 3328
Carroll, Gary (GC248)                                  +43 662 46 911 420
Carroll, James (JC198)          4carroll_j@SPCVXA.SPC.EDU   201-843-1970
Carroll, Jim (JC718)            jcarroll@jacc.com        +1 416 274 5605
Carroll, Jim (JC33)             carrollj@WM-MERCER.CA     416-868-7013
Carroll, Jim (JC443)            jcarroll@SCOTIA-MCLEOD.COM  416 862 3904
Carroll, Jim (JC69)             jimc@JTS.COM             (416) 512 8910
Carroll, Johnny (JC579)         CARROLL@DEPT.CSCI.UNT.EDU  (817) 565-2279
Carroll, Leo (LC1)         (301) 862-8744 862-8764 (DSN) 326-3512 ext 8744
Carroll, Michael [Sgt] (MC475)  lowry@LWR3B201.AF.MIL
                                  (303) 676-5121 (DSN) 926-5121
Carroll, Russ (RC502)           RUSSC@RWC.COM            (619)689-2321
Carroll, Thomas R. (TRC7)       tcarroll@SNOW.NOHRSC.NWS.GOV (612) 725-3039
Whois:
```

The WHOIS database can also be accessed through a Gopher search. Accessing it using the Pipeline For Windows software, you'll see that you can search the WHOIS database as well as do three other types of searches:

- an x.500 lookup;

- a search of the Netfind database;

- a search of the DS WHOIS database.

Each of these are different sources for information concerning users of the Internet.

We accessed the database using the service known as Gopher. This particular site has been accessed using the software Pipeline For Windows through a Toronto Internet service provider, InfoRamp:

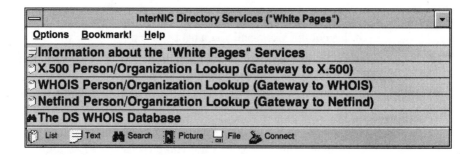

Performing a search on the name "Kramer" in the DS WHOIS database lists the following response:

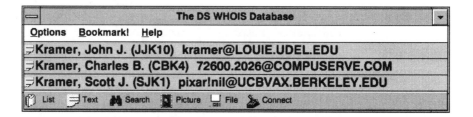

A search of WHOIS and related databases can be useful — however, 99% of the people on the Internet are not listed on WHOIS, which is what makes it such a limited tool.

As a result, a tool like the InterNIC WHOIS should only be used to look up organizations, or contacts for particular companies.

TO ACCESS WHOIS AT THE INTERNIC

Using Gopher	
Site:	ds.internic.net
Path:	Select:
	InterNIC Directory and Database Services (AT&T)
	InterNIC Directory Services ("White Pages")
	The DS WHOIS Database
Instructions:	Enter name of person you wish to do search on

POSTMASTER

When it's really important, you can usually send a message to the postmaster at a particular location to ask how you might get in touch with someone at their organization. Most locations on the Internet have a postmaster account for their organization; i.e., **postmaster@epo.gov.on.ca**.

Obviously, this won't work if you try to ask the question of a postmaster at an extremely large organization or commercial on-line e-mail system; i.e., **postmaster@ibm.com** or **postmaster@compuserve.com**.

Use such queries with discretion, since you should remember that there is an individual at the other end of the system who might be swamped with requests. And if they do respond, remember common courtesy, and send them a thank you.

YELLOW PAGES

There are a variety of information services around the Internet which provide "white" or "yellow" pages of companies registered on the Internet.

The *Directory of Canadian Organizations with Registered Internet Domains* in Appendix P includes a listing of various white and yellow page listings across Canada.

One example is the *NSTN White Pages*, which lists organizations registered under the Canadian (**.ca**) domain. When you access the Gopher, you are presented with a menu through which you can choose to list all Canadian organizations or search through the listing. Once again, we use Gopher through Pipeline For Windows to access the White Pages.

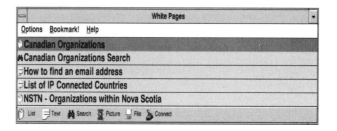

You can also choose to list all Canadian organizations

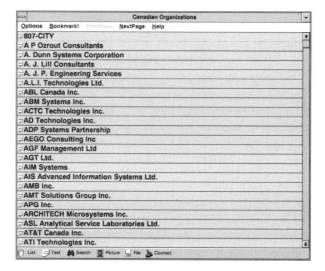

and then see the full registration details on any particular one:

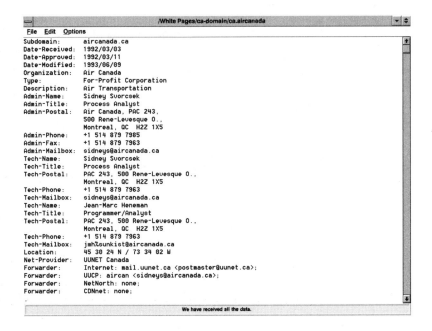

TO ACCESS THE *NSTN WHITE* PAGES

Using Gopher	
Gopher address:	gopher.nstn.ns.ca
Path:	Select:
	NSTN Cybrary
	Internet Search Facilities
	White Pages

OTHER INFORMATION SERVICES

Check with your Internet provider, as they might provide a service that helps to locate Internet e-mail addresses.

For example, the InfoRamp service in Toronto provides a good way to search for the names of Internet users by performing a search of postings made to USENET newsgroups.

By choosing the item "Find someone on the Internet," you are presented with a box asking you to type in the name. To search for the name, Caston, for example:

Once you press OK, you are notified that the service will go off and search USENET postings to get you a list of ID's that include the name Caston:

Several minutes (or hours later, depending on the time of day) you will receive a message back containing the results of your search.

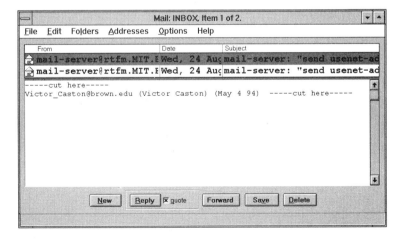

The InfoRamp search uses a database built at the Massachusetts Institute of Technology. The document describing the database notes that it "contains one-line entries consisting of names and E-mail addresses culled from the Reply-To or From lines of USENET postings."

If you only have electronic mail, you can query the system through e-mail, as detailed below:

Using E-mail	
Send message to:	mail-server@rtfm.mit.edu
In text of message, type:	send usenet-addresses/keyword.
Special Instructions:	Replace 'keyword' with the surname of the person you are looking for.

Various Internet service providers are trying to establish new and innovative methods to help you identify users of the Internet. As a result, you should always check with your Internet provider to determine if they have made a new method of looking up people on the Internet.

PERIODIC POSTINGS

A good starting point to the techniques used to try to locate a particular e-mail address is the document *How to find people's E-mail addresses* by Jonathon Kames.

The document is posted on a regular basis to several USENET newsgroups, such as **news.answers**. You can also retrieve it by using FTP or through e-mail. Chapter 7 describes how documents can be retrieved using FTP.

Using Anonymous FTP	
FTP site:	rtfm.mit.edu
Directory (on one line):	pub/usenet-by-group/news.answers
File:	finding-addresses

Using E-mail	
Send message to:	mail-server@rtfm.mit.edu
In text of message, type (on one line):	send usenet/news.answers/finding-addresses

When you retrieve it through e-mail, you should receive the document back in an e-mail message within a few hours. This uses a capability of Internet e-mail known as "query by mail" or "file-retrieval by e-mail," which is also discussed in Chapter 7.

USEFUL E-MAIL TOOLS

With the emergence of the Internet, e-mail has become increasingly sophisticated, and there are a number of tools which you might consider to be useful as you consider joining the network, or expanding the capabilities that you already have.

E-MAIL FILTERS

With the growth in the use of Internet e-mail has come the inability for some people to deal with massive volumes of messages. One practical way to deal with this is through the use of e-mail filters.

You can think of a filter as an electronic program on your e-mail system or computer that reads your e-mail before you do. It then acts upon those messages, depending on a set of rules that you have defined beforehand.

For example, you might belong to an Internet service that regularly sends you, via e-mail, a newsletter. You notice that the message always arrives with the subject, "Newsletter- (YY/MM/DD)."

Using a filter, you could specify that any messages that you receive containing the subject "Newsletter" should be automatically moved to a folder in your e-mail system called "newsletters." You can choose to go to this folder at any time to read the messages stored there, rather than seeing this particular newsletter arrive with your regular messages.

The e-mail software Pegasus, for example, permits the use of a number of e-mail filters. With these filters, you can specify certain actions to be performed on incoming messages based upon the contents of the To:, From:, Subject: or other fields, including:

- automatically moving them or copying them to a particular file folder, or automatically deleting certain messages;

- replying to every message with an automatic response; i.e., "I am a little behind on my e-mail, and it will take me about three days to respond — don't fret";

- automatically forwarding an incoming message to a particular person.

E-mail filters are a convenient method of automatically filing messages you might receive from a particular mailing list. For example, the following screen shows the method used in Pegasus Mail to ensure any messages received that were posted to the Enterprise-l list (a list sponsored by NSTN discussing the commercial use of the Internet) are automatically moved to the folder "Enterprise Discussion."

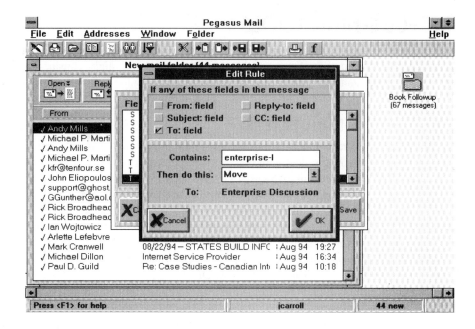

E-mail filters are not available in all e-mail systems or software linked to the Internet but are certainly a desirable feature.

"MAIL ROBOTS"

Often, the Internet solves unique problems through the simplest of methods.

One problem on the Internet has to do with providing to those people who only have an e-mail link to the Internet the ability to retrieve files or documents.

To solve the problem, the Internet came up with the concept of the "mail-robot." E-mail filters can be used to implement a simple and effective "mail robot," so that messages sent to a certain ID are automatically replied to with certain text.

A "mail-robot" is a program that runs at the receiving e-mail location, takes apart an incoming message, and mails back some type of response automatically. Organizations are using e-mail robots to permit individuals from throughout the Internet to easily request information from a company.

Try one out: for an up to date message concerning the *Canadian Internet Handbook,* send a message to **info@handbook.com**. You will receive an automatic response via e-mail, usually within hours.

"Mail robots" can be implemented quite easily with many popular e-mail systems, and can be implemented by many Internet service providers as well. "Mail robots" are close cousins to "listservs," which are discussed in Chapter 7.

MIME

As organizations began to exchange Internet e-mail around the globe and with each other, it was soon realized that there was no standard method to exchange computer files. Today, e-mail on the Internet is still very much a technology that simply permits people to exchange plain text. Standards like "uuencode" discussed previously are used here and there but are by no means universal.

MIME, the emerging *Multimedia Internet Mail Extensions* standard, intends to change that.

Begun as a grassroots initiative on the Internet, it is poised to emerge as a global standard for the exchange of e-mail between different systems and platforms in which messages can contain voice, sound, video, binary files, images or any other type of item.

Imagine receiving an e-mail message containing digitized video with the text "Here's a video of the conference proceedings; in particular, check out what happened to Dan when the podium collapsed on him!"

Even though the sender and recipient are on completely different computer platforms, MIME will permit the easy exchange of such a message with all information about the particular file format remaining intact.

This is a huge advance over current technology . . . since it would let the recipient immediately view the video file if that particular video application were supported on the recipient PC system, merely by clicking on the attachment with a mouse.

Imagine receiving an e-mail message with the text, "Hey, here's a document that I thought you should look at." With MIME, the message doesn't contain the actual document, but merely a pointer back to the document. By clicking on the pointer in the message, a program is invoked that goes to retrieve the file! MIME does this by supporting such items as Telnet and FTP commands within the body of an e-mail message. If you really want the document, your MIME mail reader will go off and get it: but *only when and if you want it.*

MIME will also see the emergence of "hypertext" e-mail messages . . . for example, a message which contains a questionnaire, with the questionnaire that is presented to you changing depending on the answers that you provide.

The arrival of MIME will cause a massive change in the role of e-mail, and will permit the development of many new applications that people are only just beginning to discover.

PROBLEMS WITH INTERNET E-MAIL

Finally, if you plan on using Internet e-mail in your organization, there are a number of important considerations that you should think of:

- Internet e-mail is not necessarily secure

    The Internet is a cooperative global network, built upon a protocol (TCP/IP) which involves the routing of information through different paths in the network. This means that mail is sometimes routed through various systems on the network — any point at which your e-mail message could be compromised.

An Internet e-mail message is subject not only to possible access by third parties somewhere in its travels, but its contents could also be changed.

- Internet e-mail doesn't necessarily guarantee delivery

There is nothing to ensure that an Internet message is received. Sometimes systems disappear, and sometimes they go down. The result is that your message might not be sent. In some cases, you will be told of the failed delivery, and in other cases you might not be.

Although you can request a "receipt" for messages that you have sent with some Internet e-mail systems, you are not guaranteed that you will get such a receipt back.

The result is that if you need a business application that guarantees you delivery of e-mail with proof of delivery the Internet is not what you are looking for.

- Internet e-mail can be forged

It is relatively easy for a person familiar with Internet e-mail protocols to forge e-mail. An experienced user could send you a message from **president@whitehouse.gov,** and you might be thrilled to receive such a message, but it is unlikely that Bill Clinton would decide to send you a message.

There is no mechanism in Internet e-mail to prove the authenticity of the sender.

These issues result in reluctance by some organizations in the use of Internet e-mail for anything more than casual messaging.

To solve the problem, some organizations on the Internet are using software that encrypts inbound and outbound messages, both to protect their contents and to ensure their authenticity. Such a capability does exist, but does involve some extra expense.

Mike Martineau, President of NSTN, thinks the security issue is overblown. "It is quite possible for an organization to use a package like Pegasus (with built-in encryption) and delivery confirmation to build a secure e-mail system over the Internet. As well, encryption and authentication standards are in development and will be used by companies such as NSTN, who are aiming their services at small- and medium-size business, businesses which cannot afford to set up their own private networks and for whom the Internet offers a cost-effective alternative."

The reality is that, despite the shortcomings, the use of Internet e-mail continues to explode. In the same way that people continue to use cellular phones, people continue to use Internet e-mail.

In your case, if you have a great deal of sensitive e-mail, you should encrypt your e-mail. If you don't, you should always be cognizant of some of these fundamental concerns.

---

1 . *Matrix News,* December 1993. Volume 3, No. 12.

2 . For example, an organization that has linked its LAN e-mail system to the Internet might not have told everyone that they can send and receive e-mail to the Internet.

3 . It should be noted that organizations which want to implement gateways from their LAN- based e-mail systems to the Internet should appreciate the technical complexity of the project. Many of the current Internet gateways for popular LAN-based e-mail systems do not function well unless set up correctly, and to set them up correctly, you must have a good working knowledge of the Internet, and in particular, Internet messaging.

4 . Note that the actual appearance of the message will depend on the type of computer you are using, the e-mail software found on that computer, the type of link that you have to the Internet, and the type of Internet service provider that you use. The definitive work that discusses the components of an Internet e-mail message is *The Internet Message*, by Marshall T. Rose (Prentice-Hall, 1993), which takes an in-depth look at the message from a detailed technical perspective.

5 . The:Net Mail has a very complex method of addressing from the respect of the Internet due to the use of what is known as X.400 (discussed later in this chapter.) The example shown is a much simplified example and uses what is known as the "registered X.400 first name and last name" of the recipient on The:Net Mail. Other possibilities can be used — you should check with Resonet for more information. It is hoped that The:Net Mail will fix this rather poor way of requiring complex Internet addresses sometime in the near future.

6 . This issue also has much to do with what you should consider when purchasing various e-mail gateways. Any gateway should be examined closely to determine the impact that it will have on simple, straightforward addressing.

7 . One of the authors has on file about 70 megabytes of messages, representing e-mail messages sent/received since October 1985.

C H A P T E R   6

. . . .

TOOLS FOR KNOWLEDGE NETWORKING

Children with a computer and a modem have access to more information in an evening than their parents had in a lifetime.

*Computers enhance the opportunity to write, publish books,
Kitchener Waterloo Record, Sat 09 Jul 94*

Internet mailing lists and USENET are the two primary methods by which you can "knowledge network" through the Internet.

THE BENEFIT OF KNOWLEDGE NETWORKING

If you have the need to be an expert on a particular topic, or wish to bring yourself up to date on a certain issue, or wish to find an answer to a question, you can often use the Internet as a means to "knowledge network."

"Knowledge networking" is the term used to describe the ability to harness on-line information, either by regularly tracking information on a particular topic by receiving information on that topic, or by seeking information or answers to questions by discussing a topic with others on-line.

By participating in Internet knowledge networks found in mailing lists and USENET newsgroups, you can receive information on specific topics on a regular basis, and join discussion topics with other people. The unique cooperative nature of the Internet means that information is available to you on thousands of topics and from thousands of sources.

For example, you can:

- subscribe to formal or informal electronic journals and newsletters, published by individuals or organizations from around the world;

- join mailing lists that will send you announcements of concerts, events, new publications or new products, or information about new initiatives by various organizations and governments;

- participate in discussions with thousands of other people from around the world on a variety of topics, ranging from the serious to the ridiculous.

A QUICK DEFINITION

A mailing list is a collection of e-mail addresses. Any message sent to the address of the mailing list is automatically sent to the address of every other member of the mailing list. There are thousands of mailing lists on all kinds of topics, and you can choose to join practically any list by sending a specially formatted e-mail message to a system which manages the list.

The result is that mailing lists are a quick and easy method of distributing information, whether it is a newsletter or a question from a member of the list. Information that you receive from mailing lists comes in with your regular Internet e-mail — no special software is required to read a message sent to a mailing list, although special software is used to manage the mailing list itself.

USENET, on the other hand, is a global system for the exchange of information on thousands of topics, referred to as "newsgroups." Individuals can choose to subscribe to any particular newsgroup, read information sent to the newsgroup, and add or "post" information to the newsgroup. Each posting is referred to as a "news article."

There are also "followups" and "replies" in USENET. A "followup" is a comment made to a previous post, while a "reply" is an e-mail message that you send to someone directly.

USENET is like a massive global bulletin board with thousands of different information resources.

You read the USENET newsgroups that you belong to with "newsreader" software, which also permits you to post messages to USENET.

WHAT'S THE DIFFERENCE?

Although the mechanics of a mailing list and USENET differ, both permit you to join a particular group and receive information or converse with people concerning the topic within the group.

Anyone with an Internet e-mail address can choose to join any number of mailing lists: your only constraint will be the volume of information that you can read during the day.[1]

USENET is another method of knowledge networking. Since you can obtain USENET news through most Internet service providers, you can choose to subscribe to the newsgroups which interest you. Given that current estimates are that some 100 megabytes of information is posted to USENET each day, you will have to be selective with respect to which newsgroups you subscribe to.

USENET newsgroups are not much different in concept from mailing lists. The major differences are:

- USENET information is more structured, with individual postings filed into particular newsgroups. In contrast, e-mail messages from mailing lists are part of your general e-mailbox, unless you have some type of special filtering software. (This is the benefit of e-mail filtering software, as discussed in Chapter 5.)

- Most USENET newsgroups undergo a series of steps of approval before they become widely distributed through the USENET system. On the other hand, anyone can start a mailing list on any topic if they have the right software.

- USENET has a culture that frowns upon networking for commercial purposes. Mailing lists can be used for anything, as long as you do not abuse the primary purpose for which a particular mailing list was established.

- USENET news articles have a limited life span. Because of the large number of USENET messages, many sites will delete messages beyond a certain date (usually two weeks, and sometimes much less). Messages sent to mailing lists will last as long as messages last in your mailbox.

- USENET news articles are not sent to personal mailboxes, but are received in batches of postings which are then made available for reading through newsreader software.

- USENET was designed as a mechanism to permit the re-broadcasting of information on a very wide basis. Any USENET article goes out to all the Internet hosts on the planet that wish to receive that specific newsgroup, or that don't refuse that newsgroup. E-mail, on the other hand, was designed as a point-to-point method of communicating, and even with mailing lists, suffers from some problems in trying to be a broadcast tool.

Other than this, USENET is very similar in concept to mailing lists, by permitting people to participate in knowledge networking with others from around the globe on a variety of topics.

To make matters more complex, there are also some "bi-directionally gated newsgroups" within USENET. Any news article sent to such a USENET newsgroup is also distributed automatically to others via a mailing list, meaning that even if you don't have access to USENET, you might be able to receive copies of postings to a particular newsgroup through your e-mail account.

INTERNET MAILING LISTS

Internet mailing lists are a convenient method for people on different computer systems to discuss particular topics or share information concerning specific issues. A mailing list might consist of as few as two people, or it might contain several thousand.

With thousands of different mailing lists on the Internet, you can choose to join any particular one that interests you, as long as it is a public, or open, list. Once you have joined, you will receive any message sent to the list.

Simply put, an Internet mailing list operates as shown in Figure 6.1.

FIGURE 6.1: INTERNET MAILING LISTS

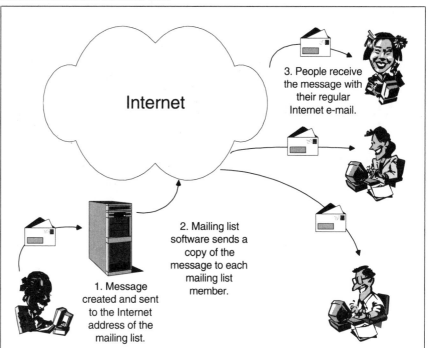

With the growing number of e-mail systems that have the capability to send messages to and receive messages from the Internet, it is no surprise that there are thousands of Internet mailing lists on virtually every topic imaginable.

Mailing lists have emerged as a new method of publishing, with a number of journals, newsletters and other information summaries available to anyone with Internet e-mail access.

TYPES OF LISTS

Mailing lists on the Internet differ by their purpose; some are used for discussion, while others are used for newsletters, and yet others are used to summarize information that has appeared in other lists or in USENET newsgroups.

An example of the types of mailing lists throughout the Internet would include those that are:

- moderated

  Lists are moderated in order to ensure that messages sent to the list are tightly focused on the list topic.

  In a moderated list, any message sent by you goes to the moderator, who determines if it should be redistributed to the list. This helps to keep the list on topic.

  Moderated lists are managed by an individual who takes on responsibility for sending messages to the list. The moderator takes on an active role in determining what should be sent to the list, ensuring that only those messages relevant to the topic of the list are received by subscribers.

  Moderated lists are most often used for newsletters and journals. Moderated lists also result in on-line "discussions" that are very focused on a particular topic, due to the involvement of the moderator in posting only those messages directly related to the topic at hand.

- unmoderated

  In an unmoderated list, any message sent by you immediately goes to everyone on the list.

  An unmoderated list might permit anyone to send to it, or it might be restricted, permitting only members to send to it.

- closed

  The Internet is a very diverse place; this results in some lists that simply are not open to everyone.

  You must meet some type of qualification to join the list — even to receive messages sent to the list. These lists are often used to restrict access to members of a particular organization.

USING LISTS — THE MECHANICS

The mechanics of Internet mailing lists are quite straightforward.

You subscribe or join an Internet mailing list by sending an e-mail message to an Internet address established for the purposes of list maintenance.

Once your message has been received at the destination, your request to be added to or deleted from a list is:

- processed manually by the list owner;

or

- processed by a specialized piece of software (called a list manager, but also regularly referred to as a listserver), which automatically makes the change to the appropriate list.

There are several automatic list managers throughout the Internet, including the programs **majordomo**, **listserv** and **mailserv**, all of which have their own unique method for joining and leaving a list.

For example, the following message is a copy of an original request to subscribe to a mailing list called **net-happenings**, a list which summarizes new Internet announcements. It has been sent a **majordomo** list manager.

```
Date: Thu, 09 Sep 1993 07:22:52 edt
Reply-To: jcarroll@jacc.com
From: jcarroll@jacc.com (Jim Carroll)
To: majordomo@is.internic.net
Cc:

subscribe net-happenings Jim Carroll
```

When this message was received at **majordomo@is.internic.net**, a program called **majordomo** processed the details of the message, and the Internet e-mail address **jcarroll@jacc.com** was added to the list.

We have reprinted, in Appendix Q, a document by James Milles of the Saint Louis University Law Library (**millesjg@sluvca.slu.edu**) which summarizes most of the popular mail servers, and the commands to use with each of them to join or leave a list.

You can obtain the most recent copy of this document by e-mail:

Using E-mail	
Send message to:	listserv@ubvm.cc.buffalo.edu
In text of message, type:	get mailser cmd nettrain f=mail

STARTING YOUR OWN LIST

One of the greatest benefits of the Internet comes through the fact that anyone can establish their own Internet mailing list.

Your Internet service provider might be able to provide you with your own Internet mailing lists. If so, you can establish a mailing list on a particular topic, and invite your friends and peers to join the list. Over time, you might find that the list begins to gain recognition throughout the Internet.

In addition, it has become increasingly possible to establish automatic list servers through e-mail software. Pegasus Mail for DOS and Windows, for example, includes this feature.

Many Internet lists began informally, yet have emerged to become the global "home" for a particular topic. Given the power of global knowledge networking, establishing your own mailing list on a topic of importance to you could become one of your most useful Internet resources.

INFORMATION ON LISTS

The obvious question is "how do I find a particular list?"

Often, you will hear about a mailing list by word of mouth, or it will be mentioned in some Internet resource that you track. In particular, a few USENET newsgroups as discussed within the next section are often used to announce new lists.

There are a number of resources available on the Internet which provide details on mailing lists. A sample entry, from the document *Publicly Accessible Mailing Lists* described below, details information for the mailing list concerning Canada's favorite baseball team [2]:

```
Toronto Blue Jays
Contact: stlouis@unixg.ubc.ca  (Phill St-Louis)
Purpose: Discussion of the Toronto Blue Jays Baseball Club
including player transactions, predictions, game commen-
tary, etc.  Everyone welcome!
```

The same list is described in the *List of Interest Groups* document described below:

```
jays@hivnet.ubc.ca
[Last Updated 9/92]
This is a mailing list for fans of the
Toronto Blue Jays baseball team.  Scores and highlights of
games, player transactions, draft picks, and status of ri-
val teams will be discussed on this group.
This list is not archived.
To join:
Please send all requests to jays-request@hivnet.ubc.ca or
to
phill@hivnet.ubc.ca
Coordinator: Phill St-Louis (phill@hivnet.ubc.ca or
stlouis@unixg.ubc.ca)
```

MAJOR SOURCES

You can retrieve several definitive summaries of available mailing lists on the Internet. Some of the more popular sources are detailed below.[3]

If retrieving these documents by e-mail, keep in mind that these documents are quite large — for example, the List of Interest Groups described below is over 1.2

megabytes in size. If you are using a commercial e-mail provider which charges on a per character basis, be prepared for a rather hefty bill!

None of these sources are comprehensive — since new lists are being added throughout the Internet on a regular basis, these summaries are a good starting point to get an idea of the lists that are out there.

BITNET LISTS

BITNET is a global network that is separate from the Internet, yet it links academic institutions and research organizations worldwide. It is fair to say that although BITNET is not disappearing, it is rapidly merging into and becoming part of the Internet.

BITNET provides global electronic mail and mailing list capabilities (and in fact, is where the **LISTSERV** program originated). It is home to some of the most diverse and interesting mailing lists available. Internet users can join any of these mailing lists.

The document *"List of all LISTSERV lists known to LISTSERV@BITNIC"* (a summary of all BITNET mailing lists) provides a comprehensive summary of over 4,000 special interest lists.

TO OBTAIN THIS LISTING

Using E-mail	
Send message to:	listserv@bitnic.cren.net
In text of message, type:	list global

PUBLICLY ACCESSIBLE MAILING LISTS
(Currently maintained by Stephanie da Silva.)

This is the definitive summary of Internet lists. Revised monthly, the list contains a detailed description of each list, as well as information on how to subscribe.

TO OBTAIN THIS LISTING

Using E-mail	
Send message to:	mail-server@rtfm.mit.edu
In text of message, type:	
	send /pub/usenet/news.answers/mail/mailing-lists/part01
	send /pub/usenet/news.answers/mail/mailing-lists/part02
	send /pub/usenet/news.answers/mail/mailing-lists/part03
	send /pub/usenet/news.answers/mail/mailing-lists/part04
	send /pub/usenet/news.answers/mail/mailing-lists/part05
	send /pub/usenet/news.answers/mail/mailing-lists/part06
	send /pub/usenet/news.answers/mail/mailing-lists/part07
	send /pub/usenet/news.answers/mail/mailing-lists/part08
	send /pub/usenet/news.answers/mail/mailing-lists/part09
	send /pub/usenet/news.answers/mail/mailing-lists/part10
	send /pub/usenet/news.answers/mail/mailing-lists/part11
	send /pub/usenet/news.answers/mail/mailing-lists/part12
	send /pub/usenet/news.answers/mail/mailing-lists/part13
	send /pub/usenet/news.answers/mail/mailing-lists/part14

Using Anonymous FTP	
FTP site:	rtfm.mit.edu
Directory:	pub/usenet/news.answers/mail/mailing-lists
Files:	part01, part02, part03, etc.

DIRECTORY OF ELECTRONIC JOURNALS AND NEWSLETTERS

This directory details a number of journals and newsletters which you can subscribe to via e-mail. Although heavily academic and research oriented, it does give an excellent overview of the wide diversity of topics that you can subscribe to via mailing lists.

TO OBTAIN THIS LISTING

Using E-mail	
Send message to:	listserv@acadvm1.uottawa.ca
In text of message, type:	get ejournl1 directry
	get ejournl2 directry

LIST OF INTEREST GROUPS

This document refers to itself as the "List of lists" — a listing of special interest group mailing lists available on the Internet.

TO OBTAIN THIS LISTING

Using E-mail	
Send message to:	mail-server@sri.com
In text of message, type:	send netinfo/interest-groups

Using Anonymous FTP	
FTP site:	sri.com
Directory:	netinfo
File:	interest-groups

NEW-LIST MAILING LIST

This is a mailing list for announcements of new mailing lists, primarily for those based upon the **LISTSERV** software.

TO OBTAIN THIS LISTING

Using E-mail	
Send message to:	listserv@vm1.nodak.edu
In text of message, type:	sub new-list firstname lastname
Special Instructions:	Replace firstname lastname above with your own firstname and lastname.

THE DIRECTORY OF SCHOLARLY ELECTRONIC CONFERENCES

The Directory of Scholarly Electronic Conferences contains descriptions of electronic mailing lists on topics of interest to scholars. The Directory is organized by academic subject area.

TO OBTAIN THIS LISTING

Using E-mail	
Send message to:	listserv@kentvm.kent.edu
In text of message, type:	GET ACADLIST INDEX
	GET ACADLIST FILE1
	GET ACADLIST FILE2
	GET ACADLIST FILE3
	|
	|
	GET ACADLIST FILE9

Using Anonymous FTP	
FTP site:	ksuvxa.kent.edu
Directory:	library
File:	acadlist.index,
	acadlist.file1
	acadlist.file2
	|
	|
	acadlist.file9

Using Gopher	
Gopher address:	gopher.usask.ca
Path:	World Wide Information
	Directory of Scholarly Electronic Conferences
File:	acadlist.index,
	acadlist.file1
	acadlist.file2
	|
	|
	acadlist.file9

Caution: Since each of these files is large, it is recommended that you first retrieve the ACADLIST INDEX file, and then request the files you want, rather than retrieve all 9 files at once. The ACADLIST INDEX file will tell you which files contain which subject areas.

LIST OF USENET GROUPS THAT ARE AVAILABLE AS MAILING LISTS
This is a list of USENET groups that are available as mailing lists.

TO OBTAIN THIS LISTING

Using E-mail	
Send message to:	mail-server@rtfm.mit.edu
In text of message, type:	send pub/usenet/news.answers/mail/news-gateways/part1

Using Anonymous FTP	
FTP site:	rtfm.mit.edu
Directory:	pub/usenet/news.answers/mail/news-gateways
File:	part1

NET-HAPPENINGS LIST
If you really want to track what is going on with the Internet, you should join the **net-happenings** list.

TO OBTAIN THIS LISTING

Using E-mail	
Send message to:	majordomo@is.internic.net
In text of message, type:	subscribe net-happenings firstname lastname
Special Instructions:	Replace firstname lastname above with your own firstname lastname.

This list has about 15-20 messages per day. Announcements concerning new mailing lists and other Internet resources are sent to this list on a regular basis throughout the day. As well, information that even remotely impacts the Internet, such as initiatives relating to the "information highway" or "national information infrastructure," are often sent to the list.

The result is a continuous stream of messages that are wide ranging and varied, but somehow relate to the Internet.

You should only join this list if you have a desire to receive a lot of e-mail and you want to track what is going on with the Internet. *This list is for hard core Internet junkies only.*

SEARCHING LISTS OF LISTS

It is possible to search several of these lists of lists. For example, you can search the Bitnet lists database by sending a specially formatted e-mail message.

TO SEARCH THE BITNET LIST DATABASE

Using E-mail	
Send message to:	listserv@bitnic.cren.net
In text of message, type:	list global/keyword
Special Instructions:	replace keyword above with the word you wish to do search on.

For example, if you are looking for a list on honey bees, you could send the following command to **listserv@bitnic.cren.net**:

                    `list global/bee`

A search will be performed on the Bitnet lists database, and an automatic reply will be mailed back to you containing the names of all the BITNET mailing lists that contain the word "bee." The automatic reply will look like this:

```
From: BITNET list server at BITNIC (1.8a)
  <LISTSERV@BITNIC.CREN.NET>
Subject: File: "LISTSERV LISTS"

Excerpt from the LISTSERV lists known to LISTSERV@BITNIC
on 29 Aug 1994 16:07

Search string: BEE

* * * * * * * * * * * * * * * * * * * * * * * * * * * * * * * * * * * * * * * *

* To subscribe, send mail to LISTSERV@ LISTSERV.NET with
the following command in the text (not the subject) of
your message:
SUBSCRIBE listname                                  *

*
*

Replace 'listname' with the name in the first column of
the table.


Network-wide ID  Full address and list      description

- - - - - - - - - - - - - -    - - - - - - - - - - - - - - - - - - - - - - - -

BEE-L     BEE-L@ALBNYVM1.BITNET
          Discussion of Bee Biology

BEEF-L    BEEF-L@WSUVM1.BITNET
          Beef Specialists
```

```
BEER-L      BEER-L@UA1VM.BITNET
            Homebrew Digest Redistri   bution List
LDP-CS      LDP-CS@ERS.
            ERS-USDA Beef and Sheep    S&O Monthly Update
ULTIMATE    ULTIMATE@PUCC.BITNET
            Princeton Ultimate Fris    bee List
```

The first mailing list item is BEE-L, a mailing list for the discussion of bee biology. The other mailing lists are not bee-related at all. They were returned to you because they contained the letters "bee."

USENET

USENET is described by many people as the "world's largest bulletin board system," even though it is definitely not a Bulletin Board System.

USENET consists of several thousand topic areas known as newsgroups, with topics ranging from locksmithing to pyrotechnics to religion to C++ computer programing.

As a user of the Internet, you can choose to subscribe to any of the USENET newsgroups that your Internet service provider carries. Not all providers carry all newsgroups.

Some USENET newsgroups are moderated in ways similar to mailing lists. However, since most USENET newsgroups are unmoderated, you can send (referred to as "posting") to any newsgroup as well.

NEWSGROUP CATEGORIES

Newsgroups within USENET belong to a series of categories. The major (global) newsgroup categories are:

CATEGORY	TOPIC
biz.	Business oriented topics
comp.	Computer oriented topics
misc.	Stuff that doesn't fit elsewhere
news.	News and information concerning the Internet or USENET
rec.	Recreational activities, i.e., bowling, skiing, chess, etc.
sci.	Scientific topics
soc.	Sociological issues
talk.	Debate oriented topics

There is also an **alt**. group. What can you find in **alt**. groups? You name it, **alt**. groups likely discuss it. Anyone can start an **alt**. group without approval, but not all sites carry all **alt**. groups. The result is a somewhat free-wheeling atmosphere, with some of the most controversial newsgroups being located in the **alt**. category.

SUBTOPICS

Each category consists of several hundred or thousand topics, organized into sub-categories.

For example, the newsgroup category **rec**. (recreation topics), includes the sub-categories:

- **rec.arts**

- **rec.audio**

- **rec.music**

and below this, a further categorization can be found, for example:

- **rec.arts.poems**

- **rec.arts.misc**

- **rec.arts.bonsai**

For very popular topics, another level of categorization might be found. For example, because of the popularity of science fiction within the Internet, there are several science fiction newsgroups within the **rec.arts.sf** category, including:

- **rec.arts.sf.misc**

- **rec.arts.sf.movies**

- **rec.arts.sf.science**

An individual could choose to subscribe to all the **rec.arts.sf** groups (getting all three above as well as others), or could choose to subscribe to only the **rec.arts.sf.movies** group.

CANADIAN NEWSGROUP CATEGORIES

Bruce Becker (**news@gts.org**) maintains a list of Canadian news groups. The categories within this list for major locations (excluding specific university categories) include:

Categories	Topics	Categories	Topics
ab	Alberta	mtl	Montreal
atl	Atlantic	nf	Newfoundland
bc	British Columbia	ns	Nova Scotia
calgary	Calgary	ont	Ontario
can	Canadian	ott	Ottawa
edm	Edmonton	qc	Quebec
hfx	Halifax	tor	Toronto
kingston	Kingston	van	Vancouver
kw	Kitchener/ Waterloo	wpg	Winnipeg
man	Manitoba		

MAJOR CANADIAN NEWSGROUPS

Some of the more popular Canadian newsgroups include:

- **can.general**. Discussion of general Canadian issues. A wide ranging number of topics.

- **can.jobs**. A surprising number of job postings are made to this group; perhaps 20 a week. Most are for people having computer expertise, with a particular emphasis on UNIX systems.

- **can.politics**. Deficits, governments, and all the related topics are discussed in here. A very busy newsgroup. Be prepared to argue.

- **ont.general**. Discussion of topics relevant to Ontario. For example, there has been much discussion recently of the Karla Homolka/Paul Teale trial ban, with banned articles concerning the trial often being posted here.

- **can.domain**. Discussion of policies and procedures relevant to registration under the **.ca domain**, and technologies and other issues affecting domain registration in Canada. A good place to track Internet issues in Canada.

As well, several communities in Canada are very active with their local Internet newsgroups, including those within the **kw.** (Kitchener Waterloo), **ott.** (Ottawa) and **tor.** (Toronto) newsgroups.

A SAMPLE USENET MESSAGE

A USENET message looks like an e-mail message, with some subtle differences. The primary difference is that a newsgroup message includes a reference to the newsgroups the information was posted to. As seen below, this item was posted to the **can.general** group.

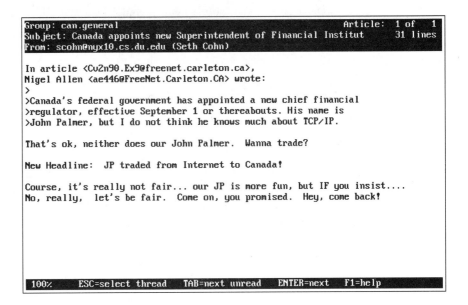

```
Group: can.general                                        Article:  1 of   1
Subject: Canada appoints new Superintendent of Financial Institut    31 lines
From: scohn@nyx10.cs.du.edu (Seth Cohn)

In article <Cv2n90.Ex9@freenet.carleton.ca>,
Nigel Allen <ae446@FreeNet.Carleton.CA> wrote:
>
>Canada's federal government has appointed a new chief financial
>regulator, effective September 1 or thereabouts. His name is
>John Palmer, but I do not think he knows much about TCP/IP.

That's ok, neither does our John Palmer.  Wanna trade?

New Headline:  JP traded from Internet to Canada!

Course, it's really not fair... our JP is more fun, but IF you insist....
No, really,  let's be fair.  Come on, you promised.  Hey, come back!



100%      ESC=select thread    TAB=next unread    ENTER=next    F1=help
```

HOW DOES USENET WORK?

To understand what USENET is and how it works, consider the newsgroup **rec.sport.football.canadian**.

Formed a number of years ago, it was established to provide a convenient discussion forum for the Canadian version of the sport.

CREATING A NEWSGROUP

The process through which **rec.sport.football.canadian** was created sheds some light on how USENET operates currently. Note that this process applies for the "big-7 hierarchy," i.e., for the **comp.**, **rec.**, **sci.**, **news.**, **soc. talk**.and **misc.** newsgroups. Procedures for other hierarchies might vary.

- The individual who wanted to start the newsgroup sent a message to the moderator of the USENET newsgroup **news.announce.newgroups** as well as to several other newsgroups, indicating why such a newsgroup should be formed. The message contained a "charter" for the group; that is, the reasons for the group, and an overview of what the group would be used for (the discussion of Canadian football). The message was posted to **news.announce.new-groups** by the moderator of that group.

- A period of discussion concerning the merits of having a special group devoted to Canadian football took place within the newsgroup **news.groups** for a month or so. Anyone could have participated in this discussion.

- Once the period of discussion was complete, a "call-for-votes" went out for people to vote on whether the group should be created. A designated period of time was set aside for voting, and an individual volunteered to be the official vote-taker. Anyone is permitted to vote.

- Once the period of time was up (usually 21-30 days), the votes were tabulated, and the group was found to have met the standard USENET acceptance criteria (the standard rule is that there are at least 100 more yes votes than no votes; and at least 2/3 of the votes had voted yes).

- Since the group "passed," a "newsgroup control message" was sent out by David Lawrence,[4] the moderator of the **news.announce.newgroups** newsgroup, advising all USENET sites that **rec.sport.canadian.football** was now considered to be on the "official" USENET list. The "newsgroup control message" provides the group with "official status."

- Had **rec.sport.canadian.football** not passed the vote, a newsgroup control message to create the group would not have been sent out by David Lawrence, and the group would not be an official group. The result would have been that most USENET locations would refuse to carry the group, since it hadn't passed the vote. (And in fact, it could even end up on a list of invalid newsgroups).

  Those who ignore the guidance over how to establish a new newsgroup will almost certainly fail in their attempt.[5]

- One other factor is that even though it is now an official newsgroup, any USENET site has the choice as to whether it will or will not carry the **rec.sport.football.canadian** newsgroup.

It is this global co-operative effort concerning the establishment of new newsgroups that is at the heart of USENET.

NEWSGROUPS IN THE CANADIAN HIERARCHY

The process above applies to the main USENET newsgroups; i.e., **comp, news, soc, rec,** etc. The process does not apply to newsgroups in the Canadian hierarchy (i.e. **ca., ont.** and others).

In fact, there is no formal process for the creation of newsgroups in Canada. Instead, a method has evolved in which proposals for new topics are posted and discussed in the newsgroup **can.general**. If there are no major objections, and if the consensus is that the group should be created, then a control message is propagated by the individual seeking creation of the group, and the group is created.

This informal process of creation is strengthened through the circulation of periodic "checkgroup messages" which detail the Canadian newsgroups which have more or less been accepted by the Canadian USENET community. In addition, individuals involved in managing the Canadian Internet service providers tend to be a very agreeable lot, as they are generally consistent in the news groups they carry. This has lead to a high degree of consistency in what are accepted as the "official" Canadian USENET newsgroups.

In August 1994, a special newsgroup, **can.config**, was created as a place to discuss the formation and propagation of Canadian USENET newsgroups.

A complete list of Canadian newsgroups as of December 1993 is provided in Appendix G, in the document *Directory of Canadian USENET Newsgroups*, reprinted with the permission of Bruce Becker. Bruce posts the message on a regular basis to a number of Canadian newsgroups, including **can.general**. Corrections and updates concerning Canadian newsgroups can be sent to Bruce at `news@gts.org.`

READING NEWS

Once the newsgroup **rec.sport.football.canadian** was approved, people could subscribe to the newsgroup and could begin posting information to it.[6]

Hence, upon approval:

- Messages posted to **rec.sport.canadian. football** are now transmitted throughout the USENET system.

- Individual users of USENET choose what newsgroups they want to belong to. Those with an interest in the CFL choose to belong to the **rec.sport.canadian.football** list.

- Each user then reads their USENET groups using newsreader software.

NEWSREADER SOFTWARE

Some individuals read USENET "on-line," i.e., while linked to the computer of their Internet service provider by modem or some other link.

Others read it "off-line," i.e., all USENET articles for groups they belong to are transferred to their computer or local network, and are read locally while not linked to another computer.

Newsreader software differs depending on the Internet service provider and the method used to retrieve USENET news, and on whether you are reading it on-line or off-line.

Newsreader software organizes each newsgroup into listings by newsgroup topic. For example, within the DOS program SNEWS (an off-line reader for PC's), the newsgroups subscribed to by one of the authors appear as follows:

```
        Select Newsgroup  (Simple NEWS 1.91)  [499k]


    >    1. alt.internet.services                    12 (74)
         2. can.jobs                                    (1)
         3. comp.groupware                              (1)
         4. comp.infosystems                            (1)
         5. comp.internet.library                       (0)
         6. comp.mail                                   (0)
         7. comp.mail.mime                            2 (3)
         8. comp.mail.misc                            4 (16)
         9. comp.mail.multi-media                       (1)
        10. comp.mail.sendmail                        1 (17)
        11. comp.mail.uucp                            1 (5)
        12. comp.protocols.iso.x400                     (3)
        13. comp.risks                                  (0)
        14. comp.security.misc                          (0)
        15. junk                                        (5)
        16. news.announce.newgroups                     (0)
        17. news.announce.newusers                      (0)
        18. news.sysadmin                               (0)
        19. ont.general                                (23)

        ESC=quit   TAB=next unread group   ENTER=read group   F1=help
```

Within each topic, individual postings are listed. For example, within the **comp.infosystems** newsgroup on August 24, 1994, the following articles appeared.:

```
        Select Thread  (Simple NEWS 1.91)  [440k]
 Group: comp.infosystems                              53 articles
                                                      53 unread

    >   1.    2    2 Loading Share.exe
        2.    1    1 The HiTek Report
        3.    1    1 MultiPlatform Software Testing & Porting Facility in SJ, CA
        4.    2    2 What ever happened to whois++?
        5.    3    3 AD - Keep up with the times!
        6.    1    1 Need Profnet info
        7.    3    3 Women in Computing
        8.    1    1 CFP: GODDARD CONF ON SPACE APPLICATIONS OF AI & EMERGING INF
        9.    1    1 Donna Cox's video at SIGGRAPH--where can I get a copy ?
       10.    1    1 whois server implementation
       11.    1    1 PACBELL's ISDN
       12.    1    1 BISC Conference in Barbados September 29 and 30
       13.    1    1 Seminar: Groupware in Action
       14.    1    1 Measuring IS Departments
       15.    2    2 MCI/SPRINTMAIL Gateways
       16.    1    1 CALL FOR PAPERS: 1st Special Issue of ISR
       17.    4    4 World Wide Web Frequently Asked Questions (FAQ), Part 1/2
       18.    1    1 SOFTWARE WORLD USA Announcement
       19.    1    1 Calling All Gopher Architects and Web-Setters

        ESC=select group   TAB=next unread   ENTER=next article   F1=help
```

Of course, users of other newsreader software will likely see a completely different presentation of USENET. As an example, consider the same newsgroup on the same day, as seen through the Pipeline for Windows software through the Toronto-based Internet provider InfoRamp.

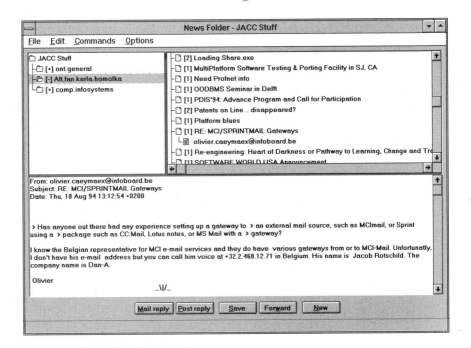

In Chapter 9, we discuss how to get connected to the Internet, and examine some of the options available to you in finding various types of USENET newsreader software.

USENET – WHAT IT'S NOT!

There are some things that you should know about USENET:

- It isn't the Internet.

  USENET happens to be carried over the Internet, as well as other networks.

  Yet, it has come to be so closely identified as an "Internet resource" that most people think of USENET as being a fundamental part of the Internet.[7]

- It isn't owned by anyone, nor is there one central authority that runs it.

  USENET exists because of the co-operative efforts of thousands of people around the globe: first and foremost, the thousands of UNIX systems and news administrators of subscribing systems from around the world; and secondly, through the efforts of a wide number of volunteers who catalogue USENET resources, conduct votes, post information and participate in countless other ways.

  The result is an on-line system which is managed through the co-operative effort of literally thousands of people from around the globe. Some call it organized or cooperative anarchy.

- It isn't for commercial use.

There is no surer way to receive streams of on-line abuse than by abusing USENET for what is clearly a profit-oriented activity.

USENET was developed to support the exchange of knowledge and information. There are thousands of topics — yet with all the millions of news articles posted to USENET, it maintains a certain culture. Even as the Internet becomes more commercialized, USENET seems to be maintaining its status as a system not to be blatantly used for commercial purposes, even though there are some buy-and-sell newsgroups.

- It is used to a limited extent for commercial purposes.

Even though USENET isn't for commercial use, there are some newsgroups that exist for distribution of information concerning certain products, and for service announcements from system vendors.

What does this mean? You might use USENET with regard to your business, "I am trying to get my computer to do this; does anyone have any hints," but you certainly shouldn't use USENET to try to drum up business. "Hey, I've started a consulting firm. Call me if you need help — my rates are $120 an hour."

NETWORK ETIQUETTE

The most important things you can learn about USENET are that:

- It has a unique on-line culture.

- Those who do not respect this culture do so at their own peril.

The culture includes procedures and guidance concerning topics such as newsgroup creation (as described above); what the network can be used for (i.e., non-commercial activity); how to post news articles; newsgroup names; official vs. non-official newsgroups; chain letters; inappropriate postings; and hundreds of other issues of etiquette.

The easiest way to learn about USENET culture is to:

- Join several newsgroups and watch how they work for some time.

In particular, if you are interested in how USENET newsgroups are established, subscribe to the groups **news.announce.newgroups** and **news.groups.**

News.announce.newgroups is the place where proposals for new groups are posted. **News.groups** is the place where these proposals are debated.

Be prepared to be shocked by what you might see in a debate: sometimes simple proposals for a new newsgroup degenerate into raging debates, with emotions getting out of hand and insults and accusations flying with fury. Why? It's the culture of USENET.

There is no better way to understand the culture of USENET than to belong to **news.groups** for a few months.

- Documents such as *A Primer on How to Work with the USENET Community* and *Rules for Posting to USENET* are posted regularly to the groups **news.newusers.questions** and **news.answers**, and can also be retrieved from a number of FTP locations.

USING USENET

The method that you use to subscribe to and read news articles will depend on how you access the Internet; there are far too many methods to describe here.

You should seek instructions from your service provider on the specific steps you should follow.

However, there are several things to keep in mind regardless of how you access USENET:

- If you respond to a posting within a USENET newsgroup, you can choose to post a follow-up message that goes to the newsgroup, or you can choose to send an e-mail message to the original poster.

- You should have some type of method of saving an article to your own computer.

  If you encounter a message that looks like gibberish, it might be a "uuencoded" file. If it isn't, it could be a ROT-13 message. ROT-13 is a simple method of changing characters in a message (A turns into N, B turns into O, etc.), and is used for controversial postings, offensive jokes, or other postings that skirt the line.

- People ROT-13 a message to warn you that it might be of questionable taste. Your news software likely has a method to de-ROT-13 the posting.

- Many USENET newsgroups periodically post a FAQ or Frequently Asked Question list. The purpose is twofold: to help out new users, but also to avoid the situation where new users continually post the same question over and over again and again every time they subscribe to a group.

  FAQ's are archived in many locations, and are available via FTP. The best source is known as **rtfm.mit.edu.**

TO OBTAIN FAQ'S

FTP site:	rtfm.mit.edu
Directory:	pub/usenet/news.answers

For example, a FAQ, prepared in conjunction with the newsgroup **rec.sport.football.canadian,** describes many of the special aspects of Canadian football. It can be found in the document **canadian-football** at the FTP site above.

LISTS OF NEWSGROUPS

Listings of USENET newsgroups in the major categories above can be found within the document List of Active Newsgroups, posted to the groups **news.announce.newusers** on a frequent basis.

You should also check with your Internet service provider to obtain a list of the newsgroups they provide. Not all providers distribute all newsgroups.

Finally, when you are on-line with an Internet service provider, you can often search for specific newsgroups by name. Once again, taking a look at Pipeline for Windows through InfoRamp, we can search for any newsgroups containing the word "highway."

KNOWLEDGE NETWORKING AND THE INTERNET

Internet mailing lists and USENET newsgroups are a tremendous asset to any individual or organization in that they provide new methods and new capabilities to obtain answers to questions, to seek knowledge or to track topics.

With the explosion of use of the Internet in Canada and across the world, the number of topics available will certainly continue to increase. As you learn how to use the Internet, always keep in mind that if a topic you would like to track doesn't exist today, it could very easily exist tomorrow.

---

1. Individuals on commercial and consumer oriented services that have links to the Internet (i.e., Compuserve, ATTMail, etc), should be careful in subscribing to mailing lists. These services, which charge either on a per character basis or time basis, might result in substantial charges to receive messages from mailing lists with a large number of messages.

2. Of course, given the performance of the Jays during the 1994 season, it could be argued that the Montreal Expos are rapidly becoming Canada's favorite baseball team!

3. References to file locations and information retrieval on the Internet sometimes changes, as systems shut down and as new organizations take on efforts previously undertaken by someone else. The Internet is a constantly evolving place: as a result, these instructions, while current as of September 1994, are not guaranteed to always work.

4. In this role, David Lawrence comes the closest to being a central authority for USENET. He maintains his position as the result of having built up a large amount of trust and respect from all members of the USENET community through the years.

5. One of the authors knows this is true, from personal experience.

6. If their Internet service provider provides USENET service and if the provider chose to carry that particular news group.

7. In fact, you can probably join a USENET newsgroup in which you could debate whether USENET is really part of the Internet or not. The discussion has gone on in some groups for months and years . . .

·····································

REMOTE ACCESS APPLICATIONS TELNET, FTP, ARCHIE

Try as you may, you cannot imagine how much data is available on the Internet.

The Internet and your business
Fortune Magazine, Mon 07 Mar 94

In this chapter, we take a look at two tools which let you access other computers on the network, and an additional tool that helps you locate files on the Internet.

Telnet and FTP are two Internet resources, similar in concept but different in function. Both let you sign on to other computers on the Internet; while Telnet lets you run programs on the other computer, FTP permits you to retrieve files from the other computer.

Archie is a program that will be useful to you as you work with FTP. Archie is a very useful tool to locate particular files in various FTP file archives.

TELNET, FTP AND ARCHIE CLIENTS

The particular method by which you might use Telnet, FTP or Archie could differ depending on the Internet service provider that you use, and depending on the type of client software you have available.

In this chapter, we present the use of each of these applications, first through a dial-up shell account, and again through Windows-based software on an account that is directly linked to the Internet. You will see that each application is quite different depending on the type of system from which you are accessing the Internet.

In the most basic form, through a "shell account," you will find it necessary to type in a series of commands to access a particular Telnet resource, FTP file location or to perform an Archie search.

Alternatively, if you have a direct network connection to the Internet, or can access it via a dial-up SLIP or PPP account, you can simply "point and click" to retrieve files or access specific Telnet resources, access and browse FTP archives, and perform an Archie search.

TELNET

Telnet opens your world to other Internet resources by providing you with the capability to run programs on other computers on the Internet. These programs might let you search or retrieve information such as a catalog of books in a local or remote library.

There are a number of locations throughout the Internet which you can Telnet to and use without charge. In each case, you are actually signing into a computer located somewhere else on the Internet.

In Canada, these locations include:

- links to the on-line catalogues of various libraries, such as the Vancouver Public Library, in order to search for particular books or other materials. A complete listing of libraries in Canada which you can access through the Internet can be found in Appendix M, in the *Directory of Internet-Accessible Library Catalogues in Canada*;

- Free-Net's (currently established in Victoria, Ottawa, Halifax, Toronto and elsewhere), to access local community information;

- access to pay-per-use database services such as CompuServe, Dialog and Nexis, if you have an account already set up with these services.[1]

As well, you can reach any other Telnet resource worldwide from your Canadian Internet account (if your account provides Telnet service), such as the "Weather Underground" system at the University of Michigan, which includes details on Canadian weather.

Once you reach a location by Telnet, you will be able to:

- directly access the resource, if no "login" or "sign-in" ID is required;

- access the resource by providing a public user ID; or

- access the resource by providing a valid user ID and password for a system that has generally restricted its access.

TELNET ACCESS — VIA A SHELL ACCOUNT

In a shell account, the Telnet program is accessed from your Internet host by typing **telnet**. Once you have accessed the Telnet command, you will see the prompt TELNET> on the screen.

Once at that prompt, you can use the **open** command with an Internet address to establish a link to a particular Internet resource, or you can use other Telnet commands to change your terminal type or perform other activities.

The Internet address that you use in the Telnet command could be the domain name or the actual domain address. For example, to link to the University of Western Ontario library, you would

- type **telnet** to get to the telnet prompt, and then type **open library.uwo.ca** at this prompt (**telnet>**);

- or, to take a short cut, type **telnet library.uwo.ca** to go there directly;

- or, you could use the actual IP address: i.e., by typing **telnet 129.100.2.18**

On occasion, you will be advised to use the domain name with a particular "port" number. This is required when you are accessing a system on the Internet in which the port directs you to a particular application. You are usually told when a particular port address is required. Type the port number after the Telnet address, when a port number is required.

For example, access to the University of Michigan Weather Underground system, which includes Canadian weather details, requires a port number. In this case, you are advised to telnet to the address **downwind.sprl.umich.edu 3000**, where 3000 is the port number used for this particular application.

SAMPLE TELNET SESSION – SHELL ACCOUNT

The following session details the steps taken to Telnet to the Vancouver Public Library, which like many libraries across Canada has made its on-line catalog available to the Internet.

The session uses a login ID of **netpac**, and a password of **netpac1**. These are provided by the library as the general IDs for public access, as detailed within the listing of *Directory of Internet-Accessible Library Catalogues in Canada* in Appendix M of this book.

```
                                          E:94% VT100 ↕   00:00:53  7:57a
$ telnet
telnet> open vpl.vancouver.bc.ca
Trying 134.87.100.1...
Connected to vpl.vancouver.bc.ca.
Escape character is '^]'.
Sequoia Telnet Server Ver 3.5
login: netpac
Password:
Copyright (c) 1989 Sequoia (All Rights Reserved)
******************************************************************************
*                Welcome to the Sequoia at Vancouver Public Library!        *
******************************************************************************
NETPAC,NETPAC1
```

Note that you could also, at the Unix $ prompt, just type **telnet vpl.vancouver.bc.ca,** rather than typing **telnet,** waiting for the prompt and then typing **open vpl.vancouver.bc.ca**.

Once attached to the library, you are prompted to indicate the type of terminal that you are using. In most cases, you would indicate VT-100, assuming that you had this capability on the communications software in your PC.

```
                                          E:94% VT100 ↕   00:00:56  7:57a




Please indicate which terminal you are using.

 1. ANSI Emulation
 2. ADDS Viewpoint emulation
 3. ADDS Viewpoint 60 Emulation
 4. VT52 Emulation
 5. VT100 Emulation
 6. Wyse 30
 7. Wyse 50
 8. Wyse 50 Terminal, ADDS VP Enhanced Mode
 9. Wyse 60
10. Wyse 75
11. Wyse 150
12. ADDS Regent 25
13. Quit (Logoff)

   Enter Selection>
```

Once you have indicated your terminal type, you see some copyright information, and are then presented with the main menu of the Vancouver Public Library system.

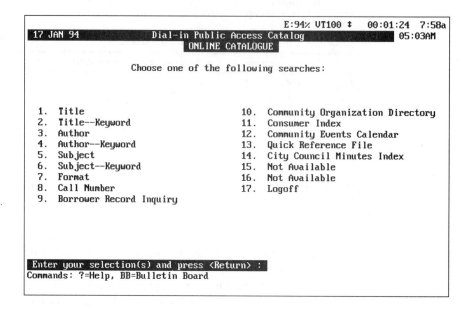

```
                                          E:94% UT100 ↕  00:01:24  7:58a
  17 JAN 94            Dial-in Public Access Catalog           05:03AM
                            ONLINE CATALOGUE

                   Choose one of the following searches:


     1.  Title                       10.  Community Organization Directory
     2.  Title--Keyword              11.  Consumer Index
     3.  Author                      12.  Community Events Calendar
     4.  Author--Keyword             13.  Quick Reference File
     5.  Subject                     14.  City Council Minutes Index
     6.  Subject--Keyword            15.  Not Available
     7.  Format                      16.  Not Available
     8.  Call Number                 17.  Logoff
     9.  Borrower Record Inquiry




   Enter your selection(s) and press <Return> :
  Commands: ?=Help, BB=Bulletin Board
```

From this point, you could search for a particular book, by title, author, keyword, subject or other criteria, or access community-related information put up by the Vancouver Public Library.

TELNET ACCESS – VIA A DIRECT ACCOUNT

The same session, when accessed through an account that is directly linked to the Internet, is not really all that much different.

Using the software Trumpet Telnet through a SLIP account, we are first prompted to enter the Telnet address that we want to link to:

```
                       telnet

   Host

   vpl.vancouver.bc.ca

              OK          Cancel
```

Having done this, we are then linked to the Vancouver Public Library, to a screen that looks almost identical to what we saw through a shell account:

```
┌─┬──────────────────── Telnet - [vpl.vancouver.bc.ca] ──────────────┬───┬─┐
│─│                                                                  │ ▼ │▲│
├─┴──────────────────────────────────────────────────────────────────┴───┼─┤
│  File   Edit   Connect   Special   Window   Help                        │▲│
├─────────────────────────────────────────────────────────────────────────┤
│                                                                       │▲│
│ HP-UX vplmkii A.09.04 U 9000/887 (ttyie)                               │ │
│                                                                        │ │
│ login: netpac                                                          │ │
│ Password:                                                              │ │
│ Please wait...checking for disk quotas                                 │ │
│ ***********************************************************************│ │
│ *                                                                    * │ │
│ *        Welcome to the NEW (!!) Vancouver Public Library System     * │ │
│ *                                                                    * │ │
│ ***********************************************************************│ │
│                                                                        │ │
│ UniVerse Command Language 7.3                                          │ │
│ (c) Copyright 1993 Vmark Software Inc. - All Rights Reserved           │ │
│ ACC.DI logged on: Wed Aug 24 13:15:29 1994                             │ │
│                                                                        │ │
│ Notify the System Administrator of the following error:               │ │
│                                                                        │ │
│     Could not locate vt102 in TERM.XREF.                              │ │
│                                                                        │ │
│     CHECK.LOGIN                                                        │ │
│                                                                        │ │
│ Press any key when ready...                                            │▼│
└─────────────────────────────────────────────────────────────────────────┘
```

In this case, the Windows application in use, Trumpet Telnet, merely wraps a friendly Windows interface around what is still a basic "terminal" session. It doesn't really make it any easier for us.

When using Telnet, you should always keep in mind that you are accessing other computers on the Internet, and as a result you are "pretending" to be directly linked to them through "terminal emulation."

"Terminal emulation" when using Telnet is one of the necessary evils of the Internet. When using Telnet, you could be linking into all kinds of different computers around the globe, each of which might run differently. Your computer has to pretend to be the proper type of "terminal" for each system that it might access, and given the different number of systems out there, it can't pretend to be everything to everyone.

What does this mean? Likely, that you will experience some frustration with Telnet due to the use of "terminal emulation," and due to the fact that every system that you Telnet to could operate differently and present you with a completely different way of doing things.

The result of this is that Telnet is not, nor can it ever be, a completely friendly, mouse-driven application.

SPECIAL NOTES ABOUT TELNET

When using Telnet, you should keep in mind that:

- Some applications that you access will ask you to specify the terminal type that you are using.

  Be sure that you understand the various types of terminals that your communications software supports, and how to switch to any particular terminal-type when you are on-line. Most services will support, at a bare minimum, the popular terminal type VT-100.

- Be aware of any special instructions that might apply to certain Internet resources.

For example, if you review the *Directory of Internet-Accessible Library Catalogues in Canada,* you will see that some libraries require you to use an access method known as TN3270, which is a variation of Telnet modified for special terminal types. The Directory includes the special instructions that you should use when accessing these locations.

- Remember the "escape character" for your particular Internet provider.

There is nothing worse than traveling somewhere on the Internet without having an understanding of how to get back to where you started.

In our link to the Vancouver Public Library, we were told once we had signed in that our **`Escape character is '^]'`**. That means to press the ctrl key and] together on your computer, when you are ready to leave this particular Telnet site.

The escape character permits you to exit from a particular Telnet session in case the service you have linked into doesn't make it obvious how to exit, or if your current session seems to "hang" or "freeze."

TELNET RESOURCES

A number of Canadian-based Telnet-accessible resources are included in Appendix L in the *Directory of Canadian Internet Resources,* as well as in *the Directory of Internet-Accessible Library Catalogues in Canada.*

Additional resources can be found throughout the Internet, with new ones continually added. One of the best sources is "Scott Yanoff's Internet Services List," which details various global Internet resources.

TO OBTAIN "SCOTT YANOFF'S INTERNET SERVICES LIST"

Using Gopher	
Gopher site:	gopher.uwm.edu
Path:	Select: Remote Information Services
	Special Internet Connections (Yanoff List)

Using Anonymous FTP	
FTP site:	csd4.csd.uwm.edu
Directory:	pub
File:	inet.services.txt

Using World Wide Web	
WWW site:	http://www.uwm.edu/Mirror/inet.services.html

FTP

The Internet contains a treasure trove of computer programs, documents and images that you can retrieve for your own use.

Many of these items are available through file servers located throughout the Internet by using FTP (file transfer protocol). The types of resources that you can retrieve include:

- public domain and shareware software; i.e., software written by people and released for general use by anybody. In some cases, a fee or donation is required in order to comply with the terms provided with the software.

- documents discussing the Internet or virtually any topic imaginable, in text form or specialized word processor form. In other cases, documents are available in "Postscript" format, which requires a printer with Postscript capability.

- images from NASA and other organizations in a variety of formats. You will need a file viewer compatible with the particular file type in order to view the image.

- sound files; i.e., CBC radio programs are now available via the Internet. You will need sound capability on your system in order to deal with the file.

USING FTP

As you start to use the Internet, you will often see reference to documents or other information that is available by FTP. The reference will usually contain three pieces of information that will help you retrieve the information mentioned, including:

- the domain address or domain name;

- the file location, in terms of the directory location;

- the file name.

You'll use all three pieces of information to retrieve the particular document.

For example, you might come across a phrase, "To obtain a copy of the New Brunswick provincial budget, use anonymous FTP to access 'ftp.gov.nb.ca' and look in the directory nb.gov.info/legislature/budget94."

Translated, this means that you should:

- use FTP to access the system ftp.gov.nb.ca;

- once there, log in to the system with the user ID anonymous;

- once logged in, move to the directory **nb.gov.info/legislature/budget94**, which contains the document **budget.zip**.

Once there, you will use the FTP `get` command to retrieve the file if you are using a shell account, or you will simply point and click to retrieve the file if you are using graphical software and have a direct or SLIP/PPP-based connection to the Internet.

FTP BASICS

There are a few things to remember when using FTP on the Internet:

- Many services permit "anonymous" logins; that is, they allow anyone on the Internet to access them, by providing a user ID of `anonymous`.

  When you use the anonymous ID, you are asked for a password. As a courtesy, you should send your own e-mail address as the password. In some cases, the FTP server will only permit a connection if you do identify yourself in this way. Some even validate what you supply.

- Most of the services you will access with FTP on the Internet are UNIX-based, and will be running software that is case-sensitive. In other cases, you might be retrieving files from a non-UNIX machine, with file names in upper case. In that instance, filenames are not case-sensitive.

  File names must usually match the case exactly as seen within the directory or as specified in the note that you read about the file.

- Many of the domain names that you will use with FTP are preceded by the word FTP or some other unique name; i.e., the FTP site at the domain `dal.ca`, will actually be `ftp.dal.ca`.

- If you are retrieving anything other than a text file, you must use the `binary` command, to ensure that the file is sent to you in the proper format. You do this by typing `binary` once you have reached an FTP site.

  More people get frustrated by fetching a file in the wrong format when using FTP. If the file doesn't have **.TXT** or **.PS** in its name, or if it isn't named README, it is likely a binary file.

- Common courtesy on the Internet suggests that you should only use FTP archives during non-working hours, in order not to cause network congestion and to avoid causing resource problems on the FTP archives that you are accessing. You should remember that the computers hosting an FTP archive are often used for many other purposes during the day. Although in many cases, there is nothing to prevent you from accessing a particular archive during the day, please remember that the Internet often functions because of common courtesy. You should also be aware that many archive sites now explicitly restrict access during normal working hours.

FILE RETRIEVAL – A ONE- OR TWO-STEP PROCESS?

If you have a direct connection or SLIP/PPP link to the Internet, file retrieval will be a one-step process – merely access an FTP site, choose a file by double-clicking on it with your mouse, and it will be transferred from the remote FTP archive directly to your computer.

However, if you are accessing the Internet using a "shell account" (i.e., you are not directly connected to the Internet), your retrieval of any file by FTP might be a two-step process, as seen in Figure 7.1

In the first step, you use FTP to retrieve a particular file from a remote system on the Internet. This transfers the file back to the system of your Internet service provider.

In the second step, you invoke a process to transfer the file from your Internet service provider to your own computer. What you do in this step will vary by service provider, and hence it is important for you to check with your Internet service provider to make sure that you understand what is involved.

Finally, it should also be noted that this second step might not be required with the shell accounts of some Internet service providers: the file transfer might occur directly to your own computer when you type the **get** command.

FIGURE 7.1: TWO-STEP FILE RETRIEVAL

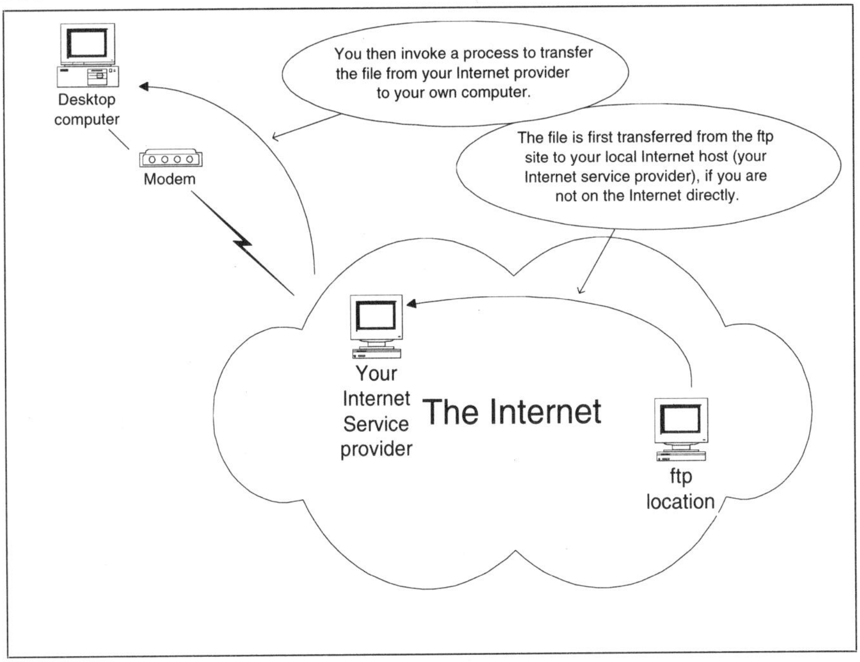

FTP ADDRESSES

Like Telnet, the FTP command can be issued by itself to enter the FTP program, or it can be used with an address to directly access a computer on the Internet.

More often than not, you will type the command `ftp` followed by the address of the particular Internet site; for example, `ftp ftp.usask.ca`.

A SAMPLE FTP SESSION – SHELL ACCOUNT

When using FTP through a shell account, you must become familiar with some of the commands used to navigate through an FTP archive and to retrieve files.

Once you are linked to another computer, you can use the `get` command to retrieve particular files, the `dir` command to look at file directories, and the `cd` command to change directories. Other commands are available, as detailed below.

In this sample FTP session, we take the following steps.

- We link to the site **ftp.cdnnet.ca,** using the command `ftp`
  `ftp.cdnnet.ca`

- Once there, a login name of **anonymous** is used, and a password is entered (matching the e-mail address of the user). The password is usually not echoed (i.e., shown on the screen) as it is typed.

```
                                      E:94% VT100 ‡   00:02:28  7:59a
$ ftp ftp.cdnnet.ca
Connected to relay.cdnnet.ca.
220 relay.cdnnet.ca FTP server (Version 2.1WU(2) Sat May 15 15:39:16 PDT 1993) r
eady.
Name (ftp.cdnnet.ca:jcarroll): anonymous
331 Guest login ok, send your complete e-mail address as password.
Password:
230-
230-Welcome to the anonymous FTP archives at CDNnet Headquarters.
230-
230-This is an experimental FTP server.  If your FTP client crashes or
230-hangs shortly after login please try using a dash (-) as the first
230-character of your password.  This will turn off the informational
230-messages that may be confusing your FTP client.
230-
230-You can get in touch with the maintainers of this archive by sending
230-a message to HQ@CDNnet.CA.
230-
230-The local time is Mon Jan 17 05:05:37 1994.
230-
230 Guest login ok, access restrictions apply.
Remote system type is UNIX.
Using binary mode to transfer files.
ftp>
```

- Once we have "logged in" and are at the **ftp** prompt, the command `cd` `ca-domain` is typed to move to the `ca-domain` directory. Once there, a directory is requested by typing `dir`, as seen below. (These two steps are not shown here.)

- The command **get application-form** is then typed to retrieve that particular file.

  Upon completion, the FTP session indicates that the file was successfully transferred. (If you are directly on the Internet, this will have transferred the file to your own computer system; if not, this indicates that the file has been copied to the file of your Internet service provider.)

- Once the file is successfully transferred, the **quit** command is entered to return to your local Internet host.

```
                                         E:94% VT100 ↕  00:04:16  8:01a
total 198
-rw-rw-r--  1 2009    2000          21845 Jan 15 22:50 application-form
lruxrwxrwx  1 2009    103              26 Jul 12  1993 ca -> registrations-hierar
 hical
-rw-rw-r--  1 2009    103            4142 Dec 29 00:19 committee-members
-rw-rw-r--  1 2009    103           40510 Jan  2 20:34 graph.ps
-rw-rw-r--  1 2009    103            1603 Jan 16 22:05 index
-rw-rw-r--  1 2009    103           54206 Jan 16 22:05 index-by-organization
-rw-rw-r--  1 2009    103           40921 Jan 16 22:05 index-by-subdomain
-rw-rw-r--  1 2009    2000           8685 Feb  2  1993 introduction
drwxrwxr-x  2 2009    103           18432 Jan 16 22:02 registrations-flat
drwxrwxr-x 14 2009    103            5120 Jan 16 21:35 registrations-hierarchical
-rw-rw-r--  1 2009    103            2258 Jan 16 22:05 statistics
226 Transfer complete.
ftp> get application-form
local: application-form remote: application-form
200 PORT command successful.
150 Opening BINARY mode data connection for application-form (21845 bytes).
226 Transfer complete.
21845 bytes received in 4.6 seconds (4.6 Kbytes/s)
ftp> quit
221 Goodbye.
$ mv application-form app.txt
$ sz app.txt
```

In the screen above, since the session occurred in a shell account, two more procedures were necessary once we left the FTP archive:

- in order that the file can be saved to a DOS machine, the file **application-form** is renamed **app.txt**, using syntax specific to the local UNIX host (**mv application-form app.txt**)

- the command **sz app.txt** is then typed to transfer the file from the system of the Internet service provider to a local PC, using the Zmodem protocol.[2]

A SAMPLE FTP SESSION – DIRECT ACCOUNT

Using FTP through an account that has a direct network link provides us the first taste of how much easier the Internet can be.

In this example, we will go to the exact same FTP archive. However, rather than navigating our way by typing commands, we can type in all of our navigation information in advance, in a simple Windows program.

In this case, using the program Trumpet Winsock WS_FTP, we merely type in the host address, the user ID (anonymous), our password (in this case, our e-mail address) and the directory location that we want to go to:

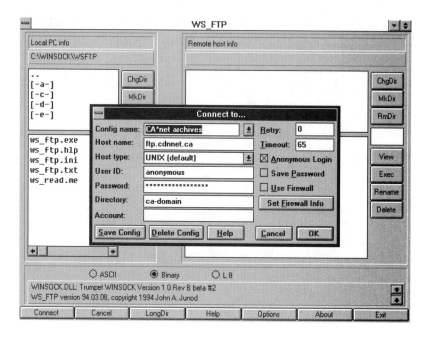

This invokes a session directly to the CA*net file archive.

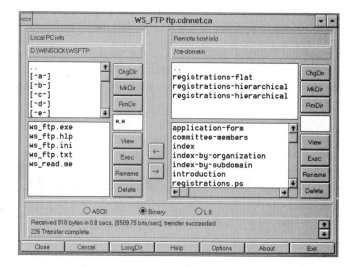

With this software, notice how the left side details the directory of the PC or local network that we are using, while the right side details the directory of the files on the remote FTP archive. Through this type of design, the concept of FTP file retrieval is made more straightforward, as it more closely resembles the way that we might work with files through the Microsoft Windows File Manager program or Finder on a Macintosh.

Once we reach the CA*net archive, we can highlight the file we want with our mouse, and click on the left arrow key to transfer the file to our PC.

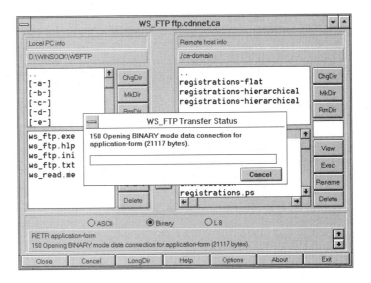

What could be easier?

FTP DIRECTORIES

When using FTP, you are most often interacting with an archive that is based upon UNIX, and hence, are working with the UNIX file directory structure.

Although these directories can seem simple when using FTP through an account directly linked to the Internet, as seen above, it is still important to have a good grasp of how they work. Although they are similar to DOS directories, there are some subtle differences.

For example, as seen above, you can see that UNIX directories include information on the type of file, the status of the file and information concerning the "owner" of the file.

For the uninitiated, these directories can seem a little bit overwhelming at first, unless you remember a couple of key pointers:

- Entries that begin with a **d** are directories. The DOS user can think of them as subdirectories beneath the directory currently shown.

- Entries beginning with anything else are usually files.

Consider the following two directory listings taken from an experimental CBC FTP site within the Department of Communications, available at **debra.dgbt.doc.ca.**

First, a command is issued to switch to the directory **pub/cbc,** where the directory is then listed by typing **dir.**

```
                                    E:94% VT100 ‡   00:00:55  8:02a
250 CWD command successful.
ftp> dir
200 PORT command successful.
150 Opening ASCII mode data connection for /bin/ls.
total 4396
drwxr-xr-x  2 114      114         512 Jan 13 15:55 .cap
-rw-r--r--  1 114      1          1523 Jan  6 16:59 README
drwxr-xr-x  3 114      114        1024 Dec 23 17:55 basic-black
drwxr-xr-x  3 114      114         512 Dec 23 17:55 canada
-rw-r--r--  1 114      1          1402 Jan 12 23:10 cbc.html
drwxr-xr-x  3 114      114         512 Jan  5 20:29 front-porch
-rw-r--r--  1 114      114         369 Jan 12 23:04 more-info.html
-rw-r--r--  1 114      114     4457122 Jan 12 23:08 ottawa-story.au
drwxr-xr-x  2 114      1          1024 Jan 13 23:08 pix
-rw-r--r--  1 114      114        3494 Dec 23 23:17 press-release
-rw-r--r--  1 114      1          6361 Jan 14 21:13 product-list
drwxr-xr-x  3 114      1           512 Dec 23 16:26 quirks-and-quarks
-rw-r--r--  1 114      1          1616 Jan 13 23:01 radio.html
-rw-r--r--  1 114      114         424 Dec 17 00:13 sounds.by.gopher
drwxr-xr-x  6 114      114         512 Dec 23 17:55 sunday-morning
drwxr-xr-x  2 114      114         512 Dec 30 16:00 tools
drwxr-xr-x  3 114      1           512 Jan 14 21:16 transcripts
226 Transfer complete.
ftp>
```

The listing above shows a number of directories (preceded with the letter d), as well as a number of files (without a d). This includes the directories **front-porch** and **quirks-and-quarks,** as well as the files **press-release** and **product-list.**

The command to switch to the directory **canada** is then typed (**cd canada** — not shown here), and a listing of the **canada** directory is requested.

```
                                    E:94% VT100 ‡   00:01:18  8:03a
250-  it was last modified on Thu Dec  9 20:38:18 1993 - 39 days ago
250 CWD command successful.
ftp> dir
200 PORT command successful.
150 Opening ASCII mode data connection for /bin/ls.
total 16932
drwxr-xr-x  2 114      114         512 Dec  9 23:08 .cap
-rw-r--r--  1 114      114        3262 Dec  9 20:38 README
-rw-r--r--  1 114      114      930021 Dec  9 19:06 all.that.freedom.au
-rw-r--r--  1 114      1         78007 Dec 23 15:29 canada.gif
-rw-r--r--  1 114      1          1370 Dec 23 16:31 canada.html
-rw-r--r--  1 114      1         11274 Dec 23 15:29 canada.small.gif
-rw-r--r--  1 114      1          3387 Dec 23 15:29 canada.tiny.gif
-rw-r--r--  1 114      114     2319631 Dec  9 19:06 counterpoint.au
-rw-r--r--  1 114      114     3215717 Dec  9 19:07 je.suis.moitie.moitie.au
-rw-r--r--  1 114      114     3604605 Dec  9 19:07 my.canada.au
-rw-r--r--  1 114      114     1242175 Dec  9 19:08 northern.reflections.au
-rw-r--r--  1 114      114     3058919 Dec  9 19:08 quebec.poetry.and.protest.
u
-rw-r--r--  1 114      114      934202 Dec  9 19:09 speak.english.speak.french
au
-rw-r--r--  1 114      114     1819780 Dec  9 19:09 stories.that.bind.au
226 Transfer complete.
ftp>
```

This directory shows a number of files, such as **canada.gif** and **je.suis.moitie.moitie.au**, as well as a directory named **.cap.** The files in the directory are quite large, ranging from 512 bytes to 3.6 megabytes in size (3,604,605 bytes, for the file **my.canada.au**). [3]

BASIC FTP COMMANDS

As with any resource on the Internet, there are several commands that you can use at the FTP prompt when in a shell account. The most often used commands to retrieve files and view directories are as follows:

COMMAND	MEANING	EXAMPLES
cd	change directory	**cd public**, to switch to the directory public
		cd /, to return to the top directory
		cd .. to go up one directory level
dir	list the directory	**dir**, for a basic directory listing. Can also use **ls** on most systems
get	retrieve a file	**get filename**, to retrieve a particular file
mget	get multiple files	**mget new*.***, to get any files beginning with the letters new
quit	leave the FTP site	

If you have the right to leave files at a particular Internet site, you can use the **put** and **mput** commands to transfer files to that site.

More information on the above, and other FTP commands, can be obtained by typing **help** at the FTP prompt.

When using an account that is directly linked to the Internet and software like Trumpet FTP as seen above, you move through the directories in a different manner.

For example, the following screen shows an FTP link to the CBC archives mentioned previously:

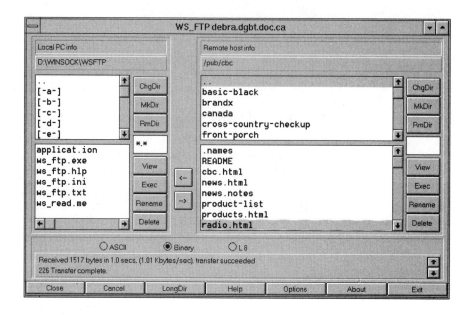

The top part of the screen lists directory information, while the bottom part of the screen lists file names. To move to another directory below the current one (i.e., cross-country-checkup), we would click on the directory names in the top half. To move up a directory level, we could click on the . . (just above basic-black.)

OTHER FTP ISSUES

There are two other issues that you will have to deal when you begin retrieving files using FTP.

FILE TYPES — FORMAT

Obviously, to use particular files that you obtain on the Internet, you must have a program capable of dealing with the format of the retrieved file.

You can't load a WordPerfect document from a PC into a Macintosh unless you have a program that will convert it to the format of your Macinstosh word processor. You can't deal with a Postscript file unless you have a Postscript printer, or if you have a program that can view or convert a Postscript file. You can't run a compiled UNIX program on an MSDOS computer — and so on.

Since the topic of file format and file types is far beyond the topic of this book, keep in mind that while the Internet might make available a lot of files, you must have appropriate programs to deal with them.

FILE TYPES — COMPRESSION

In order to speed up the file transfer process, many of the files throughout the Internet have been compressed or combined.

Files with the extensions .zip, .arc, .Z or .z, .tar, .lzh, .sit or .cpt are compressed or combined or both. The most common type of file extension is

.Z, indicating a file that has been compressed using the UNIX program `compress`. You will need appropriate software to uncompress or uncombine the file that you retrieve.

Many FTP sites on the Internet include an uncompress program. If you don't have an uncompress program available, obtain one from your Internet service provider.

Make sure that you have appropriate tools to uncompress or uncombine files that you might retrieve. The following table indicates some of the more popular compression programs, the file extension used, and the probable computer environment that the file is from.

EXTENSION	PROGRAM	PLATFORM
.zip	Pkzip/Pkunzip	DOS/Windows
.arc	Arc	DOS/Windows
.sit	Stuffit	Macintosh
.cpt	Compresslt	Macintosh
.z	Compress	Unix
.lzh	LZH	DOS/Windows

FILE RETRIEVAL VIA E-MAIL

Finally, it is possible to retrieve many of the files that are available via FTP, via e-mail instead, through a few FTP archives.

This is done by sending an e-mail message containing the file name that you want, including the directory details, to a specific e-mail address at the FTP archive site. At the FTP archive, a "mail robot" takes apart your request, obtains the selected file, and sends it back to you via e-mail. The requests are handled on a very low priority basis, and as a result you might not receive the file for several hours or even several days.

One of the most popular of these sites is a server at the Massachusetts Institute of Technology (MIT), which has an FTP site containing information about the Internet.

For example, to retrieve a document from this site that details how to use the ftp-by-mail service:

- create a message to **mail-server@rtfm.mit.edu**.

- in the text of the message, you type a command that will send a help file, or will retrieve specific files that might otherwise have been available via FTP.

For example, to obtain help, send an e-mail message as follows:

```
Date: Thu, 30 Dec 1993 08:41:24 est
Reply-To: jcarroll@jacc.com
From: jcarroll@jacc.com (Jim Carroll)
To: mail-server@rtfm.mit.edu
```

```
Cc:

help
```

To obtain actual files, use the send command within the body of the message, i.e.:

```
Date: Thu, 30 Dec 1993 08:43:06 est
Reply-To: jcarroll@jacc.com
From: jcarroll@jacc.com (Jim Carroll)
To: mail-server@rtfm.mit.edu
Cc:

send /pub/usenet/news.answers/mail/mailing-lists/part01
send /pub/usenet/news.answers/mail/mailing-lists/part02
send /pub/usenet/news.answers/mail/mailing-lists/part03
send /pub/usenet/news.answers/mail/mailing-lists/part04
send /pub/usenet/news.answers/mail/mailing-lists/part05
send /pub/usenet/news.answers/mail/mailing-lists/part06
```

This will result in e-mail messages being sent to you which summarize some of the mailing lists available on the Internet.

There are quite a number of sites throughout the Internet that permit file retrieval via e-mail. Although there might be minor variations in the method, the concept is consistent from location to location. If in doubt, obtain the help file first.

ARCHIE – THE TOOL TO FIND FILES

The Internet contains many millions of computer programs, files, documents, sound files, images and other information that you can access using FTP. Part of the challenge, however, is finding a particular program or document.

Most times, you will read about a specific document or file in a document that mentions the actual FTP archive, including the directory location and filename.

However, in other cases, you might know of a program but have no idea where to go to find it.

Archie, a program developed in Canada at McGill University and now marketed and supported worldwide by a Canadian company, Bunyip Information Systems, permits you to search file archives around the Internet by file name.

You can run Archie:

- directly from your shell, if Archie is one of the service offerings;

  or

- by Telnet to an Archie site. Some of the more popular sites include:

  ```
  archie.rutgers.edu 128.6.18.15 (Rutgers University)
  ```

  ```
  archie.unl.edu 129.93.1.14 (University of Nebraska in
  Lincoln)
  ```

archie.sura.net 128.167.254.179 (SURAnet archie server)

archie.ans.net 147.225.1.2 (ANS archie server)

archie.au 139.130.4.6 (Australian server)

archie.funet.fi 128.214.6.100 (European server in Finland)

archie.doc.ic.ac.uk 146.169.11.3 (UK/England server)

archie.cs.huji.ac.il 132.65.6.15 (Israel server)

archie.wide.ad.jp 133.4.3.6 (Japanese server)

In this case, you use the Telnet command to get to one of the sites above, and run the Archie program from that site;

or

- run Archie directly on your own computer if you have a direct network link to the Internet.

SAMPLE ARCHIE SESSION – SHELL ACCOUNT

In the following example, Archie is run directly from a shell account, using the Archie program available on the computer of the Internet service provider.

First, we establish whether we can run Archie on this system by typing **archie**. Archie responds with details on how it can be used.[4]

```
                                        E:94% VT100 *   00:00:00  9:39a
$ archie
Usage: archie [-acelorstvLV] [-m hits] [-N level] string
          -a : list matches as Alex filenames
          -c : case sensitive substring search
          -e : exact string match (default)
          -r : regular expression search
          -s : case insensitive substring search
          -l : list one match per line
          -t : sort inverted by date
     -m hits : specifies maximum number of hits to return (default 95)
 -o filename : specifies file to store results in
     -h host : specifies server host
          -L : list known servers and current default
     -N level : specifies query niceness level (0-35765)
$
```

When you use Archie, you can have it search any one of the available Archie servers worldwide. Typing **archie -L** gives us a listing of the archie servers that are available worldwide, and indicates that our archie queries will use the server at **archie.sura.net**. You should always try to use a server that is closest to your actual location.

```
                                          E:94% VT100 *   00:00:00  9:39a
$ archie -L
Known archie servers:
        archie.ans.net (USA [NY])
        archie.rutgers.edu (USA [NJ])
        archie.sura.net (USA [MD])
        archie.unl.edu (USA [NE])
        archie.mcgill.ca (Canada)
        archie.funet.fi (Finland/Mainland Europe)
        archie.au (Australia)
        archie.doc.ic.ac.uk (Great Britain/Ireland)
        archie.wide.ad.jp (Japan)
        archie.ncu.edu.tw (Taiwan)
 * archie.sura.net is the default Archie server.
 * For the most up-to-date list, write to an Archie server and give it
   the command `servers'.
$
```

Finally, we run an archie query to look for any programs containing the phrase **uupc** (in this case, looking for the program UUPC, which is a popular off-line method of using e-mail and USENET for MSDOS computers).

We do so by typing **archie -r uupc**. Archie responds with a listing of sites and filenames, as seen below.

```
                                          E:94% Pause!!   00:00:00  9:49a
$ archie -r uupc

Host swdsrv.edvz.univie.ac.at

    Location: /novell/pegasus/misc
        FILE -r--r--r--   214425   Sep  9 15:41   uupc11xd.zip
        FILE -r--r--r--    54399   Sep  9 15:41   uupc11zn.zip
        FILE -r--r--r--   204283   Sep  9 15:42   uupc11zo.zip
        FILE -r--r--r--   173696   Sep  9 15:43   uupc11zr.zip
    Location: /os2/hobbes/all/comm
        FILE -r--r--r--   214425   Sep 13 07:23   uupc11xd.zip
        FILE -r--r--r--   177679   Sep 13 07:23   uupc11z2.zip
        FILE -r--r--r--   187602   Sep 13 07:23   uupc11z3.zip
        FILE -r--r--r--    55313   Sep 13 07:22   uupc11z4.zip
        FILE -r--r--r--   309935   Sep 13 07:22   uupc11za.zip
        FILE -r--r--r--   374904   Sep 13 07:22   uupc11zb.zip
        FILE -r--r--r--   112300   Sep 13 07:22   uupc11zc.zip
```

We can then choose to use FTP to reach these sites to retrieve any of these program files, using the server name and directory path provided. For example, we know that we could open an FTP session to **swdsrv.eduz.univie.ac.at** (the site listed above), and in the directory **/novell/pegasus/misc**, find a variety of uupc files.

SAMPLE ARCHIE SESSION – DIRECT ACCOUNT

Once again, the process is completely different using Windows software on an account that has a direct link to the Internet.

In this case, we have used the WinSock Archie program. We are looking for the program **pmail301.zip** (a recent version of Pegasus Mail), and have chosen the Canadian Archie archive at **archie.uqam.ca**:

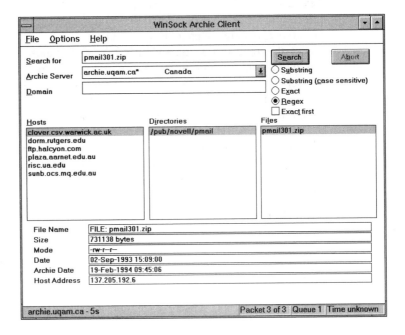

After a moment or two, Archie returns with a list of hosts that have the software, details the directory location and the file name, as seen above.

At this point, if you click on the file name in the rightmost of the three columns you will invoke an FTP session to grab the file for you!

TYPES OF ARCHIE SEARCHES

When performing an Archie search, there are several options:

- an exact match; i.e., the search must match exactly what you have typed;

- a substring search; i.e., the search will find, for the search air*, the files airways, airline, air.zip and other variations. This can be made sensitive to upper/lower case if required;

- a "regex" search, or Unix regular expression search.

In a shell account, you can choose the type of search through the command line, while in a direct connection, using software such as WS_Archie, you can choose the type of search by clicking one of the options directly on the screen.

THE DECLINING ROLE OF TELNET AND FTP

Telnet and FTP could be considered the "granddaddy" of Internet applications, as they have been used for many years.

There are a number of resources throughout the global Internet that you can Telnet to, and there are many FTP sites available.

Yet, the trend in Canada and elsewhere is that most organizations setting up new Internet information resources are using the increasing sophistication of the Gopher and World Wide Web/Mosaic applications, reviewed in Chapter 8.

The result is that Telnet and FTP seem to be falling in disfavor, as general, day-to-day applications for most Internet users.

However, it is important that you learn about them, as there are still a number of resources throughout the Internet which you can access through these two capabilities. We can expect to see many FTP sites throughout the Internet, particularly as methods to retrieve files from these sites using Gopher and World Wide Web/Mosaic emerge.

---

1. Often, accessing these services via the Internet is less expensive than accessing them via regular data services like Datapac or Tymnet.
2. These two steps, and the commands used, are specific to the Internet service provider used in this example — the procedure used on your particular provider will vary.
3. Any file with an .au extension are audio or voice files. The files in this particular example are actual audio files of various CBC radio programs. Refer to the Internet Resources list for more information on this particular ftp site.
4. If Archie doesn't run at this point, it probably means that your Internet service provider doesn't make it directly available. If this is the case, then you can telnet to one of the addresses above to access an Archie client.

. . . .

TOOLS FOR KNOWLEDGE AND INFORMATION RETRIEVAL

Mosaic – an easy way to travel through a zillion documents, reading the footnote to the footnote; this is the first working part for the library of libraries.

Originally from The Guardian, and reprinted in
The Ottawa Citizen, Sun 26 Jun 94

In this chapter, we take a look at some of the tools that can be used for information retrieval on the Internet — ways of extending your capabilities to locate and retrieve knowledge on particular topics.

THE EFFECT OF THE GLOBAL INTERNET ON INFORMATION

The Internet is making the world a smaller place when it comes to obtaining information from or about companies, organizations or governments.

With the emergence of the Internet, several things are happening:

- Companies are establishing locations on the Internet that you as a potential customer can travel to in order to obtain information about the company, their products or their services. You can obtain information on how to place an order for a product, or can order directly through the Internet. "Shopping malls" are springing up on line, providing new ways for you to find products and services.

In Canada, for example, NSTN has established a "Cybermall" which serves as a convenient point of entry to companies in Nova Scotia and elsewhere doing business on the Internet. This can be reached using Mosaic or some other World Wide Web browser at **http://www.nstn.ca**.

- Schools and educational institutions are placing information resources on the Internet which can be accessed by students and educators alike. Internet information resources promise to revolutionize the process of education in Canada and around the world by making national and global knowledge more accessible to students.

The SchoolNet Gopher, for example, provides a centralized location where educational institutions in Canada can post requests to participate in "global projects," and is an area where educators are providing information about methods of teaching children about the use of cyberspace. You can access this location with Gopher at the address **schoolnet.carleton.ca**.

- Research and scientific institutions are establishing information services that provide a convenient entry point into major knowledge resources. Entire scientific projects are now occurring supported through centralized information databases in which study information is quickly made available and shared.

The Atlantic Geoscience Centre, located at the Bedford Institute of Oceanography, is a marine geoscience organization specializing in marine and petroleum geology, geophysics, geochemistry, and geotechnology. The Centre has established a Gopher summarizing its activities and making some of its research information available. You can reach this using Gopher at **agcgopher.bio.ns.ca**.

- Public organizations are placing information about themselves and their services on-line for review by people throughout the Internet. Charitable organizations and other institutions performing a public service are finding that the Internet is a convenient method of making available their public information, and in effect helps them in the delivery of their services.

The National Adult Literacy Database has been established by Canada's Adult Literacy Information Network. The mission of the non-profit organization is to "facilitate the continued delivery of literacy programs in Canada by providing a communication network and a central clearinghouse of adult literacy information to service and support individuals, organizations, and government policy setters and decision makers in the field."

You can access the Gopher for the organization at the location **nald.fanshawec.on.ca**.

- Governments are establishing Gopher and World Wide Web servers as a means of making information available to their public. In addition, some governments have realized that the global Internet is a powerful tool that can help achieve some economic objectives.

For example, the Province of New Brunswick has established a World Wide Web site which details information for companies considering relocating to the province. The Open Government Project in Ottawa is an effort to provide a one-stop information resource of federal government information. (Access each of these with Mosaic or some other World Wide Web browser at the addresses **http://www.gov.nb.ca** and **http://www.debra.dgbt.ca.**)

BENEFITS OF INFORMATION RETRIEVAL

The Internet is rapidly evolving to become a standard means of accessing information from organizations across Canada and around the world. Part of this has to do with the fact that information retrieval tools are becoming more sophisticated.

Even though tools like Telnet and FTP are at your disposal as outlined in the previous chapter, they aren't the easiest systems by which to discover Internet resources.

Instead, programs like Gopher, Hytelnet, Finger, WAIS and the World Wide Web provide easy access to global information, and are on the cutting edge of information retrieval.

These tools provide you with new ways of searching, browsing, and reviewing information from around the world. Using them, you can discover niches of information that might be relevant to your particular needs.

In order to help you understand information retrieval on the Internet, we explore the network very much as a tourist with a camera in this chapter. We do this both as a user of a simple dial-up shell account, and again through an account that is directly linked to the Internet, using some of the sophisticated retrieval programs available such as Winsock Gopher and Mosaic.

GOPHER

If you read various computer magazines, you might come across the term "net-surfing."

Gopher could be best described as one of the main surf-boards for the Internet (the other being Mosaic.)

Gopher solves the problem of resource discovery by providing an easier method to explore the Internet. Developed at the University of Minnesota, it provides a menu-based view of Internet resources, guiding you to a variety of locations on the Internet and permitting you to view and retrieve documents or files.

P. Copley, Ph.D., a founder of The Electronic University in San Francisco (**ror@netcom.com**), had this to say about Gopher in a posting made to the network (reprinted with permission).

```
The Internet gopher is the express elevator of the Inter-
net, capable of cutting through layer upon layer of infor-
mation quickly. It permits you to traverse the world's
data banks. You can be viewing a color photograph of an
ancient Chinese vase stored on a computer in Taiwan and,
on a moment's notice, "be" in the UK, downloading a data-
base of historical names and dates. It enables you to eas-
ily retrieve all sorts of information and to connect to
many other services. Invented at the University of Minne-
sota, home of the "Golden Gophers" sports teams (hence the
name), the gopher program connects many of the major In-
ternet computers together into one unified information
service or "gopher space."
```

In a matter of little more than three and a half years, Gopher has sprung up from one installation on the University of Minnesota campus to well over 7,000 around the world. One key to Gopher's success has been that it is not overly complicated. It's easy to use, and, moreover, makes an orderly, logical presentation out of dissimilar and scattered "chunks" of information from all over the Internet.

Given the size and range of the Internet, Gopher is also proving to be a wonderful way to get yourself lost on the Internet.

ACCESSING GOPHER

Once again, keep in mind where you might run Gopher from:

- on your Internet service provider, through a dial-up shell account;

- by using Telnet to access a site at which you can run a Gopher client; or

- on your own PC or network, if you have a direct link to the Internet, using software such as Winsock Gopher (a public domain version) or WinGopher (a commercial version).

The easiest way to understand Gopher is to review a couple of Gopher sessions. To do so, we will review the use of Gopher first through a shell account and again with an account linked directly to the Internet.

GOPHER THROUGH A SHELL ACCOUNT

Using a shell account, we access Gopher by typing **gopher** at the $ prompt. This presents us with the main Gopher menu for this particular Internet service provider. [1]

```
                                                VT100 ‡    00:01:35  1:50p
                      Internet Gopher Information Client 2.0 pl3

                      Root gopher server: nic.hookup.net

  -->  1.  BBS and Information Documents/
       2.  Electronic Texts/
       3.  HookUp Communication Corp..
       4.  HookUp Services/
       5.  Internet Resources/
       6.  Michigan Gopher and Information Server/
       7.  National Weather Service Forecasts/
       8.  Other Gopher and Information Servers/
       9.  Southern Ontario Weather.
      10.  University of Minnesota Gopher Server/
      11.  University of Waterloo (UWInfo)/




  Press ? for Help, ? to Quit, ? to go up a menu          Page: 1/1
```

If your Internet service provider has not installed a local Gopher client, typing Gopher at the prompt will not work. In this case, you must access a Gopher by using Telnet to link to a location that offers a public Gopher client. Instructions on how to do this can be found in Appendix E, *Directory of Gopher Servers and Campus-Wide Information Systems in Canada.*

In addition, the Gopher menu of any particular Internet service provider or Internet host will be different, and will change over time. The prompts used within the Gopher session on your Internet provider might differ from the prompts used in this example.

As a result, the sample menu above is not exactly what you would see on any other provider or Gopher site.

Notice as well that the prompt --> is placed at the first entry on the screen. To choose an item, you type its corresponding number or move the prompt with your cursor keys.

The menu item *Other Gopher and Information Services* is a good place to discover the breadth of Internet information resources. Choosing this item presents us with a menu of Gopher servers by country:

```
                                              VT100 ‡   00:01:50  1:51p
                    Internet Gopher Information Client 2.0 pl3

                        Other Gopher and Information Servers

     -->  1.  All the Gopher Servers in the World/
          2.  Search All the Gopher Servers in the World <?>
          3.  Search titles in Gopherspace using veronica/
          4.  Africa/
          5.  Asia/
          6.  Europe/
          7.  International Organizations/
          8.  Middle East/
          9.  North America/
          10. Pacific/
          11. Russia/
          12. South America/
          13. Terminal Based Information/
          14. WAIS Based Information/
          15. Gopher Server Registration. <}


 Press ? for Help, ? to Quit, ? to go up a menu            Page: 1/1
```

Choosing North America, and then Canada from the menus, presents us with a list of some Canadian Gopher servers.

```
                                              VT100 ‡   00:02:36  1:52p
                    Internet Gopher Information Client 2.0 pl3

                                   Canada

     -->  1.  Acadia University Gopher/
          2.  Achilles Internet Services/
          3.  Alberta Research Council gopher/
          4.  Algonquin College of Applied Arts and Technology, Nepean, ON, Cana../
          5.  Atlantic Geoscience Centre - Geological Survey of Canada/
          6.  B.C. Teachers' Federation Gopher/
          7.  Bedford Institute Of Oceanography (Canada)/
          8.  Bishop's University/
          9.  British Columbia Institute of Technology/
          10. Brock University, St. Catharines, Ontario, Canada/
          11. CANARIE Gopher/
          12. CANARIE Inc. Gopher/
          13. CUFA/BC Post-Secondary Education Information Service/
          14. Camosun College School of Business/
          15. Camosun College, Victoria B.C. Canada/
          16. Canada's Coalition for Public Information Gopher/
          17. Canadore College, North Bay, Ontario, Canada/
          18. Carleton University/

 Press ? for Help, ? to Quit, ? to go up a menu            Page: 1/7
```

GOPHER THROUGH A DIRECT ACCOUNT

Using Winsock Gopher, a public domain program, we can see a much more graphical view of a Gopher server.

The SchoolNet gopher, a site which details information about Canada's initiative to link schools across the country to the Internet, is shown below. (You can access this server at the gopher site **schoolnet.carleton.ca.**).

Rather than using numbers to move your way through the menus, you select one of the menu items above by moving your cursor to an item with your mouse and double clicking.

Using Gopher through a direct account can be a lot of fun given how easy it is to move from menu item to menu item and from server to server across Canada and around the world.

Another innovative approach to Gopher is found with the Pipeline for Windows software, as seen here through the Internet service provider InfoRamp based in Toronto. In this case, we are viewing a Gopher which details access to government information.

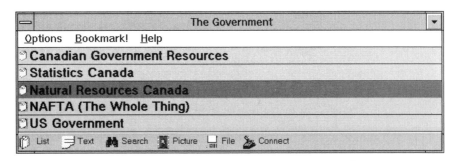

NAVIGATION TOOLS

Depending on the service and software that you are using, Gopher menus might show symbols to indicate what you will find behind a particular menu item.

- In a shell account, these symbols include **?** for a menu item that will lead you to a search prompt; **/** to indicate that the menu is followed by another menu; and **<TEL>** to indicate that the menu item will link you to another site via Telnet.

- In Winsock Gopher and other software used to access Gopher through a SLIP account, various icons are used beside each menu item to detail the type of information that the menu item will lead to. Binoculars, for example, signify that the item will perform a search for information when selected.

- The Pipeline software, as shown above, shows a series of icons at the bottom of the screen which match the icon used beside a particular Gopher menu item as a way of identifying the type of information.

USING GOPHER

Gopher helps you discover many resources on the Internet that you might not be readily aware of, or that might have been difficult to find using Telnet and FTP. For example, Gopher will assist you in finding:

- information on Internet resources

  Many Gopher sites will point you to resources which help to locate USENET FAQ's (Frequently Asked Questions) and other documents about various Internet services.

- complete guides to the Internet, and documents on how to use various Internet services

- particular mailing lists or USENET newsgroups, by allowing you to search some of the documents mentioned in the chapter on mailing lists and USENET

- locations of software within particular FTP sites (although Archie, described below, is the industrial-strength file finder of the Internet world)

- in addition, with the increasing trend toward commercial use of the network, we are seeing an increasing trend toward the establishment of on-line "stores" based on Gopher.

Many Gopher menus are linked to other Gopher menus, meaning that you can often start out in one location, and quickly travel to another location somewhere else in Canada or around the world.

In addition, there are a number of ways in which Gopher can be an invaluable tool in discovering Internet information resources. There are a number of special capabilities that make the use of Gopher more convenient. These include:

- Gopher Jewels, an initiative in which the "best" Gopher servers are categorized by information;

- Veronica, a program that helps you search global "gopherspace" for particular words;

- the ability to search for documents in particular Gopher databases;

- the ability to send a document that you have found with Gopher, to yourself or someone else via e-mail;

  and

- the use of Gopher bookmarks so that you can easily find your way back to a location that you have visited.

Each of these capabilities is reviewed here in depth. Keep in mind that not all Gopher software or Gopher servers will support all capabilities.

GOPHER JEWELS

The massive growth in the number of Gopher sites and services brought together a group of people who believed that they should index some of the more interesting sites on the Internet.

The result was Gopher Jewels, a service accessible from many Gopher services. Information within Gopher Jewels is categorized by topic.

Your Internet service provider might or might not provide access to Gopher Jewels. If access is provided, the location within the menu could be different for each service provider. The easiest way to find out if you have access to Gopher Jewels on your local client is to look around through the menus; and if you cannot find it, ask your Internet service provider for help.

You can also access the main Gopher Jewels site directly from within Winsock Gopher. Do this by choosing to "open" a new Gopher site, and type in the address **cwis.usc.edu** (the main "home" for the Gopher Jewels project).

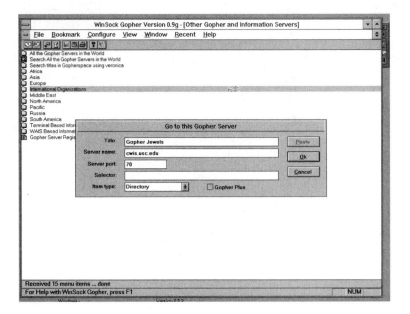

From the menu which is presented, choose the item "Other Gopher and Information Servers." The next screen will detail a number of choices, including the item Gopher Jewels. By selecting that, we are presented with a screen which categorizes global Gopher resources according to type of resource:

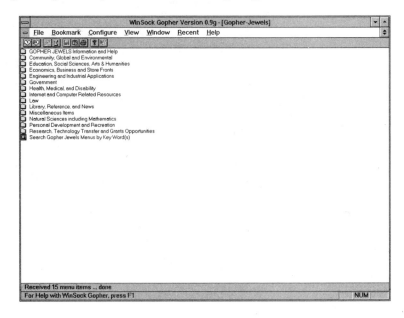

You can also join a mailing list about new Gopher jewels by e-mail, as follows:

Using E-mail	
Send message to:	listproc@einet.net
In text of message, type:	subscribe gopherjewels firstname lastname
Special Instructions:	Replace firstname and lastname with your own firstname and lastname.

You might also check into "The Clearinghouse for Subject-Oriented Internet Resource Guides." This site includes details about new Gopher databases. You can use Gopher to access these guides as follows:

Using Gopher	
Site:	gopher.lib.umich.edu
Path:	Select:
	What's New and Featured Resources
	The Clearinghouse for Subject-Oriented Internet Resource Guides

SEARCHING FOR INFORMATION IN "GOPHERSPACE"

It is also possible to use Veronica, a program that lets you search global Gopher menus for particular topics or phrases.

Veronica is available on many Gopher servers. Choosing it, you are presented with a number of locations in which you can perform the Veronica search. After choosing one, you can type in the text you are searching for, and are then presented with a list of Gopher menus that matches your search phrase.

In the following screen, for example, we have chosen to search for information on Canadian resources, and are presented with a menu of three hits or matches.

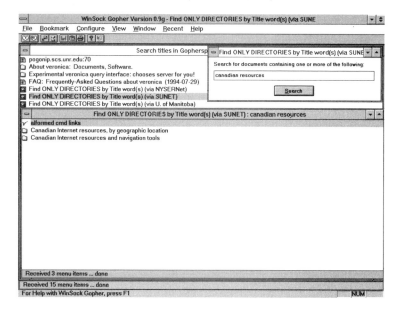

Clicking on "Canadian Internet Resources, by geographic location," will actually take us to the Gopher server at the National Library of Canada, which has undertaken an effort to try and index many of the Canadian Internet information resources. (The National Library Gopher is actually a very good place to visit for information on the Canadian Internet — you can get there directly using the Gopher address **gopher.nlc-bnc.ca**.)

You should keep in mind that Veronica is a very popular service, and as a result, you might rarely be able to use it during the day — you will be told that there are "too many connections." Your only choice is to try another Veronica server, or to try again later.

SEARCHING FOR INFORMATION IN GOPHER

In addition to search menus throughout Gopherspace, an increasing number of Gopher servers are also supporting the ability for you to search for information within a particular Gopher site based on a term that you specify.

For example, when accessing the Industry & Science Canada Gopher (at **debra.dgbt.doc.ca**) you can choose the menu item "Search Industry Canada Documents." When you do so, you are presented with a dialog box in which you specify your search term.

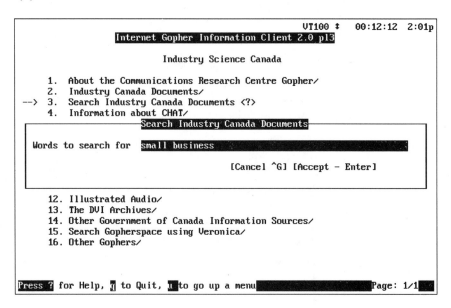

In this case, having asked for any documents mentioning the phrase "small business," we are presented with a menu of documents. We can choose to view any document by typing its corresponding number (or choosing it with our mouse, if we are using a graphical Gopher software package.)

```
                                      UT100 ‡   00:12:42  2:02p
                   Internet Gopher Information Client 2.0 p13

                  Search Industry Canada Documents: small business

  -->  1.  english    ..Information.Highway/Info.Highway.Advisory.Council/study/.
       2.  convergence.report.e   /isc/.
       3.  videotheque.library.eng   /isc/.
       4.  02-19-94.e   /isc/gazette/.
       5.  manley.speech.may12-94.txt   /isc/Industry.Canada.News.Releases/.
       6.  manley.speech.may11-94.txt   /isc/Industry.Canada.News.Releases/.
       7.  couriers.txt   /isc/Industry.Profiles/english/.
       8.  April-29-94.txt   /isc/Industry.Canada.News.Releases/.
       9.  isc.programs.english   /isc/.
      10.  02-19-94.f   /isc/gazette/.
      11.  rpt-fnl.txt   ..n.Information.Highway/Info.Highway.Advisory.Council/.
      12.  Building.Canada's.Info.Infrastructure.April94.txt   ..ation.Highway/.
      13.  technology.brokers.and.consultants   ../Technology.Networking.Guide/.
      14.  budget_e.asc   ../Industry.Canada.News.Releases/Federal Budget 1994/.
      15.  management.consultants.txt   /isc/Industry.Profiles/english/.
      16.  trading.houses.txt   /isc/Industry.Profiles/english/.
      17.  ostry.report.feb.1994   /isc/Canadian.Information.Highway/.
      18.  meeting.one   ..n.Information.Highway/Info.Highway.Advisory.Council/.

 Press ▓ for Help, ▓ to Quit, ▓ to go up a menu            Page: 1/15
```

MAILING A GOPHER DOCUMENT

Another nice feature of most Gopher systems is the ability to:

- download the document immediately to your own computer. You can only do this if the technical setup of your service provider, Gopher site and personal computer software, support this (working in unison);

- transfer the file to your Internet service provider, to save it for downloading later (the method you would use if you couldn't use the download method above); or

- have a document that you are viewing sent to you via e-mail (if neither of the methods above work).

For example, in the Industry & Science Gopher above, we can obtain a copy of the document by e-mail by choosing (m)to mail. When we do so, we are prompted for the Internet e-mail address that we want to send the document to.

```
                                          VT100 ↕  00:13:37  2:03p
            Internet Gopher Information Client 2.0 p13

              Search Industry Canada Documents: small business

      1.  english    ..Information.Highway/Info.Highway.Advisory.Council/study/.
      2.  convergence.report.e  /isc/.
      3.  videotheque.library.eng  /isc/.
      4.  02-19-94.e  /isc/gazette/.

  ┌────────────────────────────────────────────────────────────────┐
  │  Mail current document to: │jcarroll@jacc.com             │     │
  │                                                                  │
  │                             [Cancel ^G] [Accept - Enter]         │
  └────────────────────────────────────────────────────────────────┘

  -->  12.  Building.Canada's.Info.Infrastructure.April94.txt    ..ation.Highway/.
       13.  technology.brokers.and.consultants    ../Technology.Networking.Guide/.
       14.  budget_e.asc    ../Industry.Canada.News.Releases/Federal Budget 1994/.
       15.  management.consultants.txt   /isc/Industry.Profiles/english/.
       16.  trading.houses.txt   /isc/Industry.Profiles/english/.
       17.  ostry.report.feb.1994   /isc/Canadian.Information.Highway/.
       18.  meeting.one   ..n.Information.Highway/Info.Highway.Advisory.Council/.

  Press ? for Help, ? to Quit, ? to go up a menu        Receiving file..|
```

GOPHER BOOKMARKS

Finally, another useful aspect of Gopher is the ability to use bookmarks.

When you have used Gopher to locate a particular Internet resource, and you want to go back to access it again, you might find that you have a difficult time finding it. Remembering which menus you worked your way through is not the easiest thing to do.

Gopher bookmarks permit you to keep track of particular Gopher resources, and to access them through your own personal Gopher menu.

In a shell account, there are four basic bookmark commands:

a	add an item to your bookmark list
A	add the current search to the bookmark list. For example, you might have run a search within Gopher and retrieved a list of documents. Typing A will save the search to your personal Gopher menu so that you can quickly return there.
v	view your current bookmark list
d	delete a bookmark

In a SLIP account, and software such as Winsock Gopher, it is a very straightforward matter to add an item to your bookmark list — merely click on the "add bookmark" icon, which is found at the top left on the row of icons:

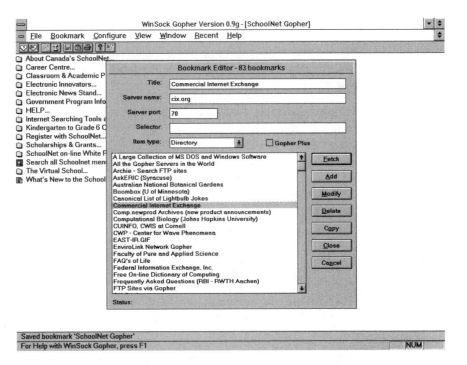

Doing so presents you with a box in which you can change the name for your bookmark or modify other details. You can then click on the "bookmark" icon (the second button from the top left) at any time to travel to one of your "bookmarked" locations.

THE GROWTH OF GOPHER

By one estimate, the number of Gopher servers on the Internet is increasing at an annual rate of 997%.[2]

One of the primary reasons why the number of Gopher servers is increasing at such a dramatic rate is that any institution connected to the Internet can establish its own Gopher server, mount information on it and make it accessible to anyone else in the world with Gopher.

Many organizations on the Internet are actively encouraging the use of Gopher. For example, York University encourages student groups to put information on Gopher and make it available to the rest of the campus and around the world.

As a result, Gopher is rapidly becoming an important information dissemination tool throughout the Internet.

HYTELNET

Hytelnet is a Canadian program, originally written by Peter Scott of the University of Saskatchewan Libraries with assistance from Earl Fogel of the same institution.

Hytelnet summarizes information available on Internet resources worldwide.

Although you can use a Telnet session to a site that has Hytelnet (for example, Telnet to **access.usask.ca** to run it to the Hytelnet client at that location), it is far more convenient to run it on your own computer. Versions of Hytelnet are available for Amiga, MSDOS, Macintosh, UNIX and VMS systems.

TO OBTAIN HYTELNET FOR A PC

Using Anonymous FTP	
FTP site:	ftp.usask.ca
Directory:	Select: pub/hytelnet/pc/latest
File:	hyteln*.zip (* = version number)

The following screens provide a brief tour of Hytelnet, as run on an MSDOS system.

SAMPLE HYTELNET SESSION

The introductory screen indicates the types of information that are available. The two key entries are "**Library catalogs**" and "**Other Resources.**"

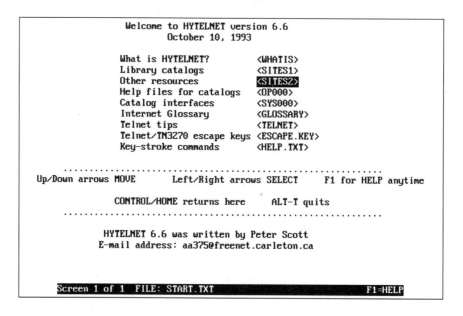

```
              Welcome to HYTELNET version 6.6
                    October 10, 1993

            What is HYTELNET?        <WHATIS>
            Library catalogs         <SITES1>
            Other resources          <SITES2>
            Help files for catalogs  <OP000>
            Catalog interfaces       <SYS000>
            Internet Glossary        <GLOSSARY>
            Telnet tips              <TELNET>
            Telnet/TN3270 escape keys <ESCAPE.KEY>
            Key-stroke commands       <HELP.TXT>

  .................................................................
 Up/Down arrows MOVE      Left/Right arrows SELECT     F1 for HELP anytime

            CONTROL/HOME returns here      ALT-T quits
  .................................................................

            HYTELNET 6.6 was written by Peter Scott
            E-mail address: aa375@freenet.carleton.ca


    Screen 1 of 1  FILE: START.TXT                        F1=HELP
```

By moving to **<SITES2>** with the cursor key and pressing return, we see a menu of various resources available by Telnet.

```
                    Other Telnet-accessible resources

              <ARC000>  Archie: Archive Server Listing Service
              <CWI000>  Campus-wide Information systems
              <FUL000>  Databases and bibliographies

              <DIS000>  Distributed File Servers (Gopher/WAIS/WWW)
              <BOOKS>   Electronic books
              <FEE000>  Fee-Based Services

              <FRE000>  FREE-NETs & Community Computing Systems
              <BBS000>  General Bulletin Boards
              <HYT000>  HYTELNET On-line versions

              <NAS000>  NASA databases
              <NET000>  Network Information Services
              <DIR000>  Whois/White Pages/Directory Services

              <OTH000>  Miscellaneous resources




   Screen 1 of 1  FILE: SITES2                              F1=HELP
```

Choosing the **Databases and bibliographies** entry shows the following screen:

```
                   Databases and Bibliographies

   <FUL035> AAtDB: An Arabidopsis thaliana Data Base
   <FUL041> ABSEES: American Bibliography of Slavic & East European Studies
   <FUL043> Arizona State Economic Development Database
   <FUL031> Bank of England Quarterly Bulletin Time Series Data
   <FUL001> BLAISE-LINE (British Library's On-Line Service)
   <FUL002> British Library Document Supply Centre
   <FUL055> CARL System Database Gateway
   <FUL029> Central Statistical Office Macro-Economic Time Series Data
   <FUL046> Coalition for Networked Information Server
   <FUL004> CONSER database (journal/serial/periodical indexes)
   <FUL005> Constitutional Documents (USA)
   <FUL006> Court of Appeals of Ohio, Eighth District, County of Cuyahoga
   <FUL007> Dartmouth Dante Project
   <FUL024> Earth Images Catalogue LEDA
   <FUL025> Earth observation satellite data inventory service
   <FUL033> Einstein On-Line Service
   <FUL049> Electronic Periodic Table of the Elements
   <FUL008> Environmental Education Database
   <FUL009> ERIC (Educational Resources Information Center Documents)
   <FUL048> Eureka Example screens (Research Libraries Group)
   <FUL044> EX-USSR data files
   <FUL010> General Accounting Office Documents
   ↓↓  Screen 1 of 3  FILE: FUL000                          F1=HELP
```

Choosing the entry **<FUL055>** provides details concerning how to Telnet to the **CARL** service.

```
                    CARL System Database Gateway

TELNET DATABASE.CARL.ORG or 192.54.81.76
Select 5 for vt100

                 WELCOME TO THE CARL SYSTEM DATABASE GATEWAY

CARL Systems, Inc. is proud to present our Shopping List of Databases.
Many of the databases included require a password.  If you would like to
look at one of these restricted databases, please contact CARL Systems,
Inc. at database@carl.org or 303/758-3030.  If you have already been
given a password to a database, please enter your password when
prompted.  There are a number of library catalogs and free databases
available, please feel free to look around.

     1.  UnCover
         (Article Access and Delivery)
     2.  Information Access Company Databases
         (including Business Index, Magazine Index and others)
     3.  Grolier's Academic American Encyclopedia
     4.  Facts on File
     5.  H.W. Wilson Databases
         (including Library Literature)
     6.  Other Information and Article Databases
 ↓↓  Screen 1 of 2  FILE: FUL055                              F1=HELP
```

Hytelnet was originally written for use by librarians, and hence includes a separate section on library resources. Examining the entry for Canada (several levels down from the <SITES1> entry on the starting point above), we see a listing of these libraries.

```
<CA040> Ottawa Public Library
<CA001> Queen's University
<CA016> Saint Mary's University
<CA049> Saskatoon Public Library
<CA029> Simon Fraser University
<CA024> St. Boniface General Hospital Library
<CA017> Technical University of Nova Scotia
<CA027> Trent University
<CA045> Universite de Moncton - Bibliotheque Champlain
<CA037> Universite de Sherbrooke
<CA019> University College of Cape Breton
<CA051> University of Alberta
<CA022> University of British Columbia
<CA003> University of Calgary
<CA052> University of Guelph
<CA020> University of Kings College
<CA034> University of Lethbridge
<CA023> University of Manitoba Libraries
<CA002> University of New Brunswick
<CA047> University of Ottawa
<CA012> University of Prince Edward Island
<CA008> University of Saskatchewan
<CA005> University of Toronto
<CA035> University of Victoria
 ↓↓  Screen 2 of 3  FILE: CA000                              F1=HELP
```

Choosing **Saskatoon Public Library**, we are provided with a screen which details the Telnet address and other information necessary to sign into the library service.

```
                    Saskatoon Public Library

TELNET CHARLY.PUBLIB.SASKATOON.SK.CA or 192.197.206.1
Username: PUBLIC
At the PAC >>> prompt, type  pac

OPAC = DRA <OP004>

To exit, type EXIT
At the PAC >>> prompt, type  quit

 Screen 1 of 1  FILE: CA049                        ·F1=HELP
```

An on-line Hytelnet session looks almost identical. For example, if we Telnet to **access.usask.ca,** and login with the ID **hytelnet**, we see the following screen:

```
                                  VT100 ‡   00:15:02  2:04p
              Welcome to HYTELNET version 6.7.x
                Last update   July 11, 1994

        What is HYTELNET?           <WHATIS>
        Library catalogs            <SITES1>
        Other resources             <SITES2>
        Help files for catalogs     <OP000>
        Catalog interfaces          <SYS000>
        Internet Glossary           <GLOSSARY>
        Telnet tips                 <TELNET>
        Telnet/TN3270 escape keys   <ESCAPE.KEY>
        Key-stroke commands         <HELP>

 ...............................................
 Up/Down arrows MOVE     Left/Right arrows SELECT    ? for HELP anytime

      m returns here     i  searches the index     q quits
 ...............................................
        HYTELNET 6.7 was written by Peter Scott
        E-mail address: aa375@freenet.carleton.ca
        Unix and VMS software by Earl Fogel
```

Which is, of course, almost identical to the screen we get with the PC-based version.

You can also access Hytelnet using Gopher.

Using Gopher	
Site:	liberty.uc.wlu.edu
Path:	Select:
	Explore Internet Resources
	Telnet To Sites (Hytelnet)

Regardless of how we might access it, Hytelnet is a simple, effective and quick way to track Internet resources.

Since updates are released fairly regularly, it is highly recommended.

TO JOIN A MAILING LIST THAT ANNOUNCES NEW HYTELNET RESOURCES.

Using E-mail	
Send message to:	listserv@kentvm.kent.edu
In text of message, type:	subscribe hytel-l firstname lastname
Special Instructions:	Replace firstname and lastname with your own first name and last name.

WORLD WIDE WEB/MOSAIC

Mosaic is, as some people say, an application whose time has come.

Many people believe that the very future of the Internet lies in the application World Wide Web when used with Mosaic client software. The reason for this is that Mosaic presents you with a graphical view into Internet resources through which you can access locations that contain not only text, but images, voice, sounds and even moving pictures, should you have a fast network link into the Internet.

Mosaic and World Wide Web work hand in hand so it is important that you understand the role each plays.

WORLD WIDE WEB

World Wide Web, developed in Europe at CERN, the European Laboratory for Particle Physics, is an Internet initiative which promises much easier browsing of Internet resources, and a type of indexing of Internet information.

World Wide Web servers (or WWW as they are often referred to) provide access to information from throughout the Internet using a unique "hypertext" link. Each WWW screen can include pointers to other WWW screens, with some pointers eventually leading you to specific bits of information and knowledge. Not only that, but a WWW screen can include pointers to documents that link not only to a document on the server you are currently linked to, but documents located on any other WWW server worldwide!

Using WWW is a little like following a maze; you can take a lot of different turns, and each time you are not sure where you are going to end up. At one moment, you might be in Paris, and the next in Australia. With a click of your mouse, you travel the globe, discovering information resources of such breadth and diversity that you will be truly astounded by what you discover.

MOSAIC

Mosaic is the client software that you use to access and browse World Wide Web servers.

Mosaic was developed at NCSA (the National Centre for SuperComputing Applications) and released to the Internet early in 1993. Its usage has exploded since then — according to the Internet Index by Win Treese, usage in terms of the volume of information accessed increased by some 2,500% from June 1993 to June 1994.[3]

Mosaic provides access to World Wide Web servers through a graphical interface, and makes it easy to select information merely by moving to a highlighted word or icon with a mouse and double-clicking.

Some people call the combination of Mosaic and WWW "hypermedia," a combination of hypertext and multimedia. Information can be organized in a graphical manner, such as geographical maps. Click on a city on the map, and you go to a page that shows information about that city! It is this graphical representation that makes the Mosaic/WWW combination so powerful, and makes information on the Internet so easy to navigate.

Mosaic, available for Windows, Macintosh and UNIX systems, is an excellent tool to discover the full diversity of the Internet. Spend a little time with Mosaic, and you will come away with a new appreciation, and a sense of awe, for the power of the global Internet.

NAVIGATING WITH MOSAIC

There are a couple of key points that you should keep in mind as you begin to work with World Wide Web and Mosaic.

WWW/Mosaic makes use of a Uniform Resource Locator (or URL) to define the address of a particular page.

As you begin to explore the Internet, you will often see reference made to WWW addresses in the form of URL's. For example, consider this article which discussed a bookstore in Vancouver now doing business on the Internet:

> In real life, the air of creativity and vision is unmistakable in the offices of
> Duthie Books that wrap around the company's warehouse in Kitsilano. Celia
> Duthie, the enlightened hand at the helm of one of Canada's most successful
> independent book operations, recognized the Internet's potential for building
> business early on. Already a successful player in the mail-order business,
> Duthie saw the Internet as a way of expanding and speeding up her order ful-

fillment. More than a year ago she was talking about ways to build a ``virtual bookstore."

Given that level of insight, and the company's capacity for bright ideas, it's no surprise that it has its own site on the World Wide Web. Duthie's virtual bookstore, lodged on the server at Wimsey – point your browser to: **http://www.wimsey. com/Duthie/** – will carry 50,000 titles in 150 different subject areas once it's completed – books and some audios and videos that are either in stock or on order at the real-world bookstores.

Bookstore is a virtual reality
Vancouver Sun, Sat 09 Jul 94

The article provides the URL in the form of the address **http://www.wimsey.com/Duthie/**. This is what you will use with Mosaic to go to the Duthie virtual bookstore.

Most often, Internet WWW servers refer to this as the "home page," or the default page that you see when you access that particular location. The "home page" for a particular server is like a table of contents for information at that location.

In addition, you can specify a URL that will take you to a specific page or resource buried deep within the server. For example, this article, which announces a new on-line service by the *Halifax Daily News*, provides a pointer to their service, which is certainly several levels down in this particular WWW site:

If you're using a WWW browser (which are available free on-line through the Internet) specify the following URL: **http://www.cfn.cs.dal.ca/Media/TodaysNews/TodaysNews.html**. The system is fussy about upper and lower case, so type carefully.

Two ways to connect to us on-line
The Daily News (Halifax), Tue 02 Aug 94

An interesting point is that the concept of Uniform Resource Locator's (URL's) is becoming common throughout the Internet as a means of describing all information resources, not just WWW resources. Over time, we should see FTP archives, Gopher sites and other services listed with URL's instead of the types of descriptions that they use now.

A SAMPLE MOSAIC/WWW SESSION

Let's take a look at the World Wide Web page for the Halifax Daily News as mentioned above:

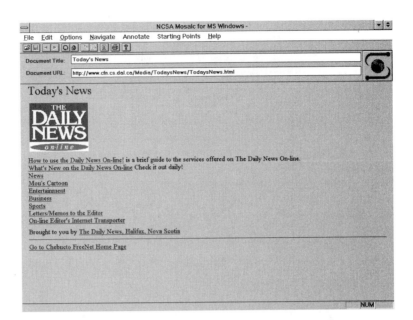

The screen provides the logo for the newspaper, as well as some information as to what is available. Choices are highlighted on the screen in a different color.

We can choose any of these items by moving to it and "double-clicking" with our mouse. For example, if we choose the "On-line Editor's Internet Transporter," we see the following page.

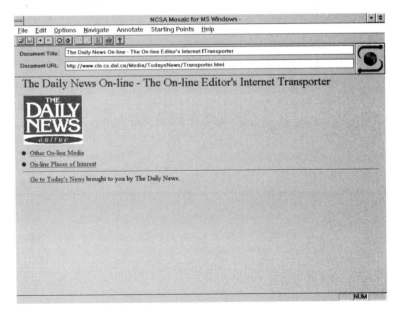

Here is where it gets interesting. If we choose the item "Other On-line Media," we get a listing of other World Wide Resources:

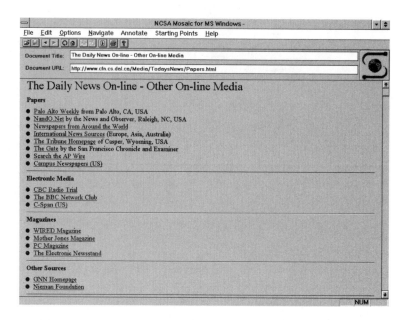

If we choose the "CBC Radio Trial," we are then linked (or transported, as this service calls it) to the CBC World Wide Web site in Ottawa.

In other words, Mosaic choices link to other pages of information — but those pages could be located anywhere on the globe!

EXPLORING MOSAIC

A good place to start out with many Mosaic explorations is the "home page" for an Internet service provider in Canada, or the "home page" of an organization that has established an Internet resource. *The Directory of WWW Servers in Canada* provides a number of these World Wide Web locations.

Let's take a look at the home page for Wimsey, a BC- based Internet service provider. The address for the home page is **http://www.wimsey.com**. To go there, we choose File Open in Mosaic, and type in the URL:

This takes us to the Wimsey home page. Like many "home pages," Wimsey always provides current information on new items. On August 18, 1994, the home page listed the following items:

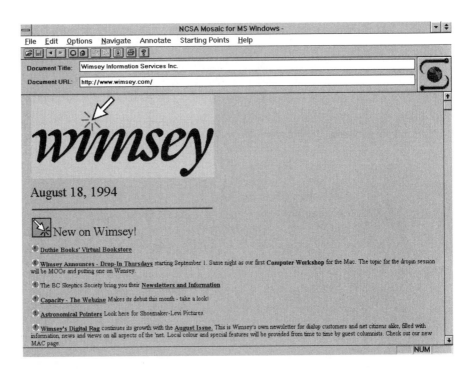

Paging down the "home page" a bit, we see a menu item that points to the main Wimsey WWW directory, referred to as "WIMSEY's Inside Pages":

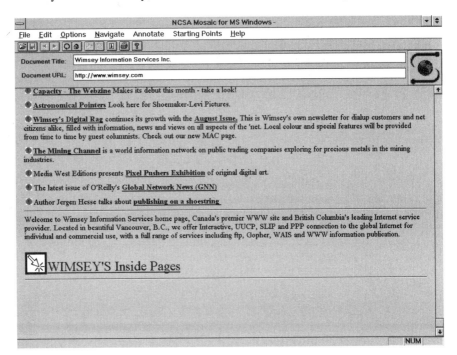

Choosing that item, we can see some of the business and other resources available on the Wimsey WWW server:

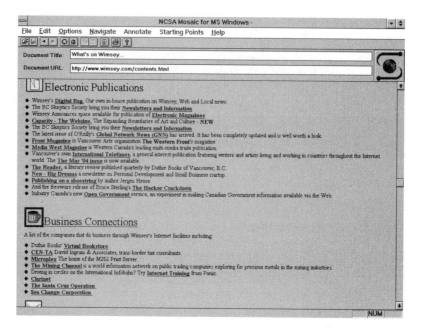

which fills at least two pages:

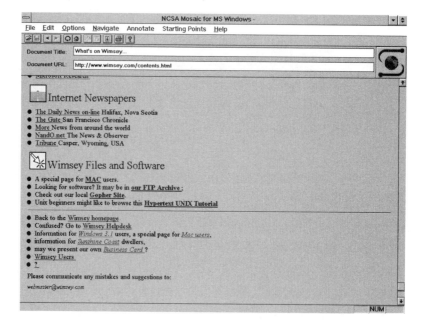

SAMPLE WWW SESSION – SHELL ACCOUNT

Although you can't really use WWW effectively through a shell account, you can try it out by using Telnet to reach a site that has a screen-based WWW client available. For example, to try out a World Wide Web server, Telnet to `info.cern.ch`. No additional login is required.

After navigating a couple of screens that detail where to find more information about WWW, we are presented with an introductory screen.

```
                                              VT100 :   00:01:11 11:14a
                                                       Overview of the Web
                         GENERAL OVERVIEW OF THE WEB

   There is no "top" to the World-Wide Web. You can look at it from many points
   of view. Here are some places to start.

   by Subject[1]            The Virtual Library organises information by subject
                            matter.

   List of servers[2]       All registered HTTP servers by country

   by Service Type[3]       The Web includes data accessible by many other
                            protocols. The lists by access protocol may help if
                            you know what kind of service you are looking for.

   If you find a useful starting point for you personally, you can configure
   your WWW browser to start there by default.

   See also: About the W3 project[4] .
      [End]



  1-4, Back, Up, Quit, or Help:
```

Note that the WWW screen includes numbers next to each item. As you dig further into WWW, you will find that complete sentences contain a variety of numbers, each of which points to a different Internet resource. This is the equivalent of highlighted text when WWW is accessed through Mosaic.

As you can see, there really is no comparison when it comes to the use of World Wide Web through a dial-up shell account, compared to using it with Mosaic through a dial-up SLIP account or an account that has a direct network link to the Internet.

FRUSTRATIONS WITH MOSAIC

Given what it can do, many people believe that Mosaic is the future of the Internet.

"Many companies are stepping up to WWW as THE technology with which to present info on the Internet — companies like Novell, Quarterdeck and QMS," says Michael Martineau, the President of NSTN Inc.

"Telnet and FTP are, in my opinion, dying applications. They are hard to use and understand," Michael comments, when asked about the future of information retrieval on the Internet. "WWW can fully replace Telnet, FTP, Gopher and WAIS. It handles information in a variety of forms and is capable of being the only information retrieval system that people need to use. Mosaic is available today, for Windows, MACs and Unix systems."

Yet, there is a real limitation to the use of Mosaic — to really take advantage of it and to enjoy its use, you must have a good, high-speed connection to the Internet.

Although you can use Mosaic through a dial-up modem, you really can't do so at speeds less than 9600 baud — it is simply too slow. Even with a 9600 baud or 14400 baud modem, Mosaic can be infuriating. The reason for this is that World Wide Web sites send all kinds of information — and when you start receiving images, sound or other files, it can quickly overwhelm even the fastest modem link.

As a result, to truly appreciate Mosaic, you need a high-speed, direct network link to the Internet. (Direct network links are discussed in the next chapter.)

The reality of Mosaic is that some people will struggle to use it with a dial-up modem, but we really need to wait for the emergence of faster telecommunication links to really take advantage of what it offers.

OTHER INFORMATION UTILITITIES

FINGER

Finger is a utility originally used in the UNIX world to list users on a local system, or to list users located at another location on the Internet.

Some locations on the Internet are now using Finger as a simple method of making information available. For example, if you are in a shell account that has a Finger client, you can obtain recent information on auroral (Northern Lights) activity in Canada by typing:

```
finger aurora@xi.uleth.ca
```

If you have a direct connection to the Internet, you can use Winsock Finger, a public domain Finger client.

Accessing the site above, for example, shows you the following:

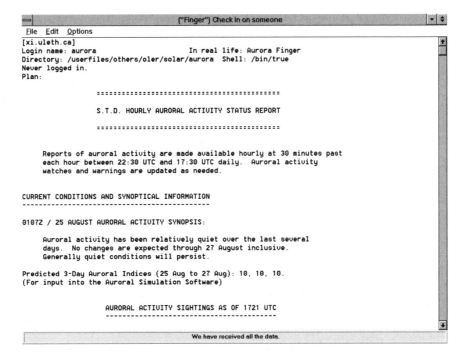

```
                              ("Finger") Check in on someone

File  Edit  Options
[xi.uleth.ca]
Login name: aurora                        In real life: Aurora Finger
Directory: /userfiles/others/oler/solar/aurora   Shell: /bin/true
Never logged in.
Plan:

          ===============================================

          S.T.D. HOURLY AURORAL ACTIVITY STATUS REPORT

          ===============================================


     Reports of auroral activity are made available hourly at 30 minutes past
     each hour between 22:30 UTC and 17:30 UTC daily.  Auroral activity
     watches and warnings are updated as needed.


CURRENT CONDITIONS AND SYNOPTICAL INFORMATION
---------------------------------------------

0107Z / 25 AUGUST AURORAL ACTIVITY SYNOPSIS:

     Auroral activity has been relatively quiet over the last several
     days.  No changes are expected through 27 August inclusive.
     Generally quiet conditions will persist.

Predicted 3-Day Auroral Indices (25 Aug to 27 Aug): 10, 10, 10.
(For input into the Auroral Simulation Software)

          AURORAL ACTIVITY SIGHTINGS AS OF 1721 UTC
          -----------------------------------------

                        We have received all the data.
```

IRC

Although not really an information retrieval utility, Internet Relay Chat does deserve some mention.

IRC is best described as a "CB radio" for the Internet. Using IRC, you can participate in on-line discussions in real time with other Internet users. Discussions are either open or private.

To use IRC, you must have either:

- a direct connection to the Internet and have the IRC client software on your own system; or

- use a version located on your Internet service provider.

In both cases, you will also need an IRC server location to access. Your Internet service provider might automatically link to a site. The major Canadian location is at **ug.cs.dal.ca**.

To check if you have IRC access, type IRC at your Internet service provider prompt.

A listing of IRC servers in Canada can be found in Appendix I, in the document *Directory of IRC Servers in Canada.*

WAIS

WAIS (Wide Area Information Server) is another tool used to locate information throughout the Internet. WAIS runs on everything from a supercomputer at its developer, Thinking Machines, to many other types of computers throughout the Internet.

However, there seem to be fewer WAIS servers throughout the Internet that are readily accessible, compared to Gopher and World Wide Web. In addition, few sites seem to be adopting it for general use to the same degree that Gopher and World Wide Web are being deployed.

Given its limited use throughout the Internet, it's not really believed to be a technology that you will want to take the time to learn.

LIMITATIONS OF INTERNET INFORMATION SOURCES

Internet is not a solution to all your information needs.

If you have come to the Internet to look for market research reports, or to be able to perform in-depth research on particular topics based on major industry magazines or publications, or to find financial statements or other corporate information, you've come to the wrong place.[4]

Using the tools described in this chapter can often be frustrating and difficult. Finding the information resources on the Internet that you need can be a harrying experience.

In many situations, you will become frustrated because you cannot find the information that you are looking for.

The Internet is not a magic bullet when it comes to information access. There are several problems when it comes to locating information on the Internet:

- You must remember that the Internet had its roots in research and academic communities. As a result, a lot of the available Internet information sources tend to be from those communities, and will not be the type of information that you are seeking.

- Some people suggest that the Internet is a vast, unindexed *data swamp*. In some ways, this is true — since there is no "master index" for the Internet, it can be very difficult to locate the type of information that you seek.

- Information resources on the Internet are not always permanent — a resource that you access and find useful today might not be there tomorrow. Information resources established on the Internet are often put up through volunteer efforts or are established as part of some backroom, unsupported corporate initiative. This means that Internet information resources are not the most reliable services in the world.

- The reliability of information on the Internet can sometimes be called into question. Since anyone can establish an Internet resource, you really have no way of knowing the quality of the information, unless you take the time to determine the background of the author, and attempt to judge its validity. This means that you really should treat any information from the Internet with a degree of healthy skepticism.

Although the range and breadth of information available on the Internet is constantly growing and can be astounding, you should keep in mind that it is not a solution to all of your information needs. There are other information solutions available to you which might more adequately meet your particular information needs.

COMMERCIAL INFORMATION SERVICES

There are many other research tools available through networked systems, including those that you pay a usage fee for over and above any Internet access charge.

These include systems like Dow Jones News Retrieval, Dialog and Nexis, massive warehouses of information. For example, Dialog and Nexis each contain up to fifteen years' worth of the full text of major magazines and newspapers from around the world. Search rates range from $50 to several hundred dollars per hour. These services are all accessible from the Internet, although you must separately arrange for a user ID and password on each system, and must make appropriate billing arrangements.

In Canada, major on-line research systems include Infoglobe and Infomart, which carry the full text of such publications as *The Globe and Mail*, *The Financial Post*, *The Ottawa Citizen* and other major daily newspapers. In addition, these services carry corporate profiles, market research reports, stock prices (delayed) and other types of information. At this time, neither Infoglobe or Infomart are accessible via the Internet. Rates for usage of these databases also vary, but are usually in the range of $100/hr and up.

THE USE OF HOME PAGES

We mentioned the concept of a home page when describing the use of WWW/Mosaic.

Many Internet service providers are now spending time to establish well-organized home pages for both Gopher and WWW.

You can freely explore cyberspace on your own in search of information, or start with a home page that somehow organizes cyberspace. A well-organized home page is an important service that a provider can offer its customers. So important, in fact, that some providers have hired librarians to bring order to the chaos — an extremely positive step, indeed!

MULTIPLE SOURCES OF INFORMATION

When it comes to information, there is a simple rule that you must remember — you get what you pay for.

The limited range of Internet databases is but one type of available on-line information. If information research is key to your activities, consider examining the alternatives available in commercial on-line databases as described above, but keep in mind that you must be willing to pay for that information.

THE FUTURE OF INFORMATION RETRIEVAL ON THE INTERNET

Certainly, Mosaic and Gopher continue to best portray the future of information retrieval on the Internet.

The frustrations of using Mosaic through a modem connection means that Gopher will be around for some time to come. Gopher is accessible by people on the Internet from both shell accounts and direct accounts, and hence can be accessed by many people throughout the Internet. It is a tool that can be used by those without a sophisticated connection to the Internet.

Mosaic, on the other hand, requires a direct network connection. For the next several years at least, this will limit its use to those people who purchase SLIP accounts, or who link their internal networks directly to the Internet, as discussed in the next chapter. This limits the number of people who can use World Wide Web somewhat. Although Mosaic is on the leading edge as the primary method to access WWW servers, it will take some time for it to be fully deployed.

Clearly, however, with tools such as Gopher and Mosaic, the Internet is proving to be an ever more useful tool for the retrieval of national and global information.

---

1 . Through a Gopher client, you can also connect directly to a Gopher server without going through all the menus. For example, you could have typed GOPHER NSTN.NS.CA to link directly to a Gopher server at the Nova Scotia Technology Network.

2 . The Internet Index, compiled by Win Treese (treese@crl.dec.com), 7/8/93, revised: 12/16/93

3 . Contact treese@openmarket.com for more information.

4 . In a significant development, the U.S. government has decided to make available information filed with the Securities and Exchange Commission via the Internet, rather than via a pay-per-use on-line commercial database. This occurred after an intense grassroots campaign by Internet supporters for such information to be publicly available.

C H A P T E R   9

. . . .

CONNECTING TO THE INTERNET

As you have seen in the preceding chapters, the way that you access the Internet will have an effect on what you can do with it, and how easy it will be for you to use.

In particular, if you are "directly connected" to the Internet, your use of the system will differ from those who are not, as you will be able to take advantage of many of the more sophisticated software programs available to use various applications on the Internet.

Yet, even this simple rule about a direct connection is becoming less true, particularly with the arrival of new software such as Pipeline for Windows, which permits easy navigation of most Internet services without the need for a direct connection.

In this chapter, we examine some of the technical methods by which you or your organization might link yourself to the Internet:

- an indirect, electronic mail only connection;

- an indirect, e-mail and USENET only connection, using UUCP;

- an indirect connection via access through a "shell" account;

- a permanent TCP/IP connection;

- a temporary TCP/IP connection via a modem, using SLIP/PPP.

In order to clarify your options, we examine in the first section of this chapter what you can do with the Internet as an individual with a modem, and in the second section, what you can do as an organization via a modem or a more direct network link.

The possible connections are shown in Figure 9.1.

FIGURE 9.1: INTERNET CONNECTIVITY

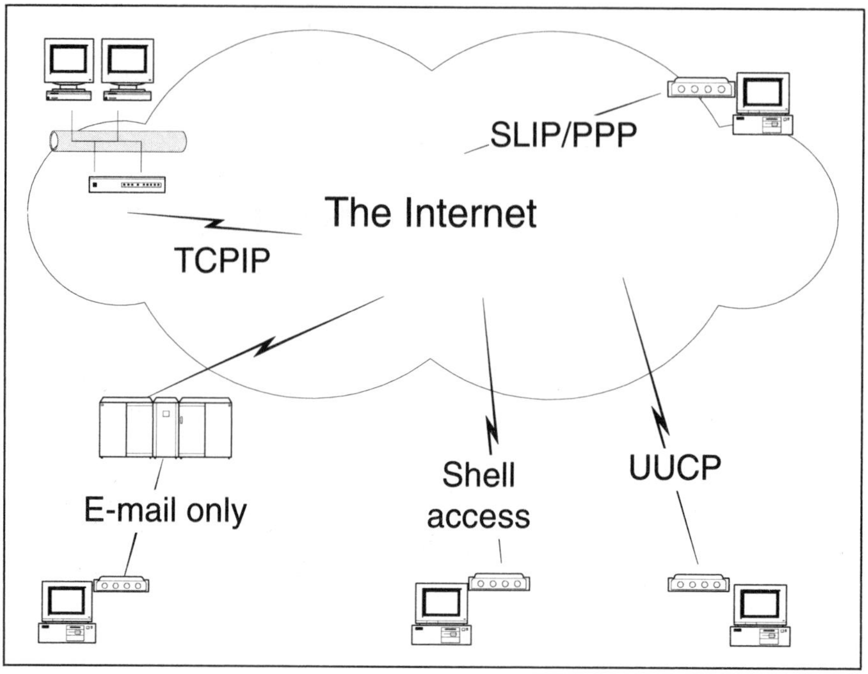

INTERNET SERVICE PROVIDERS

Appendix C includes the *Directory of Canadian Internet Service Providers,* which details the range of services offered by these companies. As you review the listings, you will appreciate that there are many methods to link into the Internet in Canada.

Some of these providers provide UUCP, shell, permanent and temporary SLIP/PPP access to the network; others provide only one or two of these options; while several others provide only e-mail access to the Internet.

Part of the art for you is to figure out what type of connectivity you need and for what purpose. What is appropriate in your circumstances depends upon:

- your particular communication needs;

- the technical effort you are willing to put in to participate in the network;

- the amount of money that you are willing or have available to spend;

- the hardware and operating system platform in which you operate.

Keep in mind that providers come and go. Obviously, some might not be here later, and new ones will appear. At least two providers listed in the 1994 edition of the *Canadian Internet Handbook* had disappeared within a few months of the book having hit bookstores.

As you review the listings of providers in Appendix C, keep in mind that the list is current as of September 1994. As a result, new providers might have appeared on the local or national scene, or existing providers might have gone out of business.

INDIVIDUAL ACCESS

Many people in organizations choose to first access the Internet as individuals in order to explore it and understand it better. More often than not, they might be doing this from a PC at home, or in other cases, through their office.

This section details methods by which you can access the Internet on your own, usually through a dialup-based modem connection. This includes examination of how to get simple e-mail-only access to the Internet, the use of UUCP-based programs to use Internet e-mail and USENET news, and "shell" or SLIP/PPP accounts for access to most Internet services.

ELECTRONIC MAIL ACCESS ONLY

With the growing popularity of Internet e-mail, it is evident that many people want to have an "Internet e-mail address" without having to take the step of establishing a full connection to the Internet. You might find that you have a need to send and receive Internet e-mail, yet you can't wait for the technical department in your company to put in place a network link.

To establish e-mail-only access to the Internet, you can subscribe on your own to a commercial electronic mail or on-line service.

The *Directory of Canadian Internet Service Providers* includes references to a number of commercial e-mail and on-line services which have established links to Internet e-mail. These systems include U.S. commercial e-mail services such as ATTMail and MCIMail, on-line services such as CompuServe and Genie, and the Canadian TheNet:Mail system (formerly known as Envoy 100/iNet 2000) and Mpact Immedia.

If you simply want to have an Internet e-mail address and don't want or need access to other Internet services, you might consider joining a service such as CompuServe, or one of the commercial e-mail providers mentioned such as MCIMail.

Many of these services come with, or make available, special communications software that makes it easy to send and receive e-mail messages.

Using a software package such as CompuServe Information Manager, available for both Windows and Macintosh, sending and receiving Internet e-mail is made much easier. The following screen shows a message being created destined for someone on the Internet:

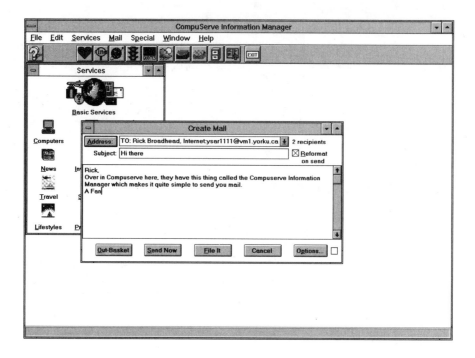

Using a service such as CompuServe or MCIMail provides you with your own unique Internet address that can be used to receive Internet messages, and provides you with the capability to send e-mail to anyone with an Internet e-mail address.

There is one main concern with this approach, and that is cost. Some commercial e-mail services charge for messages sent to and received from the Internet on a per-kilocharacter basis – i.e., for every 1,000 characters sent or received. With rates reaching as high as 25¢ per kilocharacter, you might find yourself spending a lot of money very quickly.

As a result, if you take this approach, it is suggested that you closely examine and fully understand the cost of the alternative. And in particular, it is suggested that you be very careful about joining any mailing lists, since the volume of e-mail you might receive as a result could easily end up costing you a lot of money!

E-MAIL AND USENET VIA UUCP

The second method of establishing your own personal link to the Internet is to use the "UUCP" protocol, and to purchase or find software that uses this protocol.

By using UUCP, you can participate in Internet e-mail and USENET newsgroups, but you can't use any other Internet services such as Gopher or WWW/Mosaic.

Strictly speaking, since you're not directly connected to the Internet, and do not have an IP address, you are not "on" the Internet.

UUCP EXPLAINED

Many Internet service providers provide UUCP service — that is, they permit users to send and receive Internet e-mail and USENET news using the UUCP protocol.

UUCP stands for Unix-to-Unix Copy Protocol, which is a "store-and-forward" file transfer utility found within most UNIX systems. UUCP takes on responsibility for copying e-mail and USENET postings to and from your Internet service provider. Using UUCP, you are only intermittently connected to your Internet service provider.

To use UUCP, you will need:

- a UUCP program for your system;

and

- an e-mail program and newsreader software that work with your version of UUCP. This often comes with the UUCP program you are using.

There are commercial and public domain versions of UUCP available for both DOS/Windows and Macintosh systems.

HOW DOES UUCP WORK?

UUCP is a batch-oriented system — that is to say:

- any messages you create are not sent to your Internet service provider immediately, but are sent the next time you make a UUCP call to your provider;

- any messages sent to you are only received by you when you make a UUCP call to the provider;

- USENET news is delivered to you, for the groups you choose to belong to when you make a UUCP call to your provider.

UUCP PUBLIC DOMAIN SOFTWARE

There are many implementations of UUCP for popular operating systems available in the "public domain" or as shareware. This means that you can either use the program for free, or are requested to pay a fee to use the software.

It's often necessary to mix and match the following components to get a full working system in place:

- a basic UUCP system to send and receive e-mail and news to and from your Internet service provider. The basic UUCP system sometimes includes rudimentary e-mail and news programs;

and

- more full-featured e-mail and/or newsreader software.

For example, UUPC for MSDOS (do not confuse UUPC with UUCP) comes with a simple program that permits you to send and receive Internet e-mail, and has the capability to receive USENET news. However, it does not have a newsreader: a program that permits you to read the USENET news you receive. In this case, you need newsreader software such as SNEWS in addition to your UUPC software. SNEWS and UUPC have been modified by their authors to work closely together.

You should only explore the use of public domain or shareware software if you have a technical bent and want the maximum degree of flexibility in your use of Internet e-mail and USENET news, as it can take a little bit of playing to get a full configuration working correctly. However, once you do get it working, you might find it to be a tremendously valuable way to use the Internet.

One of the co-authors of this book now uses a combination package for stand-alone purposes that consists of:

- UUPC, a UUCP program for DOS computers that dials up his Internet service provider and sends/receives e-mail and USENET news;

- Pegasus Mail for Windows, a full-featured, LAN-based e-mail system (used on a stand-alone basis);

- SNEWS, a simple, effective DOS newsreader program;

- SNUUPM, a program developed to permit a straightforward implementation of all three pieces of software above.

Pegasus Mail for Windows provides a very straightforward means to send and receive Internet e-mail.

Another very popular DOS/Windows-based UUCP combination consists of Waffle, a program that handles the UUCP connection, combined with Helldiver, a Windows-based program that provides an excellent front-end to e-mail and USENET news collected by Waffle.

In the Macintosh world, you can look for Mac/gnuucp or uupc 3.0 for the Macintosh to send and receive your UUCP batches, and for ToadNews, rnMac or TheNews-UUCP to read your USENET news.

In addition, some shareware packages have bundled both the UUCP and e-mail/USENET news components into one simple, straightforward package. An interesting piece of software is WinNET, a Windows program available for $99 U.S. that combines e-mail and news software into one friendly, easy-to-configure package. Originally programed to work with a particular Internet provider in the U.S., it will also work with any other UUCP provider as long as the shareware fee is paid.

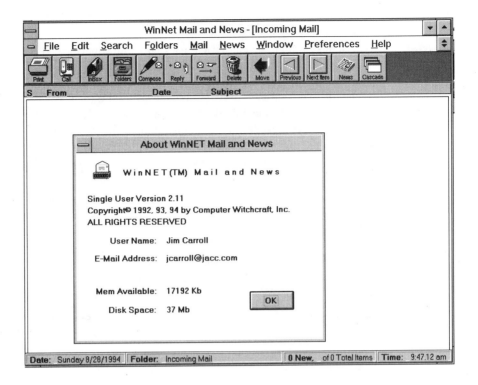

You can obtain a listing of various public domain UUCP alternatives from one of the main "Frequently Asked Questions" FTP archives on the Internet, as follows:

Using Anonymous FTP	
FTP site:	rtfm.mit.edu
Directory:	pub/usenet/news.answers/msdos-mail-news
Files:	intro
	software

Using E-mail	
Send message to:	mail-server@rtfm.mit.edu
In text of message, type:	send /pub/usenet/news.answers/msdos-mail-news/intro
	send /pub/usenet/news.answers/msdos-mail-news/
	software

You can get more information about WinNet by sending an e-mail message.

Using E-mail	
Send message to:	winnet@win.net

COMMERCIAL *UUCP* PACKAGES

A number of commercial UUCP packages with sophisticated e-mail and USENET newsreader software are now coming to market.

The best-known is MKS Internet Anywhere, a package developed in Kitchener, Ontario. The software provides Windows-based e-mail, news and other programs to help manage your Internet access via UUCP. The program manager for MKS Internet Anywhere shows the various components of the program.

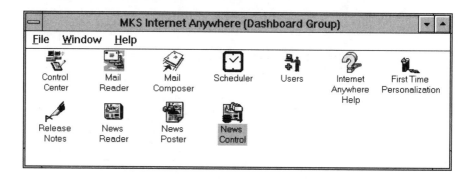

In the Macintosh world, take a look for UUCP/Connect, a full-featured UUCP package.

ACCESS VIA A SHELL ACCOUNT

If you would like to do more than Internet e-mail and USENET news, you can buy a "shell account" from an Internet service provider. "Shell account" access is available through either a Canadian Internet provider, or through one of the major commercial on-line services based in the U.S.

Most Internet service providers offer shell access, and since it can be the easiest method from a technical perspective to access the Internet, shell access is recommended for most individuals who are curious about the Internet and want to explore what it offers.

Keep in mind, however, that many of these same Internet service providers are now also offering SLIP/PPP access (discussed in the next section), which allows use of simple Windows- or Macintosh-based point-and-click navigation tools.

As a result, although it can be easy to get a shell account, it's not necessarily the easiest way to access the full range of Internet services – for that, you want a SLIP or PPP account.

ACCESSING A SHELL ACCOUNT

You access a shell account like you would any other on-line computer service.

Using communications software, you dial your Internet service provider and sign in to an account with your user ID and password. You're then presented with a menu from which to choose Internet services, or are presented directly with a prompt from which you can access various Internet services.

When using a shell account, keep in mind that you're using terminal emulation which, as discussed in Chapter 4, results in a number of limitations on how you can use the Internet.

THROUGH A CANADIAN INTERNET PROVIDER

Many of the Internet service providers in Canada offer shell access. There is also a derivative of shell access, known as TAC, that provides access to some but not all of the Internet services accessible through shell access.

FIGURE 9.2: SHELL ACCESS VIA CANADIAN INTERNET SERVICE PROVIDERS

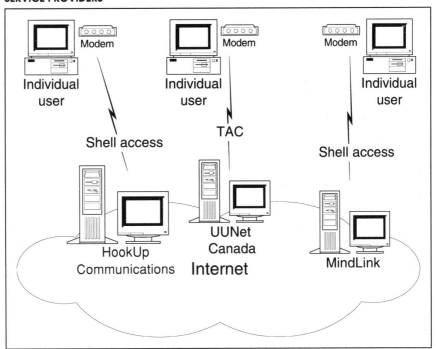

For example, HookUp Communications, which provides access in Toronto, Kitchener and other major centers, as well as 1-800 access, allows you to dial in to its system and directly access Internet services via a shell account.

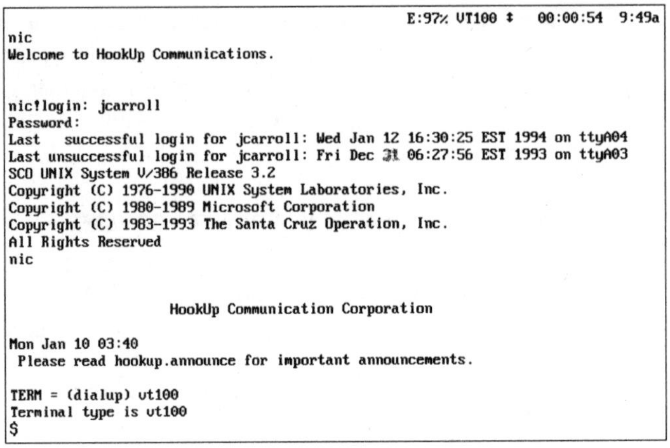

```
                                      E:97% VT100 ‡   00:00:54  9:49a
nic
Welcome to HookUp Communications.


nic!login: jcarroll
Password:
Last    successful login for jcarroll: Wed Jan 12 16:30:25 EST 1994 on ttyA04
Last unsuccessful login for jcarroll: Fri Dec 31 06:27:56 EST 1993 on ttyA03
SCO UNIX System V/386 Release 3.2
Copyright (C) 1976-1990 UNIX System Laboratories, Inc.
Copyright (C) 1980-1989 Microsoft Corporation
Copyright (C) 1983-1993 The Santa Cruz Operation, Inc.
All Rights Reserved
nic


                  HookUp Communication Corporation

Mon Jan 10 03:40
 Please read hookup.announce for important announcements.

TERM = (dialup) vt100
Terminal type is vt100
$
```

When you dial in, you are prompted to enter your login name, password and terminal type (usually vt-100, if your communications software supports this).

At the $ prompt at the bottom of the screen, you can use Telnet or FTP. In addition, since Gopher and Archie are resident on the HookUp system, using these two applications is faster than using them via Telnet to some other computer on the Internet.

VIA A COMMERCIAL ON-LINE SERVICE

Several major commercial on-line services that provide on-line conferences, games, research libraries and other services, also provide full or partial access to the Internet.

FIGURE 9.3: INTERNET VIA COMMERCIAL ON-LINE SERVICES

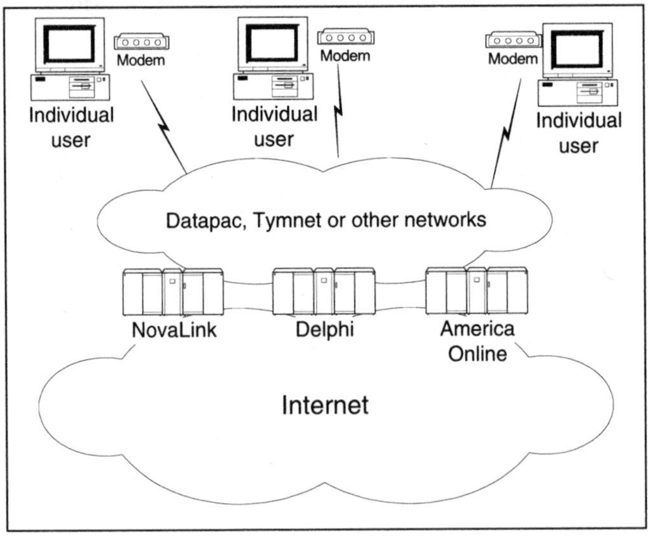

Systems like Delphi, BIX and America Online all offer access to the Internet, and since they are available via major communication networks such as Datapac, SprintNet and Tymnet, they are often accessible via a local telephone call within Canadian cities and towns.

An example of such a service is NovaLink, based out of Shrewsbury, Massachusetts. NovaLink is accessible via a local call in Toronto, Vancouver, Ottawa, Montreal and Calgary (via the CompuServe data network), and provides access to Internet e-mail, USENET news, FTP and Telnet, in addition to other services.

When you dial into Novalink and access Internet from the main menu, you'll see the following:

```
                                       E:94% UT100 *   00:00:00  2:35p
Menu choice (or 'X' for previous): i

9/27/93 NovaLink has just installed a QWK mail program.  Please be
advised that until this message disappears, this feature is in beta,
_use_at_your_own_risk_.  If you have any problems, questions or remarks
please email Bulloney.

Please see the Internet Help Desk topic message #90 in the Internet
Bulletin Board for a note on QWK mail reader compatability.

Email Clufkin for Internet and UNIX help!

Page: INTERNET
14:39:28 EST, 10-JAN-94

     A ... About the Internet Connection
     B ... Internet Bulletin Board
     F ... Feedback to Internet/Unix Admn
     L ... Library of Internet Help Files
     N ... Netmail & UseNet News
     S ... Shell (Telnet, FTP, etc.)
     T ... Internet Teleconference

Menu choice (or 'X' for previous):
```

Choosing N for Netmail & UseNet News provides an additional menu that permits you to send and receive Internet e-mail, join and read newsgroups, and post messages to newsgroups.

Another menu choice leads you to shell access, which lets you use Telnet and FTP. In addition, since NovaLink runs Gopher and Archie directly on its own system, these services are fast and responsive.

```
                                       E:94% UT100 *   00:00:00  2:35p
     L ... Library of Internet Help Files
     N ... Netmail & UseNet News
     S ... Shell (Telnet, FTP, etc.)
     T ... Internet Teleconference

Menu choice (or 'X' for previous): n

Internet Netmail & UseNet News
NovaMail Version 2.00
(C)1993 Inner Circle Technologies, Inc.

Your mailbox: explorer@novalink.com <Rick Broadhead>

J ... Join Newsgroup
P ... Post News
Q ... QWK-Mail Transfer
R ... Read private NetMail
S ... Scan Newsgroups
U ... Unjoin Newsgroup
W ... Write private NetMail
Z ... Special features
X ... Exit

Option:
```

Access via systems like NovaLink, Delphi or America Online is often an easy way to access Internet services, and works well for those who don't have inexpensive access through a local Internet service provider. In addition, the range of other on-line services available, such as forums, games and on-line research libraries makes them an attractive alternative for your communication needs.

However, since you're using services based in the U.S., you do end up paying a bit of a premium to use the Internet this way. With the growing number of Canadian Internet providers providing 1-800 access, there's even less incentive to use a U.S.-based service.

SLIP/PPP CONNECTIONS

Direct connections for use by individuals to the Internet are supported by the use of the SLIP or PPP protocols.

SLIP (Serial Line Interface Protocol) and PPP (Point to Point Protocol) provide full TCP/IP capabilities to the casual dial-up user, and hence allow you to be "directly connected" to the Internet.

Networks directly linked to the Internet have a registered Internet IP address, and are able to link directly to any other computer on the Internet. When using a SLIP or PPP connection, you are using a registered Internet IP address, albeit on a temporary basis.

BENEFITS OF A DIRECT CONNECTION

More and more people across Canada are buying SLIP/PPP connections to the Internet rather than shell accounts, due to the fact that you can run more Internet software (such as Mosaic) in a much friendlier environment. As we saw in Chapter 4, a direct connection lets you use all Internet services, most often with a point-and-click interface.

Individuals with a direct connection to the Internet are directly using the TCP/IP "protocol stack." The result is that the applications they run interact much more closely with other computers throughout the Internet, without the limitations imposed on a shell account by using terminal emulation. The result is that these individuals can take advantage of the wealth of new software emerging for Internet applications, such as Windows versions of Mosaic and Gopher, as seen in Chapter 8.

This results in a substantial lessening in complexity of the Internet, and a significant increase in the usefulness of the network.

SLIP/PPP FOR CASUAL MODEM CONNECTION

Dialup modem connections via SLIP/PPP usually involve a speed of 14,400 bits per second (14.4kb) or 19.2kb.

To use SLIP or PPP, you will require software that supports SLIP or PPP. There are a number of implementations of SLIP and PPP available for most operating system platforms.

A popular alternative in the DOS/Windows world is the use of Chameleon, for which there is a sampler in the "public domain." Chameleon permits fairly straightforward SLIP access to the Internet through a Windows interface. To get information on where you can get the sampler, send a message to **sales@netmanage.com**.

Trumpet Winsock is another alternative. A public domain SLIP program, it is rapidly gaining favor throughout the Internet as a method of providing SLIP access from Microsoft Windows. You can download Trumpet Winsock from many locations throughout the Internet, including the one detailed below.

Using Anonymous FTP	
FTP site:	ftp.utas.edu.au
Directory:	pc/trumpet/winsock
File:	twsk*.zip (* = version number)

For Macintosh users, there are a number of SLIP packages, including InterSLIP, MacSLIP and MacPPP for PPP access.

FOR INTERSLIP

Using Anonymous FTP	
FTP site:	ftp.intercon.com
Directory:	InterCon/sales/InterSLIP
Files:	InterSLIPInstaller
	InterSLIPInstaller1.0.1.hqx

FOR MACSLIP

Using E-mail	
Send message to:	info@hydepark.com

FOR MACPPP

Using Anonymous FTP	
FTP site:	merit.edu
Directory:	pub/ppp
File:	macppp2.0.1.hqx

If you plan to implement such a package, be prepared for a bit of a technical journey, as you'll be required to gain a bit more familiarity with TCP/IP issues, although in many cases your Internet service provider might have already configured the program for you.

For example, the configuration screen for Trumpet Winsock requires the following types of information:

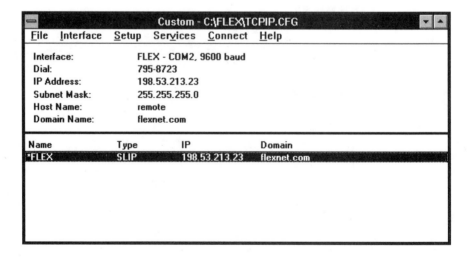

The Chameleon Sampler, configured for access through Fleximation, a Toronto Internet service provider, requires the following information:

Usually, to use such a package, you will need the guidance of your Internet service provider for the required information, which includes an IP address, domain name, name server and other tidbits.

BUNDLED SOFTWARE

An alternative is that some vendors are providing "bundled" software to casual dial-up users, to make it easier to use the Internet using SLIP/PPP.

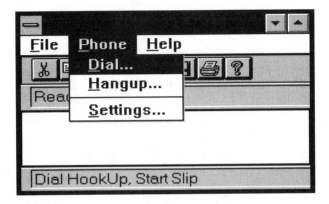

HookUp Communications, for example, provides users with "HookUp Dialer for Windows," a program that will provide a simple SLIP connection to their service. Establishing the SLIP connection is as simple as choosing a menu item. Once you click on Dial, HookUp Dialer for Windows takes care of invoking the Trumpet Winsock application for you, isolating you from some of the complexity.

HookUp also provides access to several other Internet tools, making them available from within Microsoft Windows.

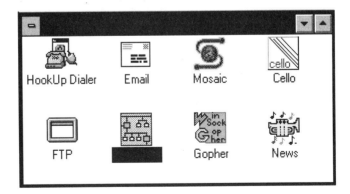

Many Internet service providers are beginning to bundle such tools together into one "package," thus making it easier than ever to access the Internet via a SLIP connection.

NEW LEADING-EDGE SOFTWARE

An interesting alternative to a standard dialup shell account or SLIP account is the use of Pipeline for Windows.

This software uses a proprietary computer protocol that is not SLIP, yet provides many of the benefits of a SLIP connection.

The protocol, which the Pipeline folks call "Pink Slip," provides a very effective, very easy to use interface into most Internet services through what is really a dial-up shell account. It does this by performing a number of nifty background tricks while it's on-line.

In Canada, the Pipeline software has been already licensed for use in the Toronto area by a new Internet service provider, InfoRamp.

The Pipeline software provides one program access to pretty well every Internet feature, except for Mosaic. When you load the Pipeline software, you see a single screen which provides simple access to news, e-mail and other services. Clicking on Connect!, you are linked into Inforamp through a dial-up call.

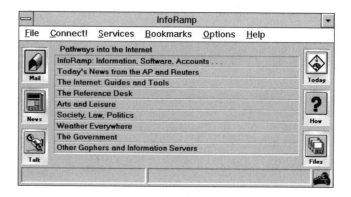

The Services menu item lists additional services that you can reach, such as IRC, Veronica and Archie:

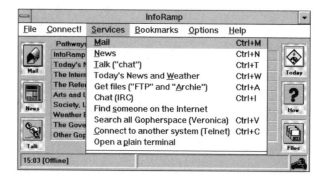

The center of the screen is an entry point to Gopher resources. Choosing any one of the menu items by double clicking on it presents a Gopher menu, albeit in a very straightforward graphical environment.

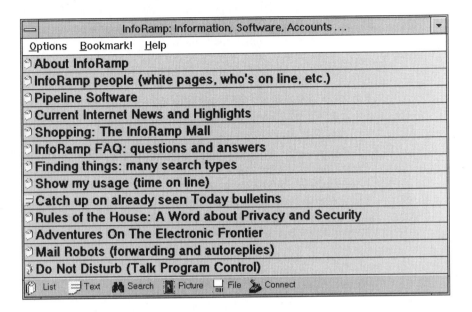

The Pipeline software is a highly effective tool for new users of the Internet, given that it wraps together many of the Internet applications discussed in this book (with the exception of Mosaic) into a simple package that can be used with any modem. Pipeline intends to provide a Mosaic equivalent by the end of 1994.

Given the sophistication now found with the arrival of the Pipeline software, we can only expect the Internet to become even easier to use in the years to come.

QUESTIONS TO ASK YOUR PROVIDER

You should shop around when looking for a dialup account. Be careful to ensure that you understand what you are buying, and spend a little time to determine what type of support, service and help you might get. Be sure you know what type of interface you're buying with a shell account or a SLIP account.

Keep in mind as well that the Internet is growing quickly, and sometimes service providers and telephone lines get very busy. There is nothing more frustrating than trying to dial into your Internet account and continually encountering busy signals, or trying to reach your service provider and being placed on hold.

If you are considering a certain Internet provider, don't hesitate to ask around for references — friends, counterparts or others might be willing to share their experiences with you. If you already have access to the Internet and are looking for another provider, consider posting your question to some of the USENET newsgroups that discuss Internet providers (in particular, **alt.internet.services**, or a regional group; i.e., **ont.general** or **bc.general**).

The questions you should be trying to answer include:

- Find out how many phone lines your provider provides. When choosing a provider, determine if they guarantee a maximum number of accounts per phone line. Determine what kind of guarantee it is — is it a service promise, or is it a contract item? Another way to check performance is to ask about "consecutive busy minutes," which provides a direct measure of what you might actually encounter.

- How do they link to the outside world of the Internet? What type of throughput do they support to the outside world — do the links get congested and slow? Do they have any acceptable use policies in place? Are there any restrictions on your use? Do they spell out your rights and responsibilities as a customer?

- Is the service busy? Ask around — does the Internet service provider have a reputation for a slow server, lousy support, system crashes, unreliability? How often are they down for maintenance?

- How much help will you get from them? Do they have a good support team? Are their staff knowledgeable? Do they have an on-line group that you can read to determine if people are complaining about their service? Do they have manuals or other documents to make your access easier?

- What is the cost of the connection? Are there any hidden extras?

Taking a little bit of time in understanding some of these issues will help you select the best possible vendor.[1]

CORPORATE OR ORGANIZATION ACCESS

Beyond simple dial-up access for an individual, there is a link to the Internet for an entire corporation or organization.

There are a number of business benefits that result from a direct Internet link which are discussed in greater depth in Chapter 10. In a nutshell, it has become clear to many people that a direct link to the Internet is quickly becoming as necessary for a company or organization as telephones and fax machines.

As the business and organizational benefits of a link to the Internet become clearer, many organizations will want to move beyond a few simple dialup accounts used by individuals and establish a more direct link to the network.

This section includes examination of the methods to provide access to the Internet for many people within a company or an organization, most often from a local area network. These include:

- linking the corporate e-mail network to the Internet, via a simple gateway. This might or might not include the ability to receive and read USENET news;

- a permanent TCP/IP network link to the Internet, either via a permanent dialup SLIP/PPP link to an Internet service provider, or via more direct network links involving leased lines or other methods. This provides the ability to use all Internet services, not just e-mail and USENET news.

E-MAIL ONLY

A direct e-mail or network link to the Internet will support communications and activities with trading partners, computer system vendors, suppliers and customers.

Many organizations would like to link their internal corporate e-mail system to the Internet without having to establish a full, dedicated Internet connection. In this case, there is no perceived need or benefit from the ability of using Gopher, Mosaic or other Internet tools.

There are several types of e-mail gateways which can be put in place from a corporate e-mail system so that the organization has the ability to send and receive Internet messages. These include:

- a gateway to a commercial e-mail service, or some other type of on-line service that has e-mail connectivity to the Internet;

- a UUCP gateway directly from the e-mail system in use within the company to an Internet service provider;

- an SMTP-based gateway, directly from the corporate e-mail system to an Internet service provider.

VIA A COMMERCIAL OR ON-LINE SERVICE

It's possible to link a local area network-based e-mail system or other e-mail system in your organization to a commercial e-mail system or on-line service, and from there communicate with people on the Internet.

This is usually done by implementing an e-mail "gateway," purchased or provided directly by the e-mail service or purchased from a third party. The method of establishing such a link range from the technically simple to the technically complex.

For example, it's possible to link a corporate local area network e-mail system, cc:Mail, to a commercial e-mail service, MCIMail, using a cc:Mail "gateway" provided by MCIMail. Since MCIMail has connectivity to and from Internet e-mail, individuals on the cc:Mail network are effectively linked to Internet e-mail.

Many organizations already linked to a major commercial e-mail service such as GEQuickcomm, MCIMail, ATTMail, The:Net Mail, Immedia or other systems might be pleased to discover that they already have access to and from Internet e-mail!

WHAT'S INVOLVED

There are several things you need to put in place. These include:

- Gateway software. Mpact Immedia will, for example, provide you with gateways at no charge for many popular LAN-based e-mail systems such as cc:Mail, MSMail and MHS to their service.

- An account or registration on the commercial e-mail provider into which the gateway links.

- A connection to the commercial e-mail provider, either via a dialup modem or via some type of leased line or other connection.

THINGS TO WATCH FOR

If you link your corporate e-mail system to the Internet, there are several important things to keep in mind. These include ensuring that you have a good understanding of what you will pay for such a link, and ensuring that you select a service which has straightforward, simple addressing.

- Several of the commercial e-mail vendors mentioned charge for e-mail sent and received based on the number of kilocharacters. With rates as high as 25¢ for every thousand characters, you could quickly find yourself spending a fortune for your e-mail link to the Internet.

  Be careful to ensure that you know the definition of what constitutes a kilocharacter – is it charged for just the message sent through the Internet, or for every person on the Internet that the message is sent to?

  For example, at the rate of 25¢ per thousand characters, what would happen if you sent a message via the Internet that was 30,000 bytes in size? If you sent the message to one person, the charge would be $7.50. If you sent it to 10 people on the Internet, the charge could be $7.50 or $75.00, depending on whether the service charges you for each Internet message recipient or not. The numbers add up quickly!

  Also determine if you will be responsible for paying a fee for each inbound Internet message, and if so, how the fee is calculated. If you plan to use the account to receive mailing lists, for example, you could find yourself spending a fortune as the volume of inbound e-mail increases.

  Some commercial e-mail services charge on the basis of time spent on-line as opposed to the number of characters sent. CompuServe is an excellent choice as a service to link your e-mail network to, as it charges on the basis of a flat hourly fee.

  Bottom line — carefully examine the cost of the alternatives.

- Clearly understand what you'll be faced with in terms of inbound and outbound Internet addressing.

For example, if you have Microsoft Mail on your local area network you'll find that it comes with a gateway to the commercial e-mail service AT&TMail, and that this is promoted as a method to reach the Internet.

Yet, people who receive messages from you will get a message from an ID that looks like:

org!org!name@attmail.com

On the other hand, if you link your internal local area network e-mail system to CompuServe, your Internet address might be in the form: `name@company.compuserve.com`, which is nice and straightforward, and is recognizable to the Internet community.

Bottom line — carefully understand how you will send messages to and receive messages from the Internet, to ensure that it's straightforward both ways.

- If the link from the commercial e-mail service to the Internet involves X.400, stay away! Your Internet address will likely consist of a combination of X.400 and Internet addressing. Since few people on the Internet accept X.400 style addressing, you will likely find that this is not a workable solution.

For example, if you have a gateway to the Sprintmail service, messages received from you by people on the Internet will appear as an ugly mixture of X.400 and Internet addressing.

Imagine receiving a message on the Internet from an organization which has linked its e-mail network to Sprint, which has a link to the Internet:

/G=Michael/S=Nettleton/O=EDS/ADMD=TELEMAIL/PRMD=DIAM ONDNET/C=US/DD.ID=osipc1d.mnettl01/@SPRINT.COM

This ID is rather incomprehensible to mere mortals!

With this type of alphabet soup address, you can see why it is important to carefully consider your options!

THROUGH AN INTERNET SERVICE PROVIDER

The second method of establishing a link to Internet e-mail from a corporate e-mail system is to establish an e-mail link directly to an Internet service provider. There are several methods to do this, including gateways based on the UUCP protocol or SMTP. If neither of these alternatives work for your current internal e-mail system, you might consider adopting one that does work with the Internet.

UUCP METHOD

As outlined earlier in this chapter, UUCP is a protocol which permits the batching of e-mail to and from an Internet service provider. Some LAN-based e-mail systems provide a UUCP gateway that allows a quick, effective link to Internet e-mail. Such gateways are available from the LAN e-mail vendor or third parties, and include:

- UUCPLINK, a product sold by Lotus for use with the popular Lotus cc:Mail e-mail system. Information concerning this product can be obtained through Lotus Canada, or through many software resellers for as low as $500.

- TFS Gateways, a product written by TenFour Sweden AB. The product provides simple UUCP-based gateways to Lotus cc:Mail, Lotus Notes, Microsoft Mail and Word Perfect Office 4.0a. TenFour Sweden AB can be reached by sending a message to **info@tenfour.se**.

When examining a UUCP solution like this, keep in mind that the product might provide you with e-mail only; i.e., UUCPLINK does not provide for your organization to receive USENET news.

SMTP METHOD

You can put in place a gateway from your e-mail system to an Internet service provider by using an SMTP gateway.

SMTP stands for Simple Mail Transport Protocol, and is the e-mail system that is at the heart of many UNIX operating systems. It is also the e-mail system that is at the heart of the transfer of e-mail throughout the Internet.

There are a variety of gateways to SMTP-based e-mail from many other e-mail systems. For example, you can purchase a cc:Mail to SMTP gateway, or an MSMail to SMTP gateway, either directly from Lotus and Microsoft or from various third parties. There are ways to link minicomputer and mainframe-based e-mail systems to Internet e-mail through SMTP gateways as well.

Although these gateways are readily available, you should be aware of a number of complexities in implementing them:

- To implement such a gateway, you must have a working SMTP-based e-mail system. Unless you already have a direct network connection to the Internet, and a fully functioning UNIX server running SMTP, you will be out of luck.

  An alternative, if you have neither, is to convince an Internet service provider to act as your SMTP server, and to accept a modem-based **SLIP/PPP** call.

- It seems that few technical people on the Internet have anything pleasant to say about some of the available SMTP gateways. For example, although Microsoft has an SMTP gateway for MSMail, people in the USENET newsgroup **comp.misc.mail** can rarely say anything nice about it. It would seem that some of these gateways are not yet reliable, stable systems, and you could expect some frustration in implementation and ongoing maintenance.

Organizations which desire to link systems such as MSMail or cc:Mail to SMTP must appreciate the complexity of the undertaking. SMTP is recognized throughout the Internet world as one of the most demanding software programs ever developed.

Accordingly, should you wish to establish this type of e-mail connectivity, be sure that you obtain adequate technical advice or resources, either internally or from external organizations.

IMPLEMENTING OTHER E-MAIL SOFTWARE

The final option is to implement some other type of LAN e-mail software which has a direct or indirect link to Internet e-mail. If you don't have a LAN-based e-mail system, but would like to put one in place that has a link to the Internet, you could consider Pegasus Mail or other alternatives.

Pegasus, which works primary on Novell networks, has a number of available UUCP gateways and an SMTP gateway called Mercury that runs directly on a Novell File Server. It enjoys substantial use throughout the global college and university community.

You can find out more about Pegasus by locating it in the FTP archive detailed below, or you can retrieve a FAQ (Frequently Asked Question summary) which details other locations where you can find it.

Using Anonymous FTP	
FTP site:	risc.ua.edu
Directory:	/pub/network/pegasus/
Files:	pmail*.zip and winpm*.zip (where * is current version number)
Special Instructions:	Check the file name; new versions are regularly released. Pegasus Mail can also be found on other file servers around the world.

Using E-mail	
Send message to:	maiser@pmail.gen.nz
In text of message, type:	send version.faq

A FULL NETWORK CONNECTION

The final or ultimate state of Internet connectivity is a direct link from the network in use at your organization to an Internet service provider.

In this case, your network is linked directly to the Internet via some type of low- or high-speed part-time or dedicated link using either Ethernet or the PPP protocol, and you are running the TCP/IP protocol directly on your network workstations.

Your computers are considered to be "hardwired" to the Internet. You should also note that you could put in place a direct link from your network to the Internet via SLIP/PPP using a modem, which would be considered a casual Internet network connection.[2]

HARDWIRED CONNECTION

A hardwired connection to the Internet is usually through a dedicated communications line of speeds from 19,200bps, 56kbps, up to T1 and T3 speeds, using Ethernet or PPP.

Consider a portion of ONet, the research and academic Internet network in Ontario.

Figure 9.4, which presents but a small part of ONet, indicates that networks at the University of Western Ontario, Sheridan College, the National Research Council and the University of Waterloo are directly connected to the University of Toronto using a variety of permanent communication lines (which are known as 56 or 128 kilobits per second lines, and T1 lines which handle 1.544 megabits per second, or about twelve times more capacity than a 128 kbps line. These measurements are expressed in terms of "bits per second." In relative terms, a 14400 modem is 14,400 bps, a 56 kbps line is 56,000 bps, and a T1 line is 1,544,000 bps.). In addition, a dedicated link to NSFNet via CA*net exists. Together, these links make up a portion of the Canadian Internet.

FIGURE 9.4: PART OF ONET [3]

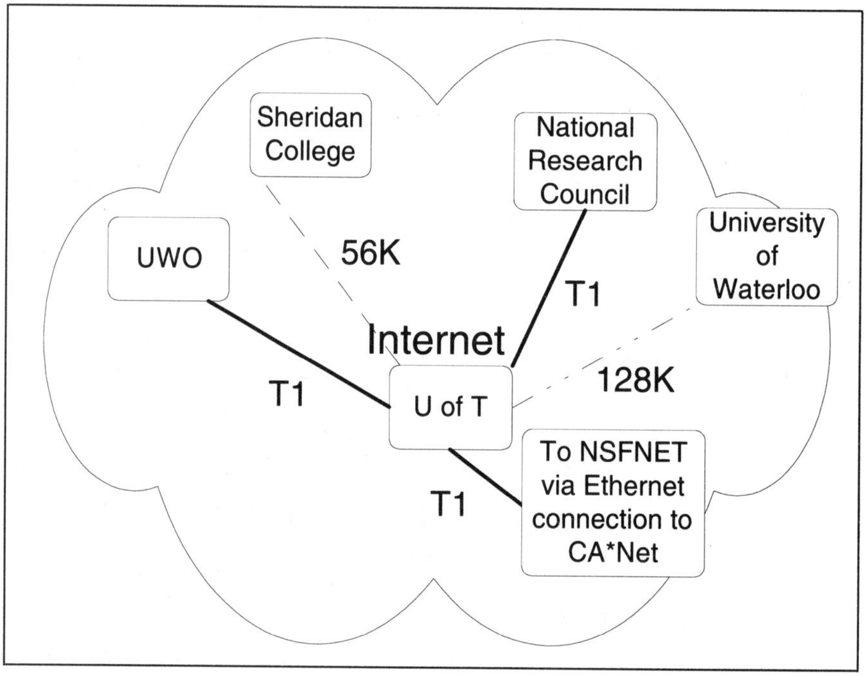

Computers at these locations are considered to be permanently attached to the Internet, since their networks are open to the Internet at all times. Individuals on networks at these locations are considered to be directly connected to the Internet.

WHAT'S INVOLVED?

Establishing a hardwired connection to the Internet is not necessarily a trivial undertaking.

At the risk of *greatly simplifying* a complex matter, connectivity in the DOS environment would involve several components:

- Each PC on the network must load software which provides the PC with the ability to "talk TCP/IP" (referred to as the TCP/IP protocol stack), the main protocol of the Internet.

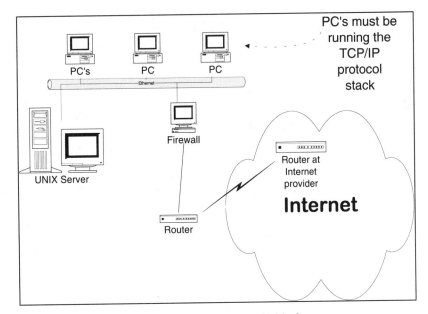

There are many TCP/IP software packages available for most computer platforms. For DOS/Windows, for example, you can purchase packages from Beame & Whiteside BW-NFS, Frontier Technologies Super TCP/NFS for Windows, FTP Software PC/TCP, IBM TCP/IP for DOS/Windows, NetManage Chameleon NFS for Windows, and Walker, Richer & Quinn Reflection/TCP Connection. These are only a few of the TCP/IP software packages available for the DOS/Windows environment. In addition to these, there are public domain versions available as well.

There are a number of alternatives for Macintosh systems, including MacTCP from Apple, and TCP/Connect II, as well as some public domain and shareware programs.

- Your network must be linked into the Internet service provider, usually via a device known as a router or network bridge.

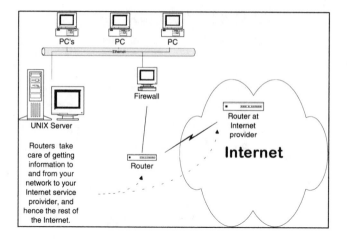

The router at your location links to the router at your Internet service provider, and does what it suggests — it routes traffic from your network to your Internet provider and hence to the global Internet, and vice versa. It routes this traffic according to the TCP/IP protocol, using your IP address as your fundamental link to the outside world.

• Dedicated lines must be brought into the organization to support the network connection to your Internet service provider.

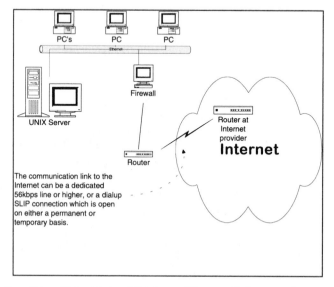

Most often, this will involve a 56kb leased line, or higher speed connections up to T1 (1.544mbps, or megabits per second). As an alternative to connectivity via a permanent line, you can also put in place a dedicated link via a dialup SLIP or PPP connection and permit people on your network to access the Internet, but you must recognize that this slow speed will certainly impact how they can use the Internet.

- A server or servers at your location to support the Internet applications you plan to implement within your organization. Most often, this server will be UNIX-based. [4]

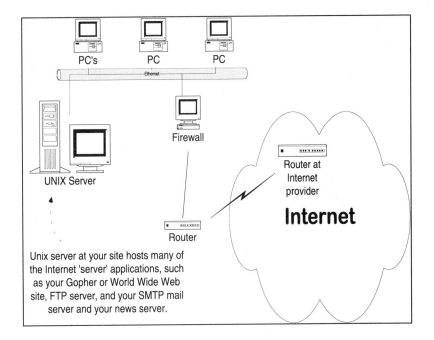

This might include an SMTP server to support e-mail to the Internet (as discussed earlier), an NNTP server to support the receipt and posting of USENET news directly through your Internet link, a Gopher, Archie, FTP or a World Wide Web server to support Internet applications.

- If you link your network directly to the Internet, you must consider security. To properly understand the risk that you might face, you should engage the services of someone who is thoroughly familiar with Internet security issues.

Once you connect your network to the Internet, anything on your network is accessible to anyone on the Internet, if you do not properly prevent access to it.

If you put in place a direct connection to the Internet and ignore security, you deserve everything that hackers on the network might throw at you.

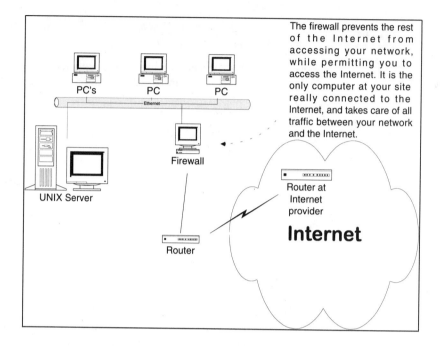

The firewall prevents the rest of the Internet from accessing your network, while permitting you to access the Internet. It is the only computer at your site really connected to the Internet, and takes care of all traffic between your network and the Internet.

To handle security, you should consider implementing a "firewall," a system which protects your network from access by people on the Internet. A firewall is either hardware, software or both.

You should also keep in mind that while firewalls are certainly valuable, they are still quite expensive, require very specialized knowledge to implement and often end up inhibiting your use of the Internet.

Alternatives to firewalls are available.

Internet security is just like office security, in that you need to properly assess the risk and the cost to protect against the risk.

• Client software to access the applications above, and to access other Internet services.

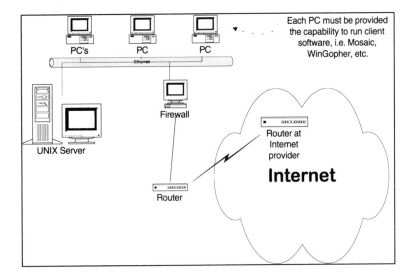

This includes client software to access Gopher and World Wide Web servers on the Internet (such as WinGopher and Mosaic), the client software for your e-mail system (i.e., MSMail if you are linked through an SMTP gateway, or Eudora if you are using SMTP directly.)

Bundle it all together, and you can see that you have a project on your hands. The scope of establishing TCP/IP connectivity directly to the Internet is far beyond the capabilities of this book. Many excellent sources and reference guides exist.

A number of Internet service providers take on an active role in assisting an organization to establish a direct, hardwired or permanent connection to the Internet. In addition, across Canada there are a number of excellent consultants who have implemented dedicated connectivity for many organizations.

Ask around, and you can probably quickly discover who they are.

INFORMATION TIPS!

Where else can you find information if you want to pursue direct connectivity to the Internet? If you're in the DOS environment, a good source for information is the PC TCP/IP "Frequently Asked Question" summary, or FAQ.

OBTAINING THE PC TCP/IP FAQ

Using Anonymous FTP	
FTP site:	rtfm.mit.edu
Directory:	Select: pub/usenet/news.answers/ibmpc-tcp-ip-faq
File:	part1
	part2
	part3

Using E-mail	
Send message to:	mail-server@rtfm.mit.edu
In text of message, type:	send /pub/usenet/news.answers/ibmpc-tcp-ip-faq/part1
	send /pub/usenet/news.answers/ibmpc-tcp-ip-faq/part2
	send /pub/usenet/news.answers/ibmpc-tcp-ip-faq/part3

Although no comparable document exists for Macintosh networks, a document about communications in the Mac environment does address TCP/IP connectivity issues.

OBTAINING THE MAC COMMUNICATIONS DOCUMENT

Using Anonymous FTP	
FTP site:	rtfm.mit.edu
Directory:	Select: pub/usenet/comp.sys.mac.comm
	comp.sys.mac.comm_Frequently_Asked_Questions_(1_4)
	comp.sys.mac.comm_Frequently_Asked_Questions_(2_4)
	comp.sys.mac.comm_Frequently_Asked_Questions_(3_4)
	comp.sys.mac.comm_Frequently_Asked_Questions_(4_4)

Using E-mail	
Send message to:	mail-server@rtfm.mit.edu
In text of message, type:	send /pub/usenet/news.answers/macintosh/comm-faq/part1
	send /pub/usenet/news.answers/macintosh/comm-faq/part2
	send /pub/usenet/news.answers/macintosh/comm-faq/part3
	send /pub/usenet/news.answers/macintosh/comm-faq/part4

QUESTIONS TO ASK YOUR INTERNET SERVICE PROVIDER

Finally, when looking at a dedicated link into the Internet for your organization, there are some things you should keep in mind when talking to various service providers:

- What is the true through-put, and will you encounter congestion as you try to link to various sites on the Internet through your service provider because of limitations at your service provider?[5] If you put a dedicated 56kb line in place to your network, are you getting 56kb throughput, or 56kb access? There can be a difference — make sure you know what you are buying.

- How much support do they provide you with? How is troubleshooting handled, should there be a problem with your network link to the Internet? Do they provider 24-hour-a-day, 7-day-a-week support?

- What's involved in upgrading your network link to faster speeds in the future, and how much will it cost? Are there cheaper upgrade paths available?

- Do they help with security issues, implementation, and other matters?

Keep in mind that establishing a direct link to the Internet is a project, not a purchase, and hence involves more time, more effort, and definitely more research in advance. Take time to understand your options, particularly when it comes to selecting an Internet service provider.

THE FUTURE OF INTERNET ACCESS

There are a lot of alternatives in Canada by which you can access the Internet. If you put in place a dedicated link to the network, you can enjoy most Internet services, including access to voice, sound, image and even film databases using Mosaic.

Yet, for many individuals accessing the Internet from the home or office with a modem, the Internet is simply too slow for use of Mosaic.

We will see this change in the years to come, with fiber optic cables being brought to the home, the use of a high-speed technology known as ISDN which uses standard telephone wires, and methods to access the Internet through your home cable TV link.

SUMMARY

Each method discussed in this chapter differs in complexity, cost, functionality and ease of use. What is appropriate for you depends on your own circumstances.

If you merely want the ability to send and receive Internet e-mail messages, examine the alternatives to establish e-mail-only access, either as an individual or by linking the e-mail system of your organization to the network.

If you're interested in exploring the Internet, a dialup shell account is one method of establishing access quickly and easily. Yet, recognize that there will be limitations on how you can navigate the Internet as a result of your use of terminal emulation through a shell account.

Using SLIP/PPP via a dialup connection is increasingly attractive, particularly as organizations begin to bundle such software into nice, simple solutions. Check with the providers in your area to see if they offer SLIP or PPP, and if you have a Macintosh or run Microsoft Windows, go for this option.

Finally, if you discover that the Internet is right for you, establishing a permanent or hardwired connection for your organization could be the next step. Related to this will be the need to convince management of your organization of the need for a dedicated Internet connection. In the next chapter we put into perspective some of the strategic applications of the Internet.

Keep in mind as you explore your options, that Canada continues to see substantial growth in the number of Internet service providers, as detailed in Appendix C in the *Directory of Canadian Internet Service Providers.*

---

1. Of course, this section is written with a typical central-Canada perspective, in which, in the Metro Toronto area, there are all kinds of choices when it comes to Internet providers. Elsewhere, you might have only one or two choices available. It doesn't hurt for you to get an understanding of these issues in any case, since it might help your use of the service down the road or ease frustration.

2. A SLIP/PPP connection might be temporary, used only during a particular dialup session, or it might be in place on a permanent basis, giving the appearance of direct, permanent connectivity to the Internet. However, for purposes of this discussion, we are trying to differentiate between those who have a full-time connection to the Internet from their local area network, and those who casually-access a direct connection to the Internet as a dialup user.

3. This is a greatly simplified diagram. Apologies are made to technical staff at ONet for stripping it down to such a degree.

4. The days of needing a UNIX server are slowly coming to a end. There are an increasing number of servers (Gopher, WWW, FTP, etc.) that run under Windows, OS/2 and Windows NT, as well as modules that load onto Novell file servers. As the Internet gains prominence as a serious wide area network alternative, major software companies such as Novell and Microsoft are including Internet support in their software.

5. Keep in mind that certain locations on the Internet will always experience some congestion, regardless of what type of through-put you have.

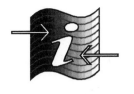

C H A P T E R   1 0

· ·

WHY THE INTERNET?

Create your own show, series or electronic art. Eventually a billion people will be on the "net" as potential customers or suppliers! No matter how weird your product, among the millions there have to be 50,000 that like your style. That's enough for a good business.

The Network: Say good night to television, by Frank
Ogden, from The Daily News (Halifax), Sun 12 Jun 94

. . . the most compelling argument for connecting is that the Internet is the biggest and earliest manifestation of the way business is going to be conducted from now on. Networked information and communication are the standard for the future.

The Internet and your business
Fortune Magazine, Mon 07 Mar 94

Quite clearly, we are witnessing the birth of the truly connected organization — one that can not only harness, access and archive organizational knowledge, but one that can also harness, access and archive global knowledge through the Internet.

If we're becoming networked, we must understand how we can operate through this new technology. In this chapter, we take a look at issues of doing business on the Internet, the impact of the Internet on education, and the role that the Internet can play in reshaping government.

It's easy to get carried away with the Internet, and to become excited with its possibilities. Yet, if you examine it with a critical eye, it's clear that the Internet will have a profound impact on the way that all organizations work in the future.

It will reshape the way that companies do business with each other. Through it, students will learn new methods of obtaining knowledge. It will help reshape government.

It will change everything that it touches.

COMPUTER TRENDS AND THE INTERNET

In one way, the organizations in which we work, whether business, education or government, have spent many years in order to learn how to take advantage of information technology effectively.

Our investment in personal computers, local area networks and software such as electronic mail, groupware and other systems, have taught us to make internal knowledge available throughout our organizations, and have provided a high degree of efficiency in our internal communications.

Information, knowledge and ideas traverse from one end of the organization to the other through sophisticated networking technologies. Organizations, whether schools, business or government, have become truly "networked" and are able to support themselves through the intelligent use of computer technology.

Yet, an organization doesn't just communicate internally. On any given day, an organization receives any number of telephone calls, faxes, letters, parcels, cellular phone calls and other types of communications. Day-to-day activity involves communications with trading partners, customers, business associates, students, teachers, regulatory and government authorities, consumer watchdog agencies, business advisors and any number of other people.

What is happening all around us today is that many of these day-to-day communications are now being supported through the Internet.

THE NEXT STEP IN THE EVOLUTION OF COMPUTER SYSTEMS

The Internet is the next logical step in the evolution of computer systems.

Through the last ten years, particularly with the arrival of personal computers, we have networked our offices, our factories, our warehouses, our schools and our government departments. We have built local area networks, metropolitan area networks, and wide area networks. Yet, all we have learned is how to use computers to support our own particular need for internal communications within our organizations.

It's as if we had invested in a telephone system that only lets us call someone else in our organization, and doesn't let us call anyone outside. What a waste!

The Internet is the next logical step in the evolution of organizational computer systems, for it is the first step in linking our internal networks to networks of other organizations.

The Internet permits our internal computer systems to participate in global computer communications, much as our phone systems can participate in global voice communications.

Simply put, we're entering an era of inter-organizational networking – that is, networking from one organization to another.

The Internet is leading the way to a world of interlinked computer networks.

THE "INFORMATION AGE"

It's an overused phrase, and has been around longer than that "other" overused phrase, the "information highway." For many years, the popular press has told us that we are entering an era in which we will be "knowledge workers." With the Internet, this is finally true.

An organization can finally participate in the "information age" by extending global communication and research capabilities directly to the desk of every employee or student. The Internet is the gateway into the "information age" for your organization — whether for employees, management staff or students.

The Internet opens up a grab bag of information capabilities, from knowledge networking, to global research, to global communications.

Use of the Internet greatly expands the knowledge capabilities of its members, and hence of the organizations that they work for.

The Internet is a fundamental first step for an organization seeking to entering the "information age."

THE "GLOBAL LIBRARY"

The Internet is quickly emerging as the largest single repository of human knowledge that has ever existed.

Corporate, government and educational information and knowledge is being archived throughout the Internet in Gopher and World Wide servers, as well as traditional FTP document servers.

Quite simply, the Internet is a massive library of information – all of which is available to an organization that chooses to participate in the "information age."

DOING BUSINESS ON THE INTERNET

Growth of the Internet is exploding because it is directly linked to many of the trends that are shaping our economy today.

Many of these trends have a direct impact on the usefulness of the Internet to a business.

- Canadian companies must learn to compete globally.

  Read any number of articles, and you're told that the forces of globalization are causing Canadian organizations to rethink their traditional place in the world.

  Not only do we have to compete with our mighty neighbors to the south, but we must be able to compete with the economic powerhouses emerging in Asia.

Canadian companies are trying to seek out new markets and new opportunities in a world that's increasingly competitive.

The Internet directly helps a company faced with the trend to globalization because it helps to make the world a smaller place. A presence on the Internet is global in scope, and extends the reach of any organization well beyond Canada for an extremely low cost. The Internet eliminates global time barriers to doing business abroad, and makes people and organizations on five continents as accessible as someone down the hall.

The simple fact is that Canadian companies participating in the Internet are selling products and services worldwide as a result of their presence on the Internet, and are learning to collaborate globally.

The Internet is quickly becoming a fundamental requirement for an organization seeking to do business around the world.

• The nineties have become the "decade of the customer."

Terms like "total quality," the "customer is king," and "customer responsiveness" have become paramount to the mission of an organization. Clearly, organizations are scrambling to ensure that the highest possible degree of customer support is available.

Leading-edge organizations are discovering that the Internet is an extremely powerful tool.

A link to the Internet is an invaluable customer service tool. A company can encourage direct customer feed-back through Internet e-mail, and thus ensure that it will hear directly from customers about quality or other concerns. Organizations can monitor particular USENET newsgroups that might relate to the products and services they sell, in order to gauge customer reaction and attitudes. Organizations can establish Gopher and World Wide Web resources that encourage customer feedback.

Organizations which have learned to make effective use of Internet e-mail realize that this is a tool that permits direct communications to and from their customer base. A direct e-mail link is a vehicle for establishing a continuing relationship with a customer, and over the long term can be used to enhance and develop that customer relationship, with a direct impact on future sales opportunities.

By establishing on-line information resources using such tools as Gopher or World Wide Web, an organization can make available help manuals, support information and any number of documents helpful to the customer. Making this information readily available makes it easier for the customer to get answers to questions — resulting directly in a much more satisfied customer.

Simply put, by linking itself to the Internet, an organization can make a statement to customers in the Internet community. Companies should also realize that the lack of Internet accessibility will increasingly become a hindrance in today's high-tech, networked world, in which an ever greater number of current and potential customers are "Internet citizens."

The Internet is a fundamental tool for a company seeking to provide the highest possible degree of customer service.

- Organizations are finding it necessary to establish joint ventures, partnerships and new methods of working with other organizations.

The Internet directly supports these inter-organizational partnerships. Whether a company is involved in a joint product development project, or is working with another company in order to have access to skills it doesn't currently have available in-house, the sheer efficiency of Internet communications makes sense.

The Internet has become one of the key tools to support such inter-company and inter-organization networking.

- The demand for intercompany networked communications will increase.

It's not only joint ventures and projects that are supported by Internet communications — many believe we are entering an era in which "doing business" via computer networks will become a necessity as opposed to an opportunity.

Over time, companies will discover that all kinds of intercompany communications can be supported through the Internet — whether it's access to price lists, general day-to-day correspondence, project reports, knowledge exchange or the exchange of transactional information.

The Internet offers a common electronic mail link between companies, and provides standard methods to access corporate information via Gopher, World Wide Web and other information services.

- Canadian companies are finding it necessary to establish new methods of marketing product and services in an increasingly competitive environment.

The Internet has become a new marketing resource, permitting not only local but global marketing efforts.

There is a lot of misconception when it comes to the Internet and marketing. While it's not acceptable to send unsolicited information to people on the Internet who have not asked for that information, it has become perfectly acceptable to put up information resources that are available to anyone. By establishing an Internet resource, you can make it easier for an existing or potential customer to obtain information about the products and services offered by your organization.

Establishing an on-line information resource on the Internet with such technologies as Gopher or World Wide Web/Mosaic allows an organization to establish an on-line "store front" which current and potential customers can access through the Internet at their leisure. We will see an explosion of new, marketing-oriented Internet resources based on World Wide Web/Mosaic and Gopher in the years to come.

The Internet has become an invaluable global marketing resource.

- Companies are increasingly sensitive to telecommunications costs, and are looking for cost savings.

As Canada enters a deregulated telecommunications environment, there are any number of opportunities for cost savings. One of the most significant is a simple Internet link, as it offers substantial reductions in communication costs.

The Internet is having a profound impact on the pricing of information services around the world, for the reason that organizations or individuals can often buy access to the Internet for a "flat fee." Once you have paid for your basic link to the Internet, you can use it for whatever you want — electronic mail, access to Internet databases, information servers or other services.

With high-speed dedicated Internet access costing as little as $600 a month in major metropolitan areas, you could, if you wanted, send e-mail all day long, with no additional charge for any particular message.

People are becoming used to a communications environment in which there are no incremental charges for each additional minute spent doing something on the Internet. Purchasing access to the Internet for a flat fee is resulting in a communications market in which the cost for national and global communications are being completely rewritten.

Clearly, the Internet is becoming as fundamental to a business as a telephone and fax machine.

Indeed, given the fact that the Internet links you to the world, many organizations are discovering that the Internet has quickly become an integral part of their day-to-day operations.

CAN I DO BUSINESS ON THE INTERNET?

One of the questions most often asked by organizations has to do with whether you can use the Internet to sell product, services and information.

If you're wondering if you can do business on the Internet, the answer is yes, as long as you understand and respect the unique culture of the Internet.

THE CULTURE OF THE INTERNET

There is a clear and simple rule when it comes to doing business on the Internet — advertising doesn't work, but marketing does. This is perhaps the most fundamental aspect of the unique Internet culture. The important thing is to recognize that there are distinct differences between advertising and marketing.

The best thing that you can do if you decide you want to do business through the Internet is to work with the Internet for at least six months in order to learn about, and respect, its unique on-line culture.

Once you understand the unique culture, you can then learn how to work within the culture in a subtle way to successfully market your product or service.

ACCEPTABLE USE POLICIES

You might have heard that in some areas of the Internet, acceptable use policies do not permit you to do business.

In Chapter 3, we reviewed the status of Acceptable Use Policies (AUPs) in Canada and put into perspective that even where they exist, they have quickly become irrelevant.

However, the Internet in Canada continues to evolve, and some providers are still evolving with it. The least you can do is understand that if you plan on doing business on the Internet, ensure that your Internet service provider does not have a restrictive AUP in place.

ADVERTISING DOESN'T WORK ON THE INTERNET

Many organizations, when they think about the potential of business on the Internet, wonder why they can't just send out an advertising flyer. If it works in the real world, why can't it work on the Internet they ask?

There's one key cultural rule related to marketing on the Internet that you must respect — *no one wants information they have not asked for*. Unsolicited information does not work.

The Internet considers this to be "advertising." Companies that try to advertise on the Internet are spectacularly unsuccessful.

There are several reasons why you won't be successful if you abuse the culture of the Internet, and send "junk mail" out on the system. The Internet culture is a strong, global force, and really can't be fooled with. You abuse it at your own risk.

- The Internet can shut you down if you play with it, and the Internet will fight back.

  If you send out an advertisement on the Internet, either via e-mail or through USENET, you'll guarantee yourself an *extremely* negative reaction from your potential customers. So negative, in fact, that you might discover that the Internet has reacted by effectively shutting down access to your account — by sending you several million e-mail messages of protest. Such is the penalty for real abuse of the Internet.

Even if you post a single message to a USENET newsgroup or mailing list that is considered to be "advertising" in nature, you might find that you have unleashed a storm of protest.

You have to keep in mind that people on the Internet refuse to gracefully accept information that they have not asked for.

- Unlike the fact that we receive e-mail for free in the "real world," you have to recognize that many people receiving e-mail and USENET news are paying to do so.

People get particularly upset when they have to pay to get junk mail. They react differently, often with anger.

- By abusing the culture of the Internet, you upset your potential customer, rather than getting their attention.

This is a fundamental breach of the first rule of Marketing 101 — never, never upset your customer. Why expend the energy, if you are doomed to fail in your approach in the first place?

Simple fact – if you plan to use the Internet to send junk mail, the authors of this book and the balance of the Internet community will have no respect or sympathy for your actions. You deserve whatever the Internet community might throw at you.

A strong statement, but such is the reality of the Internet.

HOW TO MARKET ON THE INTERNET

Marketing is different from advertising.

Marketing implies a subtle campaign to make information available to the potential customer in an unobtrusive fashion. It implies a carefully thought out strategy on how to get the attention of the customer while respecting the feelings of the customer on certain issues. It's quite different than merely sending out junk mail haphazardly.

Marketing on the Internet involves choice — and respects the fact that people on the Internet should have a choice as to whether they want to receive your information or not.

As the Internet has continued to evolve in the last two years from an academic network to a commercial network, it has become completely acceptable to put up information resources that people can choose to access. In particular, there has been an explosion of interest in the commercial potential use of Gopher and World Wide Web/Mosaic information services in order to market products and services.

When it comes to marketing on the Internet, it really is quite simple: unsolicited information won't work. Establishing information resources will. We'll see what this means when we look at marketing tools later in this chapter.

WHAT TO CONSIDER IN YOUR MARKETING PLAN

The Internet is at a very early stage when it comes to marketing opportunities, yet it promises a full-fledged revolution in access to the provision of information to the potential customer and consumer.

There are several things to keep in mind if you consider using the Internet as part of the marketing strategy for your organization:

- It has established standards for information access that are global in nature.

  The Internet has quickly become a common means for individuals at one company to access information from another company. This means that if an organization establishes a new Internet resource which includes product information, price lists and other marketing information, it can be quickly and inexpensively accessed by individuals and companies from around the world. This opens new opportunities for product sales, and avoids the development of specialized, customized computer programs to support inter-company networking.

  Simply put, Mosaic, which some people are calling the "killer application for the Internet," has emerged overnight to become the standard *global* method to make available full product catalogues, including voice, graphics, images and sound. It is a standard that cannot be ignored.

- The Internet is rapidly attaining critical mass from around the world.

  A survey by the Network Information Centre at InterNIC found that over 40% of Fortune 500 companies had registered on the network by the summer of 1994.

  In Canada, a review of the Canadian domain registry, and a review of organizations registering directly with the InterNIC, indicates that a large number of corporations, including many Fortune 500's, are joining the Internet.

  With such rapid growth and massive global interest, the Internet has already reached a point where it *is* the backbone to global commerce.

- The Internet is seeing the emergence of a new marketing target — the "cyberyuppie."

  This individual, rather than watching television, watches the Internet. There are millions of people around the globe who love nothing better than to "surf" the Internet, looking for information, accessing new information sources and exchanging information about what they've found. Given their attention to the Internet, they're a prime target for a marketing message — but to be successful, you have to respect that they do not, and will not tolerate, receiving information that they haven't asked for.

  This calls for innovative marketing methods, the best of which is the establishment of on-line information resources which will appeal to the "cyberyuppie." Nifty, innovative, high-tech on-line Internet locations are what will get their attention.

- People are already looking for your company on the Internet.

Not a day goes by that someone doesn't ask, somewhere on the Internet, for information on how to reach a particular company. If you are an organization, you should know that your customers are looking for you. Consider this posting:

```
Newsgroups: can.general
Subject: Help:  EDDIE BAUER catalogue?
Message-ID: <1994Aug8.152634.1@admin.cabot.nf.ca
From: jnoel@admin.cabot.nf.ca
Date: 8 Aug 94 15:26:34 +1000
Nntp-Posting-Host: admin.cabot.nf.ca
Lines: 13

I couldn't see a better group for this, so here goes....

I need an Eddie Bauer catalogue ("need", of course, being
a relative term).

They do mail-order, don't they?  Does anyone have an ad-
dress, 1-800 #, etcetera?  Please don't tell me to check
my local store - there isn't one in this province, hence
the need for the catalogue to begin with!  (I think I've
seen them advertise in _the Globe_, but this seems a
less hit-and-miss way to get the info.)

Thanks for the help.

JoAnne
jnoel@admin.cabot.nf.ca
```

Having a presence on the Internet will become fundamental as more and more people migrate to it, and use it in this way to try to find you.

It's quite common for people to use the Internet to try to find product information for a particular company. If you haven't made it available, you might have lost the sales opportunity!

If you aren't there, think of the opportunities that you might be missing!

- The Internet is resulting in a technologically savvy audience. If you aren't using the Internet, you run the risk of looking unsophisticated.

Simply put, if you try to market a product or service to a high-tech audience and don't make use of the Internet, you lose out on a real opportunity to build a rapport with your target customer. In particular, given that most of the high-tech sector in Canada is on the Internet, you need to pay particular attention to the Internet in your approach to this sector of the economy.

A perfect example of an organization that has failed to understand the opportunity in marketing through the Internet can be found with one of our major Canadian banks. Early in 1994, the Royal Bank announced through full-page ads in the *Globe and Mail Report on Business* and other publications that they were ready to provide focused banking services to the high-tech industry across Canada. In their advertisements, they provided pictures, names and phone numbers of the various account managers assigned responsibility for the task.

Nowhere did the Royal Bank mention how these individuals could be reached via the Internet (and in fact, they couldn't be), nor did it establish an on-line resource summarizing the new banking services. This was a mistake, because many of the people the Royal Bank were trying to reach through the advertising campaign have made the Internet a regular part of their daily working life. *An approach which used the Internet in the marketing strategy could have paid off nicely.*

The key goal of the Royal Bank advertisement was to encourage high-tech industries in Canada to contact one of their identified individuals to discuss how the Royal Bank could meet their banking needs.

Think of how it could have been more powerful in reaching this goal if it had an effective link to the Internet!

If the Royal Bank had indicated how the various account managers could be contacted by Internet e-mail, had identified a World Wide Web home page providing more information on its new high-tech industry banking services, and had established a "mail robot" through which people could obtain more information, it would have established a more effective rapport with the potential customer.

As it was, it appeared as just another tired public relations advertisement, and it missed a golden opportunity to market itself electronically.

BUSINESS ON-LINE

Today, you can find a number of companies which have discovered or are exploring how to do business on the Internet. Many of them are doing this by establishing Internet-based information servers.

Canadian Airlines, for example, has established a World Wide Web server at **http://www.cdnair.ca** which contains information about the company and its services. Although the server is preliminary at this stage, the organization has high hopes for it.

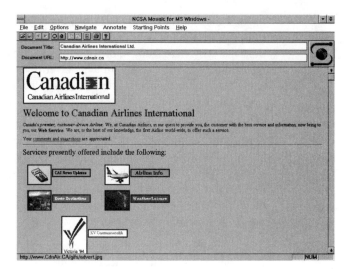

The system includes a method to access information on destinations and flight schedules through a graphical interface.

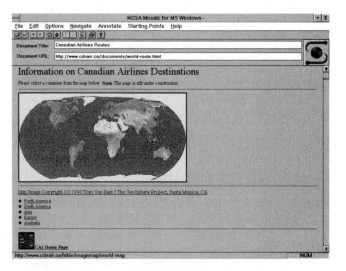

TOOLS FOR MARKETING ON THE INTERNET

There are a number of Internet tools which can be used to effectively market products or services. These tools include Gopher, World Wide Web/Mosaic, mailing lists and "mail robots" (also known as listservs.)

Each can be used in a different way. For example, through the use of simple "mail robots," individuals from around the world can contact your company for information. Through Internet mailing lists, you can establish an area where customers can choose to receive regular product and service information from you.

Through a Gopher server, you can establish an Internet site containing price lists, product information, press releases, and other background information. Individuals "surfing Gopherspace" can access this site from anywhere in the world.

A World Wide Web server can be accessed with sophisticated software such as Mosaic, and permits the ultimate level in Internet information retrieval. You can make available detailed information about your company, your products and your mission. Order forms can be placed on-line. Sounds, graphics, images can be used to add pizzazz to your on-line presentation.

Clearly, these Internet tools can be used to great advantage in a new type of marketing campaign – the "cybermarket."

USING INTERNET TOOLS FOR MARKETING PURPOSES

Let's consider how you can use these tools to implicitly market through the Internet.

- You can permit individuals to automatically retrieve an order form via an Internet e-mail message, with a "mail robot."

  For example, it's quite straightforward to create a "mail robot" using your existing e-mail software so that a message sent to *order@yourdomain.com* returns a simple text-based order form that can be returned by fax or e-mail. Voila: anyone from around the world can easily obtain an order form from you.

- You can permit individuals to request more information about your product, service or company via a "mail robot."

  For example, using a mail robot, you can set up your system such that a message sent to the ID *info@yourdomain.com* returns a message that contains an index of information that you make available via the Internet — including price lists, product information and ordering information.

  The potential customer can then retrieve any of these documents by sending a message to your mail-robot, and by including the name of the document from the index in their message.

  You can easily add additional information postings to the mail robot at any time, making this a very flexible and attractive option for marketing through the Internet.

- You can establish a mailing list that anyone can join so that customers and others can receive product, support and other updates directly from you, as well as other information postings.

  In doing so, you can effectively build a captive audience that is receptive to receiving information from you.

  Individuals can join and leave this list on a selective basis, and since only those who choose to belong to your list receive postings to it, you're not violating the unique Internet culture of sending unsolicited information.

You can use this list to post announcements concerning new releases of your products, information about product updates or other significant announcements or information of interest to the participants. The mailing list can be archived on a periodic basis, such as once each month, so that the full text of past postings can be retrieved by e-mail.

Microsoft Canada has established an Internet mailing list for use by key third party developers across the country, with the objective of reducing the cost of getting information to these people on a more timely basis, and in order to keep them up to date on important developer issues.

To join the list, a developer simply sends a message to *mscdndev@microsoft.com*, with the subject *register*. Once the message is received and a few preliminaries go back and forth, the developer is added to the mailing list. Through this list, Microsoft Canada has an up-to-date, effective method of reaching developers right across Canada. Today, over 2,600 people belong to the Microsoft Canada developer mailing list.

• You can provide a place to visit for those individuals "surfing the Internet," and allow them to request additional information about your products and services. In effect, you can establish an Internet "storefront" in order to market your products and services through the Internet, while respecting the unique culture of the Internet.

For example, you could establish a Gopher and World Wide Web site that could contain the following information

⇒ an overview of your company
⇒ a description of products or services available
⇒ press releases
⇒ a listing of major customers
⇒ a price list
⇒ testimonials from several customers
⇒ information on how to order products via e-mail and fax
⇒ information on how to contact you via e-mail and fax.

Through a World Wide Web server, you could take it one step further and provide on-line forms, in order to provide interactive communications directly to the potential customer. For example, you could include on your Web server:

⇒ an order form which is automatically sent to you via Internet e-mail when completed
⇒ a form to request more information from your company. The form, when completed, would be sent to you via e-mail, and would permit you to directly contact the potential customer.

As an example of an on-line "market," the World Real Estate Listing service offered by a company called Westcoast Interchange based in Victoria, BC, details information on properties located across the country. (**http://interchange.idc.uvic.ca/wrels/index.html**).[1]

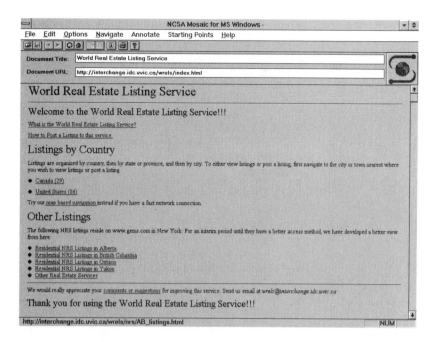

The location includes descriptions of the properites. With little effort, the site could include a picture of the property, as has been done with real estate sites elsewhere.

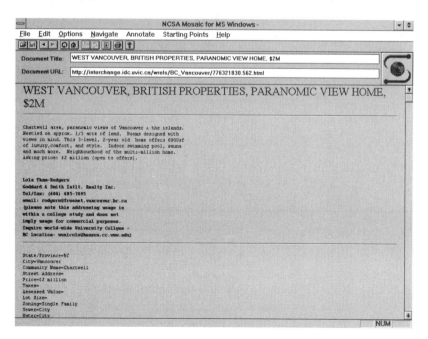

- You can establish an Internet "storefront" using Gopher or World Wide Web through an existing Internet provider.

We are seeing the emergence of a number of on-line Internet "shopping malls" or "storefronts." These services, often organized and sponsored by a particular Internet provider, categorize and make available marketing and sales information from many other companies.

The "storefront" includes access to information located at that particular Internet service provider, as well as direct access to other Internet storefront resources.

For example, Cyberstore, an Internet service provider located in New Brunswick, has established a World Wide Web storefront at the address **http://www.csi.nb.ca**:

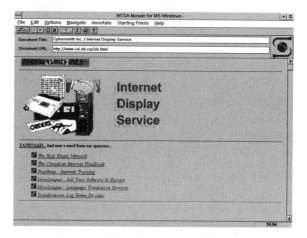

The Cyberstore Web server includes up-to-date information about the *Canadian Internet Handbook*, including order information, press releases and other background information.

NSTN Inc. has established a Nova Scotia-based "storefront" which can be accessed using Gopher at **gopher.nstn.ns.ca**. At this location, you will find access to a variety of companies.

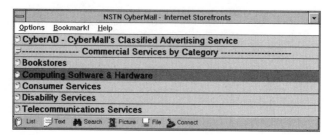

NSTN has also established a World Wide Web storefront with information from many of the same companies available in a much more graphical format.

MAKE PEOPLE AWARE OF YOUR RESOURCE

Once you establish your on-line presence on the Internet, it will be important for you to get word out on the Internet to attract "visitors" without attracting charges of advertising.

A key thing to keep in mind is that there are many people and many organizations who spend their time "indexing" the Internet, whether in magazines, books or on-line. It is to your benefit to have your Internet resource added to one of these indexes, and hence you want to try to get the attention of these people.

This can be done in several ways:

- Information about your new World Wide Web site should be posted to **comp.infosystems.www**; and information about your new gopher site should be posted to **comp.infosystems.gopher**. Check these USENET newsgroups to see what an acceptable posting should be like — it should be short, succinct, and right to the point. Posting to these groups will draw people to your location, and might help you to get indexed in other locations.

- Consider sending your press release to Gleason Sackman (**sackman@plains.nodak.edu**), to see if he is interested in posting information about it to the **net-happenings** list. If he does decide to post it, this will go to one of the premier announcement lists on the Internet, and news of your new Internet resources will travel the globe in a flash.

- Get listed in the master list of commercial World Wide Web sites at the Massachtusetts Institute of Technology. Check out the Web site at **http://tns-www.lcs.mit.edu/commerce.html** for full details.

- See if you can get your Gopher and/or World Wide Web site cross-indexed at other locations. There is a tendency for one Gopher or World Wide Web server to add increasing sophistication by offering "links" or pointers to other Gophers and WWW servers — which could include a pointer to your server.

- Consider a press release, for distribution to the general media, concerning this *new Internet initiative*. For a period of time, there will be an interest in new, significant Internet initiatives.

The key point to play up in the press release is that your new Internet resource is a product that is being carefully marketed on the Internet, without upsetting the unique culture of the Internet forbidding advertising. The press release should include information concerning the resources that you have brought on-line.

- Consider a brief announcement of your new resource in your e-mail signature. Just list the address. People will use it to visit your site when they have to.

Consider the signature for Tod Maffin at Haibeck Communications, which lists details on the WWW site for the company.

```
------------------------------------------------------------
Tod K. Maffin, Account Exec.   "One of the city's most
Haibeck Communications Inc.    Effective marketing and public
Vancouver BC  Canada           relations "firms." --
Offices: 604.683.7996          David Baines
                               The Vancouver Sun
------------------------------------------------------------
Visit our WWW site:
http://infomatch.com/0h/docs/users/haibeck
```

- Consider adding your Internet resource information to your regular marketing information. List Internet e-mail addresses on your business cards, or even your WWW server address. Consider how you can make customers aware through your traditional media campaigns about your Internet resources. A T-shirt company has gone so far as to print their e-mail address in their advertisements!

SUMMARY

The Internet is changing business in slow and subtle ways. There are opportunities for marketing on the Internet, opportunities to sell your products and services globally, and opportunities for efficiencies in your operations. Clearly, the above outline provides only a hint of what is possible on-line. The only real way to discover what works best for you is to get on-line, learn about the Internet and use it and understand it in order to determine how it might best fit your particular circumstances.

EDUCATION AND THE INTERNET

The Internet promises to revolutionize education in Canada by teaching students that knowledge comes not only from books, libraries and teachers, but that it also comes from millions of people and thousands of knowledge resources from throughout the world.

Already, in Canada, we are seeing the impact of the Internet on education — an impact that is wildly successful. SchoolNet, an initiative of Industry and Science Canada, had hoped to see 300 schools linked to the Internet by September 1994. However, as the result of efforts across the country, some related to the SchoolNet initiative but many due to local and provincial initiatives, over 3,000 schools were participating by that time.

It's a trend that is expected to continue, as many provinces, including New Brunswick, Ontario and British Columbia have announced plans to link schools throughout each province to the Internet.

EDUCATIONAL TRENDS

Education in Canada is in a difficult period of transition, particularly as public spending comes under continued constraints across the country.

Yet, for every difficulty there is an opportunity for use of the Internet. The Internet certainly presents opportunities in the field of Canadian education, particularly with respect to the following issues:

- There are fewer dollars available for education in Canada.

  The result is that education budgets are under pressure and educators are being forced to do more with less. One real impact of the budget crunch in education in Canada is that books in school libraries and books and materials for use in classrooms are becoming old and outdated. Schools are finding it difficult to ensure that information available for learning is current and up to date.

  It is difficult for a student to learn from materials that might seem so old they are perceived as irrelevant.

  The Internet solves this problem for the educator by providing the students with access to the world's largest storehouse of knowledge.

  "The Internet is current and up to date. It provides fresh resources. It provides unlimited information, and allows a school to get a huge bang for the buck," says Rachel Welch, responsible for Policy and Content Development at SchoolNet (**rwelch@ccs. carleton.ca**).

  Indeed, given the relatively low cost of access to the Internet compared to other knowledge sources, it truly is a bargain!

- Classroom sizes are growing, directly due to budget cutbacks.

  As classroom sizes grow, students get less attention from educators. "The Internet helps here, since it facilitates self-directed learning." states Rachel.

  Through the Internet, a student can spend time to explore and find knowledge from the world — on their own initiative and with little direction.

- Students have become less interested in education, yet the Internet helps to restore their interest.

  With the arrival of Nintendo and Sega games and with television and VCR's, there are even more distractions in the way of education today. To many, education can seem dull compared to the high-tech gee-whiz excitement of Super Mario Bros or the availability of Jurassic Park on video. Who wants to learn when there is so much fun stuff out there?

The experience of educators who expose their children to the Internet is that it makes them excited about learning again. It restores enthusiasm to the educational process.

"The Internet is exciting because it helps students to discover that there is an entire world out there," states Rachel.

It's very true, since it can get the student directly involved in issues. Rather than reading about the evolution of democracy in a book, a student can communicate with a counterpart in Russia to talk directly about what it is like to be in a chnging society. Rather than just preparing a report on the role of space exploration by reading a book, a student can communicate directly with a scientist at NASA. Rather than reviewing science books about human chromosomes, a student can access the complete Human Genome database on the Internet to look at the most recent research.

"The Internet is not the same as a book or television," says Rachel. "The student gets more of a feeling that what they are dealing with through the Internet is real. It has a bit more of a reality factor." And it is this reality factor that makes the student more interested in learning.

Educators who have brought their classroom into the Internet in this way have discovered that kids get enthusiastic about using the Internet, and implicitly, regain their interest in learning.

- Science education has suffered in this country and elsewhere yet the Internet promises an opportunity to return it to the forefront.

It's acknowledged by many in the educational field that our focus on science education has suffered through the past decade, and governments have announced palns to try to combat the problem. Yet, for all the talk about the problem, solutions do not seem to be readily at hand.

Yet, the Internet is changing that. It's a system that has its roots in the scientific and research communities around the world. It is full of scientific information and full of scientific debate.

The Internet is changing science, and as a result, it is changing science education. In an article called "How the Net Caught Science" in the June 16, 1993, issue of the *Globe and Mail*, it was reported that "in forging intimate new ties among researchers around the globe, computer networks are rapidly replacing old intellectual traditions with new ways of doing science. Up to four million scientists around the world are thought to be wired into a maze of over 11,000 interconnected networks, which are collectively known as the Internet – or sometimes just The Net."

The global scientific community is migrating to the Internet in massive numbers. It only makes sense for science education to take advantage of this fact. Much of the information available on the Internet is scientific in nature, and thus represents an invaluable mother lode of information to a science teacher.

- Schools have struggled for years to discover the best method to teach students about technology.

Rather than just teaching kids about word processors or spreadsheets, children learn about the use of computers as a tool. By using the Internet, educators are not teaching children how to use technology, but instead are teaching them how to use technology to learn. There is a big and fundamental difference.

Children learning on the Internet discover that rather than devices that let you type or print, computers are magical tools which can be used to explore, to find information, to ask questions, to probe for knowledge and to debate.

Which is what computers should be used for in the first place.

EDUCATION RESOURCES

It's hard to describe the extent of educational resources on the Internet, and this book certainly can't hope to provide a comprehensive summary. "There are fantastic resources out there," notes Rachel Welch. Indeed it is challenging to think of what the Internet can provide when used in education.

- Access to knowledge through mailing lists and USENET newsgroups.

Name a topic, and a mailing list probably exists. Do you plan to have your class do a project on ozone depletion? How about the USENET newsgroup **sci.environment**? Or the Ozone "Frequently Accessed Question" document, available in many FTP sites, which summarizes much of the information on the complex topic.

- Access to information through databases, databases, and more databases.

We stated before that the Internet has become the world's largest library.

There are absolutely massive volumes of information on almost any topic imaginable. As tools like Gopher and Mosaic become available, the knowledge of the world is available from your own computer screen.

- The ability to let students work on joint projects with peers somewhere else in the world.

A popular trend on the Internet is to link a classroom in one country with a class in another. Together, the two can work on a joint project through Internet e-mail. Each participant learns a little bit more about the people, the culture, the science, the art, the history, and humanity at the other side.

Imagine assigning a class to do a project about Poland. Why not link the classroom to a school in Poland — the information the students obtain with their peers will be much more relevant than any text book!

- Access to topic experts.

  Within SchoolNet, this is referred to as the "electronic innovators" project. Volunteer experts are asked to answer questions from students and teachers that relate to their area of specialty. Already, the project has linked space education projects in schools to scientists in the Canadian Space Agency and NASA. Since anyone can volunteer, the innovators project has unlimited potential.

- Fun through "scavenger hunts."

  Often, a teacher will assign a class with a project to "discover" particular information from the global Internet. The "hunt" becomes a learning exercise, as well as a way to have a bit of fun.

Through all of these activities, children are made to think about new ways of finding information, a skill that will become increasingly important as computer networks continue to evolve.

On-line resources don't stop there. There are newsgroups, databases and other information sources designed to help teachers understand their role of computers in education, how the Internet can be used in the classroom, on global class projects.

SchoolNet

There is so much information about education available on the Internet that, like many things, it can be difficult to find. Often, the complexity of the Internet presents a barrier to its use.

The enthusiastic SchoolNet initiative has the goal of helping schools and educators jump this hurdle, and has become one of the primary methods of getting elementary and high schools across Canada onto the Internet. As an initiative of Industry and Science Canada, it has aggressively planned to see every school across the country linked to the Internet within the next few years.

SchoolNet isn't charged with the mandate of actually linking schools to the network. Rather, it has the mandate of building an environment that will make it easier for a school to join. Once a school joins, it can look to SchoolNet for assistance and guidance on how to best use the Internet for educational purposes.

As a result, SchoolNet is not a place, so to speak, but an initiative to encourage the use of the Internet in education. It does this by doing several things, including:

- helping schools and educators understand why they should plug into the Internet and how they can do so;

- sponsoring a special USENET hierarchy, **can. schoolnet**, which students and teachers alike can use to network for knowledge. These newsgroups are detailed in the Appendix item *Directory of Canadian USENET Newsgroups*;

- sponsoring a mailing list for the discussion of USENET and mailing list topics;

- organizing information to make it easier for educators to get linked to the Internet in Canada, and to learn how to use it within the classroom;

- summarizing useful information that can be used within an education program, such as the "100 best locations" on the Internet.

Visiting the SchoolNet Gopher (use Gopher to go to **gopher.schoolnet. carleton.ca**) is a visit to a goldmine of information about using the Internet for education. It includes, among many other items:

- access to files and documents concerning the use of the Internet and computers in education;

- information about SchoolNet, who to contact and how to join;

- access to discussions on the SchoolNet USENET newsgroups and the SchoolNet initiative, so that you can get an idea of what the Internet is being used for in education across Canada;

- a "career Centre," with information about career planning, training information, information on university and college courses, and links to other on-line job and career Gophers;

- a place that summarizes "Classroom and Academic Projects," opportunities for your class to participate in an Internet-based education project:

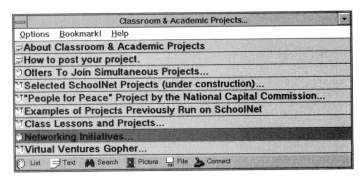

Consider the listing of projects as posted in September 1994:

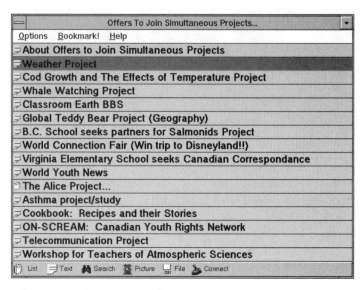

• access to electronic innovators, which provides details on how you link your classroom to specialists in particular fields.

SchoolNet is an extremely positive development in the educational scene in Canada. You can send basic questions to SchoolNet at **schoolnet-admin@carleton.ca.**

Yet, it is by no means the only initiative. In Newfoundland, Stem~Net provides similar assistance and information pointers through its World Wide Web server (at **http://calvin.stemnet.nf.ca).** It also provides a Gopher server.

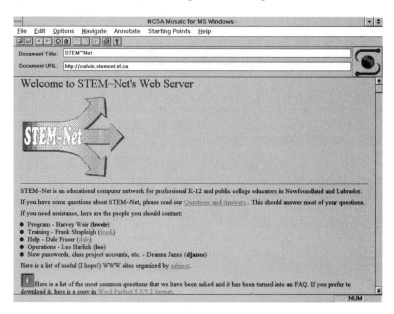

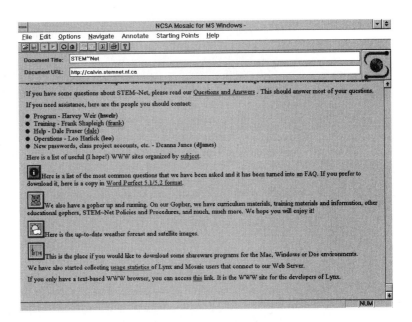

The *Directory of Gopher Servers and CWIS systems in Canada* found in Appendix E provides details on "*Canadian Educational Networking Gophers*," which includes useful pointers to provincial initiatives similar to the national SchoolNet initiative.

GOVERNMENT ON THE INTERNET

Governments in Canada are in the midst of a period of change.

The deficit continues to rise, the public demands service cutbacks and more services at the same time, public spending is under strain, cutbacks are imminent and public servants are stressed.

Terms like "re-engineering government" have entered our popular language.

All in all, it doesn't make for a pretty picture:

- Spending cutbacks are a reality.

  Like a drunken gambler, Canada has been spending beyond our means and beyond our wealth. The party is starting to end. As much as our national, provincial and municipal politicians might like to delude themselves, Canada has overspent its credit, and we will soon have no choice but to rein in our spending dramatically.

Like it or not, we seem to be headed to an era of shrinking federal and provincial budgets. With less money to go around, inevitably government has to begin to downsize and consider saving money through efficiencies.

The Internet offers some opportunities for cost savings and efficiencies in the delivery of services. Electronic mail between governments and their citizens offers an opportunity for savings. As more people begin to use the Internet, and as more government departments join the network, there is an opportunity for citizens and public servants to communicate more directly.

Through "information centres" or "information kiosks" established with World Wide Servers or Gopher servers, governments can make information available to the Internet community at a fraction of the cost of the print equivalent.

- Efficiency in the delivery of services to the public is increasingly important.

Today, obtaining information from the government can be an exercise in futility and frustration. How many of us have spent minutes and hours trying to find the right person, in the right department, in the right location, to try and find some piece of information?

Several governments in Canada have announced initiatives to provide a one-stop, one-place contact through which citizens will begin to be able to access information and services on-line – through the Internet.

- Citizens are demanding electronic access, and will continue to do so.

As many people continue to discover the power and scope of the global Internet, they will begin to demand access to their government and government services electronically.

In the United States, grassroots efforts in California led to a law which requires that certain state government information be made available at no charge. This initiative is detailed in further depth below. It is only a matter of time before similar initiatives in Canada gain momentum.

GOVERNMENT IN CANADA ON THE INTERNET

Certainly across Canada the Internet is gaining attention within government departments, and certainly within cabinet and legislative meetings.

There are several good examples in Canada where the Internet is being seriously explored.

THE OPEN GOVERNMENT PILOT, OTTAWA

As noted in its on-line World Wide Web site, "the Open Government Pilot is a demonstration project that is being developed by the Communications Development Directorate of Industry Canada. It is an Internet-based service that provides single-window access to the various segments of the federal government including: the House of Commons; the Senate; the Supreme Court; and, federal departments and agencies."

To this point, the Open Government Pilot includes access to information from a variety of sites within the federal government as well as from sites around Canada.

"Information that is available from these sites includes: contact information and information about members of Parliament; information about the Supreme Court, including its rulings; contact information for several government departments and agencies; and, constitutional documents. Links are now also provided to important government documents and treaties, provincial governments and other national governments around the world," states the on-line introduction.

The "home page" for the Open Government Pilot appears as follows:

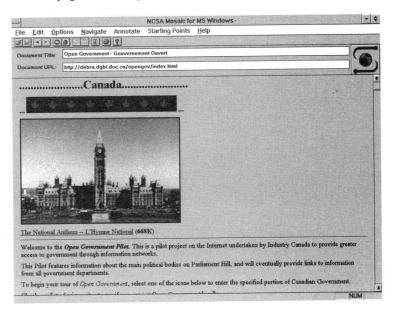

The site also includes access to departmental information, and has access to provincial government servers:

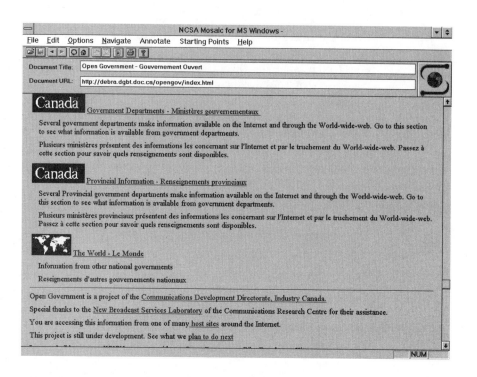

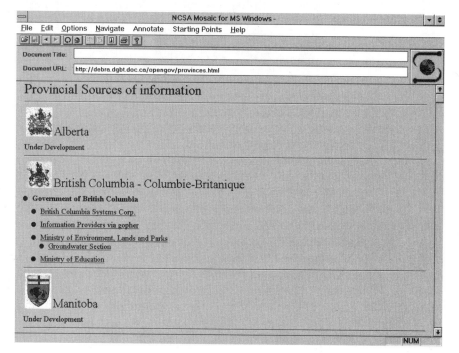

The important thing about the Pilot is that although it might not yet offer much access to information, it establishes a solid infrastructure (a popular word in

Ottawa!) upon which a single-entry point into Canadian government information can be built. Without a heavy investment in feasibility studies, project examination and other matters which take so much time, the project has already demonstrated that it is possible for the government to establish a one-stop, electronic "shopping mall" for access to government services and information.

Industry and Science Canada is known in the Canadian Internet community as being particularly aggressive and knowledgeable with Internet technology. Certain individuals at the Communications Development of Industry and Science Canada such as Andrew Stephens (**stephens@clark.dgim.doc.ca**) and Tyson Macaulay (**tyson@debra.dgbt.doc.ca**) have gained the respect of the Internet community for their efforts in Ottawa. Through their efforts, Industry and Science Canada has seen its role evolve to be one of assisting with the evolution of the Internet in Canada. They should be commended for their efforts!

In particular, the Open Government Pilot FAQ notes that "many government departments and agencies are in the process of establishing a presence on the global Internet. Industry Canada will provide some of the software tools and will share its experience in building the Open Government Pilot. Once new sites have been established and are accessible to the public, they will be made available under Open Government on a voluntary basis.

The possibilities for the Open Government Pilot are endless, and might include:

- e-mail access to Members of Parliament, Senators and other government officials;

- white and yellow page directories;

- resource pointers to other government information locations;

- simultaneous release of government documents to the Internet, including federal and provincial budget documents, economic statements, policy papers and other information.

The Open Government Pilot is by no means the only federal Internet initiative. Indeed, various federal departments have established their own Gopher servers, mailing lists and World Wide Web servers, many of which are detailed in the various directories in the appendices of this book.

NEW BRUNSWICK

Premier Frank McKenna of New Brunswick understands the Internet. In announcing his e-mail ID to the world in early 1994, he knew that he was setting an example of a politician who understood the significance of the Internet.

His goal with the Internet, as is his goal with the use of all high-tech communications, is simple — Internet connectivity plugs New Brunswick into the world, and hence represents an unparalleled opportunity for New Brunswick companies to participate in the global economy.

Through his initiatives, he is fostering an environment which encourages the use of the Internet and other high-tech communication capabilities throughout the economy of New Brunswick.

As for government services, New Brunswick has several Internet initiatives underway, including:

- the N.B. World Wide Web server, which provides access to information from various provincial departments;

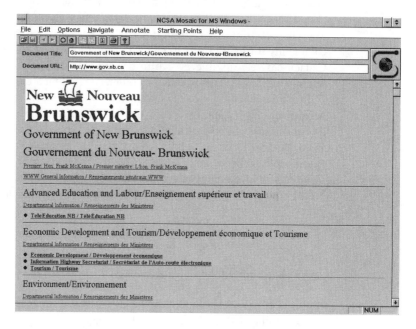

- an increasing use of Internet e-mail throughout various provincial departments;

- an FTP site, through which budget documents and other legislative information are made available.

INCREASING MOMENTUM

The move to "re-engineer" the delivery of government services in Canada will come as the result of government initiative. If government is slow, it will still come as the result of pressure from citizens.

This is certainly what happened in California. The document, "*A Guide for Accessing California Legislative Information Over Internet,*" as prepared by the Legislative Counsel Bureau of the State of California, notes in its introduction that "information regarding matters pending before the Legislature has been available to the citizens of California in printed form since 1849. That same information is now available by way of a computer network called Internet. AB 1624 (Chapter 1235/Statutes of 1993), authored by Assembly Member Debra

Bowen, D-Marina del Rey, requires that legislative information be made available to the public by way of the largest nonproprietary, non-profit cooperative public computer network. This phrase refers to the computer network known as Internet."

The same document goes on to note that "AB 1624 required that for each current legislative session, the following information be made available on Internet:

- The legislative calendar

- The schedule of legislative committee hearings

- A list of matters pending on the floors of both houses of the Legislature

- A list of the committees of the Legislature and their members

- The text of each bill introduced, including each amended, enrolled, and chaptered form of each bill

- The history of each bill introduced and amended

- The status of each bill introduced and amended

- All bill analyses prepared by legislative committees in connection with each bill

- All vote information concerning each bill

- Any veto message concerning a bill

- The California Codes

- The California Constitution

- All statutes enacted on or after January 1, 1993."

Much of the California initiative was due to a grassroots effort by citizens of the state.

It is only a matter of time before the California model will be picked up in Canada. It might not be that far off. David Schreck, a BC MLA, issued the following press release on August 29, 1994:

```
From: David Schreck <davids@yvr.cyberstore.ca>
Newsgroups: can.infohighway
Subject: BC Access to Legislative Documents
Date: Mon, 29 Aug 1994 22:43:24 -0700
Organization: Cyberstore Systems
Lines: 58
Message-ID:
<BK.BW.778225404.377401575.davids@yvr.cyberstore.ca>

NNTP-Posting-Host: yvr.cyberstore.ca
Mime-Version: 1.0
Content-Type: TEXT/PLAIN; CHARSET=US-ASCII
For Immediate Release
```

Computer hobbyist and Internet enthusiast, David Schreck, MLA for North Vancouver Lonsdale, announced today that he is lobbying government to make all legislative documents from orders of the day through statutes available without charge over the Internet. "I hope that my advice will be followed," said Schreck, "but in the event that further debate is necessary I am prepared to introduce a private member's bill modelled after what is already law in California."

In British Columbia it is already possible to use a home computer and a modem to access the Queen's Printer Bulletin Board for no more than the cost of a local phone call. Schreck is annoyed because part of that electronic bulletin board is off limits unless a user fee of $125 a year is paid in order to access the electronic version of Hansard, Bills, Statutes and other legislative documents. In California, Assembly Member Debra Bowen (Democrat - Marina del Rey) sponsored a bill which is now Chapter 1235/Statutes of 1993 which makes it the law in California to provide legislative documents free of charge over the Internet. Schreck "downloaded" Bowen's bill and provided it to his legislative colleagues as a model for British Columbia.

"I'm pleased with the general direction of government on issues involving Freedom of Information and the Information Highway," said Schreck. "It is possible to access a lot of government information with today's technology of a home computer and a modem. I hope to see government make the fact that it is open through the Internet more widely known." Schreck said his disappointment is with what is known as legislative information, documents that fall under the purview of the legislature rather than under the control of government. "It is not right," said Schreck, "that at the same time government is working to make information more easily available, legislative documents like Hansard and Bills which are already in electronic form remain subject to the barrier of a user fee." Schreck agrees that some documents should be subject to fees, but he said it will be a cold day in a hot spot before anyone thinks they can collect $125 a year for people to read speeches of politicians - the content of Hansard.

Background:

In Vancouver, the Queen's Printer BBS can be reached through modem at 660-1264
Other government services can be reached through the Internet by gopher to bcsc02.gov.bc.ca
The California legislative documents are available by FTP to leginfo.public.ca.gov
This release is also being posted to usenet.bc.generalFor Further Information Contact: David Schreck
    office 986-2254
    res. 984-8344

davids@cyberstore.ca or David_Schreck@Mindlink.bc.ca

Like everything it touches, the Internet promises to change government in Canada. That, from the perspective of many people, can only be a positive thing.

JUSTIFYING THE INTERNET

Patricia Seybold, a leading US information technology consultant, has stated that *"if you're not an active Internet citizen by the mid-1990's, you're likely to be out of business by the year 2000."*

Although this might overstate the facts somewhat, there is no doubt that the impact of the Internet is such that the world of business, education and government is changing rapidly and dramatically before our eyes.

Yet many organizations in Canada still find it necessary to educate senior management about the need for an Internet connection, and to justify the costs for a link to the network.

This is a strange state of affairs — after all, how many organizations found it necessary to justify those other fundamental business tools — the telephone and fax machine?

MOVING FROM SIMPLICITY TO COMPLEXITY

In the last two years, many individuals have signed up with one of the Internet service providers listed in this book, and have spent time on the network using a dial-up modem in order to try to understand the opportunities related to the Internet.

It is easy to go out and buy an individual dial-up account to access the Internet. Linking your organizational network to the Internet is a challenging task, however.

Part of the challenging task many people in Canada now face is the need to convince senior management that it is important for the organization to have a direct link to the Internet. And as we discussed, it is much more complex to have a direct link to the Internet than simple dial-up access.

In order to develop the strategic case for a direct link to the Internet, you need to think about several things:

- Approach the issue of the Internet not from a technology perspective, but from a strategic perspective.

   Examine the key strategy objectives for your organization. Relate how those objectives can be met through practical implementation of the Internet.

   Translate organizational goals into Internet activities. Speak the language that management understands!

   Nothing will turn management off more than technical solutions to strategic problems. What management wants are strategic solutions to strategic problems — so ensure that you are speaking the right language!

- Understand what the Internet opportunities are for your organization. How are other, similar organizations using the Internet? What is your business competition doing? What are other schools doing? What are similiar government bodies doing?

This requires a fundamental, critical look at your organization in light of the opportunities presented by the Internet, and means that you must determine which of your activities, such as with your customers, could be supported through a link to the Internet.

If you are a business, think about whether you sell your product internationally. If not, why not — has the high cost of selling internationally prevented you from marketing in this way? Is there an opportunity to provide better customer service via the Internet? How might making customer support information available via the Internet improve business opportunities?

If you are a school, are your students learning about computers, or are they using computers to learn? If a government, do you have plans to use communications technology to reach your "customers," the citizens of this country?

- Determine if you are "inter-network" capable, or determine what you need to do to get there.

Are you running or utilizing TCP/IP networking in your organization? If not, why not? What technology investments could you begin making to start on the road to Internet connectivity?

- Don't overhype the Internet.

When it comes to the Internet and business, you should be realistic about the opportunities it presents, particularly when dealing with management.

The Internet is changing the world of business, education and government. However, in many ways, it is a slow and subtle change, and won't happen overnight.

- Be realistic about expectations.

Don't promise sudden riches, or expect revolutionary results. Instead, help the organization recognize that the Internet is a long-term investment as opposed to a short-term initiative.

Plugging into the Internet will start you on the long road to discovering how to do business via networked systems in the years to come.

- Understand its limitations.

The Internet is but one technology tool to help your organization. Understand the role of all communications technologies in your organizations from a strategic, business perspective — not just the Internet.

- If you're looking for a lot of case studies on organizations successfully doing business on the global Internet, don't hold your breath.

There are a lot of organizations on the Internet experimenting, establishing resources, putting up mail robots, mailing lists, Gopher and Mosaic sites. Some are discovering what works, while others are discovering what doesn't work.

There is no magic formula with respect to how to do business on the Internet, and there likely won't be for some time. What the Internet represents is nothing less than a completely new method of doing business, which means that it will be some time before we see major, significant success stories.

- The Internet will take time to mature.

For example, the World Real Estate Listing service is an excellent example of a sophisticated information service on the Internet — yet, on August 8, 1994, there were less than 100 listings from throughout Canada on the entire service — certainly not enough to indicate that the service is an overwhelming success.

Simply put, the Internet, even as it grows in tremendous leaps and bounds, has a long way to go before it is a ubiquitous system with regular, everyday access by regular, everyday people.

- Not everyone can use Internet tools.

Many of the people linked to the Internet have simple e-mail access to Internet services. Many more have never signed on to a Gopher server. Fewer still have the high-speed access necessary to run the graphically oriented Mosaic.

The simple reality is that until high-speed information pipelines to homes and businesses become common across the country, and until more organizational networks are linked to the Internet, the number of people surfing the Internet, particularly using Mosaic, will remain somewhat low.

- Not everyone will adopt to the Internet.

To be fair, the Internet remains, even with tools such as Mosaic, a little "geeky." Basic Internet tools need to mature before they are useable by the "rest of us."

All indications are that the Internet is a fundamental revolution in the way business, education and government is conducted around the world.

When it comes to the Internet and your organization, keep in mind that even if you're not there, your competition and counterparts in the rest of the country and around the world will be. The most important thing to think about is that in order to avoid falling into a state of "competitive disadvantage," it's important for you to determine how you should participate now.

---

1. This is not the only Canadian real estate venture; a similar service has been established by Celerity Enterprises of Fredericton, New Brunswick. The service can be found on the Cyberstore "storefront" described in this chapter.

··································

PUTTING THE FUTURE OF THE INTERNET INTO PERSPECTIVE

Vinton Cerf, a codesigner of the Internet and now president of the nonprofit Internet Society, predicts there will be more than 100 million Internet users by the end of the decade. "You have to imagine that this kind of reaching out from anywhere in the world to anywhere else in the world, at your fingertips, has got to change the way we think about our world," Cerf said.

20 million drive the information highway; It's time to open the Internet to every
computer user, planners say
Montreal Gazette, Sat 02 Jan 93

To tell you the truth, I feel a little better knowing we have a Vice President who seems to know what the Internet is. But I also have the sneaking suspicion that the information highway is not as immediate an issue as everybody seems to think–and that our federal government and our leading technology companies are setting expectations that cannot ever match reality.

Hope you brought something to read during info highway wait
Los Angeles Times, Sun 24 Apr 94

The Internet in Canada has gained incredible momentum through 1994, and continues to evolve.

At the same time, a public policy discussion is taking place in Canada through the focus on the "information highway."

The two issues seem to be related so closely, yet the Internet does not yet seem to be part of the focus in Canada.

It should be.

PRESS COVERAGE IN 1994

We opened this book with several quotes about the Internet and the information highway.

It's good to take a look at the press coverage which resulted in 1994, for the media helps shape our attitudes and perspectives.

You couldn't pick up a magazine or newspaper in 1994 without hearing about the Internet or the information highway. *Maclean's* magazine featured the Internet prominently in a cover story about the "wired world" in February. *Time Magazine* did a cover story about the Internet in August 1994. *Forbes, Business Week* and the *New York Times* gave the network prominent coverage. *The Globe and Mail* mentioned the Internet 149 times from January to August 1994.

Part of the reason for the extensive coverage was due to the incredible hype that bubbled in late 1993 and boiled over in 1994 about the "information highway." The coverage was even more intense around the world.

A search of the Infomart database showed that the phrase "information highway" was mentioned at least 205 times from January to August 1994 in stories released on the major Canadian newswires, and at least 640 times (!) in major city newspapers such as the *Vancouver Sun,* the *Calgary Herald*, the *Toronto Star* and the *Halifax Daily News.*

Canadians were inundated with news and articles about the Internet and the information highway.

MAJOR CORPORATE INITIATIVES

There were a lot of corporate initiatives with respect to the information highway in Canada.

Stentor, the consortium of phone companies across the country, burst forth with the Beacon initiative, an ambitious ($8 billion) plan to wire every home and business across the country with high-speed network links. The CEO's at the press conference in which Beacon was announced said all the right things about "multimedia" and "interactive" and "networks of networks."

Yet, Stentor couldn't seem to figure out how to post information about the initiative to the Internet, leaving most Canadian users of the network puzzled as to whether this was another case of a major organization making promises about something it didn't really understand.

To its credit, Stentor is a participant in CANARIE and is involved in high-speed networking initiatives in Canada. Yet, when it comes to the Internet, it still seems to have a long way to go.

Rogers Communications launched a takeover bid for Maclean Hunter, promising to form Canada's largest cable organization. The bid caused a focus on the issue of telephone vs. cable company competition in Canada, leading to the inevitable charges and counter-charges between Stentor and Rogers.

Rogers also announced a high-profile deal with Bill Gates, chairman of Microsoft, to participate in the testing of Microsoft's entry into the TV-based information highway, which seemed to be some type of high-tech video server. Rogers also provided funding to the Toronto Free-Net, and indicated an interest in supplying access to the Internet via the cable wire.

Yet, like Stentor, Rogers seemed to focus on the hype promised by the future rather than by the reality of the Internet today.

The UBI initiative in Quebec was a far-reaching, grand scheme to wire that province with a high-tech, TV-based system to bring the future to Canadians. Consider this:

A group of Quebec businesses and a U.S. publishing empire have set out to build the first leg of Canada's information highway and it's a fascinating or frightening project – depending on how you look at it.

This network of cable-television and computer systems, unveiled Monday, will allow people to use television remote-control devices in their homes to order movies, pay their utility bills, buy goods from stores, read their electronic mail or order food from restaurants.

It will be beamed next year into 34,000 homes in Chicoutimi and Jonquiere, Que., 150 km north of Quebec City.

By the year 2002, it could be in Halifax, Quebec City, Montreal, Toronto and Edmonton. After that, the world.

It will cost $750 million to build over the next five to eight years, but should create 1,000 jobs for computer specialists.

The system will be available at no charge to cable customers – although there might be charges for some of the services provided on the system, such as movies and video games.

The companies building and using the system will foot all the bills for setting up and installing the system in homes.

A PROMOTIONAL VIDEO shows a typical Quebec family sitting around the set watching a hockey game. During a break in the play, a voice comes on and tells them that they can order St. Hubert chicken by just pushing a button.

Dad pushes the button, a menu from St. Hubert appears on the screen. He orders, and in the next scene the family is still watching the game, but now they are surrounded by St. Hubert delivery boxes.

One presumes they had to get off the couch to answer the door.

In a later scene, however, mother and son are scanning the items on sale at Sears when the son decides he wants a Walkman. Mom orders it and uses her bank card to pay for it – the system comes equipped with individual automated teller machines.

They never leave the couch.

Andre Chagnon, chairman of the Le Groupe Videotron – the cable television company that is spearheading the project – said the project won't turn us into a nation of couch potatoes.

Clicker consumerism no longer remote prospect
Windsor Star, Tue 25 Jan 94

It's scary, isn't it!

CANADIAN ACTIVITIES ON THE INTERNET

As much as we might bemoan the hype given to the "information highway," and even perhaps the hype surrounding the Internet, both did enter the public consciousness in a very big way in 1994.

We have seen some positive steps taken by government in Canada. Industry Minister John Manley and Secretary of State Jon Gerrard deserve applause for the fact that they seem to be truly trying to make an effort in understanding the role that the Internet can take in this country.

The public clamored to join the network, with Internet service providers indicating a very high number of new registrations. The number of organizations registered in the Canadian domain grew by some 62% in the first eight months of 1994 alone, going from 767 registered organizations to 1,249. Most were for commercial organizations, as corporate connectivity to the Internet continued to increase at a steady pace. Seminars about the Internet across the country filled to overflowing.

Mosaic burst to the forefront as "the" Internet application, the one that would make the network take off and truly become the backbone of global commerce. Internet storefronts and new initiatives for commerce on the Internet burst forth, some of which will be successful and some of which will be doomed to fail. Everywhere you went, you couldn't help but hear about "doing business on the Internet," and of the commercialization of the network.

YET . . . . .

Yet, something still seems to be wrong in Canada when it comes to the Internet.

Canada as a nation is in a precarious state. We have a significant budget deficit problem. Our ongoing constitutional crisis threatens to fester once again. We seem to be finally emerging from the recession, but the recovery is shaky at best. Canadians continue to be frustrated with their governments, their public figures and generally the status of everything as a whole.

We are, it would seem, a rather grumpy lot.

Even given our current grumpiness, it's clear that we as a nation must continue to learn to compete in the global economy. We must learn to introduce efficiencies to our work methods. We must learn how to compete with many of the leading-edge nations on earth.

Consider the competition. The nation-state of Singapore, in a far-reaching public policy paper called "Vision of an Intelligent Island – Singapore in the 21st Century," has proposed a networked national system that binds together industry, education and government. Access to the Internet forms a key part of that plan, as does the implementation of many other networking technologies. Singapore has proposed a system which will expand its global commercial capabilities, encourage research and development and improve the knowledge skills of its citizens. Already, out on the Internet we are seeing a number of people from Singapore learn how to access and harness global knowledge.

In Chapter 1 of this book, we focused on the fact that the discussions about the so-called "information highway" in Canada were being dominated by major telecommunication companies, and were focused on a vision of the "highway" which was based around the television. Examine the discussions closely, and you will see that part of it focuses on a device added to your television that will let you run your credit card through it. Reread the article about UBI above. Understand the promotional video that they are showing.

Canada seems intent on building an information highway that will let us order fried chicken through our TV. Home shopping, and the riches that it promises, seems to be the focus of our Canadian efforts.

Yet, many citizens of the Internet wonder if we as a country have it all wrong. Should we not focus on what we need to do to compete with a nation-state like Singapore?

THE INTERNET NEEDS HIGH-LEVEL REPRESENTATION

Aside from tentative efforts in Ottawa, few of those in positions of influence yet understand or appreciate the significance of what is happening on the global Internet.

Take a look at the United States, where Al Gore has made the Internet a fundamental part of his plans to reshape government. He regularly encourages a number of Internet initiatives with the full support of Bill Clinton. In a report on a speech he gave in early 1994, it was reported that:

> Just a few weeks later, Vice President Al Gore makes a speech in which he explicitly says the information highway should look more like the Internet than cable television.

> *Los Angeles Times- Sun 24 Apr 94*

Canada doesn't have an equivalent to Al Gore, and desperately needs someone as an equivalent to shape the public debate in this country. We need to get the Internet more fully into the debate.

Telecommunications companies have recognized that they need debate. Before the Federal Information Highway Committee was formed, Stentor was in the forefront of calls to action:

> Several of the major telecommunication companies indicate we need a debate about the information highway in Canada.

"We need champions," said Jocelyn Cote-O'Hara, president of Stentor Telecom Policy Inc., the lobby arm of Canada's telephone companies.

"We need an Al Gore. We need a national debate," she said, referring to the U.S. vice-president who made computers and high-speed communications a national issue three years ago when he was still a senator.

Technology group calls for political support
The Toronto Star, Tue 28 Sep 93

Yet, we also need to ensure that the debate includes the Internet in the forefront and not in the background.

The Internet is a global revolution no less profound than the invention of the printing press, and perhaps even more far-reaching than the invention of the telephone. The Internet binds the citizens of planet Earth together into a globally wired network in which knowledge and information spans the globe, and in which national politics become world politics.

The Internet can be the foundation for a network for Canada which will lead to significant opportunities for us to improve our capabilities as a nation.

It boils down to a fundamental question — how can we as a nation expect to thrive, to prosper and to compete in the global economy against a nation-state like Singapore if we as a nation are concentrating on building an information highway that lets us order fried chicken through our televisions?

SPEAK OUT!

Public policy discussions in Canada continue with respect to the so-called "information superhighway." Developments will continue through the next several months and years.

Every participant in the Internet has an opportunity to help shape those developments. The Internet community, having experienced first-hand the benefits that can accrue from being plugged into the knowledge of the world through the computers on their desks and in their homes, is rightly alarmed at the current state of affairs.

It's important that you get involved and speak out.

If you're new to the Internet, take the time to learn it, but more importantly, take the time to understand the significance of what it means. The Internet is not so much a "thing" as it is an "experience" — an experience in which you will discover how the world has become a smaller place, and in which world knowledge is being made freely accessible.

If you are an experienced Internet user, use your talents to ensure that your views are known. Use the Internet to help others become involved in getting the Internet onto the public policy agenda.

Make your views known to those involved in public policy discussions in Canada. Become aware of what is happening at the federal, provincial and municipal levels. Help your local politicians understand the Internet. Encourage them to adopt it and use it. Get involved with the information highway committee. Understand what the highway means today, and what it might mean tomorrow. Help federal and provincial politicians learn about the network. Encourage them to use it.

There is no doubt that there will be some wonderful capabilities as computers are married to television, and that this future high-tech system that everyone is talking about will offer some marvelous tools.

But good heavens, let's not let the idea of a couch-potato system continue to be our focus! Let's make sure that whatever we build provides us access to the huge capabilties of the Internet.

It is only through a concerted effort that Canada can really learn to exploit the significant capabilities that can be found in the Internet.

We welcome your views. Send us an e-mail message at **handbook@uunet.ca**. Since this address is an electronic mailing list, your message will reach both of us.

We'll be working away on the 1996 edition of the *Canadian Internet Handbook*, and doing what we can to ensure the Internet gets the proper degree of attention in Canada.

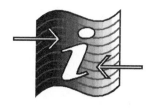

A P P E N D I X   A

······································

THE CANADIAN INTERNET TIMELINE

Notable Dates and Events in Canadian Networking
Version 1.3
Researched and compiled by Rick Broadhead

This timeline identifies key dates and events in the development of the Internet in Canada. It is an attempt to permanently record notable events in Canadian networking before they are lost to history, forever.

HOW TO SUBMIT INFORMATION FOR THE CANADIAN INTERNET TIMELINE:
Contributions to this timeline are encouraged! Please contact the authors at **<handbook@uunet.ca>** if you would like to submit an item for inclusion in future versions of the timeline.

This timeline would not have been completed if it were not for the generous assistance of numerous people across the country. We gratefully acknowledge contributions from the following individuals:

- Eric Carroll, University of Toronto (NOS)
  `<eric@enfm.utcc.utoronto.ca>`

- John Demco, CA Domain Registrar/CDNnet
  `<demco@cs.ubc.ca>`

- Alan Emtage, Bunyip Information Systems
  `<bajan@bunyip.com>`

- Ken Fockler, CA*net
  `<fockler@canet.ca>`

- Berni Gardiner, PEInet
  `<gardiner@bud.peinet.pe.ca>`

- Jim Hancock, University of PEI
  `<hancock@upei.ca>`

- Richard Lawrence, YukonNet Operating Society
  `<richard@north.nugyt.yk.ca>`

- Jack Leigh, University of British Columbia
  `<jack.leigh@ubc.ca>`

- David Macneil, University of New Brunswick
  `<dgm@unb.ca>`

- Michael Martineau, NSTN
  `<martineau@nstn.ca>`

- Rory O'Brien, WEB
  `<robrien@web.apc.org>`

- Tim Symchych, Department of Defense
  `<symchych@nrnsinc.on.ca>`

- Roger Taylor, National Science Foundation
  `<rotaylor@nsf.gov>`

- Vincent Taylor, Department of Defense
  `<vincent.taylor@sparky.crad.dnd.ca>`

- Mario Vachon, CRIM
  `<mario.vachon@crim.ca>`

- Roger Watt, University of Waterloo
  `<rwwatt@dcs1.uwaterloo.ca>`

1970

October	New Brunswick Educational Computer Network is formed, and later renamed the New Brunswick/Prince Edward Island Educational Computer Network. It is still operating.

1971

August	Science Council of Canada Report 13 is titled "A Trans-Canada Computer Communications Network."

1972

May 17

CANUNET, The Canadian Universities Network, is designed for the Federal Department of Communications, but the project is never funded.

1981

October

New Brunwsick/Prince Edward Island Educational Computer Network establishes an electronic mail system called "Mercury."

1982

May 14

The Canadian and U.S. Defense Departments agree on a project proposal which will link computer networks in the two countries. The Canadian Defense Department's network will be called DREnet.

1983

October

DREnet (Defense Resarch Establishment Network) is created, linking Defense Research Establishments in Ontario and Nova Scotia. The network consists of a 9600 bps link between the Communication Research Centre in Ottawa and the Defense Research Establishment Atlantic in Nova Scotia.

1984

March 1

CDNnet officially starts as a test network. CDNnet's purpose is to provide network services to Canada's research and education communities.

April

OUNET, the Ontario Universities Network, is launched. Six Ontario universities plus Humber College and Ryerson Polytechnical Institute (now Ryerson Polytechnic University) participate in the network that linked the central computers at each of the eight institutions.

June

OUNET is renamed NetNorth because several non-Ontario educational institutions have asked to join the OUNET network.

Fall

NetNorth establishes a connection to Cornell University in the U.S., linking NetNorth to BITNET (Because Its Time Network).

Fall

NetNorth organizes into three "regional" networks — one in Central Canada, one in Atlantic Canada, and one in Western Canada.

December 31

CDNnet (see March 1, 1984) has 14 hosts at 12 institutions.

1985

January

NetNorth's link to Atlantic Canada is established at the University of New Brunswick. IBM grants $60,000 per year for three years to help develop the network.

February	DREnet connects to ARPAnet in the U.S., a U.S. Defense Department network connecting several U.S. universities. The DREnet-ARPAnet link is a 56Kbps line connecting the Communication Research Centre in Ottawa to the University of Rochester in New York. The University of Rochester was chosen because it was the closest ARPAnet site to Ottawa. This event is important for two reasons. First, the ARPAnet eventually evolved into the Internet. Second, this was the first Canadian connection to the ARPAnet. Use of the Canada-U.S. link was restricted to people involved in authorized research programs. This restriction was lifted in June 1987.
February 25	New Brunswick/Prince Edward Island electronic mail system is linked to NetNorth.
June	NetNorth's link to Western Canada is established at the University of Alberta.

1986

Mid-1986	The Canadian end of the DREnet link to ARPAnet is moved from the Communication Research Centre in Ottawa to the Defense Research Establishment in Ottawa.
October	CRIM (Computer Research Institute of Montreal) establishes a computer network linking five universities and two research centres with 56Kbps lines. The participating institutions are the University of Quebec (Montreal), University of Montréal, Concordia University, École Polytechnique de Montréal, McGill University, SIRICON, and the Computer Research Institute of Montreal.
October 4	BCnet (British Columbia Regional Network) receives start-up funding.
November	John Demco (now the Registrar of the CA Domain) organizes a group to oversee the creation of a CA Domain for Canada.

1987

May	Web, a Canadian computer network, is launched with $20,000 in start-up funding from Environment Canada. Web was created to link environmentalists and other social-change activists across the country who were interested in issues of peace, environment, human rights, social justice, and international development. Web continues to exist today.
May	The CA top-level domain (.ca) is registered.
June	As a result of a Defense Department policy change, anyone on the DREnet is now permitted to use the DREnet-ARPAnet link for communications. Prior to this date, use of the DREnet-ARPAnet connection was restricted to authorized individuals only.
June 16	The first Canadian Networking Conference is held at the University of Guelph in Guelph, Ontario. Approximately 81 people attend.
September	The CRIM Network (see October 1986) is linked to CSnet (Computer and Science Research Network) in Cambridge, Massachusetts. The speed of the link is 9600 bps.

October 26	The National Research Council hosts a meeting in Ottawa to plan a national research network for Canada. Representatives from Canadian research institutions, computer networks and universities attend.
October	BCnet (British Columbia Regional Network) activates its first interorganization connection (between Simon Fraser University and the University of British Columbia).
November 25	The University of Prince Edward Island becomes the first Canadian organization to submit an application for a subdomain under the CA top-level domain.

1988

January 7	CDNnet requests a connection to the National Science Foundation Network (NSFnet) in Washington.
April - May	Representatives from two of Ontario's provincial centres of excellence (Information Technology Research Centre and the Institute for Space and Terrestrial Science) and from four Ontario universities (Queen's, University of Waterloo, University of Western Ontario, and the University of Toronto) begin to plan a computer network to interconnect their respective institutions. The network is initially called ORNet (Ontario Research Network), and later renamed ONet (Ontario Network).
May 26	BCnet and CDNnet establish a 19.2Kbps link to the NSFnet in Washington. The link is shared between BCnet and CDNnet.
May 31	The second Canadian Networking Conference is held in Fredericton, New Brunswick, at the University of New Brunswick. Over 100 people attend.
June 10	BCnet (British Columbia Regional Network) officially opens.
June 19	Roger Taylor and Allan Heyworth of the National Research Council deliver a paper at the 1988 Supercomputing Symposium entitled "NRCnet: A National Network for Canada's Research Community." This is the first "public" announcement of the plan to develop a Canada-wide computer network.
Summer	The National Research Council decides to change the name of Canada's national computer network from NRCnet (National Research Computer Network) to NRNet (National Research Network).
August	CDNnet has 175 hosts at 32 institutions. CDNnet's busiest host is processing 5,000 messages per day.
August	Fifty-seven institutions are participating in NetNorth.
August	ONet (Ontario Regional Network) connects its first institutions. Connections were first installed between the University of Western Ontario, the University of Toronto, the University of Waterloo, and Queen's University. Connections were established at York University and McMaster University shortly thereafter.
October	The University of Toronto establishes a 56Kbps link to the NSFnet at Cornell University.
October	The University of Toronto establishes a connection to the ARPAnet.

November	CRIM (Computer Research Institute of Montreal) establishes a 19.2Kbps link to CSNET (Computer Science Network) in Cambridge, Massachusetts.

1989

June	The third annual Canadian Networking Conference is held at Concordia University in Montreal. Approximately 157 people attend.
June 19	Roger Taylor and Allan Heyworth of the National Research Council present an update on NRNet at the 1989 Supercomputing Symposium in Toronto.
June 20	*The Globe and Mail* publishes an article about NRNet.
September	The CRIM Network (see October 1986) is replaced by a Quebec regional network called RISQ. The founding members are McGill University, École des Hautes Études, Université Laval, Université de Sherbrooke, Université de Montréal, Concordia University, Hydro-Quebec, Computer Research Institute of Montréal, Université du Québec a Montréal, École Polytechnique de Montréal, AES-Dorval, and Siège social de l'Université du Québec.
September	RISQ (Quebec regional network) is connected to NYSERnet (New York State Education and Research Network). The speed of the link is 56Kbps.
October	A meeting is held to form NBNet, a regional computer network for New Brunswick. The meeting is held in Moncton, New Brunswick, and hosted by the New Brunswick/Prince Edward Island Educational Computer Network.
November	Nova Scotia Technology Network (NSTN) is incorporated to provide Internet access in Nova Scotia.
November	RISQ (Quebec regional network) is connected to ONet (Ontario regional network). The speed of the link is 56Kbps.
November 23	A press release is issued, announcing plans for a high-speed national research network in Canada called the "National Research Network" (NRNnet).

1990

January	"CA*net" is chosen as the new name for Canada's soon-to-be-launched high-speed national research network. The name was suggested by John Curley of the National Research Council at an NRNet Board meeting.
January	NetNorth reaches its peak in membership with sixty-five members.
January	ARnet (Alberta Regional Network) begins with three members.
March	RISQ (Quebec regional network) is connected to NSTN (Nova Scotia Technology Network). The speed of the link is 19,200 bps.
March	Alan Emtage places the first prototype of "archie" on the Internet, at McGill University in Montreal. Archie is an Internet tool that helps users locate files on the Internet. The name "archie" is derived from the word "archive".

May 15	The Atlantic Canada Opportunities Agency approves funding for a link between CA*net and Prince Edward Island.
June	The 4th annual Canadian Networking Conference is held at the University of Victoria in British Columbia.
June	Documents are signed to create CA*net (Victoria).
June	Representatives from Web and six other national and regional networks sharing the same vision (see May 1987), and serving similar communities, meet in San Francisco. The result is the formation of the Association for Progressive Communications – an international organization representing computer networks that link social change activists. Web is a founding member of the APC.
June 15	New Brunswick/Prince Edward Island Educational Computer Network (Fredericton) establishes a link to CA*net.
June 12	The fourth annual Canadian Networking Conference is held at the University of Victoria in Victoria, British Columbia.
July 30	The first international Internet Engineering Task Force meeting, hosted by John Demco, is held at the University of British Columbia.
August	Nova Scotia Technology Network starts to connect its first clients.
October 25 12:00 Noon	CA*net, Canada's high-speed national research network, is officially opened in Toronto by the University of Toronto and the National Research Council. It is announced that the network will connect regional computer networks in each Canadian province. It is also announced that CA*net users will have access to research networks in Canada and throughout the world through three links to the National Science Foundation Network, (NSFnet) in the United States. The CA*net<==>NSFnet links will be from Toronto, Ontario to Ithaca, New York; Montreal, Quebec to Princeton, New Jersey; and Vancouver, British Columbia to Seattle, Washington. These links still exist today.
October	The Nova Scotia Technology Network (NSTN) is officially launched.
October 25	In Albuquerque, New Mexico, members of the Coordinating Committee for Intercontinental Research Networks (CCIRN) drink a champagne toast to celebrate the opening of CA*net.
November 20	The University of New Brunswick becomes the first university in Canada to establish a public on-line library catalogue on the Internet.

1991

January	The first version of Hytelnet is released by Peter Scott <scottp@herald.usask.ca> at the University of Saskatchewan. Hytelnet is a program that provides links to dozens of Telnet-accessible sites on the Internet, including library catalogues, community computer networks, campus-wide information systems, and databases.
March	A second archie server (see March 1990) is established on Finland's national computer network (FUNET). The FUNET server is the first archie site outside of Canada. The number of archie servers on the Internet has since grown to over twenty.

April 23	A consortium is formed to operate NBnet (see October 1989).
June	NetNorth announces its intention to wind down its operations.
June	The fifth annual Canadian Networking Conference is held at Queen's University in Kingston, Ontario. Approximately 203 people attend.
September	The link from CA*net in Vancouver to the NSFnet in Seattle, Washington is upgraded from 56Kbps to 112Kbps.
September	CA*net is carrying 27 Gigabytes of traffic per week— 10% of the load of the NSFnet T1 backbone at the time.
October	Toronto-based Web (see May 1987) begins to provide electronic communications to several computer networks in Cuba, giving Cubans Internet-based e-mail for the first time. The link is still maintained today.

1992

January 3	The link from CA*net in Vancouver to the NSFnet in Seattle, Washington is upgraded from 112Kbps to 224Kbps.
January 7	Peter Deutsch and Alan Emtage form Bunyip Information Systems Inc. to develop new versions of archie and other Internet tools. (See March 1990)
January 28	NB*net (New Brunswick Regional Network) is formally launched to provide Internet access in New Brunswick.
January 31	Total traffic on CA*net for the month of January 1992 is 160.3 megabytes.
February 29	Average growth rate on CA*net since August 1991 is 14 gigabytes per month.
April	The first commercial version of archie is released.
May 5	The link from CA*net in Toronto to the NSFnet in Ithaca, New York is increased from 224Kbps to 1.544 Mbps (T1 speed).
May 29	The link from CA*net in Montreal to the NSFnet in Princeton, New Jersey is increased from 112Kbps to 224Kbps.
June 2	The sixth annual Canadian Networking Conference is held at the Memorial University of Newfoundland in St. John's.
November	Canada's first Free-Net is launched in Victoria, British Columbia.
November 16	The NeXT User Group in the Yukon Territory becomes the first site in the Yukon to receive a domain in the .yk subdomain.
December	The can.domain USENET newsgroup is created to discuss issues pertaining to the CA Domain.
December 31	The total traffic carried by CA*net in 1992 is 271.53 megabytes.

1993

January 1	CA*net hires its first full-time staff member, an Executive Director.
January 14	The Polar Bear BBS in Rankin Inlet, Northwest Territories becomes the first site in the Northwest Territories to receive a domain in the .nt (Northwest Territories) subdomain.
March 5	CANARIE (The CAnadian Network for the Advancement of Research, Industry, and Education) is established as a not-for-profit corporation. Its goal is to assist in the development of a communications infrastructure in Canada that will improve Canada's competitiveness in the information age.
March 31	National Research Council funding for CA*net terminates.
March 31	The original CA*net agreements with the University of Toronto (to maintain and operate the network) and INSINC (to supply long-distance telephone service) terminate. These agreements are later renewed.
March 31	The link between DREnet and the U.S. is upgraded from 56Kbps to 1.544Mbps.
March 31	CDNnet terminates its activities.
April	NetNorth's membership is down to forty-one members.
June 15	The seventh annual Canadian Networking Conference is held at McGill University in Montreal.
June 21	CANARIE is officially launched. (See March 5, 1993)
August	PEInet is officially incorporated to provide commercial Internet access in Prince Edward Island. Plans are initiated to transfer control of the regional network from the University of Prince Edward Island to PEInet, a joint venture between IslandTel (PEI's telephone company) and On-Line Support, (PEI's largest consulting and development firm).
October 15	SchoolNet, a cooperative initiative among federal, provincial, and territorial governments, and the private sector, is launched. SchoolNet's mission is to connect elementary and secondary schools to the information highway
December 31	The total amount of traffic carried by CA*net in 1993 is 680.16 megabytes. This is a growth of 250% in one year.

1994

January	The Nova Scotia Technology Network expands beyond provincial borders, the first CA*net regional network to do so. NSTN opens a Point-of-Presence in Ottawa.
January	The CA*net Board admits the Government of Canada (GTIS) as a member of CA*net.
January 4	PEInet officially opens in Charloftetown, Prince Edward Island.
January 13	The YukonNet Operating Society is incorporated in Whitehorse, Yukon Territory, to provide commercial Internet services to residents of the Yukon Territory.

January 20	Premier Frank McKenna of New Brunswick announces the appointment of a Minister responsible for the electronic highway. New Brunswick is the first province in Canada to appoint a cabinet minister responsible for the development of the electronic information highway.
January 20	Premier Frank McKenna of New Brunswick publicly announces his Internet address <premier@gov.nb.ca> in a speech given to the Fredericton Chamber of Commerce. Premier McKenna becomes the first Canadian Premier to have a public Internet address.
March 17	Federal Industry Minister John Manley announces the government's intention to create an Advisory Council to help implement a Canadian strategy for the Information Highway.
April 19	Federal Industry Minister John Manley announces the membership of the National Advisory Council on the Information Highway.
April 19	Federal Industry Minister John Manley releases a discussion paper called "The Canadian Information Highway - Building Canada's Information and Communications Infrastructure." This paper explains why it is essential for Canada to have an information highway, provides an overview of Canada's existing communications and network infrastructure, and identifies some key policy issues that need to be addressed.
May	CA*net completes its upgrade to T1 speeds.
May 7	The *Canadian Internet Handbook* reaches the #1 position on the *Toronto Star*'s National Bestsellers List. It is the first Internet book to reach the #1 position on a general bestseller list.
June	The CA*net Board approves connections to the Yukon Territory and Northwest Territories.
June	The CA*net Board approves a 1994-1998 Strategic Plan for CA*net. It is available by anonymous FTP from **ftp.cc.umanitoba.ca** in pub/plan94.txt.
June	NetNorth's membership is down to twenty-five members: British Columbia Systems Corporation, TRIUMF, University of Alberta, University of Manitoba, Natural Resources Canada, Lakehead University, York University, University of Toronto, University of Waterloo, Concordia University, École Polytechnique de Montréal, University of Victoria, University of Ottawa, British Columbia Institute of Technology, University of Calgary, University of Regina, Humber College, Queen's University, École des Hautes Études Commerciales de Montréal, McGill University, Université Laval, Université de Sherbrooke, Mount Allison University, Université de Moncton, University of New Brunswick.
June 20	The eighth annual Canadian Networking Conference is held at The University of Saskatchewan in Saskatoon.
July 2	The *Canadian Internet Handbook* reaches the #1 position on the *Financial Post's Bestseller List*.
July 7	The Prince Edward Island Crafts Council in Charlottetown, Prince Edward Island becomes the first institution on the island to officially launch a World Wide Web server.

July 20   The ONet Association is disbanded and replaced
                  by the ONet Networking corporation, which assumes
                  responsibility for ONet.

July 25   Internet is on the cover of *Time* magazine.

July 31   The NetNorth consortium ceases funding of its National
                  Administrative Centre at the University of Toronto.

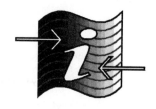

A P P E N D I X   B

·····································

HISTORY OF THE DEVELOPMENT OF CA*net: 1986-1990

Printed with the permission of Roger Taylor. Roger Taylor co-led the movement to establish CA*net, Canada's national research and education network.

©Roger Taylor
Division of Networking and Communications Research and Infrastructure
National Science Foundation
4201 Wilson Blvd., Room 1175
Arlington, VA 22230
Internet: rotaylor@nsf.gov

In August 1986 I was appointed Director (title later changed to Director General) of the newly created Division of Informatics at the National Research Council (NRC). NRC is a national science and engineering research institution with laboratories located across Canada, the majority being in Ottawa. In accepting that appointment, I had to make the transition from fundamental research in theoretical physics at NRC to taking charge of the central computing and communications services, the Computation Centre being the major component. And with that came the task of overseeing the development and operation of an NRC-wide network, originally proposed in 1984 by Larry Bradley of the Computation Centre as a link for the Ottawa laboratories, and widely discussed in the ensuing two years. This network would of course be connected to NetNorth, the Canadian arm of BITnet. NetNorth and CDNnet were the only two networks linking the academic research community within Canada at that time.

My first act was to appoint John Curley as the Networks Manager for NRC, reporting to me. John's previous position was Head of the Customer Service Section of the Computation Centre. Needless to say, he and I very quickly started discussing how we would set up a network linking all the components of NRC.

There would, of course, have to be a local network linking the Ottawa labs together which we decided should be an ethernet. But there was the additional necessity of linking labs literally from coast to coast, from the Dominion Astrophysical Observatory (DAO) on Vancouver Island to the Institute of Marine Dynamics in St. John's, Nfld. I don't know who came up with it first, but from one of our early conversations came the thought that if we had to go coast to coast, why restrict ourselves to NRC labs? Why not link every research institution, government, academic or private — in the whole country?

Ideas like that need a gestation period to allow us to think about them and figure out how to pull them off. We talked about it through the fall and winter while starting to monitor what was happening with NSFNET. Andy Woodsworth of DAO filled us in on plans being developed by Peter Shames (of NASA's Space Telescope Science Institute) for the distribution of and access to data from the forthcoming Hubble Telescope. DAO would be an official repository of CD-ROMs containing Hubble Telescope data, the intention being that they could be accessed remotely. So in March 1987, we headed south to Baltimore, where we met with Peter and also Steve Wolff, Director of NSF's Division of Networking and Communications Research and Infrastructure. Steve, of course, was responsible for the funding of NSFNET. Our objective was to get a better understanding of the types of applications that the network should support and to learn more about NSFNET and its plans for the future. From them we received many words of advice, lots of encouragement to go ahead with the project, and promises of cooperation. Of course, they were not being totally altruistic. I know that Steve was concerned about the possibility of Canadian institutions setting up north-south connections to link up with NSFNET, and using it to carry Canadian internal traffic. That would not sit well with Congress, who might wonder why *they* were funding a network to be used by Canadians for their own purposes. And Peter wanted to ensure good access to the planned data repository at DAO, so having an equivalent backbone network in Canada was deemed to be a good thing. Nevertheless, the cooperation we received from NSFNET went well beyond the minimum necessary to ensure that our network got up and running.

Shortly after that visit I presented our proposed program plans to the NRC Management Committee, and included the national network as a new initiative. The reaction was one of surprise, but eventually it was agreed to set up a Network Committee consisting of John Curley (chairman), Morven Gentleman, Art Hunter and Andy Woodsworth. By September the committee had drafted a report and had put together plans for a one-day meeting on October 26, 1987. The objective was to get together network gurus from across Canada to discuss the concept and to get a feeling for whether or not they would support it. The following were able to attend:

Larry Bradley, Division of Informatics, NRC
Dennis Crabtree, Herzberg Institute of Astrophysics, NRC
John Curley, Informatics Division, NRC
John Demco, University of British Columbia, CDNnet
Frances De Verteuil, Centre de Recherche Informatique de Montreal

Paul Dirksen, University of Waterloo, NetNorth
Ron Elliott, Department of Communications.
Dave Farber, University of Delaware, NSFnet
Ed Froes, University of British Columbia, BCnet
Morven Gentleman, Division of Electrical Engineering, NRC
Allan Heyworth, University of Toronto
Art Hunter, Industry Development Office, NRC
Ron Kieffer, University of Calgary
Dave Macneil, University of New Brunswick, NB/PEI network
Dave McPherson, Atomic Energy of Canada Limited
Ross Pottie, Executive Vice President, NRC
Peter Shames, NASA Space Telescope Science Institute
Ian Sinclair, Treasury Board Secretariat
Henry Spencer, University of Toronto, USEnet
Roger Taylor, Director, Informatics Division, NRC
Brad Tipler, Software Kinetics, DREnet
Mario Vachon, Centre de Recherche Informatique de Montreal, CRIM
Janet Walden, NSERC
Andy Woodsworth, Herzberg Institute of Astrophysics, NRC

That October 26 meeting was a major turning point. The participants were uniformly enthusiastic in their support for the proposal and fully agreed that NRC was the appropriate agency to lead the charge. I had fortunately persuaded Ross Pottie, Executive Vice President for NRC, to open the meeting with some words of welcome and to stay on for a while. He later told me that he was most impressed by what he heard and was fully supportive of the notion that NRC should lead the project. Another key person at that meeting was Dave Farber from the University of Pennsylvania. Dave filled us in on what was happening with NSFNET and had many words of advice, particularly concerning the management of the network. NSFNET had started off life with decentralized management, and that had not worked out well. Dave told us to make sure that we set it up in a central fashion, advice which we had no hesitation in heeding.

We followed that up with another meeting on October 30 to solicit opinions from others from within the federal government. One concern we had was to make sure that we were not intruding on the perceived mandate of such organizations as the Canadian Government Telecommunications Agency. No problem. Again the feeling was that NRC was the appropriate agency to lead the way.

By November, the Network Committee report was complete and it was presented to the NRC Management Committee on December 1, where it was given approval in principle, and where we were assigned the task of preparing a business plan (eventually put together by John Curley). At that point, Assistant Vice President Bill Coderre became our point of contact on the committee. He promptly dubbed the network NRCnet, the National Research Computer network. This was, of course, just a way of getting the initials "NRC" into the name without explicitly calling it the National Research Council network and we all cheerfully agreed to it.

John Curley then organized two further committee meetings, one in December 1987 at the University of British Columbia and the other in February 1988 at the University of Toronto, where Allan Heyworth and Eugene Siciunas presented an offer from the University of Toronto to run phase 1 of a national backbone network. They costed out routers, a four or five node topology, staff and other details. This was particularly helpful in the development of the business plan.

In March 1988 I presented the NRCnet proposal and business plan to the NRC Major Initiatives Committee. This was a committee to make recommendations to the Management Committee concerning any proposed new major initiatives. Key elements of the proposal were that NRC should contribute $2 million to the network as seed money to get it up and running, and that it would not require further funding; it would be self-supporting thereafter. The presentation was received very well by the committee and soon thereafter the NRC Management Committee committed the $2 million, subject to Treasury Board approval. Earl Dudgeon was the VP given the task of overseeing the project and Andy Woodsworth, on our recommendation, was appointed Project Manager to put flesh on the bones and to assemble the boiler plate needed to get things through the Treasury Board.

Shortly thereafter, John Curley and I attended a meeting of the SUPERNET Management Board, a group set up to provide researchers in government and academia with remote access to the Cray 1/S supercomputer located in the Atmospheric Environment Service Computing Center in Dorval, Quebec. At that meeting we outlined our plans for NRCnet and suggested that it could become a vehicle for the implementation of SUPERNET. One of the attendees was Peter MacKinnon, who was then on secondment to Industry Science and Technology Canada (ISTC) from Cognos Inc. Peter quickly saw our proposal as a prototype for a network that could strongly enhance the effectiveness of many components of industry in Canada. Those ideas were the genesis of what eventually became known as CANARIE (CAnadian Network for the Advancement of Research, Industry and Education), a project which evolved in parallel with CA*net, as NRCnet eventually became known.

Our first truly public announcement concerning the network came via a paper co-authored by Allan Heyworth of the University of Toronto that I presented to the 1988 Supercomputing Symposium, held at the U of Alberta, June 19-21, 1988. The paper, entitled "NRCnet: A National Network for Canada's Research Community," appears on page 351 of the proceedings of that conference. In that paper, the then current status of Canadian networks is summarized and attention is drawn to the existence of BCnet and the CRIM network in Montreal, the only two regional nets operational at that time. The concept of a backbone network linking regional nets across Canada was delineated along with the decision to go with TCP/IP. Mine was the last presentation at the Supercomputing Symposium, allowing me the opportunity to close the conference on an upbeat note.

That summer we changed the name of the network to NRNet, the feeling being that we were being a little crass to call it NRCnet, particularly since it would be operated by the Canadian networking community, not NRC.

Following the lead of NSFNET, it was decided to solicit bids via an RFP (Request For Proposal) to operate the network, anticipating that we might get bids from one or more consortia similar to the Merit-MCI-IBM consortium operating NSFNET. It was not the intention of the NRC to operate the network. The first step was the issuance of an RFI (Request For Information) in September of 1988 to get some feeling for the types of proposals that we might receive in response to our RFP. Nine responses were received. The NRNet Implementation Committee under the chairmanship of Jack Leigh of UBC was then set up to evaluate those responses, to prepare the RFP document, and to select the winning bid.

Getting a proposal like that through the Treasury Board was a far from trivial exercise. A major political hassle concerned our commitment to TCP/IP (Transmission Control Protocol/Internet Protocol) when the Canadian Government had adopted the OSI (Open Systems Interconnect) religion. It took a lot of fancy footwork to step our way through that one. We also had to make the case that it was within NRC's mandate to support the startup of NRNet, not too difficult, fortunately. Then, of course, we needed to make sure that it was understood that the community was behind us. Hence I never missed an opportunity to publicize the project and I visited several university campuses with the object of building up the momentum until it was unstoppable. I also started attending meetings of the CCIRN (Coordinating Committee for Intercontinental Research Networks) and the NACCIRN (North American Coordinating Committee for International Research Networks) where I gave updates on the progress of the project to an international community. Meanwhile Andy Woodsworth was writing and rewriting the Treasury Board submission and John Curley was aiding and abetting both of us, in addition to getting out to visit the major carriers and organizing meetings with potential partners, most notably IBM.

We failed in our attempt to get the submission on the Treasury Board agenda before the end of the fiscal year in March, 1989. Meanwhile, I attended the June 1989 Supercomputing Symposium in Toronto to give an update on the network. The paper, co-authored by Andy Woodsworth and entitled "National Research Network: An Update," appears on page 59 of the proceedings. This time *The Globe and Mail* interviewed me extensively and gave the project a good write-up in the Business section the next day (June 20). Interest was definitely building.

Finally, approval came from the Treasury Board in the early summer of 1989, allowing us to issue the RFP. Responses were due in August, 1989. Again nine were received. The winning bid came from a consortium led by the University of Toronto Computing Services and also involving IBM and INSINC, a Canadian reseller of bandwidth (i.e., they buy transmission capacity in bulk and resell it in smaller amounts at discount prices).

Shortly thereafter the NRNet Board of Directors was established, with representatives from each province, NetNorth, CDNnet and NRC. The list is as follows:

Jack Leigh (UBC), alternate Mike Patterson (BCnet)
Walt Neilson (Alberta Research Council)
Glenn Peardon (U. of Regina), alternate Dean Jones (U. of Sask)
Gerry Miller (U. of Manitoba)
Andy Bjerring (UWO)
Bernie Turcotte (CRIM)
Dave Macneil (UNB)
Jim Hancock (UPEI)
Peter Jones (Dalhousie U.), alternate Mike Martineau (NSTN)
Wilf Bussey (Memorial U.)
John Demco (UBC), CDNnet representative
Alan Greenberg (McGill U.), NetNorth representative
Roger Taylor (NRC), alternate John Curley (NRC)

NRC membership was non-voting. John and I both attended the early meetings. As we moved towards a timetable of a September 1990 implementation, large numbers of discussions took place via e-mail over NetNorth and in face-to-face meetings. Cost sharing was a very difficult problem, to be confirmed because of the vast disparities in resources and numbers of potential users from province to province. I remember being tremendously impressed with the goodwill displayed by the various board members as they struggled to find a fair formula while wondering how they would manage to pay their share when the NRC $2 million initial funding ran out. We at NRC could only sit back and let them work it out. But we contributed in other ways.

In general, people were not impressed with the generic name NRNet and our American friends pointed out that it sounded too much like NREN (National Research and Education Network), a program that had just been approved within the U.S. So, at a Board meeting in January 1990, John Curley unveiled the now familiar CA*net logo and instantly sold everyone on the name CA*net. I am convinced that the key was the brilliant red maple leaf which grabbed every Canadian heartstring in the room. At that same meeting, as I listened to heated discussions concerning network configurations with built-in redundancy, it suddenly occurred to me that everyone's suggestion was topologically equivalent to a pair of interlocking rings. So at lunchtime I drew a picture on a napkin with Montreal and Toronto at the ring intersections, with the western provincial sites distributed on one ring, and the Atlantic Canadian sites on the other. Everybody liked it because it minimized the number of hops from one node or site to another and at the same time it ensured that the network would continue to function if one node were to go down.

I was asked to chair the international committee and was given the responsibility of negotiating a cost-sharing agreement with NSF for three links to NSFNET. I completed that task in April 1990 when I spent a day in Washington working over some numbers with Steve Goldstein of NSF. That was one of the most pleasant negotiations I have ever taken part in. By agreeing that each side would pay for the cost of bringing a line to the border, we managed to get costs squeezed within Steve's budget and well within what I was authorized to spend by the CA*net Board. We both agreed that it was a win-win situation. Little did I know at that time that I was destined to move to NSF and work with Steve in the Division of Networking and Communications Research and Infrastructure.

Those were heady times as CA*net came closer and closer to reality. Official documents were signed in Victoria at a Board meeting in June, 1990. The provincial regional nets were building. We would hear how difficult it was to get 56Kbps to a particular campus, but we kept moving ahead. Then sites began to come up and finally we had full operation in September.

The official opening of CA*net took place in a ceremony at Hart House at the University of Toronto on October 25, 1990. A pretty happy bunch of people assembled to join in the celebrations and see Science Minister William Winegard officially cut the ribbon at 12:00 noon. He also delivered a very upbeat speech which was good to hear. Later on, we received a message from the CCIRN meeting in Albuquerque, New Mexico. It said that the minutes recorded that at 10:00 a.m. on October 25 (noon Toronto time) the CCIRN meeting was adjourned and the members drank a champagne toast to celebrate the opening of CA*net. What a warm feeling that gave us. The international networking community is pretty terrific.

Although several of us at NRC played key roles in bringing CA*net to fruition, once the project began to gather momentum many people from every province worked very hard to help bring it off, and their contributions were vital. Of particular importance was the NRNet Implementation Committee consisting of Jack Leigh (chairman, UBC), Bob Cavanaugh (Queen's University), John Curley (NRC), Paul Dirksen (U. of Waterloo), John Gilbert (Government Telecommunications Agency), Chris Hughes (Energy Mines and Resources), Peter Jones (Dalhousie University), Dave Macneil (UNB), Bernie Turcotte (CRIM), Ron Watkins (ISTC) and Andy Woodsworth (NRC). Of equal importance was the original CA*net Board of Directors, headed by chairman Peter Jones, and the University of Toronto implementation and operations team led by Warren Jackson and Eugene Siciunas. Two others who deserve special mention are Allan Heyworth (University of Toronto), who was tremendously supportive in the early stages as we developed the business plan, and John Demco (UBC), founder of CDNnet, who provided technical expertise and encouragement throughout the project. It was a truly Canadian effort that crossed every boundary and was a wonderful step on the way to the Internet connectivity that so many people enjoy today.

Dr. Roger Taylor is no longer with the National Research Council. He has moved to the National Science Foundation in Arlington, Virginia, where he is executive officer for the Division of Networking and Communications Research and Infrastrucure.

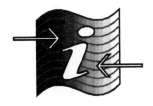

A P P E N D I X   C

....

THE DIRECTORY OF CANADIAN INTERNET SERVICE PROVIDERS

This is a comprehensive directory of dozens of organizations that provide Internet services in Canada. In this directory, we cover the entire spectrum of Internet service providers, from those offering only dial-up mail services, to those offering high-speed dedicated connections. Whether you are looking for an individual Internet connection, or a connection for your business, this directory will help you locate a suitable Internet service provider in your local calling area. An organization's appearance in this directory does not represent an endorsement of the organization by the authors of the *Canadian Internet Handbook*.

The directory is organized into three sections. The first section lists Internet service providers by province. The second section is an alphabetical list of Internet service providers that operate in more than one province. The third and last section is a list of American Internet providers that have local access numbers in Canada.

Each entry in this directory is structured like this:

Name of the organization or service

Town or city where the organization is located

The organization's Internet domain

Mailing address and telephone number of the Internet service provider. If the organization has a fax number and/or an Internet address for general queries, this information will be provided here.

Brief description of the organization or service. Most of the descriptions that appear in this directory were provided by the Internet service providers. They should not be taken as an endorsement of the service by the authors.

Service Area:	Indicates locations where customers can access the service with a local telephone call.
1-800 Service:	Indicates whether customers can access the provider's on-line service using a 1-800 number. If known, the cost of 1-800 service is indicated.
PDN Service:	Indicates whether customers can access the service using a public data network. Public data networks allow you to access computers in another city with a local telephone call. For example, CompuServe, a commercial on-line service located in Ohio, has local telephone numbers in several Canadian cities. When you call these numbers, your call is routed through a public data network to CompuServe's computers in Ohio. Public data networks can be cheaper than making a long-distance call, but they can still be expensive. Public data networks in Canada include BT Tymnet and Datapac.
Connection via:	Indicates who the Internet service provider buys its Internet connection from, and if known, the speed of the Internet connection.
Leased Line Service:	Indicates whether the Internet service provider offers leased line service. Leased lines are used when an organization requires a dedicated (i.e., 24 hour, 7-day-a-week) connection to the Internet. Most Internet providers support a specific range of leased line speeds. If known, the range of leased line speeds supported by the provider is listed. This box will also indicate if the Internet provider supports ISDN service.
Dedicated Dial-Up Service:	Indicates whether the Internet service provider offers "dedicated dial-up" service, where the customer has access to a telephone line for his/her exclusive use. A dedicated dial-up connection can be used on a casual dialup basis, or the connection can be held open 24 hours a day.
SLIP/PPP Service:	Indicates whether the Internet service provider offers SLIP/PPP service. This box will also indicate if the provider supplies any freeware, shareware, or commercial SLIP/PPP software. The software may be supplied on a disk, or it may be available on-line for downloading. Check with the provider for details. When shareware is distributed by an Internet service provider, customers are responsible for paying the appropriate shareware fees.
UUCP Service:	Indicates whether the Internet service provider offers UUCP service.

Interactive Accounts:	Indicates whether the Internet service provider offers dial-up (terminal emulation) accounts on a host that is either directly or indirectly connected to the Internet. The Internet services offered are listed. This box will also indicate the types of interfaces supported by the provider, and whether off-line readers are supported. The three main types of Internet interfaces are Unix shell (users enter Internet commands from a Unix prompt), menu-driven interface (users select Internet services from a menu), and graphical interface (users select Internet services by pointing and clicking using a mouse).
Maximum Casual Dial-Up Speed:	Indicates the maximum dial-up modem speed that the Internet service provider supports.
USENET News:	Indicates whether the Internet service provider offers USENET News. If known, the approximate number of newsgroups carried by the provider is listed. If the Internet service provider offers ClariNet news, it will be indicated.
Local File Archives:	Indicates whether the Internet service provider maintains local files for customers.
Domain Registration Service:	Indicates whether the Internet service provider offers "full" or "limited" domain registration service. There are two steps to domain registration. The first step is completing the form. The second step is submitting the form. "Full service" means that the Internet service provider will help customers with the paperwork *and* submit the registration form on the customer's behalf. "Limited service" means that the Internet service provider will only do one of these tasks, but not both. There may be an extra fee for domain registration service. If the fee is known, it is indicated in this box.
Domain Park Service:	Indicates whether the Internet service provider operates a **Domain Park**. This means that the Internet service provider will allow you to become a subdomain under their domain. For example, if the Internet service provider's domain is **north.net**, your system could become **your_system_name.north.net**. This is an alternative to registering your own domain.
Consulting Services:	Indicates whether the Internet service provider offers consulting services. Areas of specialization are listed.
DNS Service:	Indicates whether the Internet service provider supplies primary and/or secondary nameservers for a customer's domain. In order to register an Internet domain, you must have two independent domain nameservers. Domain nameservers are machines on the Internet that can answer queries from other domain nameservers about your domain.
Commercial Traffic:	Indicates whether the Internet service provider allows message traffic that is not related to research or education. Many Internet service providers have Acceptable Use Policies (AUPs) which prohibit certain types of message traffic on their system. Check with each Internet service provider for specific guidelines.
Additional Comments:	Other items of interest relating to the provider (optional).

HOW TO SIGN UP

If the Internet service provider allows "on-line" registration (i.e. you can sign up using your computer and your modem), instructions will be provided here. This includes registration over the Internet, if such capability exists. If the Internet service provider does not permit on-line registration, you will be told to contact the organization for registration instructions. If you already have Internet access, the organization may be able to send you a registration form by electronic mail or by fax.

Rates

Prices for a selection of the Internet provider's services are listed here. Rates may have certain conditions attached. Furthermore, rates are subject to change without notice, and the authors assume no responsibility for errors or omissions. Contact the Internet service provider directly for complete pricing information.

For More Information

If the Internet provider distributes service and/or pricing information by FTP, Gopher, the World Wide Web, or Telnet, it will be noted here.

HOW TO SUBMIT INFORMATION FOR THE DIRECTORY OF CANADIAN INTERNET PROVIDERS:

If you are a commercial Internet Access Provider or a commercial BBS that provides access to the Internet, and you would like to appear in future editions of this directory, please contact the authors at **<handbook@uunet.ca>** to obtain a copy of our questionnaire.

YUKON TERRITORY

YukonNet

Whitehorse, Yukon
yukonnet.yk.ca

YukonNet
c/o Northern Research Institute
Yukon College
Box 2799
Whitehorse, Yukon
Y1A 5K4
Voice: (403) 668-8735
Fax: (403) 668-8734
Internet: richard@north.nugyt.yk.ca (Richard Lawrence)

YukonNet was established to get the Yukon connected to Canada's electronic "information highway" - to bring the Yukon to the world, and the world to the Yukon. YukonNet is the regional service provider for the Yukon Territory.

Service Area:	Whitehorse.
	Planning to expand to other communities in the Yukon during 1995-1996.
1-800 Service:	No.
PDN Service:	No.

Connection via:	CA*net. 56Kbps.
Leased Line Service:	Planned. Up to 56Kbps.
Dedicated Dial-Up Service:	Yes.
SLIP/PPP Service:	Yes. SLIP and PPP.
UUCP Service:	Planned.
Interactive Accounts:	Yes. Direct connection to the Internet. 1 MB permanent storage per user. Users can pay for additional storage space (call for pricing). Telnet, TN3270, FTP, Gopher, WAIS, World Wide Web, Internet Relay Chat, Hytelnet, Archie. Menu-driven interface and shell access.
Maximum Casual Dial-Up Speed:	14,400 bps.
USENET News:	Planned.
Local File Archives:	Planned.
Domain Registration Service:	Yes. Full service. Call for pricing.
Domain Park Service:	Call for information.
Consulting Service:	No.
DNS Services:	Yes. Primary nameservers only.
Commercial Traffic:	Yes.
Additional Comments:	World Wide Web servers for the Yukon Chamber of Mines and Yukon Tourism are under development.

HOW TO SIGN UP

Registration is over the telephone. Please call to register.

Rates
INDIVIDUAL PACKAGES
One-time setup fee of $35.00.
Special Lite
$20.97/month. Includes 15 hours per month. $3.00/hr for additional use. Dial-up ratio =1:50.
Off Hours
$37.97/month. Monday-Saturday from 6:00 p.m. - 8:00 a.m. and Sunday Dial-up ratio =1:15.
Business Hours
$48.97/month. Monday to Saturday from 8:00 a.m. to 6:00 p.m. Dial-up ratio =1:15.
All Hours
$59.97/month. Dial-up ratio=1:15

COMMERCIAL PACKAGES
Level 1
$104.86/month. $75.00 one-time set-up fee. Dial-up ratio =1:10.

Level 2
$220.89/month. $75.00 one-time set-up fee.
Dial-up ratio =1:5.
Level 3
$441.75/month. $250.00 one-time set-up fee.
Dial-up ratio =1:1.
Custom
Custom monthly fee. $500.00 one-time set-up fee.
Dial-up ratio = 1:1.

NORTHWEST TERRITORIES

NTnet Society
Yellowknife, Northwest Territories
ntnet.nt.ca

Box 1976
Yellowknife, Northwest Territories
X1A 2P5
Voice: (403) 669-7284
Fax: (403) 669-7286
Internet: info@ntnet.nt.ca

NTNet Society is a non-profit society dedicated to providing low-cost public networking and reasonable-cost commercial networking in the Northwest Territories.

Service Area:	Yellowknife.
	Planning to expand to Inuvik, Iqaluit, Rankin Inlet, Hay River.
1-800 Service:	No.
PDN Service:	No.
Connection via:	CA*net. 56Kbps.
Leased Line Service:	Yes.
Dedicated Dial-Up Service:	No.
SLIP/PPP Service:	Yes.
UUCP Service:	Yes. Mail and news feeds.
Interactive Accounts:	Yes. Direct connection to the Internet. 10 MB permanent disk space per user (fixed, not expandable). Telnet, FTP, Gopher, WAIS, World Wide Web, Internet Relay Chat, Archie. Menu-driven interface and shell access.
Maximum Casual Dial-Up Speed:	14,400 bps.
USENET News:	Yes.
Local File Archives:	No.

Domain Registration Service:	Yes.
Domain Park Service:	Yes.
Consulting Services:	No.
DNS Service:	Yes. Primary and secondary nameservers.
Commercial Traffic:	Yes.

HOW TO SIGN UP
Please call for information.

Rates
Call for pricing.

BRITISH COLUMBIA

BCnet
Vancouver, British Columbia
bc.net

BCnet Headquarters
515 West Hastings Street
Vancouver, British Columbia
V6B 5K3
Voice: (604) 291-5209
Fax: (604) 291-5022
Internet: info@BC.net

BCnet is a wide-area data communications network (WAN) that interconnects local-area networks (LANs) in British Columbia. It interconnects the organization-wide LANs of British Columbia's universities, the majority of its community colleges, most of its major research laboratories, and many schools, government offices, non-profit organizations, research-oriented organizations, and commercial companies. In addition, BCnet provides these organizations with access to the world-wide Internet.

Service Area:	Vancouver, Victoria, Nanaimo, Courtenay, Kelowna, Kamloops, Trail.
1-800 Service:	No
PDN Service:	No
Connection via:	CA*net. 4 T1 lines.
Leased Line Service:	Yes. Up to 10Mbps. ISDN service is available.
Dedicated Dial-Up Service:	Yes. Leased lines only.
SLIP/PPP Service:	Yes. SLIP and PPP. Dedicated service only.
UUCP Service:	No.
Interactive Accounts:	No.

Maximum Casual Dial-Up Speed:	No casual dial-up services.
USENET News:	Call for information.
Local File Archives:	No.
Domain Registration Service:	Yes. Full service. Free if ordered as part of a connection. $50.00 charge otherwise.
Domain Park Service:	No.
Consulting Services:	No.
DNS Service:	Yes. Primary and secondary nameservers.
Commercial Traffic:	Yes.

HOW TO SIGN UP

Call or send electronic mail for information.

Rates
Call for information.

For More Information
FTP:
ftp.bc.net

Cyberstore Systems Inc.

Vancouver, British Columbia
cyberstore.ca, cyberstore.com, cyberstore.net

Suite 201 - 601 West Broadway
Vancouver, British Columbia
V3L 3C5
Voice: (604) 873-1101
Fax: (604) 872-6095
Internet: info@cyberstore.ca

Cyberstore Systems Inc. is dedicated to providing highly available Internet connectivity services to organizations and individuals at reasonable prices. Product offerings include educational and consultant services.

Service Area:	Vancouver, Victoria, and Kelowna.
	Planning to expand to Kamloops, Prince George, Whistler, and Nanaimo.
1-800 Service:	No.
PDN Service:	No.
Connection via:	Sprint. T1.
Leased Line Service:	Yes. 56Kbps - 10Mbps. ISDN service is available.

Dedicated Dial-Up Service:	Yes.
SLIP/PPP Service:	Yes. SLIP and PPP. Software supplied to customers.
UUCP Service:	No.
Interactive Accounts:	Yes. Direct connection to the Internet. 3 MB permanent storage/user (fixed - not expandable). Mail, Telnet, TN3270, FTP, Gopher, WAIS, World Wide Web (Sentience Software Lynx), Internet Relay Chat, Hytelnet, Archie. Sentience for Unix "browsers" for specific periodicals for information sources. Menu-driven interface, graphical "point-and-click" user interface, and shell access. RIPTERM for DOS provided to customers free-of-charge.
Maximum Casual Dial-Up Speed:	28,800 bps.
USENET News:	Yes. 4,800+ newsgroups. ClariNet News is available.
Local File Archives:	Yes. Shareware and freeware TCP/IP applications for Windows, Mac, OS/2, software shipped by members of the Association of Shareware Professionals.
Domain Registration Service:	Yes. Full service. Minimum $100.00 fee.
Domain Park Service:	Yes.
Consulting Services:	Yes. Connectivity; hardware, software, and bandwidth requirements; organization implementation and training.
DNS Service:	Yes. Primary and secondary nameservers.
Commercial Traffic:	Yes.

HOW TO SIGN UP

INTERNET:
Telnet to **cyberstore.ca**, login as **guest**, no password required.

MODEM:
Vancouver: *(604) 526-3676, V.32bis V.terbo, login as **guest**, no password required.*
Victoria: *(604) 384-3911, V.32bis V.terbo, login as **guest**, no password required.*
Kelowna: *(604) 862-8143, V.32bis V.terbo, login as **guest**, no password required.*

Rates

1. *Premier Internet Access (1 year)* *$149.00*
   The simple way to get started. Full access to Internet facilities using a Graphical User Interface with mouse support. (Our free GUI client requires MS/DOS.)
   For the one flat fee, you may use the system for up to 75 minutes per day, for 365 days. There are no usage fees.

2. *Premier Internet Access (6 months)* *$79.00*
   As above, only for a period of six months.

3. *Premier Internet Access (3 months)* *$49.00*
   As above, only for a period of three months.

4. *Premier Plus Internet Access (1 year)* *$249.00*
   As above, for 1 year but with 150 minutes per day of access time.

5. Account Set-Up and Registration $20.00
This is a one-time only charge for new accounts, and applies to individual dial-up TCP/IP accounts as well.

Individual Dial-Up TCP/IP Services

1. Internet Starter Kit (MS Windows) $99.00
An excellent way for the MS Windows user to get plugged into the 'Net directly. The package includes:
   - *"Navigating the Internet, Deluxe Edition" by Gibbs & Smith including direct Internet access software*
   - *additional freeware applications (including Mosaic)*
   - *35 hours of Cyberstore connect time*
   - *Dial-Up IP account set-up and registration*

2. Internet Starter Kit (Macintosh) $99.00
An excellent way for the Macintosh user to get plugged into the 'Net directly. The package includes:
   - *"Internet Starter Kit for Macintosh" by Adam C. Engst including direct Internet access software*
   - *additional freeware applications (including Mosaic)*
   - *35 hours of Cyberstore connect time*
   - *Dial-Up IP account set-up and registration*

3. 50 Hours of Dial-Up TCP/IP Connect Time $90.00

4. 150 Hours of Dial-Up TCP/IP Connect Time $249.00

5. Additional hours $2.00

Organization Services

1. Internet Ethernet - Full Time LAN Connectivity @ 14,400 bps $699.00
This is the complete solution for the Novell Local Area Network connection to the Internet. It includes all hardware and software components necessary for up to 10 users, all set-up and installation, and maintenance for all components for the life of the contract.
(Per month price is based upon a one (1) year contract.)

2. Internet Ethernet - Full Time LAN Connectivity @ 56,000 bps $1,749.00
This is the same type of solution offered for larger LANS, or those requiring higher performance. It also includes all hardware and software (for up to 25 users), set-up and installation, and maintenance.
Please note that this item is subject to the availability of 56Kbps digital services at your address.
(Per month price is based upon a one (1) year contract.)

3. Internet Ethernet - Full Time LAN Connectivity @ 128,000 bps $1,899.00
This is the same type of solution offered for larger LANS, or those requiring higher performance. It also includes all hardware and software (for up to 25 users), set-up and installation, and maintenance.
Please note that this item is subject to the availability of ISDN at your address.
(Per month price is based upon a one (1) year contract.)

For More Information
FTP:
ftp.cyberstore.ca
Directory: info

Telnet:
cyberstore.ca
Login: **guest**

Gopher:
gopher.cyberstore.ca

World Wide Web:
http://www.cyberstore.ca

DataFlux Systems Limited
Victoria, British Columbia
DataFlux.bc.ca

1281 Lonsdale Place
Victoria, British Columbia
V8P 5L3
Voice: (604) 744-4553
Fax: (604) 652-4520
Internet: info@dataflux.bc.ca

Dataflux Systems is a full-service Internet connection provider. Our services include Internet consulting and planning, education and classes, and connections and technical support. Gopher and WWW pages can be created and placed on our high-speed file server for the world to access. Contact us for any of your Internet connection needs.

Service Area:	Victoria, Shawnigan Lake, Duncan.
	Expansion is planned to Nanaimo and Prince George.
1-800 Service:	No.
PDN Service:	No.
Connection via:	BCnet. 10Mbps.
Leased Line Service:	Yes.
Dedicated Dial-Up Service:	Yes.
SLIP/PPP Service:	Yes. SLIP and PPP. SLIP/PPP software is supplied at no additional charge.
UUCP Service:	Yes. Mail and news services. Newsgroup changes must go through a service person.
Interactive Accounts:	Yes. Direct connection to the Internet. Permanent storage is available and additional storage is free on request. Telnet, FTP, Gopher, WAIS, World Wide Web (Lynx), Internet Relay Chat, Hytelnet, Archie, MUD client. Shell access.
Maximum Casual Dial-Up Speed:	28,800 bps.
USENET News:	Yes. Approximately 3,500 newsgroups. ClariNet news is available.
Local File Archives:	Yes. Macintosh and IBM/PC SLIP applications; Internet help files.
Domain Registration Service:	Yes. Full service. $50.00 charge.
Domain Park Service:	Yes.
Consulting Services:	Yes. Network connectivity; wide area and local area networks; Unix systems management; custom hardware and software engineering and implementation.
DNS Service:	Yes. Primary and secondary nameservers.
Commercial Traffic:	Yes.

HOW TO SIGN UP

Call or send electronic mail for information.

Rates

Basic:
$9.95/month. No free hours.
$4.50/hour from 8:00a.m. to 5:30p.m.
$3.00/hour from 5:30p.m. to 8:00a.m. and weekends
$1.50/hour from 11:30p.m. to 8:00a.m.

Personal Connection:
$19.95/month (includes 10 free hours)
Additional hours:
$4.50/hour from 8:00a.m. to 5:30p.m.
$3.00/hour from 5:30p.m. to 8:00a.m. and weekends
$1.50/hour from 11:30p.m. to 8:00a.m.

Personal + Package:
$35.95/month (includes 20 free hours)
Additional hours:
$4.50/hour from 8:00a.m. to 5:30p.m.
$3.00/hour from 5:30p.m. to 8:00a.m. and weekends
$1.50/hour from 11:30p.m. to 8:00a.m.

Business Connection:
$49.95/month (includes 30 free hours)
Additional hours:
$3.00/hour from 5:30p.m. to 8:00a.m. and weekends
$1.50/hour from 11:30p.m. to 8:00a.m.

Business+ Connections:
$199.95 (unlimited use)

UUCP Feeds:
One-time registration fee
$39.95/month for up to 40 hours.

For More Information

Gopher:
gopher.dataflux.bc.ca

World Wide Web:
http://www.dataflux.bc.ca

Designed Information Systems Corporation (DISC)

Burnaby, British Columbia

aurora.net, aurora-net.com, disc-net.com

5065 Anola Drive
Burnaby, British Columbia
V5B 4V7
Voice: (604) 294-4357
Fax: (604) 294-0107
Internet: sales@aurora.net

Since 1981, DISC has designed and integrated local and wide area networks for business, education, and the professions. Our business is data networking and we excel in offering multi-platform integration services. DISC is a Novell Authorized Service Centre, Gold Authorized Reseller and a UNIXWare Master. auroraNET is DISC's commercial Internet service. auroraNET offers reliable, easy-to-use connections to the Internet.

Service Area:	Lower Mainland of British Columbia.
	Planning to expand to all major Canadian cities.
1-800 Service:	No.

PDN Service:	No.
Connection via:	fONOROLA. T1.
Leased Line Service:	Yes. Up to 1.544 Mbps. ISDN service will be available in late 1994.
Dedicated Dial-Up Service:	Yes.
SLIP/PPP Service:	Yes. SLIP and PPP. Software supplied.
UUCP Service:	Yes. Mail and news feeds. Newsgroup changes must go through a service person.
Interactive Accounts:	Yes. Direct connection to the Internet. Permanent storage is available. Storage is billed on amounts greater than 1 megabyte. Extra storage space costs $0.01/MB/day. Mail, Telnet, FTP, Gopher, WAIS, World Wide Web (Lynx), Internet Relay Chat, Hytelnet, Archie. Shell access.
Maximum Casual Dial-Up Speed:	28,800 bps.
USENET News:	Yes. 6,700 newsgroups.
Local File Archives:	Yes. SLIP/PPP software for Windows; graphical point-and-click software for use with Windows; Novell NetWare documents, information, patches and fixes; SVR4.2 UnixWare 1.1.1 software.
Domain Registration Service:	Yes. No charge if ordered with most services. $50.00 for additional domains.
Domain Park Service:	Yes.
Consulting Services:	Yes. Network design and implementation, network auditing, network troubleshooting, Internet server configuration, network management, router installation and configuration.
DNS Service:	Yes. Primary and secondary nameservers.
Commercial Traffic:	Yes.

HOW TO SIGN UP

Registration is done by fax or telephone. Call or send electronic mail for information.

Rates
MHS or UUCP:
Individual*: $75.00 set-up charge. $25.00/month includes connection time. Unused time cannot be accumulated. Additional time is billed at $5.00/hour in 6-second increments. See below for hourly rates.*
Corporate*: $350.00 set-up charge. $100.00/month includes connection time. Unused time cannot be accumulated. Additional time is billed at $5.00/hour in 6-second increments. See below for hourly rates.*

Internet Access:
Individual: *$75.00 set-up charge. $50.00/month includes connection time. 1 MB of storage. Unused connection time cannot be accumulated. See below for hourly rates.*
Corporate: *$100.00 set-up charge. Set-up includes two login IDs.*
$50.00/month includes connection time. 1 MB of storage. Unused connection time cannot be accumulated. Additional login IDs are $25.00 each. See below for hourly rates.

Dial-up SLIP/PPP:

Individual: *$75.00 set-up charge. $50.00/month includes connection time. Unused connection time cannot be accumulated. Domain name registration and network addresses are included in the setup. See below for hourly rates.*

Corporate: *$100.00 set-up charge. $50.00/month includes connection time. Unused connection time cannot be accumulated. Domain name registration and network addresses are included in the setup. Additional login IDs are $25.00 each. See below for hourly rates.*

Dedicated Services:

19,200Kbps:	*$800.00 set-up charge.*
	$500.00/month includes no limit on connect time.
	$300.00 set-up fee is waived with a one-year contract.
56Kbps:	*$1500.00 set-up charge.*
	$1000.00/month includes no limit on connect time.
	$500.00 set-up fee is waived with a one-year contract.
LAN Connection:	*Parking of servers on DISC's premises and connected to the Internet through auroraNET's LAN via Ethernet. Pricing is based on requirements.*

Primary Domain Service:
$50.00/domain. $5.00/node for more than 10 nodes.

Secondary Domain Service:
$50.00/domain.

Hourly Rates:

6:00a.m. to 6:00p.m.	*$5.00 per hour*
6:00p.m. to 12:00a.m.	*$3.00 per hour*
12:00a.m. to 6:00a.m.	*$2.00 per hour*

All rates are tracked in 6 second increments.

For More Information
World Wide Web:
http://www.aurora.net

Deep Cove Bulletin Board Systems Ltd.

White Rock, British Columbia
deepcove.com

#5 - 15273 24th Avenue
White Rock, British Columbia
V4A 2H9

Voice:	(604) 536-5855
Fax:	(604) 536-7418
Internet:	wayne.duval@deepcove.com (Wayne Duval)

Deep Cove BBS is an on-line communications service and Internet service provider owned and operated by Deep Cove Bulletin Board Service Ltd. It has been in operation since May 1985 and is one of the most popular systems of its kind in Western Canada. Deep Cove is a multi-line system operated on a Novell network using IBM Compatibles (486/66) and The Bread Board System (TBBS) Information Manager and a host of related software modules. It is a subscription service but offers a number of features that can be accessed by any member of the public (after registration) without the need to purchase a membership. The system has over 10 GB of files and shareware for DOS, Windows, OS/2, Macintosh and Amiga, as well as an extensive collection of GIF and JPEG images. Deep Cove also offers comprehensive Internet services to its members and has very competitive membership fees and hourly access rates for Internet access. SLIP and PPP connections were recently added as a service and further expansions are planned for 1994/1995. In 1994, Deep Cove BBS was voted the #6 BBS in North America (#1 in Canada) by the readers of Boardwatch Magazine.

Service Area:	Vancouver, Richmond, Surrey, White Rock, West Vancouver, North Vancouver, Burnaby, Delta, Abbotsford, Cloverdale, Port Moody, Coquitlam, New Westminster, Lanley, Maple Ridge, Matsqui.
	Planning to expand to Kamloops, Williams Lake, Vernon.
1-800 Service:	No.
PDN Service:	No.
Connection via:	BCnet. 56Kbps.
Leased Line Service:	No.
Dedicated Dial-Up Service:	No.
SLIP/PPP Service:	Yes. SLIP and PPP. Preconfigured freeware/shareware is supplied to customers.
UUCP Service:	No.
Interactive Accounts:	Yes. Gateway connection to the Internet for mail. Permanent storage is available for $0.35/MB/month. Mail, Telnet, FTP, Gopher, World Wide Web (Lynx). Menu-driven interface and shell access. Communications software (Telix) supplied to customers. QWK-compatible off-line readers supported. Shareware off-line readers are available for download. E-mail-to-fax gateway for the local calling area. Deep Cove supports full RIP graphics interface on its BBS lines.
Maximum Casual Dial-Up Speed:	28,800 bps.
USENET News:	Yes. 2,900 newsgroups.
Local File Archives:	Yes. 8 gigabytes of shareware, freeware, upgrades, and graphic image files for IBM, Macintosh, OS/2, Novell, and Amiga operating systems. There are also 3 CDROMs on-line.
Domain Registration Service:	No.
Domain Park Service:	No.
Consulting Services:	No.
DNS Service:	No.
Commercial Traffic:	Yes.

HOW TO SIGN UP

Customers can register on-line or by telephone.

MODEM:
(604) 536-5889, v.32bis/v.34, login as yourself and choose a password.
(604) 536-5859, v.32bis/HST, login as yourself and choose a password.
(604) 536-5885, v.22, login as yourself and choose a password.

Rates
Annual Membership Fee (Adult):
$90.00.
Interactive Internet Services (non-SLIP/PPP):
$0.20 to $0.40 per hour.
SLIP/PPP:
$25.00 registration fee. $0.75 to $1.25 per hour.

Digital Ark
Courtenay, British Columbia
ark.com

Cortec Communications Corp.
P.O. Box 3310, 3906 Island Highway
Courtenay, British Columbia
V9N 5N5
Voice: (604) 334-1662
Internet: brianf@mars.ark.com

The goal of Digital Ark is to provide North Vancouver Island with high quality, cost-effective solutions to a wide variety of network needs. Through partnerships with regional training centres, a variety of seminars are available to those interested in learning more about the many services, resources, and tools accessible through the Internet.

Service Area:	Courtenay, Comox, Cumberland.
	Planning to expand to Campbell River, Port McNeill, and Gold River.
1-800 Service:	No.
PDN Service:	No.
Connection via:	INSINC.
Leased Line Service:	Planned for 1st quarter 1995.
Dedicated Dial-Up Service:	Yes.
SLIP/PPP Service:	Yes. SLIP.
UUCP Service:	Planned for 1st quarter 1995.
Interactive Accounts:	Yes. Direct connection to the Internet. Permanent storage space. Telnet, FTP, WAIS, WWW, Gopher, Archie, Talk. Shell access. Plans for menu-driven interface.
Maximum Casual Dial-Up Speed:	28,800 bps.
USENET News:	Yes. Approximately 1,500 available with plans to expand to full service in 1st quarter 1995.
Local File Archives:	Yes.
Domain Registration Service:	Yes.
Domain Park Service:	Yes.

Consulting Services:	Yes.
DNS Service:	Yes.
Commercial Traffic:	Yes.

HOW TO SIGN UP

On-line registration is not available. Please call or send electronic mail for information on how to register.

Rates

Basic Service - Terminal/Shell:
$50.00 set-up fee. $180.00 per year for 1 hour per day.
Enhanced Service - SLIP:
$140.00 set-up fee. $100.00 per month for 50 hours per month.

Helix Internet

Vancouver, British Columbia
helix.net

#902-900 West Hastings Street
Vancouver, British Columbia
V6C 1E6
Voice: (604) 689-8544
Fax: (604) 685-2554
Internet: info@helix.net

Helix Internet provides Internet access to individuals and businesses in the Vancouver region through terminal and dial-up SLIP/PPP. We strive to be the most cost-effective service in the region.

Service Area:	Vancouver region.
1-800 Service:	No.
PDN Service:	No.
Connection via:	BCnet. 56Kbps.
Leased Line Service:	Yes. Up to 28,800 bps.
Dedicated Dial-Up Service:	Yes.
SLIP/PPP Service:	Yes. SLIP and PPP. Freeware/shareware for IBM/Macintosh is available on-line.
UUCP Service:	Yes. Mail and news feeds. Freeware/shareware UUCP software is available on-line.
Interactive Accounts:	Yes. Direct connection to the Internet. Soft limit of 4 MB of permanent storage per user. Additional storage space is available for $0.25/MB/month. Mail, Telnet, TN3270, FTP, Gopher, WAIS, World Wide Web (Lynx), Internet Relay Chat, Hytelnet, Archie, MUD (tf, tintin). Menu-driven interface and shell access. E-mail-to-fax gateway for the local calling area.

Maximum Casual Dial-Up Speed:	28,800 bps.
USENET News:	Yes. 3,000+ newsgroups.
Local File Archives:	Yes. Shareware for Macintosh and IBM.
Domain Registration Service:	Full service, but only for dedicated SLIP/PPP customers. Cost is negotiated on a per-case basis (part of set-up charge).
Domain Park Service:	No.
Consulting Services:	Yes. Macintosh consulting and Internet connectivity.
DNS Service:	Yes. Primary and secondary nameservers.
Commercial Traffic:	Yes.

HOW TO SIGN UP

Customers can register on-line for a trial account. Customers must mail or fax in a form to activate a full-access account.

INTERNET:
Telnet to **helix.net***, login as* **guest** *(no password required).*

MODEM:
(604) 689-8577,V.32bis V.34, login as **guest** *(no password required).*

Rates
Standard Flat Fee Accounts - Terminal Dial-Up Only:
Time limit of 60 hours per month. Time limit per call imposed during peak hours. No calls per day limit. No other usage charges at all.
One Week Trial: *Free*
One Month: *$20.00.*
Three Months: *$55.00*
Student Four-Month Rate: *$60.00.*
Six Months: *$100.00.*
One Year: *$190.00.*
Time-Rated Accounts - Terminal/SLIP/PPP:
Includes 15 hours of usage per month. Additional time is charged at $1.20 per hour.
One Month: *$20.00*
Three Months: *$55.00*
Six Months: *$100.00*
One Year: *$190.00*

For More Information
FTP:	**Telnet:**	**World Wide Web**
ftp.helix.net	*helix.net*	*http://www.helix.net*
Directory: pub/info	*Login:* **guest**	

Gopher:
gopher.helix.net

ICE ONLINE

Burnaby, British Columbia
iceonline.com

Box 30606
#201 Lougheed Hwy.
Burnaby, British Columbia
V5C 6J5
Voice: (604) 298-4346
Fax: (604) 298-0246
Internet: info@iceonline.com

Service Area:	Vancouver, Victoria.
1-800 Service:	No.
PDN Service:	No.
Connection via:	UUNET Canada. 56Kbps.
Leased Line Service:	No.
Dedicated Dial-Up Service:	Yes.
SLIP/PPP Service:	Yes. SLIP and PPP. Shareware collection of client software is provided to customers.
UUCP Service:	Yes. Mail and news feeds. Newsgroup changes must go through a service person.
Interactive Accounts:	Yes. Direct connection to the Internet. 10 MB permanent storage per user. Mail, Telnet, TN3270, FTP, Gopher, World Wide Web (Lynx), Internet Relay Chat, MUD (Majic-Realm). Menu-driven interface with shell access. Telix and ZTERM communications software are available for customers.
Maximum Casual Dial-Up Speed:	28,800 bps.
USENET News:	Yes. 1,600 newsgroups. Clarinet News is available.
Local File Archives:	Yes. Windows, MSDOS, Amiga, Mac, Simtel software.
Domain Registration Service:	Yes. Full service. $75.00 fee.
Domain Park Service:	Yes.
Consulting Services:	Yes. Unix, networking, Internet connectivity, World Wide Web pages.
DNS Service:	Primary and secondary nameservers.
Commercial Traffic:	Yes.
Additional Comments:	ICE ONLINE writes its own entertainment software. A graphics MUD will be available in November 1994.

HOW TO SIGN UP

INTERNET:
Telnet to **iceonline.com** and login in as **bbs** (no password required).

MODEM:
Vancouver:

(604) 298-8411	28,800 bps	login as **new**
(604) 298-7655	14,400 bps	login as **new**
(604) 298-7529	2,400 bps	login as **new**

Victoria:

(604) 727-3230	2,400 bps	login as **new**
(604) 727-0206	9,600 bps/14,400 bps	login as **new**

Rates
$15.00-$20.00 per month for 1 hour per day.
Additional time at $1.00-$1.60 per hour.

For More Information

FTP:	Telnet:	World Wide Web
iceonline.com	iceonline.com	http://www.iceonline.com
Directory: pub	Login: **bbs**	
File: ICE_ACCESS.TXT		

InfoMatch Communications Inc.
Burnaby, British Columbia
infomatch.com

143-9632 Cameron Street
Burnaby, British Columbia
V3J 7N3
Voice: (604) 421-3230
Fax: (604) 421-3230
Internet: accounts@infomatch.com

InfoMatch Communications is Canada's leading producer of Windows-based consumer Internet software, and is committed to the development of user-friendly Internet software and systems for commercial and home use.

Service Area:	Vancouver, Burnaby.
	Planning to expand to Seattle, Washington.
1-800 Service:	No.
PDN Service:	No.
Connection via:	BCnet. ISDN.
Leased Line Service:	No.
Dedicated Dial-Up Service:	Yes.
SLIP/PPP Service:	Yes. SLIP only. Software supplied to customers at no charge.
UUCP Service:	No.

Interactive Accounts:	Yes. Direct connection to the Internet. 5 MB permanent storage per user. Free additional storage space is available for temporary periods only. Mail, Telnet, FTP, Gopher, WAIS, World Wide Web (Lynx), Internet Relay Chat, Archie. Menu-driven interface or shell access. Communications software is supplied to customers (Telix, Unicom).
Maximum Casual Dial-Up Speed:	28,800 bps.
USENET News:	Yes. 2,200 newsgroups.
Local File Archives:	Yes. Macintosh, DOS, Windows, BSDI Unix files.
Domain Registration Service:	Yes. Full service. $40.00 fee.
Domain Park Service:	Yes.
Consulting Services:	Yes. Systems design and implementation.
DNS Service:	Yes. Primary and secondary nameservers.
Commercial Traffic:	Yes.

HOW TO SIGN UP

INTERNET:
*Telnet to **infomatch.com**, login as **guest**, no password required.*

MODEM:
*(604) 421-3277, V.32, login as **guest**, no password required.*

Rates
SLIP or Dial-Up:
$139.00 for 1 year. Includes 210 minutes of connect time per week. Additional time is $1.20 per hour. Pro-rated 1-month, 3-month, and 6-month accounts are available.

For More Information

Telnet:	***Gopher:***	***World Wide Web:***
infomatch.com	infomatch.com	http://infomatch.com:70
Login: **guest**		

InterLink On-Line Services Inc.
Victoria, British Columbia
interlink.bc.ca

4252 Commerce Circle
Victoria, British Columbia
V8Z 4M2
Voice: (604) 385-4302
Fax: (604) 727-6418
Internet: info@interlink.bc.ca

InterLink provides turn-key value-added Internet services, by low-cost leased lines, ISDN and switched 56Kbps, and state-of-the-art wireless connections.

Service Area:	Victoria. Expansion is planned to other cities with point-of-presence BCnet or another provided by mid-level or regional network
1-800 Service:	No.
PDN Service:	No.
Connection via:	BCnet.
Leased Line Service:	Yes. 300-28,800 bps over a voice-grade line. Higher speeds available on request.
Dedicated Dial-Up Service:	Yes.
SLIP/PPP Service:	Yes. SLIP and PPP. Dedicated service only.
UUCP Service:	No.
Interactive Accounts:	No.
Maximum Casual Dial-Up Speed:	N/A.
USENET News:	Yes. Full feed.
Local File Archives:	No.
Domain Registration Service:	Yes. Full service.
Domain Park Service:	Yes.
Consulting Services:	Yes. Turn-key solutions to inter-networking.
DNS Service:	Yes. Primary and secondary nameservers.
Commercial Traffic:	Yes.

HOW TO SIGN UP

Call or send electronic mail for information.

Rates
Call or send electronic mail for information.

Internet Direct
Vancouver, British Columbia
direct.ca

1628-555 West Hastings
Vancouver, British Columbia
V6B 4N6
Voice: (604) 691-1600
Fax: (604) 691-1605
Internet: info@direct.ca

Service Area:	Lower Mainland of British Columbia.

1-800 Service:	No.
PDN Service:	No.
Connection via:	Call for information. T1.
Leased Line Service:	Yes. Up to 1.544Mbps. ISDN service is available.
Dedicated Dial-Up Service:	Yes.
SLIP/PPP Service:	Yes. SLIP and PPP. A free disk of shareware/freeware Internet applications with a TCP/IP stack is supplied to customers. The software automatically configures for Internet Direct's system.
UUCP Service:	No.
Interactive Accounts:	Yes. Direct connection to the Internet. 2 MB of permanent storage per user. Additional storage is available for $5.00/MB/month. Mail, Telnet, FTP, Gopher, World Wide Web (Lynx), Internet Relay Chat, Archie. Shell access. E-mail-to-fax gateway for the local calling area.
Maximum Casual Dial-Up Speed:	14,400 bps.
USENET News:	Yes. Approximately 5,000 newsgroups. ClariNet News is available.
Local File Archives:	Yes. PC, Macintosh, Unix archives. Freeware.
Domain Registration Service:	Yes. Full service. $75.00 charge.
Domain Park Service:	Yes.
Consulting Services:	Yes. Unix, networking, Internet connectivity.
DNS Service:	Yes. Primary and secondary nameservers.
Commercial Traffic:	Yes.

HOW TO SIGN UP

INTERNET:
*Telnet to **direct.ca** and login as **signup** (no password required).*

MODEM:
*(604) 684-3733, 14,400 bps, login as **signup** (no password required).*

Rates
Subject to change.
Dial-Up Access (Shell/SLIP/PPP):

One-time administration fee:	*$25.00*
5 hours per month:	*$9.95*
10 hours per month:	*$14.95*
20 hours per month:	*$29.95*

Additional hours are $1.50/hour. Hours are billed in quarterly installments.

Dedicated Services (14,400 bps - T1):
Call for pricing information.

For More Information

FTP:	*Gopher:*	*World Wide Web:*
ftp.direct.ca	*gopher.direct.ca*	*http://www.direct.ca*

The Internet Shop Inc.
Kamloops, British Columbia
netshop.bc.ca

1160 8th Street
Kamloops, British Columbia
Voice: (604) 376-3710
Fax: (604) 376-5931
Internet: info@netshop.bc.ca

The Internet Shop is a comprehensive Internet service provider offering Internet access, consulting, marketing, training, research, and sales and service of Internet-related hardware, software, and books.

Service Area:	Kamloops, Barriere, Pritchard, Savona, Chase, Logan Lake, Westwold, Douglas Lake. Planning to expand to Prince George, Williams Lake, Quesnel, Kelowna, Salmon Arm, Cache Creek.
1-800 Service:	Coming soon.
PDN Service:	Coming soon.
Connection via:	INSINC. 57Kbps. ISDN service is available.
Leased Line Service:	Yes. 2.4Kbps-57Kbps.
Dedicated Dial-Up Service:	Yes.
SLIP/PPP Service:	SLIP and PPP. Commercial software is available to customers at regular retail prices.
UUCP Service:	Yes. Mail and news feeds.
Interactive Accounts:	Yes. Direct connection to the Internet. Permanent storage available. Mail, Telnet, TN3270, FTP, Gopher, WAIS, World Wide Web (Lynx), Hytelnet, Archie, MUD. Menu-driven interface or shell access.
Maximum Casual Dial-Up Speed:	28,800 bps.
USENET News:	Yes.
Local File Archives:	Call for information.
Domain Registration Service:	Yes. Full service. Call for pricing.
Domain Park Service:	Yes.
Consulting Services:	Yes. Internet marketing, training, advertising, research, education, recreation.
DNS Service:	Yes. Call for information.

Commercial Traffic:	Yes.

HOW TO SIGN UP

Call for information.

Rates

Call for information.

Island Internet

Nanaimo, British Columbia
island.net

515b Campbell Street
Nanaimo, British Columbia
V9R 3G9
Voice: (604) 753-1139
Fax: (604) 753-8542
Internet: info@island.net

Island Internet serves the central and northern region of Vancouver Island. Island Internet's mandate is to provide cost-effective, reliable Internet access and network services to the people of Vancouver Island. Island Internet's aim is to provide a high level of customer support and to expand its services and its service area. Island Internet was the first commercial Internet service provider in the Central Vancouver Island area.

Service Area:	Nanaimo, Parksville, Qualicum Beach, Nanoose, Bowser, Chemainus, Crofton, Ladysmith, Cedar, Cassidy, Duncan, Lantzville.
	Planning to expand to Courtenay, Comox, Port Hardy, Port Alberni, Campbell River.
1-800 Service:	No.
PDN Service:	No.
Connection via:	BC Systems Corporation. T1.
Leased Line Service:	Yes. 14,400 bps - 57Kbps.
Dedicated Dial-Up Service:	Yes.
SLIP/PPP Service:	Yes. SLIP. PPP is available on special request. Shareware software is supplied to customers.
UUCP Service:	Yes. Mail and news feeds. Newsgroup changes must go through a service person.
Interactive Accounts:	Yes. Direct connection to the Internet. 5 MB of permanent storage per user. Additional storage space, when available, costs $1.00/MB/month. Mail, Telnet, TN3270, FTP, Gopher, World Wide Web (Lynx), Internet Relay Chat, Archie. Numerous RIP applications produced by Island Internet (RIP-elm, RIP-tin, RIP-Gopher, RIP-lynx, RIP-menu, RIP-joe). Menu-driven interface and shell access. Ripterm and Telix communications software is available to customers. QWK-compatible off-line readers supported. Shareware version of WINQWK is available to customers. E-mail-to-fax gateway for the local calling area.

Maximum Casual Dial-Up Speed:	19,200 bps. 28,800 bps in early 1995.
USENET News:	Yes. 3,500 newsgroups.
Local File Archives:	Yes. Windows SLIP software, Ripterm and Telix, locally developed applications, files requested by users.
Domain Registration Service:	Yes. Full service. $75.00.
Domain Park Service:	Yes.
Consulting Services:	Yes. Limited Novell Network, Unix administration, Internet networking, PC Networking, general PC repair and consulting, information server design, remote network management, Internet and general Unix training.
DNS Service:	Yes. Primary and secondary nameservers.
Commercial Traffic:	Yes.
Additional Comments:	Island Internet is currently developing RIP-based applications.

HOW TO SIGN UP

Registration is by telephone or fax. Please call or send electronic mail for information.

Rates
PERSONAL ACCOUNTS:
Shell Accounts:
Setup: $30.00
Usage: $1.00 per hour. 20 hours/month minimum.
            OR-
$199.00/year. 75 minutes per day.
$119.00/6 months. 75 minutes per day.
$1.50 for each additional hour.

SLIP Accounts:
Setup: $50.00
Usage: $1.50 per hour. 20 hours/month minimum.
       - OR-
$299.00/year. 75 minutes per day.
$169.00/6 months. 75 minutes per day.
$2.00 for each additional hour.

E-Mail Only:
Setup: $10.00
Usage: $5.00 /month
(Actually $1.25/hour. Minimum 4 hours/month)

E-Mail Only (with E-mail-to-Fax forwarding):
Setup: $15
Usage: $6.00 /month
(Actually $1.50/hour. Minimum 4 hours month)

COMMERCIAL ACCOUNTS:
Shell Accounts:
Setup: $50.00
Usage: $1.50 per hour. 20 hours/month minimum.
       - OR-
$299.00/year. 90 minutes per day.
$169.00/6 months. 90 minutes per day
$2.00 for each additional hour.

SLIP Accounts:
Setup: $100.00
Usage: $2.00 per hour. 20 hours/month minimum.
            -OR-
$399.00/year. 90 minutes per day.
$269.00/6 months. 90 minutes per day.
$3.00 each additional hour.

E-mail Only:
Setup: $20.00
Usage: $10.00/month.
(Actually $2.50/hour. Minimum 4 hours/month)

E-Mail Only (with E-mail-to-Fax forwarding):
Setup: $30.00
Usage: $6.00/month
(Actually $3.00/hour. Minimum 4 hours/month)

UUCP Mail/News Accounts:
Setup: $25.00
Usage: $1.00 per hour. 10 hours/month minimum.

For More Information
Gopher: **World Wide Web:**
epaus.island.net   http://www.island.net/

ISLAND NET
Victoria, British Columbia
amtsgi.bc.ca, islandnet.com

P.O. Box 6201, Depot 1
Victoria, British Columbia
V8P 5L5
Voice: (604) 479-7861
Fax: (604) 479-7343
Internet: mark@islandnet.com (Mark Morley)

At Island Net, our goal is to be the best all around Internet provider there is. We strive to offer the widest range of services, the lowest prices, and the best customer support. Our system has been designed and developed in-house.

Service Area:	Victoria, Shawnigan Lake, Cobble Hill, Colwood, Langford, Sooke, Metchosin.
	Planning to expand to Nanaimo, Vancouver, Duncan, Gulf Islands.
1-800 Service:	No.
PDN Service:	No.
Connection via:	BCnet. 56Kbps.
Leased Line Service:	Planned. Up to 56Kbps.
Dedicated Dial-Up Service:	Yes.
SLIP/PPP Service:	Yes. SLIP and PPP. DOS/Windows/Mac software is provided to customers. $10.00 for a SLIP manual including the software.

UUCP Service:	Yes. Mail and news feeds. UUCP software not supplied, but assistance is provided with selection of software. Customers can modify their own newsgroup subscriptions.
Interactive Accounts:	Yes. Direct connection to the Internet. Permanent storage space is available. Mail, Telnet, TN3270, FTP, Gopher, WAIS, World Wide Web (Lynx), Hytelnet, Archie, MUD (TinTin), Ping, Traceroute, WHOIS. Menu-driven interface and shell access. QWK- and SOUP- compatible readers supported. MultiTerm communications software supplied at no cost.
Maximum Casual Dial-Up Speed:	28,800 bps.
USENET News:	Yes. Approximately 1,100+ newsgroups.
Local File Archives:	Yes. Games, fonts, virus protection software, etc.
Domain Registration Service:	Yes. Full service. No charge.
Domain Park Service:	Yes.
Consulting Services:	Yes. "How-to" sessions, network planning, Internet training for individuals and businesses. Computer labs on-site, which are directly connected to the Internet. Standard and custom courses available.
DNS Service:	Yes. Primary and secondary nameservers.
Commercial Traffic:	Yes.
Additional Comments:	Island Net is planning to introduce a 1-800 number for business customers on the road, dedicated leased line service, and a satellite feed of over 6,000 newsgroups. Every account has the ability to create WWW home pages without any additional charges. Every account is able to create its own FTP directory. Courses are available to help users with these tasks.

HOW TO SIGN UP

Account creation is immediate. Just dial or Telnet in, answer the questions, and then call us back. New customers are given 30 minutes of free time so they can start exploring the Internet right away.

INTERNET:
*Telnet to **islandnet.com**, login as **new**, no password required.*

MODEM:
*(604) 477-5163, V.32bis V.FC, login as **new**, no password required.*

Rates
Hourly Plan:
Members buy 10 or more hours at a time, then use it whenever and however they want.
10-24 hours: $2.50 per hour
25-49 hours: $2.25 per hour
50+ hours: $2.00 per hour

Monthly Plan:
Members pay a certain amount each month for a fixed amount of time each day. If a member does not call one day, then the time for that day is lost. Members may bank an unused portion of their time and use it to extend their time on another day.

20 minutes per day: $10.00 per month
60 minutes per day: $20.00 per month
110 minutes per day: $30.00 per month
170 minutes per day: $40.00 per month
240 minutes per day: $50.00 per month
10% discount if you buy 3 months at a time.
20% discount if you buy 6 months at a time.
30% discount if you buy 9 months at a time.
40% discount if you buy 12 months at a time.

For More Information

Telnet:	**Gopher:**	**FTP:**
islandnet.com	*gopher.islandnet.com*	*ftp.islandnet.com*
Login: **guest** or **new**		Directory: *IslandNet*

World Wide Web:
http://www.islandnet.com

KB's BBS
Courtenay, British Columbia
kbsbbs.com

RR#4 Site 425 Comp-4
Courtenay, British Columbia
V9N 7J3
Voice: (604) 337-2021
Fax: (604) 337-2023
Internet: postmaster@kbsbbs.com

KB's BBS is a multi-node general interest BBS specializing in electronic mail. Internet e-mail and USENET news is available by subscription.

Service Area:	Comox Valley and Campbell River (via a call-back door).
1-800 Service:	No.
PDN Service:	No.
Connection via:	HoloNet.
Leased Line Service:	No.
Dedicated Dial-Up Service:	No.
SLIP/PPP Service:	No.
UUCP Service:	No.
Interactive Accounts:	Yes. Gateway connection to the Internet. Up to 20MB of storage per user. Internet mail. QWK-compatible off-line readers supported. Menu-driven interface and point-and-click graphical user interface.
Maximum Casual Dial-Up Speed:	28,800 bps.

USENET News:	Yes. 150 newsgroups.
Local File Archives:	Yes. General purpose shareware and freeware IBM/PC files.
Domain Registration Service:	No.
Domain Park Service:	No.
Consulting Services:	No.
DNS Service:	No.
Commercial Traffic:	Yes.

HOW TO SIGN UP

MODEM:
(604) 337-2023   *V.32bis/HST*
(604) 337-2024   *V.32bis/V.FC/V.34*
Login using your real name, and select a password.

Rates
Preferred user access is a flat rate of $60.00 per year.

MINDLINK! Communications Corporation
Langley, British Columbia
mindlink.bc.ca

105 - 20381 62nd Avenue
Langley, British Columbia
V3A 5E6
Voice: (604) 534-5663
Fax: (604) 534-7473
Internet: info@mindlink.bc.ca

MINDLINK's mission is to provide high-quality access to on-line communications at a price affordable to the general public.

Service Area:	Lower Mainland of British Columbia:
	Abbotsford, Aldergrove, Beach Grove, Bowen Island, Bridgeview, Cloverdale, Coquitlam, Fort Langley, Haney, Ladner, Langley, Mission, Newton, Pitt Meadows, Port Coquitlam, Port Moody, Richmond, Vancouver (East, North, South, West), Whalley, White Rock, Whonnock.
	Outside the Lower Mainland:
	Price George
	Planning to Expand to:
	British Columbia (Kamloops, Kelowna, Osoyoos, Vernon, Victoria), Alberta (Calgary, Edmonton), Saskatchewan (Saskatoon), Manitoba (Winnipeg), Quebec (Montreal), Ontario (Ottawa, Toronto), Washington (Seattle).

1-800 Service:	No.
PDN Service:	No.
Connection via:	BCnet.
Leased Line Service:	Yes. Up to 56Kbps.
Dedicated Dial-Up Service:	Yes.
SLIP/PPP Service:	Yes. SLIP and PPP.
UUCP Service:	Yes. E-mail and news feeds. Newsgroup changes must go through a service person.
Interactive Accounts:	Yes. Direct connection to the Internet. Telnet, TN3270, FTP, IRC, Archie, Gopher, WAIS, World Wide Web (Lynx client). Permanent storage. Additional storage is available for approx. 10 cents/megabyte/week. Menu-driven interface. Shell access available. Off-line mail readers supported. Local and international e-mail-to-fax gateway.
Maximum Casual Dial-Up Speed:	19,200 bps (28,800 bps in Winter, 1994).
USENET News:	Yes. 1,700 newsgroups through custom interface. All English-language groups through Unix and SLIP/PPP interface. ClariNet news is available.
Local File Archives:	Yes. More than 19 gigabytes of utilities, spreadsheet programs, games, gifs, text files, etc. Files for most platforms, including MSDOS, Windows, OS/2, Unix, Linux, Macintosh, Amiga, Atari, etc.
Domain Registration Service:	Yes. $25.00 charge.
Domain Park Service:	Yes.
Consulting Services:	Yes.
DNS Service:	Yes. Primary and secondary nameservers.
Commercial Traffic:	Yes.
Other Comments:	Hard-copy user's guide is available at no additional charge.

HOW TO SIGN UP

INTERNET:
Telnet to **mindlink.bc.ca**, login as **guest**, no password required.

MODEM:

(604) 576-1214	V.32bis	login as **guest**, no password required.
(604) 576-1683	HST	login as **guest**, no password required.

Rates
Full Internet Service, One Month Trial: $10.70
One month trial plus 1.5 hour introduction class: $21.35
Full Internet Membership:
$105.93/year or $70.62 for 6 months.
Internet Plus Membership:
$170.13/year or $105.93 for 6 months.
Unix Plus Membership:
$234.33/year or $141.28 for 6 months.
Corporate Membership:
$321.00/year or $186.18 for 6 months.
Corporate Unix Membership:
$410.88/year or $243.96 for 6 months.

For More Information
Telnet:
mindlink.bc.ca
Login: **guest**

World Wide Web:
http://www.mindlink.bc.ca

Nanaimo SchoolsNET
Nanaimo, British Columbia
sd68.nanaimo.bc.ca

Curriculum Resource Centre
420 Selby Street
Nanaimo, British Columbia
V9R 2R7
Voice: (604) 755-2147 (Mike Silverton)
            (604) 741-5289 (Brian Kuhn)
Internet: msilverton@sd68.nanaimo.bc.ca
            bkuhn@sd68.nanaimo.bc.ca

Nanaimo SchoolsNET exists to provide students, teachers, other district staff and the public with an Internet-based information service. The focus is both educational and administrational. Educational primarily for the students and teachers, but also for all others. Administrational in that this service will be used to support the Freedom of Information legislation handed down by the B.C. legislature. Public users seeking information about the school district will find it here. The Nanaimo SchoolsNET is a public service of the Nanaimo School District, managed by volunteer staff. There is no charge for use, and hence no official support to users.

Service Area:	Nanoose, Lantzville, Nanaimo, Ladysmith.
1-800 Service:	No.
PDN Service:	No.
Connection via:	BCnet. 56Kbps.

Leased Line Service:	No.
Dedicated Dial-Up Service:	No.
SLIP/PPP Service:	Yes. SLIP and PPP.
UUCP Service:	No.
Interactive Accounts:	Yes. Direct connection to the Internet. Permanent storage space is available. Mail and other Internet services. Menu-driven interface. No shell access.
Maximum Casual Dial-Up Speed:	14,400 bps.
USENET News:	Yes. 1,200+ newsgroups.
Local File Archives:	No.
Domain Registration Service:	No.
Domain Park Service:	No.
Consulting Services:	No.
DNS Service:	No.
Commercial Traffic:	Yes.

HOW TO SIGN UP

Users must download a registration form, complete it, and mail it in.

MODEM:
(604) 754-3630   *2,400 bps*   *login as **GUEST**, no password required.*
(604) 754-9578   *14,400 bps*   *login as **GUEST**, no password required.*

INTERNET:
*Telnet to **bbs.sd68.nanaimo.bc.ca**, login as **GUEST**, no password required.*

Rates
Services are free.

For More Information
Gopher: **Telnet:**
bbs.sd68.nanaimo.bc.ca   *bbs.sd68.nanaimo.bc.ca*
                                     *Login: **GUEST***

World Wide Web:
http://bbs.sd68.nanaimo.bc.ca:8001/welcome.html

Pro.Net Communications Inc.
Vancouver, British Columbia
pro.net, pronet.bc.ca

890 West Pender Street, Suite 410
Vancouver, British Columbia
V6C 1J9
Voice: (604) 688-9282
Fax: (604) 688-9229
Internet: info@pro.net

Pro.Net sells value-added services to customers over the Internet. Pro.Net provides access, publishing and marketing services that satisfy the information needs of market segments found throughout the global on-line community. Pro.Net plans to ensure that users enjoy simple "first-time" access to the Internet when using Pro.Net by providing an adequate number of access lines and installing reliable communications equipment; by automating the installation of client software; by simplifying the procedure of issuing user-ids, accounts and passwords; and by providing friendly, prompt customer support representatives.

Service Area:	Greater Vancouver area.
1-800 Service:	No.
PDN Service:	No.
Connection Via:	Sprint. 1.5 Mbps
Leased Line Service:	Yes. Up to 1.5 Mbps. ISDN service is available.
Dedicated Dial-Up Service:	Yes
SLIP/PPP Service:	Yes.
UUCP Service:	No.
Interactive Accounts:	No.
Maximum Dial-Up Speed:	28,000 bps.
USENET News:	Yes. Full Feed. ClariNet News is available.
Local File Archives:	No.
Domain Registration Service:	Yes. Full Service. $25 charge.
Domain Park Service:	Yes.
Consulting Services:	Yes. Security/firewall; marketing on the Internet; connecting to the Internet; World Wide Web server setup and configuration; creation of World Wide Web pages.
DNS Service:	Yes. Primary and secondary nameservers.
Commercial Traffic:	Yes.

HOW TO SIGN UP

Call for information.

Rates
Call for information.

For More Information
FTP:
ftp.pro.net
Directory: /pub/
File: pro.net.info

World Wide Web:
http://www.pro.net

Simon Fraser University
External Services
Burnaby, British Columbia
sfu.ca

External Services
Academic Computing Services
Simon Fraser University
Burnaby, British Columbia
V5A 1S6
Voice: (604) 291-3946
Fax: (604) 291-4242
Internet: devlin@sfu.ca (Tim Devlin)

Service Area:	Greater Vancouver.
1-800 Service:	No.
PDN Service:	Yes. Datapac.
Connection via:	BCnet.
Leased Line Service:	No.
Dedicated Dial-Up Service:	No.
SLIP/PPP Service:	SLIP and PPP.
UUCP Service:	No.
Interactive Accounts:	Yes. Direct connection to the Internet. 1 MB permanent storage per user. Users can pay for additional storage space if required. Mail, Telnet, TN3270, FTP, Gopher, WAIS, Archie. Menu-driven interface and shell access.
Maximum Casual Dial-Up Speed:	14,400 bps.
USENET News:	Yes. Full feed.
Local File Archives:	Yes. Internet client software.
Domain Registration Service:	Yes. Limited service. No additional cost when ordered with an Internet account.
Domain Park Service:	Yes.
Consulting Services:	No.
DNS Service:	Yes. Primary nameservers only.
Commercial Traffic:	Yes.

HOW TO SIGN UP

Call for information.

Rates
Call for information.

Sir HackAlot's Castle BBS
Port Alberni, British Columbia
hakatac.almanac.bc.ca

2366 14th Avenue
Port Alberni, British Columbia
V9Y 8A3
Voice: (604) 724-1436
Internet: rthomas@hakatac.almanac.bc.ca (Robb Thomas)

Sir HackAlot's Castle BBS provides Internet e-mail and newsfeed access.

Service Area:	Port Alberni, Ucluelet.
1-800 Service:	No.
PDN Service:	No.
Connection via:	Malaspina College.
Leased Line Service:	No.
Dedicated Dial-Up Service:	No.
SLIP/PPP Service:	No.
UUCP Service:	Yes. Newsgroup changes must go through a service person.
Interactive Accounts:	Yes. Running Waffle 1.65. Gateway connection to the Internet. 1-2 MB of permanent storage per user (fixed, not expandable). Users can send and receive Internet mail. Multi-line chat. Menu-driven interface. Public domain communications software (Kermit) provided to customers. Off-line readers supported (Helldiver, BlueWave, QWK, Zipnews). Helldiver supplied to customers.
Maximum Casual Dial-Up Speed:	14,400 bps.
USENET News:	Yes. 3,000 newsgroups.
Local File Archives:	No.
Domain Registration Service:	No.
Domain Park Service:	No.
Consulting Services:	No.
DNS Service:	No.
Commercial Traffic:	No.

HOW TO SIGN UP

MODEM:

(604) 724-0067	*V.32bis/ v.42bis*	*login as **bbs***
(604) 724-9975	*HST/MNP5/2400*	*login as **bbs***
(604) 724-9976	*PEP/MNP5/2400*	*login as **bbs***

Rates

BBS access is currently free, and at sysop's discretion. News/mail feeds currently free to local calling area, and at sysop's discretion.
News/mail feeds outside the local calling area are $2.00/hour or free if another local site will feed you. List of other sites will be provided upon request.

UNIServe Online

Aldergrove, British Columbia
uniserve.com

27009 Fraser Highway
Aldergrove, British Columbia
V4W 3L6
Voice: (604) 856-6281
Fax: (604) 856-7796
Internet: netinfo@gumby.uniserve.com

UNIServe Online is owned by Technovision Systems Inc. UNIServe Online provides many services to the public. Internet and SLIP/PPP accounts are only a few of them. Technovision Systems Inc. will soon be a public company and will be listed on the VSE. Our goal is to offer the best possible services for the best possible cost. UNIServe is currently expanding in leaps and bounds and we hope to be known and used by people all around the world.

Service Area:	North and West Vancouver, Greater Vancouver area, Delta, Langley, Aldergrove, Chilliwack, Sardis.
1-800 Service:	Yes. $4.00 per hour.
PDN Service:	No.
Leased Line Service:	Yes. Up to 56Kbps. ISDN service is available.
Dedicated Dial-Up Service:	Yes.
SLIP/PPP Service:	Yes. SLIP and PPP. Freeware and commercial software is available to customers.
UUCP Service:	Yes. Mail and news feeds.
Interactive Accounts:	Yes. Users do not have access to local storage. Mail, Telnet, TN3270, FTP, Gopher, WAIS, World Wide Web (Lynx), Archie. Menu-driven interface or shell access. Communications software is available to customers (DC Term, Telix). Blue Wave off-line reader supplied to customers. E-mail-to-fax gateway for the local calling area.
Maximum Casual Dial-Up Speed:	28,800 bps.
USENET News:	Yes. 4,600 newsgroups.

Local File Archives:	Yes. Games; pictures; files for Windows, OS/2, DOS, Novell, Unix.
Domain Registration Service:	Yes. Full service. $50.00
Domain Park Service:	Yes.
Consulting Services:	Yes. Internet consulting.
DNS Service:	Yes. Primary and secondary nameservers.
Commercial Traffic:	Yes.

HOW TO SIGN UP

MODEM:
(604) 856-8008, 14,400 bps or 28,800 bps, login using your first and last name.

Rates
Dial-up
SLIP/PPP: *$100.00 set up fee (on-site software install)*
              $25.00 set up fee (download software)
              $15.00 maintenance fee per mailbox per year
              $1.00/hour. $10.00 minimum to start.
Full Internet Access via BBS:
              $99.00/year for 2 hours/day and 5 MB download/day.
              $59.40/year for 1 hour/day and 3.5 MB download/day.

Victoria Free-Net
Victoria, British Columbia
freenet.victoria.bc.ca

Victoria Free-Net Association
203-1110 Government Street
Victoria, British Columbia
V8W 1Y2
Voice: (604) 727-7057
Fax: (604) 384-8634
Internet: vifa@freenet.victoria.bc.ca

The Victoria Free-Net is a community-based computer system available at no cost to residents and visitors of the Greater Victoria region. Our service goals include: computer-mediated communications among Victoria Free-Net users; easy access to information posted by community organizations, individuals, businesses, and government; community events information; worldwide e-mail and access to selected on-line public access resources throughout the world. The Victoria Free-Net is run by a core of dedicated volunteers belonging to the Victoria Free-Net Association, a non-profit society formed on June 17, 1992.

Service Area:	Victoria.
1-800 Service:	No.
PDN Service:	No.
Connection via:	Camosun College.
Leased Line Service:	No.
Dedicated Dial-Up Service:	No.
SLIP/PPP Service:	No.
UUCP Service:	No.
Interactive Accounts:	Yes. Internet mail, Gopher, World Wide Web. Telnet service to other Free-Nets. Permanent disk space. No shell access.
Maximum Casual Dial-Up Speed:	14,400 bps.
USENET News:	Yes.
Local File Archives:	Yes. Community information.
Domain Registration Service:	No.
Domain Park Service:	No.
Consulting Services:	Yes.
DNS Service:	No.
Commercial Traffic:	No.

HOW TO SIGN UP

INTERNET:
Telnet to **freenet.victoria.bc.ca**, login as **guest**, no password required.

MODEM:
(604) 595-2300, V.32bis, login as **guest**, no password required.

Rates
All services provided by the Victoria Free-Net are free to the user.

For More Information
Telnet:
freenet.victoria.bc.ca
Login: **guest**

Gopher:
freenet.victoria.bc.ca

World Wide Web:
http://freenet.victoria.bc.ca/vifa.html

Wimsey Information Services Inc.

Burnaby, British Columbia

wimsey.com, wimsey.bc.ca, wis.net

Wimsey Information Services
8523 Commerce Court
Burnaby, British Columbia
V5A 4N3
Voice: (604) 421-4741
Fax: (604) 421-4742
Internet: info@wimsey.com

Wimsey is the oldest commercial Internet service in Western Canada. Wimsey's Internet service was started in 1986 by its founder, Stuart Lynne, as an adjunct to his successful computer software business. Since that time, it has provided Internet e-mail and USENET news to virtually every BBS in Vancouver, and provided interactive access to computer professionals and other individuals on its central Unix systems. In late 1993, Wimsey expanded its operations to allow and foster the use of the emerging "point and click" Mosaic-based Internet access software through the addition of dial-up networking hardware and software. In addition to providing access, Wimsey has created an on-line facility for publishing electronic publications throughout its servers. The expanded emphasis of these World Wide Web facilities and services has meant a tremendous growth in the company and its user base.

Service Area:	Greater Vancouver, Kelowna.
	Planning to expand to other major centres in British Columbia and Montreal, Quebec.
1-800 Service:	No.
PDN Service:	No.
Connection via:	BCnet. 128Kbps. Cyberstore. 128Kbps.
Leased Line Service:	Yes. Up to 128Kbps. ISDN service is available.
Dedicated Dial-Up Service:	Yes.
SLIP/PPP Service:	Yes. SLIP and PPP. Preconfigured freeware/shareware packages for Macintosh and Windows are provided to customers.
UUCP Service:	Yes. Mail and news. Users can modify their own newsgroup subscriptions automatically. Free/shareware UUCP software is provided to customers.
Interactive Accounts:	Yes. Directly connected to the Internet. 1 MB permanent storage per user. Additional storage available for $0.02/MB/day. Mail, Telnet, FTP, Gopher, WAIS, World Wide Web (Lynx and Xmosaic), Internet Relay Chat, Hytelnet, Archie. Menu-driven interface and shell access. E-mail-to-fax gateway for the local calling area.
Maximum Casual Dial-Up Speed:	14,400 bps (28,800 bps as soon as the standard is ratified).
USENET News:	Yes. Approximately 4,700 newsgroups. ClariNet News is available.
Local File Archives:	Yes. Software and Internet documentation.
Domain Registration Service:	Yes. Full service. $50.00 fee.

Domain Park Service:	Yes.
Consulting Services:	Yes. SCO Unix setup and administration; INN setup and administration; e-mail setup and administration; World Wide Web (httpd) setup and administration; Mosaic (html) publishing.
DNS Service:	Yes. Primary and secondary nameservers. Secondary nameservers limited to direct customers.
Commercial Traffic:	Yes.
Additional Comments:	Wimsey is planning to introduce e-mail gateways for various PC LAN mail systems, including cc-Mail, Lotus Notes, etc. A MS-Mail gateway is already in place and running.

HOW TO SIGN UP

MODEM:
Port Moody:
*(604) 937-7411, v32/v32bis v42/v42bis, login as **help**, press the **<enter>** key at the password prompt*
Burnaby:
*(604) 420-0483, v32/v32bis v42/v42bis, login as **help**, press the **<enter>** key at the password prompt*
*(604) 420-1194, 28,800bps, login as **help**, press the **<enter>** key at the password prompt*

INTERNET:
*Telnet to **wimsey.com**, login as **help**, press the **<enter>** key at the password prompt*

Rates
Individual Hourly Account:
$15.00 one-time set-up charge. $1.80 per hour (Burnaby).
$1.60 per hour (Port Moody - No UUCP).
10% discount between 1:00a.m. and 7:00a.m.
10% surcharge between 7:00p.m. and 1:00a.m.
Accounts must be prepaid in amounts of $100.00.
Other conditions apply. Call for details.

Individual Annual Account:
$15.00 one-time set-up charge. $1.00 per hour access charge. Available for any number of hours over 15 per month ($180.00 per year). Hours in excess of prepaid per month will be charged at normal hourly rate. No discount or surcharge for peak/off-peak hours for prepaid hours (normal discount/surcharge is applicable to excess hours).
Other conditions apply. Call for details.

Non-Profit Association:
$50.00 set-up charge. Includes "business card" in Mosaic under the appropriate heading. Separate domain name, directory structure, and group ID available for a fee. Each user account must be set up individually and billed to the individual as per the individual accounts above. Hourly or annual access charge for each account may be chosen. Other conditions apply. Call for details.

Commercial Account:
$250.00 set-up charge. $150.00 per year for subsequent years. Up to 10k of text in Mosaic under appropriate heading. Includes setup and administration of separate domain if requested. Includes up to 10 user-IDs set up at the time the account is opened. Additional user-IDs are $15.00 each. Hourly access charge only available for each account. Other conditions apply. Call for details.

Corporate Account:
$450.00 set-up charge. $350.00 per year for subsequent years. Includes 10k of text and/or graphics in Mosaic under appropriate heading. Includes setup and administration of separate domain name if requested. Includes use of separate home directory structure and group ID if requested. Up to 50 user-IDs set up at the time the account is opened. Additional user-IDs are

$15.00 each. Hourly access charge only available to each account. Other conditions apply. Call for details.

BBS UUCP Account:
$75.00 set-up charge includes domain registration. $25.00 per year. $2.00 per hour or annual contract (prepaid) $3,600.00 (regular dial lines) or annual contract (prepaid) $4,200.00 (dedicated dial line). Includes an interactive account on Wimsey for the system administrator to use. Account must be prepaid in amounts of $100.00. Other conditions apply. Call for details.

MS-Mail Gateway Account:
(Internet SMTP gateway to/from dedicated MS-Mail Customer)
$375.00 set-up charge. No annual fee. $100.00 set-up per additional post office through same gateway. $4.00 per hour connect time. $25.00 minimum per month per post office, no message fee (one-minute increments). Includes registration of domain if requested. Other conditions apply. Call for details.

On-line Publishing Services:
Call for details.

Consulting Fees:
Phone consulting: $200.00 per hour. 20 minute minimum.
On Site: $200.00 per hour. 2 hour minimum.
Interactive Dialup: $1.25/hour
Dialup SLIP/PPP: $1.25/hour
Dialup UUCP: $2/hour
Extra login ID's over 4: $5 per ID.

For More Information

Telnet:	**Gopher:**
wimsey.com	wimsey.com

Login: **help**
Password: press **<enter>**

World Wide Web:
http://www.wimsey.com/

ALBERTA

Alberta SuperNet Inc.
Edmonton, Alberta
supernet.ab.ca

#325 Pacific Plaza
10909 Jasper Avenue
Edmonton, Alberta
T5J 3L9
Voice: (403) 441-3663
Fax: (403) 424-0743
Internet: info@supernet.ab.ca

Alberta SuperNet provides economical Internet access to the public.

Service Area:	Edmonton.
	Planning to expand to Calgary, Lethbridge, Red Deer and Medicine Hat.
1-800 Service:	No.

PDN Service:	No.
Connection via:	ARnet. 56Kbps.
Leased Line Service:	Yes. Up to 64Kbps. ISDN service will be available in January 1995.
Dedicated Dial-Up Service:	Yes.
SLIP/PPP Service:	Yes. SLIP and PPP. Freeware software provided.
UUCP Service:	Yes. Mail and news feeds. Newsgroup changes must go through a service person.
Interactive Accounts:	Yes. Direct connection to the Internet. Permanent storage available (amount varies with account type). Telnet, TN3270, FTP, Gopher, WAIS, World Wide Web (Lynx and other clients), Internet Relay Chat (ircII), Archie, MUD (tiny fugue). Menu-driven interface and shell access. QWK-, SOUP-, and ZIPNEWS compatible off-line readers supported.
Maximum Casual Dial-Up Speed:	19,200 bps (28,800 bps in January 1995).
USENET News:	Yes. Approximately 3,900 newsgroups. ClariNet news is available.
Local File Archives:	Yes. Utilities.
Domain Registration Service:	Yes. Full service.
Domain Park Service:	Yes.
Consulting Services:	Yes. Networking.
DNS Service:	Yes. Primary and secondary nameservers.
Commercial Traffic:	Call for information.

HOW TO SIGN UP

Registration is by telephone or fax. Please call or send electronic mail for information.

Rates

E-Mail Feed (UUCP):
$35.00/month plus installation fee.

USENET and E-Mail Feed (UUCP):
$75.00/month plus installation fee.

Host Dial-up Account with Unix Shell - Individual Server Plan:
Installation fee plus $10.00 month for 7 hours of connect time/month. Additional connect time is $12/hour from 7a.m. to 6p.m and $6.00/hour from 6p.m.-7a.m. 2 MB storage/user. Additional storage is $1.00/MB/day.

Host Dial-up Account with Unix Shell - Individual Gateway Plan:
Installation fee plus $30.00/month for 20 hours of connect time/month. Additional connect time is $3.00/hour. 5 MB storage/user. Additional storage is $1.00/MB/day.

Host Dial-up Account with Unix Shell - Group Terminal Access (1-5 Users):
Installation fee plus $100.00 per month includes 60 hours of connect time/month. Additional time is $3.00 per hour. 3 MB of storage per user. Additional storage is $1.00/MB/day.

Personal Network Connection - SLIP/PPP:
$60.00/month plus $5.00 per hour. Includes 20 free hours.

9600/14400 SLIP Dial-up - Dedicated Port:
$350.00 set-up fee plus $450.00 per month.

9.6KB SLIP Leased Line:
Installation fee plus $550.00 per month.

19.2KB SLIP Leased Line:
Installation fee plus $750.00 per month.

56KB Leased Line:
Installation fee plus $1500.00 per month.

For More Information:
World Wide Web:
http://www.supernet.ab.ca

ARnet
Edmonton, Alberta
arc.ab.ca

ARnet
c/o Alberta Research Council
Box 8330
Edmonton, Alberta
T6H 5X2
Voice: (403) 450-5189
           (403) 450-5197
Fax: (403) 461-2651
Internet: ARnet@arc.ab.ca
           penno@arc.ab.ca (Ralph Penno)

ARnet is a non-profit, provincial computer-based communications network, specifically oriented to meeting the needs of Alberta's research and education communities in both public and private sectors.

Service Area:	Lethbridge, Calgary, Alberta, Athabasca
	ARnet is planning to expand its service throughout the province.
1-800 Service:	No.
PDN Service:	No.
Connection via:	CA*net. 1.544Mbps.
Leased Line Service:	Yes. Up to 1.544Mbps. ISDN Service is available.
Dedicated Dial-Up Service:	Yes.
SLIP/PPP Service:	Yes. Dedicated service only.
UUCP Service:	No.
Interactive Accounts:	No.
Maximum Casual Dial-Up Speed:	N/A.
USENET News:	Yes. Full feed.

Local File Archives:	No.
Domain Registration Service:	Yes. Full service. Provided free-of-charge.
Domain Park Service:	Yes.
Consulting Services:	Yes. Network configuration, implementation, and setup.
DNS Service:	Yes. Secondary nameserver only.
Commercial Traffic:	Yes.

HOW TO SIGN UP

Call or send electronic mail for information.

Rates
Full Membership:
$42,400.00/year.

Associate Membership:
The fee is based on the speed of the connection line.

Line Speed:	Annual Fee:
9,600 bps	$5,000.00
19,200 bps	$5,000.00
56Kbps	$12,500.00
1.544Mbps	$42,400.00

CADVision Development Corp.

Calgary, Alberta
cadvision.com

Suite 1590
300 5th Avenue SW
Calgary, Alberta
T2P 3C4
Voice: (403) 777-1300
Fax: (403) 777-1319
Internet: info@cadvision.com

CADVision provides Internet business solutions to corporations. We help our clients maximize the potential of the Internet for their business. CADVision works with clients to identify how the Internet can be used in their organizations. CADVision provides the needs analysis studies, Internet connections, training, software, support, and virtual storefronts.

CADVision's focus is to create a professional image for our clientele. CADVision's objective is to be a turn-key solution provider. CADVision provides solutions, not just connections.

Service Area:	Calgary.
	Planning to expand to Victoria, Edmonton, Red Deer, Lethbridge, and Winnipeg.
1-800 Service:	Yes.
PDN Service:	No.
Connection via:	INSINC. T1.

Leased Line Service:	Yes. ISDN service is available.
Dedicated Dial-Up Service:	Yes.
SLIP/PPP Service:	Yes. SLIP and PPP. Commercial and shareware software is available to customers.
UUCP Service:	Yes. Mail and news feeds. Newsgroup changes must go through a service person. UUCP software is available to customers.
Interactive Accounts:	Yes. Direct connection to the Internet. 10 MB permanent storage per user. Extra storage space is available for $2.00/MB/month. Telnet, TN3270, FTP, Gopher, WAIS, World Wide Web, Internet Relay Chat, Archie, Finger, NSLOOKUP, WHOIS. Shell access. Qmodem communications software (shareware) is available to customers. E-mail-to-fax gateway for the local calling area.
Maximum Casual Dial-Up Speed:	28,800 bps.
USENET News:	Yes. 5,000 newsgroups.
Local File Archives:	No.
Domain Registration Service:	Yes. Full service. No charge for a dedicated line.
Domain Park Service:	Yes.
Consulting Services:	Yes. Needs analysis, tutorials, competitive intelligence services, developing implementation plans.
DNS Service:	Yes. Primary and secondary nameservers.
Commercial Traffic:	Yes.
Additional Comments:	CADVision has created a large virtual city on its network, which houses malls, parks, government, academia and schools.

HOW TO SIGN UP

Registration takes place over the telephone. Please call for information.

Rates

Personal Internet Connection - STANDARD:
Dial-up access to the Internet. $50.00 set-up fee. $50.00 monthly. $4.00 hourly. 1:12 modem:user ratio. 5 MB of storage. Bundled public domain software included in the installation fee. Trial period of 15 free hours. $50.00 discount on enrollment in CADVision's Internet Basics course.

Personal Internet Connection - PRO:
Same as standard package (above) but includes custom login ID's, helpline for two weeks, Chameleon TCP/IP software for Windows. $300.00 set-up fee. $65.00 monthly. $4.00 per hour. 10 MB of storage.

Dedicated Business Analog Internet Connection for Modems:
14,400 bps: $350.00 set-up fee. $350.00 monthly.
28,800 bps: $500.00 set-up fee. $450.00 monthly.

Dedicated Business Digital Internet Connection:
56Kbps: $800.00 set-up fee. $900.00 monthly.

ISDN Service:
$2,500.00 set-up fee. $1,200.00 monthly.

Internet Courses:
Call for pricing.

For More Information
World Wide Web:
http://www.cadvision.com/top.html

Calgary Unix Users' Group
Calgary, Alberta
cuug.ab.ca

300 5th Avenue SW, Suite 1590
Calgary, Alberta
T2P 3C4
Voice: (403) 265-2289
Fax: (403) 266-1804
Internet: postmaster@cuug.ab.ca

Objectives of the Calgary Unix Users' Group:

The Calgary Unix Users' Group will promote and increase the knowledge and understanding of Unix to its members and associates by:

(a) *Collaborating with universities, colleges, technical institutions and any other special-interest groups.*

(b) *Publishing and distributing technical and other information such as public domain software.*

(c) *Exchanging information between members and other similar associations with emphasis on the use of electronic media such as mail or UUCP.*

(d) *Coordinating presentations on matters of interest to the association and its members.*

(e) *Developing an understanding of and promoting Unix in the community.*

(f) *Establishing technical competency through the development of a regular meeting program, sponsoring meetings, conferences, special technical sessions, and supporting special interest groups.*

Service Area:	Calgary.
1-800 Service:	No.
PDN Service:	No.
Connection via:	INSINC. 56Kbps.
Leased Line Service:	No.
Dedicated Dial-Up Service:	No.
SLIP/PPP Service:	Yes. SLIP and PPP. Public domain Unix software provided at no cost.
UUCP Service:	Yes. Mail and news feeds. Customers can automatically modify their own newsgroup subscriptions. Public domain Unix software supplied at no cost.
Interactive Accounts:	Yes. Direct connection to the Internet. Permanent storage space available. Mail, Telnet, TN3270, FTP, Gopher, WAIS, World Wide Web, Internet Relay Chat, Archie, MUD. Shell access.
Maximum Casual Dial-Up Speed:	14,400 bps.

USENET News:	Yes. 2,000 newsgroups.
Local File Archives:	Yes. Unix public domain: GNU, Net client/servers, X-windows.
Domain Registration Service:	No.
Domain Park Service:	Yes.
Consulting Services:	No.
DNS Service:	Yes.
Commercial Traffic:	Yes.
Additional Comments:	Users must be 18 years of age or older.
	CUUG is run entirely by volunteers. There were 925 members as of August 1994. CUUG is in its fifth year of operation.

HOW TO SIGN UP

Registration takes place over the telephone or in person. Please call for information.

Rates
Membership is $100.00 per year. Services are provided as a convenience to club members and no guarantees about services are offered.

For More Information
World Wide Web:
http://www.cuug.ab.ca:8001

CCI Networks
Edmonton, Alberta
ccinet.ab.ca

4130 - 95 Street
Edmonton, Alberta
T6E 6H5
Voice: (403) 450-6787
Fax: (403) 450-9143
Internet: info@ccinet.ab.ca

CCI Networks is Alberta's premier supplier of IP-level access to customers in the province. Our mission is to provide cost-effective, high-quality access to the Internet, backed up by excellence in customer support and training. The parent company, Corporate Computers, has been involved in selling, installing, and supporting computer systems and networks for more than 10 years. CCInet's long-term goal is to provide local-call dial-up access to the Internet for most Albertans.

Service Area:	Calgary and Edmonton.
	Expansion is planned to Fort McMurray, Grand Prairie, Medicine Hat and Lethbridge.
1-800 Service	No.
PDN Service:	No.

Connection via:	ARnet. 2*56Kbps.
Leased Line Service:	Yes. Up to 64Kbps. ISDN service is available.
Dedicated Dial-Up Service:	Yes.
SLIP/PPP Service:	Yes. SLIP and PPP. SLIP/PPP software is available from CCInet. Help sheets are supplied to help with the set-up of SLIP/PPP software.
UUCP Service:	Yes. Mail and News feeds. Newsgroup changes must go through a service person.
Interactive Accounts:	No.
Maximum Casual Dial-Up Speed:	14,400 bps (28,800 bps when the standard is ratified).
USENET News:	Yes. Approximately 3,800 newsgroups. ClariNet News is available. An AP ClariNet feed will be available to all subscribers in 1995.
Local File Archives:	Yes. Internet access software for Macintosh and Windows; other software for Macintosh and Windows users; documents relating to the Internet.
Domain Registration Service:	Yes. Full service. For dedicated and network connections, domain registration is provided at no additional cost. For other types of connections, a fee may apply. Call for details.
Domain Park Service:	Yes.
Consulting Services:	Yes. Set-up and maintenance of Macintosh, Windows, and Unix machines for e-mail and news. Hands-on training for all levels of Internet use from novice to expert.
DNS Service:	Yes. Primary and secondary nameservers.
Commercial Traffic:	Yes.
Other Comments:	CCInet has a significant long-term interest in providing access to the Internet for two distinct groups in Alberta - Education and Healthcare. Call CCInet for details about our projects in these areas.

HOW TO SIGN UP

On-line registration is not available. Call or send e-mail for information.

Rates

UUCP:
$40.00 registration fee. $20.00/month plus $2.00 per hour for bulk overnight news transfer. Up to six calls allowed during the daytime for low-volume e-mail transfer.

Shared SLIP/PPP:
$40.00 registration fee. $40.00/month plus $5.00 per hour of connect time. 15 free hours with an initial sign-up of four months. Registration fee is waived plus five additional free hours if customer takes hands-on Internet training course for $99.00.

Dedicated SLIP/PPP:
$350.00 registration fee. $450.00/month. No connect time charges.

Network Connection:
$750.00 registration fee plus $750.00/month for 56Kbps access. Customer supplies link and router on his or her premises. Call to discuss requirements.

For More Information
FTP:
ftp.ccinet.ab.ca
Directory: pub/CClnet

World Wide Web:
http://www.ccinet.ab.ca

Cybersurf Internet Access (CIA)
Calgary, Alberta
cia.com

Box 81–Bay 5
4404-12 Street N.E.
Calgary, Alberta
T2E 6K9
Voice: (403) 777-2000
Fax: (403) 777-2003
Internet: info@cia.com

Cybersurf's target market is the **average** *home user who wants to get set up on the Internet with ease. Cybersurf provides users with true, easy Windows access to the Internet, even if the user's machine cannot run Windows. Cybersurf's system does not run Unix anywhere. The customer types a single command at the DOS prompt, which evokes a pre-configured program that dials Cybersurf. Customers can run their own Windows environment directly connected to the Internet.*

Service Area:	Calgary.
1-800 Service:	No.
PDN Service:	No.
Connection via:	fONOROLA. 56Kbps.
Leased Line Service:	Yes.
Dedicated Dial-Up Service:	Yes.
SLIP/PPP Service:	No.
UUCP Service:	Yes.
Interactive Accounts:	Yes. 2 MB permanent storage per user. Additional storage costs $1.00/month/MB. Telnet, TN3270, FTP, Gopher, World Wide Web, Internet Relay Chat, Archie. Menu-driven interface or "point-and-click" graphical user interface. Pre-configured software is supplied to customers free of charge.
Maximum Casual Dial-Up Speed:	14,400 bps.
USENET News:	Yes. 5,500 newsgroups.
Local File Archives:	Yes. Windows freeware/shareware, games, drivers, popular shareware games for DOS.
Domain Registration Service:	No.
Domain Park Service:	No.

Consulting Services:	Yes. Helping businesses to understand how the Internet can be used in business; training end-users to effectively use their time on the Internet.
DNS Service:	No.
Commercial Traffic:	Yes.

HOW TO SIGN UP

Registration is over the telephone. Please call to register.

Rates
One-Time Sign-Up Fee:
$50.00. Includes manuals and software for home computer.
Subscription:
$300.00 per year. Includes 60 hours of connect time per month.
Dedicated Line:
$300.00 per month.

InterNode Networks
Calgary, Alberta
internode.net

112 Rivergreen Cr. SE
Calgary, Alberta
T2C 3V6
Voice: (403) 296-1190
Fax: (403) 279-9581
Internet: info@internode.net

InterNode Networks provides a variety of inexpensive Internet dial-up accounts in the Calgary area. We offer unlimited access SLIP or PPP connections for a flat monthly fee to businesses and individuals. Our Remote Access services allow Microsoft Windows for WorkGroup and Windows NT users to connect to our network using utilities built into the operating system. Users can then run programs from our server or download files by simply using the File Manager. MS Mail and multi-player games are supported. We specialize in entertainment, education and multi-player games.

Service Area:	Calgary.
1-800 Service:	No.
PDN Service:	No.
Leased Line Service:	No.
Dedicated Dial-Up Service:	Yes.
SLIP/PPP Service:	Yes. SLIP and PPP. Shareware software is available for download.
UUCP Service:	Yes. Mail and news feeds. Newsgroup changes must go through a service person. Shareware UUCP software is available for download.
Interactive Accounts:	Yes. Direct connection to the Internet. 5 MB of permanent storage per user. Additional storage is available for $2.00/MB/month. Mail, Telnet, FTP, Gopher, WAIS, World Wide Web (Lynx), Internet Relay Chat, Archie, MUD (Tinymud etc.). Shell access.

Maximum Casual Dial-Up Speed:	28,800 bps.
USENET News:	Yes. Full feed.
Local File Archives:	Yes. Internet client software. Internet utility software.
Domain Registration Service:	Yes. Limited service. $40.00 fee.
Domain Park Service:	Call for information.
Consulting Services:	No.
DNS Service:	Yes. Primary and secondary nameservers.
Commercial Traffic:	Yes.

HOW TO SIGN UP

Registration is over the telephone. Call to register.

Rates
UUCP:
$50.00 set-up. $20.00 for 25 newsgroups.
SLIP (1 User):
$25.00 set-up. $15.00 monthly fee. No hourly charges.
SLIP (Family):
$25.00 set-up. $25.00 monthly fee. No hourly charges.
SLIP (Businesses):
$25.00 set-up. $40.00 monthly fee. No hourly charges.
Interactive Host:
$25.00 set-up. $15.00 monthly fee. No hourly charges.
Remote Access:
$25.00 set-up. $15.00 monthly fee. No hourly charges.
Mail Only:
$25.00 set-up. $5.00 monthly fee.

For More Information
FTP: **World Wide Web:**
ftp.internode.net   http://www.internode.net

The Network Centre
Calgary, Alberta
tnc.com

300, 555 4th Avenue S.W.   BKB Engineering
Calgary, Alberta   11211 76th Avenue
T2P 3E7   Edmonton, Alberta
Voice: (403) 262-3880   T6G 0K2
Fax: (403) 266-1837   Voice: (403) 438-2531
Internet: tncinfo@tnc.com

The Network Centre, established by a group of information technology specialists, provides wide-area data and internetworking services to the Alberta business community. We provide complete networked communications solutions including direct and dial-up Internet connections. Our seasoned staff work with our customers to ensure that business objectives are achieved through cost-efficient and effective use of the latest communications technology.

Service Area:	Edmonton, Calgary.
1-800 Service:	No.
PDN Service:	Yes. Datapac.
Connection via:	fONOROLA. 56Kbps.
Leased Line Service:	Yes. 9,600 bps - T1. ISDN service is available in Calgary only.
Dedicated Dial-Up Service:	Yes.
SLIP/PPP Service:	Yes. SLIP and PPP. Commercial software is available for purchase.
UUCP Service:	No.
Interactive Accounts:	No.
Maximum Casual Dial-Up Speed:	14,400 bps.
USENET News:	Yes. Full feed. ClariNet News is available.
Local File Archives:	No.
Domain Registration Service:	Yes. Full service. Call for pricing.
Domain Park Service:	Yes.
Consulting Services:	Yes. Internet connectivity, applications, and information retrieval; business on the Internet; Wide Area Networking.
DNS Service:	Yes. Primary and secondary nameservers.
Commercial Traffic:	Yes.

HOW TO SIGN UP
Registration is over the telephone. Call to register.

Rates
Call for current pricing.

Telnet Canada Enterprises, Ltd.
Calgary, Alberta
tcel.com

Penthouse
1812, 4th Street SW
Calgary, Alberta
T2S 1W1
Voice: (403) 245-1882
Fax: (403) 228-9702
Internet: info@tcel.com

Telnet Canada Enterprises is committed to providing affordable Internet connections, education and consulting services, and marketing facilities to users of the Internet. From casual dial-up to dedicated connections, and marketing services from our server, or yours, we provide Internet solutions, not just Internet service.

Service Area:	Calgary.
	Planning to expand to Regina, Saskatoon, Winnipeg, Vancouver, Edmonton, Red Deer.
1-800 Service:	No.
PDN Service:	No.
Connection via:	INSINC. 56Kbps. T1 as of January 1995.
Leased Line Service:	Yes. Up to 56Kbps. T1 in January 1995. ISDN service is available.
Dedicated Dial-Up Service:	Yes.
SLIP/PPP Service:	Yes. SLIP and PPP. Freeware/shareware software provided to customers at no charge.
UUCP Service:	Yes. Mail and news feeds. Newsgroup changes must go through a service person. MKS Internet Anyware is available for purchase.
Interactive Accounts:	Yes. Direct connection to the Internet. 1024 KB of permanent storage per user. Additional storage is available for $20.00/MB/month. Telnet, TN3270, FTP, Gopher, World Wide Web (Lynx), Internet Relay Chat, Archie. Menu-driven interface or shell access.
Maximum Casual Dial-Up Speed:	28,800 bps.
USENET News:	Yes. 6,000 newsgroups. ClariNet News is available.
Local File Archives:	Yes. Internet access tools.
Domain Registration Service:	Yes. Full service. $75.00 fee.
Domain Park Service:	Yes.
Consulting Services:	Yes. Internet security/firewalls, Internet marketing strategies, WAN planning and implementation, e-mail system integration, LAN-Internet integration.
DNS Service:	Yes. Primary and secondary nameservers.
Commercial Traffic:	Yes.

HOW TO SIGN UP

Registration is over the telephone. Call to register.

Rates
From $14.95 per month for casual dial-up.
From $250.00 per month for dedicated access.

For More Information

FTP:	**Gopher:**	**World Wide Web:**
ftp.tcel.com	*gopher.tcel.com*	*http://www.tcel.com*
Directory: pub/info		

WorldGate

Edmonton, Alberta
worldgate.edmonton.ab.ca

16511 - 85 Avenue
Edmonton, Alberta
T5R 4A2
Voice: (403) 481-7579
Fax: (403) 444-7720
Internet: info@worldgate.edmonton.ab.ca

WorldGate was started to provide the people of Edmonton with reasonably-priced access to the Internet. We currently provide a very well-rounded shell-level (dumb terminal) environment, and plan to upgrade our network link to ISDN and provide SLIP/PPP service.

Service Area:	Edmonton local calling area.
1-800 Service:	No.
PDN Service:	No.
Connection via:	CCInet. 28Kbps.
Leased Line Service:	Planned for January 1995. ISDN service planned for January 1995.
Dedicated Dial-Up Service:	Yes.
SLIP/PPP Service:	Planned for October 1994.
UUCP Service:	Yes. Mail and news feeds. Newsgroup changes must go through a service person. Shareware UUCP software (UUCP) is available on-line.
Interactive Accounts:	Yes. Direct connection to the Internet. 5 MB of permanent storage per user. Additional storage space is available for $5.00/MB/year. Mail, Telnet, FTP, Gopher, WAIS, World Wide Web (Lynx), Internet Relay Chat, Hytelnet, Archie. Menu-driven interface or shell access. Freeware/shareware communications software (Kermit (DOS) and Mac-Layers are available for download). QWK-, SOUP-, and ZipNews compatible off-line readers are supported.
Maximum Casual Dial-Up Speed:	28,800 bps.
USENET News:	Yes. 3,414 newsgroups.
Local File Archives:	Yes.
Domain Registration Service:	Yes. Full service. $20.00 per hour.
Domain Park Service:	No.
Consulting Services:	Yes. Wide area network connectivity for individuals and small businesses. "Free UNIX" (Linux and FreeBSD) consultation and administration. WorldGate sells and administers PC-based TCP/IP router devices and preconfigured BSD/386, FreeBSD, and Linux PCs.
DNS Service:	Primary and secondary nameservers planned for October 1994.

Commercial Traffic:	Yes.

HOW TO SIGN UP

Registration takes place over the telephone. Please call to register.

Rates
PERSONAL TERMINAL ACCOUNTS:
All new accounts are charged a one-time set-up fee of $20.00.
Occasional Use:
$10.00 per month. Includes 10 hours on-line per month.
Additional time is $2.00 per hour.
Moderate Use:
$25.00 per month. Includes 30 hours on-line time per month.
Additional time is $2.00 per hour.
Frequent Use:
$35.00 per month or $150.00 every 6 months. Includes 50 hours on-line time per month.
Additional time is $2.00 per hour.
Unlimited Use:
$130.00 per month or $550.00 every 6 months. Unlimited time.
GROUP RATES:
Individual Accounts:
Groups of 3 or more members receive a discount of 30% on individual accounts.
Dedicated Line:
$200.00 per month or $840.00 every six months. The group is assigned a modem and a single dedicated phone number. Time is unlimited. Perfect for small businesses.

For More Information
FTP:
valis.worldgate.edmonton.ab.ca
Directory: pub/worldgate
Telnet:
valis.worldgate.edmonton.ab.ca
*Login: **new***
Gopher:
valis.worldgate.edmonton.ab.ca
World Wide Web:
http://valis.worldgate.edmonton.ab.ca/

SASKATCHEWAN

SASK#net
Saskatoon, Saskatchewan
Regina, Saskatchewan
sasknet.sk.ca

SASK#net
Computing Services
Room 56, Physics Building
University of Saskatchewan
Saskatoon, Saskatchewan
S7N 0W0
Voice: (306) 966-4817 (Saskatoon)
              (306) 585-4023 (Regina)
Fax: (306) 966-4938

Internet: consulting@usask.ca (Saskatoon - Help Desk)
exner@max.uregina.ca (Regina - Art Exner)

SASK#net provides Internet access within Saskatchewan.

Service Area:	Prince Albert, Regina, Saskatoon.
1-800 service:	No.
PDN Service:	No.
Connection via:	CA*net. T1.
Leased Line Service:	Yes. Up to T1. ISDN service is available.
Dedicated Dial-Up Service:	Yes.
SLIP/PPP Service:	Yes. SLIP and PPP. Software supplied to PC and Macintosh customers.
UUCP Service:	No.
Interactive Accounts:	Yes. Direct connection to the Internet. 10 MB permanent storage/user (fixed - not expandable). Telnet, TN3270, FTP, Gopher, WAIS, World Wide Web (Lynx), Hytelnet, Archie. Menu-driven interface and shell access. Kermit communications software supplied at no cost.
Maximum Casual Dial-Up Speed:	14,400 bps.
USENET News:	Yes. Full feed.
Local File Archives:	No.
Domain Registration Service:	Yes. Full service. No charge.
Domain Park Service:	No.
Consulting Services:	Yes. One day of consulting is provided to potential customers at no cost. SASK#net will assist customers in choosing the hardware and software required to connect to SASK#net.
DNS Service:	Yes. Primary and secondary nameservers.
Commercial Traffic:	Yes.

HOW TO SIGN UP

On-line registration is not available. Please call for information on registration procedures.

Rates
Dedicated Access:
The annual membership fee ranges from $3,700 (9,600 bps access, 1-10 people in the organization) to $99,700 (256Kbps access, 2001-4000 people in the organization). Some conditions apply. The annual membership fee is based on the speed of the connection (9,600 bps - 256Kbps) and the size of the organization making the connection. There is no connection-time charge.

Shared Access Service:
Shared access service is not sensitive to organizational size. Regardless of organization size, 9,600 bps (or less) dial-in service is $30.00 per month plus $3.00 per hour after the first two hours per month. This provides an account on a SASK#net Unix server. There is a $100.00 set-up charge.
SLIP/PPP:
$20.00 per month. POP mail services are available for SLIP/PPP customers for an additional $10.00 per month.

For More Information
FTP:
ftp.usask.ca
Directory: pub/net-info/sasknet

Gopher:
gopher.usask.ca
Choose Computing
Choose SASK#net

UNIBASE Telecomm Ltd.
Regina, Saskatchewan
unibase.com

3002 Harding Street
Regina, Saskatchewan
S4V 0Y4
Voice: (306) 789-9007
Fax: (306) 761-1831
Internet: leigh@unibase.unibase.com (Leigh Calnek)

UNIBASE Telecomm Ltd. focusses on providing Internet access to schools, small libraries, and a variety of not-for-profit agencies. It currently operates 23 sites located in New York, Saskatchewan, and Manila. It attempts to provide Internet access to organizations that do not have the technical support or resources but do have a definite need for access to resources and communications tools.

Service Area:	Regina, Saskatoon, Prince Albert.
	Planning to expand to Moose Jaw and Yorkton/Melville.
1-800 Service:	No.
PDN Service:	Yes. Datapac.
Connection via:	INSINC. 56Kbps.
Leased Line Service:	Yes. 9600 bps - 56Kbps.
Dedicated Dial-Up Service:	Yes.
SLIP/PPP Service:	Yes. SLIP only.
UUCP Service:	Yes. Mail and news feeds. Newsgroup changes must go through a service person.
Interactive Accounts:	Yes. Direct connection to the Internet. Permanent storage space. Mail, Telnet, TN3270, FTP, Gopher, WAIS, World Wide Web (Lynx), MUD (tiny fugue). Unichat is also available (network-wide interactive conference software similar to Internet Relay Chat). Menu-driven interface and shell access. Local and international e-mail-to-fax gateway.
Maximum Casual Dial-Up Speed:	28,800 bps.

USENET News:	Yes. Satellite feed.
Local File Archives:	Yes. Public domain software.
Domain Registration Service:	Yes. Full service.
Domain Park Service:	Yes.
Consulting Services:	Yes. Limited to network users. Internet connectivity and training.
DNS Service:	Yes. Primary and secondary nameservers.
Commercial Traffic:	Yes.

HOW TO SIGN UP

INTERNET:
Regina: Telnet to **unibase.unibase.com**, login as **bbs**, no password required.
Saskatoon: Telnet to **bailey2.unibase.sk.ca**, login as **bbs**, no password required.
Prince Albert: Telnet to **gdipa.unibase.sk.ca**, login as **bbs**, no password required.

MODEM:
All numbers accept a login of "bbs"

Regina:
(306) 789-0709, 9600 bps
(306) 789-0715, 9600 bps, PEP
(306) 789-0729, 14400 bps
(306) 761-2482, 14400 bps
(306) 761-1384, 9600 bps
(306) 761-2958, 14400 bps

Saskatoon:
(306) 652-9491, 9600 bps
(306) 652-9492, 9600 bps
(306) 652-9493, 14000 bps

Prince Albert:
(306) 922-8800, 2400 bps

Rates
Single User Dial-in:
$25.00 per month
Education SLIP:
$250.00 per month
Commercial SLIP:
$300.00 per month

For More information
Telnet:
unibase.unibase.com
Login: **netguest** (15 min. Browse period)

Gopher:
unibase.unibase.com

World Wide Web:
http://cdrom1.unibase.com/welcom.html

MANITOBA

MBnet
Winnipeg, Manitoba
MBnet.MB.CA

MBnet
c/o Computer Services
University of Manitoba

15 Gillson Street
Winnipeg, Manitoba
R3T 2N2
Voice: (204) 474-7235
Fax: (204) 275-5420
Internet: info@MBnet.MB.CA

MBnet is Manitoba's regional data network, supporting education, research and development, and technology transfer. It is currently administered by the University of Manitoba.

Service Area:	Winnipeg.
1-800 Service:	No.
PDN Service:	Yes. Datapac.
Connection via:	CA*net. 1.544 Mbps.
Leased Line Service:	Yes. Up to 1.544 Mbps. ISDN service planned for late 1994.
Dedicated Dial-Up Service:	Yes.
SLIP/PPP Service:	Yes. SLIP and PPP.
UUCP Service:	Yes. Mail and news feeds.
Interactive Accounts:	Yes. Direct connection to the Internet. Menu-driven system. Shell access. 2MB permanent storage/user. $3.00 for each additional MB of storage. Telnet, TN3270, FTP, Gopher, WAIS, World Wide Web, Hytelnet, Archie, Internet Relay Chat. QWK-compatible off-line readers supported. E-mail-to-fax gateway for the local calling area.
Maximum Casual Dial-Up Speed:	14,400 bps.
USENET News:	Yes. Approximately 4300 newsgroups.
Local File Archives:	Yes.
Domain Registration Service:	Yes. Full service. $100.00 fee.
Domain Park Service:	Yes.
Consulting Services:	No.
DNS Service:	Yes. Primary and secondary nameservers.
Commercial Traffic:	Yes.

HOW TO SIGN UP

INTERNET:
*Telnet to **access.mbnet.mb.ca**, login as **guest**, no password required*

MODEM:
Set your communications software to VT100, 8 data bits, 1 stop bit
(204) 275-6100, 2400 bps

(204) 474-7100, 9600/14,400 bps

Press <return> once connected.
At the Enter classname prompt, type mbnet and press <return>
At the login: prompt, type guest and press <return>
There is a menu item for registering online.

Rates
Dial-up accounts (individuals):
$25.00 one-time registration fee (includes 5 hours of connect time for exploration). $50.00/year for 25 hours of connect time and 2MB of disk space. Additional connect time is $1.00/hour. Additional disk space is $3.00/MB.

Dial-up accounts (Business or Organization):
$100.00 one-time charge for domain name set-up and all user accounts (includes 20 hours of connect time for exploration). There is no registration fee. Account charges are the same as for individual accounts. The initial connect time allocation for each user account is shared among all users. An account may be set up to be polled via UUCP. A UUCP account has a $50.00/year surcharge.

Datapac access is provided for users at a surcharge of $5.00/hour of connect time. This applies to all connect time including the initial allocation.

Direct Network Connection:
A direct connection has two cost components. A port charge and access charges.
(i) Port Charge
  $3,000.00 per year for a leased synchronous line. The user pays for the communication line and modems. 56Kbps to 1.5 Mbps lines are supported.
  $1,500.00/year for an asynchronous dial port. This covers the cost of the modem and dedicated phone line located at the MBnet node. V.32(bis)/V.42(bis) modems are used.
(ii) Access Charges
  Access charges are based on the number of potential MBnet users. The number would be the total of all users with permission to use Internet-connected computers. Fees range from $3,000/year (25 users on a 56Kbps line to $26,000/year (8000 users on a 1.544 Mbps line).

For More Information
Telnet:
access.mbnet.mb.ca
Login: guest

Gopher:
gopher.mbnet.mb.ca

World Wide Web:
http://www.mbnet.mb.ca

Winnipeg PC User Group Inc.
Winnipeg, Manitoba
wpcusrgrp.mb.ca

P.O. Box 3149
Winnipeg, Manitoba
R3C 4E6
Voice: (204) 488-9796
Internet: roger.buchanan@wpcusrgrp.mb.ca (Roger Buchanan)

The Winnipeg PC User Group is a non-profit organization with many benefits for its over 1,300 members. These benefits include a 32-page newsletter; the multi-line, high-speed BBS; the monthly meeting; special interest groups; and the group's purchasing power. All these benefits bring substantial value to a user's membership. The Winnipeg PC User Group is an organization that is dedicated to helping people get the most from their computer. Our motto sums it all up:

"Run by users, for the benefit of users"

Though we only provide dial-up mail service to the Internet, we offer many things to the user who wants an Internet account. We offer training on how to do things, from getting a unique account to working with the World Wide Web. We offer support to users so that they don't have to do it themselves.

Service Area:	Winnipeg.
1-800 Service:	No.
PDN Service:	No.
Connection via:	MBnet. 14,400 bps.
Leased Line Service:	No.
Dedicated Dial-Up Service:	No.
SLIP/PPP Service:	No.
UUCP Service:	No.
Interactive Accounts:	Yes. Gateway connection to the Internet. Internet mail (via gateway to PC Board).
Maximum Casual Dial-Up Speed:	19,200 bps.
USENET News:	No.
Local File Archives:	Yes. Patches, games, drivers.
Domain Registration Service:	No.
Domain Park Service:	No.
Consulting Service:	Yes. General Internet help.
DNS Service:	No.
Commercial Traffic:	Yes.

HOW TO SIGN UP

MODEM:
*(204) 958-7280, 14,400 bps, login as "**new user**", no password required*
*(204) 958-7285, 14,400 bps, login as "**new user**", no password required*

Rates
$45.00 for a one-year membership.

ONTARIO

Achilles Internet
Gloucester, Ontario
achilles.net

Dennis J. Hutton Associates Ltd.
1810 Thornecrest
Gloucester, Ontario
K1C 6K7
Voice: (613) 830-5426
Fax: (613) 824-2342
Internet: office@dragon.achilles.net

Achilles Internet is bringing dial-up Internet access as well as 14,400 bps and 28,800 bps access into an affordable price range. We have equipped our facilities with the specialized hardware needed to do the job reliably, and we do not believe in cutting corners on reliability or accessibility.

Service Area:	Gloucester, Ottawa, Nepean, Kanata, Alymer, Hull, Gatineau.
1-800 service:	No.
PDN Service:	No.
Connection via:	fONOROLA. 2*56Kbps.
Leased Line Service:	Yes. ISDN service is available.
Dedicated Dial-Up Service:	Yes.
SLIP/PPP Service:	Yes. SLIP and PPP.
UUCP Service:	Yes. Mail and news feeds. Newsgroup changes must go through a service person, but soon customers will be able to add and delete newsgroups automatically.
Interactive Accounts:	Yes. Direct connection to the Internet. 5 MB of permanent storage per user. Additional storage space is $1/MB/month. Mail, Telnet, FTP, Gopher, WAIS, World Wide Web (Lynx), Internet Relay Chat, Hytelnet, Archie, MUDs (lpmudr, tinyfugue, tt++). Menu driven interface and shell access. Communications software supplied free-of-charge (Telix for PC users, Z-term for Macintosh users). QWK-compatible off-line readers supported.
Maximum Casual Dial-Up Speed:	14,400 bps.
USENET News:	Yes. Approximately 4000 newsgroups.
Local File Archives:	Yes. Microsoft Windows Internet clients, Linux distributions, GNU source, and generic file archives.
Domain Registration Service:	Yes. Full service. $50.00 charge.
Domain Park Service:	Yes.
Consulting Services:	Yes. World Wide Web, WAIS, E-mail gateways, dedicated connections, network configuration and installations.

DNS Service:	Yes. Primary and secondary nameservers.
Commercial Traffic:	Yes. Commercial users must choose the Business Access plan.

HOW TO SIGN UP

On-line registration is not available. Call or send electronic mail for information.

Rates
Personal Access:
$250.00/year or $25.00/month paid bi-monthly. Includes 50 hours per month. Additional hours are $0.50/hour up to 100, and $1.00 per hour thereafter. 20:1 ratio maximum on large modem pool of 14,400 bps modems.

Business Access:
$500.00/year for the first account and $250.00 for each additional account, or $45.00/month per individual. Includes 50 hours per month. Additional hours are $0.50/hour up to 100 hours, and $1.00/hour thereafter.

Dedicated 14,400 bps Access:
$300.00/month. No start-up fee. User may supply approved modem. Typically a 1-2 day wait to go on-line.

Dedicated 28,800 bps Access:
$650.00/month. No start-up fee. Typically a 2-day wait period to go on-line.

For More Information
Gopher:
gopher.achilles.net

World Wide Web:
http://www.achilles.net

Babillard Synapse Inc.
Gatineau, Quebec
synapse.net

22 Beloeil
Gatineau, Quebec
J8T 7G3
Voice: (819) 561-1697
Fax: (613) 564-2924
Internet: daniel.coulombe@bbs.synapse.net

Babillard Synapse Inc. offers full Internet services to individuals or organizations in the Ottawa/Gatineau/Hull area.

Service Area:	Ottawa, Hull, Alymer, Kanata, Gloucester, Nepean, Cumberland.
1-800 service:	No.
PDN Service:	No.
Leased Line Service:	No.
Dedicated Dial-Up Service:	Yes.
SLIP/PPP Service:	Yes. SLIP and PPP. Freeware/shareware software supplied at no cost.
UUCP Service:	Yes. Mail and news feeds. UUCP-PC software supplied if required.

Interactive Accounts:	Yes. Direct connection to the Internet. 10 MB of permanent storage per user. Additional storage is available on request, at no cost, subject to space availability. Mail, Telnet, TN3270, FTP, Gopher, WAIS, World Wide Web (Lynx), Internet Relay Chat, Archie. Menu-driven interface to the Internet. Shareware communications software supplied to customers upon request (Telix, Intellicom).
Maximum Casual Dial-Up Speed:	14,400 bps.
USENET News:	Yes. 7,000 newsgroups.
Local File Archives:	Yes. General interest files. Text files related to the Internet.
Domain Registration Service:	Yes. Full service. $10.00 charge.
Domain Park Service:	No.
Consulting Services:	No.
DNS Service:	Yes. Primary and secondary nameservers.
Commercial Traffic:	Yes.

HOW TO SIGN UP

MODEM:
*(819) 561-4321, V.32bis, login as **INTERNET SERVICE**, password is **REGISTER***

Rates
Individual BBS Accounts:
$1.00 per hour. Payable in advance in $15.00 (minimum) increments.
*Includes terminal access to the Internet via the BBS *Uniboard).*
Individual SLIP Accounts:
Monthly flat rate of $25.00, including the first 100 hours of access. Additional hours are available for $0.25 per hour. No set-up fee. Maximum monthly charge of $200.00.
Corporate Dedicated Line Accounts:
Initial set-up fee of $250.00. Monthly flat rate of $250.00.
UUCP Accounts:
Initial set-up fee of $25.00. Minimum monthly charge of $10.00, which includes the first 10 hours of access. Additional hours are $1.00 per hour.

For More Information
FTP:
ftp.synapse.net

Baudeville BBS
Scarborough, Ontario
bville.gts.org

Ian Evans Communications
4352 Kingston Road
Box 1135
Scarborough, Ontario
M1E 2M8
Internet: info@bville.gts.org

Baudeville BBS is known to its members as The Economical E-mail Emporium. It provides access to 2300+ USENET newsgroups as well as over 2000 message areas in other e-mail networks.

Service Area:	Metropolitan Toronto.
1-800 Service:	No.
PDN Service:	No.
Leased Line Service:	No.
Dedicated Dial-Up Service:	No.
SLIP/PPP Service:	No.
UUCP Service:	No.
Interactive Accounts:	Yes. Gateway connection to the Internet. No local storage. Users can send and receive Internet mail. Menu-driven interface. QWK-based off-line readers are supported.
Maximum Casual Dial-Up Speed:	28,800 bps.
USENET News:	Yes. 2300+ newsgroups.
Local File Archives:	Yes. Over 1 gigabyte of DOS, Windows, and OS/2 files.
Domain Registration Service:	No.
Domain Park Service:	No.
Consulting Services:	No.
DNS Service:	No.
Commercial Traffic:	Certain areas only.

HOW TO SIGN UP

Modem:
(416) 283-0114, v.32bis, login using your real name

Rates
$36.00 per year for 1 hour and 1 MB of files daily
$48.00 per year for 2 hours and 4 MB of files daily

CRS Online
Etobicoke, Ontario
canrem.com

24-12 Steinway Blvd.
Etobicoke, Ontario
M9W 6M5
Voice: (416) 213-6000
          1-800-563-2529

Fax: (416) 213-6038
Internet: info@canrem.com

CRS Online provides value-added access to on-line information and the Internet. Our powerful Windows client software, FRONTIER, makes the usually technical task of setting up a direct Internet connection a simple one-minute installation. CRS also provides, at no extra charge, access to a vast software library, Reuters and UPI news feeds, and stock market results. Free seminars and telephone support are provided to help our users get the most out of their on-line time.

Service Area:	Hamilton, Stoney Creek, Dundas, Lynden, Brantford, Burlington, Milton, Caledon East, Orangeville, Hespeler, Guelph, Kitchener-Waterloo, Brampton, Georgetown, Toronto and surrounding areas, Aurora, Newmarket, Barrie, Moonstone, Orillia, Midland, Ajax, Oshawa, Bowmanville.
	Planning to expand to the Niagara region and London and Ottawa in the first half of 1995.
1-800 service:	No.
PDN Service:	Yes. Datapac and INET 2000.
Connection via:	UUNET Canada. 128Kbps.
Leased Line Service:	No.
Dedicated Dial-Up Service:	No.
SLIP/PPP Service:	Yes. FRONTIER software uses a PPP connection. FRONTIER software is supplied free-of-charge to subscribers.
UUCP Service:	No.
Interactive Accounts:	No.
Maximum Casual Dial-Up Speed:	28,800 bps.
USENET News:	Yes. Full feed.
Local File Archives:	Yes. Public domain archive of over 100,00 files for all computer types.
Domain Registration Service:	No.
Domain Park Service:	No.
Consulting Services:	No.
DNS Service:	No.
Commercial Traffic:	Yes.
Additional Comments:	FRONTIER software is a powerful client tool that integrates access to all basic Internet functions (news, mail, Gopher, World Wide Web, Archie, WAIS etc.).

HOW TO SIGN UP

INTERNET:
*Telnet to **canrem.com** (no login or password required)*

MODEM:
(416) 213-6004 (V.32, V.32bis, V.34, V.FC)

Rates
FRONTIER ACCESS:
$40.00 per year, with time purchased in blocks. Block time does not expire. It is not a monthly amount that is lost if unused.
10 hours: $20.00
25 hours: $40.00
50 hours: $75.00

1-month Trial Subscription:
$15.00 (includes 5 hours and FRONTIER access)

For More Information
Gopher:	Telnet:
canrem.com	*canrem.com (no login or password required)*

CIMtegration Inc.
Toronto, Ontario
cimtegration.com

4850 Keele Street
North York, Ontario
M3J 3K1
Voice: (416) 665-3566
Fax: (416) 554-1815
Internet: info@cimtegration.com

CIMtegration provides complete Internet services. In addition to providing Internet access services for both commercial and consumer customers, we offer full consulting services including Internet software installation and configuration and custom programming services.

Service Area:	Toronto and surrounding area.
1-800 service:	No.
PDN Service:	No.
Leased Line Service:	No.
Dedicated Dial-Up Service:	Yes.
SLIP/PPP Service:	Yes. PPP service only. PPP software is supplied for $150.00 (Frontier Technology Super Highway Access).
UUCP Service:	Yes. E-mail feeds only.
Interactive Accounts:	Yes. Direct connection to the Internet. 500 Kb permanent storage space per user. Extra storage space is $4/MB/month. Shell access. Mail, Telnet, FTP, WAIS, World Wide Web (Lynx), Internet Relay Chat, Archie. Kermit communications software supplied at no charge.

Maximum Casual Dial-Up Speed:	28.800 bps.
USENET News:	Yes. Full feed.
Local File Archives:	Yes. Games, PC software, popular public domain and shareware software for PC and Unix platforms.
Domain Registration Service:	Yes. Full service. Fee is included as part of the Internet installation service.
Domain Park Service:	Yes.
Consulting Services:	Yes. Internet system installation for Unix platforms, network consulting services for TCP/IP environments, World Wide Web marketing services.
DNS Service:	Yes. Primary and secondary nameservers.
Commercial Traffic:	Call for information.

HOW TO SIGN UP:

MODEM:
*(416) 665-3669, 28,000 bps, login as **guest**, no password required.*

Rates
$20.00 per month at 14,400 bps (includes 4 hours connect time)
$30.00 per month at 28,800 bps (includes 4 hours connect time)

For More Information
FTP:
ftp.cimtegration.com

World Wide Web:
http://www.cimtegration.com

Ernst and Young Inc.
Montreal, Quebec
ey.ca, sobeco.com

1 Place Alexis Nihon
3400 De Maisonneuve Blvd. West
Montreal, Quebec
H3Z 3E8
Voice: (514) 935-5101
Fax: (514) 935-9008
Internet: lavalle@ey.ca (Mario Lavallee)
               stacy@sobeco.com (Stacy Millions)

Area Served: Toronto
See main entry under Province of Quebec

Fleximation Systems Inc.

Mississauga, Ontario
flexnet.com, flexnet.ca

1495 Bonhill Road
Units 1 and 2
Mississauga, Ontario
L5T 1M2
Voice: (905) 795-0300
               1-800-263-8733
Fax: (905) 795-0310
Internet: admin@flexnet.com

Fleximation's mission is to provide leading-edge quality system integration solutions that meet the needs of our present and future customers. Fleximation offers complete Internet connectivity solutions from dial-up to dedicated leased lines, as well as Internet marketing services.

Service Area:	Metropolitan Toronto and surrounding area.
	Planning to expand to Vancouver, Calgary, Winnipeg, Guelph, Kitchener, Ottawa, Montreal, and Halifax within the next year.
1-800 service:	Yes. $0.65 per minute.
PDN Service:	No.
Connection via:	fONOROLA. 128 Kbps.
Leased Line Service:	Yes. Up to 1.544 Mbps. ISDN service available.
Dedicated Dial-Up Service:	Yes.
SLIP/PPP Service:	Yes. SLIP and PPP. NetManage software supplied for an additional fee.
UUCP Service:	Yes.
Interactive Accounts:	No.
Maximum Casual Dial-Up Speed:	19,200 bps (28,800 bps as soon as the standard is ratified).
USENET News:	Yes. Approximately 2,500 newsgroups. ClariNet News is available.
Local File Archives:	No.
Domain Registration Service:	Yes. Full service. Free to customers with leased line service.
Domain Park Service:	Yes.
Consulting Services:	Yes. Internet services; LAN/WAN integration; Network Maintenance, management and monitoring; X.25 and Frame Relay connectivity; Electronic Data Interchange.
DNS Service:	Yes. Primary and secondary nameservers.
Commercial Traffic:	Yes.

HOW TO SIGN UP

INTERNET:
Telnet to **alfa.flexnet.com** *login as* **new**, *no password required.*

Rates
(1) Corporate On-Line
For users who require constant access with instant e-mail and database needs on a 24 hour, per day basis. Features include:

- *dial-up speeds up to 14,400 bps (customer ratio 1:1)*
- *Multiple user-ID's on the Internet*

Service Fee: $250.00/month (unlimited use per connection)
One-Time Set-Up Fee: $250.00

(2) Corporate Dial-Up
This package is for users who need access on an occasional basis and have limited users accessing the Internet. Features include:

- *dial-up speeds up to 14,400 bps (customer ratio of 1:10)*
- *multiple user-ID's on the Internet*

Service Fee: $60.00/month (includes 30 hours per month)
                                -or- $20.00 for 10 hours
One-Time Set-Up Fee: $50.00
Rate for Additional Hours: $2.00/hour between 8:00 a.m. and 6:00 p.m.
                                 $1.00/hour between 6:00 p.m. and 8:00 a.m.

(3) Corporate Custom
For customers with line speed requirements of 56Kbps or greater. Features include:

- *line speeds up to T1 (customer ratio 1:1)*
- *multiple user-ID's on the Internet*

Service Fee: Custom
One-Time Set-Up Fee: Custom
Rates for Additional Hours: Custom

For More Information

FTP:	Gopher:	World Wide Web:
ftp.flexnet.com	*gopher.flexnet.com*	*http://www.flexnet.com*

Global-X-Change Communications Inc.

Ottawa, Ontario
globalx.net

709-170 Laurier Avenue West
Ottawa, Ontario
K1P 5V5
Voice: (613) 235-6865
Fax: (613) 232-5285
Internet: info@globalx.net

Global-X-Change Communications Inc. strives to be the leading provider of innovative, customer-driven Internet business solutions. The company fosters the use of the Internet as a standard business tool by delivering Internet products and services to private and public sector individuals and organizations in the National Capital Region. Global-X-Change offerings include service bureau facilities, connectivity products and services, training, site configuration, graphics design and consulting.

Global-X-Change hosts GLOBAL MONITOR, Ottawa's definitive computer magazine on-line. Global-X-Change is also home to Ottawa's Silicon Valley North Hi-Tech Directory, a listing of over 500 high-tech firms in the National Capital Region.

Service Area:	Ottawa, Kanata, Nepean, Gloucester, Cumberland, Hull, Aylmer, Gatineau, Wakefield, Kemptville, Osgoode, Stittsville, Rockcliffe Park, Orleans
1-800 Service:	No.
PDN Service:	No.
Connection via:	INSINC 56Kbps.
Leased Line Service:	Yes. 14,400 bps - 56Kbps.
Dedicated Dial-Up Service:	Yes.
SLIP/PPP Service:	Yes. SLIP and PPP. Freeware/shareware software is provided to customers.
UUCP Service:	No.
Interactive Accounts:	No.
Maximum Casual Dial-Up Speed:	28,800 bps.
USENET News:	Yes. 6,500 newsgroups.
Local File Archives:	No.
Domain Registration Service:	Yes. Full service. $50.00 fee.
Domain Park Service:	No.
Consulting Services:	Yes. Site configuration, software installation, enterprise strategies, application development, business process design.
DNS Service:	Yes. Primary and secondary nameservers.
Commercial Traffic:	Yes.

HOW TO SIGN UP

Registration takes place over the telephone. Call to register.

Rates
From $0.68 per day and up. Call for complete pricing.

For More Information
World Wide Web:
http://www.globalx.net/

HookUp Communications
Oakville, Ontario
hookup.net

1075 North Service Road West
Suite 207
Oakville, Ontario, Canada
L6M 2G2
Voice: Toll-Free Canada-Wide: 1-800-363-0400
         Direct Dial: (905) 847-8000
Fax: (905) 847-8420
Internet: info@hookup.net

HookUp provides affordable, dial-up and digital access to the Internet. HookUp is proud of its leadership position in offering professional, best-value, full Internet access using the latest technology, security, and back-up systems.

Service Area:	56Kbps dedicated access across Canada. Local dial-up access in much of the 519, 416, 905, and 613 area codes.
1-800 Service:	Yes. Call for pricing.
PDN Service:	No.
Connection via:	Sprint. T1.
Leased Line Service:	Yes. 56Kbps - T1. ISDN service is available.
Dedicated Dial-Up Service:	Yes.
SLIP/PPP Service:	Yes. SLIP and PPP. Software is provided free of charge to customers (HookUp Dialer, developed in-house).
UUCP Service:	Yes. Mail and news feeds. Newsgroup changes must go through a service person.
Interactive Accounts:	Yes. Direct connection to the Internet. 1MB permanent storage/user. Additional storage space is available for $15/MB/yr. Mail, Telnet, FTP, Gopher, WAIS, World Wide Web, Internet Relay Chat, Hytelnet, Archie, MUD (tf). Shell access. QWK-compatible off-line readers supported.
Maximum Casual Dial-Up Speed:	14,400 bps.
USENET News:	Yes. 4,000+ newsgroups. ClariNet News is available.
Local File Archives:	Yes. Software for SLIP/PPP and Internet applications for most operating systems.
Domain Registration Service:	Yes. Full service. No charge.
Domain Park Service:	Yes.
Consulting Services:	Available in 2nd quarter 1995.
DNS Service:	Yes. Primary and secondary nameservers.
Commercial Traffic:	Yes.

HOW TO SIGN UP

Customers can register by telephone, fax, or electronic mail. Call or send electronic mail for information.

Rates

INDIVIDUAL PACKAGES

Residential Lite Plan:
$35.00 one-time set-up fee. $14.95/month for 5 hours of connect time per month. Additional hours are $3.00/hour.

Residential Plan:
$35.00 one-time set-up fee. $34.95/month for 15 hours of connect time per month. Additional hours are $1.00/hour.

Individual Access Plan:
$35.00 set-up fee. $299.95/year for 50 hours of connect time per month. Additional hours are $0.50/hour.

CORPORATE PACKAGES

Corporate Dial-up:
$50.00 one-time set-up fee. $59.95/month for 30 hours of connect time per month. Additional hours are $0.50/hour. Includes multiple user ID's on the Internet.

Corporate On-line:
$295.00 one-time set-up fee. $249.95/month (unlimited connection). Includes multiple user ID's on the Internet.

Corporate Custom:
Call for consultation. Packages are available for businesses requiring line speeds of 56k or greater and other custom set-ups, including custom applications.

For More Information

FTP:
ftp.hookup.net
Directory: pub/info

Gopher:
gopher.hookup.net

World Wide Web:
http://www.hookup.net

InaSec Inc.
Ottawa, Ontario
inasec.ca

29 Beechwood Avenue
Suite 320
Ottawa, Ontario
K1M 2M1
Voice: (613) 746-3200
Fax: (613) 747-2046
Internet: mike@inasec.ca (Michel Paradis)

InaSec Inc. provides LiveWire Online (adults only BBS) and GenX (teens only BBS) and many custom business/private solutions. InaSec Inc. also offers graphical (pictures) databases, on-line services/BBSes, as well as several other private on-line systems. We are establishing a physical presence in all major cities.

Service Area:	Major Canadian cities. Call for information.
1-800 Service:	No.

PDN Service:	Yes. Datapac.
Connection via:	fONOROLA.
Leased Line Service:	No.
Dedicated Dial-Up Service:	Yes.
SLIP/PPP Service:	Yes. SLIP and PPP. Shareware software is available to customers.
UUCP Service:	Yes. Available October 1994. Shareware software will be available to customers.
Interactive Accounts:	Yes. 5 MB permanent storage per user. Additional storage space is available if required (call for pricing), Mail, Telnet, FTP, Gopher, WAIS, World Wide Web, Internet Relay Chat, Archie, MUD (Tiny Fugue). Shell access. Off-line mail readers supported on the LiveWire Online system (off-line readers not supported on the Unix site). Shareware off-line readers are available to customers. E-mail-to-fax gateway for the local calling area.
Maximum Casual Dial-Up Speed:	28,800 bps.
USENET News:	Yes. 1000 newsgroups. Expanding to a full feed in Winter 1994.
Local File Archives:	Yes.
Domain Registration Service:	Yes. Limited service.
Domain Park Service:	Yes.
Consulting Services:	Yes. On-line services, custom on-line services, graphical databases, networking.
DNS Service:	Yes. Primary and secondary nameservers.
Commercial Traffic:	Yes.

HOW TO SIGN UP

Registration takes place on-line or over the telephone.

INTERNET:
Telnet to **198.53.239.3** *(LiveWire Online), login as* **guest**, *no password required*

MODEM:
(613) 746-2001 (LiveWire Online), 14,400 bps
(613) 746-7007 (GenX), 14,400 bps

Rates
Full Internet account - $25.00 per 30 days.

For More Information
FTP:
inasec.ca
File: InaSec_Info.README

Gopher:
inasec.ca

InfoRamp Inc.
Toronto, Ontario
inforamp.net

134 Adelaide Street East
Suite 207
Toronto, Ontario
M5C 1K9
Voice: (416) 363-9100
Fax: (416) 363-3551
Internet: staff@inforamp.net

InfoRamp's mission is to provide the best Internet service possible. As a service company, InfoRamp is constantly investing in new ways to improve our service, to implement new technologies, and to make your time on the network more enjoyable and more productive. As part of our service commitment, we strive to provide you with tools which simplify the use of the Internet, the power and resources which allow you to make effective use of the Internet, and friendly customer support to answer your questions whenever necessary. Customers receive a free copy of Pipeline, an award-winning graphical interface to the Internet. Pipeline is the winner of the PC Magazine Network Edition Editor's Choice Award for interfaces to the Internet.

Service Area:	Toronto and surrounding area.
	Planning to expand nation-wide by mid-1995.
1-800 Service:	No.
PDN Service:	No.
Connection via:	fONOROLA. 56Kbps.
Leased Line Service:	No.
Dedicated Dial-Up Service:	Yes.
SLIP/PPP Service:	Planned for 4th quarter, 1994.
UUCP Service:	No.
Interactive Accounts:	Yes. Direct connection to the Internet. 5 MB permanent storage per user. Users can buy additional disk space for $1.00/MB/month. Mail, Telnet, FTP, Gopher, WAIS, World Wide Web (Lynx), Internet Relay Chat, Archie. A Mosaic-style client will be available in the third quarter of 1994. All customers receive a free copy of either Pipeline for Windows or Pipeline for Macintosh. This software includes terminal emulation along with an easy-to-use, powerful point-and-click interface. The Pipeline software allows mail and FTP transfers to go directly to the customer's desktop computer. Shell access or point-and-click graphical interface. Pipeline supports off-line mail and news reading using a friendly graphical user interface.
Maximum Casual Dial-Up Speed:	19,200 bps.
USENET News:	Yes. 8,000+ newsgroups. ClariNet News is available.
Local File Archives:	Yes. Archives of popular shareware programs are planned.
Domain Registration Service:	Yes. Limited service. No charge.

Domain Park Service:	Yes.
Consulting Services:	No.
DNS Service:	Primary and secondary nameservers.
Commercial Traffic:	Yes.

HOW TO SIGN UP

Registration takes place over the telephone. Please call to register.

Rates
One-time connect fee of $35.00. $29.95 per month for 25 hours or $19.95 per month for 5 hours. Additional hours are $1.50 each.

For More Information

Gopher:	*E-mail:*	*World Wide Web:*
inforamp.net	*info@inforamp.net (automatic reply)*	*http://www.inforamp.net*

Interlog Internet Services

Toronto, Ontario
interlog.com

1235 Bay Street
Suite 400
Toronto, Ontario, Canada
M5R 3K4
Voice: (416) 975-2655
Fax: (416) 975-2655
Internet: internet@interlog.com

Interlog's mission is to provide low-cost, reliable connectivity to the Internet for individuals and businesses. We provide an AUP-free environment, and place absolutely no restrictions on the use or content of the connections we provide. We work to provide the best possible user support. Our goal is to keep end-user costs as low as possible while ensuring reliable service.

Service Area:	Metropolitan Toronto.
1-800 service:	No.
PDN Service:	No.
Connection via:	fONOROLA. 56Kbps.
Leased Line Service:	Yes. ISDN service is available.
Dedicated Dial-Up Service:	Yes.
SLIP/PPP Service:	Yes. SLIP and PPP. Freeware/shareware software is provided to customers.
UUCP Service:	No.

Interactive Accounts:	Yes. Direct connection to the Internet. 2 MB permanent storage per user. Additional storage is available for $0.50/MB/month. Mail, Telnet, TN3270, FTP, Gopher, WAIS, World Wide Web (Lynx), Internet Relay Chat, Hytelnet, Archie. Shell access. QWK- and SOUP-compatible off-line readers are supported.
Maximum Casual Dial-Up Speed:	14,400 bps.
USENET News:	Yes. 9400 newsgroups.
Local File Archives:	Yes. Internet-related software for DOS, Macintosh, and Windows.
Domain Registration Service:	Yes. Full service. No charge.
Domain Park Service:	Yes.
Consulting Services:	Yes. Complete turn-key Internet connection solutions. Security, training, system administration, network connectivity.
Nameserver Service:	Yes. Primary and secondary nameservers.
Commercial Traffic:	Yes.

HOW TO SIGN UP

Registration is available on-line.

MODEM:
*(416) 515-1414, v.32bis, login as **guest**, no password required*

INTERNET:
*Telnet to **gold.interlog.com**, login as **guest**, no password required*

Rates
Personal Accounts:
$22.50/month. $15.00 one-time set-up fee.
90 hours per month. Access using SLIP/PPP or shell login.
Extra time (above 90 hours) is $0.30/hour.
Group Rate Account:
Available for groups of 5 or more. Each member of the group has a full personal account. $20.00 per month per person. $10.00 per person set-up fee.
Dedicated Dial-Up:
$200.00/month for 14,400 bps SLIP/PPP. $300.00 set-up fee.
$325.00/month for 28,800 bps SLIP/PPP. $500.00 set-up fee.
Set-up fee is $100.00 if customer supplies an appropriate modem.
ISDN and Leased Line Service:
Call for pricing.

For More Information
FTP:	**Telnet:**	**Gopher:**
ftp.interlog.com	*gold.interlog.com*	*gopher.interlog.com*
Directory: pub/info	*Login: **guest***	

World Wide Web:
http://www.interlog.com

Internet Access Inc.
Ottawa, Ontario
ottawa.net

1678 Ortona Avenue
Ottawa, Ontario
K2C 1W7
Voice: (613) 722-7335
Fax: (613) 722-2778
Internet: info@ottawa.net

Internet Access is an Ottawa-based full-service Internet provider. Internet Access was formed as a partnership and consortium of several companies who needed, but could not get, painless access to the Internet. Now, Internet Access provides Internet access to these companies, other companies, and private individuals. To provide a full service to their clients, Internet Access is now allied with training centers, consulting firms, Unix/PC/Mac vendors, and Internet service providers. Internet Access is in the business of providing painless access to the Internet.

Service Area:	Ottawa, Nepean, Gloucester, Kanata, Orleans, Kemptville, Hull, Gatineau, Rockland.
	Planning to expand to Arnprior, Renfrew, and Smiths Falls.
1-800 service:	No.
PDN Service:	No.
Connection via:	fONOROLA. T1.
Leased Line Service:	Yes. 2400 bps - T1. ISDN service is available.
Dedicated Dial-Up Service:	Yes.
SLIP/PPP Service:	Yes. SLIP and PPP. Freeware/shareware/commercial software is available to customers.
UUCP Service:	Yes. Mail and news feeds. Customers can add and delete newsgroups automatically. Shareware/freeware and commercial UUCP software is available to customers.
Interactive Accounts:	Yes. Direct connection to the Internet. Permanent storage space is available. Additional storage space is available (call for pricing). Mail, Telnet, FTP, Gopher, World Wide Web. Menu-driven interface and shell access. Shareware/freeware and commercial communications software is provided to customers (e.g. Telix, Qmodem etc.).
Maximum Casual Dial-Up Speed:	28,800 bps.
USENET News:	Yes. Full feed.
Local File Archives:	Yes. Community information, hints and lists for Internet surfing.
Domain Registration Service:	Yes. Full service. Call for pricing.
Domain Park Service:	Yes.

Consulting Services:	Yes. Planning, providing, installing, and configuring clients' equipment for Internet access; maintaining/supporting Internet software, hardware, and circuits.
Nameserver Service:	Yes. Primary and secondary nameservers.
Commercial Traffic:	Yes.

HOW TO SIGN UP

On-line registration is not available. Call or send electronic mail to find out how to register.

Rates
Internet Lite (Dial-Up):
$19.98/month plus 9 to 19 cents per quarter-hour. Usage fee depends on time of day.
Group Internet Lite:
Large discounts are available for groups as small as 6 people.
Internet Regular (Leased/Dial-Up):
$199.00/month plus 1 to 4 cents per MB transfered. Circuit is extra.
Internet Deluxe (Leased):
$698.00/month plus 1 to 4 cents/MB. Router included. Circuit extra.

For More Information
Gopher:	**World Wide Web:**
shop.net	*http://shop.net*

Internex Online
Toronto, Ontario
io.org

1 Yonge Street
Suite 1801
Toronto, Ontario
M5E 1W7
Voice: (416) 363-8676
Fax: (416) 369-0515
Internet: support@io.org

Internex Online (IO) is Toronto's first public-access Internet provider. Full access to all Internet services through modem dialup as well as SLIP and PPP is available at a very reasonable cost. IO offers a variety of interfaces, including UNIX shell access, a full-screen menu system and GUI applications for SLIP/PPP users. Accounts can be configured to suit each user's needs for on-line time, disk storage and Internet services. This lets the user pay for only the services that he or she requires. Accounts start at less than $8/month for full Internet access. Free trial accounts are also available (contact support@io.org for more information). 120 high-speed modems on four dedicated terminal servers are available to all our paid members.

Service Area:	Toronto.
1-800 service:	No.
PDN Service:	No.
Connection via:	UUNET Canada. T1.

Leased Line Service:	No.
Dedicated Dial-Up Service:	No.
SLIP/PPP Service:	Yes. SLIP and PPP. Shareware clients for Windows, Macintosh, Amiga, and OS/2 are available for download from Internex Online's FTP site.
UUCP Service:	No.
Interactive Accounts:	Yes. Direct connection to the Internet. 5 MB permanent storage per user. Additional storage is available for $10.00/5MB/year. Telnet, TN3270, FTP, Gopher, World Wide Web (Lynx), Hytelnet, Archie, MUD (tinyfugue). Menu-driven interface and shell access. Popular shareware communications programs are available for download. QWK- and SOUP- compatible off-line readers are supported.
Maximum Casual Dial-Up Speed:	19,200 bps. 28,800 bps in December 1994.
USENET News:	Yes. Approximately 8,600 newsgroups.
Local File Archives:	Yes. Public domain and shareware files for Amiga, Apple II, Atari ST, Linux, Macintosh, MSDOS, and Unix.
Domain Registration Service:	No.
Domain Park Service:	No.
Consulting Services:	No.
Nameserver Service:	Yes. Primary and secondary nameservers.
Commercial Traffic:	Yes.

HOW TO SIGN UP

Customers can register on-line, or over the telephone.

INTERNET:
*Telnet to **io.org**, login as **new**, no password required.*

MODEM:
*(416) 363-4151, V.32bis, login as **new**, no password required.*

Rates
Basic Internet Account:
$95.00 per year includes 1 hour per day and 5 MB of storage.
Each additional hour per day = $45.00 per year.
Each hour over daily limit = $0.36 per hour.
Each five additional megabytes = $10.00 per year.

Unlimited Time Access:
$175.00 per month.

SLIP/PPP Set-Up Fee:
$35.00 one-time.

For More Information
World Wide Web:
http://www.io.org/

Lightning Communications Corporation

Nepean, Ontario
lightning.ca

57 Auriga Drive
Suite 102
Nepean, Ontario
K2E 8B2
Voice: (613) 225-5932 (9 a.m. - 4 p.m. est Mon-Fri)
         (613) 797-1729 (After Hours Sales)
         (613) 797-1728 (After Hours Sales & Technical Support)
Fax: (613) 224-4460
Internet: info@lightning.ca

Lightning Communication's purpose is to provide inexpensive, easy access to the Internet. We believe that everyone should be connected to the Internet to help facilitate communications between individuals, corporations, and governments in hopes that this brings about the necessary changes to benefit society. Information = Knowledge = Understanding.

Service Area:	Ottawa-Carleton, Stittsville, Carp, Blackburnhamlet, Orleans, Manotick, Kars, North Gower, Hull (Quebec), Aylmer (Quebec), Gatineau (Quebec), Rockland, Dunrobin, Greely. Planning to expand to Montreal and Toronto.
1-800 service:	Yes. $0.16-$0.28 per minute.
PDN Service:	No.
Connection via:	fONOROLA. 56Kbps.
Leased Line Service:	No.
Dedicated Dial-Up Service:	Yes.
SLIP/PPP Service:	Yes. SLIP and PPP. Shareware software provided to customers.
UUCP Service:	Yes. Mail and news feeds. Customers can add and delete their own newsgroups. Shareware UUCP software is available to customers.
Interactive Accounts:	Yes. Direct connection to the Internet. 4MB of permanent storage space per user. Additional storage space is $10.00 per megabyte. Mail, Telnet, TN3270, FTP, Gopher, WAIS, World Wide Web, Internet Relay Chat, Hytelnet, Archie. Menu-driven interface and shell access. Communications software is supplied to customers (Telix, Procomm). Graphical user interface software is available to access extended services.
Maximum Casual Dial-Up Speed:	28,800 bps.
USENET News:	Yes. 6500 newsgroups. ClariNet news is available.
Local File Archives:	Yes. Internet help documentation; TCP/IP packages for DOS, Macintosh, Amiga; Unix communication packages.
Domain Registration Service:	Yes. Full service. $20.00 fee.
Domain Park Service:	Yes.

Consulting Services:	Yes. Network set-up, administration and repair related to connecting to the Internet.
Nameserver Service:	Yes. Primary and secondary nameservers.
Commercial Traffic:	Yes.

HOW TO SIGN UP

MODEM:
*(613) 225-6957, v.32 v.42 V.Fast, login as **new**, no password required*

INTERNET:
*Telnet to **lightning.ca**, login as **new**, no password required*

Rates
$30.00 for 50 hours. Each additional hour is $0.50.
$50.00 for 100 hours. Each additional hour is $0.25.
Dedicated Dial-Up:
Set-up fee: $395.00 for the first line and $150.00 for each additional line.
Monthly rate: $300.00 for the first line and $95.00 for each additional line.
UUCP Feeds:
$25.00 and a set-up fee of $20.00.
Connect Time Charges:
There is an hourly rate of $2.00 that must be bought in increments of
$48.00. Please note that time carries over to subsequent months until it is used.

Magi Data Consulting Incorporated
Ottawa, Ontario
magi.com

20 Colonnade Road
Nepean, Ontario
K2E 7M6
Voice: (613) 225-3354
Fax: (613) 225-2880
Internet: info@magi.com

MAGI has been providing systems development, client server, training and consulting services to the National Capital Region (NCR) for over ten years. MAGI has also worked with McDonnell Douglas Information Systems in distributing ProKit Workbench (CASE tool) and PRO IV (4th Generation Language) throughout Ontario for the past four years.

MAGI has worked very closely with the Canadian Radio-television and Telecommunications Commission (CRTC) for the past eight years developing most of the systems used to monitor and track the telecommunications industry. In so doing, MAGI has recently completed a system to monitor and track all programming aired on television. Our requirement to distribute information and updates of this system to the broadcast industry sparked our interest in some of the possibilities in using the Internet to achieve the same results. MAGI subsequently decided to establish itself as an Internet access provider in the NCR. Our desire is to provide our clients with reasonable access fees, to continually develop information features and overall, to become a customer-driven service organization for our Internet users.

Service Area:	National Capital Region (Ottawa, Hull).
1-800 service:	No.

PDN Service:	No.
Connection via:	fONOROLA. 56Kbps.
Leased Line Service:	No.
Dedicated Dial-Up Service:	Yes.
SLIP/PPP Service:	Yes. SLIP and PPP. Shareware software supplied to customers.
UUCP Service:	Yes. Mail and news feeds. Newsgroup changes must go through a service person.
Interactive Accounts:	Yes. Direct connection to the Internet. 3 MB of permanent storage per user. Additional storage is available for $0.02/MB/month. Mail, Telnet, FTP, Gopher, World Wide Web (Lynx), Internet Relay Chat, Archie, MUD (tinyfugue). Menu-driven interface and shell access. Telix communications software is available to customers.
Maximum Casual Dial-Up Speed:	28,800 bps.
USENET News:	Yes. Full feed.
Local File Archives:	Yes. Shareware.
Domain Registration Service:	Yes. Full service. Call for pricing.
Domain Park Service:	Yes.
Consulting Services:	Yes. Training, planning, connectivity.
Nameserver Service:	Yes. Primary nameservers only.
Commercial Traffic:	Yes.

HOW TO SIGN UP

Customers can register by telephone, or on-line.

MODEM:
*(613) 225-4000, V.Fast, login as **new**, no password required*

INTERNET:
*Telnet to **magi.com**, login as **new***
      - or-
http://www.magi.com/magi/new.user.html

Rates
Call for pricing.

For More Information
FTP:	**Gopher:**	**World Wide Web:**
fred.magi.com	*gopher.magi.com*	*http://www.magi.com/*

Mindemoya Computing and Design
Sudbury, Ontario
mcd.on.ca

180 Countryside Drive
Sudbury, Ontario
P3E 5A4
Voice: (705) 523-0243
Fax: (705) 523-2109
Internet: info@mcd.on.ca

MCD*Net is an on-line communication service which provides modem users and organizations with access to electronic mail, USENET news, freely distributable software, and mail and news feeds.

Service Area:	Sudbury.
1-800 Service:	No.
PDN Service:	No.
Connection via:	UUNET Canada.
Leased Line Service:	No.
Dedicated Dial-Up Service:	No.
SLIP/PPP Service:	No.
UUCP Service:	Yes. Mail and news. Customers can modify their own newsgroup subscriptions. MKS Internet Anywhere (commercial UUCP software) is available for purchase.
Interactive Accounts:	Yes. Gateway connection to the Internet for mail. 500k permanent storage/user. Each additional 500k is $5.00/month. Mail, Telnet, FTP, Gopher, World Wide Web, Archie. Menu-driven interface or shell access. Telix (MS-DOS) or Zterm (Mac) communications software is available to customers. SOUP- compatible readers supported. YARN (MS-DOS off-line reader) supplied to customers.
Maximum Casual Dial-Up Speed:	14,400 bps.
USENET News:	Yes.
Local File Archives:	Yes. MSDOS and Macintosh archives.
Domain Registration Service:	Yes. Limited service.
Domain Park Service:	Yes.
Consulting Services:	No.
DNS Service:	No.
Commercial Traffic:	Yes.

HOW TO SIGN UP

A subscription form is available on-line. The subscription form must be postal-mailed for full registration.

MODEM:

*(705) 523-2109,14,400 bps, login as **guest**, no password required*

Rates
Access Accounts
$2.50 per hour.

National Capital FreeNet
Ottawa, Ontario
freenet.carleton.ca

National Capital FreeNet
Carleton University
1125 Colonel By Drive
Ottawa, Ontario
K1S 5B6
Voice: (613) 788-3947
Internet: info-request@freenet.carleton.ca
             ncf@freenet.carleton.ca
             office@freenet.carleton.ca

The National Capital Free-Net is a computer-based information service designed to meet the present information needs of the people and public agencies in the region, and to prepare the community for full and broadly based participation in rapidly changing communication environments. The National Capital Free-Net is incorporated as a non-profit community utility that is free to everyone in the community, and will neither charge nor pay for any information or other services it provides.

Service Area:	National Capital Region (Ottawa, Hull, Nepean, Gloucester, Orleans, Kanata, Gatineau, etc.).
1-800 Service:	No.
PDN Service:	No.
Connection via:	Carleton University.
Leased Line Service:	No.
Dedicated Dial-Up Service:	No.
SLIP/PPP Service:	No.
UUCP Service:	No.
Interactive Accounts:	Yes. Direct connection to the Internet. 1 MB permanent storage per user (fixed - not expandable). Mail, Gopher, Telnet service to limited sites, World Wide Web (Lynx), Local Internet Relay Chat. Menu-driven interface. No shell access.
Maximum Casual Dial-Up Speed:	14,400 bps.
USENET News:	Yes. 4,800 newsgroups.

Local File Archives:	Yes. Community information provided by government and organizations in the community. Organizations in the National Capital Region are encouraged to provide information on the system. Call the National Capital Free-Net for details.
Domain Registration Service:	No.
Domain Park Service:	No.
Consulting Services:	Yes. Training on how to use the Free-Net.
DNS Service:	No.
Commercial Traffic:	Yes.

HOW TO SIGN UP

Customers can register on-line, but customers must sign a membership agreement before the account is activated. Anyone can log on as a guest and browse and read most things on the Free-Net. Only registered users can post to discussion groups and send/receive e-mail.

INTERNET:
Telnet to **freenet.carleton.ca**, *login as* **guest**, *no password required.*
Telnet to **freenet3.carleton**.ca, *login as* **guest**, *no password required.*

MODEM:
(613) 564-3600, 2400 bps, login as **guest**, *no password required.*
(613) 564-0808, 14,400 bps, login as **guest**, *no password required.*

Rates:
All services offered by the National Capital Free-Net are free to the user. Donations are solicited and encouraged.

For More Information
Telnet:
freenet.carleton.ca
Login: **guest**

Gopher:
freenet.carleton.ca

NetAccess Systems Inc.
Hamilton, Ontario
netaccess.on.ca

Suite E
231 Main Street West
Hamilton, Ontario
L8P 1J4
Voice: (905) 524-2544
Fax: (905) 524-3010
Internet: info@netaccess.on.ca

NetAccess provides Internet access and Internet training and consulting in the Greater Hamilton and Burlington area. Our primary purpose is to provide high-quality access and service and support at affordable rates. NetAccess is committed to work with business, government, library, service, and not-for-profit sectors, along with educators and information providers, to encourage the innovative use of computer technology for the benefit of the whole community. We believe access to the tremendous resources of computer-based communications and information systems is a key to personal and corporate productivity in the 90s. We seek to give our clients an edge in this rapidly changing environment.

Service Area:	Greater Hamilton-Burlington area.
	Expansion is planned in the Niagara Peninsula to St. Catharines, Niagara Falls, and Welland.
1-800 Service:	No.
PDN Service:	No.
Connection via:	WorldLinx.
Leased Line Service:	No.
Dedicated Dial-Up Service:	Yes.
SLIP/PPP Service:	Yes. SLIP and PPP. Shareware/freeware software is available for download.
UUCP Service:	Yes. Mail and news feeds. Newsgroup changes must go through a service person. UUCP freeware is available for download.
Interactive Accounts:	Yes. Direct connection to the Internet. 1MB permanent storage/user. Up to 10MB of storage is available temporarily. Telnet, TN3270, FTP, Gopher, WAIS, World Wide Web, Internet Relay Chat, Hytelnet, Archie. Menu-driven interface and shell access. E-mail-to-fax gateway for the local calling area.
Maximum Casual Dial-Up Speed:	19,200 bps.
USENET News:	Yes. Approximately 3000 newsgroups.
Local File Archives:	Yes. PC/Macintosh software.
Domain Registration Service:	Yes. Full service. Price is included in the set-up fee.
Domain Park Service:	Yes.
Consulting Services:	Yes. Evaluation of client options for initial Internet connections and management; consulting and Internet training.
DNS Service:	Yes. Primary and secondary nameservers.
Commercial Traffic:	Yes.

HOW TO SIGN UP

Registration takes place over the telephone. Call for information.

Rates
Bronze Package:
$14.95/month. Includes 5 free hours. Additional hours are $1.95/hour.
Silver Package:
$24.95/month. Includes 15 free hours. Additional hours are $1.49/hour.
Gold Package:
$39.95/month. Includes 30 free hours. Additional hours are $0.99/hour.

For More Information
Gopher:
gopher.netaccess.on.ca

World Wide Web:
http://netaccess.on.ca/welcome.html

Nova Scotia Technology Network Inc. (NSTN)
Dartmouth, Nova Scotia
nstn.ca

201 Brownlow Avenue
Dartmouth, Nova Scotia
B3B 1W2
Voice: (902) 481-NSTN (6786)
          1-800-336-4445 (Toll-Free Canada-Wide)
Fax: (902) 468-3679
Internet: info@nstn.ca (Automated)
          sales@nstn.ca (Sales/Marketing Team)

Area Served: Ottawa and Toronto
See main entry under Province of Nova Scotia

ONet Networking
Toronto, Ontario
onet.on.ca

ONet Networking
Network Registrar
University of Toronto
4 Bancroft Avenue BC103C
Toronto, Ontario
M5S 1C1
Voice: (416) 978-4589 (Herb Kugel)
Fax: (416) 978-6620
Internet: info@onet.on.ca

ONet's mission is to facilitate the exchange of information among research, development, technology transfer, education, training, health care, library, and public sector communities throughout Ontario, and to provide Ontario-based researchers with access to Canadian and international sources of information. ONet enables its members to meet their objective of leading the way in finding new and innovative ways to make life-long learning a reality.

Founded in 1988, ONet is Ontario's longest operating Internet Service Provider. ONet provides a high bandwidth backbone with exceptionally wide coverage of the Province of Ontario.

With over 110 high-speed members, a 24 hour Network Operations Centre, a substantial network engineering and operations staff and a superior operational record, ONet provides high quality Internet connectivity to organizations with demanding Internet access needs. ONet provides Internet access for organizations such as Newbridge, BNR, Gandalf, IBM, NRC, all Ontario colleges and universities, and many government, health, community groups and business research consortia. ONet's participation in CA*net provides a solid foundation for ensuring the success of a Canadian Internet infrastructure, and it ensures high bandwidth access to other Canadian Internet service providers across the country and into the United States.

When an organization becomes a member of ONet, it is established as a voting representative in ONet Networking, a provincial not-for-profit corporation. This enables the member to participate in the business of the corporation and the election of the ONet Board of Directors at an Annual General meeting and other designated meetings of the corporation.

Service Area:	ONet provides dial-up access to the local calling areas around Toronto, Kitchener-Waterloo, North Bay, and Ottawa.
	ONet Networking has Points of Presence in Barrie, Belleville, Brockville, Chalk River, Deep River, Kingston, Kitchener-Waterloo, North Bay, Oakville, Ottawa, Guelph, Hamilton, London, Peterborough, St. Catharines, Sarnia, Sault Ste. Marie, Sudbury, Toronto, Thunder Bay, Welland, and Windsor.
1-800 Service:	No
PDN Service:	No
Connection via:	CA*net.
Leased Line Service:	Yes. 19,200 bps - T1.
Dedicated Dial-Up Service:	Yes.
SLIP/PPP Service:	Yes. SLIP and PPP. Casual dial-up is planned for first quarter 1995.
UUCP Service:	No.
Interactive Accounts:	No.
Maximum Casual Dial-Up Speed:	19,200 bps is planned for 1995.
USENET News:	Yes. Full feed.
Local File Archives:	Yes. ONet documents.
Domain Registration Service:	Yes. Full service. No charge.
Domain Park Service:	No.
Consulting Services:	Yes. Limited initial consultation for network configuration for Internet connectivity, mail, news, and nameservice set-up.
DNS Service:	Yes. Primary nameservers provided for entry level services at no charge. Secondary nameservers provided for all levels of service at no charge.
Commercial Traffic:	Yes.

HOW TO SIGN UP

Call or send electronic mail for information.

Rates
1994-95 Fee Schedule:
LEASED LINE SERVICES
(A) Initiation Fee
$6,000.00. $3,100.00 for two years.
(B) Organizational Budget Charge
$2,250 $0M -- $50M
$5,750 $50M -- $150M
$12,75 $150M or over

(C) Required Connectivity Speed

$5,000	19.2 Kbps	$22,000	448 Kbps
$10,000	56 Kbps	$24,000	512 Kbps
$12,000	128 Kbps	$26,000	576 Kbps
$14,000	192 Kbps	$28,000	640 Kbps
$16,000	256 Kbps	$30,000	704 Kbps
$18,000	320 Kbps	$32,000	768 Kbps
$20,000	384 Kbps	$34,500	1.536 Mbps

DEDICATED DIAL-UP SERVICE

Dedicated Line, Premium Managed Service: $5,400/year
Dedicated Line, Standard Service $4,100/year

For More Information

FTP: **World Wide Web:**
onet.on.ca   http://onet.on.ca/onet/index.html
Directory: onet

Online Systems of Canada

London, Ontario
onlinesys.com

383 Richmond Street
Suite 900
London, Ontario
N6A 3C4
Voice: (416) 642-0731
Fax: (416) 642-0733
Internet: bruce.asquith@onlinesys.com (Bruce Asquith)

Online Systems of Canada has been providing data communications services to business, education, government, military, and computer hobbyists for over 5 years. We have built our business and reputation by word of mouth with an exceptional blend of services and customer support. Our services connect DOS, Unix, and Macintosh computer platforms. Most recently, we have become a partner with the Canadian Information Access Council, whose mandate is to work with both government and Canadian business to develop the Canadian information highway.

Service Area:	London, Woodstock, Sarnia, Toronto.
	Planning to expand to Windsor, Chatham, Kitchener, Stratford, Hamilton, Ottawa, Kingston.
1-800 Service:	No.
PDN Service:	No.
Connection via:	UUNET Canada. 56Kbps, upgrading soon to T1.
Leased Line Service:	Yes.
Dedicated Dial-Up Service:	Yes.
SLIP/PPP Service:	Fourth quarter 1994.
UUCP Service:	Yes. Mail and news feeds. Customers can add and delete newsgroups automatically.

Interactive Accounts:	Yes. Permanent storage space available. Gateway connection to the Internet. Additional storage space is $5.00/megabyte/month. Mail, Telnet, Gopher, FTP. Off-line readers supported (1st Reader is supplied for $30.00).
Maximum Casual Dial-Up Speed:	28,800 bps.
USENET News:	Yes. 5,000+ newsgroups.
Local File Archives:	Yes. Topics: business, CAD/CAM, communications, database, genealogy, education, games, medical, hobby, music, OS/2, networking, religion, programming, science, security, Windows, Windows-NT, word processing, desktop publishing, and more.
Domain Registration Service:	Yes. Limited service. $50.00 charge.
Domain Park Service:	Yes.
Consulting Service:	Yes. Turnkey solutions to business, government, and education for internal and dial-up services.
DNS Service:	No.
Commercial Traffic:	Yes.

HOW TO SIGN UP

MODEM:
(519) 642-0700 through (519) 642-0730 (28,800 bps).

Rates
Basic Account:
$60.00/year. Includes 1 hour of on-line time, and 1 MB of files.
Regular Account:
$100.00/year. Includes 2 hours of on-line time and 2 MB of files.
Premium Account:
$130.00/year. Includes 3 hours of on-line time and 3 MB of files.
Corporate Account:
$250.00/year. Includes 7 hours of on-line time and 7 MB of files.
Optional Telnet/FTP Access Accounts:
$3.00 for 1 hour of FTP/Telnet, or choose a package below.
Personal Account: *$60.00/year. Includes 25 hours of FTP/Telnet.*
Home/Office Account: *$100.00/year. Includes 50 hours of FTP/Telnet.*
Business Dial-up: *$150.00/year. Includes 100 hours of FTP/Telnet.*
Corporate Dial-up: *$300.00/year. Includes 300 hours of FTP/Telnet.*

ONRAMP Network Services Inc.
Markham, Ontario
onramp.ca

570 Hood Road
Markham, Ontario
L3R 4G7
Voice: (905) 470-4064
Fax: (905) 477-4808
Internet: info@onramp.ca

For the individual, ONRAMP provides easy telephone access to a full Internet connection and various Internet tools. We specialize in users running Windows-based personal computers. We provide corporations with a World Wide Web authoring and hosting service giving their company information worldwide visibility.

Service Area:	Ontario: Metropolitan Toronto, Markham, Newmarket.
	British Columbia: Vancouver, Richmond.
1-800 Service:	No.
PDN Service:	No.
Leased Line Service:	Yes.
Dedicated Dial-Up Service:	Yes.
SLIP/PPP Service:	Yes. SLIP and PPP.
UUCP Service:	No.
Interactive Accounts:	No.
Maximum Casual Dial-Up Speed:	28,800 bps.
USENET News:	Yes.
Local File Archives:	Yes.
Domain Registration Service:	Call for information.
Domain Park Service:	Call for information.
Consulting Services:	Yes. Internet connectivity for business.
DNS Service:	Call for information.
Commercial Traffic:	Yes.

HOW TO SIGN UP

Call or send electronic mail to register.

Rates
Call for information.

For More Information
Gopher:　　　　　**World Wide Web:**
onramp.ca　　　　*http://onramp.ca*

Passport Online
Toronto, Ontario
passport.ca

173 Dufferin Street
Suite 302
Toronto, Ontario
M6K 3H7
Voice: (416) 516-1616
Fax: (416) 516-1690
Internet: info@passport.ca

The Passport Philosophy:

*Our technical expertise and connectivity are second to none, but to us the Internet is much more than data and bandwidth. It's people: personalities, ideas, and meaningful interaction. It's **alive**. We're striving to create the most friendly and vibrant community on the 'Net. And we'd like you to join us. Being a Passport 'Net-setter' ™ means using the critically-acclaimed Pipeline software. It's so much fun, you'll fall in love with the 'Net the first time you log in. It means there's a friendly knowledgeable **human** voice on the other end of our exclusive help-line, whenever you need it. It also means you're connected to a system where personal service is a priority. Our enthusiastic staff are all 'Net fanatics, and love turning people on to what's out there, so when you call Passport, you'll get assistance. And while we're attracting some of the most fascinating and worthwhile people in cyberspace, we're also constantly working to develop new and innovative ways to serve them better, which means that you'll always be on the leading edge when it comes to new features and higher performance. Call Passport Today, and join the "Net Set" ™. Help us build the coolest place in cyberspace.*

Service Area:	Metropolitan Toronto and surrounding area.
	Planning to expand to all major Canadian cities by the end of 1995.
1-800 Service:	No.
PDN Service:	No.
Connection via:	fONOROLA. 56Kbps.
Leased Line Service:	Yes. Up to 128Kbps. ISDN service is available.
Dedicated Dial-Up Service:	Yes.
SLIP/PPP Service:	Yes. SLIP and PPP. Pipeline software is supplied free of charge to customers. Pipeline provides dynamic SLIP-like functionality in an easy-to-use graphical point-and-click interface.
UUCP Service:	No.
Interactive Accounts:	Yes. Direct connection to the Internet. 1 MB permanent storage space per user. Additional storage space is $1.50/MB/month based on daily average. Mail, Telnet, TN3270, FTP, Gopher, WAIS, World Wide Web (Lynx), Internet Relay Chat, Hytelnet, Archie, MUDs (NET TREK and SIM CITY), MOOs. On-line stock market quotations, Associated Press, UPI (United Press International), USA Today, Complete Oxford English Dictionary, Encyclopedia Brittanica, Compendium of Pharmaceuticals and Specialties, Cds. "Point and click" interface and shell access. Pipeline client software is supplied free of charge to customers. Pipeline automatically downloads all e-mail and FTP transfers to the user's personal computer.

Maximum Casual Dial-Up Speed:	19,200 bps.
USENET News:	Yes. 6500 newsgroups.
Local File Archives:	Yes. CD-ROMs of PC and Macintosh shareware, Unix support files, OS/2 and NeXT files, graphics files, text files.
Domain Registration Service:	Yes. Full service.
Domain Park Service:	Yes.
Consulting Services:	Yes. Unix and mainframe technologies, architecture and maintenance of Unix platforms, security, data integrity and recovery, client/server software design, networking, internetworking and TCP/IP.
DNS Service:	Yes. Primary and secondary nameservers.
Commercial Traffic:	Yes.
Additional Comments:	Users must be 18 years of age or older.

HOW TO SIGN UP

Users can apply on-line, but their credit card must be approved before full access is granted. New users can download the client software right away and browse the system for fifteen minutes at a time using the DEMO account.

MODEM:
*(416) 588-3838, 19,200 bps, login as **guest**, password is **guest***

INTERNET:
*Telnet to **passport.ca**, login as **guest**, password is **guest***

Rates
$39.95 per month for 30 hours per month. $0.95 per hour after 30 hours.
Subscribe for 12 months, pay for 10 months. Group or corporate rates available. Call for details.

For More Information

FTP:	**Telnet:**	**Gopher:**
ftp.passport.ca	*passport.ca*	*gopher.passport.ca*
	Login: **guest**	
	Password: **guest**	

RESUDOX Online Services
Nepean, Ontario
resudox.net

P.O. Box 33067
Nepean, Ontario
K2C 3Y9
Voice: (613) 567-6925
Fax: (613) 567-8289
Internet: admin@resudox.net

We are a locally-owned organization responding to the needs of the high-tech and educational communities. Our mission: To provide an affordable dial-up service for Internet access to individuals and companies in the National Capital Region, to provide an alternative link to the Free-Net community, and to contribute to the development of Internet and Free-Net access in the Ottawa-Carleton region.

Service Area:	Ottawa, Orleans, Nepean, Kanata, Hull, Gloucester.
1-800 Service:	No.
PDN Service:	No.
Connection via:	fONOROLA. 56Kbps.
Leased Line Service:	No.
Dedicated Dial-Up Service:	Yes.
SLIP/PPP Service:	Yes. SLIP and PPP. Winsock public domain software supplied at no extra charge.
UUCP Service:	Yes. Mail and news feeds.
Interactive Accounts:	Yes. Direct connection to the Internet. 5 MB of permanent storage per user. Mail, Telnet, FTP, Gopher, WAIS, World Wide Web (Lynx), Internet Relay Chat, Hytelnet, Archie. Shell access or menu-driven interface.
Maximum Casual Dial-Up Speed:	19,200 bps.
USENET News:	Yes. Approximately 2200 newsgroups.
Local File Archives:	Yes. Internet software.
Domain Registration Service:	Yes. Full service. $25.00 charge.
Domain Park Service:	No.
Consulting Services:	Yes. Hardware/software selection and set up, set up of World Wide Web servers.
DNS Service:	Yes. Primary and secondary nameservers.
Commercial Traffic:	Yes.

HOW TO SIGN UP

INTERNET:
*Telnet to **resudox.net**, login as **new**, no password required*

MODEM:
*(613) 567-1714, V.32bis, login as **new**, no password required*

Rates
Free-Net Access Account:
$17.00/month plus $1.00/hour (includes 10 free hours per month). $2 of each subscriber's monthly subscription fee will be donated to the National Capital Free-Net in Ottawa.
Full Internet Access Account:
$19.00/month plus $2.00/hour (includes 10 free hours per month).
Corporate Account:
$35.00/month plus $2.00/hour.

Dial-Up SLIP/PPP Service Account:
$25.00/month plus $2.00/hour (includes 5 free hours).
Macintosh or Windows clients are provided.
UUCP:
$35.00/month plus $2.00/hour.

For More Information

FTP:	***Gopher:***	***Telnet:***
resudox.net	*resudox.net*	*resudox.net*
Login: **new**		

World Wide Web:
http://www.resudox.net

Sentex Communications Corporation

Guelph, Ontario
sentex.net

727 Speedvale Avenue West
Unit #6
Guelph, Ontario
N1K 1E6
Voice: (519) 822-9970
Fax: (519) 822-4775
Internet: info@sentex.net

Sentex Communications is an Ontario-based commercial on-line service provider with a full connection to the Internet. We provide a full complement of Internet services for both novice and sophisticated users. Our system is designed to be powerful and yet easy to use. We have our own integrated MS Windows-based environment to make accessing the Internet easy.

Service Area:	Kitchener, Waterloo, Cambridge, Guelph, Toronto.
	Planning to expand to Burlington, Hamilton, London, Niagara.
1-800 Service:	No.
PDN Service:	No.
Leased Line Service:	Yes. Up to 56Kbps. ISDN service available on demand.
Dedicated Dial-Up Service:	Yes.
SLIP/PPP Service:	Yes. SLIP and PPP.
UUCP Service:	Yes. Mail and news feeds. Newsgroup changes must go through a service person.
Interactive Accounts:	Yes. 1 MB of permanent storage per user. Mail, Telnet, TN3270, FTP, Gopher, WAIS, World Wide Web, Archie, Menu-driven interface, "point-and-click" interface, shell access. Proprietary integrated MS Windows-based interface supplied to customers.
Maximum Casual Dial-Up Speed:	28,800 bps.
USENET News:	Yes. 5,500+ newsgroups.

Local File Archives:	Yes. Public domain MS Windows/DOS Archives, Linux and other Unix-based Internet software, Internet documentation.
Domain Registration Service:	Yes. Full service. No charge for corporate customers. Non-corporate customers: $25.00 with DNS support.
Domain Park Service:	Yes.
Consulting Services:	Yes. Unix, MS Windows, Wide Area Networking, Local Area Networking, TCP/IP.
DNS Service:	Yes. Primary and secondary nameservers.
Commercial Traffic:	Yes.

HOW TO SIGN UP

MODEM:
*(519) 822-2099, 14,400 bps, login as **new***

INTERNET:
*Telnet to **granite.sentex.net**, login as **new***

Rates
All accounts are full "shell" accounts with access via SLIP/PPP if required.
Individual non-corporate accounts :
$ 29.95/month for 45 hours/month
$159.95/6 months for 45 hours/month
$299.95/year for 45 hours/month
Additional hours are $1/hour.
Individual corporate accounts :
$ 59.95/month for 45 hours/month
Additional hours are $1/hour.

For dedicated accounts and full corporate accounts please contact
info@sentex.net.

For More Information
Telnet: **Gopher:**
granite.sentex.net   gopher.sentex.net
*Login: **new***

World Wide Web:
http://www.sentex.net/info/sentex.html

The Wire
Toronto, Ontario
the-wire.com

12 Sheppard Street
Suite 421
Toronto, Ontario
M5H 3A1
Voice: (416) 214-WIRE (9473)
Fax: (416) 862-WIRE (9473)
Internet: sysadm@the-wire.com

The Wire provides dependable, secure, affordable access to the Internet. We specialize in graphically-interfaced access and strive to provide the highest quality of customer support and service. We support NCSA's Mosaic and provide custom home-page and hypertext-linked FTP facilities. We are specialists in state-of-the-art encryption technology to facilitate the transmission of sensitive information over public data lines. The Wire has its own Internet training facility and is home to Audio-OnLine, Canada's first one-stop information and distribution center for this country's independent music industry.

Service Area:	Metropolitan Toronto.
1-800 Service:	No.
PDN Service:	No.
Connection via:	fONOROLA. 56Kbps.
Leased Line Service:	No.
Dedicated Dial-Up Service:	Yes.
SLIP/PPP Service:	Yes. SLIP and PPP. Freeware/shareware software supplied at no cost.
UUCP Service:	No.
Interactive Accounts:	Yes. Direct connection to the Internet. Permanent storage space is provided. Mail, Telnet, FTP, Gopher, WAIS, World Wide Web, Internet Relay Chat, Hytelnet, Archie. Menu-driven interface and shell access.
Maximum Casual Dial-Up Speed:	14,400 bps.
USENET News:	Yes. Approximately 9,300 newsgroups.
Local File Archives:	Yes. Internet interface software, Internet documentation.
Domain Registration Service:	No.
Domain Park Service:	No.
Consulting Services:	Yes. Commercial use of the Internet, data encryption, research, training.
DNS Service:	Yes. Primary and secondary nameservers.
Commercial Traffic:	Yes.
Additional Comments:	Customers must be over the age of 18.

HOW TO SIGN UP

Call or send electronic mail for information.

Rates
Simple Access:
$75.00/year. $30.00/three months. $45.00/six months. E-mail and USENET. 30 minutes per day,
Full Internet:
$200.00/year. $80.00/three months. $120.00/six months. 90 minutes per day.
SLIP/PPP Account:
Call for information.

For More Information
World Wide Web:
http://the-wire.com

The Usual Suspects
London, Ontario
suspects.com

430 Loverage Street
London, Ontario
N5W 4T7
Voice: (519) 451-4364
Internet: info@suspects.com

The Usual Suspects provides cost-effective information retrieval services, mediated Internet services, electronic storefront services, and customized information administration. We also provide our customers with access to the Internet via accounts on our systems. This includes electronic mail services, USENET news, FTP, Telnet, and Gopher. We will set up UUCP nodes for clients who want to receive mail, news, and other information on their desktop.

Service Area:	London, Ottawa, Guelph.
	Planning to expand to Toronto, Windsor, and Rockville, Maryland.
1-800 Service:	Yes. Call for details.
PDN Service:	No.
Connection via:	UUNET Canada.
Leased Line Service:	No.
Dedicated Dial-Up Service:	No.
SLIP/PPP Service:	No.
UUCP Service:	Yes. Newsgroup changes must go through a service person. Shareware UUCP software is provided.
Interactive Accounts:	Yes. Direct connection to the Internet. 5 MB permanent storage per user. User can pay for more storage space in 5 MB increments. Additional storage space costs $10.00 per month per 5 MB increment. Mail, Telnet, FTP, Gopher, WAIS, World Wide Web, Internet Relay Chat, Archie. Menu-driven interface and shell access.
Maximum Casual Dial-Up Speed:	19,200 bps.
USENET News:	Yes.
Local File Archives:	Yes.
Domain Registration Service:	Yes. Limited service.

Domain Park Service:	Yes.
Consulting Services:	Yes. Database design and administration, Internet information profiles for business and research, Internet connectivity options and setup.
DNS Service:	Yes.
Commercial Traffic:	Yes.

HOW TO SIGN UP

MODEM:
(519) 472-8559, 14,400 bps, login as **new**

Rates
Full Internet Shell Accounts:
$45.00 per month.
Electronic Mail/USENET News:
$15.00 per month.
UUCP Node:
$200.00 plus $15.00/month.
Base Consulting Rates:
$55.00 per hour.

UUISIS
Nepean, Ontario
uuisis.isis.org

81 Tartan Drive
Nepean, Ontario
K2J 3V6
Voice: (613) 825-5324
Internet: rjbeeth@uuisis.isis.org (Rick Beetham)

Our mandate is to deliver affordable access to the Internet for organizations, businesses, and individuals through the use of regular phone lines. Our mission is to remain stable and cost-effective for the customer and to deliver mail in as timely a manner as possible without being directly connected.

We do not attempt to be a major Internet provider but rather an affordable way for small companies and organizations to access the Internet for mail and information. All accounts utilize dial-up modem access.

Service Area:	Ontario: Gloucester, Kanata, Nepean, Ottawa, Orleans, Vanier
	Quebec: Hull, Gatineau, Aylmer.
1-800 Service:	No.
PDN Service:	No.
Connection via:	UUNET Canada. 19,200 PEP.

Leased Line Service:	No.
Dedicated Dial-Up Service:	Yes.
SLIP/PPP Service:	No. Planned.
UUCP Service:	Yes. Mail and news feeds. Customers can modify their own newsgroup subscriptions. MKS Internet Anyware is available for $125.00. Shareware UUCP software is also available.
Interactive Accounts:	Yes. Gateway connection to the Internet. 1 MB/user permanent storage for personal files. Internet mail, USENET, FTP by mail, Archie, Telnet. Menu-driven interface.
Maximum Casual Dial-Up Speed:	19,200 bps (PEP).
USENET News:	Yes. Approximately 2,300 newsgroups.
Local File Archives:	Yes.
Domain Registration Service:	No.
Domain Park Service:	Yes.
Consulting Services:	No.
DNS Service:	Yes. Primary and secondary nameservers.
Commercial Traffic:	Yes.

HOW TO SIGN UP

MODEM:
(613) 823-6539 (2400 MNP5, 9,600 bps, 19,200 bps PEP)
Login: **BBS**   *Password:* **NEW**

Rates
Premium:
$180.00/year for 600 minutes/month UUCP or login
$200.00/year for 600 minutes/month UUCP and login
$180.00/year for SLIP/PPP (when available)
Additional time is $0.08/minute/month.
Economy:
$100.00/year for 40 minutes/day UUCP or login
$135.00/year for 40 minutes/day UUCP and login
$180.00/year for SLIP/PPP (when available)
Additional time is $0.10/minute/day.
Telnet and FTP (when available):
$70.00/year (Premium) or $85.00/year (Economy).
Telnet and FTP require a login account.

UUNorth International Inc.
Willowdale, Ontario
north.net

3555 Don Mills Road
Unit 6-304
Willowdale, Ontario
M2H 3N3
Voice: (416) 225-8649
Fax: (416) 225-0525
Internet: info@uunorth.north.net

UUNorth International is an Internet service provider, offering not only connectivity to both the individual and corporate user, but also education, training, consulting, network management, network design, and applications development.

UUNorth International Inc., along with its sister affiliates, Canadian Internetworking Services and Network Wide Applications, provides a complete networking solution for individuals as well as corporations.

Service Area:	Metropolitan Toronto.
	Planning to expand to other cities across Canada in 1995.
1-800 Service:	No.
PDN Service:	No.
Connection via:	Call for information.
Leased Line Service:	Yes. ISDN service is available.
Dedicated Dial-Up Service:	Yes.
SLIP/PPP Service:	Yes. SLIP and PPP.
UUCP Service:	Yes. Mail and news feeds. Users can modify their own newsgroup subscriptions.
Interactive Accounts:	Yes. Direct connection to the Internet. Permanent disk space available. Mail, Telnet, FTP, Gopher, WAIS, World Wide Web, Internet Relay Chat, Hytelnet, Archie. Menu-driven interface. No shell access.
Maximum Casual Dial-Up Speed:	19,200 bps. 28,800 bps in 1995.
USENET News:	Yes. 6,000+ newsgroups.
Local File Archives:	Yes.
Domain Registration Service:	Yes. Full service. $75.00 fee.
Domain Park Service:	Yes.
Consulting Services:	Yes. Training, network management, network design, network security, facility-based management services, Internet connectivity procurement, applications design and management.
DNS Service:	Yes. Primary and secondary nameservers.
Commercial Traffic:	Yes
Additional Comments:	Users must be 18 years of age or older.

HOW TO SIGN UP

Registration is by telephone or fax. Please call to register.

Rates:
Call for pricing.

WINCOM

Windsor, Ontario
wincom.net

4510 Rhodes Drive
Unit 903
Windsor, Ontario
N8W 5K5
Voice: (519) 945-9462
Fax: (519) 944-6610
Internet: info@wincom.net

WINCOM's mission is to provide the population of Windsor and Essex County with local access to the Internet community.

Service Area:	Windsor, Pleasant Park, McGregor, Emeryville, Belle River, Kingsville, Lasalle, Tecumseh, Amherstburg, Maidstone, Essex, Stoney Point, Leamington, Harrow. Planning to expand to Chatham.
1-800 Service:	No.
PDN Service:	No.
Connection via:	ANS. 56Kbps.
Leased Line Service:	Yes. Up to 56Kbps.
Dedicated Dial-Up Service:	Yes.
SLIP/PPP Service:	Yes. Call for information.
UUCP Service:	Call for information.
Interactive Accounts:	Yes. Direct connection to the Internet. 10 MB permanent storage per user. Telnet, TN3270, FTP, Gopher, WAIS, World Wide Web, Hytelnet, Archie. Shell access. E-mail-to-fax gateway for the local calling area.
Maximum Casual Dial-Up Speed:	19,200 bps.
USENET News:	Yes.
Local File Archives:	Call for information.
Domain Registration Service:	No.
Domain Park Service:	Yes.
Consulting Services:	Yes.

DNS Service:	Yes. Primary and secondary nameservers.
Commercial Traffic:	Yes.

HOW TO SIGN UP

Registration is over the telephone. Please call to register.

Rates
Call for pricing.

QUEBEC

Acces Public LLC

Quebec City, Quebec
llc.org

CP 11
Station B
Quebec City, Quebec
G1K 7A1
Voice: (418) 692-4711
Fax: (418) 656-8212
Internet: info@llc.org

A non-profit organization, Acces Public LLC wishes to provide an Internet connection to all, at the lowest cost possible. We offer all standard Internet services, as well as our own World Wide Web page and our own FTP site, which provides Quebec's offerings in shareware, electronic magazines and demos.

Service Area:	Greater Quebec City area.
1-800 Service:	No.
PDN Service:	No.
Connection via:	UUNET Canada, 56Kbps.
Leased Line Service:	No.
Dedicated Dial-Up Service:	Yes.
SLIP/PPP Service:	Yes. SLIP and PPP. Shareware software is supplied to customers.
UUCP Service:	Yes. Mail and news feeds. Newsgroup changes must go through a service person. Freeware/shareware UUPC software is available to customers.

Interactive Accounts:	Yes. Direct connection to the Internet. 2 MB permanent storage space per user. Extra storage space costs $0.75/MB. Mail, Telnet, FTP, Gopher, WAIS, World Wide Web (CERN), Internet Relay Chat, Archie, MUD (Dinky MUD, in French). Majordomo for mailing lists. Menu-driven interface and shell access. Shareware communications software is available to customers (e.g. Telix, Telemate). UQWK-, YARN-, and SOUP- compatible off-line readers are supported. Shareware off-line readers are available to customers.
Maximum Casual Dial-Up Speed:	28,800 bps.
USENET News:	Yes. 8600 newsgroups.
Local File Archives:	Yes. Internet shareware software. Text files on the Internet.
Domain Registration Service:	Yes. Limited service. No charge.
Domain Park Service:	No.
Consulting Service:	Yes. Security, networking, Unix installation, Internet connectivity.
DNS Service:	Yes. Primary nameservers only.
Commercial Traffic:	Yes.

HOW TO SIGN UP

On-line registration is not available. Please call to register.

Rates
Basic User Rate:
$30.00 per month for 10 hours per week or $100.00 for four months.
SLIP/PPP:
$45.00 per month for 10 hours a week or $160.00 for four months.
Other Services:
Please call for pricing.

For More Information
FTP: **World Wide Web:**
ftp.llc.org   *http://www.llc.org*

Communications Accessibles Montreal Inc.

Montreal, Quebec
cam.org

2055 Peel, Suite 825
Montreal, Quebec
H3A 1V4
Voice: (514) 288-2581
Fax: (514) 288-3401
Internet: info@cam.org

Communications Accessibles Montreal is a non-profit corporation offering affordable Internet connectivity in the 514 (Montreal) area code. We offer complete access to all Internet resources in real time. We operate a network of Unix servers with 40+ dial-up lines and a dedicated T1 link to the Internet. A sophisticated online help system is available to help new users. Text-based environments include such popular favourites as pine, elm, tin, nn, trn, WWW, gopher, WAIS,

Archie, IRC, and Telnet. A fax gateway with Postscript support is also available free of charge (local calls only). We are a not-for-profit system and reinvest 100% of the profits back into the system.

Service Area:	Montreal, Laval, South Shore.
1-800 Service:	No.
PDN Service:	No.
Connection via:	UUNET Canada. 56Kbps, to be upgraded to 128Kbps or 256Kbps in late 1994.
Leased Line Service:	No.
Dedicated Dial-Up Service:	Yes.
SLIP/PPP Service:	Yes. SLIP and PPP. Freeware/shareware software is available for download.
UUCP Service:	Yes. Mail and news feeds. Customers can modify newsgroup subscriptions automatically.
Interactive Accounts:	Yes. Direct connection to the Internet. 4MB of permanent storage/user. Additional storage space is available for $5.00/MB/month. Telnet, FTP, Gopher, WAIS, World Wide Web (Lynx), Internet Relay Chat, Hytelnet, Archie. Shell access. QWK-compatible off-line readers are supported. Shell access. E-mail-to-fax gateway for the local calling area.
Maximum Casual Dial-Up Speed:	14,400 bps.
USENET News:	Yes. 9000+ newsgroups available.
Local File Archives:	Yes. SLIP/PPP software for PC and Macintosh users.
Domain Registration Service:	Yes. Full service. $100.00 fee.
Domain Park Service:	No.
Consulting Service:	No.
DNS Service:	Yes. Primary and secondary nameservers.
Commercial Traffic:	Yes.

HOW TO SIGN UP

Registration takes place over the telephone. Please call to register.

Rates
Interactive Shell Access:
$25.00/month (1,200 -14,400 bps).
Limit of 10 hours of connect time per week.
Dial-up SLIP/PPP + Interactive Account:
$30.00/month (9600-14,400 bps).
Dedicated SLIP/PPP + Interactive Account:
$150.00/month (9600-19200 bps).

UUCP Services:
Call for information.

For More Information

FTP:	**Telnet:**	**Gopher:**	**Finger:**
ftp.cam.org	*cam.org*	*gopher.cam.org*	*info@cam.org*
file: CAM.ORG-info	Login: **info**		

World Wide Web:
http://www.cam.org

Communications Inter-Acces

Montreal, Quebec
interax.net

5475 Pare, Suite 104
Montreal, Quebec
H4P 1R4
Voice: (514) 367-0002
Fax: (514) 368-3529
Internet: info@interax.net

Inter-Acces provides complete Internet connectivity via SLIP or PPP connections. The software required to access the Internet via a Macintosh or an IBM PC-compatible can be downloaded directly from our system. Inter-Acces also provides dedicated Internet connectivity at speeds of up to 64Kbps and above. Inter-Acces also provides consulting services to help corporate clients set up and operate Internet networks.

Service Area:	Montreal.
	Expansion is planned to Toronto and Quebec City.
1-800 Service:	No.
PDN Service:	No.
Leased Line Service:	Yes. ISDN service is available.
Dedicated Dial-Up Service:	Yes.
SLIP/PPP Service:	Yes. SLIP and PPP. Trumpet, Chameleon and Morningstar TCP/IP software is available. Extra costs may apply.
UUCP Service:	Yes. Mail and news feeds. Customers can add and delete newsgroups automatically. UUCP software is supplied (Taylor UUCP, UUPC). MKS UUCP is available for approx. $250.00.
Interactive Accounts:	No.
Maximum Casual Dial-Up Speed:	28,800 bps.
USENET News:	Yes. Approximately 7,000 newsgroups.
Local File Archives:	Yes. Internet software.
Domain Registration Service:	Yes. Full service. Free for dedicated clients. $50.00 for dial-up clients.

Domain Park Service:	Yes.
Consulting Service:	Yes. Internet gateway installation and maintenance; Internet WANs - installation, maintenance and monitoring; Internet security; Unix-Novell integration.
DNS Service:	Yes. Primary and secondary nameservers.
Commercial Traffic:	Yes.

HOW TO SIGN UP

On-line registration is not available. Call or send electronic mail for information.

Rates
Call or send electronic mail for information.

For More Information
Gopher:
gopher.interax.net

Communications Vir

Montreal, Quebec
vir.com

17 Laurier Court
Montreal, Quebec
H9W 4S7
Voice: (514) 933-8886
Fax: (514) 630-9047
Internet: info@vir.com

Communications Vir is a public Internet access provider. We provide access via SLIP, PPP and interactive accounts. We will introduce you to the Internet in a friendly way. For our more advanced users, we will help you design World Wide Web documents and provide a fast and reliable server.

Communications Vir est un fournisseur d'access à l'Internet. Nous offrons l'acces via des comptes SLIP, PPP, et Interactive. Nous pouvons vous introduire à l'Internet d'une façon simple et amicale. Pour nos clients plus avancés nous avons un server World Wide Web stable et rapide et pouvons vous assister à la construction de vos documents.

Service Area:	Greater Montreal area.
1-800 Service:	No.
PDN Service:	No.
Leased Line Service:	No.
Dedicated Dial-Up Service:	Yes.
SLIP/PPP Service:	Yes. SLIP and PPP. PC shareware is supplied to customers at no cost with a proprietary install program for Windows. Macintosh shareware and other public domain implementations are also supplied at no cost.
UUCP Service:	Mail and news feeds to be available in 1995.

Interactive Accounts:	Yes. Direct connection to the Internet. 2 MB permanent storage (10 MB temporary) per user. Additional storage space is available (call for pricing). Mail, Telnet, FTP, Gopher, Internet Relay Chat, Archie. Menu-driven interface and shell access (POSIX environment). Shareware communications software available to customers. QWK-, SOUP-, and Zip-News compatible off-line readers supported. Shareware off-line readers available to customers.
Maximum Casual Dial-Up Speed:	14,400 bps.
USENET News:	Yes. 8,000 newsgroups.
Local File Archives:	Yes. Freeware/shareware for PCs, Macintosh and Unix; Internet guides; Internet client software.
Domain Registration Service:	Yes. Full service. No charge.
Domain Park Service:	No.
Consulting Services:	Yes. Web page building and serving, Internet marketing and information gathering, Internet access.
DNS Service:	Yes. Primary and secondary nameservers.
Commercial Traffic:	Yes.

HOW TO SIGN UP

Registration is available on-line, but payment must be arranged by mail, telephone, or fax.

MODEM:
(514) 933-0000, 14,400 bps.

Rates
Full Access Plan:
$25.00 per month. Complete SLIP access. 10 hours per week. $2.00 for each additional hour.
News and E-Mail Plan:
$12.50 per month. SLIP access. Limited to news and e-mail. 45 minutes per day. $0.50 for each additional 15 minutes.
Family Plan:
$40.00 per month. Complete SLIP access. 15 hours per week. No adult newsgroups. Up to 4 e-mail addresses can be specified for this account. $2.00 for each additional hour.
Corporate Accounts:
Call for pricing.

For More Information
FTP: **World Wide Web:**
ftp.vir.com   *http://www.vir.com/index.html*

Ernst and Young Inc.
Montreal, Quebec
ey.ca, sobeco.com

1 Place Alexis Nihon
3400 De Maisonneuve Blvd. West
Montreal, Quebec
H3Z 3E8
Voice: (514) 935-5101
Fax: (514) 935-9008

Internet: lavalle@ey.ca (Mario Lavallee)
stacy@sobeco.com (Stacy Millions)

Ernst and Young is a partnership of professional consultants specialized in accounting, actuarial studies, information technologies, and human resources.

Service Area:	Ontario: Toronto
	Quebec: Montreal, Quebec City
1-800 Service:	No.
PDN Service:	No.
Connection via:	UUNET Canada. 56Kpbs.
Leased Line Service:	Yes. Up to 56Kbps.
Dedicated Dial-Up Service:	Yes.
SLIP/PPP Service:	Yes. SLIP and PPP. Some SLIP/PPP software supplied at no charge.
UUCP Service:	No.
Interactive Accounts:	Yes. 20MB permanent storage per user (fixed). Mail, Telnet, TN3270, FTP, Gopher, World Wide Web (Lynx), Hytelnet. Menu-driven interface and shell access.
Maximum Casual Dial-up Speed:	28,800 bps.
USENET News:	Yes. Approximately 3700 newsgroups. ClariNet News is available.
Local File Archives:	Yes. Mirrors of FTP sites (Dos, Windows, Mac software).
Domain Registration Service:	Yes. Limited service.
Domain Park Service:	No.
Consulting Services:	Yes.
DNS Service:	Yes. Secondary nameservers only.
Commercial Traffic:	Yes.

HOW TO SIGN UP

MODEM:
Montreal: (514) 395-0739 (V.32bis, PEP) login as: **seynet**
Toronto: (416) 360-1901 (V.32bis, PEP) login as: **seynet**
Quebec City: (418) 647-2110 (V.32 bis, PEP) login as: **seynet**
*You may need to press the **<enter>** key several times to get the login prompt. If you receive the MTL1 prompt, type **netserv** to get the login prompt.*

Rates
Text-based service: $4.00 per hour. Free 15-day trial period.
Graphical access: $250.00 per month. $400.00 registration fee.

INFOPUQ

Sainte-Foy, Quebec
infopuq.uquebec.ca

INFOPUQ
Université du Québec
2875, boulevard Laurier
Sainte-Foy, Québec
G1V 2M3
Voice: (418) 657-4422
Fax: (418) 657-2132
Internet: infopuq@uquebec.ca

INFOPUQ's first goal is to promote and support the use of telematics tools throughout the University of Quebec community. Furthermore, INFOPUQ offers its services to the general public throughout the Province of Quebec.

La principale mission d'INFOPUQ est de promouvoir et de supporter l'utilisation de moyens télématiques au sein de la communauté de l'Université du Québec. En plus, INFOPUQ rend ses services accessibles à un public plus large à la grandeur du Québec.

Service Area:	Chicoutimi, Hull, Montreal, Quebec City, Rimouski, Rouyn-Noranda, Trois-Rivières.
1-800 Service:	No.
PDN Service:	Yes. DATAPAC.
Connection via:	RISQ. 128Kbps.
Leased Line Service:	No.
Dedicated Dial-Up Service:	No.
SLIP/PPP Service:	No.
UUCP Service:	No.
Interactive Accounts:	Yes. Direct connection to the Internet. 2 MB of permanent storage per user (fixed, not expandable). Mail, Telnet, TN3270, FTP, Gopher, World Wide Web (Lynx). Menu-driven interface. Shell access on request.
Maximum Casual Dial-Up Speed:	19,200 bps.
USENET News:	Yes. Full feed.
Local File Archives:	No.
Domain Registration Service:	No.
Domain Park Service:	No.
Consulting Service:	No.
DNS Service:	No.
Commercial Traffic:	Yes.

HOW TO SIGN UP

Users must complete a paper registration form. Call to register.

Rates

$35.00 set-up fee. $5.00 per month (individual). $10.00 per month (organization). 60 minutes free connect time each month. Connect time charges are $8.00/hour between 7:00a.m. and 5:00p.m. and $6.00/hour between 5:00p.m. and 7:00a.m.

Packages:

Individual:	*$20.00/month for 5 hours*
Organization:	*$60.00/month for 15 hours*

For More Information

Gopher:

gopher.uquebec.ca

Login Informatique

Pierrefonds, Quebec

login.qc.ca, safe.org

4363 Jacques Bizard
Pierrefonds, Quebec
H9H 4W3
Voice: (514) 626-8086
Fax: (514) 626-1700
Internet: Diane.Nolet@login.qc.ca (Diane Nolet)

The main purpose of Login is to relay news, mail, and data throughout the Montreal area. Its mission is to provide reliable electronic communications to individuals and small businesses.

Service Area:	Montreal.
1-800 Service:	No.
PDN Service:	No.
Connection via:	RISQ. 56Kbps.
Leased Line Service:	No.
Dedicated Dial-Up Service:	Yes.
SLIP/PPP Service:	Yes. SLIP only. Software supplied.
UUCP Service:	Yes. Mail and news feeds. Customers can modify their own newsgroup subscriptions. UUCP software supplied.
Interactive Accounts:	Yes. Direct connection to the Internet. 5 MB of permanent storage per user. Telnet, TN3270, FTP, Hytelnet. No Internet mail. Shell access.
Maximum Casual Dial-Up Speed:	28,800 bps.
USENET News:	Yes. 4,000+ newsgroups.
Local File Archives:	No.
Domain Registration Service:	Yes. Full service. $40.00 fee.

Domain Park Service:	Yes.
Consulting Services:	Yes. Local network to Internet integration, Mosaic space design.
DNS Service:	Yes. Primary and secondary nameservers.
Commercial Traffic:	Yes.

HOW TO SIGN UP

Call or send electronic mail to register.

Rates

Basic Service:
$48 for 4 months. Mail and news via UUCP. You can receive electronic mail and an average volume of 2MB of USENET News per day. Your electronic mail address will be a simple extension of the domain login.qc.ca. An average of 45 minutes UUCP system connection time per day is allowed. This allowance can be extended to 60 minutes in "quota overflow" mode.

MX Service:
$80 for 4 months. Mail and news via UUCP. This service provides the same volumes as the Basic Service, but includes an MX domain name registration.   An average of 45 minutes UUCP system connection time per day is allowed. This allowance can be extended to 90 minutes in "quota overflow" mode.

PLUS Service:
$120 for 4 months. Mail, news and FTP. This service entitles you to one interactive account. Data transferred using FTP will be sent directly to your site in the directory of your choice. Up to 75 minutes direct Internet access time in any one day, renewable in increments of 15 minutes per day. An average of 90 minutes UUCP connect time per day is allowed. This allowance can be extended to 270 minutes in "quota overflow" mode.

COMPANY Service:
$300 for 6 months. This service entitles you to four interactive accounts. Data transferred using FTP will be sent directly to your site, in the directory of your choice. Each account may have a separate destination; the UUCP link is common to all accounts. Up to 105 minutes direct Internet access time in any one day, renewable in increments of 35 minutes per day. An average of 90 minutes UUCP connect time per day is allowed. This allowance can be extended to 270 minutes in "quota overflow" mode. The company has the use of anonymous FTP space available under the company's official domain name.

Free fifteen-day trial periods are available.

For More Information

FTP:
login.qc.ca
Directory: /pub/Login

World Wide Web:
http://www.safe.org

Metrix Interlink Corporation

Montreal, Quebec
interlink.net, rezonet.net, interlink.ca

500, boul. Rene-Levesque Ouest
Suite #1004
Montreal, Quebec
H2Z 1W7
Voice: (514) 875-0010
Fax: (514) 875-5735
Internet: info@interlink.net

Metrix Interlink is a full-service Internet provider operating in Eastern Canada with Points of Presence in Montreal, Toronto, and Quebec City. We offer high performance, commercial-grade

Internet access to government, large and small business, individuals and organizations, as well as a full range of services. Our services include turnkey Internet connection solutions, on-site installation, on-site training, strategic consulting, application development including WWW server development and Gopher server development. We also sell Black Hole Internet firewall solutions for high security and private virtual networking. In operation over a year, we have quickly built up a reputation for the performance and reliability of our network, as well as our responsiveness to customer requests.

Service Area:	Montreal, Toronto, Quebec City.
	Planning to expand to Sherbrooke, Trois-Rivières, and Ottawa.
1-800 service:	Yes. $10.00 per hour.
PDN Service:	No.
Connection via:	ANS and Sprint. T1.
Leased Line Service:	Yes.
Dedicated Dial-Up Service:	Yes.
SLIP/PPP Service:	Yes. SLIP and PPP. Freeware/shareware and commercial software is available to customers.
UUCP Service:	Yes. Mail and news feeds.
Interactive Accounts:	Yes. Direct connection to the Internet. 1 MB permanent storage per user. Additional storage is available for $1.00/MB. Mail, Telnet, TN3270, FTP, Gopher, WAIS, World Wide Web, Internet Relay Chat, Hytelnet, Archie, MUD. Menu-driven interface and shell access. Off-line mail readers supported. E-mail-to-fax gateway for the local calling area, and to Montreal, Toronto, and Quebec City.
Maximum Casual Dial-Up Speed:	28,800 bps.
USENET News:	Yes. 10,000 newsgroups. ClariNet News is available.
Local File Archives:	Yes. Windows, Unix, Macintosh, and OS/2 client software.
Domain Registration Service:	Yes. Full service. Free for permanently connected customers.
Domain Park Service:	Yes.
Consulting Services:	Yes. LAN connections to the Internet, WAN Configurations, router management, strategic use of the Internet, secure Internet connections, turnkey Internet gateway solutions, dial-up service outsourcing, custom training, on-site installation.
Nameserver Service:	Yes. Primary and secondary nameservers.
Commercial Traffic:	Yes.

HOW TO SIGN UP

Customers can register by e-mail, telephone, or fax.

Rates

Dial-Up SLIP/PPP:
$29.00 per month for 30 hours of connect time.
$99.00 one-time charge.
$1.00 per hour for additional connect time each month beyond 30 hours.

Permanent SLIP/PPP:

9.6Kbps:	*$250.00 set-up fee.*	*$250.00 per month.*
14,400 bps:	*$350.00 set-up fee.*	*$350.00 per month.*
28,800 bps:	*$525.00 set-up fee.*	*$525.00 per month.*
56Kbps/64Kbps:	*$1600.00 set-up fee.*	*$1000.00 per month.*

Consulting Services:
$400.00-$1000.00 per day.

For More Information

Gopher:
gopher.interlink.net

World Wide Web:
http://www.interlink.net

PubNIX Montreal

Cote St-Luc, Quebec
pubnix.qc.ca, pubnix.net

P.O. Box 147
Cote St-Luc, Quebec
H4V 2Y3
Voice: (514) 948-2492
Internet: info@pubnix.net

PubNIX Montreal provides affordable Internet connections to people and businesses in the Greater Montreal area.

Service Area:	Greater Montreal area.
1-800 Service:	No.
PDN Service:	No.
Connection via:	Metrix Interlink.
Leased Line Service:	No.
Dedicated Dial-Up Service:	No.
SLIP/PPP Service:	Planned for January 1, 1995.
UUCP Service:	Yes. Mail and news feeds. Newsgroup changes must go through a service person. Waffle for PCs is supplied at no charge.
Interactive Accounts:	Yes. Direct connection to the Internet. 10MB permanent storage space per user. Mail, Telnet, FTP, Gopher, WAIS, World Wide Web (Lynx), Internet Relay Chat, Archie. Shell access.
Maximum Casual Dial-Up Speed:	14,400 bps (28,800 bps. in 1995).
USENET News:	Yes. 8,000 newsgroups.
Local File Archives:	Yes. GNU software, XFree, other Unix software.

Domain Registration Service:	Yes. Full service. $100.00 charge.
Domain Park Service:	No.
Consulting Service:	No.
DNS Service:	Yes. Primary and secondary nameservers.
Commercial Traffic:	Yes.
Additional Comments:	Customers must be 18 years of age or older.

HOW TO SIGN UP

A registration form must be completed and returned to PubNIX along with a payment covering the first three months of service. Call or send electronic mail for further information.

Rates
Personal Account:
$25.00 per month. No sign-up fee.
Corporate Account:
$75.00 per month. No sign-up fee.
Special Services:
Rates available on request.

RISQ (Reseau Interordinateurs Scientifique Quebecois)

Montreal, Quebec
risq.net

Attention: Centre d'information du RISQ
1801 McGill College Avenue, Suite 800
Montreal, Quebec
H3A 2N4
Voice: (514) 398-1234
Fax: (514) 398-1244
Internet: cirisq@risq.net

Créé en 1989, le RISQ est un réseau provincial de communications informatisées voué à la recherche et l'enseignement. Le RISQ relie présentement plus de 100 organisations dont plusieurs universités et centres de recherche publics et privés oeuvrant au Québec.

Founded in 1989, RISQ is a provincial, computer-based communications network dedicated to research and education. RISQ presently provides networking for both the public and private research communities operating within Quebec.

Service Area:	Montreal, Quebec City, Sherbrooke.
	Planning to expand to Chicoutimi in Fall, 1994 and other cities in 1995.
1-800 Service:	No.
PDN Service:	No.
Connection via:	CA*net. T1 speed.
Leased Line Service:	Yes. Up to T1.

Dedicated Dial-Up Service:	Yes.
SLIP/PPP Service:	Yes. SLIP and PPP. Dedicated service only. Freeware/shareware software provided to customers.
UUCP Service:	No.
Interactive Accounts:	No.
Maximum Casual Dial-Up Speed:	No casual dial access.
USENET News:	Yes. Full feed.
Local File Archives:	Yes. Public software. RISQ information.
Domain Registration Service:	Yes. Full service. No charge.
Domain Park Service:	No.
Consulting Services:	Yes. Internet integration. RISQ operates a Network Information Center.
DNS Service:	Yes. Primary and secondary nameservers.
Commercial Traffic:	No.

HOW TO SIGN UP

Registration takes place over the telephone. Please call for information.

Rates

SLIP/PPP:

9600 bps:	*$250/month (without routing), $350/month (with routing)*
14,400 bps:	*$350/month (without routing), $550/month (with routing)*
28,800 bps:	*$650/month (without routing), $950/month (with routing)*

Dedicated Lines - Enterprises and Associates:

128Kbps or 112Kbps:	*$30,000/year (router included, line by member)*
56Kbps:	*$20,000/year (router included, line by member)*
19.2Kbps:	*$15,000/year (router included, line by member)*

Dedicated Lines - Enterprises and Associates, Members of CRIM:

128Kbps or 112Kbps:	*$27,000/year (router included, line by member)*
56Kbps:	*$18,000/year (router included, line by member)*
19.2Kbps:	*$13,000/year (router included, line by member)*

Education Organizations:

56Kbps or 19.2 Kbps:	*$15,000/year (router and line included)*
19.2Kbps/56Kbps:	*$5,000/year (router included)*

For more information

FTP:	**Gopher:**
risq.net	*risq.net*

Vircom Inc.

Laval, Quebec

vircom.com, gamemaster.qc.ca

2075 Dumouchel
Laval, Quebec
H7S 2H4
Voice: (514) 990-2532
Internet: sysop@vircom.com

Vircom is operating a BBS (The Gamemaster) that has a mission to build an on-line community at the lowest cost possible for our members in the Montreal area.

Service Area:	Montreal.
1-800 Service:	No.
PDN Service:	No.
Connection via:	RCO.
Leased Line Service:	No.
Dedicated Dial-Up Service:	Yes.
SLIP/PPP Service:	No.
UUCP Service:	No.
Interactive Accounts:	Yes. Direct connection to the Internet. Permanent storage is available. Mail, Telnet, FTP, Gopher, WAIS, World Wide Web (Lynx), Archie. Menu-driven interface. Point-and-click graphical user interface. RIPTERM software is provided to customers at no cost. QWK-compatible off-line mail readers are supported.
Maximum Casual Dial-Up Speed:	14,400 bps.
USENET News:	Yes.
Local File Archives:	No.
Domain Registration Service:	No.
Domain Park Service:	No.
Consulting Services:	Yes. Major BBS integration with Internet.
DNS Service:	No.
Commercial Traffic:	Yes.

HOW TO SIGN UP

MODEM:
(514) 875-6650   *2,400-14,400 bps*   *login as* **NEW**

Rates
From $0.25-$0.525 per hour.

NOVA SCOTIA

Chebucto FreeNet
Halifax, Nova Scotia
cfn.cs.dal.ca

Metro*CAN Society/Chebucto FreeNet
c/o Department of Mathematics, Statistics, and Computing Science
Dalhousie University
Halifax, Nova Scotia
B3H 3J5
Voice: (902) 494-2449
Internet: cfn@cfn.cs.dal.ca

The Chebucto FreeNet's Vision:

Every Nova Scotian will have free access to a Community Access Network, as part of a province-wide electronic network linked to the world-wide Internet.

The Chebucto FreeNet Mission Statement:

To achieve our vision, the Metro Community Access Network Society will:

- *Establish a Community Access Network for the Halifax-Dartmouth Metro area, which will:*
    - *help meet personal and professional information needs of people;
    foster communication among individuals and the institutions that serve them;*
    - *support community groups in their efforts at professional development, outreach and community service;*
    - *enhance opportunities for sustainable, community-based economic development; and,*
    - *create a favorable environment for business and employment growth.*
- *Cooperate with other groups to foster and support the development and linking of Community Access Networks in other parts of Nova Scotia, Atlantic Canada, the rest of Canada and the world.*

Service Area:	Halifax, Dartmouth, Bedford, Municipality of Halifax County
1-800 Service:	No.
PDN Service:	No.
Leased Line Service:	No.
Dedicated Dial-Up Service:	No.
SLIP/PPP Service:	No.
UUCP Service:	No.
Interactive Accounts:	Yes. Users have access to the World Wide Web and Internet mail.
Maximum Casual Dial-Up Speed:	14,400 bps.
USENET News:	Yes. 1370 newsgroups.
Local File Archives:	Yes. Community information.
Domain Registration Service:	No.
Domain Park Service:	No.
Consulting Services:	No.
DNS Service:	No.

Commercial Traffic:	No.

HOW TO SIGN UP

On-line registration + mail in a signed copy of the Chebucto FreeNet user agreement + mail in proof of your identification.

MODEM:
(902) 494-8006, 2400 bps-14400 bps, login as **guest**

INTERNET:
Telnet to **cfn.cs.dal.ca***, login as* **guest**

Rates
The Chebucto Free-Net services are free to the community.

For More Information

Telnet:
cfn.cs.dal.ca
Login: **guest**

World Wide Web:
http://www.cfn.cs.dal.ca/

Internet Services and Information Systems Inc.

Halifax, Nova Scotia
isisnet.com

Suite 1501
Maritime Centre
1505 Barrington Street
Halifax, Nova Scotia
Voice: (902) 429-4747
Fax: (902) 429-9003
Internet: info@isisnet.com

isis is working to bring low-cost, easy-to-use Internet access to Nova Scotia, for both individuals and organizations. isis offers quick and helpful support, LAN and WAN consulting services, and information technology solutions in association with local and international firms.

Service Area:	Halifax/Dartmouth Metropolitan area, including Sackville and Bedford.
1-800 Service:	No.
PDN Service:	No.
Connection via:	UUNET Canada. 224Kbps.
Leased Line Service:	Yes. 56Kbps to T1.
Dedicated Dial-Up Service:	Yes.
SLIP/PPP Service:	Yes. SLIP and PPP. Shareware/freeware software for DOS, Windows, Macintosh, Amiga, etc. is available for download.
UUCP Service:	Yes. Mail and news feeds. Newsgroup changes must go through a service person. Freeware/shareware UUCP software is available to customers.

Interactive Accounts:	Yes. Direct connection to the Internet. 2 MB permanent storage per user. Additional storage is available for $3.00/MB/month. Mail, Telnet, TN3270, FTP, Gopher, WAIS, World Wide Web (Lynx), Internet Relay Chat, MOO. Menu-driven interface and shell access. E-mail-to-fax gateway for the local calling area.
Maximum Casual Dial-Up Speed:	14,400 bps. 28,800 bps planned for December 1994.
USENET News:	Yes. 5,000 newsgroups.
Local File Archives:	Yes. SLIP/PPP software, popular shareware and freeware games, applications and utilities, FAQ archive.
Domain Registration Service:	Yes. Full service. No charge.
Domain Park Service:	Yes.
Consulting Services:	Yes. LAN and WAN networking, information retrieval, Internet searches/librarianship, telecommuting and information retrieval at a distance.
DNS Service:	Yes. Primary and secondary nameservers.
Commercial Traffic:	Yes.

HOW TO SIGN UP

Users can register by telephone or on-line.

MODEM:
*(902) 496-9054, 14,400 bps, login as **new**, press **<enter>** when prompted for password.*

INTERNET:
*Telnet to **ra.isisnet.com**, login as **new**, press **<enter>** when prompted for password.*

Rates

Personal connection, SLIP/PPP or terminal dial-up, 2hrs/day	*$25/month*
Personal connection, to Unix prompt with compiler access	*Phone*
14.4Kbps SLIP/PPP line (24 hour/day connection)	*$250/month*
including (year) lease of routes	*$550/month*
19.2Kbps SLIP/PPP line (24 hour/day connection)	*$325/month*
28.8Kbps SLIP/PPP line (24 hour/day connection)	*$425/month*
57.6Kbps v.35 leased line, router extra	*$1200/month*
256Kbps leased line	*Phone*
1.544Mbps leased line	*Phone*
30 frame/second video conferencing equipment	*$20,000/site*
WAN/LAN connectivity	*Phone*
Larger/custom connectivity pricing available.	*Phone us!*
UUCP mail feed (allocated polling times)	*$12/month*
UUCP news feed (15 newsgroups, no BBSs please)	*$6/month*
Extra 1MB disk space, personal connection (default, 2MB)	*$3/month*
Extra hour access per day	*$10/month*
Consultancy work (Internet searches, LAN/WAN networking)	*$50/hour*
	(plus initial fee)

EXTRA SERVICE OPTIONS FOR BUSINESS CUSTOMERS

Regular isis Service <included in monthly cost> .... *$Free*

- *Guaranteed 12 working hour response to questions/requests*
- *Monthly site visit*
- *4-hour emergency response 9a.m. - 6p.m. Monday - Friday*

isis *Bronze service* *$100/month*
- *Guaranteed 8 working hour response to questions/requests*
- *9a.m. to 5p.m. Monday - Friday telephone technical support*
- *Monthly site visit*
- *4 hour emergency response 8a.m. - 8p.m. Monday - Friday.*

isis *Silver service* *$200/month*
- *Guaranteed 4 working hour response to questions/requests*
- *8a.m. to 8p.m. Monday - Friday and 9a.m. - 5p.m. Saturday telephone tech support*
- *Site visit every two weeks*
- *3 hour emergency response 8a.m. - 8p.m. weekdays, 9a.m. - 5p.m. Saturday*
- *Limited emergency response beyond normal hours*

isis *Gold service* *$400/month*
- *Guaranteed 2 working hour response to questions/requests*
- *Reduced consultancy fees ($42/hour)*
- *8 a.m. to 8p.m. weekdays, 9a.m. to 6p.m. Saturday telephone technical support*
- *Site visit every week or every two weeks (client's choice)*
- *2-hour emergency response available 24 hrs/day 7 days/week*

Nova Scotia Technology Network Inc. (NSTN)

Dartmouth, Nova Scotia

nstn.ca

201 Brownlow Avenue
Dartmouth, Nova Scotia
B3B 1W2
Voice: (902) 481-NSTN (6786)
           1-800-336-4445 (Toll-Free Canada-Wide)
Fax: (902) 468-3679
Internet: info@nstn.ca (Automated)
           sales@nstn.ca (Sales/Marketing Team)

NSTN is more than simply a place to plug into. We are committed to providing the most affordable access to the Internet, in a manner that is practical, professional, and painless for our clients.

Service Area:	Nova Scotia: Amherst, Truro, Halifax, Bridgewater, Yarmouth, Kentville, Greenwood, Sydney.
	New Brunswick: Moncton, Dieppe, Riverview, Salisbury.
	Ontario: Toronto, Ottawa.
	Planning to expand to Vancouver, Calgary, Edmonton, Montreal, Saint John, Fredericton.
1-800 Service:	Under development. Call for information.
PDN Service:	No.
Connection via:	CA*net.
Leased Line Service:	Yes. 9600 bps - T1. ISDN service is available.
Dedicated Dial-Up Service:	Yes.

SLIP/PPP Service:	Yes. SLIP and PPP. DOS, Windows, or Macintosh SLIP/PPP software is available to customers. The software has a customized script to connect to any NSTN point-of-presence.
UUCP Service:	Yes. Mail and news feeds. Newsgroup changes must go through a service person.
Interactive Accounts:	No.
Maximum Casual Dial-Up Speed:	14,400 bps.
USENET News:	Yes. 3700 newsgroups.
Local File Archives:	Yes. SLIP software and assorted other documents and files of interest.
Domain Registration Service:	Yes. Full service. Cost is included in the installation fee.
Domain Park Service:	Call for information.
Consulting Services:	Yes. Network management, Internet consulting, Internet librarian.
DNS Service:	Yes. Primary and secondary nameservers.
Commercial Traffic:	Yes.

HOW TO SIGN UP

Registration is by telephone, fax, or e-mail. On-line registration is not available.

Rates
Dial-Up SLIP:
$35.00 installation charge (includes DOS software).
$25.00 per month. Includes 20 hours of use.
Additional hours are $1.00 per hour.
Dedicated Access:
From $250.00 per month.

For More Information
FTP:
ftp.nstn.ca
Directory: nstn-documentation

World Wide Web:
http://www.nstn.ca

Gopher:
gopher.nstn.ca

NEW BRUNSWICK

NBNet
Saint John, New Brunswick
nbnet.nb.ca

New Brunswick Telephone Company Ltd. (NBTel)
One Brunswick Square
P.O. Box 1430
Saint John, New Brunswick
E2L 4K2

Voice: 1-800-561-4459 (New Brunswick)
             (506) 458-1690
Internet: info@nbnet.nb.ca

NBTel is New Brunswick's local and long-distance telephone service provider.

Service Area:	All of New Brunswick.
1-800 service:	Yes (New Brunswick residents only).
PDN Service:	No.
Connection via:	CA*net
Leased Line Service:	Yes. From 56Kbps-10Mbps.
Dedicated Dial-Up Service:	No.
SLIP/PPP Service:	Yes. SLIP and PPP. Only to a shared modem pool on a non-dedicated line. Software is supplied for $20.00 (CommSet, produced by Cybernetic Control in Sackville, New Brunswick).
UUCP Service:	No.
Interactive Accounts:	No.
Maximum Casual Dial-Up Speed:	14,400 bps.
USENET News:	Yes. Approximately 3,500 newsgroups. ClariNet News is available.
Local File Archives:	No.
Domain Registration Service:	Yes. Full service. No charge.
Domain Park Service:	No.
Consulting Services:	No.
DNS Service:	Yes. Primary and secondary nameservers.
Commercial Traffic:	Yes.

HOW TO SIGN UP

Call or send electronic mail for information.

Rates
Dial-up Service:
Between 8:00a.m. and 6:00p.m.:	*$6.00/hour*
Between 6:00p.m. and 11:00p.m.:	*Save 20%*
Between 11:00p.m. and 8:00a.m.:	*Save 50%*
Minimum Charge:	*$5.00/month*
Maximum Charge:	*$200.00/month*
One-time Connection Service Charge:	*$17.50*

Connect time is billed on a minute-by-minute basis ($0.10 per minute).

CommunityNet Rates:
Flat rate, unlimited usage	*$35.00/month*
One-time Connection Service Charge:	*$17.50*

Dedicated Service:
Call for pricing.

For More Information
Gopher:
gopher.nbnet.nb.ca

Maritime Internet Services
Saint John, New Brunswick
mi.net

1216 Sand Cove Road
P.O. Box 6477
Saint John, New Brunswick
E2L 4R9
Voice: (506) 652-3624
Fax: (506) 652-5451
Internet: info@mi.net

Maritime Internet Services wants to bring you the world for a cost that everyone can afford. We can give you a point-and-click graphical user interface that will let you connect to hundreds of services all over the world. Or, if you prefer the power, we can get you up and running on SLIP or PPP. In addition to providing SLIP access, Maritime Internet Services offers a separate point-and-click graphical service with access to the Internet by clicking on desired applications.

Service Area:	Saint John, New Brunswick
1-800 service:	No.
PDN Service:	No.
Leased Line Service:	Yes. Up to 56Kbps.
Dedicated Dial-Up Service:	Yes.
SLIP/PPP Service:	Yes. SLIP and PPP.
UUCP Service:	Yes. Mail and news feeds. Newsgroups changes must go through a service person.
Interactive Accounts:	Yes. Direct connection to the Internet. Shell access available. Permanent storage space. 1MB soft quota. 5MB hard quota to be removed within 5 days. Additional storage space is available for an additional cost. Telnet, TN3270, FTP, Gopher, World Wide Web (Lynx), Archie, Internet Relay Chat, on-line games. RIPTERM software is supplied for free. QWK-compatible off-line mail readers are supported. Shareware copies of Bluewave are available. E-mail-to-fax gateway for local calling area only.
Maximum Casual Dial-Up Speed:	19,200 bps (28,800 bps soon).
USENET News:	Yes. 3500 newsgroups.
Local File Archives:	Yes. Communications programs, programming utilities, games, recipes, windows utilities, virus protection software etc.
Domain Registration Service:	Yes. Full service. No additional fee.
Domain Park Service:	Yes.

Consulting Services:	Yes. Internet training, network installations.
DNS Service:	Yes. Primary and secondary nameservers.
Commercial Traffic:	Yes.

HOW TO SIGN UP

MODEM:
(506) 635-5458, 14,400 bps

INTERNET:
Shell Access:
*Telnet to **itchy.mi.net** login as **new**, no password required.*

Rates
Corporate 56*PLUS
Call for pricing.

Corporate 14*PLUS
$250.00/month, unlimited 14,400 bps access.
$500.00 set-up fee.
Domain registration assistance included.

Corporate 14*LITE
$60.00 per month for 35 hours per month.
$1.50 per hour for additional hours.
$50.00 set-up fee.
Includes multiple accounts if arranged during set-up.

Individual Subscription:
$300.00/year or $170.00 for six months (includes 50 hours of connect time per month).
$0.50 per hour for additional hours.
$15.00 set-up fee.

Individual Lite:
$18.50 per month (includes 15 hours of connect time per month).
$1.15 per hour for additional hours.
$15.00 set-up fee.

Individual Regular:
$25.00 per month (includes 30 hours of connect time per month).
$0.75 per hour for additional hours.
$15.00 set-up fee.

Student Rate (available to students until grade 12 graduation):
$16.50 per month (includes 20 hours of connect time per month).
$0.60 per hour for additional hours.
$15.00 set-up fee.

Regular Rates (pay per usage):
$1.50/hour usage rate.
$5.00 minimum monthly charge.
$15.00 set-up fee.

Individual Heavy:
$85.00 per month (includes 140 hours/month).
$0.55/hr for additional hours.
$15.00 set-up fee.

Individual Plus:
$35.00/month (includes 45 hours/month).
$0.60/hour for additional hours.
$15.00 set-up fee.

For More Information

FTP:	**Telnet:**	**Gopher:**
ftp.mi.net	*itchy.mi.net*	*gopher.mi.net*
Directory: /pub/info	*Login:* **info**	

World Wide Web:
http://www.mi.net

Nova Scotia Technology Network Inc. (NSTN)

Dartmouth, Nova Scotia
nstn.ca

201 Brownlow Avenue
Dartmouth, Nova Scotia
B3B 1W2
Voice: (902) 481-NSTN (6786)
               1-800-336-4445 (Toll-Free Canada-Wide)
Fax: (902) 468-3679
Internet: info@nstn.ca (Automated)
               sales@nstn.ca (Sales/Marketing Team)

Areas Served: Moncton, Dieppe, Riverview, Salisbury
See main entry under Province of Nova Scotia

PRINCE EDWARD ISLAND

PEINet Inc.

Charlottetown, Prince Edward Island
peinet.pe.ca

P.O. Box 3126
Charlottetown, Prince Edward Island
C1A 7N9
Voice: (902) 892-PEINet (7346)
Fax: (902) 368-2446
Internet: admin@peinet.pe.ca

PEINet is Prince Edward Island's Wide Area Network providing connectivity to CA*net and the Internet. Our mission is to provide an information network for PEI to facilitate the connection of users to services. The long-range goal of PEINet is to develop a broad range of network services, to deliver value-added information services and access to external databases, and to provide the environment for the development and promotion of new, local information sources.

Our rates and services are structured so that we can provide connectivity to all levels of clientele from large organizations to the individual dial-up user. We feel it is important to provide uniform, local access province-wide so that we can facilitate technology growth and provide a platform for the Internet industry on Prince Edward Island.

Service Area:	Complete local access across Prince Edward Island.
1-800 Service:	No.
PDN Service:	No.
Connection via:	CA*net. 1/2 T1.
Leased Line Service:	Yes. Up to 56Kbps.
Dedicated Dial-Up Service:	Yes.
SLIP/PPP Service:	Yes. SLIP and PPP. Software supplied for DOS and Windows users at no extra cost.
UUCP Service:	No.
Interactive Accounts:	Yes. Direct connection to the Internet. 2MB permanent storage/user. Additional storage is available for an additional cost. Telnet, FTP, Gopher, World Wide Web (Lynx), Archie, WAIS. Menu-driven with shell access.
Maximum Casual Dial-Up Speed:	28,800 bps.
USENET News:	Yes. Approximately 2,000 newsgroups. ClariNet News is available.
Local File Archives:	No.
Domain Registration Service:	Yes. Full service. No additional cost.
Domain Park Service:	No.
Consulting Services:	Yes. Connectivity for LANs and WANs, advertising on the Internet, information dissemination on the Internet.
DNS Service:	Yes. Primary and secondary nameservers.
Commercial Traffic:	Yes.

HOW TO SIGN UP

Call or send electronic mail for information.

Rates

Dial-up accounts:
$20.00/month. Includes 20 hours free usage. Additional hours are $5.00/hour from 6a.m. to 6p.m. and $2.00/hour from 6p.m.-6a.m.

Dial-in SLIP:
$50.00/month. Includes 100 hours free usage. Additional hours are $5.00/hour from 6a.m. to 6p.m. and $2.00/hour from 6p.m.-6a.m.

Dedicated Access:
Cost depends on speed and number of users. Call for consultation.

For More Information

Gopher:
gopher.peinet.pe.ca

World Wide Web:
http://bud.peinet.pe.ca

Raven Information Systems

Charlottetown, Prince Edward Island
raven.net

P.O. Box 2906
Charlottetown, Prince Edward Island
C1A 8C5
Voice: (902) 894-4946
Internet: Dale_Poole@raven.net

Raven Information Systems offers an on-line information system using established BBS technology.

Rather than pursuing the newest graphical interfaces, a familiar Bulletin Board System interface is used to seamlessly integrate mail and news, as well as other services - callers can experience the excitement of communicating with the rest of the world, on their very first call!

Raven Information Systems can also custom design an on-line service for other groups, and provide a mail and news feed using UUCP technology.

Service Area:	Charlottetown.
1-800 Service:	No.
PDN Service:	No.
Connection via:	UUNET Canada.
Leased Line Service:	No.
Dedicated Dial-Up Service:	No.
SLIP/PPP Service:	No.
UUCP Service:	Yes. Mail and news feeds. Newsgroup changes must go through a service person. Public domain and shareware packages are available to customers.
Interactive Accounts:	Yes. Gateway connection to the Internet. 50-100K of permanent storage per user. Internet mail, FTP-by-mail, Archie-by-mail. Local conferencing. Shareware communications software is available to customers. QWK-compatible off-line readers supported. Shareware readers are available for download.
Maximum Casual Dial-Up Speed:	19,200 bps.
USENET News:	Yes. 300-400 newsgroups. Some ClariNet groups are available.
Local File Archives:	Yes. Amiga, Mac, Internet zines, game rules archive, files from Special Interest Groups.
Domain Registration Service:	No.
Domain Park Service:	No.
Consulting Services:	Yes. On-line systems design and management, associated custom programming, Internet research and information gathering, Internet end-user training for individuals and groups.

DNS Service:	No.
Commercial Traffic:	Yes.

HOW TO SIGN UP

MODEM:
(902) 628-8475, v.32bis v.42bis, login as yourself and choose a password

Rates
Call or send electronic mail for current pricing.

NEWFOUNDLAND

The Enterprise Network Inc.
St. John's, Newfoundland
entnet.nf.ca

P.O. Box 13670
Station "A"
St. John's, Newfoundland
A1B 4G1
Voice: 1-800-563-5008
Fax: (709) 729-7039
Internet: Customer_Service@porthole.entnet.nf.ca

The Enterprise Network is an information and support service specializing in the application of information technology and the Internet for business and economic development. The network operates an on-line service specializing in business and economic development-related information as well as six walk-in electronic enterprise centers (telecenters) in Newfoundland and Labrador. The Enterprise Network is a leader in the application of information technology to regional economic development focusing on networking, information provision and teleworking, and provides consulting services on a national and international basis.

Service Area:	St. John's, Clarenville, St. Alban's, Stephenville, Baie Verte, Forteau.
	1-800 service is available elsewhere in the province.
1-800 Service:	Yes. No extra cost (included in base rates).
PDN Service	No.
Connection via:	NLnet. 56Kbps.
Leased Line Service:	No.
Dedicated Dial-Up Service:	No.
SLIP/PPP Service:	No.
UUCP Service:	No.

Interactive Accounts:	Yes. E-mail is through a gateway connection to the Internet via a CC-Mail SMTP gateway. Permanent storage space is available. Telnet, FTP, Gopher, World Wide Web (Lynx), database services. Menu-driven interface. PC Anywhere is supplied to customers at no cost with the initial sign-up kit.
Maximum Casual Dial-Up Speed:	14,400 bps.
USENET News:	Available Fall 1994.
Local File Archives:	No.
Domain Registration Service:	No.
Domain Park Service:	No.
Consulting Services:	Yes. Network design, network applications, information product development, telework implementation and management, information-sector planning and development.
DNS Service:	No.
Commercial Traffic:	Yes.

HOW TO SIGN UP

Registration is by phone or mail. Call or send electronic mail for information.

Rates
Rates are under review. Please call for current rates.

NLnet (Newfoundland Regional Network)
St. John's, Newfoundland
nlnet.nf.ca

c/o Department of Computing and Communications
Memorial University of Newfoundland
St. John's, Newfoundland
A1C 5S7
Voice: (709) 737-4555
Fax::   (709) 737-3514
Internet: support@nlnet.nf.ca

NLnet is the CA*net regional network in Newfoundland and Labrador. NLnet is an association of member organizations and is operated by the Memorial University of Newfoundland. NLnet's mission is to promote the development and use of networking throughout the province in support of education, research, and economic development.

Service Area:	St. John's, Clarenville, Corner Brook, Grand Falls/Windsor, Labrador City, Stephenville. Expansion is planned to Burin and Gander.
1-800 Service:	No.
PDN Service:	No.

Connection via:	CA*net. T1.
Leased Line Service:	Yes. 9600 bps - 64Kbps.
Dedicated Dial-Up Service:	Yes.
SLIP/PPP Service:	Yes. SLIP only. Freeware and shareware software is available to customers.
UUCP Service:	No.
Interactive Accounts:	Yes. Direct connection to the Internet. 3MB permanent storage per user (fixed, not expandable). Mail, Telnet, TN3270, FTP, Gopher, Archie. Shell access. Kermit communications software is available to customers.
Maximum Casual Dial-Up Speed:	28,800 bps.
USENET News:	Yes. Approximately 2100 newsgroups.
Local File Archives:	No.
Domain Registration Service:	Yes. Full service. No charge.
Domain Park Service:	Yes.
Consulting Services:	No.
DNS Service:	Yes. Primary and secondary nameservers.
Commercial Traffic:	Yes.

HOW TO SIGN UP

Registration is over the telephone. Call or send electronic mail for information.

Rates

Interactive Account and SLIP:
$9.95 for 10 hours per month ($1.00 per hour for additional hours).
$21.25 for 25 hours per month ($1.00 per hour for additional hours).
$33.45 for 40 hours per month ($1.00 per hour for additional hours).

Dedicated Dial:
$250.00 per month.

Leased Lines:
9600 bps - $10,000.
19,200 bps - $12,500.
38,400 bps - $17,500.
56,000 bps - $22,500.

STEM~Net
St. John's, Newfoundland
stemnet.nf.ca

STEM~Net
Memorial University of Newfoundland
E-5038, G.A. Hickman Building

St. John's, Newfoundland
A1B 3X8
Voice: (709) 737-8836
Fax: (709) 737-2179
Internet: staff@calvin.stemnet.nf.ca

The mission of STEM~Net is to provide a high-quality computer network for educators in Newfoundland and Labrador, and to support teaching, curriculum and professional development activities related to their work.

Its mandate is restricted to active Newfoundland-based public K-12 educators, rural public-college educators, Memorial University's Faculty of Education and full-time MUN Education students, and selected distance-education courses and programs. Its goals are to serve these groups by:

(i)   improving communications by K-12, college and university instructors;

(ii)   facilitating access of K-12 and rural public-college educators to a wide range of on-line resources related to their work, including the resources of Memorial University, the ACOA/Enterprise Network, SchoolNet and the Internet;

(iii)   fostering a better understanding among K-12 educators of appropriate uses of information technology, in general, and computer-mediated communications, in particular;

(iv)   contributing in meaningful and significant ways to the efforts of achievement, with special attention to the areas of mathematics, science, technology education and written communications;

(v)   addressing, within the context of STEM~Net accessibility and usage, relevant issues related to disability, ethno-cultural (including native), gender and regional equity.

Service Area:	Labrador City, Stephenville, Corner Brook, Gander, St. John's, Grand Falls-Windsor, Marystown, Clarenville.
	Planning to expand to Goose Bay, Port aux Basques, and Carbonear.
1-800 Service:	No.
PDN Service:	No.
Connection via:	NLnet. 10Mbps.
Leased Line Service:	No.
Dedicated Dial-Up Service:	No.
SLIP/PPP Service:	Yes. Freeware/shareware software is supplied to users.
UUCP Service:	No.
Interactive Accounts:	Yes. Direct connection to the Internet. 3MB of permanent storage space per user (fixed, but can be expanded if necessary - call for details). Mail, Telnet, TN3270, FTP, Gopher, World Wide Web (Lynx), Hytelnet, Archie. Menu-driven interface or shell access. Communications software is available to users (Telix and Kermit). Off-line readers supported and supplied (Yarn, WaveRider, UNOR, UniQWK, Robomail, and Alice (Mac)).

Maximum Casual Dial-Up Speed:	28,800 bps.
USENET News:	Yes. 2,100 newsgroups.
Local File Archives:	Yes. Winsock applications, virus protection software, Internet documents, training materials, off-line software, programs for DOS, Windows, and Macintosh.
Domain Registration Service:	No.
Domain Park Service:	No.
Consulting Services:	No.
DNS Service:	Yes. Primary and secondary nameservers.
Commercial Traffic:	No.

HOW TO SIGN UP

Users must complete a written application form, sign it, and return it by fax or postal mail.

Rates
There is no fee to access STEM~Net.

For More Information

Gopher:
info.stemnet.nf.ca

World Wide Web:
http://info.stemnet.nf.ca

DOMESTIC PROVIDERS SERVING MORE THAN ONE PROVINCE

Advantis Canada
Markham, Ontario
ibm.net

3500 Steeles Avenue East
Markham, Ontario
L3R 2Z1
Voice: 1-800-268-3100 (Canada-wide Toll Free)
Fax: (905) 316-6967
Internet: connect@vnet.ibm.com

Advantis Canada, a wholly-owned subsidiary of IBM Canada, includes IBM's former Network Services Company (IIN), plus the Computer and Network Services of Air Canada and The Gemini Group. Advantis Canada will be part of the IBM Global Network, a business unit that will develop and operate the world's largest high-speed voice and data network dedicated to network-centric computing.

In addition to providing a full range of Internet access and support services, Advantis Canada has offerings in the areas of Network Outsourcing, Frame Relay, EDI and e-mail.

Service Area:	Toronto, Montreal, Victoria, Vancouver, Edmonton, Calgary, Regina, Winnipeg, London, Ottawa, Quebec City, Halifax.

1-800 Service:	Yes.
PDN Service:	No.
Leased Line Service:	Yes.
Dedicated Dial-Up Service:	Yes.
SLIP/PPP Service:	Yes. SLIP and PPP. SLIP software is provided as part of the "IBM Internet Connection" included with OS/2 WARP. Applications supplied include FTP, Telnet, Gopher, Newsreader, Ultimedia Mail/2 'Lite'.
UUCP Service:	No.
Interactive Accounts:	No.
Maximum Casual Dial-Up Speed:	14,400 bps.
USENET News:	Yes. 8000 + newsgroups.
Local File Archives:	Yes.
Domain Registration Service:	Yes. Call for rates.
Domain Park Service:	No.
Consulting Services:	Yes. Call for information.
DNS Service:	Yes. Primary and secondary nameservers.
Commercial Traffic:	Yes.

HOW TO SIGN UP

OS/2 Warp registers users on-line.

Rates
Call for pricing.

For more information:
Gopher:
gopher.advantis.com

World Wide Web:
http://www.ibm.com

AT&T Mail
Toronto, Ontario
attmail.com

Unitel Electronic Commerce Services
2005 Sheppard Avenue East, Suite 215
Toronto, Ontario
M2J 5B4
Voice: Canada Toll-Free 1-800-567-4671

Whether your business manufactures a product or provides a service, your staff, clients, and vendors exchange dozens of communications each day. By eliminating the traditional obstacles of geography, time and technology, AT&T Mail can help you expand your reach, increase productivity, and dramatically streamline communications - all without your purchasing additional hardware equipment. AT&T Mail gives you connectivity options that let you reach over 20 million private and public electronic mail subscribers worldwide, as well as millions of fax machines, telex terminals, and postal addresses - all without leaving your PC.

Service Area:	Where Datapac service is available.
1-800 Service:	2nd quarter 1995.
PDN Service:	Datapac, FasPac
Leased Line Service:	Yes.
Dedicated Dial-Up Service:	Yes.
SLIP/PPP Service:	No.
UUCP Service:	No.
Interactive Accounts:	Yes. Internet mail. Fax, telex, and paper delivery services.
Maximum Casual Dial-Up Speed:	9600 bps -or- 2400 bps, depending on your location.
USENET News:	No.
Local File Archives:	No.
Domain Registration Service:	No.
Domain Park Service:	No.
Consulting Services:	No.
DNS Service:	No.
Commercial Traffic:	Yes.

HOW TO SIGN UP

Call for information.

Rates
Message Charges (Within Canada and International):
$4.00/month mailbox fee.
Up to 1000 characters: $0.70
Up to 2000 characters: $1.00
Up to 3000 characters: $1.30
Each additional 1000 characters (over 3000): $0.15
Message charges apply to outgoing messages only. Incoming mail is free.

Fax, Telex, Paper Delivery:
Call for information.

fONOROLA i*internet
Ottawa, Ontario
fonorola.net, fonorola.ca, fonorola.com

250 Albert Street, Suite 205
Ottawa, Ontario
K1P 6M1

```
Voice:    (604) 683-3666 (Vancouver)
          (403) 269-3666 (Calgary)
          (416) 364-3666 (Toronto)
          (519) 642-3666 (London)
          (519) 741-3666 (Kitchener)
          (613) 235-3666 (Ottawa)
          (514) 954-3666 (Montreal)
          (716) 856-3666 (Buffalo)
Fax:      (613) 232-4329
Internet: info@fonorola.net
          sales@fonorola.net
```

fONOROLA i*internet's mandate is to provide high-quality Internet backbone and access services to all Canadians.

Service Area:	Calgary, London, Kitchener, Montreal, Ottawa, Toronto, Vancouver. Planning to expand to Halifax.
1-800 service:	No.
PDN Service:	Upon request only.
Connection via:	ANS. T1.
Leased Line Service:	Yes. 56Kbps - T1. T2 or T3 as requested. ISDN service is available.
Dedicated Dial-Up Service:	No.
SLIP/PPP Service:	Yes. PPP. Dedicated service only.
UUCP Service:	No.
Interactive Accounts:	No.
Maximum Casual Dial-Up Speed:	N/A.
USENET News:	Yes. Full feed. ClariNet News is available.
Local File Archives:	No.
Domain Registration Service:	Yes. Full service. No charge.
Domain Park Service:	Yes.
Consulting Service:	Yes. Mail, DNS servers, information servers, corporate network planning.
DNS Service:	Yes. Primary and secondary nameservers.
Commercial Traffic:	Yes.

HOW TO SIGN UP

A signed contract is required. Call or send electronic mail for information.

Rates
Call for pricing.

For More Information
FTP: *Gopher:*
ftp.fonorola.net   *gopher.fonorola.net*

INSINC
Integrated Network Services Inc.
Vancouver, British Columbia
insinc.net

Suite 1740
P.O. Box 12095
555 West Hastings Street
Vancouver, British Columbia
V6B 4N5
Voice: (604) 687-7575 (Vancouver)
          (403) 269-3290 (Calgary)
          (416) 499-2083 (Toronto)
          (514) 354-2267 (Montreal)
          1-800-563-4744 (Canada Toll-Free)
Fax: (604) 687-7121
Internet: ed.placenis@insinc.net (Edward Placenis)

INSINC is a Canadian pioneer and leader in data network integration, providing comprehensive customized network management products and services to over 300 corporations throughout Canada and the United States. INSINC serves as the strategic single point of contact for those corporations that face an increasingly complex array of equipment and carrier options for their data networks. INSINC's success is built on its proven track record of customer satisfaction. We have the experience and ability to smoothly integrate new and existing systems as well as to provide the intelligence and foresight in planning future migration paths for our customers' growth. INSINC offers a range of value-added services to our customers, including dedicated high-speed Internet connectivity.

INSINC is positioned to provide Internet access services to corporate customers and dial-up Internet providers.

Service Area:	Wherever local telephone company digital access services are available.
1-800 Service:	No.
PDN Service:	No.
Connection via:	SPRINT. 1.5Mbps.
Leased Line Service:	Yes. 56Kbps to 1.544Mbps. INSINC provides Internet access over its frame relay network.
Dedicated Dial-Up Service:	No.
SLIP/PPP Service:	No.
UUCP Service:	No.

Interactive Accounts:	No.
Maximum Casual Dial-Up Speed:	No casual dial access.
USENET News:	Yes. Full feed.
Local File Archives:	No.
Domain Registration Service:	Yes. Full service.
Domain Park Service:	No.
Consulting Services:	Yes. Network integration consulting services for a wide range of corporate requirements.
DNS Service:	Yes. Secondary nameservers only.
Commercial Traffic:	Yes.

HOW TO SIGN UP

Registration is over the telephone. Please call for information.

Rates:
Call for pricing information.

MPACT Immedia Inc.
Montreal, Quebec
immedia.ca, mpact.ca

1155 bd. René-Lévesque Ouest/West
Suite 2250
Montreal, Quebec
H3B 4T3
Voice: (514) 397-9747
              1-800-361-7252
Fax: (514) 398-0764
Internet: service@immedia.ca

MPACT Immedia Inc., a public Canadian company, offers electronic commerce and value-added network (VAN) services worldwide to help organizations move from a paper-based world for orders, invoices, and correspondence to electronic transactions that provide high productivity, speed, and a competitive edge. Interconnections ® services can be accessed through a local call from over 1,000 cities in over 30 countries around the world using IBM PCs and Macintosh equipment. It facilitates transparent, efficient, and low-cost communications between a wide range of communications devices including personal computers, local area networks, and both mini and mainframe computers.

Service Area:	Where Tymnet and Datapac services are available. Most Canadian cities are accessible locally (depends on public data network availability).
1-800 Service:	Yes. Call for pricing.
PDN Service:	Yes. Datapac and Tymnet.

Leased Line Service:	No.
Dedicated Dial-Up Service:	No.
SLIP/PPP Service:	Coming in January 1995.
UUCP Service:	Yes. E-mail feeds only.
Interactive Accounts:	Coming in January 1995. Mail, Telnet, FTP, Gopher, WAIS, World Wide Web. Menu-driven interface and "point-and-click" graphical user interface. Communications software supplied to customers at no charge - Immedia Express Remote User Agent. Electronic commerce and EDI services also available. Local and international e-mail-to-fax gateway.
Maximum Casual Dial-Up Speed:	14,400 bps.
USENET News:	No.
Local File Archives:	No.
Domain Registration Service:	Yes. Limited service. Call for pricing.
Domain Park Service:	No.
Consulting Service:	Yes. Electronic commerce services, message-enabled applications, electronic document interchange (EDI), electronic mail, bulletin board systems, interconnection to non-Internet and commercial electronic mail systems.
DNS Service:	Yes. Primary and secondary nameservers.
Commercial Traffic:	Yes.

HOW TO SIGN UP

Registration takes place over the telephone.   Please call for information using the toll-free number.

Rates:
Call for current pricing.

UUNET Canada Inc.
Toronto, Ontario
uunet.ca

1 Yonge Street, Suite 1400
Toronto, Ontario
M5E 1J9
Voice: (416) 368-6621
                1-800-INET-123
Fax: (416) 368-1350
Internet: info@uunet.ca

UUNET Canada is the oldest nation-wide Internet service provider in Canada, and a communications leader in the emerging global village. Transportation of information through the

Internet has been our only business since we initiated our network in 1991. Today, our backbone infrastructure covers major population centres from coast to coast.

Service Area:	British Columbia: Vancouver
	Alberta: Calgary, Edmonton
	Ontario: London, Kitchener, Ottawa, Toronto
	Quebec: Montreal, Quebec City
	Nova Scotia: Halifax
	Planning to expand to Sudbury, Hamilton, and Fredericton.
1-800 Service:	No.
PDN Service:	No.
Connection via:	Alternet. T1.
Leased Line Service:	Yes. 19.2 Kbps to T1. ISDN service is available.
Dedicated Dial-Up Service:	Yes.
SLIP/PPP Service:	Yes. SLIP and PPP.
UUCP Service:	Yes. Mail and news feeds. Newsgroups changes can be made automatically. Shareware UUCP packages supplied.
Interactive Accounts:	Yes. Telnet, TN3270, FTP, Gopher, WAIS, WWW (Lynx), Archie. Shell access not available. No access to e-mail. Permanent disk space not available.
Maximum Casual Dial-Up Speed:	19,200 bps (28,800 bps when available).
USENET News:	Yes. 8,800 newsgroups. ClariNet News is available.
Local File Archives:	Yes. Internet-related utilities and files.
Domain Registration Service:	Yes. Full service. Free with all new accounts. $50 for non-customers.
Domain Park Service:	Yes.
Consulting Services:	Yes. Custom services and security.
DNS Service:	Yes. Primary and secondary nameservers.
Commercial Traffic:	Yes.

HOW TO SIGN UP

Call or send electronic mail for information.

Rates

Shared UUCP:
$20/month plus $6/hour. Shared phone line and modem.

Shared IP (SLIP/PPP):
$50/month plus $6/hour. Shared phone line and modem.

Dedicated Services:
From $500/month flat-rate and up. Call for additional information.

For More Information
FTP: **World Wide Web:**
ftp.uunet.ca   *http://www.uunet.ca*

WEB
Toronto, Ontario
web.apc.org, web.net

c/o NirvCentre
401 Richmond Street West, Suite 104
Toronto, Ontario
M5V 3A8
Voice: (416) 596-0212
Fax: (416) 596-1374
Internet: support@web.apc.org

Web is Canada's best communication and information resource on areas of social concern, with over 1,000 conferences covering social justice, international development, environment, newswires, peace, health, community economic development, human rights, and education. NirvCentre operates Web, which currently offers e-mail, computer conferencing, on-line databases, and Internet services to over 2,000 organizations and individuals across Canada. Web is the Canadian member of the Association for Progressive Communications (APC), an internationally-integrated system of eighteen regional networks providing electronic communications to over 25,000 social change groups in 133 countries.

Service Area:	Toronto, Ottawa, Montreal, Vancouver.
	Planning to expand to Edmonton, Halifax, Guelph/Kitchener/Waterloo, Hamilton, London, Sault Ste. Marie.
1-800 Service:	No.
PDN Service:	Yes. Datapac.
Connection via:	UUNET Canada (2*56Kb leased line), ONet (128Kb dedicated line), BCNet (38,400 dedicated line)
Leased Line Service:	No.
Dedicated Dial-Up Service:	No.
SLIP/PPP Service:	Yes. Both SLIP and PPP to be available in early 1995.
UUCP Service:	Yes, by request only. Mail and news feeds. Newsgroup changes must go through a service person.

Interactive Accounts:	Yes. Direct connection to the Internet. Permanent storage space available. Unlimited storage for computer conferences. First 20 kilobytes of e-mail storage is free. Additional e-mail storage is $0.05/Kb/month with no limit. No shell access. Mail, Telnet, TN3270, FTP, Gopher, WAIS, World Wide Web (Lynx). An off-line reader called Messenger is available for $50 for individuals and non-profits and for $100 for corporate and government users (IBM/compatibles only). Local, national and international e-mail-to-fax gateway.
Maximum Casual Dial-Up Speed:	19,200 bps (28,800 bps coming soon).
USENET News:	Yes. 2,600 newsgroups.
Local File Archives:	Yes. Text files are available in the form of messages that have been accumulating in public on-line conferences for up to 7 years. There are over 1000 such conferences available to users, covering topics related to social change. Topics include social justice, human rights, international development, environment, peace, education, and others.
Domain Registration Service:	No.
Domain Park Service:	Yes.
Consulting Services:	Yes. On-line networking, network customization, on-line group facilitation, international networking (particularly Africa).
DNS Service:	Yes. Primary and secondary nameservers.
Commercial Traffic:	Yes.
Additional Comments:	Hard-copy manual is supplied (cost is included in account set-up fee). Web has an on-line directory of social change organizations that are on-line in Canada and around the world. Private conferences with special facilitator privileges can be set up and linked to other networks.

HOW TO SIGN UP

On-line registration will commence in early 1995. Until then, registration is by telephone, fax, or regular mail.

Rates

SINGLE-USER ACCOUNTS
Individual/Non-profit Organization:
$25.00 account set-up.
$99.00/year subscription.
$5/hour for system usage (2 hours free each month).
Datapac (where applicable): $6.50/hour during peak hours (8a.m. - 8p.m. weekdays), $4.00/hour off-peak (8p.m.-8a.m. and weekends).

Government/Corporate/Industry Association:
$50.00 account set-up.
$99.00/year subscription.
$10.00/hour for system usage.
Datapac (where applicable): $10.00/hour.

MULTI-USER ACCOUNTS
Individual/Non-profit Organization:
$25.00 account set-up/ID.
$199.00/year subscription.

$5.00/hour for system usage.
Datapac (where applicable): $6.50/hour during peak hours (8a.m. - 8p.m. weekdays), $4.00/hour off-peak (8p.m. - 8a.m. and weekends).
Government/Corporate/Industry Association:
$50.00 account set-up/ID.
$299.00/year subscription.
$10.00/hour system usage.
Datapac (where applicable): $10.00 per hour.

TRAINING/DEMONSTRATIONS
$250.00 per 3-hour session.

For More Information
FTP:
spinne.web.net
Directory: pub
File: web-info.txt

Gopher:
spinne.web.net

WorldLinx Telecommunications
Toronto, Ontario
worldlinx.com, resonet.com

BCE Place
181 Bay Street, Suite 350
P.O. Box 851
Toronto, Ontario
M5J 2T3
Voice: (416) 350-1000
          1-800-567-1811
Fax: (416) 350-1001
Internet: info@worldlinx.com

WorldLinx is the leading national provider of enhanced and global information networking products and services. WorldLinx builds upon its expertise in software, internetworking, and telecommunications to provide standard and customized solutions for customers. WorldLinx maintains sales offices throughout Canada and is represented across Canada by BCTel, AGT, NorthWest Tel, Sasktel, Manitoba Tel, Bell Canada, QuebecTel, NBTel, MT&T, Island Tel, Newfoundland Tel, and other value-added resellers.

Service Area:	Local points-of-presence in over 300 locations across Canada.
	Access from within the U.S.A. is planned for 1995.
1-800 Service:	Yes. $24.50 per hour.
PDN Service:	Yes. Datapac for the resonet.com domain. Worldlinx.com is accessible using the WorldLinx LAN/WAN national IP network, Stentor Hyperstream frame relay, and BCTel Ubiquity ATM Network.
Leased Line Service:	Yes. 56Kbps - T1. ISDN service will be available in 1995.
Dedicated Dial-Up Service:	Yes.
SLIP/PPP Service:	Yes. PPP only.
UUCP Service:	No.

Interactive Accounts:	Yes. Direct connection to the Internet. 10 MB of permanent storage per user. Additional storage is available (call for rates). Mail, Telnet, FTP, Gopher. Shell access. E-mail-to-fax gateway is available on the resonet.com domain.
Maximum Casual Dial-Up Speed:	28,800 bps.
USENET News:	Yes. 5,000 newsgroups.
Local File Archives:	No.
Domain Registration Service:	Yes. Full service. No charge.
Domain Park Service:	Yes.
Consulting Services:	Yes. User training, Internet marketing services, system security, LAN/WAN internetworking, electronic commerce.
DNS Service:	Yes. Primary and secondary nameservers.
Commercial Traffic:	Yes.
Additional Comments:	WorldLinx maintains a national network operations center for support of the worldlinx.com domain and a national customer assistance center for the resonet.com domain.

HOW TO SIGN UP

Call or send electronic mail for information.

Rates
Call for pricing.

For More Information
FTP: **Gopher:**
ftp.worldlinx.com   gopher.worldlinx.com

World Tel Internet Canada
Vancouver, British Columbia
worldtel.com

Suite 810 - 675 West Hastings Street
Vancouver, British Columbia
V6B 1N2
Voice: (604) 685-3877
Fax: (604) 687-0688
Internet: info@worldtel.com

World Tel is an international telecommunications firm that has entered into strong strategic partnerships with U.S., South American and Far Eastern organizations to bring our corporate, professional, government and individual subscribers a high level of service on the Commercial Internet. World Tel is unique in that it concentrates on the commercialization of the internet, which is now underway. World Tel is opening offices in major centers around the world to assist businesses, professionals, governments and individuals in selling and marketing their products and services, expanding international trade and finance, entering into strategic joint venture partnerships, and securing access to relevant business and technical information. World Tel is also unique in that it was founded by a consortium of international partners and businessmen who have international marketing, international trade and finance as well as technical expertise.

World Tel welcomes enquiries from companies and individuals in various locations across Canada who are interested in participating in commercial Internet joint ventures.

Service Area:	Vancouver, Calgary, Toronto, Saskatoon, New York, Los Angeles, Caracas, Hong Kong.
	Other North American, European, Far East, and South American sites in early 1995.
	Planned:
	U.S.A. - Chicago, Denver, San Francisco, Dallas, Houston, Washington, Seattle
	Canada - Ottawa, Winnipeg, Montreal
	Latin America - Caracas, Santiago, Lima, Bogota, Buenos Aires, Nassau
	Far East - Hong Kong, Beijing, Shanghai, Kuala Lumpur, Bangkok, Jakarta
	Europe - London, Paris, Madrid, Lisbon, Frankfurt, Rome, Milan
	Mexico - Mexico City, Monterey
1-800 Service:	Planned. Call for information.
PDN Service:	Yes. Call for information.
Connection via:	SPRINT. Fractional T1.
Leased Line Service:	Yes. 56Kbps - T1. ISDN service is available.
Dedicated Dial-Up Service:	Yes.
SLIP/PPP Service:	Yes. SLIP and PPP. Software is available to customers.
UUCP Service:	Yes. Mail and news feeds. Customers can automatically add and delete newsgroups. UUCP software is available to customers.
Interactive Accounts:	Yes. Direct connection to the Internet. Permanent storage available. Mail, Telnet, TN3270, FTP, Gopher, WAIS, World Wide Web (Lynx), Internet Relay Chat, Hytelnet, Archie, MUDs. Menu-driven interface and shell access. Communications software is included in the subscription cost. Off-line readers supported. Local and international e-mail-to-fax service.
Maximum Casual Dial-Up Speed:	28,800 bps.
USENET News:	Yes. 5000 newsgroups. ClariNet News is available.
Local File Archives:	Yes.
Domain Registration Service:	Yes. Full service. Norminal fee for clients.
Domain Park Service:	Yes.

Consulting Services:	Yes. International marketing and selling; advertising and marketing on the Internet; design, development, and maintenance of Web servers; network set-up; Internet seminars and workshops for businesses.
DNS Service:	Yes. Primary and secondary nameservers.
Commercial Traffic:	Yes.

HOW TO SIGN UP

Registration is by telephone. Call to register.

Rates
Call for pricing.

For More Information
Gopher:
trianon.worldtel.com

World Wide Web:
http://www.worldtel.com

U.S.-BASED PROVIDERS

America Online Inc.
Vienna, Virginia
aol.com

8619 Westwood Center Drive
Vienna, Virginia 22182-2285
Voice: Canada Toll-Free 1-800-827-6364
Corporate Headquarters: (703) 448-8700

America Online's corporate mission is to develop "electronic communities" to meet the needs of specific market segments. Focussing on interactive communications, America Online provides its users with a wide variety of features including electronic mail, news/weather/sports, stock quotes, software files, computing support, on-line classes, and much more. The company has strategic alliances with dozens of leading hardware, software, and media and affinity organizations, including IBM, Apple, Time-Warner, CNN, Knight Ridder, and Tribune Company, to develop and market on-line services that appeal to their customers. America Online has formed a new division, the Internet Services Company, with the goal of establishing a leadership position in the emerging Internet market. The Internet Services Company intends to leverage America Online's resources, expertise, and momentum to develop a completely new and independent Internet-centric business, to lead the way in popularizing the Internet for consumers and publishers. America Online now has more than 1 million subscribers.

Service Area:	Where Tymnet service or Datapac is available. There are local Tymnet access numbers in Burnaby, Calgary, Dundas, Edmonton, Halifax, Hull, Kitchener, London, Ottawa, Toronto, Vancouver, Winnipeg and Windsor.

1-800- Service:	No.
PDN Service:	Yes. Tymnet.
Leased Line Service:	No.
Dedicated Dial-Up Service:	No.
SLIP/PPP Service:	No.
UUCP Service:	No.
Interactive Accounts:	Yes. Mail, Gopher, WAIS. Telnet and FTP scheduled to be available in 1995.
Maximum Casual Dial-Up Speed:	2400 bps in Burnaby, Dundas, Edmonton, Halifax, Kitchener, London, Quebec City, Windsor. 9600 bps in Calgary, Hull, Montreal, Ottawa, Toronto, St. Laurent, Vancouver and Winnipeg.
USENET News:	Yes.
Local File Archives:	Yes.
Domain Registration Service:	No.
Domain Park Service:	No.
Consulting Services:	No.
DNS Service:	No.
Commercial Traffic:	Yes.

HOW TO SIGN UP

Call to register. Software is required (provided at no charge). America Online supports all leading platforms including Windows, DOS, and Macintosh.

Rates

US$9.95/month. Includes 5 free hours per month. Additional hours are US$3.50/hour. When you sign up, you receive 10 free hours for your first 30 days.

Tymnet Surcharge

US$0.20/minute.

Applelink

Herndon, VA
applelink.apple.com

Apple Computer Inc.
P.O. Box 10600
Herndon, Virginia 22070-0600
Voice: (408) 974-3309
Fax: (703) 318-6701

As Apple's official on-line service, Applelink gives you 24-hour access to Apple and third-party technical support. As well, users have instant, reliable electronic mail service to more than 50,000 Apple users and vendors in 55 countries around the world, and access to late-breaking local, regional, and international news stories about Apple industry and product developments.

Service Area:	Local access numbers in the following cities: Calgary, Edmonton, Halifax, Hamilton, Hespeler, London, Montreal, Ottawa, Quebec City, Toronto-Mississauga, Vancouver, Victoria, Winnipeg.
1-800 Service:	No.
PDN Service:	Datapac.
Leased Line Service:	No.
Dedicated Dial-Up Service:	No.
SLIP/PPP Service:	No.
UUCP Service:	No.
Interactive Accounts:	Yes. Internet mail.
Maximum Casual Dial-Up Speed:	9600 bps in Calgary, Montreal, Ottawa, Toronto-Mississauga, Vancouver. 2400 bps in Edmonton, Halifax, Hamilton, Hespeler, London, Quebec City, Victoria, Winnipeg.
USENET News:	No.
Local File Archives:	Yes.
Domain Registration Service:	No.
Domain Park Service:	No.
Consulting Services:	No.
DNS Service:	No.
Commercial Traffic:	No.

HOW TO SIGN UP

Call to register.

Rates
$20.00 set-up fee. $35.00/hour. Minimum billing time of 1 hour/month.
Applelink software is required. It will be supplied at no charge upon registration.

BIX
Cambridge, Massachusetts
bix.com

Delphi Internet Services
1030 Massachusetts Avenue
Cambridge, Massachusetts 02138
Voice: (617) 354-4137

Corporate Headquarters: (617) 491-3342
Fax: (617) 491-6642
Internet: info@bix.com

BIX is geared for computing professionals and enthusiasts. While other on-line services cater to computer novices, BIX is the place for knowledgeable people to go for answers to tough questions. BIX is divided into areas called conferences, each devoted to a particular area of interest. Conferences are categorized into groups, usually referred to as "exchanges," so that you can browse through whatever exchange groups interest you and see a list of the conferences they contain.

Service Area:	Where Tymnet service is available. There are local access numbers in Burnaby, Calgary, Dundas, Edmonton, Halifax, Hull, Kitchener, London, Ottawa, Toronto, Vancouver, Winnipeg and Windsor.
	There is a list of Tymnet access numbers at the end of this directory.
1-800 Service:	No
PDN Service:	Tymnet.
Leased Line Service:	No.
Dedicated Dial-Up Service:	No.
SLIP/PPP Service:	No.
UUCP Service:	No.
Interactive Accounts:	Yes. Direct connection to the Internet. Internet mail, Telnet, FTP, Gopher, World Wide Web (Lynx), Archie, WAIS, Finger, WHOIS. Menu-driven. Shell access.
Maximum Casual Dial-Up Speed:	2400 bps in Burnaby, Dundas, Edmonton, Halifax, Kitchener, London, Quebec City, Windsor. 9600 bps in Calgary, Hull, Montreal, Ottawa, Toronto, St. Laurent, Vancouver and Winnipeg.
USENET News:	Yes.
Local File Archives:	Yes.
Domain Registration Service:	No.
Domain Park Service:	No.
Consulting Services:	No.
DNS Service:	No.
Commercial Traffic:	Yes.

HOW TO SIGN UP

MODEM:
*Set your communications software to 8 data bits, one stop bit, no parity. Call your local Tymnet number. Type the letter "o" upon connection, but do not press the <**enter**> key. At the "please log in:" prompt, type **bix**. At the "Name" prompt, type **new** (no password required).*

INTERNET:

Telnet to **x25.bix.com**. At the "Username" prompt, type **bix**. At the next prompt, type **new**.

Rates

Connect Charges:

CDN$9.00/hour 6a.m.-6p.m weekdays only. CDN$4.00/hour 6p.m.-6a.m. and weekends. Telnet access: US$1.00/hour at all times.

Membership:

US$13.00/month.

CompuServe Incorporated
Columbus, Ohio
compuserve.com

5000 Arlington Center Blvd.
Columbus, Ohio 43220
Voice: Canada Toll-Free 1-800-848-8199
        Corporate Headquarters: (614) 457-8600
Fax: (614) 457-0348 (Corporate Office)

CompuServe is committed to being an information industry leader that exceeds customer expectations, challenges its associates with opportunities, provides top-quality products and services, and applies its resources to the betterment of society. With 2.25 million members worldwide, CompuServe is the leading provider of on-line information services for personal computers worldwide. CompuServe offers nearly 2,000 databases, including information retrieval, communications, and transactional services; an on-line shopping mall featuring merchants selling everything from gourmet food to consumer electronics; and more than 600 interactive forums. CompuServe has a presence in over 150 countries and has local language support in French, German, and English.

Service Area:	Access is via the CompuServe Packet Network.
	There are local access numbers in the following Canadian cities: Calgary, Edmonton, Halifax, London, Montreal, Ottawa, Regina, Quebec City, Saskatoon, Toronto, Vancouver, Winnipeg.
	CompuServe is rapidly adding new local access numbers in Canada. Call CompuServe to determine if there is a local access number in your community.
1-800 Service:	Yes. US$9.00/hour surcharge.
PDN Service:	CompuServe Packet Network, Datapac.
Leased Line Service:	No.
Dedicated Dial-Up Service:	No.
SLIP/PPP Service:	No.
UUCP Service:	No.
Interactive Accounts:	Yes. Gateway connection to the Internet. Internet mail. Telnet and FTP will be available by the end of 1994. Gopher will be available in 1995. Menu-driven interface and point-and-click interface. CompuServe Information Manager software is supplied to customers.

Maximum Casual Dial-Up Speed:	14,400 bps in some cities.
USENET News:	Yes. Several thousand newsgroups. An off-line USENET reader is under development.
Local File Archives:	Yes.
Domain Registration Service:	No.
Domain Park Service:	No.
Consulting Services:	No.
DNS Service:	No.
Commercial Traffic:	Yes.

HOW TO SIGN UP

Registration is over the telephone. Call to register.

Rates

Basic Services:
US$8.95/month. Includes US$9.00/month mail allowance, which covers 60 messages of 7500 characters or less sent to or received from Internet, and/or sent to other CompuServe members. Text messages only to Internet. No charge for mail received from other CompuServe members.

Extended Services:
US$4.80/hour - 2400 bps
US$9.60/hour - 14,400 bps

Datapac Surcharge:
US$8/hour - 2400 bps
US$20/hour - 9600 bps

Access Through CompuServe Packet Network:
No surcharge.

For More Information:
Check out CompuServe's World Wide Web page!
http://www.compuserve.com

DELPHI

Cambridge, Massachusetts
delphi.com

Delphi Internet Services
1030 Massachusetts Avenue
Cambridge, Massachusetts 02138
Voice: (617) 491-3393 or 1-800-695-4005 (Toll-Free)
            Corporate Headquarters: (617) 491-3342
Fax: (617) 491-6642
Internet: askdelphi@delphi.com

Delphi Internet Services Corporation develops and markets interactive entertainment and communications services for consumers worldwide. Delphi's on-line service has enabled people all over the world to interact, retrieve information, compete, transact business, and play games in a friendly, computer-based environment. Delphi's primary goal is to provide an environment for electronic communities of similarly interested people to thrive and interact on a global basis.

Service Area:	Where Tymnet service is available. There are local access numbers in Burnaby (B.C.), Calgary, Dundas (Ontario), Edmonton, Halifax, Hull, Kitchener, London, Ottawa, Toronto, Vancouver, Winnipeg and Windsor.

There is a list of Canadian Tymnet numbers at the end of this directory. |
1-800 Service:	No.
PDN Service:	Yes. Tymnet.
Leased Line Service:	No.
Dedicated Dial-Up Service:	No.
SLIP/PPP Service:	No.
UUCP Service:	No.
Interactive Accounts:	Yes. Telnet, FTP, Gopher, Archie, WWW, IRC, WAIS, WHOIS, Finger, Netfind, PING, Traceroute. Menu-driven.
Maximum Casual Dial-Up Speed:	2400 bps in Burnaby, Dundas, Edmonton, Halifax, Kitchener, London, Quebec City, Windsor. 9600 bps in Calgary, Hull, Montreal, Ottawa, Toronto, St. Laurent, Vancouver and Winnipeg.
USENET News:	Yes. Approximately 3,000 newsgroups.
Local File Archives:	Yes.
Domain Registration Service:	No.
Domain Park Service:	No.
Consulting Services:	No.
DNS Service:	No.
Commercial Traffic:	Yes.

HOW TO SIGN UP

INTERNET:
Telnet to **delphi.com**, login as **joindelphi**. Use the password **info** for general information about Delphi. Use the password **free** if you want to register for a free trial offer (Tymnet surcharges still apply).

MODEM:
Using your modem, dial 1-800-365-4636. Once connected, hit the **<enter>** key several times. As the password prompt, type **free**.

For general information about Delphi, use the password **info** instead.

Rates

Membership:
10/4 Plan: US$10.00 month. 4 four hours included. Each additional hour is US$4.00/hour.

20/20 Advantage Plan: US$19.00 enrolment fee. US$20.00/month. 20 free hours included. Each additional hour is US$1.80/hour.

Internet Services Surcharge:
US$3.00/month.

Tymnet Access:
US$9.00/hour 6a.m.-6p.m. weekdays only. US$3.00/hour 6p.m.-6a.m.
weekdays and weekends.

GEnie
Rockville, Maryland
genie.geis.com

GE Information Services
P.O. Box 6403
Rockville, Maryland 20850-1785
Voice: Canada Toll-Free 1-800-638-9636
Fax: (301) 251-6421

*GEnie calls itself "diverse, dynamic, and in-depth." Users can explore over 500 distinct interest
areas, ranging from highly technical computer areas dedicated to specific computer platforms,
to powerful information tools for business, to sections with broad appeal, such as pets, movies, and
music. GEnie offers a wide variety of on-line services, including business and professional services,
investment services, real-time multiplayer games, and communications services.*

Service Area:	Local access numbers in Calgary, Edmonton, Halifax, Hamilton, Kitchener, London, Mississauga, Montreal, Ottawa, Quebec City, Toronto, Vancouver, Victoria, Winnipeg.
1-800 Service:	No.
PDN Service:	Datapac.
Leased Line Service:	No.
Dedicated Dial-Up Service:	No.
SLIP/PPP Service:	No.
UUCP Service:	No.
Interactive Accounts:	Yes. Internet mail. Gateway connection to the Internet. Worldwide e-mail-to-fax service.
Maximum Casual Dial-Up Speed:	9600 bps in Calgary, Montreal, Mississauga, Vancouver. 2400 bps in Edmonton, Halifax, Hamilton, Kitchener, London, Ottawa, Quebec City, Toronto, Victoria, Winnipeg.
USENET News:	No.
Local File Archives:	Yes. Shareware, freeware.
Domain Registration Service:	No.
Domain Park Service:	No.
Consulting Service:	No.
DNS Service:	No.
Commercial Traffic:	Yes.

HOW TO SIGN UP

MODEM:

*Set communications software for half duplex (local echo) at 2400 baud. Set communications software to 8 data bits, no parity, 1 stop bit or, if you have an IBM compatible, 7 data bits, even parity, one stop bit. Dial **1-800-387-8330**. Immediately upon connection, type: **HHH <return>**. When you see the prompt "u#=", type: **signup <return>**, and wait about 10 seconds. You will be guided through the registration process, and your password and GEnie ID will be generated by the system. Have a major credit card ready. A list of local access telephone numbers will be displayed. Allow one to two business days for the account to be activated.*

Rates

CDN$10.95/month for 4 hours connect time during non-peak hours. Additional hours are CDN$4.00/hour during non-peak hours and CDN$12.00/hour during peak hours. Peak hours are 8a.m. to 6p.m. on weekdays only. Includes electronic mail, multiplayer games, bulletin boards, chat lines, real-time conferences. CDN$8.00/hour surcharge for 9600 bps access.

Access Through Datapac:
Surcharge of CDN$6.00/hour.

Access Through a Local Access Number:
No surcharge.

HoloNet
Berkeley, California
holonet.net

Information Access Technologies Inc.
46 Shattuck Square, Suite 11
Berkeley, California, 94704
Voice: (510) 704-0160
Fax: (510) 704-8019
Internet: info@iat.mailer.net -or- support@holonet.net

Information Access Technologies (IAT) provides reliable, high-quality Internet access. IAT offers a variety of services to best meet the Internet access needs of our customers. We offer terminal emulation access to the Internet using our custom easy-to-use menu-driven system. IAT is committed to providing quality service to the Internet and we are constantly improving our service to best meet our users' communication needs.

Service Area:	Where CompuServe Packet Network numbers exist. There are CompuServe access numbers in the following Canadian cities: Calgary, Edmonton, Halifax, London, Montreal, Ottawa, Regina, Quebec City, Saskatoon, Toronto, Vancouver, Winnipeg.
1-800 Service:	No.
PDN Service:	Yes. CompuServe Packet Network.
Leased Line Service:	No.
Dedicated Dial-Up Service:	Yes.
SLIP/PPP Service:	Available in late 1994.

UUCP Service:	Yes. Mail and newsfeeds. Customers can modify newsgroup subscriptions. HoloNet supplies HoloGate gateway software that will work with the following systems: FirstClass, QuickMail, MicrosoftMail, NovaLink, SnapMail, UUCP.
Interactive Accounts:	Yes. Direct connection to the Internet. 256Kb/month permanent disk space. Additional disk space is US$1.00/MB. Telnet, FTP, Gopher, WAIS, World Wide Web, Internet Relay Chat, Hytelnet, Archie, MUD. Menu-driven interface.
Maximum Casual Dial-Up Speed:	9,600 bps -or- 14,400 bps.
USENET News:	Yes. 7,000 newsgroups.
Local File Archives:	Yes.
Domain Registration Service:	Yes. Full service. $25.00 fee.
Domain Park Service:	Yes.
Consulting Service:	No.
DNS Service:	Yes. Primary and secondary nameservers.
Commercial Traffic:	Yes.

HOW TO SIGN UP

MODEM:

Set your communications software to even parity, 7 data bits, 1 stop bit.
Dial your local CompuServe Packet Network number. There are CompuServe access numbers in the following cities:

City	Modem Number	Speed
Calgary	(403) 294-9120	2400 bps
	(403) 294-9120	9600 bps
Edmonton	(403) 466-5083	2400 bps
	(403) 440-2744	9600 bps
Halifax	(902) 457-0669	2400 bps
	(902) 457-0669	9600 bps
London	(519) 663-1880	2400 bps
	(519) 663-1880	9600 bps
Ottawa	(613) 841-0400	2400 bps
	(613) 841-0400	9600 bps
Montreal	(514) 879-8519	2400 bps
	(514) 879-5826	9600 bps
Quebec City	(418) 649-7082	2400 bps
	(418) 649-7082	9600 bps
Regina	(306) 352-7168	2400 bps
	(306) 352-7168	9600 bps
Saskatoon	(306) 242-4660	2400 bps
	(306) 242-4660	9600 bps
Toronto	(416) 367-8122	2400 bps
	(416) 367-8122	9600 bps
	(416) 367-8122	14,400 bps
Vancouver	(604) 737-2452	2400 bps
	(604) 739-8194	9600 bps
Winnipeg	(204) 489-9747	2400 bps
	(204) 489-9747	9600 bps

*Once connected, press the **<enter>** key. At the host name prompt, type **holoca**, then press*
*<enter>. Login as **guest**.*

*To find your local access number, dial **1-800-638-4656** with your modem, and enter your area*
code (14,400 bps, set your modem to 8 data bits, no parity, one stop bit).

INTERNET:
*Telnet to **holonet.net**, login as **guest**, no password required.*

Rates
Membership:
US$6.00/month or US$60.00/year.

Connect Charges:
US$6.50/hour during off-peak hours. US$8.50/hour during peak hours.
Peak hours are Monday to Friday, 8a.m. to 5p.m.
All charges are prorated in one-minute increments. One-time set-up fees are applicable for
services such as custom domain names, UUCP, and SLIP services.

MCI Mail
Washington, D.C.
mcimail.com

1133 19th Street
Washington, D.C. 20036
Voice: Canada Toll-Free 1-800-444-6245
          Direct Dial: (202) 833-8484
Fax: (202) 416-5858
Internet: 3393527@mcimail.com (MCI Mail Customer Support)

MCI Mail is a premier global electronic mail network with unparalleled value-added services. MCI
Mail is reachable by MCI Mail Global Access (direct dial to a local in-country number) in 30
countries and is available through packet-switched access in 90 countries, (including those served
by MCI Mail Global Access).

Service Area:	Where Datapac and Tymnet are available.
1-800 Service:	No.
PDN Service:	Datapac and Tymnet.
Leased Line Service:	No.
Dedicated Dial-Up Service:	No.
SLIP/PPP Service:	No.
UUCP Service:	No.
Interactive Accounts:	Yes. Internet mail. Domestic and international e-mail-to-fax and e-mail-to-telex gateways. E-mail to surface mail service.
Maximum Casual Dial-Up Speed:	9600 bps.
USENET News:	No.
Local File Archives:	No.

Domain Registration Service:	No.
Domain Park Service:	No.
Consulting Service:	No.
DNS Service:	No.
Commercial Traffic:	Yes.

HOW TO SIGN UP

Call to register.

Rates:
Annual mailbox fee: US$35.00

Message prices:
1st 500 characters: US$0.50
2nd 500 characters: add US$0.10
1,001-10,000 characters: add US$0.10/1000 characters
>10,000 characters: add US$0.05/1000 characters
Call MCI Mail for pricing on fax, telex, and paper mail services.

Datapac Access:
US$0.15/minute

Tymnet Access:
US$0.25/minute.

NovaLink Interactive Networks

Westborough, Massachusetts
novalink.com

200 Friberg Parkway - Suite 4003
Westborough, Massachusetts 01581
Voice: Canada Toll-Free 1-800-274-2814
Fax: (508) 836-4766
Internet: info@novalink.com

NovaLink is a commercial on-line service providing the finest in information, multi-player games, full Internet access and active user participation. A strong emphasis is placed on on-line gaming, including the award-winning fantasy role-playing game, "Legends of Future Past", and our on-line casino located in the Virtual Cafe. Full Internet access is included as a basic feature without additional surcharges. Many special-interest forums round out NovaLink's offerings, allowing users from around the world to share thoughts and opinions on a variety of issues. New services are constantly being added, making NovaLink an exciting experience for its users.

Service Area:	Where CompuServe Packet Network numbers exist. There are local access numbers in the following Canadian cities: Calgary, Edmonton, Halifax, London, Montreal, Ottawa, Regina, Quebec City, Saskatoon, Toronto, Vancouver, Winnipeg. NovaLink plans to have a local access number in Toronto (in addition to the CompuServe Packet Network number) in 1995.
1-800 Service:	No.
PDN Service:	CompuServe Packet Network.

Connection via:	NEARnet, T-1 circuit backed up by a 56Kbps frame relay connection.
Leased Line Service:	No.
Dedicated Dial-Up Service:	Yes.
SLIP/PPP Service:	No.
UUCP Service:	No.
Interactive Accounts:	Yes. Direct connection to the Internet. Permanent storage space. 2MB of storage per user. Additional storage is available for $2/MB/month. Telnet, TN3270, FTP, Gopher, WAIS, World Wide Web (Lynx and command-line client), IRC, Hytelnet, Archie, MUD (TinyTalk), Menu-driven. Shell access. QWK-compatible off-line mail readers supported. Qwkmail supplied at no additional charge. Local/national/international e-mail-to-fax gateway.
Maximum Casual Dial-Up Speed:	2400 bps in Ottawa. 9600 bps in Calgary, Edmonton, Montreal, Toronto, Vancouver and Winnipeg.
USENET News:	Yes. Full feed.
Local File Archives:	Yes. IBM/Macintosh. Gaming, Aviation, GIF/Artwork, Adult, Travel, Metaphysics, Paranormal, and many other topics.
Domain Registration Service:	No.
Domain Park Service:	No.
Consulting Services:	Yes. Systems integration, information systems management and implementation.
DNS Service:	No.
Commercial Traffic:	Yes.
Comments:	Membership restricted to persons over the age of 18. Regular on-line guests appear, including science-fiction, romance, and non-fiction authors; celebrities; journalists; and other public figures. On-line manual available for download.

HOW TO SIGN UP

MODEM:

Set your communications software to 7 data bits, even parity, 1 stop bit. Call your local CompuServe Packet Network number (see the list below). Press **<return>** *once connected, and type* **Nova** *at the* **<Host:>** *prompt. You will be connected to NovaLink. At the* **<User ID:>** *prompt, type* **Info**. *Follow the instructions for information on NovaLink or to create a new account.*

City	Modem Number	Speed
Calgary	(403) 294-9120	2400 bps
	(403) 294-9120	9600 bps
Edmonton	(403) 466-5083	2400 bps
	(403) 440-2744	9600 bps
Halifax	(902) 457-0669	2400 bps
	(902) 457-0669	9600 bps
London	(519) 663-1880	2400 bps
	(519) 663-1880	9600 bps

Ottawa	(613) 841-0400	2400 bps
	(613) 841-0400	9600 bps
Montreal	(514) 879-8519	2400 bps
	(514) 879-5826	9600 bps
Quebec City	(418) 649-7082	2400 bps
	(418) 649-7082	9600 bps
Regina	(306) 352-7168	2400 bps
	(306) 352-7168	9600 bps
Saskatoon	(306) 242-4660	2400 bps
	(306) 242-4660	9600 bps
Toronto	(416) 367-8122	2400 bps
	(416) 367-8122	9600 bps
	(416) 367-8122	14,400 bps
Vancouver	(604) 737-2452	2400 bps
	(604) 739-8194	9600 bps
Winnipeg	(204) 489-9747	2400 bps
	(204) 489-9747	9600 bps

INTERNET:
Telnet to **novalink.com**, login as **new**

Rates:
US$9.95/month
US$6.00/hour when accessing NovaLink through the CompuServe Packet Network. US$1.80/hour when accessing NovaLink by Telnet.

For More Information
FTP:
ftp.novalink.com
Directory: info

Telnet:
novalink.com
Login: **info**

Gopher:
gopher.novalink.com

The WELL
Sausalito, California
well.com, well.sf.ca.us

1750 Bridgeway
Sausalito, California 94965-1900
Voice: (415) 332-4335
Fax: (415) 332-4927
Internet: info@well.com

The WELL (Whole Earth `Lectronic Link) is one of the most established and eclectic on-line conference communities in the world. A full service e-mail and Internet access provider, The WELL was founded by the same organization that created the Whole Earth Catalog. The WELL's roots are decidedly Northern Californian, but it attracts over half of its users from outside California and includes an impressive overseas contingent. The WELL offers over 250 forums and provides connection to full Internet services, including over 5,500 USENET newsgroups. The WELL is a community with the goal of people-to-people interaction.

Service Area:	Anywhere there is a CompuServe Packet Network access number.
1-800 Service:	No.
PDN Service:	CompuServe Packet Network.
Connection via:	BARRNET. T1. The Little Garden. T1.
Leased Line Service:	No.

Dedicated Dial-Up Service:	No.
SLIP/PPP Service:	PPP in first quarter 1995.
UUCP Service:	No.
Interactive Accounts:	Yes. Direct connection to the Internet. 512 Kb permanent storage space per user. Additional storage space is US$20.00/megabyte/month. Mail, Telnet, FTP, Gopher, WAIS, World Wide Web (Lynx), Internet Relay Chat, Hytelnet, Archie, MUD. Picospan conferencing system. Menu-driven interface and shell access.
Maximum Casual Dial-Up Speed:	14,400 bps in some cities.
USENET News:	Yes. Approximately 5,500 newsgroups.
Local File Archives:	No.
Domain Registration Service:	No.
Domain Park Service:	No.
Consulting Service:	No.
DNS Service:	No.
Commercial Traffic:	No.

HOW TO SIGN UP

MODEM:

You must call direct to California and register on-line. A WELL support representative will call you back the next business day and provide you with information on accessing The WELL via your local CompuServe access number.
*(415) 332-6106, 2400 bps, login as **new***
*(415) 332-8410, 14,400 bps, login as **new***

INTERNET:

*Telnet to **well.com**, login as **new**, no password required*

Rates

US$15.00/month user fee. US$2.00/hour connect fee.
Surcharge for Accessing The WELL via CompuServe Packet Network:
US$6.00/hour.

For More Information

Telnet:	**Gopher:**	**World Wide Web:**
well.com	gopher.well.com	http://www.well.com
login: **guest**		

Canadian TYMNET Numbers
For Further Information: 1-800-937-2862

ALBERTA

Calgary	(403) 232-6653	2400 bps
Calgary	(403) 264-5472	9600 bps
Edmonton	(403) 484-4404	2400 bps

BRITISH COLUMBIA

Burnaby, Vancouver	(604) 683-7620	2400 bps
Vancouver	(604) 683-7453	9600 bps

MANITOBA

Winnipeg	(204) 654-4041	2400 bps
Winnipeg	(204) 654-0992	9600 bps

NOVA SCOTIA

Halifax	(902) 492-4901	2400 bps

ONTARIO

Dundas	(905) 628-5908	2400 bps
Kitchener	(519) 742-7613	2400 bps
London	(519) 641-8362	2400 bps
Hull, Ottawa	(613) 563-2910	2400 bps
Hull, Ottawa	(613) 563-3777	9600 bps
Toronto	(416) 365-7630	2400 bps
Toronto	(416) 361-3028	9600 bps
Windsor	(519) 977-7256	2400 bps

QUEBEC

Montreal/St. Laurent	(514) 747-2996	2400 bps
Montreal/St. Laurent	(514) 748-8057	9600 bps
Quebec City	(514) 647-1116	2400 bps

HOW TO GET A CURRENT LIST OF TYMNET ACCESS NUMBERS

The most recent list of BT TYMNET access numbers and other information about BT TYMNET is available on-line on BT TYMNET's Worldwide Information Service. You can access this information using your computer and your modem. Please note that in early 1994, BT TYMNET was purchased by MCI and is now part of MCI's Data Services Division.

To obtain information on TYMNET using your modem:

(1) Set your communications software to 8 data bits, one stop bit, no parity.
(2) Call your local TYMNET number.
(3) When the connection is established, type the letter **o**
(4) At the **please log in:** prompt, type **information**, then press the **<enter>** key.
(5) Make a selection from the menu.

HOW TO GET INFORMATION ABOUT DATAPAC

For general information about Datapac, call 1-800-267-6574.

A P P E N D I X   D

....

THE DIRECTORY OF WORLD WIDE WEB SERVERS IN CANADA

© 1994 Rick Broadhead and Jim Carroll

This is a directory of World Wide Web servers in Canada. Entries in this directory are structured like this:

Name of the Organization Sponsoring the World Wide Web Server
Name of Department Hosting the World Wide Web Server (if applicable)

City or Town where the World Wide Web Server is located

Access: (URL)   The URL of the Web server

HOW TO SUBMIT INFORMATION FOR THE DIRECTORY OF
WORLD WIDE WEB SERVERS IN CANADA:
Submissions to this directory are welcome. If your favourite
World Wide Web server is not listed in this directory, please
contact the authors at **<handbook@uunet.ca>** so that we can
include it in future editions of this directory.

To participate in the World Wide Web, you need three things:

(1) YOU NEED TO HAVE ACCESS TO A DIRECT INTERNET
CONNECTION AT WORK, AT SCHOOL, OR THROUGH A COMMERCIAL
INTERNET PROVIDER.

COMMERCIAL INTERNET PROVIDERS

The Directory of Canadian Internet Service Providers in Appendix C contains a comprehensive list of commercial Internet providers. Only those commercial providers with a direct Internet connection can offer World Wide Web service to their customers. For individuals, there are two ways to access the World Wide Web using a commercial Internet provider. You can access the World Wide Web using a SLIP/PPP connection or by using a dial-up Internet account on your commercial provider's machine. Some commercial providers only provide SLIP/PPP service, some only provide dial-up Internet accounts, and some provide both SLIP/PPP and dial-up Internet accounts. **The Directory of Canadian Internet Service Providers** in Appendix C can help you find Internet providers that offer SLIP/PPP service or dial-up Internet accounts.

AT WORK OR SCHOOL

If you have access to the Internet at work or at school, you may have access to the World Wide Web, providing that your organization has a direct Internet connection. How do you know if you have a direct Internet connection? If you have access to Internet services like Telnet, Gopher, and FTP, you have a direct Internet connection. Ask the computing staff if in doubt.

(2) YOU NEED TO HAVE ACCESS TO A WORLD WIDE WEB CLIENT.

A client is a program that you need to run in order to use the World Wide Web. World Wide Web clients are called **browsers.** Most commercial providers that offer dial-up interactive accounts have installed a World Wide Web client on their machine for their customers to use. **The Directory of Canadian Internet Service Providers** in Appendix C indicates which commercial providers have World Wide Web clients installed on their machines (check the box labelled **Interactive Accounts**). If you know that you have direct Internet access, and you don't have a World Wide Web client installed on the system that you are using, ask your Internet provider or your computing staff if they can install a World Wide Web client for you.

(3) YOU NEED TO HAVE ACCESS TO A WORLD WIDE WEB SERVER.

The third requirement for accessing the World Wide Web is a World Wide Web server, and that's what this directory is for! A World Wide Web server is a computer that makes information available to you, providing that you have a World Wide Web client. This directory lists dozens of Canadian World Wide Web servers that you can connect to using your World Wide Web client. Entries in this directory are organized by category (e.g. universities, colleges, government, commercial organizations, etc.).

HOW DO I ACCESS THE CLIENT?

If you know that a World Wide Web client is available on your system, how you access it will vary from one system to the next.

- If you are using a dial-up Internet account on your Internet provider's computer, and the system is menu-driven (or has a point-and-click interface), look for a menu option called "World Wide Web" or "WWW."

- If you are using a dial-up Internet account on your Internet provider's computer, and you are accessing the Internet from a Unix command prompt, typing **lynx** may work. **Lynx** is the name of a popular World Wide Web client.

- If you are accessing the Internet using a SLIP or PPP connection, or if you have a direct network connection, here are a few clients that you can choose from. You can obtain these clients using anonymous FTP, and install them on your system. You may also be able to get these clients directly from your Internet provider. Many Internet providers supply their customers with a package of shareware/freeware or commercial software when they sign up for SLIP/PPP service. Many providers also have archives of SLIP/PPP software on their systems for their customers to download. You only need one of the following clients, but you may want to obtain more than one client and see which one you like better.

SLIP/PPP Clients For World Wide Web

FOR MICROSOFT WINDOWS USERS

Name of Client:	NCSA Mosaic for Windows	
Type:	Freeware	
Anonymous ftp location:	ftp.ncsa.uiuc.edu	
Directory:	PC/Windows/Mosaic	
File Name:	wmos*.zip	*=version number

Name of Client:	Mosaic Netscape	
Type:	Freeware	
Anonymous ftp location:	ftp.mcom.com	
Directory:	pub/netscape/windows	
File Name:	nscape*.zip	*= version number

Name of Client:	ElNet WinWeb
Type:	Freeware
Anonymous ftp location:	ftp.einet.net
Directory:	einet/pc/winweb
File Name:	winweb.zip

FOR MACINTOSH USERS

Name of Client:	NCSA Mosaic for the Macintosh
Type:	Freeware
Anonymous ftp location:	ftp.ncsa.uiuc.edu
Directory:	Mac/Mosaic

Name of Client:	MacWeb
Type:	Freeware
Anonymous ftp location:	ftp.einet.net
Directory:	einet/mac/macweb

WHAT IF I DON'T HAVE A WORLD WIDE WEB CLIENT AVAILABLE TO ME?

Some Internet service providers and organizations have not installed WWW clients on their systems. If a WWW client isn't installed on the system you are using, you can still access WWW by using an Internet service called **Telnet** (see Chapter 7) to connect to one of the public WWW clients listed in the table below.

The World Wide Web clients listed below are available to anyone on the Internet, but only use these clients if you don't have access to your own WWW client. A local WWW client is much faster, and significantly reduces the drain on Internet resources. If you don't have access to a World Wide Web client on your system, make sure you ask your computing staff if they can install one before you make use of the public clients listed in the table below.

PUBLIC WORLD WIDE WEB CLIENTS THAT YOU CAN TELNET TO

Internet address of WWW Client	Location	Login
sunsite.unc.edu	University of North Carolina	lynx
www.law.indiana.edu	Indiana University School of Law	www
www.njit.edu	New Jersey Institute of Technology	www
www.lbl.gov	Lawrence Berkeley Laboratory, California	www
fatty.law.cornell.edu	Cornell Law School	www

To access the World Wide Web servers listed in this directory, your client needs to know the address of the World Wide Web server. The address is called a **URL (Uniform Resource Locator)**. Uniform Resource Locators for the World Wide Web look like this:

```
http://location_of_resource
```

where: **location_of_resource** is the location of the World Wide Web server

If you are using a SLIP/PPP World Wide Web client, check the documentation that comes with the program to find out how to input a URL.

If you are using a browser such as Lynx on a Unix account, or if you are using one of the public World Wide clients listed in the table above (most of them use Lynx), use the **Go** command to specify a URL. Once the client is running, type the letter **G**, and the client will ask you to enter the URL of the World Wide Web server that you want to connect to. For example, to connect to the World Wide Web server at Acadia University in Nova Scotia, you would enter the following URL after typing **G**:

```
http://www.acadiau.ca
```

This command tells the client program to go to the World Wide Web server at the address **www.acadiau.ca**.

WHERE CAN I FIND OUT MORE ABOUT THE WORLD WIDE WEB?

(1) WORLD WIDE WEB LIST OF FREQUENTLY ASKED QUESTIONS

This is an invaluable document. It answers dozens of the most common questions about the World Wide Web. You can retrieve the document by anonymous FTP, or on the World Wide Web itself.

USING ANONYMOUS FTP

Anonymous ftp Site:	**rtfm.mit.edu**
Directory:	**pub/usenet-by-group/news.answers/www**
File Name:	**faq**

USING THE WORLD WIDE WEB

Point Your World Wide Web Browser at:
http://sunsite.unc.edu/boutell/faq/www_faq.html

(2) USENET NEWS

The following USENET newsgroups carry discussions on the World Wide Web.
You can learn a lot just by following the discussions on a regular basis.

Name of Newsgroup	Topic
comp.infosystems.www.misc	Miscellaneous discussion about the World Wide Web (e.g. the future of Web)
comp.infosystems.www.users	Discussion for users of the World Wide Web (e.g. client software, new user questions)
comp.infosystems.www.providers	Discussion for providers of information on the World Wide Web (e.g. server software)

Canadian Universities on the World Wide Web

Acadia University
Wolfville, Nova Scotia

Access: (URL)	http://www.acadiau.ca

Brandon University
Main WWW Page
Brandon, Manitoba

Access: (URL)	http://www.brandonu.ca

Brock University
Main WWW Page
St. Catharines, Ontario

Access: (URL)	http://spartan.ac.brocku.ca/default.html

Brock University
Communications Services
St. Catharines, Ontario

Access: (URL)	http://nexus.brocku.ca

Brock University
Department of Computer Science
St. Catharines, Ontario

Access: (URL)	http://sandcastle.cosc.brocku.ca

Brock University
Department of Physics
St. Catharines, Ontario

Access: (URL)	http://www.physics.brocku.ca/

Carleton University
Main WWW Server
Ottawa, Ontario

Access: (URL)	http://www.carleton.ca

Carleton University
Admissions Department
Ottawa, Ontario

Access: (URL)	http://admissions.carleton.ca

Carleton University
Apple Research Partnership Program
Ottawa, Ontario

Access: (URL)	http://arpp1.carleton.ca

Carleton University
School of Architecture
Ottawa, Ontario

Access: (URL)	http://thrain.arch.carleton.ca

Carleton University
Civil and Environmental Engineering
Ottawa, Ontario

Access: (URL)	http://www.civeng.carleton.ca

Carleton University
Conservation Ecology Journal
Ottawa, Ontario

Access: (URL)	http://journal.biology.carleton.ca

Carleton University
Department of Electronics
Ottawa, Ontario

Access: (URL)	http://www.doe.carleton.ca

Carleton University
Department of Physics
Ottawa, Ontario

Access: (URL)	http://www.physics.carleton.ca

Carleton University
Carleton Student Engineering Society
Ottawa, Ontario

Access: (URL)	http://www.civeng.carleton.ca/CSES/cses.html

Carleton University
Department of Systems and Computer Engineering
Ottawa, Ontario

Access: (URL)	http://www.sce.carleton.ca

Dalhousie University
Main WWW Page
Halifax, Nova Scotia

Access: (URL)	http://ac.dal.ca

Dalhousie University
Department of Mathematics, Statistics, and Computing Science
Halifax, Nova Scotia

Access: (URL)	http://www.cs.dal.ca/home.html

Dalhousie University
Faculty of Management
Halifax, Nova Scotia

Access: (URL)	http://quasar.sba.dal.ca:2000/maintext.html

Lakehead University
Main WWW Page
Thunder Bay, Ontario

Access: (URL)	http://www.lakeheadu.ca/menu.html

McGill University
Main WWW Page
Montreal, Quebec

Access: (URL)	http://www.mcgill.ca

McGill University
School of Architecture
Montreal, Quebec

Access: (URL)	http://architecture.mcgill.ca

McGill University
Centre for Intelligent Machines
Montreal, Quebec

Access: (URL)	http://www.cim.mcgill.ca

McGill University
School of Computer Science
Montreal, Quebec

Access: (URL)	http://www.cs.mcgill.ca

McGill University
Department of Earth and Planetary Sciences
Montreal, Quebec

Access: (URL)	http://stoner.eps.mcgill.ca

McMaster University
Department of Physics and Astronomy
Hamilton, Ontario

Access: (URL)	http://www.physics.mcmaster.ca

McMaster University
Faculty of Science
Hamilton, Ontario

Access: (URL)	http://www.science.mcmaster.ca/

McMaster University
Titles Bookstore
Hamilton, Ontario

Access: (URL)	http://bookstore.services.mcmaster.ca

Memorial University of Newfoundland
Department of Computer Science
St. John's, Newfoundland

Access: (URL)	http://web.cs.mun.ca/welcome.html

Mount Allison University
Main WWW Page
Sackville, New Brunswick

Access: (URL)	http://www.mta.ca

Mount Allison University
Apple Center for Innovation
Sackville, New Brunswick

Access: (URL)	http://aci.mta.ca

Mount Allison University
Mathematics and Computer Science
Sackville, New Brunswick

Access: (URL)	http://cs1.mta.ca

Mount Saint Vincent University
Main WWW Page
Halifax, Nova Scotia

Access: (URL)	http://www.msvu.ca

Queen's University
Main WWW Page
Kingston, Ontario

Access: (URL)	http://info.queensu.ca/index.html

Queen's University
Department of Chemistry
Kingston, Ontario

Access: (URL)	http://www.chem.queensu.ca/

Queen's University
Computing and Information Science Department
Robotics and Perception Laboratory
Kingston, Ontario

Access: (URL)	http://quail.qucis.queensu.ca:9000/index.html

Queen's University
Department of Physics
Kingston, Ontario

Access: (URL)	http://snodaq.phy.queensu.ca

Saint Francis Xavier University
Electronic Library
Antigonish, Nova Scotia

Access: (URL)	http://cwaves.stfx.ca/

Saint Mary's University
Main WWW Page
Halifax, Nova Scotia

Access: (URL)	http://www.stmarys.ca

Saint Mary's University
Department of Astronomy and Physics
Halifax, Nova Scotia

Access: (URL)	http://mnbsun.stmarys.ca/www/smu_home.html

Simon Fraser University
Main WWW Page
Burnaby, British Columbia

Access: (URL)	http://www.sfu.ca/

Simon Fraser University
Canadian Association for the Management of Technology
Burnaby, British Columbia

Access: (URL)	http://edie.cprost.sfu.ca/canmot/canmot-role.html

Simon Fraser University
Centre for Experimental and Constructive Mathematics
Burnaby, British Columbia

Access: (URL)	http://www.cecm.sfu.ca/index.html

Simon Fraser University
Centre for Policy Research on Science and Technology
Burnaby, British Columbia

Access: (URL)	http://thumb.cprost.sfu.ca/default.html

Simon Fraser University
Department of Physics
Burnaby, British Columbia

Access: (URL)   http://techie.phys.sfu.ca/

Simon Fraser University
Faculty of Education
Exemplary Centre for Interactive Technologies in Education
(ExCITE Lab)
Burnaby, British Columbia

Access: (URL)   http://oberon.educ.sfu.ca

Simon Fraser University
Faculty of Applied Sciences
Burnaby, British Columbia

Access: (URL)   http://fas.sfu.ca/

Simon Fraser University
Faculty of Applied Sciences
Centre for Systems Science
Burnaby, British Columbia

Access: (URL)   http://fas.sfu.ca/1/css

Simon Fraser University
Faculty of Business Administration
Burnaby, British Columbia

Access: (URL)   http://www.bus.sfu.ca/

Simon Fraser University
Harbour Centre Campus
Vancouver, British Columbia

Access: (URL)   http://www.harbour.sfu.ca

Simon Fraser University
Institute of Molecular Biology and Biochemistry
Burnaby, British Columbia

Access: (URL)   http://watson.mbb.sfu.ca

Simon Fraser University
Microcomputer Store
Burnaby, British Columbia

Access: (URL)	http://microstore.ucs.sfu.ca/

Simon Fraser University
Department of Communication
Burnaby, British Columbia

Access: (URL)	http://fas.sfu.ca/1/comm

Simon Fraser University
School of Computing Science
Burnaby, British Columbia

Access: (URL)	http://fas.sfu.ca/1/cs

Simon Fraser University
School of Kinesiology
Burnaby, British Columbia

Access: (URL)	http://fas.sfu.ca/1/kin

Simon Fraser University
Workshop for Computer-Aided Tutoring in Mathematics
Burnaby, British Columbia

Access: (URL)	http://mathserv.math.sfu.ca

Technical University of Nova Scotia
Main WWW Page
Halifax, Nova Scotia

Access: (URL)	http://www.tuns.ca/index.html

Trent University
Main WWW Page
Peterborough, Ontario

Access: (URL)	http://blaze.trentu.ca

University of Alberta
Main WWW Page
Edmonton, Alberta

Access: (URL)   http://web.cs.ualberta.ca/UAlberta.html

University of Alberta
Centre for Subatomic Research
Edmonton, Alberta

Access: (URL)   http://inuit.phys.ualberta.ca/

University of Alberta
Department of Chemistry
Edmonton, Alberta

Access: (URL)   http://www.chem.ualberta.ca/

University of Alberta
Department of Civil Engineering, Water Resources Engineering
Edmonton, Alberta

Access: (URL)   http://maligne.civil.ualberta.ca/home.html

University of Alberta
Department of Computing Science
Edmonton, Alberta

Access: (URL)   http://web.cs.ualberta.ca/

University of Alberta
Department of Computing Science
First Year and Service Courses Labs
Edmonton, Alberta

Access: (URL)   http://alix.cs.ualberta.ca

University of Alberta
Department of Computing Science
Senior Undergraduate WWW Server
Edmonton, Alberta

Access: (URL)   http://ugweb.cs.ualberta.ca

University of Alberta
Department of Electrical Engineering
Edmonton, Alberta

Access: (URL)   http://nyquist.ee.ualberta.ca/index.html

University of Alberta
Department of Forest Science
Edmonton, Alberta

Access: (URL)   http://www.forsci.ualberta.ca

University of Alberta
Faculty of Law
Edmonton, Alberta

Access: (URL)   http://gpu.srv.ualberta.ca/~bpoohkay/law.html

University of British Columbia
Main WWW Page (View UBC)
Vancouver, British Columbia

Access: (URL)   http://view.ubc.ca

University of British Columbia
Department of Computer Science
Vancouver, British Columbia

Access: (URL)   http://www.cs.ubc.ca/home

University of British Columbia
Computing and Communications
Vancouver, British Columbia

Access: (URL)   http://view.ubc.ca:770/homepage.html

University of British Columbia
Faculty of Education
Vancouver, British Columbia

Access: (URL)   http://ecs.educ.ubc.ca/educ.html

University of British Columbia
Geological Sciences
Vancouver, British Columbia

Access: (URL)	http://earth.geology.ubc.ca/.index.html

University of British Columbia
Haughn/Kunst Laboratory
Department of Botany
Vancouver, British Columbia

Access: (URL)	http://kh.botany.ubc.ca/welcome.html

University of British Columbia
Institute of Applied Mathematics
Vancouver, British Columbia

Access: (URL)	http://www.iam.ubc.ca/home

University of British Columbia
Faculty of Commerce
Division of Management Information Systems
Vancouver, British Columbia

Access: (URL)	http://mis.commerce.ubc.ca/MIS.html

University of British Columbia
Mechanical Engineering
Vancouver, British Columbia

Access: (URL)	http://www.mech.ubc.ca/HomePage.html

University of British Columbia
Physics
Vancouver, British Columbia

Access: (URL)	http://www.physics.ubc.ca

University of British Columbia
Theoretical Physics
Vancouver, British Columbia

Access: (URL)	http://axion.physics.ubc.ca/home.html

University of Calgary
Main WWW Server
Calgary, Alberta

Access: (URL)   http://www.ucalgary.ca

University of Calgary
Department of Clinical Neurosciences
Calgary, Alberta

Access: (URL)   http://www.cns.ucalgary.ca/index.html

University of Calgary
Department of Computer Science
Calgary, Alberta

Access: (URL)   http://www.cpsc.ucalgary.ca/

University of Calgary
Department of Geology and Geophysics
Calgary, Alberta

Access: (URL)   http://www.geo.ucalgary.ca

University of Calgary
Department of Geology, CREWES Project
Calgary, Alberta

Access: (URL)   http://www-crewes.geo.ucalgary.ca/

University of Calgary
Medicine
Calgary, Alberta

Access: (URL)   http://mir.med.ucalgary.ca

University of Calgary
Department of Physics and Astronomy
Calgary, Alberta

Access: (URL)   http://bear.ras.ucalgary.ca/department.html

University of Calgary
Department of Physics and Astronomy, Radio Astronomy Group
Calgary, Alberta

Access: (URL)	http://bear.ras.ucalgary.ca/ras-home.html

University of Calgary
Psychology Department
Calgary, Alberta

Access: (URL)	http://www.psych.ucalgary.ca/

University of Calgary
University Computing Services, Communications
Calgary, Alberta

Access: (URL)	http://asa.acs.ucalgary.ca/

Université Laval
Main WWW Page
Quebec City, Quebec

Access: (URL)	http://www.ulaval.ca/index.html

Université Laval
Département de Génie Électrique
Quebec City, Quebec

Access: (URL)	http://www.gel.ulaval.ca

Université Laval
Recherches en Sciences de la Vie et de la Santé
Quebec City, Quebec

Access: (URL)	http://www.rsvs.ulaval.ca

University of Manitoba
Main WWW Server
Winnipeg, Manitoba

Access: (URL)	http://www.umanitoba.ca

University of Manitoba
Department of Civil and Geological Engineering
Winnipeg, Manitoba

Access: (URL)   http://www.ce.umanitoba.ca/homepage.html

University of Manitoba
Department of Computer Science
Winnipeg, Manitoba

Access: (URL)   http://www.cs.umanitoba.ca/homepage.html

University of Manitoba
Department of Electrical and Computer Engineering
Winnipeg, Manitoba

Access: (URL)   http://www.ee.umanitoba.ca/EE_homepage.html

University of Manitoba
Environmental Science
Winnipeg, Manitoba

Access: (URL)   http://www.umanitoba.ca/envirosciences/env.html

University of Manitoba
Student Linguistics Association
Winnipeg, Manitoba

Access: (URL)   http://www.umanitoba.ca/linguistics/index.html

University of Manitoba
Department of Physics
Winnipeg, Manitoba

Access: (URL)   http://www.umanitoba.ca/physics/homepage.html

University of Manitoba
Micro Resource Centre
Winnipeg, Manitoba

Access: (URL)   http://www.umanitoba.ca/mrc/mrchome.html

University of Manitoba
Winnipeg Institute for Theoretical Physics
Winnipeg, Manitoba

Access: (URL)	http://www.umanitoba.ca/physics/witp.html

Université de Moncton
Centre Universitaire Saint-Louis-Maillet (CUSLM)
Moncton, New Brunswick

Access: (URL)	http://www.cuslm.ca

Université de Montréal
Département d'Informatique et de Recherche Operationelle
Montreal, Quebec

Access: (URL)	http://www.iro.umontreal.ca

Université de Montréal
Faculty of Law
Montreal, Quebec

Access: (URL)	http://www.droit.umontreal.ca

Université de Montréal
Département de Physique
Montreal, Quebec

Access: (URL)	http://ftp.astro.umontreal.ca/physique/index.html

University of New Brunswick
Main WWW Page
Fredericton, New Brunswick

Access: (URL)	http://www.unb.ca

University of New Brunswick
Computer Services
Fredericton, New Brunswick

Access: (URL)	http://sol.sun.csd.unb.ca

University of New Brunswick
Fire Science
Fredericton, New Brunswick

Access: (URL)	http://www.fsc.unb.ca

University of Ottawa
Department of Computer Science
Ottawa, Ontario

Access: (URL)	http://www.csi.uottawa.ca

University of Ottawa
Department of Electrical and Computer Engineering
Multimedia Communications Research Laboratory
Ottawa, Ontario

Access: (URL)	http://mango.genie.uottawa.ca

University of Prince Edward Island
Main WWW Page
Charlottetown, Prince Edward Island

Access: (URL)	http://www.cs.upei.ca

Université du Québec à Montréal
Main WWW Page
Montreal, Quebec

Access: (URL)	http://www.uqam.ca

Université du Québec à Montréal
Service de l'Informatique
Montreal, Quebec

Access: (URL)	http://www.si.uqam.ca

University of Saskatchewan
Main WWW Page
Saskatoon, Saskatchewan

Access: (URL)	http://www.usask.ca

University of Toronto
Main WWW Page
Toronto, Ontario

Access: (URL)   http://www.utoronto.ca/uoft.html

University of Toronto
Bladen Library
Toronto, Ontario

Access: (URL)   http://library-gopher.scar.utoronto.ca

University of Toronto
Centre for Instructional Technology Development
Toronto, Ontario

Access: (URL)   http://library.scar.utoronto.ca/citd/citd.html

University of Toronto
Department of Chemistry
Toronto, Ontario

Access: (URL)   http://www.chem.utoronto.ca

University of Toronto
Department of Computer Science
Toronto, Ontario

Access: (URL)   http://www.cdf.utoronto.ca

University of Toronto
Department of Electrical and Computer Engineering
Toronto, Ontario

Access: (URL)   http://www.eecg.toronto.edu/Welcome.html

University of Toronto
Division of the Environment
Toronto, Ontario

Access: (URL)   http://zinnia.zoo.toronto.edu

University of Toronto
Department of Industrial Engineering
Toronto, Ontario

Access: (URL)	http://www.ie.utoronto.ca

University of Toronto
Instructional and Research Computing
Toronto, Ontario

Access: (URL)	http://www.utirc.utoronto.ca/home.html

University of Toronto
Centre for Landscape Research
Toronto, Ontario

Access: (URL)	http://www.clr.toronto.edu:1080/clr.html

University of Toronto
Department of Mathematics
Toronto, Ontario

Access: (URL)	http://www.cdf.toronto.edu/math/math-OverView.html

University of Toronto
Network and Operations Services, Computing and Communications
Toronto, Ontario

Access: (URL)	http://madhaus.utcc.utoronto.ca

University of Toronto
Department of Physics
Toronto, Ontario

Access: (URL)	http://www.physics.utoronto.ca

University of Toronto
Scarborough College
Toronto, Ontario

Access: (URL)	http://www.scar.toronto.edu

University of Victoria
Main WWW Page
Victoria, British Columbia

Access: (URL)	http://www.uvic.ca

University of Victoria
Department of Computer Science
Victoria, British Columbia

Access: (URL)	http://www-csc.uvic.ca

University of Victoria
Department of Physics and Astronomy
Victoria, British Columbia

Access: (URL)	http://info.phys.uvic.ca/uvphys_welcome.html

University of Victoria
Faculty of Engineering
Victoria, British Columbia

Access: (URL)	http://www-engr.uvic.ca

University of Waterloo
Main WWW Server
Waterloo, Ontario

Access: (URL)	http://www.uwaterloo.ca

University of Waterloo
Broadband Networks and Services Group
Waterloo, Ontario

Access: (URL)	http://bbcr.uwaterloo.ca

University of Waterloo
Computer Graphics Lab
Waterloo, Ontario

Access: (URL)	http://watcgl.uwaterloo.ca

University of Waterloo
Computer Science Club
Waterloo, Ontario

Access: (URL)   http://csclub.uwaterloo.ca

University of Waterloo
Computing Services
Waterloo, Ontario

Access: (URL)   http://dcs1.uwaterloo.ca/

University of Waterloo
Electronic Library
Waterloo, Ontario

Access: (URL)   http://www.lib.uwaterloo.ca

University of Waterloo
FASS Theatre Company
Waterloo, Ontario

Access: (URL)   http://usg.uwaterloo.ca/hypertext/jms/fass/home.html

University of Waterloo
Faculty of Arts
Waterloo, Ontario

Access: (URL)   http://watarts.uwaterloo.ca/home.html

University of Waterloo
Faculty of Environmental Studies
Waterloo, Ontario

Access: (URL)   http://cousteau.uwaterloo.ca

University of Waterloo
Faculty of Applied Health Sciences
Waterloo, Ontario

Access: (URL)   http://healthy.uwaterloo.ca

University of Waterloo
Logic Programming and Artificial Intelligence Group
Waterloo, Ontario

Access: (URL)	http://logos.uwaterloo.ca

University of Waterloo
Math Faculty Computing Facility
Waterloo, Ontario

Access: (URL)	http://math.uwaterloo.ca/

University of Waterloo
Parallel and Distributed Systems Group
Waterloo, Ontario

Access: (URL)	http://www.pads.uwaterloo.ca

University of Waterloo
Programming Languages Group
Waterloo, Ontario

Access: (URL)	http://plg.uwaterloo.ca

University of Waterloo
Unix Support Group
Waterloo, Ontario

Access: (URL)	http://usg.uwaterloo.ca/home.html

University of Western Ontario
Department of Astronomy
London, Ontario

Access: (URL)	http://phobos.astro.uwo.ca

University of Western Ontario
Space and Atmospheric Research
London, Ontario

Access: (URL)	http://aurora.physics.uwo.ca

University of Windsor
Faculty of Science
Windsor, Ontario

Access: (URL)	http://www.cs.uwindsor.ca/welcome.html

University of Windsor
School of Nursing
Windsor, Ontario

Access: (URL)	http://www.cs.uwindsor.ca/units/nurs/welcome.html

York University
Main WWW Page
Toronto, Ontario

Access: (URL)	http://www.yorku.ca

York University
Computer Club
Toronto, Ontario

Access: (URL)	http://yucc.yorku.ca

York University
Division of Humanities
Toronto, Ontario

Access: (URL)	http://guinness.huma.yorku.ca/Welcome.html

York University
Department of Earth and Atmospheric Science
Toronto, Ontario

Access: (URL)	http://unicaat.yorku.ca/home.html

York University
Office of Research Administration
Toronto, Ontario

Access: (URL)	http://ora_prt1.resadmin.yorku.ca

Canadian Colleges on the World Wide Web

Camosun College
Victoria, British Columbia

Access: (URL)	http://www.camosun.bc.ca

Canadore College of Applied Arts and Technology
North Bay, Ontario

Access: (URL)	http://www.canadorec.on.ca/index.html

Okanagan University College
Kelowna, British Columbia

Access: (URL)	http://oksw01.okanagan.bc.ca/home.html

Canadian Networking Initiatives on the World Wide Web

CA*net Networking Inc.
Victoria, British Columbia

Access: (URL)	http://www.canet.ca/canet/index.html

LARG*net-London and Region Global*network
Main WWW Page
London, Ontario

Access: (URL)	http://www.largnet.uwo.ca

SchoolNet
Main WWW Page
Ottawa, Ontario

Access: (URL)	http://schoolnet.carleton.ca/schoolnet/hmpage.html

STEM~Net
Main WWW Page
St. John's, Newfoundland

Access: (URL)	http://calvin.stemnet.nf.ca

TeleEducation New Brunswick
Main WWW Page
Sackville, New Brunswick

Access: (URL)	http://tenb.mta.ca

Canadian Libraries on the World Wide Web

St. Francis Xavier University Library
Antigonish, Nova Scotia

Access: (URL)	http://libwww.stfx.ca

University of British Columbia Library
Vancouver, British Columbia

Access: (URL)	http://unixg.ubc.ca:7001

Université Laval (Library)
Quebec City, Quebec

Access: (URL)	http://www.bibl.ulaval.ca

University of Waterloo Library
Waterloo, Ontario

Access: (URL)	http://www.lib.uwaterloo.ca

Canadian Internet Providers on the World Wide Web

Achilles Internet
Gloucester, Ontario

Access: (URL)	http://www.achilles.net

CCI Networks
Edmonton, Alberta

Access: (URL)	http://www.ccinet.ab.ca

Cimtegration
Toronto, Ontario

Access: (URL)	http://www.cimtegration.com

Communications Accessibles Montréal
Montreal, Quebec

Access: (URL)	http://www.cam.org

Cyberstore Systems Inc.
New Westminster, British Columbia

Access: (URL)	http://www.cyberstore.ca

Dataflux Systems
Victoria, British Columbia

Access: (URL)	http://dataflux.bc.ca/home.html

Fleximation Systems Inc.
Mississauga, Ontario

Access: (URL)	http://www.flexnet.com/welcome.html

Helix Internet
Vancouver, British Columbia

Access: (URL)	http://www.helix.net

HookUp Communications
Toronto, Ontario

Access: (URL)	http://www.hookup.net

ICE ONLINE
Burnaby, British Columbia

Access: (URL)	http://www.iceonline.com

InfoMatch Communications Inc.
Burnaby, British Columbia

Access: (URL)	http://infomatch.com:70

Interlink On-Line Services
Victoria, British Columbia

Access: (URL)	http://www.interlink.bc.ca/home.html

Interlog Internet Services
Toronto, Ontario

Access: (URL)	http://www.interlog.com

Internex Online
Toronto, Ontario

Access: (URL)	http://www.io.org

Island Internet
Nanaimo, British Columbia

Access: (URL)	http://www.island.net

Island Net
Victoria, British Columbia

Access: (URL)	http://www.islandnet.com

MBnet
Winnipeg, Manitoba

Access: (URL)	http://www.mbnet.mb.ca

Magi Data Consulting
Ottawa, Ontario

Access: (URL)	http://www.magi.com

Metrix Interlink
Montreal, Quebec

Access: (URL)	http://www.interlink.net

Nova Scotia Technology Network
Dartmouth, Nova Scotia

Access: (URL)	http://www.nstn.ca

ONet Networking Inc.
Toronto, Ontario

Access: (URL)	http://www.onet.on.ca/onet/index.html

PEInet
Charlottetown, Prince Edward Island

Access: (URL)	http://bud.peinet.pe.ca

The Wire
Toronto, Ontario

Access: (URL)	http://the-wire.com

Telnet Canada Enterprises
Calgary, Alberta

Access: (URL)	http://www.tcel.com

Wimsey Information Services
Port Moody, British Columbia

Access: (URL)	http://www.wimsey.com/index.html

WorldGate
Edmonton, Alberta

Access: (URL)	http://valis.worldgate.edmonton.ab.ca

UUNET Canada Inc.
Toronto, Ontario

Access: (URL)	http://www.uunet.ca

Canadian Government Bodies on the World Wide Web

Bedford Institute of Oceanography
Habitat Ecology Division
Dartmouth, Nova Scotia

Access: (URL)	http://biome.bio.dfo.ca

Government of British Columbia
Ministry of Environment, Lands, and Parks
Main WWW Page
Victoria, British Columbia

Access: (URL)	http://www.env.gov.bc.ca

Government of British Columbia
Ministry of Education
Victoria, British Columbia

Access: (URL)	http://www.etc.bc.ca/home.html

Government of British Columbia
Ministry of Environment, Lands, and Parks
Human Resources Branch
Victoria, British Columbia

Access: (URL)	http://hrbwww.env.gov.bc.ca

Canadian Broadcasting Corporation
Ottawa, Ontario

Access: (URL)	http://debra.dgbt.doc.ca/cbc/cbc.html

Canadian Forest Service
Northern Forestry Centre
Edmonton, Alberta

Access: (URL)	http://www.nofc.forestry.ca

Canadian Forest Service
Pacific Forestry Centre
Advanced Forest Technologies Program
Victoria, British Columbia

Access: (URL)   http://pine.pfc.forestry.ca/

Canadian Geographical Names Database
Ottawa, Ontario

Access: (URL)   http://www-nais.ccm.emr.ca/cgndb/geonames.html

Canadian Heritage Information Network
Ottawa, Ontario

Access: (URL)   http://www.chin.doc.ca

Communauté Urbaine de Montréal
Montreal, Quebec

Access: (URL)   http://www.cum.qc.ca

Communications Research Centre
Ottawa, Ontario

Access: (URL)   http://debra.dgbt.doc.ca

Environment Canada
Downsview, Ontario

Access: (URL)   http://cmits02.dow.on.doe.ca

City of Fredericton Tourism Department
Fredericton, New Brunswick

Access: (URL)   http://www.cygnus.nb.ca/fredericton/fredfin.html

Health Canada
Main WWW Server
Ottawa, Ontario

Access: (URL)   http://hpb1.hwc.ca

Human Resources Development Canada
Ottawa, Ontario

Access: (URL)	http://www.hrdc-drhc.gc.ca

National Research Council
Autonomous Systems Laboratory
Ottawa, Ontario

Access: (URL)	http://autsrv.iitsg.nrc.ca

National Research Council
Canada-France-Hawaii Telescope
Ottawa, Ontario

Access: (URL)	http://www.cfht.hawaii.edu

National Research Council
Canadian Astrophysical Data Center
Ottawa, Ontario

Access: (URL)	http://cadc.dao.nrc.ca/CADC-homepage.html

National Research Council
Dominion Astrophysical Observatory
Ottawa, Ontario

Access: (URL)	http://dao.nrc.ca/DAO-homepage.html

National Research Council
Dominion Radio Astrophysical Observatory
Ottawa, Ontario

Access: (URL)	http://www.drao.nrc.ca

National Research Council
Main WWW Server
Ottawa, Ontario

Access: (URL)	http://www.nrc.ca

National Research Council
Science Affairs Office
Scientific Computing Support Group
Ottawa, Ontario

Access: (URL)	http://www.sao.nrc.ca/home.page.html

National Research Council
Knowledge Systems Laboratory
Ottawa, Ontario

Access: (URL)	http://ai.iit.nrc.ca/home_page.html

National Research Council
Software Engineering Laboratory
Ottawa, Ontario

Access: (URL)	http://wwwsel.iit.nrc.ca

Natural Resources Canada
Main WWW Server
Ottawa, Ontario

Access: (URL)	http://www.emr.ca

Natural Resources Canada
Geodetic Survey of Canada
Ottawa, Ontario

Access: (URL)	http://www.geod.emr.ca

Natural Resources Canada
Canada Centre for Mapping
Ottawa, Ontario

Access: (URL)	http://ccm-10.ccm.emr.ca

Government of New Brunswick
Fredericton, New Brunswick

Access: (URL)	http://www.gov.nb.ca

Open Government Pilot
Senate of Canada, House of Commons, Supreme Court of Canada
Ottawa, Ontario

Access: (URL)	**MAIN SITE** http://debra.dgbt.doc.ca/opengov **MIRROR SITE:** http://www.culturenet.ucalgary.ca/opengov http://www.unb.ca/opengov http://www.emr.ca/opengov http://www.cs.ubc.ca/opengov http://www1.cciw.ca/opengov http://www.droit.umontreal.ca/opengov

Public Works and Government Services Canada
Ottawa, Ontario

Access: (URL)	http://www.pwc-tpc.ca

TRIUMPH
Vancouver, British Columbia

Access: (URL)	http://www.triumf.ca

Canadian Commercial Organizations on the World Wide Web

Barwise Realty
Fredericton, New Brunswick

Access: (URL)	http://www.cygnus.nb.ca/realstate/barwise.html

Canadian Airlines
Vancouver, British Columbia

Access: (URL)	http://www.cdnair.ca

Canadian Football League
Toronto,Ontario

Access: (URL)	http://www.cfl.ca

Canadian Himalayan Expeditions
Toronto, Ontario

Access: (URL)	http://www.netpart.com/che/brochure.html

Communicopia Environmental Research and Communications
Victoria, British Columbia

Access: (URL)	http://interchange.idc.uvic.ca/communicopia/index.html

Cybersmith Inc.
Sackville, New Brunswick

Access: (URL)	http://www.csi.nb.ca

Cygnus Telecom
Fredericton, New Brunswick

Access: (URL)	http://www.cygnus.nb.ca

Damon Legal Services
British Columbia

Access: (URL)	http://infomatch.com:70/0h/docs/users/dls

Darr Houssen Dog Obedience School
Moncton, New Brunswick

Access: (URL)	http://www.cygnus.nb.ca/dogtrain/doghome.html

Discribe Limited
Fredericton, New Brunswick

Access: (URL)	http://www.discribe.ca

Global-X-Change Communications
Ottawa, Ontario

Access: (URL)	http://www.globalx.net

Goose Lane Editions
Fredericton, New Brunswick

Access: (URL)	http://www.cygnus.nb.ca/glane/glogo.html

Haibeck Communications - Public Relations and Marketing
Vancouver, British Columbia

Access: (URL)	http://infomatch.com:70/0h/docs/users/haibeck

The Halifax Daily News
Halifax, Nova Scotia

Access: (URL)	http://www.cfn.cs.dal.ca/Media/TodaysNews/TodaysNews.html

Hollow Reed Book Distribution
New Maryland, New Brunswick

Access: (URL)	http://www.cygnus.nb.ca/bookstr/hollowreed/hollowreed.html

Lord Beaverbrook Hotel
Fredericton, New Brunswick

Access: (URL)	http://www.cygnus.nb.ca/travel/lbr.html

Microplex Systems Limited
Vancouver, British Columbia

Access: (URL)	http://microplex.com

The Mining Channel
Vancouver, British Columbia

Access: (URL)	http://www.wimsey.com/Magnet/mc/index.html

Online Visions Limited
Canada Net Pages
Richmond, British Columbia

Access: (URL)	http://www.visions.com/netpages/

Ponds Resort
Ludlow, New Brunswick

Access: (URL)	http://www.cygnus.nb.ca/ponds/homepond.html

Robelle Consulting Limited
Surrey, British Columbia

Access: (URL)	http://www.robelle.com

Roswell's Computer Books
Halifax, Nova Scotia

Access: (URL)	http://www.nstn.ca/cybermall/roswell/roswell.html

Sea Change Corporation
Victoria, British Columbia

Access: (URL)	http://www.seawest.seachange.com

Seaside Book and Stamp
Halifax, Nova Scotia

Access: (URL)	http://www.nstn.ca/cybermall/biz-subject/bookstores/seaside/seaside.html

Software Metrics
Waterloo, Ontario

Access: (URL)	http://www.metrics.com/info.html

Sport Card and Comic Emporium
Fredericton, New Brunswick

Access: (URL)	http://www.cygnus.nb.ca/retail/cards/homecard.html

Westcoast Interchange
Victoria, British Columbia

Access: (URL)	http://interchange.idc.uvic.ca

Wollongong Group Canada
Waterloo, Ontario

Access: (URL)	http://www.lehman.on.ca

Xenitec Consulting Services
Kitchener, Ontario

Access: (URL)	http://www.xenitec.on.ca

Canadian Free-Nets on the World Wide Web

Free-Nets Home Page at the University of Saskatchewan
Saskatoon, Saskatchewan

Access: (URL)	http://jester.usask.ca/~scottp/free.html

Chebucto Free-Net
Halifax, Nova Scotia

Access: (URL)	http://www.cfn.cs.dal.ca

National Capital Free-Net
Ottawa, Ontario

Access: (URL)	http://freenet.carleton.ca

Vancouver Free-Net
Vancouver, British Columbia

Access: (URL)	http://freenet.vancouver.bc.ca

Victoria Free-Net
Victoria, British Columbia

Access: (URL)	http://freenet.victoria.bc.ca

Canadian Not-For-Profit Organizations on the World Wide Web

Alberta Research Council
Edmonton, Alberta

Access: (URL)	http://www.arc.ab.ca

Commonwealth of Learning
Vancouver, British Columbia

Access: (URL)	http://www.col.org

International Institute for Sustainable Development
Winnipeg, Manitoba

Access: (URL)	http://www.iisd.ca/linkages

Prince Edward Island Crafts Council
Charlottetown, Prince Edward Island

Access: (URL)	http://www.crafts-council.pe.ca/index.html

Vancouver PC Users' Group
Vancouver, British Columbia

Access: (URL)	http://www.wimsey.com/~infinity/vpcus/vpcus_hp.html

Other Canadian Organizations on the World Wide Web

Institute for Space and Terrestrial Science
Main WWW Server
Toronto, Ontario

Access: (URL)	http://www.ists.ca/Welcome.html

Institute for Space and Terrestrial Science
Space Astrophysics Lab
Toronto, Ontario

Access: (URL)	http://www.sal.ists.ca/Welcome.html

Institute for Space and Terrestrial Science
Earth Observations Laboratory
Toronto, Ontario

Access: (URL)	http://www.eol.ists.ca/Welcome.html

Sports World BBS Inc.
Vancouver, British Columbia

Access: (URL)	http://debussy.media.mit.edu/dbecker/docs/swbbs.html

A P P E N D I X   E

....

THE DIRECTORY OF GOPHER SERVERS AND CAMPUS-WIDE INFORMATION SYSTEMS IN CANADA

This is a directory of Gopher servers and campus-wide information systems (CWIS) in Canada (see Chapter 8 for a discussion of Gopher). Entries in this directory are structured like this:

Name of the Organization Sponsoring the Gopher/CWIS
Name of Department Hosting the Gopher/CWIS (if applicable)
City or Town where the Gopher or CWIS is located

ACCESS: **How to access the Gopher/CWIS using Gopher, Telnet or TN3270**

HOW TO SUBMIT INFORMATION FOR THE DIRECTORY OF GOPHER SERVERS AND CAMPUS-WIDE INFORMATION SYSTEMS:
Submissions to this directory are welcome. If your favourite Gopher is not listed in this directory, please contact the authors at **<handbook@uunet.ca>** so that we can include it in future editions of this directory.

To access Gopher, you need three things:

(1) YOU NEED ACCESS TO A DIRECT INTERNET CONNECTION AT WORK, AT SCHOOL, OR THROUGH A COMMERCIAL INTERNET PROVIDER.

COMMERCIAL INTERNET PROVIDERS

The Directory of Canadian Internet Service Providers in Appendix C contains a comprehensive list of commercial Internet providers. Only those commercial providers with a direct Internet connection can offer Gopher service to their customers. For individuals, there are two ways to access Gopher using a commercial Internet provider. You can access Gopher using a SLIP/PPP connection or by using a dial-up Internet account on your commercial provider's machine. Some commercial providers only provide SLIP/PPP service, some only provide dial-up Internet accounts, and some providers provide both SLIP/PPP and dial-up Internet accounts. **The Directory of Canadian Internet Providers** can help you find Internet Providers that offer SLIP/PPP service or dial-up Internet accounts with a direct Internet connection.

AT WORK OR SCHOOL

If you have access to the Internet at work or at school, you may have access to Gopher providing that your organization has a direct Internet connection. How do you know if you have a direct Internet connection? If you have access to Internet services like Telnet and FTP, you have a direct Internet connection. Ask the computing staff if in doubt.

(2) YOU NEED ACCESS TO A GOPHER CLIENT.

The second requirement for using Gopher is a Gopher **client**. A client is a program that you need to run in order to use Gopher.

Check the **Directory of Canadian Internet Providers** in Appendix C to determine which commercial providers have installed a Gopher client on their dial-up Internet accounts. Commercial providers that have "Gopher" listed in the "Interactive Accounts" box have a Gopher client installed on their system.

If you know that you have direct Internet access, and you don't have a Gopher client installed on the system that you are using, ask your Internet provider or your computing staff if they can install a Gopher client for you.

(3) YOU NEED ACCESS TO A GOPHER SERVER.

The third requirement for accessing Gopher is a Gopher server, and that's what this directory is for! A Gopher server is a computer that makes information available to you, providing that you have access to a Gopher client. This directory lists dozens of Canadian Gopher servers that you can connect to using your Gopher client.

How do I Access the Client?

If you know that a Gopher client is available on your system, how you access it will vary from one system to the next.

- If you are using a dial-up Internet account on your Internet Provider's computer, and the system is menu-driven (or has a point-and-click interface), look for a menu option called "Gopher".

- If you are using a dial-up Internet account on your Internet Provider's computer, and you are accessing the Internet from a Unix command prompt, typing the following command from the Unix command prompt will generally work:

```
gopher server-name
```

where:
server-name is the Internet domain of the Gopher server you want to go to.

For example, if you want to connect to the Gopher server at St. Francis Xavier University in Antigonish, Nova Scotia, you would type the following command at the Unix prompt:

```
gopher gopher.stfx.ca
```

If you just type **gopher** without typing a server name, your Gopher client will connect you to a default Gopher site. The default Gopher site is often a Gopher server belonging to the site that is providing you with Internet access. For example, if you are accessing Gopher from a university, typing **gopher** should connect you to your university's Gopher server.

- If you are accessing the Internet using a SLIP or PPP connection, there are a few clients that you can choose from. You have to obtain these clients using anonymous FTP, and install them on your system. You may also be able to get these clients directly from your Internet provider. Many Internet providers supply their customers with a package of shareware/freeware or commercial software when they sign up for SLIP/PPP service. Many providers also have archives of SLIP/PPP software on their systems for their customers to download. You only need one of the following clients, but you may want to obtain more than one and see which one you like better.

SLIP/PPP Clients for Gopher

FOR MICROSOFT WINDOWS USERS

Name of Client:	WSGopher
Type:	Freeware
Anonymous FTP location:	boombox.micro.umn.edu
Directory:	pub/gopher/Windows
File Name:	wsg-*.exe * = version number

Name of Client:	HGopher
Type:	Freeware
Anonymous FTP location:	lister.cc.ic.ac.uk
Directory:	pub/wingopher
File Name:	hgopher2.3.zip

Name of Client:	Gopher Book
Type:	Freeware
Anonymous FTP location:	boombox.micro.umn.edu
Directory:	pub/gopher/Windows/gophbook
File Name:	gophbook.zip

Name of Client:	BC Gopher
Type:	Freeware
Anonymous FTP location:	boombox.micro.umn.edu
Directory:	pub/gopher/Windows
File Name:	bcg*.exe * = version number

FOR MACINTOSH USERS

Name of Client:	TurboGopher
Type:	Freeware
Anonymous FTP location:	boombox.micro.umn.edu
Directory:	pub/gopher/Macintosh-TurboGopher

WHAT IF I DON'T HAVE A GOPHER CLIENT AVAILABLE TO ME?

Some Internet service providers and organizations have not installed Gopher clients on their systems. If a Gopher client is not installed on the system you are using, you can still access Gopher by using an Internet service called **Telnet** to connect to one of the public Gopher clients listed in the table below.

The Gopher clients listed in the table below are available to anyone on the Internet, but only use these clients if you don't have access to your own Gopher client. A local Gopher client is much faster, and it significantly reduces the drain on Internet resources. If you don't have access to a Gopher client on your system, make sure you ask your Internet provider or computing staff if they can install one before you make use of the public clients listed in the table below.

To access any of the Gopher clients listed in the table below, telnet to the Internet address of the client, and log in using the login specified in the table. Passwords are not required.

PUBLIC GOPHER CLIENTS THAT YOU CAN TELNET TO

Internet Address of Gopher Client	Location	Login
ux1.cso.uiuc.edu	Illinois	gopher
fatty.law.cornell.edu	New York	gopher
uwinfo.uwaterloo.ca	Ontario	uwinfo
sunsite.unc.edu	North Carolina	gopher
una.hh.lib.umich.edu	Michigan	gopher
info.umd.edu	Maryland	--------------
r2d2.jvnc.net	New Jersey	gopher

A QUICK WORD ABOUT PORTS

As you use this directory, you will notice that the addresses of some Gopher servers specify a port. For example, the address of the ACAATO Gopher server is **info.senecac.on.ca,** port **2000**. ACAATO stands for the Association of Colleges of Applied Arts and Technology of Ontario. A port is a way of specifying a specific application at an Internet address. A port number distinguishes applications from each other, so multiple applications can be accessed on the same Internet address. To access a Gopher server that uses a port number, try placing the port number after the address of the Gopher server. For example, to access the ACAATO Gopher, you would type:

```
gopher info.senecac.on.ca 2000
```

This will work on most UNIX systems. VMS systems may require that you specify the port in a different way. On many VMS systems, you have to place **/port=** before the port number. For example:

```
gopher info.senecac.on.ca /port=2000
```

WHERE CAN I FIND OUT MORE ABOUT GOPHER?

(1) FREQUENTLY ASKED QUESTIONS ABOUT GOPHER

This document answers many of the most common questions about Gopher. You can retrieve the document by anonymous FTP, or on Gopher itself.

USING ANONYMOUS FTP

Anonymous FTP Site:	**rtfm.mit.edu**
Directory:	**pub/usenet-by-group/news.answers**
File Name:	**gopher-faq**

USING GOPHER

Gopher address:	**gopher.tc.umn.edu**
Select:	**Information About Gopher**
	Frequently Asked Questions About Gopher

(2) USENET NEWS

The following USENET newsgroup carries discussions on Gopher. You can learn a lot just by following the discussions on a regular basis.

Name of Newsgroup	Topic
comp.infosystems.gopher	General Discussion About Gopher

(3) THE GOPHER-ANNOUNCE MAILING LIST

Announcements of new Gopher products, services, and Gopher servers are distributed regularly on the Gopher-Announce mailing list. To join the Gopher-Announce mailing list, send an electronic mail message to the following Internet address:

`gopher-announce-request@boombox.micro.umn.edu`

Put the following command on the first line of the body of your message:

`subscribe gopher-announce firstname lastname`

Replace **firstname** and **lastname** with your first name and last name.

A WORD ABOUT GOPHER NAMES

Some sites have chosen a special name for their Gopher server or Campus Wide Information System. For example, Lakehead University in Thunder Bay, Ontario calls its Gopher **LUCI** — an acronym that stands for **L**akehead **U**niversity **C**ampus **I**nformation. When the Gopher or CWIS has a name, it will be indicated in brackets after the name of the organization or after the name of the department responsible for the Gopher.

Canadian Universities on Gopher

Acadia University
Wolfville, Nova Scotia

ACCESS:	Gopher: gopher.acadiau.ca

Acadia University
Computer Science Club
Wolfville, Nova Scotia

ACCESS:	Gopher: dragon.acadiau.ca port 1666

Bishop's University
Lennoxville, Quebec

ACCESS:	Gopher: venus.ubishops.ca

Brandon University
Brandon, Manitoba

ACCESS:	Gopher: gopher.brandonu.ca

Brock University
St. Catharines, Ontario

ACCESS:	Gopher: gopher.ac.brocku.ca

Carleton University
Main Gopher Server
Ottawa, Ontario

ACCESS:	Gopher: gopher.carleton.ca

Carleton University
Admissions Gopher
Ottawa, Ontario

ACCESS:	Gopher: admissions.carleton.ca

Carleton University
Conservation Ecology Journal
Ottawa, Ontario

ACCESS:	Gopher: journal.biology.carleton.ca

Carleton University
Faculty of Graduate Studies and Research
Ottawa, Ontario

ACCESS:	Gopher: gsro.carleton.ca

Carleton University
Media and Community Relations
Ottawa, Ontario

ACCESS:	Gopher: gsro.carleton.ca port 414

Concordia University
Montreal, Quebec

ACCESS:	Gopher: clonnie.concordia.ca

Dalhousie University (DalInfo)
Halifax, Nova Scotia

ACCESS:	Gopher:	ac.dal.ca
	Telnet:	ac.dal.ca
	Login:	**dalinfo**

Lakehead University (LUCI)
Main Gopher Server
Thunder Bay, Ontario

ACCESS:	Gopher: flash.lakeheadu.ca

McGill University
Campus Wide Information System
Montreal, Quebec

ACCESS:	TN3270: vm1.mcgill.ca
	Press the **<Enter>** key at the VM/ESA
	screen, then type **info**

McGill University
Main Gopher Server
Montreal, Quebec

ACCESS:	Gopher: gopher.mcgill.ca

McGill University
Electrical Engineering Department
Montreal, Quebec

ACCESS:	Gopher: gopher.ee.mcgill.ca

McGill University
Information Network and Systems Lab
Montreal, Quebec

ACCESS:	Gopher: insl.mcgill.ca

McGill University
Microelectronics and Computer Systems Labratory
Montreal, Quebec

ACCESS:	Gopher: finnegan.ee.mcgill.ca

McGill University
Telecommunications and Signal Processing Labratory
Montreal, Quebec

ACCESS:	Gopher: tsp.ee.mcgill.ca

McGill University
Research Centre for Intelligent Machines
Montreal, Quebec

ACCESS:	Gopher: gopher.cim.mcgill.ca

McGill University
Physics Department
Montreal, Quebec

ACCESS:	Gopher: nazgul.physics.mcgill.ca

McMaster University
Main Gopher Server
Hamilton, Ontario

ACCESS:	Gopher: gopher.mcmaster.ca

McMaster University
Bookstore
Hamilton, Ontario

ACCESS:	Gopher: bookstore.services.mcmaster.ca

McMaster University
Computing and Information Services
Hamilton, Ontario

ACCESS:	Gopher: offsv1.cis.mcmaster.ca

McMaster University
Faculty of Health Sciences
Hamilton, Ontario

ACCESS:	Gopher: fhs.csu.mcmaster.ca

Memorial University of Newfoundland
Main Gopher Server
St. John's, Newfoundland

ACCESS:	Gopher: cwis.ucs.mun.ca

Mount Allison University
Main Gopher Server
Sackville, New Brunswick

ACCESS:	Gopher: gopher.mta.ca

Mount Allison University
Apple Center For Innovation
Sackville, New Brunswick

ACCESS:	Gopher: aci.mta.ca

Mount Allison University
On Line Learning Centre
Sackville, New Brunswick

ACCESS:	Gopher: pringle.mta.ca

Mount Saint Vincent University
Main Gopher Server
Halifax, Nova Scotia

ACCESS:	Gopher: gopher.msvu.ca

Ontario Institute for Studies in Education
Main Gopher Server
Toronto, Ontario

ACCESS:	Gopher: gopher.oise.on.ca

Queen's University
Main Gopher Server
Kingston, Ontario

ACCESS:	Gopher: gopher.queensu.ca

Ryerson Polytechnic University
Main Gopher Server
Toronto, Ontario

ACCESS:	Gopher: gopher.ryerson.ca

Ryerson Polytechnic University
Computing and Communications Services
Toronto, Ontario

ACCESS:	Gopher: hermes.acs.ryerson.ca

St. Francis Xavier University
Main Gopher Server
Antigonish, Nova Scotia

ACCESS:	Gopher: gopher.stfx.ca

Saint Mary's University
Main Gopher Server
Halifax, Nova Scotia

ACCESS:	Gopher: gopher.stmarys.ca

Simon Fraser University
Main Gopher Server
Burnaby, British Columbia

ACCESS:	Gopher: gopher.sfu.ca

Simon Fraser University
Faculty of Applied Sciences
Burnaby, British Columbia

ACCESS:	Gopher: fas.sfu.ca

Simon Fraser University
Centre for Experimental and Constructive Mathematics
Burnaby, British Columbia

ACCESS:	Gopher: gopher.cecm.sfu.ca

Simon Fraser University
Emergency Preparedness Information Exchange
Burnaby, British Columbia

ACCESS:	Gopher: hoshi.cic.sfu.ca port 5555

Simon Fraser University
Harbour Centre Campus
Vancouver, British Columbia

ACCESS:	Gopher: hoshi.cic.sfu.ca

Simon Fraser University
Faculty of Education
Burnaby, British Columbia

ACCESS:	Gopher: bach.educ.sfu.ca

Simon Fraser University
Media and Public Relations
Burnaby, British Columbia

ACCESS:	Gopher: asmundson.mediapr.sfu.ca

Simon Fraser University
Physics
Burnaby, British Columbia

ACCESS:	Gopher: techie.phys.sfu.ca

Trent University
Peterborough, Ontario

ACCESS:	Gopher: blaze.trentu.ca

University of Alberta
Main Gopher Server
Edmonton, Alberta

ACCESS:	Gopher:	cwis.srv.ualberta.ca
	Telnet:	cwis.srv.ualberta.ca
	Login:	**gopherc**

University of Alberta
Chemistry
Edmonton, Alberta

ACCESS:	Gopher: cwis.chem.ualberta.ca

University of Alberta
Computing Science
Edmonton, Alberta

ACCESS:	Gopher: gopher.cs.ualberta.ca

University of British Columbia (VIEW UBC)
Main Gopher Server
Vancouver, British Columbia

ACCESS:	Gopher: view.ubc.ca

University of British Columbia
Chemistry Department
Vancouver, British Columbia

ACCESS:	Gopher: chem.ubc.ca

University of British Columbia
Computer Science Department
Vancouver, British Columbia

ACCESS:	Gopher: gopher.cs.ubc.ca

University of British Columbia
Computing and Communications
Vancouver, British Columbia

ACCESS:	Gopher: gopher.ucs.ubc.ca

University of British Columbia
Economics Department
Vancouver, British Columbia

ACCESS:	Gopher: gopher.econ.ubc.ca

University of British Columbia
Faculty of Education
Vancouver, British Columbia

ACCESS:	Gopher: ecs.educ.ubc.ca

University of British Columbia
Geophysics and Astronomy
Vancouver, British Columbia

ACCESS:	Gopher: gopher.astro.ubc.ca

University of Calgary
Main Gopher Server
Calgary, Alberta

ACCESS:	Gopher: gopher.ucalgary.ca

University of Calgary
Department of Computer Science
Calgary, Alberta

ACCESS:	Gopher: gopher.cpsc.ucalgary.ca

University of Calgary
Department of Electrical Engineering
Calgary, Alberta

ACCESS:	Gopher: gopher.enel.ucalgary.ca

University of Calgary
Education Technology
Calgary, Alberta

ACCESS:	Gopher: pc30.educ.ucalgary.ca

Université Laval
Main Gopher Server
Quebec City, Quebec

ACCESS:	Gopher: gopher.ulaval.ca

University of Lethbridge
Lethbridge, Alberta

ACCESS:	Gopher: gopher.uleth.ca

University of Manitoba (UMinfo)
Winnipeg, Manitoba

ACCESS:	Gopher: gopher.cc.umanitoba.ca

Université de Moncton
Moncton, New Brunswick

ACCESS:	Gopher: bosoleil.ci.umoncton.ca

Université de Moncton
Centre Universitaire Saint-Louis-Maillet

ACCESS:	Gopher: gopher.cuslm.ca

Université de Moncton
Shippagan Campus
Shippagan, New Brunswick

ACCESS:	Gopher: gopher.cus.ca

Université de Montréal
Main Gopher Server
Montreal, Quebec

ACCESS:	Gopher: gopher.umontreal.ca

Université de Montréal
Campus Wide Information System (UdeMatik)
Montreal, Quebec

ACCESS:	Telnet: udematik.umontreal.ca

Université de Montréal
Faculté de l'Aménagement
Montreal, Quebec

ACCESS:	Gopher: mistral.ere.umontreal.ca port 7070

Université de Montréal
Bibliothèque de Médecine Vétérinaire
Montreal, Quebec

ACCESS:	Gopher: brise.ere.umontreal.ca port 7070

Université de Montréal
Gopher des Bibliothèques Scientifiques
Montreal, Quebec

ACCESS:	Gopher: brise.ere.umontreal.ca

Université de Montréal
Département de Biochimie (Biochemistry)
Montreal, Quebec

ACCESS: Gopher: megasun.bch.umontreal.ca

Université de Montréal
École de Bibliothéconomie et des Sciences
de l'Information (EBSI)
Montreal, Quebec

ACCESS: Gopher: tornade.ere.umontreal.ca   port 7072

Université de Montréal
Canadian Federation of the Humanities
Montreal, Quebec

ACCESS: Gopher: tornade.ere.umontreal.ca   port 7071

Université de Montréal
Département d'Informatique et de
Recherche Operationnelle
Montreal, Quebec

ACCESS: Gopher: gopher.iro.umontreal.ca

Université de Montréal
Faculté de Droit (Law Gopher)
Montreal, Quebec

ACCESS: Gopher: gopher.droit.umontreal.ca

Université de Montréal
Gopher Litteratures
Montreal, Quebec

ACCESS: Gopher: tornade.ere.umontreal.ca   port 7070

University of New Brunswick
Main Gopher Server
Fredericton, New Brunswick

ACCESS: Gopher: gopher.unb.ca

University of New Brunswick
Unix Services
Fredericton, New Brunswick

ACCESS:	Gopher: jupiter.sun.csd.unb.ca

University of Ottawa
Main Gopher Server
Ottawa, Ontario

ACCESS:	Gopher: panda1.uottawa.ca

University of Ottawa
Department of Epidemiology and Community Medicine
Ottawa, Ontario

ACCESS:	Gopher: zeus.med.uottawa.ca

University of Prince Edward Island
Main Gopher Server
Charlottetown, Prince Edward Island

ACCESS:	Gopher: gopher.cs.upei.ca

Université du Québec
Main Gopher Server
Sainte-Foy, Quebec

ACCESS:	Gopher: gopher.uquebec.ca

Université du Québec à Montréal (INFOPUB)
Main Gopher Server
Montreal, Quebec

ACCESS:	Gopher: infopub.uqam.ca

University of Regina
Computer Science Department
Regina, Saskatchewan

ACCESS:	Gopher: gopher.cs.uregina.ca

University of Saskatchewan
Main Gopher Server
Saskatoon, Saskatchewan

ACCESS:	Gopher: gopher.usask.ca

University of Saskatchewan
Engineering Gopher
Saskatoon, Saskatchewan

ACCESS:	Gopher: dvinci.usask.ca

University of Toronto
Main Gopher Server
Toronto, Ontario

ACCESS:	Gopher: gopher.utoronto.ca

University of Toronto
Computer Systems Research Institute
Toronto, Ontario

ACCESS:	Gopher: bathurst.csri.utoronto.ca

University of Toronto
Division of the Environment
Toronto, Ontario

ACCESS:	Gopher: zinnia.zoo.utoronto.ca

University of Toronto
EPAS Computing Facility
Toronto, Ontario

ACCESS:	Gopher: alpha.epas.utoronto.ca

University of Toronto
Erindale College
Mississauga, Ontario

ACCESS:	Gopher: credit.erin.utoronto.ca

University of Toronto
Instructional and Research Computing
Toronto, Ontario

ACCESS:	Gopher: gopher.utirc.utoronto.ca

University of Toronto
Department of Physics
Toronto, Ontario

ACCESS:	Gopher: gopher.physics.utoronto.ca

University of Toronto
Scarborough Campus
Scarborough, Ontario

ACCESS:	Gopher: wave.scar.utoronto.ca

University of Toronto
VM Gopher
Toronto, Ontario

ACCESS:	Gopher: vm.utcc.utoronto.ca

University of Victoria
Main Gopher Server
Victoria, British Columbia

ACCESS:	Gopher: gopher.uvic.ca

University of Victoria
Department of Computer Science
Victoria, British Columbia

ACCESS:	Gopher: gulf.uvic.ca

University of Victoria
Faculty of Engineering
Victoria, British Columbia

ACCESS:	Gopher: gopher-engr.uvic.ca

University of Victoria
Faculty of Fine Arts
Victoria, British Columbia

ACCESS:	Gopher: kafka.uvic.ca

University of Waterloo (UWinfo)
Main Gopher Server
Waterloo, Ontario

ACCESS:	Gopher: gopher.uwaterloo.ca

University of Waterloo
Office of the Provost
Waterloo, Ontario

ACCESS:	Gopher: provost-admin.uwaterloo.ca

University of Waterloo
Faculty of Arts
Waterloo, Ontario

ACCESS:	Gopher: watarts.uwaterloo.ca

University of Waterloo
Computer Science Club
Waterloo, Ontario

ACCESS:	Gopher: csclub.uwaterloo.ca

University of Waterloo
Faculty of Engineering
Waterloo, Ontario

ACCESS:	Gopher: sail.uwaterloo.ca

University of Western Ontario
Main Gopher Server
London, Ontario

ACCESS:	Gopher: gopher.uwo.ca

University of Western Ontario
Business School
London, Ontario

ACCESS:	Gopher: gopher.business.uwo.ca

University of Windsor
Main Gopher Server
Windsor, Ontario

ACCESS:	Gopher: gopher.uwindsor.ca

University of Windsor
Faculty of Science
Windsor, Ontario

ACCESS:	Gopher: zaphod.cs.uwindsor.ca

York University
Main Gopher Server
Toronto, Ontario

ACCESS:	Gopher: gopher.yorku.ca

York University
Computer Club
Toronto, Ontario

ACCESS:	Gopher: yucc.yorku.ca

York University
UNICAAT Project
Toronto, Ontario

ACCESS:	Gopher: unicaat.yorku.ca

Canadian Colleges and Schools on Gopher

ACAATO
Association of Colleges of Applied Arts and Technology of Ontario
Ontario, Canada

ACCESS:	Gopher: info.senecac.on.ca port 2000

Algonquin College of Applied Arts and Technology
Main Gopher Server
Nepean, Ontario

ACCESS:	Gopher: gopher.algonquinc.on.ca

Camosun College
Main Gopher Server
Victoria, British Columbia

ACCESS:	Gopher: gopher.camosun.bc.ca

Camosun College
School of Business
Victoria, British Columbia

ACCESS:	Gopher: dragon.camosun.bc.ca

Canadore College
Main Gopher Server
North Bay, Ontario

ACCESS:	Gopher: mars.canadorec.on.ca

Centennial College
Main Gopher Server
Scarborough, Ontario

ACCESS:	Gopher: cenvmc.cencol.on.ca

La Cité Collégiale
Main Gopher Server
Ottawa, Ontario

ACCESS:	Gopher: gopher.lacitec.on.ca

Conestoga College
Main Gopher Server
Kitchener, Ontario

ACCESS:	Gopher: holmes.conestogac.on.ca

École des Hautes Études Commerciales
Main Gopher Server
Montreal, Quebec

ACCESS:	Gopher: gopher.hec.ca

Fanshawe College
Main Gopher Server
London, Ontario

ACCESS:	Gopher: claven.fanshawec.on.ca

George Brown College
Main Gopher Server
Toronto, Ontario

ACCESS:	Gopher: gbc.gbrownc.on.ca

Georgian College
Main Gopher Server
Barrie, Ontario

ACCESS:	Gopher: gc1.georcoll.on.ca

Humber College
Main Gopher Server
Rexdale, Ontario

ACCESS:	Gopher: admin.humberc.on.ca

Lambton College
Main Gopher Server
Sarnia, Ontario

ACCESS:	Gopher: white.lambton.on.ca

National Adult Literacy Database
Fanshawe College
London, Ontario

ACCESS:	Gopher: nald.fanshawec.on.ca

Malaspina College
Main Gopher Server
Nanaimo, British Columbia

ACCESS:	Gopher: gopher.mala.bc.ca

Niagara College
Main Gopher Server
Welland, Ontario

ACCESS:	Gopher: lundy.niagarac.on.ca

Northern College
Main Gopher Server
Kirkland Lake, Ontario

ACCESS:	Gopher: kirk.northernc.on.ca

North Island College
Main Gopher Server
Courtenay, British Columbia

ACCESS:	Gopher: matthew.nic.bc.ca

Nova Scotia Agricultural College
Main Gopher Server
Truro, Nova Scotia

ACCESS:	Gopher: ac.nsac.ns.ca

Okanagan University College
Main Gopher Server
Kelowna. British Columbia

ACCESS:	Gopher: oksw01.okanagan.bc.ca

Royal Military College
Main Gopher Server
Kingston, Ontario

ACCESS:	Gopher: gopher.rmc.ca

St. Clair College
Main Gopher Server
Windsor, Ontario

ACCESS:	Gopher: gopher.stclairc.on.ca

St. Lawrence College
Main Gopher Server
Brockville. Ontario

ACCESS:	Gopher: slcsl.stlawrencec.on.ca

Sault College
Main Gopher Server
Sault Ste. Marie, Ontario

ACCESS:	Gopher: gopher.saultc.on.ca

Seneca College of Applied Arts and Technology
Main Gopher Server
Toronto, Ontario

ACCESS:	Gopher: info.senecac.on.ca

Sheridan College
Main Gopher Server
Oakville, Ontario

ACCESS:	Gopher: gopher.sheridanc.on.ca

Sir Sandford Fleming College
Main Gopher Server
Peterborough, Ontario

ACCESS:	Gopher: gopher.flemingc.on.ca

Canadian Libraries on Gopher

Carleton University Library
Ottawa, Ontario

ACCESS:	Gopher: library3.library.carleton.ca

National Library of Canada
Ottawa, Ontario

ACCESS:	Gopher: gopher.nlc-bnc.ca

Ryerson Polytechnic University Library
Toronto, Ontario

ACCESS:	Gopher: hugo.lib.ryerson.ca

University of Alberta Data Library
Edmonton, Alberta

ACCESS:	Gopher: datalib.library.ualberta.ca

University of British Columbia Library
Vancouver, British Columbia

ACCESS:	Gopher: unixg.ubc.ca port 7001

Université Laval Library
Quebec City, Quebec

ACCESS:	Gopher: gopher.bibl.ulaval.ca

University of Toronto Library
Toronto, Ontario

ACCESS:	Gopher: robarts.library.utoronto.ca

University of Western Ontario Library
London, Ontario

ACCESS:	Gopher: zoi.lib.uwo.ca

Canadian Educational Networking Organizations on Gopher

CANARIE Inc.
Ottawa, Ontario

ACCESS:	Gopher: tweetie.canarie.ca

Community Learning Network
Sidney, British Columbia

ACCESS:	Gopher: cln.etc.bc.ca

SchoolNet
Ottawa, Ontario

ACCESS:	Gopher: gopher.schoolnet.carleton.ca

STEM~NET
St John's, Newfoundland

ACCESS:	Gopher: info.stemnet.nf.ca

TeleEducation New Brunswick
Sackville, New Brunswick

ACCESS:	Gopher: tenb.mta.ca

Canadian Government Bodies on Gopher

Atlantic Geoscience Centre
Dartmouth, Nova Scotia

ACCESS:	Gopher: agcgopher.bio.ns.ca

Bedford Institute of Oceanography (BIOME)
Habitat Ecology Division
Dartmouth, Nova Scotia

ACCESS:	Gopher: biome.bio.ns.ca

Government of British Columbia
Ministry of Environment, Lands, and Parks
Victoria, British Columbia

ACCESS:	Gopher: gopher.env.gov.bc.ca

British Columbia Systems Corporation
Victoria, British Columbia

ACCESS:	Gopher: bcsc02.gov.bc.ca

Canada Centre for Inland Waters
Burlington, Ontario

ACCESS:	Gopher: csx.cciw.ca

Communauté Urbaine de Montréal
Montreal, Quebec

ACCESS:	Gopher: gopher.cum.qc.ca

Communications Research Centre
Ottawa, Ontario

ACCESS:	Gopher: debra.dgbt.doc.ca

Environment Canada
Downsview, Ontario

ACCESS:	Gopher: cmit02.dow.on.doe.ca

Health Canada
Ottawa, Ontario

ACCESS:	Gopher: hpb1.hwc.ca

National Library of Canada
Ottawa, Ontario

ACCESS:	Gopher: gopher.nlc-bnc.ca

National Research Council
Photonic Systems Group
Ottawa, Ontario

ACCESS:	Gopher: holo.ps.iit.nrc.ca

Natural Resources Canada
Main Gopher Server
Ottawa, Ontario

ACCESS:	Gopher: gopher.emr.ca

Natural Resources Canada
Canada Centre for Mapping
Ottawa, Ontario

ACCESS:	Gopher: ccm-10.ccm.emr.ca

Natural Resources Canada
Geodetic Survey of Canada
Ottawa, Ontario

ACCESS:	Gopher: gdim.geod.emr.ca

Natural Resources Canada
Pacific Forestry Centre
Victoria, British Columbia

ACCESS:	Gopher: pfc.pfc.forestry.ca

Government of Ontario
Toronto, Ontario

ACCESS:	Gopher: govonca.gov.on.ca

Ontario Ministry of Education and Training
Toronto, Ontario

ACCESS:	Gopher: gopher.edu.gov.on.ca

Open Government Pilot
House of Commons, Senate of Canada,
Supreme Court of Canada
Ottawa, Ontario

ACCESS:	Gopher: debra.dgbt.doc.ca (Main Server)
	Gopher: gopher.emr.ca (Mirror Server)

Revenue Canada
Ottawa, Ontario

ACCESS:	Gopher: gopher.revcan.ca

Statistics Canada
Ottawa, Ontario

ACCESS:	Gopher: talon.statcan.ca

Canadian Internet Providers on Gopher

Achilles Internet Services
Ottawa, Ontario

ACCESS:	Gopher: gopher.achilles.net

Communications Accessibles Montréal
Montreal, Quebec

ACCESS:	Gopher: gopher.cam.org

Communications Inter-Acces
Montreal, Quebec

ACCESS:	Gopher: gopher.interax.net

Dataflux Systems Limited
Victoria, British Columbia

ACCESS:	Gopher: gopher.dataflux.bc.ca

Helix Internet
Vancouver, British Columbia

ACCESS:	Gopher: gopher.helix.net

HookUp Communications
Waterloo, Ontario

ACCESS:	Gopher: gopher.hookup.net

InfoRamp Inc.
Toronto, Ontario

ACCESS:	Gopher: inforamp.net

Interlog Internet Services
Toronto, Ontario

ACCESS:	Gopher: gopher.interlog.com

Internet Access Inc.
Ottawa, Ontario

ACCESS:	Gopher: shop.net

Internex Online
Toronto, Ontario

ACCESS:	Gopher: io.org

Island Internet
Nanaimo, British Columbia

ACCESS:	Gopher: epaus.island.net

Island Net
Victoria, British Columbia

ACCESS:	Gopher: gopher.islandnet.com

Magi Data Consulting
Nepean, Ontario

ACCESS:	Gopher: fred.magi.com

MBnet
Winnipeg, Manitoba

ACCESS:	Gopher: gopher.mbnet.mb.ca

Metrix Interlink Corporation
Montreal, Quebec

ACCESS:	Gopher: gopher.interlink.net

NBNet
Saint John, New Brunswick

ACCESS:	Gopher: gopher.nbnet.nb.ca

Nova Scotia Technology Network
Dartmouth, Nova Scotia

ACCESS:	Gopher: gopher.nstn.ca

PEInet
Charlottetown, Prince Edward Island

ACCESS:	Gopher: gopher.peinet.pe.ca

Resudox Online Services
Nepean, Ontario

ACCESS:	Gopher: resudox.net

RISQ
Montreal, Quebec

ACCESS:	Gopher: risq.net

Telnet Canada Enterprises
Calgary, Alberta

ACCESS:	Gopher: gopher.tcel.com

Canadian Community Networks on Gopher

807-City
Thunder Bay, Ontario

ACCESS:	Gopher: tourism.807-city.on.ca

National Capital Free-Net
Ottawa, Ontario

ACCESS:	Gopher: freenet.carleton.ca

Victoria Free-Net Association
Victoria, British Columbia

ACCESS:	Gopher: freenet.victoria.bc.ca

Canadian Commercial Organizations on Gopher

Cygnus Telecomm
Fredericton, New Brunswick

ACCESS:	Gopher: gopher.cygnus.nb.ca

Discribe Limited
Fredericton, New Brunswick

ACCESS:	Gopher: gopher.discribe.ca

Internet Shopping Network
Ottawa, Ontario

ACCESS:	Gopher: shop.net

Knowledge Plus Multimedia Publishing
Kelowna, British Columbia

ACCESS:	Gopher: basil.kplus.bc.ca

Sirius Solutions Limited
Dartmouth, Nova Scotia

ACCESS:	Gopher: sirius1.sirius.ns.ca

Software Kinetics Limited
Stittsville, Ontario

ACCESS:	Gopher: gopher.sofkin.ca

Other Canadian Organizations on Gopher

Alberta Research Council
Edmonton, Alberta

ACCESS:	Gopher: gopher.arc.ab.ca

British Columbia Electronic Library Network (InfoServ)
Victoria, British Columbia

ACCESS:	Gopher: infoserv.uvic.ca

British Columbia Institute of Technology
Main Gopher Server
Burnaby, British Columbia

ACCESS:	Gopher: bcit.bcit.bc.ca

British Columbia Institute of Technology
Technology Centre
Burnaby, British Columbia

ACCESS:	Gopher: moon.arcs.bcit.bc.ca

British Columbia Teachers' Federation
Vancouver, British Columbia

ACCESS:	Gopher: sun.bctf.bc.ca

Canadian Mathematical Society (CAMEL)
Burnaby, British Columbia

ACCESS:	Gopher: camel.cecm.sfu.ca

Chedoke-McMaster Hospitals
Hamilton, Ontario

ACCESS:	Gopher: gopher.cmh.on.ca

Coalition for Public Information
Ottawa, Ontario

ACCESS:	Gopher: gabriel.resudox.net port 1994

Confederation of University Faculty Associations of British Columbia
Vancouver, British Columbia

ACCESS:	Gopher: epix.cic.sfu.ca

Digital Ark
Comox Valley, Vancouver Island

ACCESS:	Gopher: moon.ark.com

French Embassy
Ottawa, Ontario

ACCESS:	Gopher: avril.amba-ottawa.fr

Institute for Space and Terrestrial Science
Toronto, Ontario

ACCESS:	Gopher: network.admin.ists.ca

Institute for Fisheries and Marine Technology
St. John's, Newfoundland

ACCESS:	Gopher: inseine.ifmt.nf.ca

Native Education Center
Vancouver, British Columbia

ACCESS:	Gopher: gopher.native-ed.bc.ca

Nova Scotia Research Foundation Corporation
Dartmouth, Nova Scotia

ACCESS:	Gopher: info.nsrfc.ns.ca

Prince Edward Island Crafts Council

Charlottetown, Prince Edward Island

ACCESS:	Gopher: gopher.crafts-council.pe.ca

A P P E N D I X   F

....

INTERNET FORMS

This appendix contains three forms:

(i) The application form for a domain from the CA Domain Registrar (page 530)
(ii) The application form for a domain from the InterNIC (page 542)
(iii) The application form for a Class C Network Number in Canada (page 545)

- Use the CA Subdomain application form when you want to apply for a subdomain under the **.ca** domain.

- Use the InterNIC domain application form when you want to apply for a **.com, .org, .edu, .net,** or **.gov** domain.

- Use the Class C network number application form when you want to apply for an IP number for your computer network. Organizations that are establishing permanent, dedicated connections to the Internet will need one or more IP numbers.

These forms are provided for reference purposes only. Most commercial Internet providers will fill out and/or submit these forms for you. Consult the **Directory of Canadian Internet Providers** in Appendix C to see which commercial providers offer domain registration service.

You can obtain electronic copies of these forms on the Internet, as detailed in the boxes below:

Application form for a domain from the CA Domain Registrar

Anonymous FTP Site:	ftp.cdnnet.ca
Directory:	ca-domain
File:	application-form

Application form for a domain from the InterNIC

Anonymous FTP Site:	rs.internic.net
Directory:	templates
File:	domain-template.txt

Application form for a Class C Network Number

Anonymous FTP Site:	ftp.canet.ca
Directory:	canet/templates
File:	ip-req.txt

CA SUBDOMAIN APPLICATION FORM

CA Subdomain Application Instructions (Updated 1994 August 24)

This document describes the CA subdomain application form. To apply for a subdomain, please fill out an application form and submit it to the appropriate liaison from the list below. It is recommended that you edit the sample form included below and change the information as appropriate for your organization.

Your liaison may charge a fee for the registration service, and may also require further information. Organizations applying directly to the CA Registrar may be charged a fee. Currently the registrar cannot accept telephone requests.

Please note that your application is being made on behalf of your entire organization. As such, it is important that you are authorized to speak for your entire organization in this matter and that you obtain the agreement of all interested parties within your organization prior to submission.

See below for instructions on how to obtain more information on the CA domain, such as an introduction to the domain and a list of current subdomain registrations.

Here is a description of each field of the application form:

Subdomain:

The name of the subdomain applied for. Since the CA domain
is structured according to Canadian political geography,
this will be of the form "yourorg.CA," or
"yourorg.province-or-territory.CA," or
"yourorg.locality.province-or-territory.CA."

"province-or-territory" is one of the following provincial
and territorial abbreviations, as recommended by the
Department of the Secretary of State: AB, BC, MB, NB, NF,
NS, NT, ON, PE, QC, SK and YK. "locality" is the full name
of a city, town or village. Hyphens are used to replace
spaces, e.g., Niagara-Falls, New-Westminster.

Here are requirements and guidelines to help determine the
appropriate level of subdomain name for your organization:

(1) Second (national) level — To qualify for a second-level
    domain, your organization must have offices or other
    points of presence (such as computer hosts or dial-up
    facilities) in more than one province or territory, or
    be incorporated or chartered nationally.

(2) Third (provincial or territorial) level — To qualify for
    a third-level domain, your organization must have
    offices or other points of presence (such as computer
    hosts or dial-up facilities) in more than one locality, or
    be incorporated or registered provincially or
    territorially. Provincial and territorial governments,
    referral hospitals and post-secondary degree or
    certificate-granting educational institutions such as
    universities and colleges should have third-level
    subdomain names.

(3) Fourth (municipal) level — Small organizations such as
    companies which do most of their business in one
    locality and bulletin board systems should apply for a
    fourth-level or municipal subdomain name, as should
    organizations such as local hospitals, libraries,
    municipal governments, and schools.

    When applying for anything other than a fourth-level
    subdomain name, please provide supporting information
    such as your incorporation number, office locations,
    etc.

    "yourorg" is a string that encodes the proper name of
    your organization. Determining the string is a matter
    of establishing the "corporate electronic identity" of
    your organization for years to come. This is something
    you should discuss with the individual in your
    organization whose authority includes the "corporate
    image." If the appropriate string is not immediately
    obvious to this person, then we suggest that you use the
    following steps to determine the string for which you
    are applying.

(1) Start with the full proper name by which your organization conducts its business. E.g.: "AB Systems Incorporated," "University of Waterloo";

(2) Remove all the blanks. E.g.: "ABSystemsIncorporated," "UniversityofWaterloo";

(3) Remove truly extraneous components, if there are any. E.g.: "ABSystems," "UniversityWaterloo";

(4) If it is excessively long, abbreviate by trimming the parts whose removal will result in the least loss of recognizability outside the sphere in which your organization is already well known, E.g.: "ABSystems," "UWaterloo";

(5) Please choose a descriptive abbreviation of your organization's name, and try to avoid a cryptic abbreviation that defeats the objective of step (4) above. To repeat, it is essential that your choice be approved by the person in charge of your organization's corporate image. If you are in doubt about your choice, ask your CA Domain Committee member to offer an opinion before you submit the application.

It is your responsibility to ensure that you have the right to use the name you have chosen.

Obscene names are not permitted.

Geographical place names, such as municipality and province names, are reserved.

Legal characters are letters, digits, and the hyphen. You may mix upper and lower case, or use all upper or all lower case. Software will ignore case, and users can type in whatever case they like. You should capitalize your subdomain name as you wish it to appear in machine-generated lists, such as the return address generated in your outgoing electronic mail. Hyphens may be used to separate words if necessary or consistent with normal references to the proper name of your organization.

The CA domain registrar is the final authority on all matters relating to registration and subsequent use of your subdomain name.

Your subdomain name must be approved by the CA domain registrar before it is used in network communications. If you devise further subdomains of your domain name, then you in turn will have final authority on matters relating to the use of those subdomains.

Since the CA domain was first created, the requirements and guidelines have been modified from time to time. Although all existing registrations remain in effect, some registered subdomain names might not be permitted if applied for today. New applications and voluntary applications for

re-registration will be considered using the current
guidelines.

Examples:

MegaCo.CA	National company
WidgetCo.PE.CA	Provincial company
CityAutoLtd.Melville.SK.CA	Small business
AlphaBetaU.MB.CA	University

Organization:

The full name of your organization.

Type:

Type of organization.

For example:

    For-Profit Corporation
    Non-Profit Corporation
    For-Profit Partnership
    Proprietorship
    Ph.D.-granting University
    High School
    Federal Government Branch
    Provincial Government
    Military Branch

Description:

A short paragraph describing your organization. Please
include any appropriate justification for your choice of
subdomain level. For example, please state whether your
corporation is federally or provincially incorporated, and
whether your corporation has offices in more than one
province.

    Admin-Name:
    Admin-Title:
    Admin-Postal:
    Admin-Phone:
    Admin-Fax:
    Admin-Mailbox:

The name, title, full mailing address, phone number,
facsimile number, and electronic address of an
administrative contact for the organization. This person is
within the subdomain's organization and is the contact point
for administrative and policy questions about the subdomain.
This person is responsible for this application and for any
future changes. We recommend that you choose a person who
is expected to be around and in a position of authority for
many years, and that you use a properly maintained generic
electronic address.

For example:

```
Admin-Name:     John Smith
Admin-Title:    Administrative Assistant
Admin-Postal:   Alpha Beta University
                Dept. of Computer Science
                1234 Main St.
                Hoople, Manitoba
                M1B 2C3
Admin-Phone:    +1 (204) 555 1511
Admin-Fax:      +1 (204) 555 9095
Admin-Mailbox:  admin@AlphaBetaU.MB.CA

Tech-Name:
Tech-Title:
Tech-Postal:
Tech-Phone:
Tech-Fax:
Tech-Mailbox:
```

The name, title, full mailing address, telephone number, facsimile number, and electronic address of two or more technical contacts.

This is the contact point for problems with the subdomain and for updating information about the subdomain. The registrar will verify changes by sending the current registration information back to the submitter and to the administrative contact. We recommend that you use a properly maintained generic electronic address.

Don't list people who hate to get electronic mail. One or more of the contacts must read their mail often enough to respond quickly, should a problem arise. For very small organizations, it is permissible to have only one technical contact. It is appropriate to have at least one contact corresponding to each of the forwarders within the organization. Forwarders are described below.

For example:

```
Tech-Name:      Jean Smith
Tech-Title:     Researcher
Tech-Postal:    Alpha Beta University
                Dept. of Computer Science
                1234 Main St.
                Hoople, Manitoba
                M1B 2C3
Tech-Phone:     +1 (204) 555 1512
Tech-Name:      Fred Rogers
Tech-Title:     Computing Staff
Tech-Postal:    Alpha Beta University
                Dept. of Computer Science
                1234 Main St.
                Hoople, Manitoba
                M1B 2C3
Tech-Phone:     +1 (204) 555 1513
```

```
Tech-Fax:      +1 (204) 555 9099
Tech-Mailbox:  tech@AlphaBetaU.MB.CA
```

Location:

The latitude and longitude of the subdomain. (This can be taken as the location of the main organizational machine, or the headquarters, or the contact persons; usually the machine is used.) Give as much precision as you know; if you can determine the location only to the nearest minute, or the nearest few minutes, that's satisfactory. Include "city" only if you are using the location of your city center, for which information is often available in an atlas, at a library, City Hall or a nearby airport. At a minimum, please provide the location of your city center. This field is used to draw maps.

For example:

```
52 04 05 N / 97 37 46 W
```

or

```
52 04 N / 97 37 W city
```

Net Provider:

The name of your primary network provider. Your network provider is the organization which provides your IP connectivity to the Internet. Here is a list of network providers:

```
Arnet
BC Systems
Bcnet
DREnet
fONOROLA
HookUp
Mbnet
NB*net
Nlnet
NSTN
Onet
PEInet
RISQ
SASK#net
UUNET Canada
```

If you have no IP connectivity to the Internet but do have UUCP connectivity, specify "UUCP" as your provider. If you have no connectivity but wish to apply for a subdomain name anyway, specify "none" as your provider.

The list above will be expanded as needed. If your network provider is not on the list, have them contact the CA Registrar directly before proceeding with your application.

Forwarder:

The forwarder fields describe how your organization can be reached FROM specified networks. This information is used to guide tasks such as the routing of electronic mail to your organization. (They do not describe how your organization sends traffic TO any network.) For the purposes of your application, there are two kinds of forwarders:

Organization-Internal Forwarder. Your organization has one or more computing systems that have direct Internet or UUCP connections. Also, all computing systems within your organization are internally connected. Please see the examples below for what to do in the case of a forwarder that cannot reach all recipients within your organization.

Organization-External Forwarder. Your organization is directly connected to network A; another organization is directly connected to both networks A and B, and has agreed to provide a forwarder that will accept mail from network B and forward it to your organization-internal forwarder in network A.

Within the application form, each forwarder specification appears as follows:

Forwarder: networkname: forwarder_address(comment)<reference_address>;

   or

Forwarder: networkname: none;

   or:

Forwarder: Internet: DNS;

where "networkname" is the name of the network, "forwarder_address" is the network-specific electronic address of the forwarder, "(comment)" is optional explanatory text and "reference_address" is the electronic address of an individual to whom questions regarding the use of that forwarder may be sent. For an organization-internal forwarder, the reference will be some entity within your organization subdomain; for an organization-external forwarder, it will be the entity external to your organization that has authorized your organization to use that forwarder.

Specify forwarder fields for both the Internet and UUCP, even if you do not have access to both. For historical reasons, existing registrations may have forwarder fields for CDNnet and NetNorth.

Example 1 — Internet and UUCP connections

In this case, the organization can be reached directly from both networks.

Forwarder: Internet: DNS;

Forwarder: UUCP: abunix <rob@AlphaBetaU.MB.CA>;

When DNS (Domain Name System) is specified, please provide as supplementary information the subdomain names and IP addresses of at least two nameserver hosts (one primary and at least one secondary) for the new subdomain. See the sample application form below for an example.

Example 2 — Internet-only

Here are the forwarder specifications for an organization which is directly connected to the Internet, but which has no direct UUCP connection.

Forwarder: Internet: DNS;

Forwarder: UUCP: none;

Example 3 — External Internet forwarder

Forwarder: Internet: relay.otherorg.ca <joe@otherorg.ca>;

Forwarder: UUCP: abunix <rob@AlphaBetaU.MB.CA>;

Here the organization does not have direct Internet connectivity, but joe@otherorg.ca (whose organization is on the Internet) has agreed to forward mail from the Internet to the organization. In this case, the CA nameserver administrator will put the appropriate MX records into the CA nameservers to make this work.

Example 4 — UUCP-only

Here is an example of the forwarder specification for an organization with a direct UUCP connection, but with no access to the Internet.

Forwarder: Internet: none;

Forwarder: UUCP: abunix <rob@AlphaBetaU.MB.CA>;

Note that in this case your organization will not be directly addressable from the Internet. That is, your subdomain name will not appear in the DNS.

Example 5 — No connectivity

When applying for a subdomain name for your organization's future use, specify "none" for the forwarders.

Forwarder: Internet: none;

Forwarder: UUCP: none;

Once you establish forwarders, resubmit the application with the updated information.

NOTES:

(1) In the case of direct connection to a network but lack of full organization-internal connectivity, please do

not omit the forwarder specification. If you can arrange full connectivity with the help of an external organization, specify the forwarder as above. Otherwise, specify:

Forwarder: networkname: none;

(2) Each network-administration body may have specific regulations covering the valid uses of its network. The acceptance of an application for a CA subdomain in no way alters or eliminates your obligations to adhere to the regulations for the uses of those networks.

Applications and updates may be submitted to the following contacts:

UUCP sites:
> CA Registry
> c/o XeniTec Consulting Services,
> 199 Silver Aspen Cr.
> Kitchener, Ontario
> N2N 1H5

E-mail: registry@cs.utoronto.ca, registry@utai.uucp, ...!utai!registry

UUNET Canada:
> Lynda Fincham
> UUNET Canada Inc.
> Yonge St., Suite 1400
> Toronto, ON
> Canada M5E 1J9
> E-mail: support@uunet.ca

BCnet and British Columbia:
> Darren Kinley
> BCnet Headquarters
> 413 - 6356 Agricultural Road
> Vancouver, B.C.
> V6T 1Z2
> E-mail: Darren.Kinley@BCnet.BC.CA

ARnet and Alberta:
> Chris Thierman
> University of Alberta
> Computing and Network Services
> 352 General Services Building
> Edmonton, Alberta
> Canada T6G 2H1
> E-mail: thierman@namao.ucs.ualberta.ca
> Fax: +1 (403) 492 1729
> Phone: +1 (403) 492 9318

MBnet and Manitoba:
> Gary Mills
> Networking Group, Computer Services
> Room 603, Engineering Building
> University of Manitoba

Winnipeg, Manitoba
R3T 2N2
E-mail: mills@ccu.umanitoba.ca

ONet and Ontario:
Herb Kugel
ONET Registrar
Univ. of Toronto Network Operating Services
255 Huron Street
Toronto, Ontario
M5S 1A1
E-mail: herb@gpu.utcc.utoronto.ca

RISQ and Quebec:
Francois Robitaille
Centre de récherché informatique de Montréal (CRIM)
1801, McGill College Avenue
Suite 800
Montréal (Quebec), Canada
H3A 2N4
E-mail: f_robita@crim.ca

NBnet and New Brunswick:
Brian Kaye
Computing Services
University of New Brunswick
P.O. Box 4400
Fredericton, N.B.
E3B 5A3
E-mail: bdk@unb.ca

NSTN and Nova Scotia:
Daniel MacKay
Communications Services
Dalhousie University
Halifax, N.S.
B3H 4H8
E-mail: daniel@nstn.ca

fONOROLA:
Hung Vu
Network Engineering
fONOROLA
250 Albert Street, Suite 205
Ottawa, Ontario
Canada K1P 6M1
E-mail: hungv@fonorola.com
Fax: +1 (613) 232 4329
Phone: +1 (613) 235 3666

British Columbia Systems Corporation:
Russ Forster
Interconnect Services
British Columbia Systems Corporation
4000 Seymour Place
Victoria, B.C.
Canada V8X 4S8

E-Mail: RForster@Galaxy.GOV.BC.CA
Fax: +1 (604) 389-3412
Phone: +1 (604) 389-3186

HookUp Communications:
Murray S. Kucherawy
HookUp Communications
50 Westmount Road North, Suite 220
Waterloo, Ontario
Canada N2L 2R5
E-mail: mskucher@hookup.net
Fax: +1 519 746 3521
Phone: +1 519 747 4110 x321

Other organizations:
CA Domain Registrar
c/o John Demco
Department of Computer Science
University of British Columbia
Vancouver, British Columbia
V6T 1Z4
E-mail: ca-registrar@CDNnet.CA

Information about the CA domain is available via electronic mail, anonymous FTP, and gopher.

To retrieve CA domain information via electronic mail, specify a line of the following form:

index ca-domain

or

send ca-domain <filename> [<filename> ...]

in the subject line or body of an electronic mail message to the CDNnet archive server. Send this message to:

archive-server@relay.CDNnet.CA

Example:

To: archive-server@relay.CDNnet.CA
Subject: send ca-domain Introduction Application-form

To retrieve CA domain information via anonymous FTP or gopher, use these URLs:

ftp://ftp.cdnnet.ca/ca-domain
gopher://owl.nstn.ns.ca/11/White%20Pages
gopher://gopher.fonorola.net/11/ca-domain

Here is a sample application form:
Subdomain: AlphaBetaU.MB.CA Organization: Alpha Beta University
Type: Ph.D.-granting university

```
Description:     Alpha Beta University is a degree-granting
                 academic organization widely known for its
                 program in Greek studies.

Admin-Name:      Jean Smith
Admin-Title:     Associate Director
Admin-Postal:    Alpha Beta University
                 Computing Services
                 1234 Main St.
                 Hoople, Manitoba
                 M1B 2C3
Admin-Phone:     +1 (204) 555 1511
Admin-Fax:       +1 (204) 555 9095
Admin-Mailbox:   admin@AlphaBetaU.MB.CA
Tech-Name:       John Smith
Tech-Title:      Systems Manager
Tech-Postal:     Alpha Beta University
                 Dept. of Computer Science
                 1234 Main St.
                 Hoople, Manitoba
                 M1B 2C3
Tech-Phone:      +1 (204) 555 1512
Tech-Fax:        +1 (204) 555 9099
Tech-Name:       Fred Rogers
Tech-Title:      Computing Staff
Tech-Postal:     Alpha Beta University
                 Dept. of Computer Science
                 1234 Main St.
                 Hoople, Manitoba
                 M1B 2C3
Tech-Phone:      +1 (204) 555 1513
Tech-Fax:        +1 (204) 555 9098
Tech-Mailbox:    tech@AlphaBetaU.MB.CA
Location:        52 04 05 N / 97 37 46 W
Net-Provider:    Mbnet
Forwarder:       Internet: DNS;
Forwarder:       UUCP:abunix<rob@AlphaBetaU.MB.CA>;

Nameserver information:
                 hub.alphabetau.mb.ca 199.3.2.1
                 relay.otherorg.ca 200.1.2.3
```

APPLICATION FORM FOR A DOMAIN FROM THE InterNIC

To establish a domain, the following information must be sent to the InterNIC Registration Services (HOSTMASTER@INTERNIC.NET). Either this template, or the "short form" following this template may be used.

(1) The name of the top-level domain to join (EDU, GOV, COM, NET, ORG).

1. Top-level domain:

(2) The name of the domain (up to 24 characters). This is the name that will be used in tables and lists associating the domain with the domain servers' addresses. While domain names can be quite long, the use of shorter, more user-friendly names is recommended.

2. Complete Domain Name:

(3) The name and address of the organization for which the domain is being established.

3a. Organization name:
3b. Organization address:

(4) The date you expect the domain to be fully operational.

4. Date operational:

NOTE: The key people must have electronic mailboxes (even if in the domain being registered) and "handles" (unique InterNIC database identifiers). If you have to access to "WHOIS," please check to see if the contacts are registered and if so, include only the handle and changes (if any) that need to be made in the entry. If you do not have access to "WHOIS," please provide all the information indicated and a handle will be assigned.

(5) The handle of the administrative head of the organization in (3) above or this person's name, postal address, phone number, organization, and network emailbox. This is the contact point for administrative and policy questions about the domain.

Administrative Contact

5a.   Handle (if known):
5b.   Name (Last, First):
5c.   Organization:
5d.   Postal Address:
5e.   Phone Number:
5f.   Net Mailbox:

(6) The handle of the technical contact for the doamin or this person's name, mailing address, phone number,

organization, and network mailbox. This is the contact point for problems and updates regarding the domain or zone.

Technical and Zone Contact

        6a.   Handle (if known):
        6b.   Name (Last, First):
        6c.   Organization:
        6d.   Postal Address:
        6e.   Phone Number:

NOTE: Domains must provide at least two independent servers for translating names to addresses for hosts in the domain. The servers should be in physically separate locations and on different networks if possible. The servers should be active and responsive to DNS queries BEFORE this application is submitted. Incomplete information in sections 7 and 8 or inactive servers will result in delay of the registration.

(7)   The primary server information.

        7a.   Primary Server Hostname:
        7b.   Primary Server Netaddress:
        7c.   Primary Server Hardware:
        7d.   Primary Server Software:

(8)   The secondary server information.

        8a.   Secondary Server Hostname:
        8b.   Secondary Server Netaddress:
        8c.   Secondary Server Hardware:
        8d.   Secondary Server Software:

(9)   Please briefly describe the organization for which this domain is being registered. If the domain is for an organization that already has a domain registered, please describe the purpose of this domain.

For further information contact InterNIC Registration Service:

Via electronic mail: HOSTMASTER@INTERNIC.NET

Via telephone: (703) 742-4777
Via facsimile: (703) 742-4811
Via postal mail: Network Solutions
                   InterNIC Registration Services
                   505 Hunter Park Drive
                   Herndon, VA 22070

The party requesting registration of this name certifies that, to her/his knowledge, the use of this name does not violate trademark or other statutes.

Registering a domain name does not confer any legal rights to that name and any disputes between parties over the rights to use a particular name are to be settled between the contending parties using normal legal methods. (See RFC 1591.)

1.   Top-level domain.....:

2.   Complete Domain Name..:

3a.   Organization name...:
3b.   Organization address...:

4.   Operational Date...:

Administrative Contact:
5a.   NIC Handle (if known):
5b.   Name (Last, First)...:
5d.   Postal Address..:
5e.   Phone Number..:
5f.   Net Mailbox...:

Technical/Zone Contact:
6a.   NIC Handle (if known):
6b.   Name (Last, First)...:
6d.   Postal Address..:
6e.   Phone Number..:
6f.   Net Mailbox...:

7a.   Primary Server Hostname:
7b.   Primary Server Netaddress:
7c.   Primary Server Hardware:
7d.   Primary Server Software:

8a.   Secondary Server Hostname:
8b.   Secondary Server Netaddress:
8c.   Secondary Server Hardware:
8d.   Secondary Server Software:

9.   Domain/Org Purpose/Desc.:

Notes: In Sections 3b, 5d, & 6d use multiple lines for addresses. If contacts are registered, only 5a and 6a are needed. If servers are registered, only 7a & b and 8a & b are needed. If there is more than one secondary server, just copy Section 8.

The party requesting registration of this name certifies that, to her/his knowledge, the use of this name does not violate trademark or other statutes.

Registering a domain name does not confer any legal rights to that name and any disputes between parties over the rights to use a particular name are to be settled between contending parties using normal legal methods.
(See RFC 1591.)

APPLICATION FORM FOR A CLASS C NETWORK NUMBER

CANADIAN INTERNET PROTOCOL NETWORK NUMBER APPLICATION
for
CLASS C NETWORK NUMBERS
Template [8/23/93/hck]

This template is to be used to obtain a TCP-IP number from CA*net. It makes obsolete Form [1/3/tjm] which should no longer be used.

This template is in two parts. The first part is a sample template and the second part is the template itself, which should be filled out carefully, using the guidelines in the sample template, and returned as indicated below.

Please fill in the template in EXACTLY the same format as shown in the sample. This information is scanned by software, and any errors WILL result in delays in the issuance of the number(s) to you. In this situation, EXACTLY means EXACTLY as shown, line by line, item by item, field by field. The NIC software designed to parse the application can accept no other format. Please do not change this format in any way. Do not combine fields that are on different lines and separate them with a semi-colon; the NIC software will not handle this. Please, in this case, EXACTLY really does mean EXACTLY.

Please note that the network name is not the domain name of the network. The network name may contain dashes but no other special characters and must be less than or equal to twelve characters. This name is used as an identifier for the network in the Network Information Center (NIC) "WHOIS" database and will be changed by the Network Registrar if the name is already in use.

Applications may be sent by email or by fax to:

CA*net IP Registry
Email: ipregist@canet.ca
Fax: (416) 978 6620

If possible, send your request by e.mail. E.mail submissions allow us to automatically process the application and will therefore result in the request being processed in a shorter time than if the request is submitted by fax.

Please do not send requests to the NIC in the USA. They will be forwarded by the NIC to the Canadian IP Registry office which will then process the number. You will lose a considerable amount of time if you send your request to the NIC.

Replies will be via e.mail if the request was received through e.mail and via telephone if the request was received by fax.

In the following, the "Type of Organization" should be either government, educational or commercial, while the fifth item deals with the actual number of networks being requested. In the case of Class C addresses, IP numbers are assigned in blocks to CA*net and then reassigned to specific organizations through this template. Enter the number of of Class C addresses you desire here. If you wish a Class B address, contact the IP registrar BEFORE submitting this form.

Item 6 is required for installations currently connected to or planning to be connected to one of the provincial networks such as MBnet, ARCnet, etc. It is used strictly to gather statistical information for CA*net and is not used for routing or any other technical purpose whatsoever. As this form is to be used by any organization in Canada to obtain an IP number or numbers, it should be left blank by those organizations not planning to join a regional network.

Thus, in the following example, the Pooh Software Company is requesting two Class C networks and planning to connect to ONet.

```
-------Sample Template-------
1a.  Technical Contact name (Lastname, Firstname): Smith,
     John
1b.  Technical Contact title: Sr. Programmer
1c.  Mail address:
     1230 Main Street
     Toronto, Ontario; M5S 1A1
     Canada
1d.  Phone: +1 (604) 432-8711
1e.  Net Mailbox: smith@pooh.on.ca
2.   Network name: pooh-on-ca
3a.  Postal address for main/headquarters network site:
     1280 Main Street
     Toronto, Ontario; M5S 1A1
     Canada
3b.  Name of Organization: Pooh Software Company
4.   Type of Organization: Commercial
5.   Quantity of network numbers being requested: 2
6.   Regional Network Affiliation: ONet
```

Please fill out the following carefully using the above as as
a guideline.

++

-----------Application Template---------

1a. Technical Contact name (Lastname, Firstname):
1b. Technical Contact title:
1c. Mail address:

1d. Phone:
1e. Net Mailbox:
2.   Network name:
3a. Postal address for main/headquarters network site:

3b. Name of Organization:
4.   Type of Organization:
5.   Quantity of Networks being
     requested:
6.   Regional Network Affiliation:

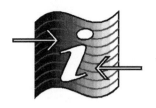

....

THE DIRECTORY OF CANADIAN USENET NEWSGROUPS

This is a master directory of Canadian USENET newsgroups. USENET News was discussed in Chapter 6. This list is maintained and updated regularly by Bruce Becker **<news@gts.org>**.

Most commercial Internet providers provide USENET news to their customers. However, the number of newsgroups carried by commercial providers varies. Some providers carry only a few hundred newsgroups, while other providers carry thousands of newsgroups. Consult **The Directory of Canadian Internet Providers** in Appendix C for data on the number of newsgroups carried by each commercial provider. If USENET is important to you, the number of newsgroups carried by a provider may be an important factor in deciding which commercial provider you choose to go with.

Very few commercial providers or organizations will carry all the newsgroups listed in this directory. If there is a newsgroup on this list that appeals to you, and your site doesn't have it, don't despair. Ask your Internet provider or your computer staff if they will obtain the newsgroup for you.

To participate in USENET, you need to use a USENET client, also known as a **newsreader**.

If you are accessing USENET from a Unix (or shell) account, there are a number of different newsreaders that you can use. The four most popular newsreaders are **nn**, **rn**, **tin** and **trn**. Most commercial providers have one or more of these newsreaders installed on their system for you to use. Check with your Internet provider if you are unsure which USENET newsreaders are available to you.

If you are accessing USENET over a SLIP/PPP or direct network connection, several USENET newsreaders that you can use are listed below. You can obtain these newsreaders using anonymous FTP. While you need only one of the following newsreaders, it is a good idea to experiment with a few different newsreaders, and then choose the one you feel most comfortable with.

SLIP/PPP CLIENTS FOR USENET

FOR MICROSOFT WINDOWS USERS

Name of Client:	Trumpet for Windows	
Type:	Shareware	
Anonymous FTP Site:	ftp.utas.edu.au	
Directory:	pc/trumpet/wintrump	
File:	wtwsk*.zip	(*=version number)

Name of Client:	WinVN	
Type:	Freeware	
Anonymous FTP Site:	ftp.ksc.nasa.gov	
Directory:	pub/win3/winvn	
File:	winvn*.zip	(*=version number)

FOR MACINTOSH USERS

Name of Client:	Newswatcher
Type:	Freeware
Anonymous FTP Site:	ftp.acns.nwu.edu
Directory:	pub/newswatcher

Name of Client:	Nuntius
Type:	Freeware
Anonymous FTP Site:	mac-dev.ruc.dk
Directory:	pub/nuntius

The listing attached is printed in its entirety as compiled by Bruce, with the exception of the exclusion of a count of articles for each newsgroup. No editing changes have been made in order to preserve the comprehensives of Bruce's effort.

```
Newsgroups:
can.general,bc.general,ab.general,man.general,ont.general,qc
.general,nb.general,ns.general,nf.config,news.groups
Distribution: can,bc,ab,man,ont,qc,nb,ns,nf
Organization: G. T. S., Toronto, Ontario
Subject: A listing of Canadian regional and school
newsgroups
From: can-reg@gts.org
Reply-To: can-reg@gts.org
Approved: can-reg@gts.org
Archive-name: can-reg-newsgroups
Last-modified: 26 August 1994 by news@gts.org
Here's a listing of Canadian regional and school newsgroups,
as it appears from here.  Some of the information is thought
to be reasonably accurate, but some hierarchies are
incomplete or perhaps even missing entirely (please note
that this list currently includes only places and schools —
newsgroups from individual computer systems may become the
subject of a separate listing in future).
There are 682 groups shown, as well as 49 aliases (indicated
by "=" beginning the text field).  The count of articles
received here so far is in the second field, if the line
describes an actual "active" file entry.
Where the text field is merely ".", no description is known
(creative suggestions are welcomed).

If there are additional such newsgroups on your system but
not in this list, e-mail to that effect would be
appreciated. Please send to "can-reg@gts.org."
Also there is a list of e-mail addresses of some of the
moderators of the moderated newsgroups, followed by a list
of e-mail addresses of moderated groups for your "mailpaths"
file. These lists are appended after the end of the
newsgroups description list below.
Thanks to all who send updates, suggestions and comments.
Your help is appreciated.
Bruce Becker-News Administration, Toronto, Ont.
Internet:    can-reg@gts.org
UUCP: ...!web!gts!can-reg
"We have the technology" - Pere Ubu

          --------- 8< --------- 8< --------- 8< ----

ab.arnet                      (Moderated).
ab.general                    Items of general interest in Alberta.
ab.jobs                       Jobs in Alberta.
ab.politics                   Discussion of politics in Alberta.
acadia.bulletin-board         Acadia University, Wolfville, N.S.
acadia.chat                   Acadia University, Wolfville, N.S.
acadia.cs.chat                Acadia University, Wolfville, N.S.
```

atl.general	Atlantic provinces (conflict with Atlanta newsgroup).
bc.bcnet	The British Columbian network.
bc.general	Items of general interest in British Columbia.
bc.news.stats	Network news statistics in British Columbia.
bc.rcbc	British Columbia.
bc.unix	Talk about Unix in British Columbia.
bc.weather	[British Columbia] Environment Canada forecasts.
bison.alt.tv.parker-lewis	U. of Manitoba - Parker Lewis mailing list.
bison.binaries	Bison binaries distribution.
bison.coco	Color computer mailing list.
bison.debate	Debate anyone.
bison.guns	Yummy... guns.
bison.newsgroups	Newsgroup discussions.
bison.sci.homebrew	How to make homebrew.
bison.wanted	Software wanted.
cabot.announcements	Cabot College, St. John's, Newfoundland.
cabot.choices_94	Cabot College, St. John's, Newfoundland.
cabot.computing_resources	Cabot College, St. John's, Newfoundland
cabot.general	Cabot College, St. John's, Newfoundland.
cabot.international	Cabot College, St. John's, Newfoundland.
calgary.general	Items of general interest in Calgary, Alberta.
can.ai	Artificial intelligence in Canada.
can.atlantic.biz	Commercial postings within Atlantic Canada.
can.atlantic.forsale	Items for sale or wanted in Atlantic Canada.
can.atlantic.general	General discussions relating to Atlantic Canada.
can.canet.d	An open forum discussing CA*net topics (Moderated).
can.canet.stats	USENET statistics from major CA*Net NNTP sites.
can.domain	Where people are supposed to be able to get even.
can.english	+CAN.POLITICS
can.followup	+CAN.GENERAL
can.forsale	+CAN.GENERAL
can.francais	About the francophone population (in French).
can.general	Items of general interest to Canadians.
can.info.highway	+CAN.INFOHIGHWAY
can.infobahn	+CAN.INFOHIGHWAY
can.infohighway	Cruisin' with the top down.
can.jobs	Jobs in Canada.
can.legal	Canadian law and legal matters.
can.motss	Gay/lesbian/bi issues in Canada.
can.newprod	New products/services of interest to Canadian readers.
can.politics	Canadian politics.
can.schoolnet.biomed.jr	Biology and medicine for elementary students.
can.schoolnet.biomed.sr	Biology and medicine for high school students.
can.schoolnet.chat.students.jr	General talk by elementary school SchoolNet students.
can.schoolnet.chat.students.sr	General talk by high school SchoolNet students.
can.schoolnet.chat.teachers	General talk by SchoolNet teachers.

can.schoolnet.chem.jr	SchoolNet Chemistry for elementary students.
can.schoolnet.chem.sr	SchoolNet Chemistry for high school students.
can.schoolnet.comp.jr	SchoolNet Computer Science for elementary students.
can.schoolnet.comp.sr	SchoolNet Computer Science for high school students.
can.schoolnet.earth.jr	SchoolNet Earth Sciences for elementary students.
can.schoolnet.earth.sr	SchoolNet Earth Sciences for high school students.
can.schoolnet.elecsys.jr	SchoolNet EE and Systems Eng.for elementary students.
can.schoolnet.elecsys.sr	SchoolNet EE and Systems Eng.for high school students.
can.schoolnet.eng.jr	SchoolNet Engineering for elementary students.
can.schoolnet.eng.sr	SchoolNet Engineering for high school students.
can.schoolnet.math.jr	SchoolNet Mathematics for elementary students.
can.schoolnet.math.sr	SchoolNet Mathematics for high school students.
can.schoolnet.phys.jr	SchoolNet physics for elementary school students.
can.schoolnet.phys.sr	SchoolNet physics for high school students.
can.schoolnet.problems	The group to gripe in about SchoolNet or find its FAQs.
can.schoolnet.projects.calls	SchoolNet CFPs, project announcements.
can.schoolnet.projects.discuss	SchoolNet project discussion.
can.schoolnet.socsci.jr	Social Sciences for elementary students.
can.schoolnet.socsci.sr	Social Sciences for high school students.
can.schoolnet.space.jr	SchoolNet Space Sciences for elementary students.
can.schoolnet.space.sr	SchoolNet Space Sciences for high school students.
can.sun-stroke	Sun Microsystems Users in Canada.
can.talk.bilingualism	+CAN.GENERAL
can.talk.smoking	+CAN.GENERAL
can.test	Like it sez.
can.usrgroup	/USR/GROUP-related information in Canada.
can.uucp	Canadian UUCP problems.
can.uucp.maps	Canadian UUCP maps are posted here. (Moderated).
can.vlsi	
can.wanted.misc	+CAN.GENERAL
carleton.chinese-news	Carleton University, Ottawa.
carleton.doe.chat	Carleton University, Ottawa.
carleton.general	Carleton University in Ottawa, Canada.
carleton.news	Carleton University, Ottawa.
carleton.scs	Carleton University, Ottawa.
carleton.scs.undergraduate	Carleton University, Ottawa.
carleton.sigs.opirg	Carleton University, Ottawa.
dal.general	Dalhousie University, Nova Scotia.
dal.test	Dalhousie University, Nova Scotia.
edm.general	Items of general interest in Edmonton, Alberta, Canada.
edm.news.stats	USENET Statistics in Edmonton, Alberta.
edm.politics	Items of political interest in Edmonton, Alberta.
edm.usrgrp	Unix Users Group in Edmonton, Alberta.
hfx.general	Halifax, N.S.

hum.general	Humber College Technology Division, Etobicoke, Ontario.
kingston.bbs	The local BBS crowd in Kingston, Ontario.
kingston.bbs.fido.users	249
kingston.eats	Anything dealing with food in Kingston, Ontario.
kingston.events	Kingston, Ontario, "Happenings."
kingston.forsale	Wanna buy/wanna sell in Kingston, Ontario.
kingston.general	Miscellaneous discussion in Kingston, Ontario.
kingston.jobs	Jobs available in Kingston, Ontario.
kingston.os.linux	Discussions of a free Unix clone.
kingston.test	1, 2, 3... for Kingston, Ontario.
kingston.uucp	Discussion of UUCP in Kingston, Ontario.
kingston.uucp.stats	UUCP statistics in Kingston, Ontario.
kingston.wanted	Stuff &/or information &/or advice wanted in Kingston.
kw.bb.sale	+KW.FORSALE
kw.birthdays	Happy birthday in Kitchener-Waterloo, Ontario.
kw.cpsr	KW branch of Computer Professionals for Social Responsibility.
kw.eats	Restaurant reviews.
kw.forsale	Things for sale.
kw.fun	Fun stuff.
kw.general	General information in Kitchener-Waterloo.
kw.housing	Rooms for rent in Kitchener-Waterloo.
kw.internet	+KW.NETWORKS
kw.jobs	Job postings for Kitchener-Waterloo.
kw.micro	Microcomputer discussion.
kw.microvax	DEC microvax users.
kw.movies	Film reviews.
kw.networks	Connectivity and networking within the KW community.
kw.news	+KW.NEWS.STATS
kw.news.stats	USENET statistics in Kitchener-Waterloo.
kw.stats	+KW.NEWS.STATS
kw.theatre	Theatre reviews, etc.
kw.uucp	+KW.NETWORKS
man.general	Manitoba.
man.linux	Manitoba.
mcgill.general	McGill University, Montreal, Quebec.
mcgill.unix	McGill University, Montreal, Quebec.
mcmaster.announce	Important McMaster announcements (Moderated).
mcmaster.buysell	Things for sale at McMaster University.
mcmaster.comp.xwindows	Computer-related discussions involving X windowing.
mcmaster.conduct	The McMaster Code of Conduct (Moderated).
mcmaster.fhs.med.news	FHS med student news.
mcmaster.fhs.med.social	FHS med student social.
mcmaster.fhs.med.student-council	Faculty of Health Science med students.
mcmaster.grad	Grad issues at McMaster University.
mcmaster.msu.clubs.computer	The McMaster Computer Club.
mcmaster.netserv.gopher	For discussions of the McMaster Gopher System.
mcmaster.news.config	For discussions of the McMaster USENET System.
mmcmaster.newuser	Instructions and Information for New Users (Moderated).
mcmaster.services.modem-pool	For discussions about access via modems.

mcmaster.talk.pagic	Discussions of the McMaster PAGIC report.
mcmaster.talk.soapbox	For lively debate on a wide range of topics.
mcmaster.test	Testing at McMaster University.
mtl.freenet.org	Montreal FreeNet/LiberTel, discussions non-téchniques.
mtl.general	General stuff in Montreal, Quebec.
mtl.test	USENET Testing in Montreal.
mun.announce	Urgent Announcements at Memorial U., Newfoundland (Moderated).
mun.arts	Faculty of Arts discussion group.
mun.arts.computing	Faculty of Arts computing issues.
mun.biochem.general	Biochemistry Department general topics group.
mun.cal	Computer-aided learning group.
mun.cc.announce	Announcements for users of C&C services (Moderated).
mun.cc.general	Discussions of general interest to C&C users.
mun.cc.maint	Software and hardware changes on C&C machines.
mun.cc.mwrc	The C&C Microcomputer/Workstation Resource Centre.
mun.chem.general	Chemistry Department general topics group.
mun.comp.hpcc	High-performance computing and communication.
mun.comp.mac	Apple MacIntosh users at MUN.
mun.comp.misc	Computing at MUN.
mun.comp.news	Discussions about USENET news at MUN.
mun.comp.pc	Discussion of IBM PCs and clones at MUN.
mun.comp.sun	Discussion and announcements for Sun users at MUN.
mun.computing	Computing at MUN.
mun.cs.club	Computer Science Club.
mun.cs.general	C.S. Dept. general discussion.
mun.cs.maint.d	Discussion of hardware and software in C.S.
mun.cs.maint.log	Log of hardware and software changes in C.S.
mun.cs.maint.todo	Things to be done in C.S.
mun.cwis	Discussion of the MUN Campus Wide Information System.
mun.engr.announce	Faculty of Engineering announcements.
mun.engr.general	Faculty of Engineering general topics group.
mun.general	
mun.gsu	Graduate Students' Union discussion.
mun.ifmt.general	Marine Institute general topics.
mun.library	Discussions relating to the MUN library.
mun.mac	Macintosh support.
mun.math.general	Math department general topics group.
mun.pc	Items relevant to PC users at MUN.
mun.physics.general	Physics department general topics group.
mun.psych.general	Psychology department general topics group.
mun.research	Bulletins from the Office of Research.
mun.safety	Announcements and discussions relating to safety.
mun.science	Faculty of Science discussion group.
mun.seminars	Event and seminar announcements.
mun.sun	Discussion and announcements for Sun users at MUN.

mun.swgc	Group for Sir Wilfred Grenfell College Corner Brook).
mun.talk	Discussion of anything and everything.
mun.test	News tests.
mun.wanted	Items wanted or for sale.
nb.biz	Commercial postings within New Brunswick.
nb.forsale	Items for sale or wanted in New Brunswick.
nb.general	General discussions relating to New Brunswick.
nf.birds	Bird lovers in Newfoundland.
nf.computing	Computing/Internet-related topics for Newfoundland.
nf.config	Nfld. USENET configuration, administration and discussion.
nf.general	General discussion for people in Newfoundland.
nf.k12	Education in Newfoundland from kindergarten to Grade 12.
nf.test	Tests of Newfoundland news network.
nf.wanted	Wanted and for-sale ads for Newfoundland.
ns.general	Items of general interest to folks in Nova Scotia.
ns.nstn.usergroup	The NSTN usergroup in Nova Scotia.
ont.archive	+ONT.ARCHIVES
ont.archives	Archives in Ontario.
ont.conditions	Current highway conditions for winter driving.
ont.events	Ontario, Canada happenings.
ont.events.macwator.ece	+ONT.EVENTS
ont.followup	+ONT.GENERAL
ont.forsale	+ONT.GENERAL
ont.general	Items of general interest in Ontario.
ont.jobs	Jobs in Ontario, Canada.
ont.micro	Microcomputer-related postings in Ontario.
ont.personals.whips.and. rubber.chickens	+ONT.SINGLES
ont.sf-lovers	Science Fiction Lovers in Ontario.
ont.singles	Singles in Ontario.
ont.test	Testing in Ontario.
ont.uucp	UUCP related postings in Ontario.
ott.events	Seminars and the like at Ottawa, Ontario, sites.
ott.for-sale	+OTT.FORSALE
ott.forsale	Things for sale/wanted in Ottawa, Ontario.
ott.general	General news local to Ottawa sites.
ott.housing	Places to live wanted, for sale or for rent.
ott.motorcycles	
ott.ncf	
ott.news	+OTT.USENET
ott.online	
ott.singles	
ott.test	
ott.usenet	USENET in Ottawa.
ott.vietnamese	Vietnamese interest group.
ott.weather	Weather forecasts for Ottawa, Ontario (Moderated).
qc.general	General interest items in Quebec.
qc.jobs	Jobs in Quebec.
qc.politique	Politics of Quebec.
qucis.announce	Queen's University, Kingston, Ontario.
qucis.chat	Queen's University, Kingston, Ontario.
qucis.events	Queen's University, Kingston, Ontario.
queens.events	Queen's University, Kingston, Ontario.

queens.forsale	Queen's University, Kingston, Ontario.
queens.soc.grad	Queen's University, Kingston, Ontario.
rye.ee.general	
rye.ee.linux	
rye.general	Articles of general interest at Ryerson, Toronto.
rye.nets	Articles on networking at Ryerson.
rye.scs.linux	
rye.test	Group for testing news at Ryerson.
sfu.general	Simon Fraser University, British Columbia.
sfu.grad	Simon Fraser University, British Columbia.
sj.general	General discussion in St. John's, Newfoundland.
sj.test	Tests of St. John's news network.
socs.jobs	McGill School of Computer Science, Montreal, Quebec.
socs.misc	McGill School of Computer Science, Montreal, Quebec.
stemnet.announce	Announcements about schools in Newfoundland.
stemnet.enterprise	Enterprise education general discussion.
stemnet.experts.all	Experts on-line Q&A.
stemnet.fam_studies	NLTA Home Economics Council.
stemnet.general	Q&A and discussion about Stemnet.
stemnet.k12.chem	Chemistry in K12 discussion.
stemnet.k12.chess	Teacher-organized chess tournaments.
stemnet.k12.cls	Q&A about Columbia library system.
stemnet.k12.comp_studies	Computer studies K12 discussion.
stemnet.k12.iclas	IBM Classroom LAN Administration Software.
stemnet.k12.lang_arts	Language arts in school.
stemnet.k12.linkway	Q&A about IBM hypertext package Linkway.
stemnet.k12.math	Mathematics in K12 discussion.
stemnet.k12.music	Music in K12 discussion.
stemnet.k12.physics	Physics in K12 discussion.
stemnet.k12.small	Small schools discussion.
stemnet.k12.tech_ed	Discussion about projects in tech education.
stemnet.learning.resources	Q&A about classroom "learning experiences."
stemnet.nltasic.coss	NLTA Special Interest Council of Special Services.
stemnet.nltasic.science	NLTA Special Interest Council — Science.
stemnet.novell.support	Q&A for novell LANs.
stemnet.primary	For primary school teachers.
stemnet.roots	Genealogy discussion for teachers and students.
stemnet.smallgroup. coplearning	Organizing small groups to work and learn.
stemnet.social_studies	Info and discussion on social studies.
stemnet.students.at_risk	STAY IN SCHOOL, discussion and resource list.
stemnet.sys.mac	Q&A for Macintosh users.
stemnet.sys.windows_ms	Discussion about MS Windows.
stemnet.teach	Used for Stemnet training.
stemnet.test	Test posting from Stemnet.
tor.arts	+TOR.GENERAL
tor.buysell	+TOR.GENERAL
tor.config	+TOR.GENERAL
tor.eats	+TOR.GENERAL
tor.forsale	+TOR.GENERAL
tor.general	Items of general interest in Toronto, Ontario.
tor.jobs	+TOR.GENERAL

tor.news	USENET in Toronto, Ontario.
tor.news.stats	USENET statistics in Toronto, Ontario.
tor.test	Testing in Toronto, Ontario.
tor.uucp	+TOR.GENERAL
ualberta.cs.general	University of Alberta.
ualberta.general	
ualberta.phys.general	
ubc.events	University of British Columbia.
ubc.forum	University of British Columbia.
ubc.general	University of British Columbia.
ubc.help	University of British Columbia.
ubc.unix	University of British Columbia.
ulaval.ariane	.
ulaval.comp.excel	University of Laval, Quebec.
ulaval.comp.mac	.
ulaval.cti	.
ulaval.fsa	.
ulaval.fsg	.
ulaval.gel	.
ulaval.marks	.
ulaval.phy	.
ulaval.rec.sports	
ulaval.rsvs	.
ulaval.rsvs.gcg	.
ulaval.test	.
ulaval.unix-ul	.
umontreal.cerca	Centre de récherche sur le calcul appliqué.
umontreal.general	General discussion at the University of Montreal.
umontreal.iro.biblio-nouveau	New acquisitions of the Comp. Science library.
umontreal.iro.incognito	Comp. Science AI Newsgroup.
umontreal.iro.info-info	General newsgroup for the Comp. Science Dept.
umontreal.iro.labs-nouveau	New software/hardware announcements.
umontreal.iro.protoco	Telecommunication Protocols Group.
umontreal.iro.seminaires	Comp. Science seminar announcements.
umontreal.iro.support	Comp. Science user support groups.
umontreal.iro.vlsi	Comp. Science VLSI newsgroup.
umontreal.si.jsp.annonces	Comp. Science undergrads newsgroup (announcements).
umontreal.si.jsp.questions	Comp. Science undergrads newsgroup (questions).
usask.general	University of Saskatchewan.
ut.16k	Discussions on the National Semi series 16000 CPU.
ut.ai	+UT.DCS.AI
ut.biz.sunproducts	
ut.cdf.announce	UofT Computing Disciplines Facility announcements (Moderated).
ut.cdf.general	UofT CDF general discussion.
ut.cdf.gripes	UofT CDF complaints.
ut.cdf.student	UofT CDF student talk.
ut.cdf.test	UofT CDF testing.
ut.chinese	University of Toronto Chinese community.
ut.cquest.general	
ut.cquest.test	.
ut.cslab.announce	Computer Science Lab.
ut.cslab.problems	
ut.cslab.system	.
ut.cslab.test	Computer Science Lab.
ut.dcs.ai	Artificial intelligence at the University of Toronto.
ut.dcs.cscw	Computer supported cooperative work.
ut.dcs.dbois	Database/office information systems.

ut.dcs.general	General messages from UofT Dept. of Computer Science.
ut.dcs.gradnews	Info for Graduates.
ut.dcs.graphics	Graphics.
ut.dcs.hci	Human-Computer Interaction.
ut.dcs.na	Numerical Analysis.
ut.dcs.seminars	Seminars.
ut.dcs.systems	Systems.
ut.dcs.theory	Theory.
ut.dcs.vision	Vision Research.
ut.ecf.comp9T5	Computer Engineering Students.
ut.ecf.engsci	Engineering Science Students.
ut.ecf.test	Test group for Engineering Computing Facility.
ut.ee	Electrical Engineering.
ut.ee.eecg.computer	System-related issues for the EE computer group.
ut.ee.eecg.news	EE computer group announcements.
ut.ee.ieee	IEEE in EE.
ut.ee.vlsi	.
ut.ee.vlsi.cadence	
ut.ee.vlsi.cmc	.
ut.ee.vlsi.cmos4s	.
ut.ee.vlsi.electric	.
ut.ee.vlsi.test	.
ut.eng.gradnews	Discussions by grad students in engineering.
ut.followup	+UT.GENERAL
ut.general	General messages.
ut.mac-users	.
ut.mathsci	.
ut.na	+UT.DCS.NA
ut.nets.reports	Net connectivity reports (Moderated).
ut.nonlinear.dynamic-sys	
ut.org.outing-club	U of Toronto outing club trips & announcements.
ut.org.seta	Students for Ethical Treatment of Animals.
ut.oriental	Asia-Pacific Association.
ut.sac	Student Administrative Council.
ut.software	.
ut.software.tex	Use of TeX at University of Toronto.
ut.software.x-windows	Three guesses.
ut.stardate	Stardates from MacDonald Observatory.
ut.supercomputer	Pray for the Cray.
ut.ta	Teaching assistants.
ut.test	Test messages.
ut.theory	+UT.DCS.THEORY
ut.unix.sysadmin	System Administration of Unix sites at U. of Toronto.
ut.unix.user	Information for Unix users.
ut.vlsi	Big Iron.
uvic.clubs	University of Victoria, B.C.
uvic.cosi.test	University of Victoria, B.C.
uvic.csc.announce	University of Victoria, B.C.
uvic.csc.coop	University of Victoria, B.C.
uvic.csc.forsale	University of Victoria, B.C.
uvic.csc.general	University of Victoria, B.C.
uvic.csc.mac	University of Victoria, B.C.
uvic.csc.mac.pascal	University of Victoria, B.C.
uvic.csc.rigi	University of Victoria, B.C.
uvic.csc.seminar	University of Victoria, B.C.
uvic.csc.system	University of Victoria, B.C.
uvic.csc.system.research	University of Victoria, B.C.
uvic.csc.union	University of Victoria, B.C.
uvic.forsale	University of Victoria, B.C.
uvic.general	University of Victoria, B.C.
uvic.jobs	University of Victoria, B.C.

uvic.jobs.adminacad	University of Victoria, B.C.
uvic.jobs.confidential	University of Victoria, B.C.
uvic.jobs.cupe917	University of Victoria, B.C.
uvic.jobs.cupe951	University of Victoria, B.C.
uvic.jobs.exempt	University of Victoria, B.C.
uvic.jobs.external	University of Victoria, B.C.
uvic.jobs.notes	University of Victoria, B.C.
uvic.jobs.specinstr	University of Victoria, B.C.
uvic.lost+found	University of Victoria, B.C.
uvic.misc	University of Victoria, B.C.
uvic.mlist.apple-ip	University of Victoria, B.C.
uvic.mlist.bcnet-info	University of Victoria, B.C.
uvic.mlist.framers	University of Victoria, B.C.
uvic.mlist.mac-sun	University of Victoria, B.C.
uvic.mlist.next-info	University of Victoria, B.C.
uvic.mlist.next.next-managers	University of Victoria, B.C.
uvic.mlist.next.nextcomm	University of Victoria, B.C.
uvic.mlist.next.nug	University of Victoria, B.C.
uvic.mlist.offcampus.seminars	University of Victoria, B.C.
uvic.mlist.sun-info	University of Victoria, B.C.
uvic.mlist.sun-managers	University of Victoria, B.C.
uvic.mlist.sunnet-manager	University of Victoria, B.C.
uvic.outages	University of Victoria, B.C.
uvic.physics.general	University of Victoria, B.C.
uvic.physics.seminar	University of Victoria, B.C.
uvic.secretariat	University of Victoria, B.C.
uvic.secretariat.board	University of Victoria, B.C.
uvic.secretariat.senate	University of Victoria, B.C.
uvic.seminar	University of Victoria, B.C.
uvic.sys.evaluation	University of Victoria, B.C.
uvic.sys.mac	University of Victoria, B.C.
uvic.sys.next	University of Victoria, B.C.
uvic.system	University of Victoria, B.C.
uvic.test	University of Victoria, B.C.
uvic.unix.questions	University of Victoria, B.C.
uw.aco.system	U. of Waterloo.
uw.ahs.general	Faculty of Applied Health Sciences news.
uw.ahs.system	Faculty of Applied Health Sciences computing systems news.
uw.ai.learning	AI stuff at U. of Waterloo, Ontario.
uw.aix.support	Support for the AIX operating system at UW.
uw.alt.fan.karla-homolka	+ALT.FAN.KARLA-HOMOLKA
uw.alt.sex.beastiality	+ALT.SEX.BESTIALITY
uw.alt.sex.bestiality	+ALT.SEX.BESTIALITY
uw.alt.sex.bondage	+ALT.SEX.BONDAGE
uw.alt.sex.stories	+ALT.SEX.STORIES
uw.alt.sex.stories.d	+ALT.SEX.STORIES.D
uw.alt.tasteless	+ALT.TASTELESS
uw.archive	.
uw.asplos	.
uw.assignments	For assignment coordination (Moderated).
uw.business-club	
uw.campus-news	Daily bulletin and other announcements.
uw.ccng.general	Computer Communications Network Group.
uw.ccng.system	Computer Communications Network Group.
uw.censorship	For equal access.
uw.cgl	Computer Graphics Lab.
uw.cgl.software	Computer Graphics Lab.
uw.cgl.system	Computer Graphics Lab.
uw.chinese	Chinese Students (Moderated).
uw.combopt	.
uw.computer-store	Computer Store (Moderated).

uw.computing.support.staff	Computing support at University of Waterloo.
uw.cong.system	
uw.cray	Nobody uses crays here, do they?
uw.cs.database	Computer Science.
uw.cs.dept	Computer Science.
uw.cs.eee	Computer Science/Electrical Engineering.
uw.cs.faculty	Computer Science.
uw.cs.general	Computer Science.
uw.cs.grad	Computer Science.
uw.cs.grad.topics	Computer Science.
uw.cs.mdbs	Computer Science.
uw.cs.theory	Computer Science.
uw.cs.ugrad	Computer Science.
uw.csc	Computer Science Club.
uw.csg	.
uw.dcs.changes	Computing Services software notices.
uw.dcs.courses	Computing Services (Moderated).
uw.dcs.gripe	.
uw.dcs.news	Computing Services (Moderated).
uw.dcs.operations	Computing Services.
uw.dcs.staff	Computing Services.
uw.dcs.suggestions	Computing Services.
uw.dcs.system	Computing Services.
uw.dcs.trc	Computing Services.
uw.dcs.watserv1	Computing Services.
uw.dcs.watshine	Computing Services.
uw.disspla	.
uw.dp.changes	.
uw.dp.staff	.
uw.dsgroup	Data Structures.
uw.dsgroup.misc	Data Structures.
uw.ee.grad	Electrical Engineering.
uw.ee.opt	Electrical Engineering.
uw.ee.sunee	Electrical Engineering.
uw.engl.phd	.
uw.english-usage	
uw.envst.general	
uw.envst.system	.
uw.fass	Faculty, alumnae, staff, students amateur theatre.
uw.feds	Federation of Students (Moderated).
uw.forsale	Items for sale.
uw.gams	.
uw.general	Whatever.
uw.gllow	Gay and Lesbian Liberation of Waterloo.
uw.gnu	FSF software for GNU at WATERLU.
uw.grad	Generic grad students.
uw.gsa	Graduate Student Association (Moderated).
uw.harmony	Harmony OS.
uw.icr	Institute for Computer Research.
uw.icr.forum	Institute for Computer Research.
uw.icr.hardware	Institute for Computer Research.
uw.ieee	IEEE at Waterloo.
uw.image-proc	Image Processing.
uw.imprint	Imprint, UW student newspaper (Moderated).
uw.jsaw	For Japanese Student Association of Waterloo.
uw.kin	Kinesiology.
uw.lang	Languages.
uw.laurel	Laurel OS.
uw.library	Library.
uw.library.journals	Library.
uw.library.new-books	Library.
uw.logic	Logic programming.

uw.lpaig	Linear Programming & Artificial Intelligence Group.
uw.lpaig.changes	Linear Programming & Artificial Intelligence Group.
uw.lpaig.nlu	Linear Programming & Artificial Intelligence Group.
uw.lpaig.system	Linear Programming & Artificial Intelligence Group.
uw.mac-users	.
uw.mail-list.biomech	Mailing list.
uw.mail-list.comp-chem	Mailing list.
uw.mail-list.csnet-forum	Mailing list.
uw.mail-list.fractals	Mailing list.
uw.mail-list.s	Mailing list.
uw.mail-list.sml	Mailing list.
uw.mail-list.sun-managers	Mailing list.
uw.maple	Maple symbolic math software.
uw.math.faculty	Math Faculty.
uw.math.grad	Math Faculty.
uw.math.tsa	Math Faculty.
uw.math.ugrad	Math Faculty.
uw.mathcad	
uw.matlab	A matrix package.
uw.mech.system	Mechanical Engineering.
uw.mfcf.bugs	Math Faculty Computing Facility.
uw.mfcf.gripe	Math Faculty Computing Facility.
uw.mfcf.hardware	Math Faculty Computing Facility.
uw.mfcf.hardware.mac	Math Faculty Computing Facility.
uw.mfcf.people	Math Faculty Computing Facility.
uw.mfcf.questions	Math Faculty Computing Facility.
uw.mfcf.software	Math Faculty Computing Facility.
uw.mfcf.software.mac	Math Faculty Computing Facility.
uw.mfcf.suggestions	Math Faculty Computing Facility.
uw.mfcf.system	Math Faculty Computing Facility (Moderated).
uw.mfcf.todo	Math Faculty Computing Facility.
uw.mfcf.updates	Math Faculty Computing Facility.
uw.minos	MINOS project.
uw.msg	Multiprocessor Systems Group.
uw.nag	.
uw.network	Network status reports.
uw.network.external	
uw.network.stats	
uw.networks	+UW.NETWORK
uw.neural-nets	Neural Networks.
uw.newsgroups	Configuration discussions.
uw.opinion	Blather.
uw.os.research	OS research.
uw.os2-users	.
uw.outers	UW Outers Club: events, activities and discussions.
uw.pami	Pattern Analysis & Machine Intelligence.
uw.pami.bsd	Pattern Analysis & Machine Intelligence.
uw.pami.gripe	Pattern Analysis & Machine Intelligence.
uw.pami.system	Pattern Analysis & Machine Intelligence.
uw.pmc	Pure Math and C&O club.
uw.progressive.conservatives. club	.
uw.psychology	
uw.recycling	Recycled discussions.
uw.rpw	.
uw.sas	
uw.scicom	Scientific Computing.
uw.science.computing	
uw.sd.grad	Systems Design.

uw.sd.smsg	Systems Design.
uw.shoshin	Shoshin project.
uw.shoshin.changes	Shoshin project.
uw.shoshin.system	Shoshin project.
uw.stats	Statistics department.
uw.stats.grad	Statistics department.
uw.stats.s	+UW.MAIL-LIST.S
uw.sun-owners	For people who have Suns.
uw.swen	.
uw.sylvan	Sylvan project.
uw.sylvan.os	Sylvan project.
uw.sys.amiga	For people with Amigas.
uw.sys.apollo	For people with Apollos.
uw.sys.atari	For people with Ataris.
uw.sytek	Sytek communication system.
uw.talks	Upcoming seminars.
uw.test	Testing.
uw.test.xxx	+UW.TEST
uw.test.yyy	+UW.TEST
uw.test.zzz	+UW.TEST
uw.tex	TEX text formatting.
uw.ucc.fortrade	University Computing Committee.
uw.ugrad.cs	Undergrads.
uw.unix	Arguments about Unix.
uw.unix.sysadmin	Campus unix admin.
uw.usystem	U-kernel and u-system.
uw.utility.shutdown	
uw.utility.shutdowns	+UW.UTILITY.SHUTDOWN
uw.uwinfo	UWinfo discussion, comments, feedback, etc.
uw.virtual-worlds	Exploring virtual reality at U Waterloo.
uw.visualization	
uw.vlsi	VLSI group.
uw.vlsi.ate	VLSI group.
uw.vlsi.cadence	VLSI group.
uw.vlsi.cmc	VLSI group.
uw.vlsi.electric	VLSI group.
uw.vlsi.industry	VLSI group.
uw.vlsi.software	VLSI group.
uw.vlsi.system	VLSI group.
uw.vlsi.vlsiic	VLSI group.
uw.vlsi.works	VLSI group.
uw.vm-migration	.
uw.vms	For people who have to use VMS.
uw.watserv1	+UW.DCS.WATSERV1
uw.watshine	+UW.DCS.WATSHINE
uw.watstar	STAR group.
uw.weef	.
uw.wira	.
uw.wordperfect.users	
uw.wpirg	(Moderated).
uw.x-hints	How to use X windows.
uw.x-windows	How to use X windows.
uwo.biomed.engrg	Biomedical Engineering Research at U. of Western Ontario.
uwo.biomed.inroads	Rehabilitation Engineering Research and Development.
uwo.ccs.changes	CCS System Change Notices.
uwo.ccs.courses	CCS course offerings.
uwo.ccs.talk	Rumors, Gripes, Comments re: CCS.
uwo.chinese	Chinese Community at U. of Western Ontario.
uwo.cogsci	Cognitive Sciences, change notices and more.
uwo.comp.epix	EpixInfo Mailing list archive (admin'd locally).
uwo.comp.general	General computer issues.
uwo.comp.helpdesk	HelpDesk management and support, hdeskl@yvnvm.bitnet.

uwo.comp.ibm.announce	Announcements from IBM Canada (Joe Potworka).
uwo.comp.micro	Micro Computer Issues (PC's, Mac's, etc.).
uwo.comp.net-status	Network Status Reports.
uwo.comp.next	U. of Western Ontario Next users groups.
uwo.comp.nupop	NUPOP Mailing list (informational).
uwo.comp.packet	Packet Drivers Mailing list (informational).
uwo.comp.pegasus	Pegasus Mailing list (informational).
uwo.comp.pine	PINE (Pine is not Elm) Mailing list (informational).
uwo.comp.progress	Progress Data Base (informational).
uwo.comp.security	Computer Security — Issues and Policy Formation.
uwo.comp.sgi.announc	Announcements from SGI Canada (Bill Stewart).
uwo.comp.snmp	Simple Network Management Protocol, snmp@nisc.nyser.net.
uwo.comp.sun-managers	Sun Managers, sun-managers@eecs.nwu.edu.
uwo.comp.sun.announce	Announcements from Sun Canada (Rick Baker).
uwo.comp.trumpet	The Trumpet PC news reader.
uwo.comp.unix	Unix issues.
uwo.comp.wais	Wide Area Information Services (mailing list fed).
uwo.comp.x500	X500 Directory, disi@merit.edu, osi-ds@cs.ucl.ac.uk.
uwo.comp.xwindows	X11 windows, problems, feedback, etc.
uwo.csd	Computer Science Department.
uwo.csd.acm	.
uwo.csd.forum	Anonymous discussion on CSD issues (Moderated).
uwo.events	Things happening around U. of Western Ontario.
uwo.forsale	Short, tasteful postings about items for sale.
uwo.general	Announcements, activities and talk at U. of Western Ontario.
uwo.iaa.international	International activities and funding.
uwo.iaa.research	U. of Western Ontario.
uwo.lahla	London Area Health Libraries Association (local).
uwo.library	Libraries.
uwo.med	Medicine — Seminars, Minutes, Jobs, etc.
uwo.med.research	Medical Research — funding opportunities, etc.
uwo.med.talk	Medicine — Problems, Answers, Gossip, etc.
uwo.news.config	U. of Western Ontario.
uwo.news.groups	U. of Western Ontario.
uwo.newsletters	Newsletters: Focus, information exchange, etc.
uwo.physics.optics	Applied optics, U. of Western Ontario.
uwo.pma	.
uwo.rri	General RRI info, network/system changes & downtimes.
uwo.rri.ctrg	Issues/chat at the clinical trials resources group.
uwo.rri.heart	Issues/chat at the heart and circulation group.
uwo.rri.irus	Issues/chat at the Imaging Research Lab.
uwo.slis	School of Library and Information Systems.
uwo.slis.clip	SLIS Computer Literacy Program.

```
uwo.slis.job                  Library and Related Job Postings.
uwo.slis.official             Official announcements and information
                              from the school.
uwo.slis.readers              A readers advisory and discussion —
                              devoted to fiction.
uwo.slis.review               GSLIS long-term review
                              conference.
uwo.sogs                      .
uwo.ssc.network               Social Sciences Centre — Network &
                              Services.
uwo.sscl.network              +UWO.SSC.NETWORK
uwo.test                      Testing, put your junk here.
uwo.westernnews               Western News (the weekly paper).
van.chatter                   Vancouver, British Columbia.
van.general                   Vancouver, British Columbia.
van.test                      Vancouver, British Columbia.
wpg.general                   Winnipeg, Manitoba.
york.announce                 Announcements at York University,
                              Toronto.
york.ariel                    .
york.calumet                  .
york.canet-status-report      +YORK.ML.CANET-STATUS-REPORTS
york.doc                      Documentation? at York Univ.
york.email                    .
york.general                  Postings of general interest at York
                              University.
york.ml.big-lan               Big-lan mailing list.
york.ml.bind                  Bind mailing list.
york.ml.canet-status-reports  Canet-status-reports mailing list.
york.ml.cmutcp                CMUtcp mailing list.
york.ml.decstation-managers   Decstation-managers mailing list.
york.ml.future                Future mailing list.
york.ml.info-pmdf             Info-pmdf mailing list.
york.ml.namedroppers          Name-droppers mailing list.
york.ml.nn                    NN mailing list.
york.ml.onet-status-reports   Onet-status-reports mailing list.
york.ml.openbook              Openbook mailing list.
york.ml.pcm-dev               PCM-dev mailing list.
york.ml.sun-managers          Sun-managers mailing list.
york.ml.texhax                Texhax mailing list.
york.onet-status-reports      +YORK.ML.ONET-STATUS-REPORTS
```

Here is a list of e-mail addresses for contacting the moderators of
some of the moderated newsgroups in the Canadian regional news
hierarchies:

```
can.uucp.maps                 pathadmin@cs.toronto.edu
uw.wpirg                      jmsellens@math.uwaterloo.ca
```

Here is a list of e-mail addresses for submitting articles to
moderated newsgroups in the Canadian regional news hierarchies:

```
ab.arnet                      .
can.canet.d                   canet-d@canet.ca
can.uucp.maps                 pathadmin@cs.toronto.edu
mcmaster.announce             .
mcmaster.conduct              .
mcmaster.newuser              .
mun.announce                  .
mun.cc.announce               .
ott.weather                   weather@aficom.ocunix.on.ca
ut.cdf.announce               clarke@csri.toronto.edu
ut.nets.reports               .
```

uw.assignments	assignments@math.uwaterloo.ca
uw.chinese	hshi@neumann.uwaterloo.ca
uw.computer-store	jwdodd@watserv1.uwaterloo.ca
uw.dcs.courses	bjhicks@watserv1.uwaterloo.ca
uw.dcs.news	editor@watserv1.uwaterloo.ca
uw.dp.changes	dp70@watserv1.uwaterloo.ca
uw.feds	feds@watserv1.uwaterloo.ca
uw.gsa	broberts@knuth.uwaterloo.ca
uw.imprint	imprint@math.uwaterloo.ca
uw.mfcf.system	operator@math.uwaterloo.ca
uw.wpirg	uw-wpirg@math.uwaterloo.ca
uwo.csd.forum	

APPENDIX H

....

THE DIRECTORY OF CSO AND WHOIS SERVERS IN CANADA

Have you ever wondered how to find someone's e-mail address on the Internet? There is no easy way to do this because there is no central authority that is responsible for keeping track of who is using the Internet. Our local telephone company can produce a phone book of everyone in the city who has a telephone number because they have a record of everyone who has local telephone service. On the Internet, there are many organizations that provide Internet service, so no single organization can produce a complete directory of all Internet users.

What organizations *can* do is place a searchable directory of their Internet users on the Internet. These directories can often provide you with detailed information about a person, including the person's full name, telephone number, e-mail address, departmental affiliation, and office location. Most Internet-connected organizations in Canada **do not** make their internal telephone/e-mail directories available on the Internet. However, several Canadian universities/colleges and other organizations have placed their telephone/e-mail directories on the Internet. You can search these directories from your own Internet account, provided that you have the right Internet tools. Keep in mind that many of these directories do not contain student e-mail addresses, so if you're looking for the e-mail address of a student, these directories may not be able to help you.

There are two common types of directory services that you will come across on the Internet. The first type is a **CSO** server. The second type of directory service is a **whois** server.

You need three things in order to use these services:

(1) YOU NEED TO HAVE ACCESS TO A DIRECT INTERNET CONNECTION AT WORK, AT SCHOOL, OR THROUGH A COMMERCIAL INTERNET PROVIDER.

Check the **Directory of Canadian Internet Providers** (Appendix C) to see which providers provide direct connections to the Internet. Commercial providers that offer Internet accounts with services such as Telnet, Gopher, and FTP have a direct Internet connection. If you have Telnet or Gopher access at work or school, then you have a direct Internet connection. You can also get a direct Internet connection using SLIP or PPP service. The **Directory of Canadian Internet Providers** will tell you which providers offer SLIP or PPP service.

(2) YOU NEED TO ACCESS AN APPROPRIATE SERVER.

To use CSO, you need to access a CSO server. To use whois, you need to access a whois server. The server is the machine that contains the directory information for users at an Internet site. There are dozens of CSO and whois servers on the Internet. This appendix contains tables of Canadian CSO and whois servers that you can connect to. Each CSO or whois server contains information on Internet users at that site only.

(3) YOU NEED THE APPROPRIATE CLIENT PROGRAM.

The client is the program you use to send an information request to the server. To use CSO, you need a client called **ph**. To use whois, you need a client called **whois**.

CSO

There are three methods of accessing a CSO server:

(1) YOU CAN USE A DIAL-UP INTERNET ACCOUNT ON YOUR INTERNET PROVIDER'S MACHINE, PROVIDING THAT YOUR INTERNET PROVIDER HAS INSTALLED A PH CLIENT THAT YOU CAN USE.

If you are not sure if you have a ph client installed on your machine, ask your Internet provider or the computing staff in your organization. If you don't have a ph client installed on your system, ask your Internet provider or your computing staff if they can install one for you.

If you know that a ph client is available on your Internet provider's system, how you access it will vary from one system to the next. If your system is menu-driven (or has a point-and-click interface), you should look for a menu option that allows you to access a ph client.

If you are using a Unix account that has a ph client installed, typing the following command will generally work:

```
ph -s ADDRESS-OF-SERVER QUERY
```
where:

ADDRESS-OF-SERVER = the domain name of the CSO server you want to query

QUERY = the last name or first name of the person you are looking for

Some organizations do not keep first names in their database, so it is best to try the person's last name first. For example, let's say I want to find the e-mail address of Joe Smith at Lakehead University in Thunder Bay, Ontario. From the table of CSO servers on page 570, I know that Lakehead University has a ph server. The address of Lakehead's ph server is **flash.lakeheadu.ca**. Therefore, I can type the following command from my Unix prompt:

```
ph -s flash.lakeheadu.ca smith
```

This command will provide me with a list of all the Smiths who are registered in the ph server at Lakehead University.

I could have also entered the following command:

```
ph -s flash.lakeheadu.ca joe
```

This command will provide me with a list of all the people with the name "Joe" who are registered in the ph server at Lakehead University.

Some ph servers may require you to enter a **port number** in addition to the server name. When a port number is required, the command changes slightly. For example, the student directory at the Technical University of Nova Scotia is on port 1050. When a port number is required, the command looks like this:

```
ph -s ADDRESS-OF-SERVER -p PORT-NUMBER QUERY
```

where:

ADDRESS-OF-SERVER = the domain name of the CSO server that you want to query

PORT-NUMBER = the port number for the CSO server you are querying

QUERY = the first or last name of the person you are looking for

For example, if I am looking for the e-mail address of Mary Brown, who is a student at the Technical University of Nova Scotia, I could type the following command from my Unix account to see if Mary is listed in the student directory (providing that a ph client has been installed on my machine):

```
ph -s newton.ccs.tuns.ca -p 1050 Brown
```

I could also try this command, if I want to search by first name:

```
ph -s newton.ccs.tuns.ca -p 1050 Mary
```

(2) YOU CAN USE A PH CLIENT ON A SLIP OR PPP CONNECTION.

Many of the commercial providers listed in the **Directory of Canadian Internet Service Providers** in Appendix C provide SLIP or PPP access. If you have SLIP or PPP access using Microsoft Windows, you can use a ph client called **Phwin**. You have to obtain this client using anonymous FTP, and install it on your system. Phwin allows you to input the name of a CSO server, and query that server directly.

Name of Client:	Phwin (for Microsoft Windows)
Type:	Freeware
Anonymous FTP location:	auck.irl.cri.nz
Directory:	pub/phone
File Name:	irlphwin.zip

(3) YOU CAN ACCESS CSO SERVERS USING GOPHER OR THE WORLD WIDE WEB.

Many Gopher and World Wide Web servers have built-in support for querying CSO servers. The following Gopher and World Wide Web sites will provide you with a list of CSO servers that you can query.

USING GOPHER

Point your Gopher client at: **gopher.nd.edu**
Select: Non-Notre Dame Information Sources
Phone Books - Other Institutions

USING THE WORLD WIDE WEB

Point your World Wide Web browser at: **http://www.uiuc.edu/cgi-bin/ph/lookup?.**

The World Wide Web site at **http://sci-ed.fit.edu/cgi-bin/phf** will provide you with an on-line form for querying a CSO server of your choice.

CSO SERVERS IN CANADA

BRITISH COLUMBIA

Province	Institution	Address of CSO Server
- - - - - - - - -	Geodetic Survey of Canada	ns.geod.emr.ca
British Columbia	Camosun College	gopher.camosun.bc.ca
British Columbia	North Island College (Staff)	nicad3.nic.bc.ca
British Columbia	North Island College (Others)	nicad4.nic.bc.ca
British Columbia	University of British Columbia	phserver.ubc.ca
British Columbia	University of Victoria	netinfo.uvic.ca

ALBERTA, MANITOBA, ONTARIO

Province	Institution	Address of CSO Server
Alberta	University of Alberta	chinchaga.ucs.ualberta.ca
Manitoba	University of Winnipeg	uwpg02.uwinnipeg.ca
Ontario	Brock University	bigmoc.cns.brocku.ca
Ontario	Carleton University	ernest.carleton.ca
Ontario	Canada Centre for Inland Waters	csx.cciw.ca
Ontario	Chedoke-McMaster Hospitals	gopher.cmh.on.ca
Ontario	Fanshawe College	admin.fanshawec.on.ca
Ontario	Lakehead University	flash.lakeheadu.ca
Ontario	Lambton College	ns.lambton.on.ca
Ontario	McMaster University	mcmail.cis.mcmaster.ca
Ontario	Niagara College	lundy.niagarac.on.ca
Ontario	Ontario Institute for Studies in Education	ns.oise.on.ca
Ontario	Queen's University	knot.queensu.ca
Ontario	Ryerson Polytechnic University	ph.acs.ryerson.ca
Ontario	Seneca College	info.senecac.on.ca
Ontario	Trent University	blaze.trentu.ca
Ontario	University of Guelph	nermal.cs.uoguelph.ca
Ontario	University of Waterloo	uwdir.uwaterloo.ca
Ontario	University of Waterloo Math Department	ns.uwaterloo.ca
Ontario	Wilfrid Laurier University	info.wlu.ca
Ontario	York University	ph.yorku.ca

QUEBEC, NEW BRUNSWICK, NOVA SCOTIA

Province	Institution	Address of CSO Server
Quebec	École des Hautes Études Commerciales	cso.hec.ca
Quebec	McGill University Research Center for Intelligent Machines	lightning.mcrcim.mcgill.edu
Quebec	Université Laval	ns.ulaval.ca
Quebec	Université Laval Genie Electrique	cso.gel.ulaval.ca
Quebec	Université du Québec à Montréal	cso.uqam.ca

New Brunswick	University of New Brunswick	ns.unb.ca
Nova Scotia	Technical University of Nova Scotia	newton.ccs.tuns.ca
Nova Scotia	Technical University of Nova Scotia Unofficial Student Directory	newton.ccs.tuns.ca port 1050

WHOIS

There are three methods of accessing a whois server:

(1) YOU CAN USE A DIAL-UP INTERNET ACCOUNT ON YOUR INTERNET PROVIDER'S MACHINE, PROVIDING THAT YOUR INTERNET PROVIDER HAS INSTALLED A WHOIS CLIENT THAT YOU CAN USE.

If you are not sure if you have a whois client installed on your machine, ask your Internet provider or the computing staff in your organization. If you don't have a whois client installed on your system, ask your Internet provider or your computing staff if they can install a client for you.

If you know that a whois client is available on your Internet provider's system, how you access it will vary from one system to the next. If your system is menu-driven (or has a point-and-click interface), you should look for a menu option that refers to "whois" searches. If you are accessing the Internet from a Unix command prompt, and a whois client is installed on your system, typing the following command will generally work:

```
whois -h ADDRESS-OF-SERVER QUERY
```

where:

ADDRESS-OF-SERVER = the domain name of the whois server you want to query
QUERY = the first or last name of the person you are looking for.

For example, let's say I want to find the e-mail address of Bob Brown at the University of New Brunswick. By consulting the list of whois servers on page 572, I know that the University of New Brunswick has a whois server. The address of the University of New Brunswick's whois server is **whois.unb.ca**. Therefore, I can type the following command at the Unix command prompt:

```
whois -h whois.unb.ca bob
```

After entering this command, I will receive a list of all the people named Bob who are registered in the whois server at the University of New Brunswick.

(2) YOU CAN ACCESS WHOIS USING A SLIP OR PPP CONNECTION.

Many of the commercial providers listed in the **Directory of Internet Service Providers in Canada** (Appendix C) provide SLIP or PPP access. If you have SLIP or PPP access using Microsoft Windows, you can use a whois client called **WinWhois**. You have to obtain this client using anonymous FTP, and install it on your system. Using WinWhois, you can input the name of a whois server and query that server directly.

Name of Client:	WinWhois (for Microsoft Windows)
Type:	Freeware
Anonymous FTP location:	net-dist.mit.edu
Directory:	pub/dos/potluck/winsock
File Name:	winwhois.zip

(3) YOU CAN ACCESS WHOIS SERVERS USING GOPHER.
The Gopher server at **sipb.mit.edu** has an alphabetical list of whois servers that you can query.

WHOIS SERVERS IN CANADA

Province	Institution	Address of whois Server
British Columbia	University of Victoria Physics and Astronomy	phys.uvic.ca
Saskatchewan	University of Saskatchewan	whois.usask.ca
Saskatchewan	University of Saskatchewan Engineering	dvinci.usask.ca
Ontario	University of Ottawa	panda1.uottawa.ca
Ontario	Queen's University	whois.queensu.ca
Ontario	University of Western Ontario	whohost.uwo.ca
New Brunswick	University of New Brunswick	whois.unb.ca

A P P E N D I X I

....

THE DIRECTORY OF IRC SERVERS
IN CANADA

WHAT IS INTERNET RELAY CHAT?

Think of Internet Relay Chat (or IRC) as an electronic version of a conference call. On IRC, you can participate in "live" discussions with other people on the Internet. You talk with other IRC participants by typing in messages on your computer. The people you exchange messages with may be in the same city, another province, or they may be in another country on another continent. At any given time on Internet Relay Chat, there can be dozens of conversations taking place on different topics. Topics are organized into discussion areas called "channels". IRC operates 24 hours a day, seven days a week, and people can join and leave "channels" at their leisure.

HOW DO I PARTICIPATE IN THE INTERNET RELAY CHAT?

To participate in the IRC, you need to have three things:

(1) YOU NEED TO HAVE ACCESS TO A DIRECT INTERNET CONNECTION AT WORK, AT SCHOOL, OR THROUGH A COMMERCIAL INTERNET PROVIDER.

COMMERCIAL INTERNET PROVIDERS

The **Directory of Canadian Internet Service Providers** in Appendix C contains a comprehensive list of commercial Internet providers in Canada. Only those commercial providers with a direct Internet connection can offer IRC to their customers. For individuals, there are two ways to access IRC using a commercial Internet provider: you can access IRC using a SLIP/PPP connection or by using a dial-up Internet account on your Internet provider's machine.

Some commercial providers only provide SLIP/PPP service, some provide only dial-up Internet accounts, and some offer *both* SLIP/PPP and dial-up Internet accounts. You can always access IRC using a SLIP/PPP connection, but some providers may choose not to offer Internet Relay Chat on their dial-up Internet accounts.

Check the **Directory of Canadian Internet Providers** to see which providers offer SLIP/PPP service and dial-up Internet accounts with a direct Internet connection.

AT WORK OR SCHOOL

If you have access to the Internet at work or at school, you may have access to Internet Relay Chat, providing that your organization has a direct Internet connection. How do you know if you have a direct Internet connection? If you have access to Internet services like Telnet, Gopher, and FTP, you have a direct Internet connection. Ask the computing staff if in doubt. Keep in mind that many organizations do not permit the use of Internet Relay Chat, so check with the computing staff if you're not sure if IRC is permitted.

(2) YOU NEED TO HAVE ACCESS TO AN IRC CLIENT.

The second requirement for using IRC is an IRC client. A client is a program that you need to run in order to use Internet Relay Chat. The **Directory of Canadian Internet Providers** will tell you which providers have installed IRC clients on their dial-up systems (check the box labeled "Interactive Accounts" to see if IRC is listed as an available service). If you know that you have direct Internet access, and you don't have an IRC client installed on your system, ask your Internet provider or your computing staff if they can install a client for you.

HOW DO I ACCESS THE CLIENT?

If you know that an IRC client is available on your system, how you access it will vary from one system to the next. If you are using a dial-up Internet account on your Internet Provider's computer, and the system is menu-driven (or has a point-and-click interface), look for a menu option called "IRC" or "Internet Relay Chat". If you are using a dial-up Internet account on your Internet provider's computer, and you are accessing the Internet from a Unix command prompt, typing **irc** will generally work.

If you are accessing the Internet using a SLIP/PPP account or a direct network connection, you need to obtain and install an IRC client on your system (if one hasn't been installed already). Listed below are some clients for Microsoft Windows and Macintosh platforms. You only need one client, but it is wise to try out several clients to see which one you like best.

SLIP/PPP CLIENTS FOR IRC

FOR MICROSOFT WINDOWS USERS

Name of Client:	WSIRC	
Type:	Shareware/Freeware	
Anonymous FTP location:	cs-ftp.bu.edu	
Directory:	irc/clients/pc/windows	
File Name:	wsirc*.zip	(*= version number, e.g., wsirc14.zip)

Name of Client:	WINIRC
Type:	Freeware
Anonymous FTP location:	cs-ftp.bu.edu
Directory:	irc/clients/pc/windows
File Name:	winirc.exe

FOR MACINTOSH USERS

Name of Client:	Homer
Type:	Shareware
Anonymous FTP location:	cs-ftp.bu.edu
Directory:	irc/clients/macintosh/homer

Name of Client:	ircle
Type:	Freeware
Anonymous FTP location:	cs-ftp.bu.edu
Directory:	irc/clients/macintosh/ircle

(3) YOU NEED TO HAVE ACCESS TO AN IRC SERVER.

The third requirement for Internet Relay Chat is an IRC server. You use your IRC client to connect to an IRC server. There are IRC servers all over the world, but to avoid wasting network resources, you should connect to the IRC server that is physically closest to you. When we speak about "physical distance," we are referring to the distance between sites on the Internet. Because traffic on the Internet often takes circuitous routes, the server geographically closest to you may not be the server that is physically closest to you. When you are setting up an IRC client, you need to tell the client which server to connect to. If an IRC client has already been installed on your system, your network administrator has probably set up your client so that it will connect to the server that is physically closest to you. You can simply start the client and not worry about choosing an IRC server. Your IRC client will connect to the default server specified by your network administrator.

If you are setting up the IRC client yourself (i.e. SLIP or PPP client), you need to determine which server to connect to. There is no rule of thumb for doing this, because the answer depends on how your system is connected to the rest of the Internet. Ask your Internet provider for guidance if you're not sure which server you should connect to. Alternatively, you can temporarily connect to one of the U.S. or Canadian servers below, and ask once you get there. There are two channels you can go to for guidance. One is **#twilight_zone**, where IRC administrators from around the world gather. Canadian IRC administrators have a channel of their own called **#ca-ops**. You can also ask there for advice if you're not sure which server to connect to. Before asking for assistance on an IRC channel, ask your Internet Service Provider or computing staff for advice.

For your guidance and general reference, the table below lists Canadian IRC servers, along with the Internet addresses of the IRC administrators for each server. The most recent version of the Canadian IRC servers list is posted to the USENET group **alt.irc** on the 15th and 30th of each month. Christopher Oates <**irc@cs.mun.ca**> of the Memorial University of Newfoundland maintains the list of Canadian IRC servers. Please note that you cannot telnet to these servers. You must use an IRC client.

Be aware that many of the sites listed in the table below restrict access to Internet sites in their area. For example, the IRC server at the Memorial University of Newfoundland is only available to Internet users in Newfoundland and Prince Edward Island.

IRC SERVERS IN CANADA

Province	Server Address	Site	Administrator
Manitoba	castor.cc.umanitoba.ca	University of Manitoba	darose@cc.umanitoba.ca
Ontario	green.ariel.cs.yorku.ca	York University	irc@ariel.cs.yorku.ca
Quebec	tsunami.cc.mcgill.ca	McGill University	yves@cc.mcgill.ca
Quebec**	montreal.qu.ca.undernet.org	École Polytechnique de Montréal	------------------------------
Quebec	irc.polymtl.ca	École Polytechnique de Montréal	ircadmin@info.polymtl.ca
Nova Scotia	elk.nstn.ca	Nova Scotia Technology Network	irc@moose.nstn.ca
Newfoundland	irc.cs.mun.ca	Memorial University of Newfoundland	irc@cs.mun.ca

** This server is part of an IRC network called "Undernet" that operates independently of the other IRC servers listed in this table.

SOME U.S. IRC SERVERS

State	Server
Massachusetts	irc-2.mit.edu
Massachusetts	irc.bu.edu
Colorado	irc.colorado.edu
Washington	alfred1.u.washington.edu

WHERE CAN I GET MORE INFORMATION ON IRC?

Before attempting to use Internet Relay Chat, consult the help files and tutorials that are available on the Internet. There are several places to go on the Internet for general information on IRC and how to use it:

(1) THE INTERNET RELAY CHAT FAQS (FREQUENTLY ASKED QUESTIONS)

These documents contain a list of frequently asked questions about IRC. There are two versions of the IRC FAQ. One version is the general IRC FAQ, and the second version is the IRC Undernet FAQ. Both are recommended reading for newcomers to IRC. You can obtain the IRC FAQs by anonymous FTP, as detailed in the boxes below.

GENERAL *IRC FAQ*

Anonymous FTP Site:	cs-ftp.bu.edu
Directory:	irc/support
File:	alt-irc-faq

UNDERNET *IRC FAQ*

Anonymous FTP Site:	rtfm.mit.edu
Directory:	pub/usenet-by-group/news.answers/irc/undernet-faq
Files:	part1 part2

(2) THE IRC PRIMER AND IRC TUTORIALS

The IRC Primer and IRC Tutorials provide an introduction to Internet Relay Chat for beginners.

IRC PRIMER

Anonymous FTP Site:	cs-ftp.bu.edu
Directory:	irc/support
File:	IRCprimer1.1.txt

IRC TUTORIALS

Anonymous FTP Site:	cs-ftp.bu.edu
Directory:	irc/support
Files:	tutorial.1
	tutorial.2
	tutorial.3

(3) USENET

The following USENET newsgroups carry discussions on IRC:

Newsgroup	Topic
alt.irc	General discussions about Internet Relay Chat (IRC)
alt.irc.ircii	Discussions about an IRC client called ircii
alt.irc.questions	Questions about Internet Relay Chat
alt.irc.undernet	Discussion about the IRC network called Undernet

Please read the IRC Frequently Asked Questions documents before posting a question to USENET.

(4) THE CANADIAN IRC USERS MAILING LIST

A mailing list called "ircusers" has been established for discussion of the IRC in Canada. Subscription is open to anyone.

To subscribe to "ircusers", send an e-mail message to **listserv@sifon.cc.mcgill.ca**, and place the following words on the first line of the body of the message:

```
subscribe ircusers <firstname> <lastname>
```

For example, if your name is John Smith, you would send the following message to listserv@sifon.cc.mcgill.ca:

```
subscribe ircusers John Smith
```

Before posting questions to this mailing list, please read the IRC Frequently Asked Questions documents. You may find the answer to your question there. The administrator of the ircusers discussion list is Yves Lepage **<yves@cc.mcgill.ca>**.

A P P E N D I X   J

....

THE DIRECTORY OF ARCHIE SERVERS IN CANADA

Archie is a Canadian-developed tool that can help you locate files on the Internet. To use archie, you need to use an archie "client." To do this, you need to have access to a direct Internet connection – either a dial-up Internet account on a commercial Internet provider's machine, a direct network connection, or a SLIP/PPP connection. Many Internet providers offer archie service on their dial-up accounts. Consult the **Directory of Canadian Internet Service Providers** in Appendix C to see which commercial providers have installed an archie client on their system (if an archie client has been installed, "archie" will be listed in the "Interactive Accounts" box of the provider's entry in the directory).

If you're accessing the Internet from a Unix command prompt, and an archie client has been installed on your system, typing **archie** from the command prompt will generally start the program.

If you are accessing the Internet using a SLIP/PPP connection, you can obtain an archie client by anonymous FTP and install it on your system.

SLIP/PPP CLIENTS FOR ARCHIE

FOR MICROSOFT WINDOWS USERS

Name of Client:	WSARCHIE	
Type:	Freeware	
Annonymous FTP Site:	polecat.law.indiana.edu	
Directory:	pub/mirror/cica/pc/win3/winsock	
File:	wsarch*.zip	(*=version number)

FOR MACINTOSH USERS

Name of Client:	ARCHIE
Type:	Shareware
Annonymous FTP Site:	ftp.hawaii.edu
Directory:	mirrors/info-mac/comm/tcp

If you don't have an archie client available on your system, you can telnet to one of the public archie servers listed in the table below. Login using the username **archie**. If an archie client isn't available on your system, ask your Internet Service Provider or local computing staff if they will install one. You will find that a local archie client is faster. It also reduces the load on the public archie servers. Many of the public archie servers are unavailable much of the time because of the high volume of users.

PUBLIC ARCHIE SERVERS (CANADA AND THE U.S.)

Server Address	Location
archie.uqam.ca	**Canada**
archie.rutgers.edu	New Jersey
archie.cs.mcgill.ca	**Canada**
archie.sura.net	Maryland
archie.ans.net	New York
archie.unl.edu	Nebraska
archie.internic.net	Virginia

You can also access archie on the World Wide Web, using one of the hypertext archie clients listed below.

CANADIAN ARCHIE SERVERS ON THE WORLD WIDE WEB*

URL	Location
http://www.csi.nb.ca/archgate.html	Cybersmith Inc., Sackville, New Brunswick
http://ricotta.ucs.ubc.ca/archie.html	University of British Columbia, Vancouver
http://www.cs.mcgill.ca/cgi-bin/archieplex.pl	McGill University, Montreal, Quebec

* The first two servers in this table require WWW browsers that have forms support.

The following site contains a master list of archie servers available on the World Wide Web. It includes a list of archie servers that require forms support, and a list of archie servers that do not require forms support. Check it out!

```
http://web.nexor.co.uk/archie.html
```

....

THE DIRECTORY OF INTERNET SERVICE BUREAUS IN CANADA

This is a directory of Canadian Internet Service Bureaus. Internet Service Bureaus are organizations that assist other organizations in placing information and services on the Internet. They specialize in helping organizations that don't have the knowledge, expertise, or resources to establish a presence on the Internet themselves. Please note that a firm's presence in this directory does not constitute an endorsement of the firm by the authors.

Keep in mind that many Internet Service Providers allow their customers to set up their own FTP directories, Gopher directories, and World Wide Web pages. This is an option that may be available to you, depending on the Internet provider you are dealing with.

The services offered by Internet Service Bureaus can include:

- Advice on establishing an Internet connection

- Purchase, set-up, configuration, and administration of the client's own Internet servers

- Rental of space on an Internet server maintained by the Internet Service Bureau

- Conversion of documents into Internet-compatible formats (Internet publishing services)

- Set-up and configuration of on-line order mechanisms

- Preparation of Internet marketing strategies

> • Public relations services to help clients announce Internet services on the Internet and through traditional media

Not all the above services are offered by every Internet Service Bureau, so when you approach an Internet Service Bureau, make sure you ask which services *are* supported, and which services are *not* supported. It is important that you ask this question, especially if many of the services listed above are important to you.

Other questions to ask include:

CAN MY INTERNET SERVICES OPERATE UNDER MY OWN DOMAIN NAME?

Some Internet Service Bureaus only make Internet services available under their own domain name or a third-party domain name (e.g. an Internet Provider). If it is important that Internet users access your Internet information using your firm's domain name, make sure that the Internet Service Bureau can accommodate this.

WHAT OTHER CLIENTS DO YOU HAVE?

Ask the Internet Service Bureau if you can see examples of the work that they have done for other clients on the Internet. This way, you can see the quality of their workmanship first-hand.

DO YOU OPERATE AN INTERNET STOREFRONT?

Many service bureaus offer "Internet storefronts" where vendors can rent space to advertise their products and services on the Internet.

To see what an Internet storefront looks like, check out the following Canadian examples:

http://www.csi.nb.ca   (Cybersmith Inc., Sackville, New Brunswick)
http://www.nstn.ca   (Nova Scotia Technology Network, Dartmouth, Nova Scotia)

Each entry in this directory is structured like this:

Name of the Service Bureau
Town or city where the organization is located.
The organization's Internet domain (optional).

Mailing address of the organization
Telephone Number
Fax Number
Internet Address

Brief description of the organization. This section is optional, since many of the organizations listed in this directory already have descriptions in the Directory of Canadian Internet Providers. Most of the descriptions that appear in this directory were provided by the Internet service bureaus for publication in this directory. The descriptions should not be taken as an endorsement of the organizations by the authors.

Set Up an Internet Mailing List	(Yes/No). Indicates whether the service bureau will set up an Internet mailing list/discussion group for a client.
Set Up a Mail Reflector	(Yes/No). Indicates whether the service bureau will set up a mail reflector for a client. A mail reflector is an Internet address that returns an automatic response (similar to a fax-back service).
Mount Information on WWW	(Yes/No). Indicates whether the service bureau will place information on the World Wide Web for a client.
Design WWW Pages	(Yes/No). Indicates whether the service bureau will design World Wide Web documents for a client.
Mount Information on Gopher	(Yes/No). Indicates whether the service bureau will place information on a Gopher server for a client.
Mount Information on FTP	(Yes/No). Indicates whether the service bureau will place information on an FTP server for a client.

RATES:
The rates for services offered by the Internet Service Bureau. Rates are subject to change without notice. Certain conditions may apply.

For More Information:
Where to get more information about the organization on the Internet.

HOW TO SUBMIT INFORMATION FOR THE DIRECTORY OF INTERNET SERVICE BUREAUS IN CANADA:
If you are a commercial organization that provides Internet marketing and consulting services to help organizations establish a presence on the Internet, and you would like to appear in future editions of this directory, please contact the authors at **<handbook@uunet.ca>** to obtain a copy of our questionnaire.

YUKON TERRITORY

YukonNet
Whitehorse, Yukon
yukonnet.yk.ca

YukonNet
c/o Northern Research Institute
Yukon College
Box 2799
Whitehorse, Yukon
Y1A 5K4

Voice: (403) 668-8735
Fax: (403) 668-8734
Internet: richard@north.nugyt.yk.ca (Richard Lawrence)

See the Directory of Canadian Internet Providers for a description of YukonNet.

Set Up an Internet Mailing List	No
Set Up a Mail Reflector	No
Mount Information on WWW	Yes
Design WWW Pages	Yes
Mount Information on Gopher	No
Mount Information on FTP	No

RATES:
Call for a quotation.

BRITISH COLUMBIA

Communicopia Environmental Research and Communications

Vancouver, British Columbia
#468 - 916 West Broadway
Vancouver, British Columbia
V5Z 1K7
Voice: (604) 875-9990
Fax: (604) 875-9584
Internet: communicopia@mindlink.bc.ca

Communicopia is the communications firm that draws together leading-edge communications technologies with environmental issues and affairs. At a time when computer networks are reshaping the way we interact, Communicopia offers consultation and services to establish an electronic presence for clients with environmental priorities.

Communicopia unites the talents of telecommunications consultants, on-line researchers, media and public relations consultants, writers, graphic artists and desktop publishers, providing a comprehensive range of services including:

- *World Wide Web home page development*

- *high-volume information distribution consultation and support*

- *information retrieval*

- *electronic media monitoring*

- *conference and corporate environmental communications*

- *traditional and electronic publishing*

Founded in 1993, Communicopia offers its services to the private and public sectors alike, with past clients including Greenpeace Canada, Environment Canada and Westcoast Energy. With close to 50 years of combined environmental experience, and using the latest telecommunications technology, Communicopia is leading the way in extending environmental visions.

Set Up an Internet Mailing List	Yes
Set Up a Mail Reflector	No
Mount Information on WWW	Yes
Design WWW Pages	Yes
Mount Information on Gopher	No
Mount Information on FTP	No

RATES:

$35.00 to $50.00 per hour for consultation and HTML development, depending on the status of the client (e.g. non-profit, government, corporate). $0.35/kilobyte/month for HTML document storage on a WWW server.

For More Information about Communicopia:

World Wide Web:
http://interchange.idc.uvic.ca/communicopia/index.html

Connectivity Technology Inc.

Vancouver, British Columbia
connectivity.com

4824 Fraser Street
Vancouver, British Columbia
Voice: (604) 874-1430
Fax: (604) 874-1431
Internet: info@connectivity.com

Connectivity Technology is a provider of Internet consulting services and facilities management. Connectivity Technology is a specialist in Internet hookups, with particular skills at more challenging configurations, custom organizational mail gateway development, Internet marketing consultation and World Wide Web services.

Connectivity Technology can provide strategic market definition and identification with respect to the Internet, development of appropriate marketing materials, conversion of documents for Gopher/World Wide Web presentation, and maintenance and monitoring of Gopher and World Wide Web servers as appropriate.

Services are available under Connectivity Technology's domain, or under the preferred domain of the client. Domain registration service is available.

Set Up an Internet Mailing List	Yes
Set Up a Mail Reflector	Yes

Mount Information on WWW	Yes
Design WWW Pages	Yes
Mount Information on Gopher	Yes
Mount Information on FTP	Yes

RATES:
Each client is quoted on an individual basis. Call for a quotation.

Cyberstore Systems Inc.

Vancouver, British Columbia
cyberstore.ca, cyberstore.com, cyberstore.net

Suite 201 - 601 West Broadway
Vancouver, British Columbia
V3L 3C5
Voice: (604) 873-1101
Fax: (604) 872-6095
Internet: info@cyberstore.ca

See the Directory of Canadian Internet Providers for a description of Cyberstore.

Set Up an Internet Mailing List	Yes
Set Up a Mail Reflector	Yes
Mount Information on WWW	Yes
Design WWW Pages	Yes
Mount Information on Gopher	Yes
Mount Information on FTP	Yes

RATES:
Call for a quotation.

For More Information about Cyberstore:

FTP:
ftp.cyberstore.ca
Directory: info

Telnet:
cyberstore.ca
*Login: **guest***

Gopher:
gopher.cyberstore.ca

World Wide Web:
http://www.cyberstore.ca

DataFlux Systems Limited

Victoria, British Columbia

dataflux.bc.ca

1281 Lonsdale Place
Victoria, British Columbia
V8P 5L3
Voice: (604) 744-4553
Fax: (604) 652-4520
Internet: info@dataflux.bc.ca

See the Directory of Canadian Internet Providers for a description of DataFlux.

Set Up an Internet Mailing List	Yes
Set Up a Mail Reflector	Yes
Mount Information on WWW	Yes
Design WWW Pages	Yes
Mount Information on Gopher	Yes
Mount Information on FTP	No

RATES:
Consulting is $50.00 per hour. Each service is individually priced thereafter. Call for a quotation.

For More Information about DataFlux:

Gopher:
gopher.dataflux.bc.ca

World Wide Web:
http://www.dataflux.bc.ca

Designed Information Systems Corporation (DISC)

Burnaby, British Columbia

aurora.net, aurora-net.com, disc-net.com

5065 Anola Drive
Burnaby, British Columbia
V5B 4V7
Voice: (604) 294-4357
Fax: (604) 294-0107
Internet: sales@aurora.net

See the Directory of Canadian Internet Providers for a description of DISC.

Set Up an Internet Mailing List	Yes
Set Up a Mail Reflector	No

Mount Information on WWW	Yes
Design WWW Pages	Yes
Mount Information on Gopher	Yes
Mount Information on FTP	Yes

RATES:
Call for a quotation.
For More Information about DISC:
World Wide Web:
http://www.aurora.net

Deep Cove Bulletin Board Systems Ltd.
White Rock, British Columbia
deepcove.com

#5 - 15273 24th Avenue
White Rock, British Columbia
V4A 2H9
Voice: (604) 536-5855
Fax: (604) 536-7418
Internet: wayne.duval@deepcove.com (Wayne Duval)

See the Directory of Canadian Internet Providers for a description of Deep Cove.

Set Up an Internet Mailing List	Yes
Set Up a Mail Reflector	Yes
Mount Information on WWW	Yes
Design WWW Pages	No
Mount Information on Gopher	Yes
Mount Information on FTP	No

RATES:
Set up Internet mailing list:
$250.00
Mount information on World Wide Web:
$100.00 to $500.00
Mount information on Gopher:
$100.00 to $500.00
Set up mail reflector:
$100.00

Helix Internet
Vancouver, British Columbia
helix.net

#902-900 West Hastings Street
Vancouver, British Columbia
V6C 1E6
Voice: (604) 689-8544
Fax: (604) 685-2554
Internet: info@helix.net

See the Directory of Canadian Internet Providers for a description of Helix Internet.

Set Up an Internet Mailing List	Yes
Set Up a Mail Reflector	Yes
Mount Information on WWW	Yes
Design WWW Pages	Yes
Mount Information on Gopher	Yes
Mount Information on FTP	Yes

RATES:
Negotiated based on usage. Helix Internet is an Internet Service Provider. Many of the above services are available to registered users at no extra charge provided that usage is light. Call for a quotation.

For More Information about Helix Internet:

FTP:
ftp.helix.net

Telnet:
helix.net
Login: **guest**

Gopher:
gopher.helix.net

World Wide Web:
http://www.helix.net

ICE ONLINE
Burnaby, British Columbia
iceonline.com

Box 30606
#201 Lougheed Hwy
Burnaby, British Columbia
V5C 6J5
Voice: (604) 298-4346
Fax: (604) 298-0246
Internet: info@iceonline.com

See the Directory of Canadian Internet Providers for a description of ICE ONLINE.

Set Up an Internet Mailing List	No
Set Up a Mail Reflector	Yes
Mount Information on WWW	Yes
Design WWW Pages	Yes
Mount Information on Gopher	No
Mount Information on FTP	Yes

RATES:

Call for a quotation.

For More Information about ICE ONLINE:

FTP:	**Telnet:**	**World Wide Web:**
iceonline.com	iceonline.com	http://www.iceonline.com
Directory: pub	Login: **bbs**	
File: ICE_ACCESS.TXT		

InfoMatch Communications Inc.

Burnaby, British Columbia
infomatch.com

143-9632 Cameron Street
Burnaby, British Columbia
V3J 7N3
Voice: (604) 421-3230
Fax: (604) 421-3230
Internet: accounts@infomatch.com

See the Directory of Canadian Internet Providers for a description of InfoMatch.

Set Up an Internet Mailing List	Yes
Set Up a Mail Reflector	Yes
Mount Information on WWW	Yes
Design WWW Pages	Yes
Mount Information on Gopher	Yes
Mount Information on FTP	Yes

RATES:

World Wide Web:

$40.00 per megabyte or portion per month based on a six-month contract. Includes free initial page design.

For More Information about InfoMatch:

Telnet:	*Gopher:*	*World Wide Web:*
infomatch.com	infomatch.com	http://infomatch.com:70
Login: **guest**		

Internet Direct
Vancouver, British Columbia
direct.ca

1628-555 West Hastings
Vancouver, British Columbia
V6B 4N6
Voice: (604) 691-1600
Fax: (604) 691-1605
Internet: info@direct.ca

Internet Direct is a leading Internet provider serving businesses and individuals in the Lower Mainland. Internet Direct offers a specific range of products and services that include the following:

* *A pre-configured MS Windows Internet access disk for individuals*
* *WWW publishing and information management solutions*
* *Development of industry-specific Internet "front ends"*
* *High-speed dedicated lines from 14.4K to 128K (ISDN)*
* *Co-location of equipment with direct access to the Internet*

Set Up an Internet Mailing List	Yes
Set Up a Mail Reflector	Yes
Mount Information on WWW	Yes
Design WWW Pages	Yes
Mount Information on Gopher	Yes
Mount Information on FTP	Yes

RATES:
Prices are on a per-case basis. Call for a quotation.

For More Information about Internet Direct:

FTP:	*Gopher:*	*World Wide Web:*
ftp.direct.ca	gopher.direct.ca	http://www.direct.ca

The Internet Shop Inc.
Kamloops, British Columbia
netshop.bc.ca

1160 8th Street
Kamloops, British Columbia
Voice: (604) 376-3710
Fax: (604) 376-5931

Internet: info@netshop.bc.ca

See the Directory of Canadian Internet Providers for a description of the Internet Shop.

Set Up an Internet Mailing List	Yes
Set Up a Mail Reflector	Yes
Mount Information on WWW	Yes
Design WWW Pages	Yes
Mount Information on Gopher	Yes
Mount Information on FTP	Yes

RATES:
Call for a quotation.

Island Internet

Nanaimo, British Columbia
island.net

515b Campbell Street
Nanaimo, British Columbia
V9R 3G9
Voice: (604) 753-1139
Fax: (604) 753-8542
Internet: info@island.net

See the Directory of Canadian Internet Providers for a description of Island Internet.

Set Up an Internet Mailing List	Yes
Set Up a Mail Reflector	Yes
Mount Information on WWW	Yes
Design WWW Pages	Yes
Mount Information on Gopher	Yes
Mount Information on FTP	Yes

RATES:

World Wide Web Server:	*$300.00 per month plus set up*	
Gopher Server:	*$200.00 per month plus set up*	
World Wide Web + Gopher:	*$400.00 per month plus set up*	
FTP Directory:	*$50-100 per month plus set up*	*$1.00/MB/month*
Mailing List:	*$25-50 per month plus set up*	
Mail Reflector:	*$25.00 per month plus set up*	

For More Information about Island Internet:

Gopher:
epaus.island.net

World Wide Web:
http://www.island.net/

ISLAND NET
Victoria, British Columbia
amtsgi.bc.ca, islandnet.com

P.O. Box 6201, Depot 1
Victoria, British Columbia
V8P 5L5
Voice: (604) 479-7861
Fax: (604) 479-7343
Internet: mark@islandnet.com (Mark Morley)

See the Directory of Canadian Internet Providers for a description of Island Net.

Set Up an Internet Mailing List	Yes
Set Up a Mail Reflector	Yes
Mount Information on WWW	Yes
Design WWW Pages	Yes
Mount Information on Gopher	Yes
Mount Information on FTP	Yes

RATES:
Island Internet is an Internet Service Provider. The services listed above are offered to registered users at no extra charge. Every account has the ability to create World Wide Web home pages and its own FTP directory.

For More Information on Island Net:

Telnet:
islandnet.com
Login: **guest** or **new**

Gopher:
gopher.islandnet.com

FTP:
ftp.islandnet.com
Directory: *IslandNet*

World Wide Web:
http://www.islandnet.com

MINDLINK! Communications Corporation
Langley, British Columbia
mindlink.bc.ca

105 - 20381 62nd Avenue
Langley, British Columbia
V3A 5E6
Voice: (604) 534-5663
Fax: (604) 534-7473
Internet: info@mindlink.bc.ca

See the Directory of Canadian Internet Providers for a description of MINDLINK!

Set Up an Internet Mailing List	Yes
Set Up a Mail Reflector	Yes
Mount Information on WWW	Yes
Design WWW Pages	Yes
Mount Information on Gopher	Yes
Mount Information on FTP	Yes

RATES:
Call for a quotation.

For More Information about MindLink!:

Telnet:	**World Wide Web:**
mindlink.bc.ca	*http://www.mindlink.bc.ca*
Login: **guest**	

Pro.Net Communications Inc.

Vancouver, British Columbia
pro.net, pronet.bc.ca

890 West Pender Street, Suite 410
Vancouver, British Columbia
V6C 1J9
Voice: (604) 688-9282
Fax: (604) 688-9229
Internet: info@pro.net

See the Directory of Canadian Internet Providers for a description of Pro.Net.

Set Up an Internet Mailing List	Yes
Set Up a Mail Reflector	Yes
Mount Information on WWW	Yes
Design WWW Pages	Yes
Mount Information on Gopher	Yes
Mount Information on FTP	Yes

RATES:
Call for a quotation.

For More Information about Pro.Net:

World Wide Web:
http://www.pro.net

Simon Fraser University
External Services

Burnaby, British Columbia
sfu.ca

External Services
Academic Computing Services
Simon Fraser University
Burnaby, British Columbia
V5A 1S6
Voice: (604) 291-3946
Fax: (604) 291-4242
Internet: devlin@sfu.ca (Tim Devlin)

See the Directory of Canadian Internet Providers for a description of Simon Fraser University External Services.

Set Up an Internet Mailing List	Yes
Set Up a Mail Reflector	Yes
Mount Information on WWW	Yes
Design WWW Pages	Yes
Mount Information on Gopher	Yes
Mount Information on FTP	Yes

RATES:
Call for a quotation.

Wimsey Information Services Inc.

Burnaby, British Columbia
wimsey.com, wimsey.bc.ca, wis.net

Wimsey Information Services
8523 Commerce Court
Burnaby, British Columbia
V5A 4N3
Voice: (604) 421-4741
Fax: (604) 421-4742
Internet: info@wimsey.com

Wimsey Information Services Inc. provides business users of the Internet with a complete production and presentation service for the World Wide Web, Gopher and WAIS. Wimsey has been a leader in building practical, cost-effective uses of these new media for businesses in many categories. In addition, Wimsey has created an exciting and well-travelled Internet site with features that draw interest from all over the world. Services include:
Conceptual refinement; design and execution of all WWW facilities; on-line order entry; statistical feedback and analysis; automated response mechanisms; implementation of designs on Wimsey's systems, customer systems on Wimsey's site (facility management), customer systems on their site (facility management), customer systems to be administered by customer; migration of systems from Wimsey's site to their own.

Set Up an Internet Mailing List	Yes
Set Up a Mail Reflector	Yes
Mount Information on WWW	Yes
Design WWW Pages	Yes
Mount Information on Gopher	Yes
Mount Information on FTP	Yes

RATES:

Hourly rates for design and execution range from $200.00 to $70.00/hour or less for longer contacts. Machine rates are on a usage basis or on a monthly contact basis depending on design objectives and projected disk and bandwidth needs. Call Wimsey's publishing department for a quotation or point your World Wide Web browser at the following URL: http://www.wimsey.com/wimsey.buscard.html

For More Information about Wimsey:

Telnet:
wimsey.com
Login: **help**
Password: press **<enter>**

Gopher:
wimsey.com

World Wide Web:
http://www.wimsey.com/

ALBERTA

Alberta SuperNet Inc.
Edmonton, Alberta
supernet.ab.ca

#325 Pacific Plaza
10909 Jasper Avenue
Edmonton, Alberta
T5J 3L9
Voice: (403) 441-3663
Fax: (403) 424-0743
Internet: info@supernet.ab.ca

See the Directory of Canadian Internet Providers for a description of Alberta SuperNet.

Set Up an Internet Mailing List	Yes
Set Up a Mail Reflector	Yes
Mount Information on WWW	Yes

Design WWW Pages	Yes
Mount Information on Gopher	Yes
Mount Information on FTP	Yes

RATES:

Call for a quotation.

For More Information about Alberta SuperNet:

World Wide Web:

http://www.supernet.ab.ca

CADVision Development Corp.

Calgary, Alberta

cadvision.com

Suite 1590
300 5th Avenue SW
Calgary, Alberta
T2P 3C4
Voice: (403) 777-1300
Fax: (403) 777-1319
Internet: info@cadvision.com

See the Directory of Canadian Internet Providers for a description of CADVision.

Set Up an Internet Mailing List	Yes
Set Up a Mail Reflector	Yes
Mount Information on WWW	Yes
Design WWW Pages	Yes
Mount Information on Gopher	Yes
Mount Information on FTP	Yes

RATES:

World Wide Web:	*$1,000.00 per set up*
	$60.00 per hour
Gopher:	*$500.00 per set up*
	$60.00 per hour

Space and computing space can be leased for $400.00 - $1,000.00 per month.

For More Information about CADVision:

World Wide Web:

http://www.cadvision.com/top.html

CCI Networks
Edmonton, Alberta
ccinet.ab.ca

4130 - 95 Street
Edmonton, Alberta
T6E 6H5
Voice: (403) 450-6787
Fax: (403) 450-9143
Internet: info@ccinet.ab.ca

See the Directory of Canadian Internet Providers for a description of CCI Networks.

Set Up an Internet Mailing List	Yes
Set Up a Mail Reflector	No
Mount Information on WWW	Yes
Design WWW Pages	Yes
Mount Information on Gopher	No
Mount Information on FTP	Yes

RATES:
Call for a quotation.

For More Information on CCI Networks:

FTP: **World Wide Web:**
ftp.ccinet.ab.ca   *http://www.ccinet.ab.ca*
Directory:
pub/CCInet

InfoHarvest Inc.
Edmonton, Alberta

11428 - 77 Avenue
Edmonton, Alberta
T6G 0L8
Voice: (403) 439-6001
Fax: (403) 439-6001
Internet: mjohnson@ccinet.ab.ca

InfoHarvest assists clients in distributing their information over the Internet by setting up pages on the World Wide Web and converting information into hypertext mark-up language. InfoHarvest also teaches people how to use the Internet and how to prepare their own hypertext mark-up files. InfoHarvest has an in-depth understanding of agricultural information. Searching for other related data sources is provided, and links to these sources can be included in a customer's World Wide Web page.

Set up an Internet Mailing List	No
Set up a Mail Reflector	No
Mount Information on WWW	Yes
Design WWW Pages	Yes
Mount Information on Gopher	No
Mount Information on FTP	No

RATES:
Search/Retrieval and translating documents into HTML: $60.00 per hour. Call for further information.

InterNode Networks
Calgary, Alberta
internode.net

112 Rivergreen Cr. SE
Calgary, Alberta
T2C 3V6
Voice: (403) 296-1190
Fax: (403) 279-9581
Internet: info@internode.net

See the Directory of Canadian Internet Providers for a description of InterNode Networks.

Set up an Internet Mailing List	Yes
Set up a Mail Reflector	Yes
Mount Information on WWW	Yes
Design WWW Pages	Yes
Mount Information on Gopher	Yes
Mount Information on FTP	Yes

RATES:
Call for a quotation.

For More Information about InterNode:

FTP:
ftp.internode.net

World Wide Web:
http://www.internode.net

The Network Centre

Calgary, Alberta
tnc.com

300, 555 4th Avenue S.W.
Calgary, Alberta
T2P 3E7
Voice: (403) 262-3880
Fax: (403) 266-1837
Internet: tncinfo@tnc.com

BKB Engineering
11211 76th Avenue
Edmonton, Alberta
T6G 0K2
Voice: (403) 438-2531

See the Directory of Canadian Internet Providers for a description of The Network Centre.

Set Up an Internet Mailing List	Yes
Set Up a Mail Reflector	Yes
Mount Information on WWW	Yes
Design WWW Pages	Yes
Mount Information on Gopher	Yes
Mount Information on FTP	Yes

RATES:
Call for a quotation.

Telnet Canada Enterprises, Ltd.

Calgary, Alberta
tcel.com

Penthouse
1812, 4th Street SW
Calgary, Alberta
T2S 1W1
Voice: (403) 245-1882
Fax: (403) 228-9702
Internet: info@tcel.com

See the Directory of Canadian Internet Providers for a description of Telnet Enterprises.

Set Up an Internet Mailing List	Yes
Set Up a Mail Reflector	Yes
Mount Information on WWW	Yes

Design WWW Pages	Yes
Mount Information on Gopher	Yes
Mount Information on FTP	Yes

RATES:

Initial Consultation:	*FREE*
World Wide Web Home Page Design:	*$50.00 per hour*
HTML Document Translation:	*$50.00 per hour*
Server Space Rental:	*$50.00/MB/month*

For More Information about Telnet Canada:

FTP:	*Gopher:*	*World Wide Web:*
ftp.tcel.com	*gopher.tcel.com*	*http://www.tcel.com*

WorldGate
Edmonton, Alberta
worldgate.edmonton.ab.ca

16511-85 Avenue
Edmonton, Alberta
T5R 4A2
Voice: (403) 481-7579
Fax: (403) 444-7720
Internet: info@worldgate.edmonton.ab.ca

See the Directory of Canadian Internet Providers for a description of WorldGate.

Set Up an Internet Mailing List	Yes
Set Up a Mail Reflector	Yes
Mount Information on WWW	Yes
Design WWW Pages	Yes
Mount Information on Gopher	Yes
Mount Information on FTP	Yes

RATES:

Rates are customized depending on requirements. Administration time is $20.00 per hour. Storage is $5.00/MB/year. Cost of bandwidth use varies.

For More Information about WorldGate:

FTP:
valis.worldgate.edmonton.ab.ca

Telnet:
valis.worldgate.edmonton.ab.ca
Login: **new**

Gopher:
valis.worldgate.edmonton.ab.ca

World Wide Web:
http://valis.worldgate.edmonton.ab.ca/

SASKATCHEWAN

UNIBASE Telecomm Ltd.
Regina, Saskatchewan
unibase.com

3002 Harding Street
Regina, Saskatchewan
S4V 0Y4
Voice: (306) 789-9007
Fax: (306) 761-1831
Internet: leigh@unibase.unibase.com (Leigh Calnek)

See the Directory of Canadian Internet Providers for a description of UNIBASE Telecomm.

Set Up an Internet Mailing List	Yes
Set Up a Mail Reflector	Yes
Mount Information on WWW	Yes
Design WWW Pages	Yes
Mount Information on Gopher	Yes
Mount Information on FTP	Yes

RATES:
Call for a quotation.

For More Information about UNIBASE Telecomm:

FTP:
udevdiv.unibase.com

Telnet:
unibase.unibase.com
Login: **netguest** *(15 min. browse period)*

Gopher:
unibase.unibase.com

World Wide Web:
http://cdrom1.unibase.com/welcom.html

MANITOBA

MBnet
Winnipeg, Manitoba
MBNET.MB.CA

MBnet
c/o Computer Services
University of Manitoba
15 Gillson Street
Winnipeg, Manitoba
R3T 2N2
Voice: (204) 474-7235
Fax: (204) 275-5420
Internet: info@mbnet.mb.ca

See the Directory of Canadian Internet Providers for a description of MBnet.

Set Up an Internet Mailing List	Yes
Set Up a Mail Reflector	Yes
Mount Information on WWW	Yes
Design WWW Pages	No
Mount Information on Gopher	Yes
Mount Information on FTP	Yes

RATES:
Call for a quotation.

For More Information about MBnet:

Telnet:
access.mbnet.mb.ca
Login: **guest**

Gopher:
gopher.mbnet.mb.ca

World Wide Web:
http://www.mbnet.mb.ca

ONTARIO

Achilles Internet

Gloucester, Ontario
achilles.net

Dennis J. Hutton Associates Ltd.
1810 Thornecrest
Gloucester, Ontario
K1C 6K7
Voice: (613) 830-5426
Fax: (613) 824-2342
Internet: office@dragon.achilles.net

See the Directory of Canadian Internet Providers for a description of Achilles Internet.

Set Up an Internet Mailing List	Yes

Set Up a Mail Reflector	Yes
Mount Information on WWW	Yes
Design WWW Pages	Yes
Mount Information on Gopher	Yes
Mount Information on FTP	Yes

RATES:
Prices are on a per-case basis. Call for a quotation.

For More Information about Achilles Internet:

Gopher: **World Wide Web:**
gopher.achilles.net   *http://www.achilles.net*

CRS Online

Etobicoke, Ontario
canrem.com

24-12 Steinway Blvd.
Etobicoke, Ontario
M9W 6M5
Voice: (416) 213-6000
                 1-800-563-2529
Fax: (416) 213-6038
Internet: info@canrem.com

See the Directory of Canadian Internet Providers for a description of CRS Online.

Set Up an Internet Mailing List	Yes
Set Up a Mail Reflector	Yes
Mount Information on WWW	Yes
Design WWW Pages	No
Mount Information on Gopher	Yes
Mount Information on FTP	No

RATES:
Call for a quotation.

For More Information on CRS Online:

Gopher: **Telnet:**
canrem.com   *canrem.com (no login or password required)*

CIMtegration Inc.

Toronto, Ontario
cimtegration.com

4850 Keele Street
North York, Ontario
M3J 3K1
Voice: (416) 665-3566
Fax: (416) 554-1815
Internet: info@cimtegration.com

See the Directory of Canadian Internet Providers for a description of CIMtegration.

Set Up an Internet Mailing List	Yes
Set Up a Mail Reflector	Yes
Mount Information on WWW	Yes
Design WWW Pages	Yes
Mount Information on Gopher	No
Mount Information on FTP	Yes

RATES:
$75.00 per hour for all services.
For More Information on CIMtegration:
World Wide Web:
http://www.cimtegration.com

e-Commerce Inc.

Mississauga, Ontario
e-commerce.com

1030 Kamato Road
Suite 201
Mississauga, Ontario
L4W 4B6
Voice: (905) 602-0863
Fax: (905) 602-8402
Internet: info@e-commerce.com

e-Commerce is a growing consulting company specializing in Internet-based application development and deployment. Leveraging available technologies, e-Commerce provides the expertise an organization requires to capitalize on the rapid growth of global information networks.

e-Commerce believes in a layered approach to Internet system construction. Functionality and services are added only after a secure, stable foundation is prepared. In this way, each piece of the framework benefits from all of the services below it and also acts as a building block for those above.

e-Commerce enables your usage of the Internet by providing expertise at many layers, including:

- *Consultation and training, building a Road Map to Internet usage*

- *Basic Internet connection set up, via an Internet Access Provider*

- *Internet Security Firewall, protecting your organization's information*

- *Electronic mail integration (Internet Mail to cc:Mail, MS Mail, and others)*

- *Application(s) that enable business goals, using World Wide Web, Gopher, WAIS, FTP, and automated electronic mail systems (mail robots)*

e-Commerce both lives the culture of the Internet and understands the tools and mechanisms applicable to marketing products and services electronically. With the client's Internet presence assembled, we will work with them to inform their market via both traditional and electronic means:

Set Up an Internet Mailing List	Yes
Set Up a Mail Reflector	Yes
Mount Information on WWW	Yes
Design WWW Pages	Yes
Mount Information on Gopher	Yes
Mount Information on FTP	Yes

RATES:

Consulting services are billed on a per diem basis. Rates vary depending on the size and scope of the project. Call for a quotation.

For More Information about e-Commerce:

Gopher:
gopher.e-commerce.com

World Wide Web:
http://www.e-commerce.com

Fleximation Systems Inc.

Mississauga, Ontario
flexnet.com, flexnet.ca

1495 Bonhill Road
Units 1 and 2
Mississauga, Ontario
L5T 1M2
Voice: (905) 795-0300
                1-800-263-8733
Fax: (905) 795-0310
Internet: admin@flexnet.com

See the Directory of Canadian Internet Providers for a description of Fleximation.

Set Up an Internet Mailing List	Yes
Set Up a Mail Reflector	Yes
Mount Information on WWW	Yes

Design WWW Pages	Yes
Mount Information on Gopher	Yes
Mount Information on FTP	Yes

RATES:

FTP Server:
$400.00 set up fee with $150.00 monthly fee.

Gopher Server:
$1,000.00 set up fee with $200.00 monthly maintenance.

World Wide Web Server:
$2,000.00 set up fee with $400.00 monthly maintenance.

For More Information about Fleximation:

Gopher:
gopher.flexnet.com

World Wide Web:
http://www.flexnet.com

Global-X-Change Communications Inc.
Ottawa, Ontario
globalx.net

709-170 Laurier Avenue West
Ottawa, Ontario
K1P 5V5
Voice: (613) 235-6865
Fax: (613) 232-5285
Internet: info@globalx.net

Global-X-Change Communications Inc. strives to be the leading provider of innovative, customer-driven Internet business solutions. The company fosters the use of Internet as a standard business tool by delivering Internet products and services to private and public sector individuals and organizations in the National Capital Region. Global-X-Change offerings include service bureau facilities, connectivity products and services, training, site configuration and consulting.

Global-X-Change will provide full marketing services, from identification of audiences and preparation of material to announcements over Internet and conventional marketing channels.

Set Up an Internet Mailing List	Yes
Set Up a Mail Reflector	Yes
Mount Information on WWW	Yes
Design WWW Pages	Yes
Mount Information on Gopher	Yes
Mount Information on FTP	Yes

RATES:
Call for a quotation.

For More Information about Global-X-Change:

World Wide Web:
http://www.globalx.net/

HookUp Communications
Oakville, Ontario
hookup.net

1075 North Service Road West
Suite 207
Oakville, Ontario
L6M 2G2
Voice: Toll-Free Canada-Wide: 1-800-363-0400
          Direct Dial: (905) 847-8000
Fax: (905) 847-8420
Internet: info@hookup.net

See the Directory of Canadian Internet Providers for a description of HookUp.

Set Up an Internet Mailing List	Yes
Set Up a Mail Reflector	Yes
Mount Information on WWW	Yes
Design WWW Pages	Yes
Mount Information on Gopher	Yes
Mount Information on FTP	Yes

RATES:
Rates are customized. Call for a quotation.

For More Information about HookUp:

FTP: *Gopher:*
ftp.hookup.net   *gopher.hookup.net*

World Wide Web:
http://www.hookup.net

InaSec Inc.
Ottawa, Ontario
inasec.ca

29 Beechwood Avenue
Suite 320
Ottawa, Ontario
K1M 2M1
Voice: (613) 746-3200
Fax: (613) 747-2046
Internet: mike@inasec.ca (Michel Paradis)

See the Directory of Canadian Internet Providers for a description of InaSec.

Set Up an Internet Mailing List	Yes
Set Up a Mail Reflector	Yes
Mount Information on WWW	No
Design WWW Pages	No
Mount Information on Gopher	Yes
Mount Information on FTP	Yes

RATES:
Call for a quotation.

For More Information about InaSec:

FTP:	*Gopher:*
inasec.ca	*inasec.ca*

InfoRamp Inc.
Toronto, Ontario
inforamp.net

134 Adelaide Street East
Suite 207
Toronto, Ontario
M5C 1K9
Voice: (416) 363-9100
Fax: (416) 363-3551
Internet: staff@inforamp.net

See the Directory of Canadian Internet Providers for a description of InfoRamp.

Set Up an Internet Mailing List	Yes
Set Up a Mail Reflector	Yes
Mount Information on WWW	Yes
Design WWW Pages	Yes
Mount Information on Gopher	Yes
Mount Information on FTP	Yes

RATES:
Rates are on a per-case basis. Call for a quotation.

For More Information about InfoRamp:

Gopher:
inforamp.net

INGENIA Communications Corporation
Ottawa, Ontario

2-44 Grove Avenue
Ottawa, Ontario
K1S 3A6
Voice: (613) 788-2600 ext. 8288
Fax: (613) 788-5682
Internet: karen@ccs.carleton.ca
           rwelch@ccs.carleton.ca

Ingenia continues to provide consulting and technical services of the highest calibre, meeting the needs and exceeding the expectations of our clients. We are continually enhancing and expanding the services we offer, to include everything from new technologies to new telecommunications policy.

Ingenia designs, configures and maintains Internet nodes, network servers, information resources and communication services. Ingenia helps clients realize the potential of operating on the world's largest computer network, providing them with the knowledge and tools necessary to face its complex challenges. Our activities cover everything from conducting training workshops, compiling background documentation and carrying out investigative studies to programming World Wide Web servers, Wide Area Information Servers and Gopher servers.

As an organization that is active in the networking community, Ingenia will advise organizations on how to market effectively on the Internet, without violating the accepted use of the Internet.

Ingenia employs computer technology experts, networking consultants and certified network designers, specializing in Internet services and applications. Based at Carleton University in Ottawa, Ingenia is also affiliated with Industry Canada, the Ottawa Carleton Research Institute, Communications Research Centre, Rogers Communications, Apple Canada, Carleton University - Faculty of Engineering and Computing and Communication Services, and the Canadian Council of Professional Engineers.

Set Up an Internet Mailing List	Yes
Set Up a Mail Reflector	Yes
Mount Information on WWW	Yes
Design WWW Pages	Yes
Mount Information on Gopher	Yes
Mount Information on FTP	Yes

RATES:
Prices vary according to the nature of the services and the amount of information to be provided. Prices are based on per diem rates for consultants, which vary from $150.00 to $700.00 depending on the technical expertise required. Rates are greatly reduced for non-profit, educational and community organizations. All rates are fully negotiable. Call for a quotation.

Interlog Internet Services
Toronto, Ontario
interlog.com

1235 Bay Street
Suite 400
Toronto, Ontario
M5R 3K4
Voice: (416) 975-2655
Fax: (416) 975-2655
Internet: internet@interlog.com

See the Directory of Canadian Internet Providers for a description of Interlog.

Set Up an Internet Mailing List	Yes
Set Up a Mail Reflector	Yes
Mount Information on WWW	Yes
Design WWW Pages	No
Mount Information on Gopher	Yes
Mount Information on FTP	Yes

RATES:
Rates are set on a case-by-case basis. Call for information.

For More Information about Interlog:

FTP:
ftp.interlog.com
Directory: pub/info

Telnet:
gold.interlog.com
Login: **guest**

Gopher:
gopher.interlog.com

World Wide Web:
http://www.interlog.com

Internet Access Inc.
Ottawa, Ontario
ottawa.net

1678 Ortona Avenue
Ottawa, Ontario
K2C 1W7
Voice: (613) 722-7335
Fax: (613) 722-2778
Internet: info@ottawa.net

See the Directory of Canadian Internet Providers for a description of Internet Access.

Set Up an Internet Mailing List	Yes
Set Up a Mail Reflector	Yes
Mount Information on WWW	Yes
Design WWW Pages	Yes
Mount Information on Gopher	Yes
Mount Information on FTP	Yes

RATES:
Set up/Preparation/Configuration Services:
US$19.00 - $44.00 per hour.

On-line Storage:
$0.01/KB/day (discounted for major clients).

For More Information about Internet Access:

Gopher:	**World Wide Web:**
shop.net	*http://shop.net*

Internex Online
Toronto, Ontario
io.org

1 Yonge Street
Suite 1801
Toronto, Ontario
M5E 1W7
Voice: (416) 363-8676
Fax: (416) 369-0515
Internet: support@io.org

See the Directory of Canadian Internet Providers for a description of Internex Online.

Set Up an Internet Mailing List	Yes
Set Up a Mail Reflector	Yes
Mount Information on WWW	Yes
Design WWW Pages	No
Mount Information on Gopher	Yes
Mount Information on FTP	Yes

RATES:

Internex Online is an Internet Service Provider. The above services are provided at no extra charge to registered users, but services are subject to disk quota limitations.

For More Information about Internex Online:

World Wide Web:
http://www.io.org/

InterWeb Internet Services Inc.
Ottawa, Ontario
interweb.com

440 Laurier Avenue West
Suite 200
Ottawa, Ontario
K1R 7X6
Voice: (613) 782-2481
Fax: (613) 782-2445
Internet: info@interweb.com

InterWeb's main goal is to facilitate the implementation of Web and Gopher servers, and all supporting services required to make it successful. Services include helping clients to define and focus their ideas; image scanning; graphics design and integration into Web pages; strategic announcement of a client's information services on the Internet.

Services can be made available under InterWeb's domain name, or the preferred domain name of the client. Domain registration service is available.

Set Up an Internet Mailing List	Yes
Set Up a Mail Reflector	Yes
Mount Information on WWW	Yes
Design WWW Pages	Yes
Mount Information on Gopher	Yes
Mount Information on FTP	Yes

RATES:
Prices vary depending on the type and volume of service. Call for a quotation.

For More Information about InterWeb:

World Wide Web:
http://www.interweb.com

Lightning Communications Corporation
Nepean, Ontario
lightning.ca

57 Auriga Drive
Suite 102
Nepean, Ontario
K2E 8B2
Voice: (613) 225-5932 (9a.m. - 4p.m. EST Mon-Fri)
            (613) 797-1729 (After Hours Sales)
            (613) 797-1728 (After Hours Sales & Technical Support)
Fax: (613) 224-4460
Internet: info@lightning.ca

See the Directory of Canadian Internet Providers for a description of Lightning Communications.

Set Up an Internet Mailing List	Yes
Set Up a Mail Reflector	Yes
Mount Information on WWW	Yes
Design WWW Pages	Yes
Mount Information on Gopher	Yes
Mount Information on FTP	Yes

RATES:
Prices vary depending on application and implementation time. Call for a quotation.

Magi Data Consulting Incorporated
Ottawa, Ontario
magi.com

20 Colonnade Road
Nepean, Ontario
K2E 7M6
Voice: (613) 225-3354
Fax: (613) 225-2880
Internet: info@magi.com

See the Directory of Canadian Internet Providers for a description of Magi Data.

Set Up an Internet Mailing List	Yes
Set Up a Mail Reflector	Yes
Mount Information on WWW	Yes
Design WWW Pages	Yes
Mount Information on Gopher	Yes
Mount Information on FTP	Yes

RATES:
Above services are free for existing clients.
In-house consultation: *$85.00 per hour*
On site consultation: *$125.00 per hour*

For More Information about Magi Data:

Gopher: **World Wide Web:**
gopher.magi.com   *http://www.magi.com/*

Mindemoya Computing and Design

Sudbury, Ontario
mcd.on.ca

180 Countryside Drive
Sudbury, Ontario
P3E 5A4
Voice: (705) 523-0243
Fax: (705) 523-2109
Internet: info@mcd.on.ca

See the Directory of Canadian Internet Providers for a description of Mindemoya.

Set Up an Internet Mailing List	Yes
Set Up a Mail Reflector	Yes
Mount Information on WWW	No
Design WWW Pages	Yes
Mount Information on Gopher	No
Mount Information on FTP	No

RATES:
Call for a quotation.

NetAccess Systems Inc.

Hamilton, Ontario
netaccess.on.ca

Suite E
231 Main Street West
Hamilton, Ontario
L8P 1J4
Voice: (905) 524-2544
Fax: (905) 524-3010
Internet: info@netaccess.on.ca

See the Directory of Canadian Internet Providers for a description of NetAccess.

Set Up an Internet Mailing List	No
Set Up a Mail Reflector	Yes
Mount Information on WWW	Yes
Design WWW Pages	Yes
Mount Information on Gopher	Yes
Mount Information on FTP	Yes

RATES:

Rates are variable. Call for a quotation.

For More Information about NetAccess:

Gopher:
gopher.netaccess.on.ca

World Wide Web:
http://netaccess.on.ca/welcome.html

Nova Scotia Technology Network Inc. (NSTN)

Dartmouth, Nova Scotia
nstn.ca

201 Brownlow Avenue
Dartmouth, Nova Scotia
B3B 1W2
Voice: (902) 481-NSTN (6786)
              1-800-336-4445 (Toll-Free Canada-Wide)
Fax: (902) 468-3679
Internet: info@nstn.ca (Automated)
              sales@nstn.ca (Sales/Marketing Team)

Area Served: Ottawa
See main entry under Nova Scotia.

ONRAMP Network Services Inc.

Markham, Ontario
onramp.ca

570 Hood Road
Markham, Ontario
L3R 4G7
Voice: (905) 470-4064
Fax: (905) 477-4808
Internet: info@onramp.ca

See the Directory of Canadian Internet Providers for a description of ONRAMP.

Set Up an Internet Mailing List	Yes
Set Up a Mail Reflector	Yes
Mount Information on WWW	Yes
Design WWW Pages	Yes
Mount Information on Gopher	Yes
Mount Information on FTP	Yes

RATES:
Call for a quotation.

For More Information on ONRAMP:

Gopher:
onramp.ca

World Wide Web:
http://onramp.ca

Passport Online
Toronto, Ontario
passport.ca

173 Dufferin Street
Suite 302
Toronto, Ontario
M6K 3H7
Voice: (416) 516-1616
Fax: (416) 516-1690
Internet: info@passport.ca

See the Directory of Canadian Internet Providers for a description of Passport Online.

Set Up an Internet Mailing List	Yes
Set Up a Mail Reflector	Yes
Mount Information on WWW	Yes
Design WWW Pages	Yes
Mount Information on Gopher	Yes
Mount Information on FTP	Yes

RATES:
Call for a quotation.

For More Information about Passport Online:

FTP:
ftp.passport.ca

Telnet:
passport.ca
Login: **guest**
Password: **guest**

Gopher:
gopher.passport.ca

RESUDOX Online Services

Nepean, Ontario
resudox.net

P.O. Box 33067
Nepean, Ontario
K2C 3Y9
Voice: (613) 567-6925
Fax: (613) 567-8289
Internet: admin@resudox.net

See the Directory of Canadian Internet Providers for a description of RESUDOX.

Set Up an Internet Mailing List	Yes
Set Up a Mail Reflector	No
Mount Information on WWW	Yes
Design WWW Pages	Yes
Mount Information on Gopher	Yes
Mount Information on FTP	Yes

RATES:
Call for a quotation.

For More Information about RESUDOX:

Gopher:
resudox.net

Telnet:
resudox.net
Login: **new**

World Wide Web:
http://www.resudox.net

Sentex Communications Corporation

Guelph, Ontario
sentex.net

727 Speedvale Avenue West
Unit #6
Guelph, Ontario
N1K 1E6
Voice: (519) 822-9970
Fax: (519) 822-4775
Internet: info@sentex.net

See the Directory of Canadian Internet Providers for a description of Sentex Communications.

Set Up an Internet Mailing List	Yes
Set Up a Mail Reflector	Yes
Mount Information on WWW	Yes
Design WWW Pages	Yes
Mount Information on Gopher	Yes
Mount Information on FTP	Yes

RATES:
Contingent on the size of the project. Call for a quotation.

For More Information about Sentex Communications:

Telnet: **Gopher:**
granite.sentex.net   gopher.sentex.net
Login: **new**

World Wide Web:
http://www.sentex.net/info/sentex.html

The-Wire
Toronto, Ontario
the-wire.com

12 Sheppard Street
Suite 421
Toronto, Ontario
M5H 3A1
Voice: (416) 214-WIRE (9473)
Fax: (416) 862-WIRE (9473)
Internet: sysadm@the-wire.com

See the Directory of Canadian Internet Providers for a description of The-Wire.

Set Up an Internet Mailing List	Yes
Set Up a Mail Reflector	Yes
Mount Information on WWW	Yes
Design WWW Pages	Yes
Mount Information on Gopher	Yes
Mount Information on FTP	Yes

RATES:
Prices are negotiated on a per-case basis. Call for a quotation.

For More Information about The-Wire:

World Wide Web:
http://the-wire.com

The Usual Suspects
London, Ontario
suspects.com

430 Loverage Street
London, Ontario
N5W 4T7
Voice: (519) 451-4364
Internet: info@suspects.com

See the Directory of Canadian Internet Providers for a description of The Usual Suspects.

Set Up an Internet Mailing List	Yes
Set Up a Mail Reflector	Yes
Mount Information on WWW	Yes
Design WWW Pages	Yes
Mount Information on Gopher	Yes
Mount Information on FTP	Yes

RATES:
Rates are negotiable. Call for a quotation.

For More Information about The Usual Suspects:

FTP:	**Gopher:**
ftp.suspects.com	*gopher.suspects.com*

UUISIS
Nepean, Ontario
uuisis.isis.org

81 Tartan Drive
Nepean, Ontario
K2J 3V6
Voice: (613) 825-5324
Internet: rjbeeth@uuisis.isis.org (Rick Beetham)

See the Directory of Canadian Internet Providers for a description of UUISIS.

Set Up an Internet Mailing List	Yes
Set Up a Mail Reflector	Yes
Mount Information on WWW	No
Design WWW Pages	No
Mount Information on Gopher	Yes
Mount Information on FTP	No

RATES:
Call for a quotation.

UUNorth International Inc.
Willowdale, Ontario
north.net

3555 Don Mills Road
Unit 6-304
Willowdale, Ontario
M2H 3N3
Voice: (416) 225-8649
Fax: (416) 225-0525
Internet: info@uunorth.north.net

See the Directory of Canadian Internet Providers for a description of UUNorth.

Set Up an Internet Mailing List	Yes
Set Up a Mail Reflector	Yes
Mount Information on WWW	Yes
Design WWW Pages	Yes
Mount Information on Gopher	Yes
Mount Information on FTP	Yes

RATES:
Call for a quotation.

WINCOM
Windsor, Ontario
wincom.net

4510 Rhodes Drive
Unit 903
Windsor, Ontario
N8W 5K5
Voice: (519) 945-9462
Fax: (519) 944-6610
Internet: info@wincom.net

See the Directory of Canadian Internet Providers for a description of WINCOM.

Set Up an Internet Mailing List	Yes
Set Up a Mail Reflector	Yes
Mount Information on WWW	Yes
Design WWW Pages	Yes
Mount Information on Gopher	Yes
Mount Information on FTP	Yes

RATES:
Call for a quotation.

QUEBEC

Acces Public LLC
Quebec City, Quebec
llc.org

CP 11
Station B
Quebec City, Quebec
G1K 7A1
Voice: (418) 692-4711
Fax: (418) 656-8212
Internet: info@llc.org

See the Directory of Canadian Internet Providers for a description of Acces Public LLC.

Set Up an Internet Mailing List	Yes
Set Up a Mail Reflector	Yes
Mount Information on WWW	Yes
Design WWW Pages	Yes
Mount Information on Gopher	No

Mount Information on FTP	Yes

RATES:
Marketing services are available on demand only. Call for a quotation.

For More Information about Acces Public LLC:

FTP: *World Wide Web:*
ftp.llc.org   *http://www.llc.org*

Communications Accessibles Montréal Inc.
Montreal, Quebec
cam.org

2055 Peel, Suite 825
Montreal, Quebec
H3A 1V4
Voice: (514) 288-2581
Fax: (514) 288-3401
Internet: info@cam.org

See the Directory of Canadian Internet Providers for a description of Communications Accessibles Montréal.

Set Up an Internet Mailing List	Yes
Set Up a Mail Reflector	No
Mount Information on WWW	Yes
Design WWW Pages	No
Mount Information on Gopher	Yes
Mount Information on FTP	Yes

RATES:
Rates are negotiable. Call for a quotation. Registered users may put up their own World Wide Web pages for free in an unsupported manner.

For More Information about CAM:

FTP: *Telnet:*   *Gopher:*   *Finger:*
ftp.cam.org   *cam.org*   *gopher.cam.org*   *info@cam.org*
File: CAM.ORG-info *Login: **info***

World Wide Web:
http://www.cam.org

Communications Inter-Acces
Montreal, Quebec
interax.net

5475 Pare, Suite 104
Montreal, Quebec
H4P 1R4

Voice: (514) 367-0002
Fax: (514) 368-3529
Internet: info@interax.net

See the Directory of Canadian Internet Providers for a description of Communications Inter-Acces.

Set Up an Internet Mailing List	Yes
Set Up a Mail Reflector	No
Mount Information on WWW	Yes
Design WWW Pages	Yes
Mount Information on Gopher	Yes
Mount Information on FTP	Yes

RATES:
Prices are on a per-case basis. Call for a quotation.

For More Information:

Gopher:
gopher.interax.net

Communications Vir
Montreal, Quebec
vir.com

17 Laurier Court
Montreal, Quebec
H9W 4S7
Voice: (514) 933-8886
Fax: (514) 630-9047
Internet: info@vir.com

See the Directory of Canadian Internet Providers for a description of Communications Vir.

Set Up an Internet Mailing List	No
Set Up a Mail Reflector	No
Mount Information on WWW	Yes
Design WWW Pages	Yes
Mount Information on Gopher	Yes
Mount Information on FTP	Yes

RATES:

$25.00 per month for World Wide Web pages, not to exceed 100KB. Statistics provided.
$25.00 per page for creation if all graphics and text are provided in electronic form.
$50.00 per page for creation if printed graphics and text are provided.
$150.00 per page if content has to be generated in its entirety.

For More Information about Communications Vir:

FTP: **World Wide Web:**
ftp.vir.com   *http://www.vir.com/index.html*

Login Informatique

Pierrefonds, Quebec
login.qc.ca, safe.org

4363 Jacques Bizard
Pierrefonds, Quebec
H9H 4W3
Voice: (514) 626-8086
Fax: (514) 626-1700
Internet: diane.nolet@login.qc.ca (Diane Nolet)

See the Directory of Canadian Internet Providers for a description of Login Informatique.

Set Up an Internet Mailing List	Yes
Set Up a Mail Reflector	Yes
Mount Information on WWW	Yes
Design WWW Pages	Yes
Mount Information on Gopher	Yes
Mount Information on FTP	Yes

RATES:
Call for a quotation.

For More Information about Login Informatique:

FTP:
login.qc.ca
Directory: /pub/Login

Metrix Interlink Corporation

Montreal, Quebec
interlink.net, rezonet.net, interlink.ca

500, boul. René-Lévesque Ouest
Suite 1004
Montreal, Quebec
H2Z 1W7
Voice: (514) 875-0010
Fax: (514) 875-5735
Internet: info@interlink.net

See the Directory of Canadian Internet Providers for a description of Metrix Interlink.

Set Up an Internet Mailing List	Yes
Set Up a Mail Reflector	Yes
Mount Information on WWW	Yes
Design WWW Pages	Yes
Mount Information on Gopher	Yes
Mount Information on FTP	Yes

RATES:
$400.00 to $1,000.00 per day.

For More Information about Metrix Interlink:

Gopher:
gopher.interlink.net

World Wide Web:
http://www.interlink.net

RISQ (Reseau Interordinateurs Scientifique Québécois)
Montreal, Quebec
risq.net

Attention: Centre d'information du RISQ
1801 McGill College Avenue, Suite 800
Montreal, Quebec
H3A 2N4
Voice: (514) 398-1234
Fax: (514) 398-1244
Internet: cirisq@risq.net

See the Directory of Canadian Internet Providers for a description of RISQ.

Set Up an Internet Mailing List	Yes
Set Up a Mail Reflector	No
Mount Information on WWW	Yes
Design WWW Pages	No
Mount Information on Gopher	Yes
Mount Information on FTP	Yes

RATES:

Call for a quotation.

For More Information about RISQ:

FTP: **Gopher:**

risq.net   *risq.net*

NOVA SCOTIA

Internet Services and Information Systems Inc. (ISIS)

Halifax, Nova Scotia

isisnet.com

Suite 1501
Maritime Centre
1505 Barrington Street
Halifax, Nova Scotia
Voice: (902) 429-4747
Fax: (902) 429-9003
Internet: info@isisnet.com

See the Directory of Canadian Internet Providers for a description of ISIS.

Set Up an Internet Mailing List	Yes
Set Up a Mail Reflector	Yes
Mount Information on WWW	Yes
Design WWW Pages	Yes
Mount Information on Gopher	Yes
Mount Information on FTP	Yes

RATES:

Gopher entry:	*$40.00 per month*
WWW/Mosaic Page:	*$150.00+ per month*
Gopher entry, local access only:	*$20.00 per month*
WWW/Mosaic page, local access only.	*Call for a quotation*
Listserv mailing list:	*$30.00+ per month*
Newsgroup:	*$40.00+ per month*
Local FTP Site:	*$150.00 per month*
Local disk space for FTP Site:	*$3.00/MB/month*
Mail reflector:	*$10.00 per month*
WWW pages designed and drawn:	*Call for a quotation*

For More Information on ISIS:

Gopher: **World Wide Web:**

ra.isisnet.com   *http://www.isisnet.com*

Nova Scotia Technology Network Inc. (NSTN)

Dartmouth, Nova Scotia

nstn.ca

201 Brownlow Avenue
Dartmouth, Nova Scotia
B3B 1W2
Voice: (902) 481-NSTN (6786)
         1-800-336-4445 (Toll-Free Canada-Wide)
Fax: (902) 468-3579
Internet: info@nstn.ca (Automated)
         sales@nstn.ca (Sales/Marketing Team)

See the Directory of Canadian Internet Providers for a description of NSTN.

Set Up an Internet Mailing List	Yes
Set Up a Mail Reflector	Yes
Mount Information on WWW	Yes
Design WWW Pages	Yes
Mount Information on Gopher	Yes
Mount Information on FTP	Yes

RATES:
Rates are customized. Call for a quotation.

For More Information about NSTN:

FTP: *Gopher:*
ftp.nstn.ca   *gopher.nstn.ca*
Directory:/nstn-documentation/

World Wide Web:
http://www.nstn.ca

NEW BRUNSWICK

Cybersmith Inc.

Sackville, New Brunswick

csi.nb.ca

83 Queen's Road
Sackville, New Brunswick
E0A 3C0
Voice: (506) 536-0134
Fax: (506) 536-0228
Internet: info@csi.nb.ca

Cybersmith Inc. specializes in producing Internet display and information packages for corporate and government organizations. We pride ourselves on our ability to deliver innovative and cost-

effective Internet marketing solutions. Cybersmith believes in being part of the community and has produced, and continues to display, a number of public access/community service information systems free of charge.

Cybersmith offers a comprehensive range of consulting services tuned specifically to our clients needs. We often find that a combination of training and market research is required. Consequently, Cybersmith provides marketing studies (Internet demographics, competitive analysis, cost/benefit breakdowns etc). Our Internet displays are designed to return sales leads and orders electronically to our clients - we offer assistance in organizing the procedures to handle this influx. Cybersmith offers its clients the necessary assistance to ensure they get the maximum advantage from their presence on the Internet.

Cybersmith is committed to continuously working with its clients to ensure they derive the maximum benefit from their Internet display investment. We offer assistance in composing press releases, and advice in tactfully using the Internet for marketing. Statistics from the server are returned to our clients weekly - we provide advice and assistance in processing this extremely useful marketing data. Cybersmith believes it is our job to ensure that our clients' information is viewed by as many people as possible per day and actively builds this traffic by placing a considerable amount of public service information on our server along with our clients' displays.

Services can operate under Cybersmith's domain name or the preferred domain name of the client. Domain registration service is available.

Set Up an Internet Mailing List	Yes
Set Up a Mail Reflector	Yes
Mount Information on WWW	Yes
Design WWW Pages	Yes
Mount Information on Gopher	Yes
Mount Information on FTP	Yes

RATES:

For larger projects involving more complicated facilities such as database search and retrieval, multiple page layouts, custom script engines or large amounts of disk space/network traffic, quotes are on a per-project basis.

For less complex displays (one or two pages with text and graphics) the price includes a nominal one-time charge to construct the display and $50.00-60.00 per month to serve it to the public. This price could also include an automated e-mail response facility that allows viewers to send orders/comments to the information provider.

For More Information about Cybersmith:

World Wide Web:
http://www.csi.nb.ca/

Cygnus Technology Limited

Fredericton, New Brunswick
cygnus.nb.ca

154 Main Street
Fredericton, New Brunswick
E3A 1C8

Voice: (506) 459-4606
Fax: (506) 452-9321
Internet: ferguson@cygnus.nb.ca

Cygnus Technology Ltd. is a small systems integrator specializing in telecommunications. Cygnus also provides commercial Internet services in the form of an "electronic mall" - a medium where a company can advertise its services and products to the world. Cygnus Technology's business activity is spread around the world - focusing at this time in Kuwait, South America, Central America and North America.

Set Up an Internet Mailing List	Yes
Set Up a Mail Reflector	Yes
Mount Information on WWW	Yes
Design WWW Pages	Yes
Mount Information on Gopher	Yes
Mount Information on FTP	Yes

RATES:

To place products and services in Cygnus Technology's Electronic Mall:
$500.00/MB start-up fee. $50.00/MB/month rental fee.
These prices are discounted for large quantities of information.

For More Information about Cygnus Technology:

Gopher: **World Wide Web:**
gopher.cygnus.nb.ca   *http://www.cygnus.nb.ca*

Maritime Internet Services

Saint John, New Brunswick
mi.net

1216 Sand Cove Road
P.O. Box 6477
Saint John, New Brunswick
E2L 4R9
Voice: (506) 652-3624
Fax: (506) 652-5451
Internet: info@mi.net

See the Directory of Canadian Internet Providers for a description of Maritime Internet Services.

Set Up an Internet Mailing List	Yes
Set Up a Mail Reflector	Yes
Mount Information on WWW	Yes
Design WWW Pages	Yes

Mount Information on Gopher	Yes
Mount Information on FTP	Yes

RATES:

Internet Mailing List:
$20.00 per month. $50.00/year/100 users.

World Wide Web Page Rental:
$20.00 per month. $120.00/year/megabyte.

World Wide Web Page Design:
$50.00 per hour includes scanning images.

Gopher Pages:
$20.00 per month. $120.00/year/megabyte.

FTP Information:
$2.00/megabyte/month or $20.00/MB/year.

Mail Reflector:
$10.00 per month. $100.00 per year per mail reflector ID.

For More Information about Maritime Internet Services:

FTP:
ftp.mi.net
Directory: /pub/info

Telnet:
mi.net
Login: **info**

Gopher:
gopher.mi.net

World Wide Web:
http://www.mi.net

Nova Scotia Technology Network Inc. (NSTN)
Dartmouth, Nova Scotia
nstn.ca

201 Brownlow Avenue
Dartmouth, Nova Scotia
B3B 1W2
Voice: (902) 481-NSTN (6786)
               1-800-336-4445 (Toll-Free Canada-Wide)
Fax: (902) 468-3579
Internet: info@nstn.ca (Automated)
               sales@nstn.ca (Sales/Marketing Team)

Areas Served: Moncton, Dieppe, Riverview, Salisbury
See main entry under Nova Scotia

PRINCE EDWARD ISLAND

PEINet Inc.
Charlottetown, Prince Edward Island
peinet.pe.ca

P.O. Box 3126
Charlottetown, Prince Edward Island
C1A 7N9

Voice: (902) 892-PEINet (7346)
Fax: (902) 368-2446
Internet: admin@peinet.pe.ca

See the Directory of Canadian Internet Providers for a description of PEINet.

Set Up an Internet Mailing List	Yes
Set Up a Mail Reflector	Yes
Mount Information on WWW	Yes
Design WWW Pages	Yes
Mount Information on Gopher	Yes
Mount Information on FTP	Yes

RATES:
Rates vary depending on requirements. Call for a quotation.

For More Information on PEINet:

World Wide Web: *Gopher:*
http://bud.peinet.pe.ca   *gopher.peinet.pe.ca*

Raven Information Systems
Charlottetown, Prince Edward Island
raven.net

P.O. Box 2906
Charlottetown, Prince Edward Island
C1A 8C5
Voice: (902) 894-4946
Internet: dale_poole@raven.net

See the Directory of Canadian Internet Providers for a description of Raven Information Systems.

Set Up an Internet Mailing List	Yes
Set Up a Mail Reflector	Yes
Mount Information on WWW	No
Design WWW Pages	No
Mount Information on Gopher	No
Mount Information on FTP	No

RATES:
Call for a quotation.

NEWFOUNDLAND

STEM~Net

St. John's, Newfoundland
stemnet.nf.ca

STEM~Net
Memorial University of Newfoundland
E-5038, G.A. Hickman Building
St. John's, Newfoundland
A1B 3X8
Voice: (709) 737-8836
Fax: (709) 737-2179
Internet: staff@calvin.stemnet.nf.ca

See the Directory of Canadian Internet Providers for a description of STEM~Net.

Set Up an Internet Mailing List	Yes
Set Up a Mail Reflector	Yes
Mount Information on WWW	Yes
Design WWW Pages	Yes
Mount Information on Gopher	Yes
Mount Information on FTP	Yes

RATES:

Free for registered STEM~Net users. Use of STEM~Net is restricted to Newfoundland-based K-12 educators, rural public-college educators in Newfoundland, members of the Memorial University of Newfoundland's Faculty of Education, and education students at the Memorial University of Newfoundland. Projects using the above services must be approved by STEM~Net's director and must meet STEM~Net's mandate and goals.

For More Information about STEM~Net:

Gopher:
info.stemnet.nf.ca

World Wide Web:
http://info.stemnet.nf.ca

DOMESTIC PROVIDERS SERVING MORE THAN ONE PROVINCE

Advantis Canada
Markham, Ontario
ibm.net

3500 Steeles Avenue East
Markham, Ontario
L3R 2Z1
Voice: Canada Toll-Free 1-800-268-3100
Fax: (905) 316-6967
Internet: connect@vnet.ibm.com

See the Directory of Canadian Internet Providers for a description of Advantis Canada.

Set Up an Internet Mailing List	No
Set Up a Mail Reflector	No
Mount Information on WWW	Yes
Design WWW Pages	Yes
Mount Information on Gopher	Yes
Mount Information on FTP	Yes

For More Information about Advantis Canada:

Gopher:
gopher.advantis.com

World Wide Web:
http://www.ibm.com

RATES:
Call for a quotation.

fONOROLA
Ottawa, Ontario
fonorola.net, fonorola.ca, fonorola.com

250 Albert Street, Suite 205
Ottawa, Ontario
K1P 6M1
Voice: (604) 683-3666 (Vancouver)
             (403) 269-3666 (Calgary)
             (416) 364-3666 (Toronto)
             (519) 642-3666 (London)
             (519) 741-3666 (Kitchener)
             (613) 235-3666 (Ottawa)
             (514) 954-3666 (Montreal)
             (716) 856-3666 (Buffalo)
Fax: (613) 232-4329
Internet: info@fonorola.net
             sales@fonorola.net

See the Directory of Canadian Internet Providers for a description of fONOROLA.

Set Up an Internet Mailing List	Yes
Set Up a Mail Reflector	Yes
Mount Information on WWW	Yes
Design WWW Pages	No
Mount Information on Gopher	Yes
Mount Information on FTP	Yes

RATES:

Gopher or Mosaic Server Application.

Purchase storage on fONOROLA's servers. Maintained by fONOROLA staff 24 hours a day, 7 days a week. Sun SPARC2 compatible.

2.4GB hard drive.

Ethernet attached to Internet:
$250.00 per month plus $300.00 set up fee.

Storage 0-5 MB:
$40.00 per month plus $1.00/MB/month transfer.

Storage 5-25 MB:
$120.00 per month plus $1.00/MB/month transfer.

Storage 25-50 MB:
$200.00 per month plus $1.00/MB/month transfer.

Storage 50-100 MB:
$300.00 per month plus $1.00/MB/month transfer.

Consulting:
(Internet Specialist, Unix Specialist, Communications Specialist, PC Specialist)
$90.00 per hour. Minimum 4 hours.

For More Information about fONOROLA:

FTP: **Gopher:**
ftp.fonorola.net   *gopher.fonorola.net*

UUNET Canada Inc.

Toronto, Ontario
uunet.ca

1 Yonge Street, Suite 1400
Toronto, Ontario
M5E 1J9
Voice: (416) 368-6621
             1-800-INET-123
Fax: (416) 368-1350
Internet: info@uunet.ca

See the Directory of Canadian Internet Providers for a description of UUNET Canada.

Set Up an Internet Mailing List	Yes
Set Up a Mail Reflector	Yes
Mount Information on WWW	Yes
Design WWW Pages	Yes
Mount Information on Gopher	Yes
Mount Information on FTP	Yes

RATES:
Call for a quotation.

For More Information about UUNET Canada:

FTP:
ftp.uunet.ca

World Wide Web:
http://www.uunet.ca/

WEB
Toronto, Ontario
web.apc.org, web.net

c/o NirvCentre
401 Richmond Street West, Suite 104
Toronto, Ontario
M5V 3A8
Voice: (416) 596-0212
Fax: (416) 596-1374
Internet: support@web.apc.org

See the Directory of Canadian Internet Providers for a description of Web.

Set Up an Internet Mailing List	Yes
Set Up a Mail Reflector	Yes
Mount Information on WWW	Yes
Design WWW Pages	Yes
Mount Information on Gopher	Yes
Mount Information on FTP	Yes

RATES:
Prices vary depending on the size and scope of the project. Call for a quotation.

For More Information about Web:

FTP:
spinne.web.net
Directory: pub
File: web-info.txt

Gopher:
spinne.web.net

WorldLinx Telecommunications
Toronto, Ontario
worldlinx.com, resonet.com

BCE Place
181 Bay Street
Suite 350
P.O. Box 851
Toronto, Ontario
M5J 2T3
Voice: (416) 350-1000
              1-800-567-1811
Fax: (416) 350-1001
Internet: info@worldlinx.com

See the Directory of Canadian Internet Providers for a description of WorldLinx.

Set Up an Internet Mailing List	Yes
Set Up a Mail Reflector	Yes
Mount Information on WWW	Yes
Design WWW Pages	Yes
Mount Information on Gopher	Yes
Mount Information on FTP	Yes

RATES:
Specialized service pricing is available on request. Call for a quotation.

For More Information on WorldLinx:

FTP: **Gopher:**
ftp.worldlinx.com   *gopher.worldlinx.com*

World Tel Internet Canada
Vancouver, British Columbia
worldtel.com

Suite 810 - 675 West Hastings Street
Vancouver, British Columbia
V6B 1N2
Voice: (604) 685-3877
Fax: (604) 687-0688
Internet: info@worldtel.com

See the Directory of Canadian Internet Providers for a description of World Tel.

Set Up an Internet Mailing List	Yes

Set Up a Mail Reflector	Yes
Mount Information on WWW	Yes
Design WWW Pages	Yes
Mount Information on Gopher	Yes
Mount Information on FTP	Yes

RATES:
Prices are on a project-by-project basis. Call for a quotation.

For More Information on World Tel:

Gopher:
trianon.worldtel.com

World Wide Web:
http://www.worldtel.com

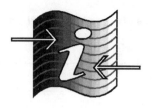

A P P E N D I X   L

....

THE DIRECTORY OF CANADIAN INTERNET RESOURCES

This is a directory of Internet resources that pertain to Canada. Each entry in this directory contains the name of the resource, a brief description of the resource, and instructions that describe how you can access the resource using the Internet, using tools such as electronic mail, USENET, the World Wide Web, Gopher, and anonymous FTP, which have been discussed in previous chapters.

HOW TO SUBMIT INFORMATION FOR THE DIRECTORY OF CANADIAN INTERNET RESOURCES:
Contributions to this directory are welcome. If your favourite Canadian Internet resource does not appear in this directory, please contact us at **<handbook@uunet.ca>** so that we can include it in future revisions of this directory.

ARCHIVAL ISSUES IN CANADA DISCUSSION FORUM

A mailing list for the discussion of Canadian archives and related subjects.

HOW TO ACCESS:

Send a message to **listserv@vm.ucs.ualberta.ca** and place the following command on the first line of the body of the message:
subscribe arcan-l <FirstName> <LastName>
e.g. subscribe arcan-1 John Smith

BEER LOVER'S GUIDE TO ONTARIO

Everything you ever wanted to know about beer in Ontario! Includes information about brewery tours in Ontario, a list of Ontario beers, and books that cover the Ontario beer industry. This guide also recommends some good pubs in Ontario. Posted regularly to the USENET newsgroup **rec.food.drink.beer**.

HOW TO ACCESS:

Available by annonymous FTP:
FTP site: **sierra.stanford.edu**
Directory: **pub/homebrew/rfdb**
File: **beer_ontario.faq.Z**

BOTANICAL ELECTRONIC NEWS MAILING LIST

Botanical Electronic News is a newsletter distributed on electronic mail. It covers the botany and plant ecology of predominantly British Columbia, Canada, and the Pacific Northwest with broader reference to planet Earth. It is published approximately once every two weeks. The newsletter is also distributed in the USENET newsgroup **bio.plants**.

HOW TO ACCESS:

Requests for subscription should be sent to the owner: Adolf Ceska, **aceska@freenet.victoria.bc.ca**.

BRITISH COLUMBIA LEGISLATURE BBS

This service is used to distribute information about the proceedings of the British Columbia Legislature.

HOW TO ACCESS:

Telnet: **bbs.qp.gov.bc.ca**
Also available by anonymous FTP:
Site: **bbs.qp.gov.bc.ca**

CANADIAN UFO SURVEY, 1992

This document, published by Ufology Research of Manitoba, documents and analyzes UFO sightings across Canada in 1992.

HOW TO ACCESS:

Gopher: **wiretap.spies.com**
Select: /Wiretap Online Library/Fringes of Reason/UFOs and Mysterious Abductions

1992 REPORT ON CROP CIRCLES AND RELATED TRACES

This document, published by the North American Institute for Crop Circle Research in Winnipeg, documents and analyzes reports of unusual ground markings (UGMs) in North America in 1992.

HOW TO ACCESS:

Gopher: **wiretap.spies.com**
Select: /Wiretap Online Library/Fringes of Reason/UFOs and Mysterious Abductions

CANADA GAZETTE MAILING LIST

This mailing list distributes excerpts from the Canada Gazette that are relevant to the communications sector of Industry Canada.

HOW TO ACCESS:

To subscribe to the mailing list, send an electronic mail message to **listserv@debra.dgbt.doc.ca**, and put the following command on the first line of the body of the message:
subscribe gazette-list <First Name> <Last Name>
e.g. subscribe gazette-list John Smith
To unsubscribe from this list, send the message:
unsubscribe gazette-list to **listserv@debra.dgbt.doc.ca**
Archives of the Gazette notices are available by anonymous FTP:
Site: **debra.dgbt.doc.ca**
Directory: **/pub/isc/gazette**

CA DOMAIN DOCUMENTS

Here you will find a complete list of organizations registered in the CA Domain (organized by name and by subdomain), a list of members on the CA Domain Committee, CA Domain Statistics, an overview and history of the CA Domain, and a CA Domain application form.

HOW TO ACCESS:

Anonymous FTP: **ftp.cdnnet.ca**
Directory: **ca-domain**

CANADIANA RESOURCES SERVER

An assortment of Internet resources that pertain to Canada.

HOW TO ACCESS:

World Wide Web:
http://www.cs.cmu.edu:8001/afs/cs.cmu.edu/user/clamen/misc/Canadiana

CBC Radio Information

The Canadian Broadcasting Corporation, in cooperation with the Communications Research Centre in Ottawa, is making programming information available over the Internet. You can retrieve a selection of CBC Radio programs in digital form ("au" format) from popular CBC shows such as Quirks and Quarks, Basic Black, Sunday Morning, Cross Country Check Up, and Brand X. Audio files of daily CBC News broadcasts are also available. You can also find program schedules for CBC Radio Ottawa, a list of transcripts available from CBC Radio, and a list of CBC Radio products.

HOW TO ACCESS:

Gopher: **debra.dgbt.doc.ca** Select: CBC Radio Trial
Anonymous FTP: **debra.dgbt.doc.ca** Directory: **/pub/cbc**
World Wide Web: **http://debra.dgbt.doc.ca/cbc/cbc.html**
Comments about this service can be sent to **cbc@debra.dgbt.doc.ca**.

Canadian Business and the Internet Discussion Forum

A mailing list has been established to discuss how Canadian businesses can make effective use of the Internet.

HOW TO ACCESS:

To subscribe to the mailing list, send an electronic mail message to **listserv@nstn.ca** and put the following command in the body of the message:
subscribe enterprise-l <First Name> <Last Name>
e.g. subscribe enterprise-l John Smith
To unsubscribe from this list, send the message:
unsubscribe enterprise-l to **listserv@nstn.ca**

Canadian Campus Radio Stations on the Internet

Several Canadian campus radio stations have a presence on the Internet. They include:
CFRC-FM 101.9 Radio Queen's University
<plunketm@qucdn.queensu.ca>
CFUV Radio, Victoria, B.C.
<cfuv@sol.uvic.ca>
<ur860@freenet.victoria.bc.ca>
CHMR-FM, Memorial University of Newfoundland
<chmr@morgan.ucs.mun.ca>
CKMS-FM, University of Waterloo
<ckmsfm@web.apc.org>
World Association of Community Radio Broadcasters (Montreal, Quebec)
<amarc@web.apc.org>

To add a campus radio station to this list, please contact the authors at **handbook@uunet.ca**

CANADIAN HEALTH LIBRARIES DISCUSSION FORUM

A mailing list for the discussion of issues that relate to Canadian health sciences libraries.

HOW TO ACCESS:

To subscribe to the mailing list, send an electronic mail message to **listserver@morgan.ucs.mun.ca**, and put the following command in the body of the message: **subscribe CANMEDLIB**
To cancel your subscription to this list, send the command: **unsubscribe CANMEDLIB** to **listserver@morgan.ucs.mun.ca**

CANADIAN GOVERNMENT INFORMATION DISCUSSION FORUM

A mailing list for the discussion of Canadian government information at all levels of government.

HOW TO ACCESS:

To join the mailing list, send an electronic mail message to **mailserv@sask.usask.ca** and place the following command on the first line of the body of the message: **subscribe govinfo <YOUR NAME>**
e.g. subscribe govinfo John Smith
To remove yourself from the GOVINFO mailing list, send an electronic mail message to **mailserv@sask.usask.ca** with the command **unsubscribe govinfo**

CANADIAN INFORMATION HIGHWAY ARCHIVE

A collection of documents relating to Canada's information highway. This site is provided by Industry Canada.

HOW TO ACCESS:

Gopher: **debra.dgbt.doc.ca**
Select: Industry Canada Documents/Canadian Information Highway

CANADIAN INFORMATION HIGHWAY MAILING LIST

A mailing list for the discussion of the development of the information highway in Canada.

HOW TO ACCESS:

To join the mailing list, send an electronic mail message to **listprocessor@cunews.carleton.ca** with the following command on the first line

of the body of the message: **subscribe Pac-Hiway <Your Name>**
e.g. subscribe Pac-Hiway John Smith

CANADIAN METEOROLOGICAL CENTRE INFORMATION

Weather forecasts, maps, forecasts, and charts, primarily for the Province of Ontario.

HOW TO ACCESS:

Gopher: **cmits02.dow.on.doe.ca**

CANADIAN GOVERNMENT DOCUMENTS

This archive contains the text of the Canadian Constitution Act, Meech Lake Accord, Charlottetown Constitutional Agreement, and excerpts from Canada's Constitutional Act.

HOW TO ACCESS:

Gopher: **wiretap.spies.com**
Select: /Government Docs (U.S. and World)/Canadian Documents

CANADIAN EDUCATION LIBRARY ISSUES MAILING LIST

For the discussion of issues affecting Canadian education libraries.

HOW TO ACCESS:

Send an electronic mail message to **listserv@dewey.ed.brocku.ca** and put the following command on the first line of the body of the message:
subscribe OTELA-L <First Name> <Last Name>
e.g. subscribe otela-l John Smith
To unsubscribe from this list, send the message **unsubscribe OTELA-L** to **listserv@dewey.ed.brocku.ca**

CANADIAN FOOTBALL - FREQUENTLY ASKED QUESTIONS

This document looks at the history and rules of the CFL. It includes a directory of CFL teams, including mailing addresses, team colours, stadium capacities, and Grey Cup wins. There is even a section on esoteric CFL records. A must-read for every CFL fan! It is updated periodically, and posted to the USENET group **rec.sport.football.canadian**. The maintainer of this document is Michael Burger **<mmb@lamar.colostate.edu>**, who describes himself as a "CFL-crazy American who just has a tad too much free time."

HOW TO ACCESS:

Anonymous FTP: **rtfm.mit.edu**
Directory: **/pub/usenet-by-group/news.answers**
File: **canadian-football**

CANADIAN FOOTBALL LEAGUE SERVER

Information on the Canadian Football League, including the television broadcast schedule, a glossary of CFL terms, referee's signals, and the history of the Canadian Football League.

HOW TO ACCESS:

World Wide Web: **http://www.cfl.ca**

CANADIAN FREE-NET DISCUSSION FORUM

A mailing list for the discussion of community computer networks in Canada.

HOW TO ACCESS:

To join this mailing list, send an electronic mail message to **listserv@cunews.carleton.ca** with the following command on the first line of the body of the message: **subscribe can-freenet <Your Name>**
e.g. subscribe can-freenet John Smith

CANADIAN GEOGRAPHICAL NAMES DATABASE

This service is sponsored by the Geographical Names Section of the Canadian Centre for Mapping, Ministry of Natural Resources. You can search Canada's official geographical names database, and obtain information about the Canadian Permanent Committee on Geographical Names (CPCGN).

HOW TO ACCESS:

World Wide Web: **http://www-nais.ccm.emr.ca/cgndb/geonames.html**

CANADIAN INFORMATION PROCESSING SOCIETY (CIPS) DISCUSSION FORUM

A discussion forum for the Canadian Information Processing Society.

HOW TO ACCESS:

To join this mailing list, send an electronic mail message to **listserv@unb.ca** with the following command in the first line of the body of the message: **subscribe cips-l <Your Name>**
e.g. subscribe cips-l John Smith

NEWSLETTER OF THE CANADIAN INSTITUTE OF RESOURCES LAW

This newsletter provides information on current resources law issues and Institute publications and programs.

HOW TO ACCESS:

World Wide Web: **http://www.waikato.ac.nz/law/resource.html**

CANADIAN INVESTMENTS DISCUSSION FORUM

A USENET group for the discussion of investment in Canadian financial markets.

HOW TO ACCESS:

USENET: **misc.invest.canada**

CANADIAN ISSUES FORUM

This is a mailing list for the discussion of political, social, cultural, and economic issues in Canada. There are over 300 subscribers.

HOW TO ACCESS:

To subscribe to this mailing list, send an electronic mail message to **listserv@vm1.mcgill.ca** and put the following command on the first line of the body of the message:
subscribe canada-l <First Name> <Last Name>
e.g. subscribe canada-l John Smith
To remove yourself from this list, send the message **unsubscribe canada-l** to **listserv@vm1.mcgill.ca**

CANADIAN SUPREME COURT DECISIONS

The University of Montreal Law Gopher contains the full text of Canadian Supreme Court decisions and Supreme Court Bulletins, and a searchable Supreme Court decisions index. The documents are available in text (ASCII) format, Macintosh MS-Word 4.0 format, and WordPerfect 5.1 format. Supreme Court decisions will be made available on this server within 24 hours of the decision being announced.

HOW TO ACCESS:

Gopher: **gopher.droit.umontreal.ca**
Select: English Version of This Gopher/Supreme Court of Canada
            (Experimental)

CANADIAN WEATHER FORECASTS

Current weather forecasts for all the provinces and territories.

HOW TO ACCESS:

Gopher: **gopher.nstn.ca**
Select: NSTN CyberMall - Information Kiosks/Canadian Weather Forecasts

CANADIAN WEATHER FORECASTS

More Canadian weather information, from the University of Illinois Weather Machine.

HOW TO ACCESS:

Gopher: **wx.atmos.uiuc.edu**
Select: Canada

CBC RADIO DISCUSSION FORUM

General discussion about CBC Radio.

HOW TO ACCESS:

USENET: **alt.radio.networks.cbc**

DIRTY LINEN FOLK MUSIC CALENDAR

Dirty Linen is a magazine of folk, electric folk, traditional and world music. Dirty Linen Magazine makes its folk music calendar available on the Internet each month. The calendar contains a list of folk music concerts in Canada and the United States, updated monthly.

HOW TO ACCESS:

Anonymous FTP: **nysernet.org**
Directory: **folk_music/dirty_linen**
File: **DLCALxxx.TXT**

where **xxx** is the monthly abbreviation e.g. DLCALFEB.TXT

DISABILITY ISSUES IN CANADIAN LIBRARIES

This is a discussion forum, sponsored by the National Library Advisory Group on Library Services for Disabled People. Its purpose is to discuss disability issues relating to library services and access to information. Canadian librarians and other interested parties are welcome to join.

HOW TO ACCESS:

To join this discussion list, send an electronic mail message to **mailserv@nlc-bnc.ca**. In the body of the message, place the command **subscribe acs-can-l** To unsubscribe from this list, send the message **unsubscribe acs-can-l** to **mailserv@nlc-bnc.ca**

EARTHQUAKES IN CANADA

What was the largest earthquake in Canada this century? How many earthquakes are recorded in Canada each year? What is the most active earthquake region in Canada? This document, prepared by the Geological Survey of Canada, answers these questions and more.

HOW TO ACCESS:

Gopher: **gopher.emr.ca**
Select: /NRCan-Info (English)/Geological Survey of Canada (GSC)/ABOUT the Geological Survey of Canada/Geophysics Division/Earthquakes in Canada

ENERGY EFFICIENT HOUSING IN CANADA

An archive of information about environmentally-responsible housing in Canada.

HOW TO ACCESS:

World Wide Web: **http://web.cs.ualberta.ca/~art/house/**

GAME SHOWS IN CANADA

A list of Canadian game shows and their hosts, posted regularly to the Usenet groups **alt.tv.game-shows**, **rec.arts.tv**, **alt.answers**, **rec.answers**, **news.answers**

HOW TO ACCESS:

Available by anonymous FTP.
Site: **rtfm.mit.edu**
Directory: **pub/usenet-by-group/news.answers/tv/game-shows**
File: **canada**

FALCON LAKE CASE

This is a survey of the research and literature surrounding the Falcon Lake Case, an incident which occurred on May 20, 1967. A person claimed to have been burned by a strange craft, just north of the town of Falcon Lake, Manitoba. A re-creation of this story was broadcast on Unsolved Mysteries in 1992 and 1993. According to the author of this research paper, "although largely unknown, the case may be the most significant in North America because of the intense investigation by the United States Air Force, the Royal Canadian Air Force, the Royal Canadian Mounted Police, and civilian groups, and because of the amount of physical evidence and physiological effects on the witness."

HOW TO ACCESS:

Anonymous FTP: **ftp.rutgers.edu**
Directory: **/pub/ufo**
File: **falcon-lake.1967.Z**
(you need to uncompress this file)

FREQUENTLY ASKED QUESTIONS ABOUT CANADA

This document is regularly posted monthly on the USENET group **soc.culture.canada**. It contains questions and answers on such topics as Canadian History (e.g. When was Canada discovered?), Canadian Politics (e.g. Who were Canada's Prime Ministers?), Canadian Society and Culture (e.g. Do Canadians use British or American spelling?, Why isn't the Canadian Thanksgiving the same day as the American Thanksgiving?), Canadian Education (e.g. What Canadian universities offer programs in Canadian Studies?), and Canadian Business (e.g. How can I start a business in Canada?). This document is maintained by Martin Savard **<ag656@freenet.carleton.ca>**.

HOW TO ACCESS:

Anonymous FTP: **rtfm.mit.edu**
Directory: **/pub/usenet-by-group/news.answers/canada-faq**
Files: **part1, part2**

GOVERNMENT INFORMATION IN CANADA ELECTRONIC NEWSLETTER

A quarterly electronic journal for the discussion and study of Canadian federal, provincial/territorial, and local government information.

HOW TO ACCESS:

World Wide Web: **http://www.usask.ca/library/gic/index.html**

GUIDE TO VEGETARIANISM IN CANADA

This guide contains a list of vegetarian restaurants, vegetarian-friendly restaurants, natural food stores, and vegetarian organizations, and other items of interest to Canadian vegetarians.

HOW TO ACCESS:

Anonymous FTP: **rtfm.mit.edu**
Directory: **/pub/usenet-by-group/news.answers/vegetarian/guide**
Files: **canada1, canada2**

HALIFAX DAILY NEWS ON-LINE

An on-line version of the Halifax Daily News, a daily newspaper in Halifax, Nova Scotia.

HOW TO ACCESS:
World Wide Web:
http://www.cfn.cs.dal.ca/Media/TodaysNews/TodaysNews.html

HEALTHNET MAILING LIST

HEALTHNET is an Internet forum for the discussion of issues surrounding high speed networking initiatives focusing on (but not specific to) Canadian health care. Potential uses of HEALTHNET include the discussion of the use of networks for health care applications (e.g. Medical Electronic Data Interchange), and announcements of programs involving computer networks and Canadian health care facilities. Anyone with an interest in the area of networking and health care (e.g. health care personnel and administrators, physicians, technologists, government officials) is invited to join the discussion.

HOW TO ACCESS:

To subscribe to the list, send an electronic mail message to **listserv@debra.dgbt.doc.ca**, and put the following command on the first line of the body of the message: **subscribe healthnet <First Name> <Last Name>**
e.g. subscribe healthnet John Smith
To remove yourself from this list, send the message **unsubscribe healthnet** to **listserv@debra.dgbt.doc.ca**

HORTICULTURE INFORMATION SERVICE

The Department of Horticulture at the University of Saskatchewan has produced over 40 fact sheets on horticultural topics. Topics include: "Earthworms: Friend or Foe?," "Facts about Potatoes," and "Saskatchewan's Edible Wild Fruits and Nuts."

HOW TO ACCESS:

Gopher: **gopher.usask.ca**
Select: /Other/Horticulture Information

INDUSTRY CANADA NEWS

Industry Canada News is a mailing list for the distribution of news releases and fact sheets issued to the public by the Communications Canada branch of Industry Canada. The news releases are information that has been issued to the public and media about decisions made by the Canadian government regarding communications policy. The fact sheets are for the announcement of developments in communications technology and related applications in Canada.

HOW TO ACCESS:

To subscribe to this list, send an electronic mail message to **listserv@debra.dgbt.doc.ca,** and put the following command on the first line of the body of the message:

subscribe iscnews <First Name> <Last Name>

e.g. subscribe iscnews John Smith

To unsubscribe from this list, send the message: **unsubscribe iscnews** to **listserv@debra.dgbt.doc.ca**

Archives of the ISCNEWS are available by anonymous FTP:

Site: **debra.dgbt.doc.ca**

Directory: **pub/isc/Industry.Canada.News.Releases**

LIBRARY JOBS IN ATLANTIC CANADA MAILING LIST

For the announcement of job openings for graduates in the field of library and information studies. All postings will be for the announcements for such positions within Atlantic Canada. Job listings received electronically, or by mail or fax directed to the School of Library and Information Studies at Dalhousie University, will be posted on the list as soon as they are received.

HOW TO ACCESS:

To subscribe to this list, send an electronic mail message to **mailserv@ac.dal.ca,** and put the following command on the first line of the body of the message: **subscribe lis-joblist**

MACLEAN'S MAGAZINE

Information about Maclean's Magazine, Canada's weekly newsmagazine, from the Internet's Electronic Newsstand. This service contains sample articles from the current issue, sample articles from past issues, pricing and subscription information, and an on-line order form. Subscribe to Maclean's Magazine on the Internet! Send a message to **macleans@enews.com** to start your subscription, and include your name and postal address.

HOW TO ACCESS:

Gopher: **gopher.enews.com**

Select: Magazines, Periodicals and Journals (all titles)/All Titles Listed
          Alphabetically/Titles from M to R/Maclean's

METEORITES IN CANADA

How much will the Geological Survey of Canada pay you if you find the first specimen of a Canadian meteorite? This document, prepared by the Geological Survey of Canada, gives an overview of meteorites and their importance, and tells you what to do if you happen to find one in Canada.

HOW TO ACCESS:

Gopher: **gopher.emr.ca**
Select: /NRCan-Info (English)/Geological Survey of Canada (GSC)/What
services we provide/Identification Services/Meteorites

MONTREAL CANADIENS MAILING LIST

A mailing list for the discussion of the Montreal Canadiens.

HOW TO ACCESS:

To join the mailing list, send a message to: **habs-request@cse.ucsc.edu** and ask
to join.

MONTREAL CANADIENS WWW PAGE

For fans of the Montreal Canadiens! This site contains vital team statistics,
uniform information, team and player nicknames, team awards, team schedules,
ticket information, and much more.

HOW TO ACCESS:

World Wide Web: **http://www.pipeline.com:80/~amir/habs/**

MONTREAL EXPOS WWW SERVER

This site contains team statistics, the team history, and general information about
the Montreal Expos.

HOW TO ACCESS:

World Wide Web: **http://www.nando.net/baseball/bbs/bbhome/mon.html**

MUSIC IN CANADA DISCUSSION FORUM

A USENET group for the discussion of the Canadian music scene.

HOW TO ACCESS:

USENET: **alt.music.canada**

NATIONAL LIBRARY OF CANADA MAILING LIST

This list is for announcements from the National Library of Canada.

HOW TO ACCESS:

To join this mailing list, send an electronic mail message to **mailserv@nlc-bnc.ca**
and place the following command on the first line of the body of the message:
subscribe info-l

To cancel your subscription to this mailing list, send an electronic mail message to **mailserv@nlc-bnc.ca** with the command **unsubscribe info-l** in the body of the message.

NORTH AMERICAN FREE TRADE AGREEMENT

The text of the North American Free Trade Agreement.

HOW TO ACCESS:

Gopher: **wiretap.spies.com**
Select: Government Docs (US and World)/North American Free Trade
          Agreement

NORTH BAY, ONTARIO WWW SERVER

Everything you ever wanted to know about North Bay, Ontario, including information about weather, history, attractions, recreational facilities, accommodations, entertainment, dining, labour statistics, economic statistics, social services, health care, transportation facilities, and much much more.

HOW TO ACCESS:

World Wide Web: **http://www.canadorec.on.ca/northbay.html**

NORTH PACIFIC MARINE SCIENCE ORGANIZATION (PICES) MAILING LIST

The Convention for the establishment of the North Pacific Marine Science Organization came into force on March 24, 1992. Canada is one of the four contracting countries. The organization is concerned with marine scientific research in the North Pacific Ocean and adjacent seas, especially north of 30 degrees north. Messages from the organization's bulletin board are periodically sent out to Internet users via the mailing list.

HOW TO ACCESS

To be added to the mailing list, send a request by electronic mail to the PICES Secretariat at **PICES@ios.bc.ca**.

NEW BRUNSWICK 1994-1995 BUDGET

The 1994-1995 budget for the Province of New Brunswick. The budget speech and other related documents are also available at the same site.

HOW TO ACCESS:

Available by anonymous FTP:
DOS/Windows:
Site: **ftp.gov.nb.ca**
Directory: **nb.gov.info/legislature/budget94**

File:	**budget.zip**
Macintosh:	
Site:	**ftp.gov.nb.ca**
Directory:	**nb.gov.info/legislature/budget94**
File:	**budget.sit.hqx**

NEW BRUNSWICK ELECTRONIC HIGHWAY DISCUSSION PAPER

This is the report of the New Brunswick Task Force on the Electronic Information Highway, released in March, 1994.

HOW TO ACCESS:

Available by anonymous FTP:

DOS/Windows:

Site:	**ftp.gov.nb.ca**
Directory:	**nb.gov.info/infohigh**
File:	**driving.zip**
Macintosh:	
Site:	**ftp.gov.nb.ca**
Directory:	**nb.gov.info/infohigh/macfiles**
File:	**mactext.sit.hqx (Text version)**

NEW BRUNSWICK BUSINESS OPPORTUNITIES INFORMATION

Thinking about moving your business to New Brunswick? Stop by this site to see what New Brunswick can offer your business. It provides general information on housing, education, research & development, and the overall quality of life in New Brunswick.

HOW TO ACCESS:

World Wide Web: **http://www.unb.ca./NB/nb_business.html**

NEW BRUNSWICK TOURING GUIDE

What body of water has the highest tides in the world? New Brunswick's Bay of Fundy, of course! Did you know that the ice cream cone was invented in New Brunswick? That New Brunswick is home to the world's largest axe? You'll find these and other tantalizing pieces of New Brunswick trivia at this site, which also offers an abundance of travel information on the province.

HOW TO ACCESS:

World Wide Web: **http://www.cuslm.ca/tourist/welcome.html**

NOVA SCOTIA SYMPHONY INFORMATION

Join us in welcoming the Nova Scotia Symphony to the Internet! Visit their Gopher site, where you'll find ticket information, concert descriptions, and an on-line order form.

HOW TO ACCESS:

Gopher: **gopher.nstn.ca**
Select: NSTN Cybermall - Information Kiosks/Symphony Nova Scotia

NORTHERN ONTARIO TOURISM SERVER

A fantastic repository of images from Thunder Bay, Ontario!

HOW TO ACCESS:

World Wide Web: **http://tourism.807-city.on.ca**

NOVA SCOTIA TOURISM SERVER

Where's the only Canadian post office run from a lighthouse? The Nova Scotia Tourism Server has the answer! Here you'll find an abundance of tourist information on Nova Scotia, including guides to shops, restaurants, and attractions. You can even take an on-line tour of some popular spots in the province.

HOW TO ACCESS:

World Wide Web: **http://ttg.sba.dal.ca/nstour**

ONET/INTERNET INSTRUCTION MANUAL

A description of the Internet using Computer Interactive Text (CIT). Developed by Doug van Vianen at Northern College in Kirkland Lake, Ontario.

HOW TO ACCESS:

Telnet: **kirk.northernc.on.ca**
Login: **vianen**

OTTAWA BICYCLE CLUB MAILING LIST

An electronic forum for the discussion of the activities of the Ottawa Bicycling Club and its members and for the discussion of cycling in eastern Ontario and western Quebec.

HOW TO ACCESS:

To join this mailing list, send an electronic mail message to **majordomo@cycling.org** with the following command in the first line of the body of the message: **subscribe obc**

OTTAWA BICYCLE CLUB WORLD WIDE WEB SERVER

Did you know that the Ottawa Bicycle Club is the oldest bicycle club in Canada? This World Wide Web server offers general information about the club, including events and programs.

HOW TO ACCESS:

World Wide Web: **http://www.sce.carleton.ca/rads/greg/obc/obc.html**

PHYSICAL ANTHROPOLOGY IN CANADA WWW SERVER

This site is sponsored by the Canadian Association for Physical Anthropology. It includes an on-line membership form for CAPA, and includes links to other Internet sites of interest to physical anthropologists.

HOW TO ACCESS:

World Wide Web: **http://library-www.scar.utoronto.ca/CAPA/CAPA.html**

PRINCE EDWARD ISLAND ELECTRONIC MAIL DIRECTORY

A list of e-mail users on Prince Edward Island.

HOW TO ACCESS:

Gopher: **gopher.crafts-council.pe.ca**
Select: **Prince Edward Island Electronic Mail Directory**

PRINCE EDWARD ISLAND CRAFTS INFORMATION SERVICE

The PEI Crafts Information Service is a service of the non-profit PEI Crafts Council. It offers solutions to crafts producers looking for information about sources of supplies, equipment, services, and expertise. The organization maintains a database of some 5,000 suppliers located across North America. They can provide references to craftspeople looking for particular products (e.g. "Where can I buy a flexishaft in Manitoba?") or general supplier lists (e.g. "Who sells weaving supplies in Canada?"). The organization can also provide information about crafts experts who offer training, education, or advice. They also track consumer experiences with suppliers. You can access the Prince Edward Island Crafts Council's databases by Gopher or World Wide Web. Internet users who do not have access to Gopher or the World Wide Web can contact the PEI Crafts Council by e-mail. General information about the services offered by the Prince Edward Island Crafts Council is available in the Craft Council's FAQ (Frequently

Asked Questions) file, which is available by anonymous FTP, and also posted every 14 days to the newsgroups **news.answers**, **rec.answers**, **rec.crafts.misc**, **rec.crafts.textiles.***. General information about the Prince Edward Island Crafts Council is also available on the Craft Council's Gopher and World Wide Web servers.

HOW TO ACCESS THE CRAFT COUNCIL'S INFORMATION SERVICES:
Gopher: **gopher.crafts-council.pe.ca**
World Wide Web: **http://www.crafts-council.pe.ca**
E-mail: **info@crafts-council.pe.ca**

HOW TO ACCESS THE CRAFT COUNCIL'S FAQ:
Available by anonymous FTP:
Site: **gus.crafts-council.pe.ca**
Directory: **pub**
File: **craftsinfo.FAQ**

PRINCE EDWARD ISLAND PICTURES
If you're in the mood for a quick visual tour of some landmarks in Prince Edward Island, this site contains colour pictures of Charlottetown City Hall, the Prince Edward Island Coastline, and the Prince Edward Island Fishing Harbour. To view these pictures, you need to use a World Wide Web browser with graphics support.

HOW TO ACCESS:
World Wide Web: **http://bud.peinet.pe.ca/homepage/info.html**

QUEBEC DISCUSSION FORUM
A USENET group for the discussion of Quebec culture.

HOW TO ACCESS:
USENET: **soc.culture.quebec**

QUEBEC NORDIQUES MAILING LIST
A mailing list for fans of the Quebec Nordiques hockey team. Potential topics for discussion include game summaries, rumors, injury reports, the playoffs, and many other interesting subjects.

HOW TO ACCESS:
To join the mailing list, send an electronic mail message to **nords-request@badaboum.ulaval.ca**, and request to be added to the discussion group.

SATURDAY NIGHT MAGAZINE

Information about Saturday Night Magazine, Canada's influential magazine of people, politics, business and the arts, from the Internet's Electronic Newsstand. This service contains sample articles from the current issue of Saturday Night, sample articles from past issues, pricing and subscription information, and an on-line order form. Subscribe to Saturday Night magazine on the Internet! Send a message to **Saturday_Night@enews.com** to start your subscription and include your name and mailing address.

HOW TO ACCESS:

Gopher: **gopher.enews.com**
Select: Magazines, Periodicals and Journals (all titles)/All Titles Listed
          Alphabetically/Titles from S to Z/Saturday Night

SASKATCHEWAN EXPATRIATES NEWSLETTER

A newsletter covering news and happenings in the Province of Saskatchewan for Saskatchewan Expatriates.

HOW TO ACCESS:

World Wide Web: **http://www.usask.ca/~scottp/saskwatch.html**

STATISTICS CANADA MAILING LIST

This mailing list is for the general discussion of Statistics Canada data.

HOW TO ACCESS:

To subscribe to this mailing list, send an electronic mail message to **listproc@statcan.ca** and place the following command on the first line of the body of the message: **subscribe statcan <Your Name>**
e.g. subscribe statcan John Smith

STATISTICS CANADA DAILY INFORMATION

A daily publication for the release of statistical data and announcements of new products and services from Statistics Canada.

HOW TO ACCESS:

To subscribe to this mailing list, send an electronic mail message to **listproc@statcan.ca** and place the following command on the first line of the body of the message: **subscribe daily <Your Name>**
e.g. subscribe daily John Smith

QUOTECOM STOCK QUOTE SERVICE

This is a commercial service providing financial market data to Internet users. For a fee, you can follow all Canadian exchanges and receive access to intraday quotes and end-of-the-day update files. Some historical data for Canadian exchanges is also available. For full information on QuoteCom's services, stop by their World Wide Web site.

HOW TO ACCESS:

For more information:
World Wide Web: **http://www.quote.com/**
Electronic Mail: **info@quote.com (automatic response)**

SUBWAY ROUTE FINDER (THE SUBWAY NAVIGATOR)

This service, located in France, will help you find your way through subway systems in cities around the world, including Montreal and Toronto.

HOW TO ACCESS:

Telnet: **metro.jussieu.fr port 10000**

TECHNICAL SERVICES IN CANADIAN LIBRARIES DISCUSSION FORUM

A mailing list for the discussion of the provision of technical services in Canadian libraries, established by the Technical Services Interest Group of the Canadian Library Association.

HOW TO ACCESS:

To join the mailing list, send an electronic mail message to **listproc@acadiau.ca** with the following command on the first line of the body of the message:
subscribe tsig-l <FIRST NAME> <LAST NAME>
e.g. subscribe tsig-l John Smith

TORONTO BLUE JAYS WWW SERVER

This site contains team statistics, the team history, and general information about the Toronto Blue Jays.

HOW TO ACCESS:

World Wide Web: **http://www.nando.net/baseball/bbs/bbhome/tor.html**

TORONTO BLUE JAYS MAILING LIST

This is a mailing list for the discussion of the Toronto Blue Jays. There are over 240 subscribers.

HOW TO ACCESS:

Subscriptions and requests for information should be sent to
jays-request@hivnet.ubc.ca

TRAVEL INFORMATION FOR CANADA

Travel guides for British Columbia, Ontario, Quebec, New Brunswick, Nova Scotia, and Newfoundland, compiled by people on the Internet.

HOW TO ACCESS:

Anonymous FTP:
Site: **ftp.cc.umanitoba.ca**
Directory: **rec-travel/north_america/canada**

TRAVEL DISCUSSION - CANADA/UNITED STATES

A USENET newsgroup for the discussion of Canadian and American travel topics.

HOW TO ACCESS:

USENET: **rec.travel.usa-canada**

UNIVERSITY OF WATERLOO ONLINE BOOKSTORE INQUIRY (WITH BUILT-IN GEOGRAPHIC INFORMATION SYSTEM!)

Users can search the inventory of the bookstore by title, author, instructor, course, or ISBN number. The system will tell you how many copies of the book are in stock, and present all the standard bibliographic information. What's nifty about this system is that you can call up a map of the bookstore on the screen, and a blinking symbol will indicate where the book is located.

HOW TO ACCESS:

Telnet: **bg1.uwaterloo.ca**
Login: **booklook**

VANCOUVER CANUCKS MAILING LIST

The Vancouver Canucks Mailing list is devoted to the discussion of the Vancouver Canucks, Vancouver's NHL team. Discussion topics include trade talks and criticism/praise of players. The list also serves as a medium to organize trips, hockey pools, and hockey games. Canuck statistics are usually posted after every game, and league/player statistics are posted on a monthly basis.

HOW TO ACCESS:

To subscribe to the mailing list, send an electronic mail message to **vancouver-canucks-request@sfu.ca**   Put **SUBSCRIBE CANUCKS** on the subject line, and put your name and electronic mail address on the first line of the body of the message.

VIRTUAL MALL PROJECT

The Virtual Mall Project is a shopping mall research study whereby catalogues of various vendors are distributed electronically over the Internet. Sponsored by the accounting firm of Dillabough Rowson, Certified General Accountants, in Thunder Bay, Ontario, the project exists as a way to help businesses reach new markets all over the world. The Virtual Mall Project currently operates as an "e-mail on demand" service, where Internet shoppers can request text-based catalogues, make queries and place orders for products and services. The project is constantly researching ethical ways of marketing over the Internet and new approaches are slowly introduced in ways such that their effectiveness can be measured. The project expects to add gopher/WWW service over the next year.

HOW TO ACCESS:

If you're interested in "checking out" the mall, send a message to **vmall@hookup.net** with the subject **Send VMALL**. The system will forward a listing of the mall merchants. If you're interested in further information about the project, you can contact the sponsoring firm:
Internet: **grant.rowson@oln.com**

Dillabough Rowson, CGAs
Attn.: R. Grant Rowson, CGA
1404 E. Moodie Street
Thunder Bay, ON P7E 4Y9
(807) 622-4995

WEST'S LEGAL DIRECTORY

An on-line legal directory that contains 675,000 profiles of law firms and branch offices and biographical records of lawyers in the U.S. and Canada. It is available without charge to Internet users.

HOW TO ACCESS:

Gopher: **wld.westlaw.com**

WHISTLER SKI REPORTS

Ski reports for Whister, British Columbia, one of Canada's most popular ski resorts.

HOW TO ACCESS:

Finger: **whistler@wimsey.com**

CITY OF WINNIPEG WWW PAGE

What does Winnipeg have to offer the visitor? Check out this World Wide Web page to find out what's waiting for you in Winnipeg.

HOW TO ACCESS:

World Wide Web: **http://www.umanitoba.ca/wpg/wpg.html**

YUKON MAILING LIST

For people interested in information and/or gossip about the Yukon Territory. A cool mailing list!

HOW TO ACCESS:

To join the discussion, send your e-mail address to:
yukon-request@cs.concordia.ca

A P P E N D I X M

....

THE DIRECTORY OF INTERNET-ACCESSIBLE LIBRARY CATALOGUES IN CANADA

© 1994 Rick Broadhead and Jim Carroll

This is a comprehensive listing of Canadian libraries that have made their Online Public Access Catalogue (OPAC) available on the Internet. An OPAC allows you to interactively search a library collection for books, authors, and/or subjects that meet your search criteria. Using the Internet, you can search the holdings of almost every university library in Canada. A number of Canadian colleges and public library systems have also connected their electronic catalogues to the Internet.

To compile the information for this directory, we surveyed librarians at university, college, and public libraries across the country. We thank the participating libraries for their support.

HOW TO SUBMIT INFORMATION FOR THE DIRECTORY OF INTERNET-ACCESSIBLE LIBRARY CATALOGUES:
Contributions to this directory are welcome. If your favourite on-line catalogue is not listed in the directory, please contact us at <handbook@uunet.ca> so that we can list it in future revisions of the directory.

Each entry in this directory contains the following information:

(1) INTERNET ADDRESS OF THE OPAC AND ACCESS METHOD

The Internet address of the catalogue, and the access method you should use.

The most common access method is Telnet. Some library catalogues require that you use a TN3270 client, which is a variant of Telnet. Many libraries make their catalogues and/or other library information available via Gopher and the World Wide Web.

Telnet may not work with library catalogues that require TN3270, unless the machine you use to access the Internet is an IBM mainframe computer. In order to use TN3270, you need to use a program called a TN3270 client. If you are accessing the Internet using a dial-up interactive account, your Internet provider (or the organization that provides you with Internet access) must first install a TN3270 client on their system for you to use. If you are not sure if a TN3270 client has been installed, ask your Internet provider or your organization's computer support personnel, or consult the Directory of Canadian Internet Providers in Appendix C. If a commercial provider has a TN3270 client installed on their system, it will be indicated in the "Interactive Accounts" box of the directory.

If a TN3270 client *has* been installed on your Internet provider's system, and if you are accessing the Internet from a Unix shell, you can start TN3270 from the Unix command prompt by typing the following command:

```
tn3270 ADDRESS-OF-OPAC
```

where: **ADDRESS-OF-OPAC** is the Internet address of the on-line library catalogue.

For example, to access the University of Regina's on-line library catalogue, you would type the following command:

```
tn3270 max.cc.uregina.ca
```

If your Internet provider's system is menu-driven, look for a menu item called "TN3270."

If you are using Microsoft Windows, and if you have a direct Internet connection or access the Internet using a SLIP/PPP connection, you can obtain a TN3270 client by anonymous FTP, as detailed in the table below. This program was written by Jim Rymerson of Queen's University, in Kingston, Ontario.

Name of Client:	QWS3270 (for Microsoft Windows)
Type:	Freeware
Anonymous FTP site:	ftp.ccs.queensu.ca
Directory:	pub/msdos/tcpip
File Name:	qws3270.zip

(2) INSTRUCTIONS
How to log into the catalogue once you have established a connection.

Once you connect to an on-line catalogue, you usually have to log in by entering a user-id and/or password, or by selecting an option off an opening menu. The procedure for logging in varies by catalogue.

Once you have successfully logged into the catalogue, the commands that you use to perform searches will vary depending on the software that the catalogue is using. Because so many different types of OPAC software are in use across Canada, we do not provide specific instructions on how to use each type of software. However, most catalogues have on-line help files that will aid you in performing searches on the catalogue. Many catalogues display the most common commands on the screen to help you with your search.

(3) HOW TO EXIT
Instructions on how to leave the catalogue when you are finished.

Occasionally, you will need to use a control sequence like CTRL-Z, CTRL-D, or CTRL-C. To use a control sequence, hold down the control key and press the specified letter at the same time. For example, to use CTRL-Z, press the CTRL key and the letter Z at the same time. If you get stuck in the catalogue at any time, you can often use the Telnet escape sequence, which is generally **CTRL-]** on UNIX systems (hold down the CTRL key and press the] key). If you are using TN3270, the escape sequence is often **CTRL-C** (hold down the CTRL key and press the letter C). When the "Telnet>" or "TN3270>" prompt appears, type **quit** and press **<enter>.**

(4) OPAC TYPE
The type of OPAC software the library is using.

Remember that the search commands for each catalogue will vary according to the software being used.

(5) SIZE OF THE COLLECTION (OPTIONAL)
The total size of the institution's library collection.

Since libraries measure collection sizes in different ways, the collection size estimates in this directory are not standardized.

(6) % CATALOGUED (OPTIONAL)
The percentage of the library's total collection that is listed on the OPAC.

(7) NOT CATALOGUED (OPTIONAL)
When you are searching an on-line catalogue, keep in mind that many libraries don't list all their holdings on the OPAC. For this reason, we indicate what items in the library's collection are *not* in the OPAC.

(8) SUBJECT STRENGTHS (OPTIONAL)
Subject strengths of the library.

Subject strengths are topical areas where the library has strong or notable collections.

(9) SPECIAL COLLECTIONS (OPTIONAL)
If the library has any special collections, they will be noted here.

(10) SPECIAL NOTES (OPTIONAL)
If the library's collection has any unique or interesting characteristics, they will be noted here.

(11) PUBLIC DATABASES (OPTIONAL)
Names of any databases on the OPAC that the public has access to.

Many libraries have databases on their OPAC that are restricted to local patrons. Databases with restricted access will not be listed.

NAMES

Many libraries have assigned a name to their on-line library catalogue. If a library has given a name to its on-line catalogue, the name is indicated in brackets after the name of the institution or organization. For example, Bishop's University in Lennoxville, Quebec, calls its OPAC **Borris**. Trent University in Peterborough, Ontario, calls its OPAC **Topcat**.

Acadia University Library System
Wolfville, Nova Scotia

ACCESS:	Telnet: **auls.acadiau.ca**
Instructions:	At the "login:" prompt, type **opac**. Type **LC** to access the library catalogue.
How to Exit:	Type **Q** to leave the library system. Type **X** to disconnect.
OPAC Type:	AULS (In-house).
Size of Collection:	500,000+ total; 450,000 print volumes; 10,000 other.
% Catalogued:	50%.
Not Catalogued:	The special collections for which Acadia is known are for the most part accessible only through the card catalogue. Most archival materials are not catalogued, and only selected government documents are included on the OPAC. However, retrospective conversion is ongoing.
Subject Strengths:	The collections of Canadian history and literature. The library subscribes to about 2300 serials and is full depository for Canadian Federal Government documents and Nova Scotia Government documents.
Special Collections:	The library is known for its special collections of Canadiana (the Eric R. Dennis Collection of Canadiana and the John D. Logan Collection of Canadian Literature, with materials on T.C. Haliburton, C.G.D. Roberts, Bliss Carman and M.M. Saunders) and for its archival collections (the Atlantic Baptist Historical Collection, the Acadia University Archives, the Annapolis Valley Regional Collection, the Mermaid Theatre Collection and others). Most titles in these collections are listed only in the card catalogue.

Public Databases:	Library Catalogue; Planter Database - A bibliography of primary documents about the New England Planters who settled in the Maritime Provinces between 1759 and 1800. The documents themselves are located in various archives throughout the Maritimes and New England. The Planter Database is a project of the Committee for Planter Studies in Acadia; Source Records Databases include - Canadiana Name Authorities, Canadiana Subject Authorities, Library of Congress Name Authorities, Library of Congress Subject Authorities, and Memorial University of Newfoundland's Government Documents (up to Aug 1993). These are accessed by selecting Search Sources from the menu of the first Library Catalogue screen.

University of Alberta (The GATE)
Edmonton, Alberta

ACCESS:	Telnet: dra.library.ualberta.ca
Instructions:	At the "Username:" prompt, type **GATE**. Type **direct** to access the library catalogue.
How to Exit:	Type **quit** to disconnect.
OPAC Type:	DRA
Size of Collection:	4,205,110 print volumes, 3,067,746 microforms, 1,403,000 maps.
% Catalogued:	90%.
Not Catalogued:	The map collection is not in the OPAC, also some government publications and several large microform sets.
Subject Strengths:	Slavic and German history and literature, northern and circumpolar (interdisciplinary), western Canadian and Americana, English and American literature, anthropology (especially Amerindian), book arts of the 19th and 20th centuries, business administration and management, European romanticism, government documents, maps, music, children's literature and Alberta curriculum, education psychology, educational research, history of education in Canada, psychological tests, neuroscience, nursing and midwifery, sports medicine, American, British and Canadian primary law, Canadian family law, communications and intellectual property law, constitutional law, international business, trade and tax law, jurisprudence, legal history, oil and gas law, entomology, geology, mathematics.
Special Collections:	Canadian Circumpolar Library.
Public Databases:	None

Athabasca University (AUCAT)
Athabasca, Alberta

ACCESS:	Telnet: aucat.athabascau.ca
Instructions:	At the "Username:" prompt, type **AUCAT**. At the "Printer Name:" prompt, press **<enter>**. Select menu item **1**.
How to Exit:	Type **m** to get back to the main menu. At the main menu, type **q** to disconnect. Type **quit** at any time to disconnect.
OPAC Type:	BUCAT
Size of Collection:	111,000 total; 108,000 print volumes; 1,375 microforms; 2,600 other.
% Catalogued:	98%.

Not Catalogued:	Distance education courses from other institutions, CD-ROM databases and indexes.
Subject Strengths:	Distance Education, Women's Studies.
Special Collections:	The Reverend Edward Checkland Collection.
Special Notes:	Students live in all parts of Canada. Library requests are received by e-mail, fax, phone and regular mail.
Public Databases:	Holdings of the Athabasca University archives.

Atlantic School of Theology (Novanet)
Halifax, Nova Scotia

ACCESS:	Telnet: novanet.dal.ca
Instructions:	A menu appears when the connection is established. Press **\<enter>**. Select '**6**' to limit search. Select '**1**' for specific libraries. Select '**14**' to limit the search to the Atlantic School of Theology.
How to Exit:	Type **end**.
OPAC Type:	GEAC
Size of Collection:	69,190 print items, 1,933 non-print items.
% Catalogued:	10%.
Subject Strengths:	Theological and related material. New Hebrides Mission Collection. Hymnody (Hymnology).
Public Databases:	None.

Bishop's University (BORIS)
Lennoxville, Quebec

ACCESS:	Telnet: library.ubishops.ca
Instructions:	At the "login:" prompt, type **lib**. At the "password" prompt, type **bishops**.
How to Exit:	At main menu choose item #7.
OPAC Type:	GEAC ADVANCE
Size of Collection:	420,000 total; 282,000 print volumes, 54,269 microforms, 14,140 other.
% Catalogued:	96% .
Not Catalogued:	Government documents, vertical file materials, Quebec clerical library, archives, maps.
Subject Strengths:	Eastern Townships History, Rare and unusual books of 17th and 18th century theology, history and literature from the personal collections of George J. Mountain, 3rd Anglican Bishop of Quebec and Victorian novelist Charles Dickens.
Special Collections:	P. H. Scowen Eastern Townships Historical Collection, Mackinnon Collection of Canadiana, Belanger-Gardner Collection (history of world civilization).
Public Databases:	None.

Brandon University (BuCAT)
Brandon, Manitoba

ACCESS:	Telnet: library.brandonu.ca

Instructions:	At the "Username:" prompt, type **libcat**. Select option **1** from the main menu.
How to Exit:	Type **m** to get back to the main menu, type **quit, end** or **exit** from the main menu to disconnect.
OPAC Type:	BUCAT
Size of Collection:	210,982 bibliographic print volume records, 366,379 bibliographic microform records, 705,910 bibliographic other records.
% Catalogued:	100% of trade monographs, 98% of microfiche monographs, 25% of government documents, 15% of journal articles.
Not Catalogued:	Many government documents and journal articles.
Public Databases:	LC, CARL.

Brandon Public Library
Brandon, Manitoba

ACCESS:	**Telnet: library.brandonu.ca**
Instructions:	At the "Username:" prompt, login as **libcat**. Select option **5**, "Other Library Catalogues." Select option **1**, "Brandon Area Libraries." At the "Service: " prompt, type **login**. At the "username:" prompt, type **libcat**.
How to Exit:	Type **m** to get back to the main menu, type **Q** from the main menu to disconnect.
OPAC Type:	BUCAT

University of British Columbia (UBCLIB)
Vancouver, British Columbia

ACCESS:	**Telnet:** library.ubc.ca **Gopher:** unixg.ubc.ca port 7001 **WWW:** http://unixg.ubc.ca:7001
Instructions:	Press the **<enter>** key at the "Enter your id:" prompt. Type **LIB** for the library catalogue.
How to Exit:	Type **main** to return to main menu. Type **stop** to exit.
OPAC Type:	In-house.
Size of Collection:	9,300,000 total: 3,400,000 books/serial volumes.
% Catalogued:	35%.
Not Catalogued:	Many government publications, microforms, cartographic materials, photos and pictures.
Subject Strengths:	All standard academic disciplines. Asian materials, Life Sciences.
Public Databases:	B.C. Archival Union List (description of holdings for B.C. archives), B.C. Newspapers (current and historical B.C. newspapers held by B.C. libraries, museums, and historical societies), Bibliographies (bibliographies compiled and maintained at UBC), Directory of Statistics in Canada (index to statistical publications from Statistics Canada and other governmental and commercial sources, updated annually), B.C. Electronic Library Network media and serials holdings, UBC Recordings, UBC Serials.

Brock University
St. Catharines, Ontario

ACCESS:	Telnet: 139.57.16.2 port 1200
Instructions:	A menu will appear when the connection is established. Press **<enter>** when asked "Press SEND to begin."
How to Exit:	Press **CTRL-D** to disconnect.
OPAC Type:	GEAC
Size of Collection:	1,200,000 total.
% Catalogued:	100%.
Subject Strengths:	Niagara Region Collection, specializing in materials about the Niagara region, and containing materials written by local residents.
Public Databases:	None.

Burlington Public Library (B.I.R.O.N.)
Burlington, Ontario

ACCESS:	Telnet: halinet.sheridanc.on.ca
Instructions:	At the "login:" prompt, type **guest**. At main menu choose **4** 'The Library," then **1** 'Public Libraries', then **1** 'Burlington Public Library', then **5** 'Search the Catalog.' Be prepared to select an appropriate terminal emulation.
How to Exit:	From main search menu select: logoff.
OPAC Type:	DYNIX
Size of Collection:	351,500 total; 330,000 print volumes, 1,500 microforms, 20,000 other materials.
% Catalogued:	99%.
Not Catalogued:	Local history archives, maps.
Special Collections:	Local History, Japanese, French and other language collections.
Public Databases:	None.

University of Calgary Library (DOBIS)
Calgary, Alberta

ACCESS:	Telnet: library.ucalgary.ca
Instructions:	Enter terminal type. Follow on-screen instructions.
How to Exit:	Use **CTRL-)** to break connection.
OPAC Type:	DOBIS/LIBIS
Size of Collection:	5,000,000 total;1,800,000 volumes; 1,300,000 other materials.
% Catalogued:	Majority.
Not Catalogued:	Detailed information for special collection records, literary archives and the Canadian Architectural Archives.
Subject Strengths:	Large collection of maps and air photos noted in the catalogue at the collection level with printed finding aids. Collection of Canadian authors' manuscripts, available in the catalogue at the collection level, with printed finding aids.
Public Databases:	None.

Camosun College (CAMCAT)
Victoria, British Columbia

ACCESS:	Telnet: camcat.camosun.bc.ca
Instructions:	At the "Username:" prompt, type **catinq**. Select option **1** from the menu.
How to Exit:	Type **exit.**
OPAC Type:	BUCAT
Size of Collection:	60,641 total; 50,078 print vol; 2,005 other.
% Catalogued:	100%.
Public Databases:	None.

Canada Centre for Mineral and Energy Technology (CANMET)
Ottawa, Ontario

ACCESS:	Telnet: canlib.emr.ca
Instructions:	At the "login:" prompt, type **opac** (lower case only).
How to Exit:	Press the **PF1** key until the initial screen is displayed. Use the arrow keys to select **Exit** from the menu.
OPAC Type:	MULTILIS
Size of Collection:	750,000 volumes.
% Catalogued:	100%.
Subject Strengths:	Mining, Minerals, Metallurgy, Energy Efficiency, Alternative Energy Technology.
Public Databases:	CANMET Technical Publications.

Canada Institute for Scientific and Technical Information (CISTI)
Ottawa, Ontario

Note: This is a fee-based service and is available as part of the National Library of Canada's DOBIS service. DOBIS is available through the Internet, but you must register and pay the appropriate fee before you can use DOBIS. DOBIS contains the holdings of the National Library of Canada and over 1000 other Canadian libraries. DOBIS will be replaced in the near future by a new information system called AMICUS.

ACCESS:	Instructions for authorized subscribers are available on the National Library of Canada's Gopher server at **gopher.nlc-bnc.ca**. To subscribe, send e-mail to **cic@nlc-bnc.ca** or telephone (819) 997-7227.
Instructions:	Commands are available in the searching manual which is provided to subscribers.
OPAC Type:	IBM-developed software, enhanced by the National Library of Canada.
How to Exit:	Commands are available in the searching manual which is provided to subscribers.
Size of Collection:	55,000 serials (16,000 current titles). Over 2 million technical reports (print and microform). Over 2 million monographs.
% Catalogued:	100% of the collection since 1978.
Not Catalogued:	Some pre-1978 monographs and technical reports and a portion of the microforms collection.
Subject Strengths:	Science, engineering, and medicine.

Special Collections:	None.
Special Notes:	Largest collection of scientific/technical information in North America. CISTI operates CAN/OLE, the Canadian Online Enquiry database service. Highly advanced document delivery technology called IntelliDoc. Paper copies of documents are delivered overnight by courier to most centres in North America.
Public Databases:	None.

University College of Cape Breton (Novanet)
Sydney, Nova Scotia

ACCESS:	**Telnet: novanet.dal.ca**
Instructions:	A menu appears when the connection is established. Press return. Select `6` to limit search, select `1` for specific libraries, select `12` the University College of Cape Breton.
How to Exit:	Type **end** to disconnect.
OPAC Type:	GEAC
Size of Collection:	275,000 volumes
% Catalogued:	30%.
Not Catalogued:	Not catalogued or partially catalogued: Statistics Canada publications, Statutes, Debates, pre-1987 acquisitions.
Subject Strengths:	Environmental Science, Psychology, Sociology, Folklore, History and Culture of Cape Breton. Gaelic Language Collection.
Public Databases:	None.

Carleton University (CUBE)
Carleton **U**niversity **B**ibliographic **E**nquiry
Ottawa, Ontario

ACCESS:	**Telnet:** library.carleton.ca **Gopher:** library3.carleton.ca
Instructions:	A menu appears when the connection is established. Press the **<enter>** key at the "OPTION:" prompt.
How to Exit:	Type **off** to disconnect.
OPAC Type:	In-house.
Size of Collection:	2,704,311 total; 1,548,140 print volumes, 988,461 microforms, 167,710 other materials.
% Catalogued:	100%.
Subject Strengths:	Social Sciences, German, Canadian and Spanish Studies, Women's Studies, Canadian and United Nations government publications.
Special Collections:	Batchinsky Collection (Ukrainian politics, 19th-20th Century), Canadian, American and British small-press poetry, French Revolution, Novosti Press Agency Photograph Files (not on CUBE), William Blake (Trianon Press).
Public Databases:	None.

Communications Research Centre
Ottawa, Ontario

ACCESS:	Telnet: hazel.dgcp.doc.ca
Instructions:	At the "login:" prompt, type **library**.
How to Exit:	Select **Exit** from the main menu.
OPAC Type:	MULTILIS

Concordia University (CLUES)
Concordia **L**ibraries' **U**sers **E**nquiry **S**ystem
Montreal, Quebec

ACCESS:	Telnet: mercury.concordia.ca
Instructions:	At the "login:" prompt, type **clues**.
How to Exit:	Type the letter **D** from the main menu.
OPAC Type:	Innovative Interfaces Inc.
Size of Collection:	1,920,501 print volumes; 414,215 microforms; 35,442 other.
Not Catalogued:	Uncatalogued government publications, technical reports and some pre-1975 monographs in Webster Library, standards.
Subject Strengths:	Cinema, Building Engineering, Women's Studies, Computer Science, Holocaust Studies.
Special Collections	Irving Layton Collection; CBC Radio Drama Archives.
Public Databases:	UnCover.

Dalhousie University (Novanet)
Halifax, Nova Scotia

ACCESS:	Telnet: novanet.dal.ca
Instructions:	A menu appears when the connection is established. Press **<return>**. Select '**6**' to limit search, select '**1**' for specific libraries, select one of '**1,2,3,4,9,11**' for Dalhousie University.
How to Exit:	Type **end** to disconnect.
OPAC Type:	GEAC GLIS
Size of Collection:	1,206,688 print volumes, 305,162 microforms, 90,260 other materials.
% Catalogued:	37% of all volumes. All current serials and all acquisitions since 1987 (except archival materials) are in the OPAC.
Not Catalogued:	Partially catalogued: dead serials, rare books, older special collection items, older maps, scores, micromaterials.
Subject Strengths:	Canadian History and Literature, Sciences, Health Sciences, Law, Oceanography, Kipling materials.
Public Databases:	None.

École des Hautes Études Commerciales
Montreal, Quebec

ACCESS:	Telnet: biblio.hec.ca

Instructions:	At the "login:" prompt, type **biblio.**
How to Exit:	Follow the instructions.
OPAC Type:	MULTILIS

École Polytechnique de Montréal
Montreal, Quebec

ACCESS:	**Telnet: cat.biblio.polymtl.ca**
Instructions:	At the "login:" prompt, type **cat.**
How to Exit:	Select item **3** from the main menu.
OPAC Type:	GEAC.

Fanshawe College (FanLib)
London, Ontario

ACCESS:	**Telnet: lib.fanshawec.on.ca**
Instructions:	At the "username:" prompt type **fclink.**
How to Exit:	Select FanLib options menu, then **quit.**
OPAC Type:	DRA
Size of Collection:	75,000 total: 62,471 print volumes, 11,287 other materials.
% Catalogued:	85%
Not Catalogued:	Periodicals; non-print (i.e. videos, films etc.), annual reports, pamphlets.
Subject Strengths:	Nursing and allied health, business, technology, applied arts, communication arts, design, hospitality.
Public Databases:	None.

Geological Survey of Canada
Ottawa, Ontario

ACCESS:	**Telnet: geoinfo.gsc.emr.ca**
Instructions:	At the "login:" prompt, type **opac.**
How to Exit:	Select **D** from the main menu.

University of Guelph (searchMe!)
Guelph, Ontario

ACCESS:	**Telnet: searchme.uoguelph.ca**
Instructions:	At the "login:" prompt, type **searchme.**
How to Exit:	To disconnect, type the letter **X** at the "Enter Choice" prompt.
OPAC Type:	In-house.
Size of Collection:	2,058,632 print volumes; 1,322,885 microform units; 71,117 cartographic materials; 8,722 audio-visual materials; 5,907 films and videos; 5,609 archives and manuscripts.

% Catalogued:	100%.
Not Catalogued:	Some microfiche from the Canadian Institute for Historic Microreproduction; all the ERIC fiche.
Subject Strengths:	Agriculture, Canadian Drama, Life Sciences, Veterinary Science, Scottish Studies.
Special Collections:	L.M. Montgomery, Scottish Collection, George Bernard Shaw, Edward Johnson and Guelph Spring Festival Collections, Ontario Theatre Archives, Adelaide Hoodless and Federated Women's Institutes of Ontario. All these collections are catalogued in the OPAC.
Public Databases:	None.

Halton Hills Public Library (The Catalog)
Halton Hills, Ontario

ACCESS:	Telnet: halinet.sheridanc.on.ca
Instructions:	At the "login:" prompt, type **guest**. At main menu choose **4** The Library, **1** Public Libraries, **2** Halton Hills Public Library, **6** Use the Catalog. Be prepared to select an appropriate terminal emulation.
How to Exit:	To disconnect, select **logoff** from the main menu.
OPAC Type:	DYNIX
Size of Collection:	90,000 print volumes; 30 microforms; 3,000 other.
% Catalogued:	98%.
Not Catalogued:	Local history archives of the Esquesing Historical Society.
Special Collections:	Local history and genealogy.
Public Databases:	Index to local newspapers (Georgetown and Acton) 26,000+ entries. Community Information and Community Events.

International Development Research Centre (IDRC)
Development Data Bases Service (DDBS)
Ottawa, Ontario

ACCESS:	Telnet: ddbs.idrc.ca
Instructions:	At the "login:" prompt, type **guest**.
OPAC Type:	MINISIS.
How to Exit:	Type **exit**.
Size of Collection:	70,000 books, reports, journals, and archives. 16,000 microform units.
% Catalogued:	97%.
Not Catalogued:	Slide imaging bank and database.
Subject Strengths:	Economic development, environment, gender, health sciences, information sciences, social policy, science and technology policy, sustainable and equitable development, technology transfer.

Special Collections:	The Brundtland Collection: the original documents and tapes of the World Commission on Environment and Development.
	Corporate Archives: IDRC-supported publications, material written by IDRC staff, publications about the IDRC and its activities, final reports of IDRC projects.
	Infoquest: Collection of files containing current material describing 2,500 organizations, research centres, and government departments located in Canada and abroad whose activities relate to IDRC interests.
Special Notes:	Slide imaging bank and database. Contact **reference@idrc.ca** for more information.
Public Databases:	1. BIBLIOL: The collection of the IDRC library.
	2. IDRIS (Inter-Agency Development Research Information System):
	Research activities of BOSTID (Board on Science and Technology for International Development), FINNIDA (Finnish International Development Agency), IDRC (International Development Research Centre), IFS (International Foundation for Science), JICA (Japan International Cooperation Agency), SAREC (Swedish Agency for Research Cooperation with Developing Countries).
	3. ACRONYM: Acronyms related to the interests of the IDRC.

University of Kings College (Novanet)
Halifax, Nova Scotia

ACCESS:	Telnet: novanet.dal.ca
Instructions:	A menu appears when the connection is established. Press **<enter>**. Select '**6**' to limit search, select '**1**' for specific libraries, select '**10**' for University of Kings College.
How to Exit:	Type **end**.
OPAC Type:	GEAC

Lakehead University
Thunder Bay, Ontario

ACCESS:	Telnet: lib.lakeheadu.ca
Instructions:	At the "Username:" prompt, type **LAKEHEAD**.
How to Exit:	Press the **PF1** key until the initial screen is displayed. Use the arrow keys to select **Exit** from the menu.
OPAC Type:	MULTILIS
Size of Collection:	600,000 books, journals and other documents. 200,000 microforms.
% Catalogued:	100%.
Subject Strengths:	Early Canadiana, Northwestern Ontario, Native Studies, Forestry and Outdoor Recreation, Education (41,000 titles).
Public Databases:	Lakehead's Northern Studies Resource Centre, with 22,000 on-line records.

Laurentian University
Sudbury, Ontario

ACCESS:	Telnet: laulibr.laurentian.ca

Instructions:	At the "Username:" prompt, type **netlib**.
How to Exit:	Press the **PF1** key until the initial screen is displayed. Use the arrow keys to select **Exit** from the menu.
OPAC Type:	MULTILIS
Size of Collection:	500,000 titles.
% Catalogued:	40%.
Subject Strengths:	Franco-Ontario, Land Reclamation, Acid Mine Drainage, Mining Environment, Rock Bursts.
Public Databases:	Mining Environment Database, Rock Burst Database.

Université Laval (Ariane)
Sainte-Foy, Quebec

ACCESS:	**Telnet:** ariane.ulaval.ca **Gopher:** gopher.bibl.ulaval.ca **WWW:** http://www.bibl.ulaval.ca
Instructions:	At the "Username:" prompt, type **ARIANE**.
How to Exit:	Press the **PF1** key until you have access to the command **Sortie/Exit**.
OPAC Type:	MULTILIS
Size of Collection:	3,000,000 total, 1,410,000 print volumes, 1,112,000 microforms, 800,000 other.
% Catalogued:	80%.
Not Catalogued:	Some documents purchased before 1975.
Subject Strengths:	French Canadian and Quebec Studies, French Canadian Folklore, Quebec Geography, French and French Canadian Literature, Civil Law, 19th century French musical press, Philosophy.
Public Databases:	None.

University of Lethbridge (Eureka!)
Lethbridge, Alberta

ACCESS:	**Telnet:** eureka.uleth.ca
Instructions:	At the "login:" prompt, type **library**.
How to Exit:	Type **D** from the main menu.
OPAC Type:	INNOPAC
Size of Collection:	1,000,000 items.
% Catalogued:	85-90%.
Not Catalogued:	Microforms and LPs.
Subject Strengths:	None.
Public Databases:	None.

Lethbridge Community College
Lethbridge, Alberta

ACCESS:	**Telnet:** holly.cc.uleth.ca

Instructions:	At the "Login:" prompt, type **LCC::** At the "Username:" prompt, type **OPAC.**
How to Exit:	Use **PF1** to scroll back to previous pages. Choose **Exit** from the main screen.
OPAC Type:	MULTILIS
Size of Collection:	60,000 titles, 77,000 items. 500 serial subscriptions.
% Catalogued:	100% of books and audiovisuals. Periodical holdings are being added.
Subject Strengths:	Trades such as Electronics and Electronic Drafting, Environmental Science, Criminal Justice, Clinical Nursing, Fashion Design, Communication Arts.
Public Databases:	None.

Malaspina College (MACAT)
Nanaimo, British Columbia

ACCESS:	Telnet: mala.bc.ca
Instructions:	At the "Username:" prompt, type **MACAT.** Select option **1** for the library catalogue.
How to Exit:	Type **m** to get to the main menu. At the main menu, type **q** to disconnect. Type **quit** at any time to disconnect from the system without returning to the main menu.
OPAC Type:	TKM
Size of Collection:	113,000 items.
% Catalogued:	100%
Subject Strengths:	Call for information.
Public Databases:	Electronic Libraries Network Media Database (all 16mm films and videorecordings held by post-secondary academic libraries in B.C.), Plays Index, University/College Calendars Collection, ELN Serials Database (periodicals held by post-secondary academic libraries in B.C. and the Vancouver Public Library).

University of Manitoba (Bridge)
Winnipeg, Manitoba

ACCESS:	Telnet: umopac.umanitoba.ca
Instructions:	When the "UML=>" prompt appears on the screen, type **be** to display the introductory screen. Type the command **set lib uml** to restrict the search to the University of Manitoba.
How to Exit:	Type **close** to disconnect.
OPAC Type:	PALS
Size of Collection:	1.6 million volumes, 480,000 government publications, 1.2 million microforms and audiovisual materials.
% Catalogued:	Almost 100%. Older government publications, some of the Slavic collection, and several gift collections are not catalogued.
Subject Strengths:	Western Canadian History and Literature, Slavic Studies, Icelandic Studies, Dental collection, slide collection.
Public Databases:	None.

McGill University (MUSE)
Montreal, Quebec

ACCESS:	TN3270: mvs.mcgill.ca
Instructions:	The "Welcome to McGill University" menu will be displayed. Select **2** for MUSE. When you see the "CICS" screen, press the **<enter>** key.
How to Exit:	Type **stop** to disconnect.
OPAC Type:	NOTIS
Size of Collection:	1,457,545 records; 2,811,083 print volumes, 1,298,576 microforms, 52,341 other.
% Catalogued:	78%.
Not Catalogued:	Please refer to the EXP MUSE screen in the MUSE system.
Subject Strengths:	Canadiana. History of Medicine, British History, Law, Medicine, Ornithology, Entomology, Islamic Studies.
Special Notes:	MUSE contains the catalogue records for the Canadian Institute for Historic Microreproductions, available at McGill on microfiche.
Public Databases:	None.

Medicine Hat College
Medicine Hat, Alberta

ACCESS:	Telnet: holly.cc.uleth.ca
Instructions:	At the "login:" prompt, type **MHCLIB::** At the "Username:" prompt, type **MHCOPAC**.
How to Exit:	Use the **PF1** key to scroll back to the main menu. Choose **Exit** from the main screen.
OPAC Type:	MULTILIS.

Memorial University of Newfoundland (FOLIO)
St. John's, Newfoundland

ACCESS:	Telnet: mungate.library.mun.ca
Instructions:	At the "login:" prompt, type **mungate**. At the "Please enter terminal type:" prompt, type **vt100**. At the "Your Response:" prompt, type **select**. Select file **2** to access the library catalogue.
How to Exit:	Type **cancel** to leave the library catalogue. Type **end** at the "Your Response:" prompt to return to the welcome screen. Type **logoff** to disconnect.
OPAC Type:	SPIRES
Size of Collection:	960,441 monographs, 80,834 documents/technical reports, 274,064 serial volumes, 9,750 serial subscriptions, 1,694,407 volume equivalents in microform. Marine Institute not included in above figures.
% Catalogued:	100% of post-1979 titles. 100% of journal titles, Centre for Newfoundland Studies, Rare Book Collection, Health Sciences Library, Sir Wilfred Grenfell College, 50% of Marine Institute collection, 50% of pre-1979 titles in main library.
Subject Strengths:	Newfoundland History, Earth Sciences, Biochemistry, Folklore, Linguistics, Irish Studies, Maritime History (trade and commerce).

Public Databases:	Archives of ANSAX-L (Anglo-Saxon Literature/Language Listserv), MUN Library Union Catalogue, Catalogue of Archival Collections in the Centre for Newfoundland Studies, Catalogue of Videotapes produced by MUN extension, Canadian Labour Bibliography, Labrador Institute for Northern Studies Catalogue, Catalogue of MUN Folklore and Language Archives, Catalogue of the Ocean Engineering Information Centre, Bibliography of journal articles concerning Newfoundland and Labrador (40,000 entries), Catalogue of Queen's College (Anglican Seminary), Catalogue of the Collection of Radical Pamphlets (20th Century), Catalogue of the Art Slide Collection at Sir Wilfred Grenfell College.

Milton Public Library (The Catalog)
Milton, Ontario

ACCESS:	**Telnet: halinet.sheridanc.on.ca**
Instructions:	At the "login:" prompt, type **guest**. At the main menu choose **4** The Library, **1** Public Libraries, **3** Milton Public Library, **5** Search the Catalog. Be prepared to select a terminal emulation.
How to Exit:	From the main menu, choose **logoff**.
OPAC Type:	DYNIX
Size of Collection:	76,000 print volumes; 12 microforms; 6,000 other.
% Catalogued:	Majority.
Not Catalogued:	Vertical files, maps, most government documents (all levels), telephone books.
Subject Strengths:	Popular materials.
Public Databases:	Community Information Directory; Community Events Calendar.

Université de Moncton (ELOIZE)
Moncton, New Brunswick

ACCESS:	**Telnet: 139.103.2.2**
Instructions:	At the "Service?" prompt, type **champ**. Follow the instructions.
How to Exit:	Type **fin** to disconnect. Type **REC** to start a new search.
OPAC Type:	GEAC
Size of Collection:	420,000 titles (55% in English, 45% in French).
% Catalogued:	42%.
Not Catalogued:	Books before 1977. Government publications before 1987 (except publications from Quebec before 1983).
Subject Strengths:	Acadian people, French and French Canadian Literature.
Special Collections:	Documents by and about Acadian people.
Public Databases:	None.

Mount Allison University (MARION)
Sackville, New Brunswick

ACCESS:	**Telnet: library.mta.ca**
Instructions:	At the "Username:" prompt, type **CATALOG**. Follow the on-screen instructions.

How to Exit:	Select **Q** under options menu.
OPAC Type:	DRA
Size of Collection:	500,000 total; 360,000 print volumes, 525,136 microforms, 22,000 other.
% Catalogued:	35%.
Not Catalogued:	Dorothy and Edgar Davidson Collection of Canadiana, Historical textbook collection. Items acquired before 1979, sheet music in Conservatory Library.
Subject Strengths:	Acadiana, Folklore, Music.
Special Collections:	Dorothy and Edgar Davidson Collection of Canadiana, Bell Collection of Acadiana, Mary Mellish Collection.
Public Databases:	None.

Mount Saint Vincent University (Novanet)
Halifax, Nova Scotia

ACCESS:	**Telnet: novanet.dal.ca**
Instructions:	A menu appears when the connection is established. Press **< return>**. Select **6** to limit search, select **1** for specific libraries, select **6** for Mount Saint Vincent University.
OPAC Type:	GEAC
How to Exit:	Type **end** to disconnect.
Size of Collection:	155,000 volumes.
% Catalogued:	80%.
Not Catalogued:	Most rare books are not catalogued. Approximately 50% of government documents are not catalogued.
Subject Strengths:	Women's Studies, Tourism and Hospitality, Public Relations. McDonald Rare Book Collection.
Public Databases:	None.

National Library of Canada (DOBIS)
Ottawa, Ontario

Note: *This is a fee-based service. You must register to use DOBIS. DOBIS contains the holdings of the National Library of Canada and over 1000 other Canadian libraries. DOBIS will be replaced in the near future by a new information system called AMICUS.*

ACCESS:	Instructions for authorized subscribers are available on the National Library of Canada's Gopher server at **gopher.nlc-bnc.ca**. To subscribe, send e-mail to **cic@nlc-bnc.ca** or telephone (819) 997-7227.
Instructions:	Commands are available in the searching manual which is provided to subscribers.
OPAC Type:	IBM-developed software, enhanced by the National Library of Canada.
How to Exit:	Commands are available in the searching manual which is provided to subscribers.
Size of Collection:	14.5 million items (National Library of Canada) (9.5 million print volumes, 5 million microform units).
% Catalogued:	80-90%.

Not Catalogued:	5% of the monographs and 20% of the foreign and international official publications.
Subject Strengths:	Canadiana and Canadian Studies, especially in the social sciences and humanities. Particular strengths include Canadian literature (especially children's literature), music in Canada, Canadian history, and library and information science.
Special Collections:	Rare books collection (rare Canadiana, early travels and explorations, native language literature, book art and illustration, livres d'artistes), literary manuscripts (manuscript collections of Canadian authors), Jacob M. Lowy Collection of Rare Hebraica and Judaica, materials for small and private presses, original art work for children's literature.
Special Notes:	The National Library of Canada houses and develops the world's foremost collection of Canadiana.
Public Databases:	None.

Natural Resources Canada
Headquarters Library
Ottawa, Ontario

ACCESS:	Telnet: hqlib.emr.ca
Instructions:	At the "login:" prompt, type **opac**.
OPAC Type:	MULTILIS
How to Exit:	Press **PF1** until the initial screen appears. Select **Exit** from the menu.

University of New Brunswick (PHOENIX)
Fredericton, New Brunswick

ACCESS:	TN3270: terra.csd.unb.ca
Instructions:	Choose menu option **8**.
How to Exit:	Type **stop** and press the **<enter>** key. Press the **<enter>** key again.
OPAC Type:	In-house.
Size of Collection:	1,045,147 print volumes and 2,002,537 equivalent volumes in microform.
% Catalogued:	Majority. Not catalogued: 20,000 titles from the regular collection, 50% of the government publications, special collections.
Subject Strengths:	Surveying engineering. Canadian history. Loyalist material. Canadian correspondence of Lord Beaverbrook.
Public Databases:	None.

University of Northern British Columbia
Prince George, British Columbia

ACCESS:	Telnet: library.unbc.edu
Instructions:	At the "Username:" prompt, type **LIBRARY**. Follow on-screen instructions.
How to Exit:	Select **Quit** from the "Options" item on the menu bar.
OPAC Type:	DRA
Size of Collection:	125,000 total; 67,000 print volumes, 57,000 microforms, 1,000 other materials.
% Catalogued:	100%.

Subject Strengths:	First Nations and Northern Literature (collection under development).
Public Databases:	None.

Nova Scotia College of Art and Design (Novanet)
Halifax, Nova Scotia

ACCESS:	Telnet: novanet.dal.ca
Instructions:	A menu appears when the connection is established. Press **return**. Select '**6**' to limit search, select '**1**' for specific libraries, select '**8**' for Nova Scotia College of Art and Design.
How to Exit:	Type **end** to disconnect.
OPAC Type:	GEAC
Size of Collection:	28,000 volumes.
% Catalogued:	95%.
Subject Strengths:	Environmental Planning, Graphic Communication and Design, Crafts, Fine Arts, Art Education. Exhibition Catalog Collection. Artists Books Collection.
Public Databases:	None.

Nova Scotia Provincial Library (NcompasS)
Nova Scotia Provincial Library and Nova Scotia Regional Library System (11 regional public libraries)
Halifax, Nova Scotia

ACCESS:	Telnet: rs6000.nshpl.library.ns.ca
Instructions:	Login as **liscat**.
OPAC Type:	MULTILIS
Size of Collection:	500,000 total.
% Catalogued:	70%.
Not Catalogued:	Mostly pre-1981 imprints and many paperbacks.
Subject Strengths:	Library and Information Science.
Special Collections:	Some regional libraries have Nova Scotia and local history collections, e.g. the Nova Scotia Collection in the Cape Breton Regional Library and the Banks Collection in the Western Counties Regional Library.
Public Databases:	None.

Oakville Public Library
Oakville, Ontario

ACCESS:	Telnet: halinet.sheridanc.on.ca
Instructions:	At the "login:" prompt, type **guest**. At the main menu choose **4** The Library, **1** Public Libraries, **4** Oakville Public Library, **5** Search the Catalog. Be prepared to select a terminal emulation.
How to Exit:	From the main menu, choose: **logoff**.
OPAC Type:	DYNIX

Ontario Institute for Studies in Education (ELOISE)
Toronto, Ontario

ACCESS:	**Telnet: eloise.oise.on.ca**
Instructions:	At the "login:" prompt, type **eloise**. Follow the instructions, and select option 1 to search the library catalogue.
How to Exit:	Press **PF1** until the initial screen appears, then select **Exit** to leave the catalogue. A menu will appear. Press **PF1** to leave the menu, and press **PF1** again to disconnect. (On PC and Mac enhanced keyboards, PF1 equals F1).
OPAC Type:	MULTILIS
Size of Collection:	251,723 print volumes, 523,686 microfiche/film, 18,595 multimedia, 30,366 bound journal volumes.
% Catalogued:	100%.
Subject Strengths:	Education and psychology. Unique collection of Ontario historical textbooks and curriculum guidelines.
Special Collections:	Ontario historical textbook collection, historical curriculum guidelines.
Public Databases:	Ontario Education Resources Information Service (ONTERIS).

Ottawa Public Library (OTTCAT)
Ottawa, Ontario

ACCESS:	**Telnet: ottlib.carleton.ca**
Instructions:	A menu will appear when the connection is established. Select **1** to search the catalogue.
How to Exit:	Press **CTRL-Z** to return to the main menu. Select option **4** to disconnect. Type **ST** to start a new search.
OPAC Type:	DRA
Size of Collection:	324,637 titles, 1,014,848 volumes. 885,889 print volumes; 253 microforms; 128,706 other materials.
% Catalogued:	95%.
Not Catalogued:	Laser videodiscs, paperbacks, maps and pamphlets.
Subject Strengths:	Ottawa Valley history, genealogy.
Special Collections:	Ottawa Room Collection - books and pamphlets by local authors and publishers, early city directories, local newspapers, maps and briefs, municipal minutes and by-laws. Talking book collection - restricted to borrowers with visual impairments.
Public Databases:	None.

University of Ottawa (ORBIS)
Ottawa, Ontario

ACCESS:	**Telnet: lib.uottawa.ca**
Instructions:	At the ">>>" prompt, type **pubmrt**. Follow the instructions.
How to Exit:	Type **B** until back at main menu, choose item **12**, then type **later.**
OPAC Type:	DYNIX
Size of Collection:	4,147,000 total; 1,070,137 print volumes, 642,173 other materials.
% Catalogued:	85%.

Not Catalogued:	Slides, air photos, archival material.
Subject Strengths:	Health Sciences, History, French and English literature, Management/Economics, Slavic Studies, Civil and Common Law, bilingual collections.
Special Collections:	Canadian Women's Movement Archives. 600 feminist periodical titles.
Public Databases:	None.

Palliser Institute SIAST Library
Moose Jaw, Saskatchewan

ACCESS:	Telnet: max.siast.sk.ca
Instructions:	At the "Username:" prompt, type **LIB**.
How to Exit:	Press **PF1**. This returns you to previous screen. Then type **LO** to logout.
OPAC Type:	MULTILIS
Size of Collection:	20,000 volumes.
% Catalogued:	100%.
Subject Strengths:	Business, Technology.
Public Databases:	None.

University of Prince Edward Island (BOBCAT)
Charlottetown, Prince Edward Island

ACCESS:	Telnet: zeus.cs.upei.ca
Instructions:	At the "Username" prompt, type **BOBCAT**.
How to Exit:	Type **exit** or **F10** to logoff.
OPAC Type:	DRA
Size of Collection:	608,888 total; 285,000 monographs, 70,000 periodicals backfiles, 162,000 government documents, 91,000 microforms, 665 videos .
% Catalogued:	85%.
Not Catalogued:	Government documents are not yet included. Serials are in process of being added. Holdings information for 50,000 monographs remain to be added. This will be completed by August 1995.
Subject Strengths:	Veterinary Medicine, Education, Social Sciences, Literature, History.
Special Collections:	PEI Collection.
Public Databases:	Reserve Book Room.

Université du Québec (BADADUQ)
Sainte-Foy, Quebec

ACCESS:	Telnet: sigird.uqam.ca
Instructions:	Once connected, choose the number corresponding to your terminal type (usually vt100). Select option **2** to search the library catalogue.
How to Exit:	Press **PF1** until the initial menu appears, then select **1** from the menu to disconnect.
OPAC Type:	SIGIRD..

Size of Collection:	1,190,802 items.
% Catalogued:	42%. Not catalogued or minimally catalogued: 690,125 titles, including 59,000 microforms, 103,000 government documents, 2,400 photographs, 21,000 musical illustrations, 21,000 sound recordings, 50,000 maps, 318,000 aerial photographs, films and videos, computer programs.
Subject Strengths:	Visual Arts, Art slides, Intercultural Education, Thanatology (study of death), Project Management, Real Estate Sciences, Sexology, Sound Archives of Radio-Canada.
Public Databases:	None.

Queen's University (QLINE)
Queen's Library Network
Kingston, Ontario

ACCESS:	TN3270: qline.queensu.ca Telnet: qlineascii.queensu.ca
Instructions:	Enter terminal type, (usually **vt100**), then follow instructions (the terminal type applies only to **qlineascii.queensu.ca**).
How to Exit:	Press **PF3** (Escape key + 3)
OPAC Type:	NOTIS
Size of Collection:	6,150,072 total; 2,917,899 print volumes; 3,232,173 microforms; 140,819 other materials.
% Catalogued:	99%.
Not Catalogued:	Art exhibition catalogues, some pamphlets and maps.
Subject Strengths:	Canadiana, U.K. 17th and 18th century political pamphlets, French history, especially political and cultural history at time of the French Revolution, Anglo-Irish Literature, First and early editions of Dickens, Economics, especially economic history of Western Europe and North America, Geological Science, South African 19th and 20th century history, Mathematics, Canadian government publications, Jewish studies, Canadian law.
Special Collections:	Lorne Pierce Collection (Canadiana), Lorne Pierce Papers (in Archives), Darwin Yarish Collection of AE (the poet George William Russell), Yeats and Cuala Press, John Buchan Collection (his library and manuscripts both literary and political), Bible Collection, Dickens Collection, McNicol Collection, Monk Gibbon Collection, Ontario Local Histories, Individual Canadian Literary Figures, e.g. Charles G.D. Roberts, Carman, Lampman, Major John Richardson, Frederick Philip Grove, Thomas Chandler Haliburton.
Public Databases:	QCAT (Queen's Library Catalogue), ARC (Queen's University Archives), MAR (Marine Museum of the Great Lakes), SAB (South African Bibliography), INF - INFOQ (Queen's campus wide information system).

Regina Public Library
Regina, Saskatchewan

ACCESS:	Telnet: opc.rpl.regina.sk.ca
Instructions:	At the central "login:" prompt, type **public**.
How to Exit:	Choose "**logoff**" from the main search menu.
OPAC Type:	DYNIX
Size of Collection:	841,083 total; 745,697 print volumes, 95,386 other materials.

% Catalogued:	90%.
Not Catalogued:	Not catalogued or partially catalogued: Serials, paperbacks, vertical files, small collections (e.g. maps), microforms, professional librarian's material.
Subject Strengths:	Mysteries, general fiction, cookery, gardening.
Special Collections:	Prairie History (Saskatchewan, Manitoba, Alberta and Northern U.S.), prairie gardening, current writings by native authors, historic works on native culture.
Public Databases:	None.

University of Regina (MURLIN)
MultiUser Regina Library Information Network
Regina, Saskatchewan

ACCESS:	**TN3270: max.cc.uregina.ca.** Wait 5-10 seconds for the connection to be established.
Instructions:	At the MAX logo screen, tab to the command line and type **d vsesp.**
	At the CICS logo screen, clear the screen, and type:
	LUUR <enter> to access the University of Regina Library.
	LULG <enter> to access the Saskatchewan Legislative Library.
	LUGD <enter> to access the Gabriel Dumont Institute.
	LUHL <enter> to access the Saskatchewan Department of Health Resource Centre, Plains Health Centre Library, the Regina General Hospital Library, Pasqua Hospital, and the Wascana Rehabilitation Centre.
	A MURLIN logo should appear. Press the **<enter>** key at the "NEXT COMMAND:" prompt.
	To change catalogues, clear the screen and type the four letter code of the library catalogue you want to search.
How to Exit:	Clear and screen and type **log.** Type **sta** to start another search.
OPAC Type:	NOTIS
Size of Collection:	Total: 2,190,500.
	University of Regina: 1,733,000 total (783,000 print volumes, 828,800 microform units, 120,750 other materials).
	Saskatchewan Legislative Library: 321,500 total (129,120 print volumes, 190,760 microform units, 1800 other materials).
	Saskatchewan Department of Health: 75,000 total (75,000 print volumes).
	Gabriel Dumont Institute: 40,000 total (39,200 print volumes, 100 microform units, 350 other materials).
	Plains Health Centre: 10,300 total (9,000 print volumes, 1,230 microform units, 200 other materials).
	Regina General Hospital: 6,000 total (5,750 print volumes, 50 microform units, 200 other materials).
	Pasqua Hospital: 2,500 total (2,500 print volumes).
	Wascana Hospital: 2,500 total (2,400 print volumes, 100 other materials).

% Catalogued:	University of Regina: 98%. Saskatchewan Legislative Library: 20%. Saskatchewan Department of Health: 60%. Gabriel Dumont Institute: 50%. Plains Health Centre: 90%. Regina General Hospital: 80%. Pasqua Hospital: 30%. Wascana Hospital: 30%.
Not Catalogued:	University of Regina: Vertical file, individual titles in micro series.
	Saskatchewan Legislative Library: fiche, maps, audiovisual.
	Saskatchewan Department of Health: Saskatchewan Alcoholism and Drug Addiction Collection.
	Gabriel Dumont Institute: Collections in Prince Albert and Saskatoon.
	Plains Health Centre: fiche.
	Regina General Hospital: fiche, serials, audiovisual.
	Pasqua Hospital: serials and 60% of monographs.
	Wascana Hospital: serials and 60% of monographs.
Subject Strengths:	University of Regina: General arts and sciences, education, administration, journalism, social work, native studies.
	Saskatchewan Legislative Library: Saskatchewan history and politics.
	Saskatchewan Department of Health: Public health, prevention, lifestyles.
	Gabriel Dumont Institute: Métis.
	Plains Health Centre: Medicine - cardiovascular, trauma, neuroscience, internal medicine.
	Regina General Hospital: Medicine - obstetrics, gynecology, pediatrics.
	Wascana Hospital: Rehabilitation, long-term care.
	Pasqua Hospital: Medicine.
Public Databases:	None.

Royal Military College of Canada
Kingston, Ontario

ACCESS:	**Telnet: pacx.rmc.ca**
Instructions:	At the "Enter class" prompt, type **library**. Follow the instructions on the screen.
How to Exit:	Type **so** to start a new search. At the main menu, select option **13** to leave the catalogue. Type **logoff** to exit the OPAC. Wait 5-10 seconds for disconnection.
OPAC Type:	DYNIX
Size of Collection:	363,431 items (March/92).
% Catalogued:	98% of books and serials. Very little catalogued: technical reports, government documents, microform, photographs, manuscripts, and prints.
Subject Strengths:	Military studies (45,010 in March/92), first editions of Canadian literature.
Public Databases:	None.

Royal Roads Military College
Victoria, British Columbia

ACCESS:	**Telnet: library.royalroads.ca**

Instructions:	At the "login:" prompt, type **library** and follow the on-screen instructions. When asked if you want to set up a default print destination, type **N** for no.
How to Exit:	Select item **11** from the main menu. Type **logoff** from the opening screen, and wait 5-10 seconds.
OPAC Type:	DYNIX.

Ryerson Polytechnic University
Toronto, Ontario

ACCESS:	Telnet: hugo.lib.ryerson.ca
Instructions:	At the "Username:" prompt, type **RYERSON.** Select 1 to access the library catalogue.
How to Exit:	Type **0** and press **<enter>.** to exit from the main menu. To exit from PAC type **stop** or **exit** and press **<enter>.**
OPAC Type:	DRA
Size of Collection:	333,000 monographs, 4,000 other materials.
% Catalogued:	90%.
Not Catalogued:	Serials, maps, vertical file materials, company annual reports and a collection of urban planning documents are not yet on the system. Serials should be on the system by the end of 1994.
Subject Strengths:	Radio and Television, Film and Photography, Fashion, Interior Design, Journalism.
Special Collections:	Bureau of Broadcast Measurement publications.
Public Databases:	None.

Saint Mary's University (Novanet)
Halifax, Nova Scotia

ACCESS:	Telnet: novanet.dal.ca
Instructions:	A menu appears when the connection is established. Press **<return>**. Select '**6**' to limit search, select '**1**' for specific libraries, select '**5**' for St. Mary's University.
How to Exit:	Type **end** to disconnect.
OPAC Type:	GEAC
Size of Collection:	301,000 volumes.
% Catalogued:	85%. All currently received periodicals are catalogued.
Not Catalogued:	25% of the dead titles (periodicals not currently received), government documents collection.
Subject Strengths:	Business, Irish Studies.
Public Databases:	None.

Saskatoon Public Library (HOMER2)
Saskatoon, Saskatchewan

ACCESS:	Telnet: charly.publib.saskatoon.sk.ca
Instructions:	At the "Username" prompt, type **PUBLIC**. At the "pac>>" prompt, type **pac**. Follow the instructions.

How to Exit:	Type **stop** to return to the "pac>>" prompt. At the "pac>>" prompt, type **quit** to disconnect.
OPAC Type:	DRA
Size of Collection:	720,000 items.
% Catalogued:	97%.
Not Catalogued:	Mass-market paperbacks, audio-cassettes, magazines, vertical file collection.
Subject Strengths:	Local history, English-language literature, History.
Public Databases:	None.

University of Saskatchewan (SONIA)
Saskatoon, Saskatchewan

ACCESS:	**Telnet: sklib.usask.ca**
Instructions:	At the "Username:" prompt, type **SONIA**. Select option **1** from the menu.
How to Exit:	Type **D** from the INNOPAC main menu. From the catalogues menu, type **Q**. From the databases menu, type **Q** again to disconnect.
OPAC Type:	INNOPAC.
Size of Collection:	1.53 million print volumes, 2.53 million microform items, 427,500 government publications and pamphlets.
% Catalogued:	97%.
Subject Strengths:	Prairie Provinces History and Culture, including the Shortt Library of Western Canadiana. 18th Century History and Enlightenment. International Human Rights. Agriculture and Agrieconomics (including cooperatives). Conrad Aiken published materials. Specialized European Documentation Centre. Russell Green Music Manuscripts.
Special Collections:	Diefenbaker Collection, Shortt collection of materials pertaining to First Nations people.
Public Databases:	Saskatoon News Index, Library Hours, Landmarks of Science, University of Saskatchewan Government Publications, University Archives, Special Collections (Canadiana Pamphlets, Manuscripts, Theses), Canadian Institute for Historical Microreproductions, Canadian Education Index, History of Photography (microfilm collection), American Periodical Series — 18th Century (microfilm collection), Saskatchewan Teachers' Federation Library, Native Resource Centre, Saskatchewan Theological Libraries Consortium, Rt. Hon. John George Diefenbaker Centre Archive, Film Library, University Archives, ERIC (Resources in Education and Current Index to Journals in Education), First and Best (honour graduates who have made noteworthy achievements).

Université de Sherbrooke (SIBUS)
Système Informatisé des Bibliothèques de l'Université de Sherbrooke
Sherbrooke, Quebec

ACCESS:	**Telnet: catalo.biblio.usherb.ca**
Instructions:	At the "login:" prompt, type **qsheru**.
How to Exit:	Press the **PF1** key until the initial screen is displayed. Use the arrow keys to select **Exit** from the menu.
OPAC Type:	MULTILIS

Size of Collection:	612,493 total.
% Catalogued:	100%.
Subject Strengths:	Call for information.
Public Databases:	None.

Simon Fraser University (SFULIB)
Burnaby, British Columbia

ACCESS:	Telnet: library.sfu.ca
Instructions:	At the "Username:" prompt, type **SFULIB**. Follow the instructions.
How to Exit:	Type **end** to disconnect.
OPAC Type:	GEAC 9000
Size of Collection:	750,000 titles, 1,000,000 print volumes, 900,000 sheets/reels, 129,646 other materials.
% Catalogued:	Almost 100%.
Not Catalogued:	Maps, special collections, manuscripts.
Subject Strengths:	Contemporary Literature, Wordsworth.
Special Notes:	Patrons and other British Columbia post-secondary library users are provided with document-requesting capabilities on-line.
Public Databases:	None.

St. Boniface General Hospital
Manitoba, Canada

ACCESS:	Telnet: umopac.umanitoba.ca
Instructions:	When the "UML=>" prompt appears on the screen, type **be** to display the introductory screen. Type the command **set lib sbh** to restrict the search to St. Boniface General Hospital.
How to Exit:	Type **close** to disconnect.
OPAC Type:	PALS

St. Francis Xavier University (Novanet)
Antigonish, Nova Scotia

ACCESS:	Telnet: novanet.dal.ca WWW: http://libwww.stfx.ca OR http://www.novanet.dal.ca/www/homepg.htm
Instructions:	A menu appears when the connection is established. Press return. Select '**6**' to limit search, select '**1**' for specific libraries, select '**15**' for St. Francis Xavier.
How to Exit:	Type **end** to disconnect.
OPAC Type:	GEAC
Size of Collection:	728,367 total: 589,341 print volumes, 137,435 microform units, 1,591 other materials.
% Catalogued:	25%.

Subject Strengths:	English literature, Theology, Celtic studies.
Special Collections:	Celtic Studies.
Public Databases:	None.

Technical University of Nova Scotia (Novanet)
Halifax, Nova Scotia

ACCESS:	**Telnet: novanet.dal.ca**
Instructions:	A menu appears when the connection is established. Press return. Select `6` to limit search, select `1` for specific libraries, select `7` for Technical University of Nova Scotia.
How to Exit:	Type **end** to disconnect.
OPAC Type:	GEAC
Size of Collection:	100,000 volumes, 35,000 monographs, 65,000 serials.
% Catalogued:	71% of all serial titles, 100% of currently received serial titles, 100% of monograph titles and graduate and Ph.D theses.
Subject Strengths:	Architecture, Urban and Rural Planning, Engineering, Computer Science, Applied Mathematics.
Public Databases:	None.

University of Toronto (UTCAT)
Toronto, Ontario

ACCESS:	**Telnet: library.utoronto.ca**
Instructions:	At the "Username:" prompt, type **utlink**. Press **<enter>** when prompted for a password.
How to Exit:	Select **EXIT/Logoff** from the "UTLink Options" option on the menu bar.
OPAC Type:	DRA
Size of Collection:	8,000,000 volumes.
% Catalogued:	98% of the holdings of the University of Toronto library.
Not Catalogued:	Some non-roman titles and some older holdings.
Subject Strengths:	All areas.
Special Notes:	Largest collection in North America. Ranks in the top 10 in North America.
Public Databases:	None.

Trent University (TOPCAT)
Peterborough, Ontario

ACCESS:	**Telnet: babel.trentu.ca**
Instructions:	At the "Username:" prompt, type **TOPCAT**. Select option **1** from the menu.
How to Exit:	Press **CTRL-Z** to return to the main menu. Type **EX** to disconnect.
OPAC Type:	DRA
Size of Collection:	600,000 total; 400,000 print volumes, 60,000 microforms, 140,000 other materials.

Subject Strengths:	Canadian studies, native studies, anthropology.
Public Databases:	None.

Vancouver Public Library
Vancouver, British Columbia

ACCESS:	Telnet: vpl.vancouver.bc.ca
Instructions:	At the "login:" prompt, type **netpac**. At the "password:" prompt, type **netpac1**. When the system asks if VT100 is okay, press **<enter>** if you are using VT100 emulation. Enter **N** to select other options.
How to Exit:	Select **Logoff** from any search menu.
OPAC Type:	DYNIX
Size of Collection:	700,000 titles, 2,090,000 items.
% Catalogued:	Serials holdings are partially catalogued.
Subject Strengths:	Business, Northwest History, Photography, Standards.
Public Databases:	Community Organization Directory, Vancouver City Council Minutes, Consumer Index, Community Events Calendar, Quick Reference File.

University of Victoria (VICTOR)
Victoria, British Columbia

ACCESS:	Telnet: mpg.uvic.ca
Instructions:	At "Enter Service Name...", type **victor**. Type **vt100** as the terminal type, Press **<enter>** when the logon screen appears.
How to Exit:	Type **stop** to disconnect. Type **sta** to return to the welcome screen.
OPAC Type:	NOTIS
Size of Collection:	1.8 million volumes, 1.7 million microforms, 42,000 sound recordings, 28,000 scores, 4,000 films and videos, 170,000 maps and aerial photographs.
% Catalogued:	Majority.
Not Cataloged:	Pre-1978 holdings of Main Library, pre-1988 holdings of Law Library, 90% of the law serials.
Subject Strengths:	Local History, Modern British Literature.
Public Databases:	None.

Victoria General Hospital Library (Novanet)
Halifax, Nova Scotia

ACCESS:	Telnet: novanet.dal.ca
Instructions:	A menu appears when the connection is established. Press return. Select '**6**' to limit search, select '**1**' for specific libraries, select '**16**' for Victoria General Hospital Library.
How to Exit:	Type **end** to disconnect.
OPAC Type:	GEAC

University of Waterloo (WATCAT)
Waterloo, Ontario

ACCESS:	Telnet: watcat.uwaterloo.ca WWW: http://www.lib.uwaterloo.ca/
Instructions:	Press **<enter>** when the welcome screen is displayed. Follow the instructions.
How to Exit:	Type **end**.
OPAC Type:	GEAC
Size of Collection:	2,829,695 total: 1,676,711 print volumes, 1,020,423 microforms, 132,561 other materials.
% Catalogued:	100%.
Subject Strengths:	Mathematics, Computer Science.
Special Collections:	Early editions of Euclid, books on the history of dance and ballet, some maps, local history material, and the personal library of George Santayana, as well as the archival collections of papers, manuscripts and correspondence of notable Canadian women.
Public Databases:	None.

University of Waterloo (WatMedia)
Waterloo, Ontario

ACCESS:	Gopher: watserv2.uwaterloo.ca
Instructions:	Choose: Departments, Faculties, Associations, Student Groups/Audio Visual Center/ WatMedia.
How to Exit:	Select the **quit** command.
OPAC Type:	SPIRES. Application software written in-house.
Size of Collection:	43,000 total, 5,500 film and video titles.
% Catalogued:	100%.
Subject Strengths:	Art History, Computer Science, Engineering, Cinema, Architecture.
Special Collections:	A collection relating to the last two years of the Franco regime and the first two years of the new monarchy in Spain, about 500 films. The Breithaupt family films, part of the Breithaupt Papers in the University Archives.
Public Databases:	None.

University of Western Ontario
London, Ontario

ACCESS:	Telnet: library.uwo.ca
Instructions:	When asked to press "send," press the **<enter>** key. Type **opc,** then press **<enter>** when asked for a selection.
How to Exit:	Press **CTRL-D** to disconnect.
OPAC Type:	GEAC 9000
Size of Collection:	6,258,589 total; 2,141,703 print volumes, 3,013,499 microforms, 1,103,387 other items.
% Catalogued:	90-95%.

Not Catalogued:	Pamphlets (catalogued prior to 1993), Regional Collection material, Microform analytics (approx. 2 million items), holdings for the affiliated colleges at UWO, Brescia, King's, Huron are not included.
Subject Strengths:	Broad-based research collection includes: Canadian, American, and British Government Publications, Canadiana, Canadian and American newspapers, Medicine, English, American History, Women's Studies, Opera, Chemistry, Sciences, Business, Law, Education, Mathematics.
Special Collections:	G. William Stuart Collection of Milton and Miltoniana, pre-Confederation Canadiana, H. G. Wells Collection.
Public Databases:	None.

Wilfrid Laurier University (QCAT)
Waterloo. Ontario

ACCESS:	Telnet: mach1.wlu.ca
Instructions:	At the "Login:" prompt, type **public**. At the first menu, select option **1**.
How to Exit:	Press **CTRL-C** to get back to the menu. Type **E**, then choose item **4**.
OPAC Type:	In-house.
Size of Collection:	1,200,000 total; 568,103 print volumes, 492,910 microforms, 62,026 other materials.
% Catalogued:	98%.
Not Catalogued:	Slides.
Subject Strengths:	Social work, business and economics, music, Lutheran material, Post World War 2 international relations.
Special Collections:	String music listening collection; Lutheran Church Archives.
Public Databases:	Ensemble Music Library.

University of Windsor (LUIS)
Library User Information System
Windsor, Ontario

ACCESS:	Telnet: library.uwindsor.ca
Instructions:	Select **1** for Main Library. Press the **<enter>** key twice and you will receive the "ENTER TERMINAL TYPE:" prompt. Type **vt100**. When a blank screen appears, press **<enter>** key several times, and the on-line catalogue will be displayed.
How to Exit:	Type **stop** to disconnect. Type **sta** to start a new search.
OPAC Type:	NOTIS
Size of Collection:	2,375,507 volumes.
% Catalogued:	90-95%.
Not Catalogued:	Chinese, Russian, and non-roman alphabet items, newspaper clippings, some archival documents, and some materials in the Curriculum Resource Centre (e.g. posters) are not catalogued.
Subject Strengths:	Asian Studies, Canadian and American Relations, Criminology, International Trade, Labour Economics, Philosophy and Religious Studies, Political Science, Psychology, Theology, Victorian Literature, Sociology, Social Work, the Great Lakes Collection (38,000 documents on the Great Lakes).
Public Databases:	None.

University of Windsor, Faculty of Law Library
Windsor, Ontario

ACCESS:	**Telnet: library.uwindsor.ca**
Instructions:	Select **2** for the Law Library. Follow the on-screen instructions.
How to Exit:	Type **stop** to disconnect.
OPAC Type:	NOTIS
Size of Collection:	186,000 total; 158,445 print volumes, 27,555 microforms.
% Catalogued:	100%.
Subject Strengths:	Canadian Law - Primary (Statutes, Regs, Law reports), as well as texts and periodicals; reasonable basic collections of British, US Federal, Michigan and a few other states for primary and texts, and some periodicals; also holdings for Australian and South African primary and texts.
Public Databases:	None.

University of Winnipeg (Bridge)
Winnipeg, Manitoba

ACCESS:	**Telnet: umopac.umanitoba.ca**
Instructions:	Type **be** at the "UML=>" prompt. Type **set lib UOW** to restrict the search to the University of Winnipeg.
How to Exit:	Type **end** to finish the session, then type **close** to disconnect.
OPAC Type:	PALS
Size of Collection:	350,000 titles, 525,000 volumes, 425,000 print volumes, 120,702 microforms.
% Catalogued:	66%.
Subject Strengths:	Theology, Science Fiction, 19th Century Canadian Fiction, Canadian History.
Public Databases:	None.

York University (YORKLINE)
North York, Ontario

ACCESS:	**Telnet: yorkline.yorku.ca** **Gopher: gamma.library.yorku.ca**
Instructions:	Press **<enter>** several times when the connection is established. At the "ENTER TERMINAL TYPE" prompt, type **vt100**. When the York screen appears, type **YORKLINE**.
How to Exit:	Type **stop**.
OPAC Type:	NOTIS
Size of Collection:	2,063,777 print volumes; 3,143,583 microform units; 2,032 films, 3,441 videocassettes, 38,075 sound recordings, 47 CD-ROMs, 8,048 pamphlets.
% Catalogued:	100%.
Subject Strengths:	Dance, Social Sciences, especially Canadian Studies, Business Administration, Psychology, Sociology, Law.
Public Databases:	None.

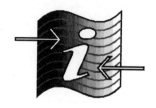

APPENDIX N

THE DIRECTORY OF INTERNET-RELATED PUBLICATIONS

In this section, we provide you with information on several publications that cover the Internet. Subscribing to one or more of the following publications will help you keep up-to-date with events on the Internet.

For each publication, we provide you with the frequency of publication, format, contact information, and subscription rates. We also indicate if the publication is sold at newsstands, or available by postal or electronic subscription.

HOW TO SUBMIT INFORMATION FOR THE DIRECTORY OF INTERNET-RELATED PUBLICATIONS:
Contributions to this directory are welcome. If you wish to add a publication to this directory, please contact the authors at <handbook@uunet.ca>.

Boardwatch Magazine
Guide to Online Information Services and Electronic Bulletin Boards
Frequency: Monthly
Format: Colour glossy
Available at newsstands or by postal subscription

Boardwatch Magazine covers electronic bulletin boards and on-line information services. Each issue contains information on BBS systems, software releases, information databases, and successful on-line systems. *Boardwatch Magazine* also provides profiles of industry players, hardware and software reviews, and tips for using your PC and modem. There are regular features on Delphi, America Online, Genie, Prodigy, CompuServe, and the Internet. There is a regular Internet section called *INTERNETICA*.

Boardwatch Magazine
8500 W. Bowles Avenue, Suite 210
Littleton, CO 80123
U.S.A.
Voice: (303) 973-6038 (Editorial)
Voice: 1-800-933-6038 (Subscriptions only)
Fax: (303) 973-3731
BBS: (303) 973-4222
Internet: subscriptions@boardwatch.com
          jack.rickard@boardwatch.com (Editor/Publisher)

U.S. and Canadian Subscriptions:
US$36.00 for a one-year subscription
US$59.00 for a two-year subscription

Overseas Subscriptions:
US$99.00 for a one-year subscription

Connect: The Modem User's Resource
Frequency: **Bimonthly**
Format: **Colour glossy**
Available at newsstands or by postal subscription

Connect has regular columns on bulletin board systems and BBS software, the Internet, and the major commercial online services such as America Online, BIX, CompuServe, Delphi, and GEnie. All varieties of computer platforms (IBM, Apple/Macintosh, Commodore/Amiga, Atari) are covered, and hardware/software reviews and industry news briefs appear regularly. *Connect* has a regular column on the Internet called "The Internet Gateway". Recent articles include:

- *Accessing the Online World of Bulletin Boards*
- *Newspapers in the Electronic Age*
- *Kids in Cyberspace*
- *How to Choose an Online Service*

Pegasus Press Inc.
3487 Braeburn Circle
Ann Arbor, Michigan 48108-2619
U.S.A.
Voice: (313) 973-8825
Fax: (313) 973-0411
BBS: (313) 973-9137 (14,400 bps)
Subscriptions: 1-800-438-2666 (credit card orders)
Internet: pegasus@cyberspace.org
Compuserve: 70007,4640

Canadian residents: US$30.00 per year (surface)
U.S. Residents: US$18.00 per year

INFORMATION highways
The Magazine for Consumers of Strategic Electronic Information
Frequency: Bi-monthly
Format: Colour glossy
Available by postal subscription only

The purpose of **INFORMATION highways** *is to provide a forum for the consumers, vendors, and publishers of electronic information services and products. Recent articles include:*

- *Canadian Federal and Provincial Government Information on the Internet*

- *Comparison Shopping: How to's on Selecting a Database*

- *Desktop Packages for Competitive Intelligence*

- *Scientists and Researchers and Electronic Information*

INFORMATION highways
c/o Database Canada Inc.
162 Joicey Blvd.
Toronto, Ontario M5M 2V2
Canada
Voice: (416) 488-7372
Fax: (416) 488-7078
Internet: infohiwy@io.org

Canadian Subscriptions:
CDN$98.00 for a one-year subscription
CDN$175.00 for a two-year subscription

Addresses Outside Canada:
US$105.00 for a one-year subscription
US$189.00 for a two-year subscription

Internet Business Advantage
Online Solutions For Business Success
Frequency: Monthly
Format: Newsletter
Available by postal subscription only

Internet Business Advantage is written for entrepreneurs and small to mid-size companies who want to learn how to do business on the Internet. Recent articles include:

- *Getting Your Business Online*

- *Advertising and Promoting Your Business Online*

- *Case Study: Polymer Wire (BBS) Targets the Plastics Industry*

- *Case Study: HotelNet Opens For Business*

- *Plugging Holes in Your Net: Keeping Online Data Safe*

Internet Business Advantage
c/o Wentworth Worldwide Media
1866 Colonial Village Lane
P.O. Box 10488
Lancaster, PA 17605-0488
Voice: 1-800-638-1639
Fax: (717) 393-5752
Internet: success@wentworth.com

Canadian and U.S. Subscriptions:
US$67.00 for a one-year subscription

The Internet Business Journal
Frequency: Monthly
Format: Paper
Available by postal subscription only

The Internet Business Journal was established to help businesses use the Internet. It provides regular coverage of commercial services and products on the Internet, and documents how large and small businesses are using the Internet for competitive advantage. Each issue contains pointers to a variety of Internet-accessible resources for business. Recent articles include:

- *The Internet in Europe*

- *Internet Publishing News*

- *Advertising on the Internet*

- *Censorship in Cyberspace*

- *Internet Store-Fronts*

Strangelove Internet Enterprises
208 Somerset Street East
Suite A
Ottawa, Ontario, Canada
K1N 6V2
Voice: (613) 565-0982
Fax: (613) 569-4433
Internet: mstrange@fonorola.net

Gopher: gopher.fonorola.net

Canadian Subscriptions:
Regular Rate:
CDN$191.53 per year
Educational Libraries and Small Business Rate:
CDN$95.23 per year

U.S. Subscriptions:
Regular Rate:
US$149.00 per year
Educational Libraries and Small Business Rate:
US$75.00 per year

Internet Business Report
Commercial Opportunities on the Global Net
Frequency: Monthly
Format: Paper
Available by postal subscription only

Recent articles include:

- *Reuters Plans Its Own Internet Mall*

- *New Internet Security Company Comes Into Being*

- *For a Drop-In-The-Bucket, Ford Gets Space on the Net*

- *Q&A: A Venture Capitalist's View of the Internet*

Internet Business Report
c/o CMP Publications Inc.
600 Community Drive
Manhasset, New York 11030
U.S.A.
Voice: 1-800-340-6485 (Subscriptions only)
Fax: (516) 733-6960 (Subscriptions only)
Internet: ibrsub@cmp.com (Subscriptions only)

Canadian and U.S. Subscriptions: **US$279.00 per year**
Overseas Subscriptions: **US$379.00 per year**

The Internet Letter
Frequency: Monthly
Format: Paper
Available by postal mail or electronic mail

Mission Statement:
The Internet Letter *covers the businesses that use the Internet, the political forces that shape it, and the information that flows across it.*

*Sample articles are available on the Electronic Newsstand's Gopher server. Point your Gopher server at **gopher.enews.com** and select The Electronic Newsstand/All Titles Listed Alphabetically/Titles From G to L/The Internet Letter.*

Jayne Levin, Editor
The Internet Letter
220 National Press Building
Washington, D.C. 20045
U.S.A.
Voice: (202) 638-6020
Fax: (202) 638-6019
Internet: netweek@access.digex.net

North American Subscriptions: **US$249.00 per year**
Outside North America: **US$295.00 per year**

Internet Research: Electronic Applications and Policy
Frequency: Quarterly
Format: Paper (black and white)
Available by postal subscription only

Internet Research is a cross-disciplinary journal that publishes research findings that describe and evaluate current and potential applications or identify and assess policy issues related to electronic networking that impact individuals, organizations, nations, or the globe. The journal also features reviews and announcments of print and electronic resources of related interest. The journal is of interest to network users, managers, and policy makers in the academic, computer, communication, library, and government communities.

Subscriptions:

Mecklermedia
20 Ketchum Street
Westport, CT 06880
U.S.A.
Voice: (203) 226-6967
Internet: info@mecklermedia.com

Editorial:

Dr. Charles R. McClure
Syracuse University
School of Information Studies
4-206 C.S.T.
Syracuse, New York 13244-4100
U.S.A.
Voice: (315) 443-2911
Fax: (315) 443-5806
Internet: cmcclure@suvm.syr.edu

Canadian Subscriptions:
U.S. $63.00 per year

Internet Society News
Frequency: Quarterly
Format: B&W glossy
Available by postal subscription only

Internet Society News provides an international forum for the exchange of information about the evolution and use of Internet technology, the growth of the global Internet and related private networks, the activities of the Internet Society and its members, and events significant to Internet Society constituents. Each issue features networking reports from around the world.

Internet Society News is free with membership in the Internet Society. Recent articles include:

- *Connecting the Caribbean*

- *Internet Developments in South Africa*

- *Becoming an Information Provider on the World Wide Web*

- *Rites of Spring: Libel Lawsuits Come to the Internet Worldwide*

Internet Society
12020 Sunrise Valley Drive, Suite 270
Reston, VA 22091
U.S.A.
Voice: (703) 648-9888
Fax: (703) 648-9887
Internet:
isoc@isoc.org (general information)
membership@isoc.org (individual membership information)
org-membership@isoc.org (organizational memberships)
Gopher: gopher.isoc.org
World Wide Web: http://info.isoc.org/home.html

Individual membership: *US$35.00 per year*
Student membership: *US$25.00 per year*

Internet World
The Magazine for Internet Users
Frequency: Monthly
Format: Colour glossy
Available at newsstands or by postal subscription

Mandate and Mission Statement: **Internet World** *is a magazine for and about the Internet user community...the primary audience is the extended user community - end-users, and people like librarians and MIS managers and system administrators who are responsible for providing services to these users, plus the information and service providers and the developers who develop the business and educational resources users use. Internet World's mission statement is "Information for the Connected and Outreach for the Interested." Recent articles include:*

- *Internet Games*

- *Sports on the Net*

- *Electronic Commerce on the Internet*

- *Visiting Museums on the Internet*

- *A Journalist's View of the Internet*

Internet World
20 Ketchum Street
Westport, Connecticut 06880
U.S.A.
Voice: 1-800-632-5537
                 (203) 226-6967
Fax: (203) 454-5840
Internet:
Subscription enquiries: iwsubs@mecklermedia.com
Editorial enquiries: iwedit@mecklermedia.com

Canadian Subscriptions:
One year subscription: *US$32.06*
Two year subscription: *US$64.12*

U.S. Subscriptions:
One year subscription: US$19.97
Two year subscription: US$39.94

Matrix News

Frequency: Monthly
Format: Paper
Available by postal subscription or electronic mail

Matrix News is a newsletter about cross-network issues in the Matrix — all computer networks worldwide that exchange electronic mail. Networks covered include USENET, UUCP, FidoNet, BITNET, Internet, and conferencing systems such as the WELL and CompuServe. Book reviews appear regularly. Recent articles include:

- *Fidonet Growth Rates*

- *A Map of the Matrix in Peru*

- *The Internet: Commercial vs. Educational*

- *Growth of Internet Resource Discovery Services*

- *The Internet Demographic Survey*

Matrix Information and Directory Services
1106 Clayton Lane
Suite 500W
Austin, Texas 78723
Voice: (512) 451-7602
Internet: mids@tic.com
World Wide Web: http://www.mids.org

Online version: *US$25.00/year (US$15 for students).*
Paper version: *US$30.00/year (US$20 for students).*
Both online and paper: *US$35.00/year (US$25 for students).*

Online Access
The Magazine that Makes Modems Work

Frequency: Monthly
Format: Colour glossy
Available at newsstands or by postal subscription

Online Access' mission is "to educate our readers about online services and how these services can benefit both their professional and personal lives". Online Access covers the full spectrum of online services from major online vendors and corporate databases to bulletin board services and the Internet. Recent articles include:

- *Managing Your E-Mail*

- *For Beginners: How to Upload and Download*

- *International BBSing*

- *Internet Mailing Lists*

- *BBSes and Shareware*

Online Access
900 North Franklin Street
Suite 310
Chicago, Illinois 60610
U.S.A.
Voice: (312) 573-1700 (Editorial enquiries)
          1-800-366-6336 (Subscriptions only)
Fax: (312) 573-0520
Internet: 70324.343@CompuServe.com

Canadian Subscriptions: **US$34.65 per year**
U.S. Subscriptions: **US$29.70 per year**
Other Countries: **US$87.15 per year**

WIRED Magazine
Frequency: Monthly
Format: Colour glossy
Available at newsstands or by postal subscription

WIRED *is a colourful magazine covering the on-line and high-tech world, with regular features on the Internet.*

Wired Magazine
520 Third Street
San Francisco, California 94107
U.S.A.
Voice: (415) 222-6200
Fax: (415) 222-6209
Internet: info@wired.com (General questions)
          subscriptions@wired.com (Subscriptions)
          editor@wired.com (Editorial correspondence)

Canadian and Mexican Subscriptions:
US$64.00 for one year, US$119.00 for two years (Individuals)
US$103.00 for one year, US$191.00 for two years (Institutions)

U.S. Subscriptions:
US$39.95 for one year, US$71.00 for two years (Individuals)
US$80.00 for one year, US$143.00 for two years (Institutions)

Foreign Subscriptions:
US$79.00 for one year, US$149.00 for two years (Individuals)
US$110.00 for one year, US$210.00 for two years (Institutions)

Information about WIRED magazine is available on the World Wide Web:
http://www.wired.com

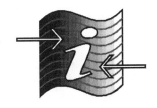

....

THE DIRECTORY OF COMMUNITY NETWORKING ORGANIZATIONS IN CANADA

© 1994 Rick Broadhead and Jim Carroll

This directory lists Canadian communities which had operational community computer systems or active organizing committees in September 1994.   Many community computer networks are known as "Free-Nets". In this book, the name "Free-Net" is synonymous with "community computer network".

WHAT IS A COMMUNITY COMPUTER NETWORK?

Most community computer networks are not-for-profit organizations, run primarily by volunteers from within the community. Community computer networks provide a wide spectrum of on-line information services to the local communities they serve. Their primary function is to provide on-line access to local information resources, but many community networks also provide limited Internet access to their users.

Community networks have traditionally been modelled on the same principle as public libraries. They provide information to the community at no charge to the end-user. Some Free-Nets have adopted a different philosophy and have chosen to impose a fee on their users.

A key element of the Free-Net concept is the participation of "information providers" – organizations from all sectors of the community that provide information to the Free-Net.

Information providers are responsible for maintaining and updating their information on the Free-Net.

HOW CAN YOU HELP?

(1) VOLUNTEER

Since volunteers are the lifeblood of most Free-Nets, Free-Nets are always seeking new volunteers. If you have experience in fund-raising, training, technical writing, public/media relations, computer networking, or volunteer management, or you just want to help out, check the directory below, and contact a Free-Net near you. Experience is not required to volunteer. Most Free-Nets are more than happy to train new volunteers.

(2) SPONSOR YOUR LOCAL FREE-NET

Free-Nets rely on government, corporate, and user support for funding. In return, sponsors receive on-line recognition of their support and contribute to the development of an important community resource. In addition to making monetary contributions, organizations can assist Free-Nets by donating expertise, services and/or equipment. Contact your local Free-Net to find out how your organization can help.

(3) BECOME AN INFORMATION PROVIDER

Free-Nets feature a wide array of information on topics such as community events, medical and health care, education, law, science and technology, social services, government, entertainment, travel and tourism, and employment. If you are an organization that has community-related information to distribute, contact your local community network to find out how you can make your information available on their system.

WHERE CAN I FIND OUT MORE?

If you would like to keep abreast of the community networking movement in Canada, we suggest that you join the **can-freenet** mailing list, which has been established for the discussion of Canadian community networking initiatives. To subscribe to the list, send a message to the following Internet address:

```
listserv@cunews.carleton.ca
```

and place the following command on the first line of the body of the message:

```
subscribe can-freenet <FIRSTNAME> <LASTNAME>
```

e.g. **subscribe can-freenet Joe Smith**

A good source of information on community networking is the University of Saskatchewan Gopher server:

gopher.usask.ca
Select: Other/Testing/Freenet_Documents.

There, you'll find papers, reports, and documentation related to community networking.

The **National Public Telecomputing Network** (NPTN) in Cleveland, Ohio is a coordinating body for Free-Net organizations worldwide. The NPTN maintains a list of Free-Nets and organizing committees on their anonymous FTP host, as well as general information about how to start a Free-Net in your city or town. You can retrieve the material by anonymous FTP, as detailed below.

Anonymous FTP Site:	**nptn.org**
Directory:	**pub/nptn**

NPTN files are in the directories **nptn.info** and **nptn.docs**.

You can retrieve a list of NPTN affiliate systems and organizing committees at the same site, as detailed in the box below:

Anonymous FTP Site:	**nptn.org**
Directory:	**pub/nptn/nptn.info**
File:	**nptn.affil-organ.list**

For further information about the National Public Telecomputing Network, you can send electronic mail to **info@nptn.org.**

An organization called **Telecommunities Canada** was formed in the summer of 1994 to represent the interests of community computer networks in Canada. Information from the founding meeting of Telecommunities Canada, and other related information, including status reports from Canadian Free-Nets, is available on the National Capital Free-Net in Ottawa, as detailed in the box below:

Telnet:	**freenet.carleton.ca**
Login:	**guest**
Select:	**About the National Capital Free-Net**
	August 1994 Community Networking Conference

BRITISH COLUMBIA

Campbell River FreeNet Association (CRFA)
Campbell River, British Columbia
Status: Organizing

Contact:
P.O. Box 123
Campbell River, British Columbia
V9W 5A7
Voice: (604) 286-4211
Fax: (604) 287-3596
Internet: ppreside@cln.etc.bc.ca (Pat Presidente)

Principal Contact:
Pat Presidente

Mission/Mandate:
To develop and operate a free, publicly accessible community computer system in
Campbell River, providing the broadest possible range of information, and
possibilities for the exchange of experience, ideas, and wisdom.

Community Information Access Organization (CIAO!)
Trail, British Columbia
Status: Open

c/o Ken McLean
School District #11 (Trail)
2079 Columbia Avenue
Trail, British Columbia
V1R 1K7
Voice: (604) 368-2233
Internet: kmcclean@ciao.trail.bc.ca (Ken McLean)
            info@ciao.trail.bc.ca

HOW TO ACCESS:
Internet:
Telnet: ciao.trail.bc.ca
Login: **guest**, no password required

Modem:
(604) 368-5764, 14,400 bps
Login: **guest**

Cranbrook Community-Net
Cranbrook, British Columbia.
Status: Organizing

Contact:
809 - 15th Street South
Cranbrook, British Columbia
V1C 5V3

Voice: (604) 426-8739
Fax: (604) 426-1815
Internet: dahumphr@cln.etc.bc.ca (David Humphrey)

Principal Contact:
David Humphrey

Mount Arrowsmith Free-Net Association

Parksville-Qualicum Beach, British Columbia
Status: Organizing

Contact:
1602 Marine Circle
Parksville, British Columbia
V9P 1Y7
Voice: (604) 752-5643
Fax: (604) 752-1911
Internet: jswanson@cln.etc.bc.ca (Jim Swanson)

Principal Contact:
Jim Swanson

Mission/Mandate:
To establish and operate a full community computer utility in District 69 of Vancouver Island.

Nanaimo SchoolsNET

Nanaimo, British Columbia
Status: Open

Contact:
c/o Brian Kuhn
School District No. 68 (Nanaimo)
Curriculum Resource Centre
420 Selby St.,
Nanaimo, British Columbia
V9R 2R7
Voice: Mike Silverton: (604) 755-2147
            Brian Kuhn: (604) 741-5289
Fax: Mike Silverton: (604) 754-7869
            Brian Kuhn: (604) 754-6511
Internet: Mike Silverton: msilverton@sd68.nanaimo.bc.ca
            Brian Kuhn: bkuhn@sd68.nanaimo.bc.ca

Principal Contacts:
Mike Silverton, District Computer Resource Teacher
Brian Kuhn, Co-ordinator of Information Systems

HOW TO ACCESS:
Internet:
Telnet: bbs.sd68.nanaimo.bc.ca
Login: **guest**

Modem:
(604) 754-3630, 2400 bps

Login: **guest**
(604) 754-9578, 14400 bps
Login: **guest**

Gopher: bbs.sd68.nanaimo.bc.ca

World Wide Web: http://bbs.sd68.nanaimo.bc.ca:8001/welcome.html

Mission/Mandate:
The Nanaimo SchoolsNET mission is to provide access to School District information, the Internet, and local community information for students, teachers, administrative staff, and the general public in our community. Such access is provided free-of-charge to any and all users in the School District and the community. The Nanaimo SchoolsNET exists to support both the School District's educational requirements and administrative needs. It is used to assist students and teachers in their use of Internet resources, and will be used to deliver information to the general public.

Prince George Free-Net
Prince George, British Columbia
Status: Open

Contact:
210 North Quinn St.
Prince George, British Columbia
V2M 3J5
Voice: (604) 562-9281
Fax :   (604) 562-8463
Internet: president@freenet.unbc.edu

Principal Contact:
Lynda Williams

HOW TO ACCESS:
Internet:
Telnet: freenet.unbc.edu
Login: **guest**

Modem:
(604) 563-3977, 14400 bps
Login: **guest**

Mission/Mandate:
The mission of the Prince George Free-Net is to raise telecomputing literacy in the region, develop local content, and provide basic Internet access in the form of electronic mail, USENET forums, and access to public information sites. The Prince George Free-Net invites local businesses to function as information providers in the interest of assisting them to gain experience with this electronic medium.

Rocky Mountain InfoNet

Sparwood, British Columbia
Status: Organizing

Contact:
Box 471
Sparwood, British Columbia
V0B 2G0
Voice: (604) 425-2605
Fax: (604) 425-7130
Internet: info@rockymtn.bc.ca

Principal Contact:
Brian Grainger, President

Mission/Mandate:
The mission of the Rocky Mountain InfoNet is to act as a community information resource for southeast B.C., southwest Alberta, and northwest Montana.

Sea to Sky Free-Net

Squamish, British Columbia
Status: Open

Contact:
Box 2539
Squamish, British Columbia
V0N 3G0
Voice: (604) 892-5531
Fax: (604) 892-5227
Internet: admin@sea-to-sky-freenet.bc.ca

HOW TO ACCESS:
Internet:
Telnet: sea-to-sky-freenet.bc.ca
Login: **guest**

Modem:
(604) 892-3500, 14,400 bps
Login: **guest**

Mission/Mandate:
The mission of the Sea-to-Sky Free-Net is to establish a community information computer system for the sea-to-sky corridor communities, which will enable members of the community to have access to information resources and electronic mail at no charge to end-users.

ValleyNet

Chilliwack, Abbotsford, and Mission, British Columbia
Status: Organizing

Contact:
The Fraser Valley Community Information Society
c/o Paul Kurucz
University College of the Fraser Valley

33844 King Road
Abbotsford, British Columbia
V2S 4N2
Voice: (604) 853-7441 Local 4360
Fax: (604) 855-7618
Internet: kuruczp@fvc.bc.ca (Paul Kurucz)

Principal Contact :
Paul Kurucz, Chairman of the Board of Directors

Mission/Mandate:
ValleyNet will act not only as an information gateway and database, but also as a tool for educating the public. By providing free access to information and technology, ValleyNet will help launch our communities into the information age.

ValleyNet is striving build a community network which will provide a graphical user interface (GUI) option along with the traditional text-based interface. This option recognizes the rapid movement to GUI Internet interfaces such as Mosaic as the natural progression to easier telecomputing.

Vancouver Regional FreeNet Association
Vancouver, British Columbia
Status: Open

Contact:
750 Burrard St.
Vancouver, British Columbia
V6Z 1X5
Voice: (604) 665-3944
Internet: eyung@freenet.vancouver.bc.ca

Principal Contact:
Brian Campbell - President

HOW TO ACCESS:
Internet:
Telnet: freenet.vancouver.bc.ca
Login: **guest**

Modem:
(604) 222-4723, 14,400 bps
Login: **guest**

Mission/Mandate:
The Vancouver Regional FreeNet Association is dedicated to the development, operation and ownership of a free, publicly accessible community computer utility in the Lower Mainland of British Columbia providing the broadest possible range of information and possibilities for the exchange of experience, ideas and wisdom.

Goals:
1. To establish a full FreeNet community computer utility in the Lower Mainland of B.C.
2. To encourage the development of a wide range of electronic community information resources.
3. To encourage the broadest possible participation of information providers in making their information available on FreeNet.
4. To work toward building a network of similar services in cities and towns internationally.

5. To work toward the widest possible public access to government and other information through FreeNet and other non-profit organizations such as libraries.
6. To work with other Canadian FreeNets to create a Canadian Computing Network.
7. To educate and encourage the public in the use of computer telecommunications and information retrieval.
8. To research ways to improve and expand public access to and use of electronic information resources and facilities.

Victoria Free-Net
Victoria, British Columbia
Status: Open

Contact :
Victoria Free-Net Association
c/o Vancouver Island Advanced Technology Center
Suite 203-1110 Government Street
Victoria, British Columbia
V8W 1Y2
Voice: (604) 727-7057
Fax: (604) 384-8634
Internet: vifa@freenet.victoria.bc.ca

HOW TO ACCESS:
Internet:
Telnet: freenet.victoria.bc.ca
Login: **guest**

Modem:
(604) 595-2300, 14,400 bps
Login: **guest**

Gopher:
freenet.victoria.bc.ca

World Wide Web:
http://freenet.victoria.bc.ca/vifa.html

Mission/Mandate:
The Victoria Free-Net is a community-based computer network available at no cost to residents and visitors of the Greater Victoria region. Modelled on the highly successful Cleveland Free-Net, the service goals of the Victoria Free-Net include:

- computer-mediated communications among Victoria Free-Net users and community members;
- easy access to information posted by community organizations, individuals, businesses, and government;
- community events information;
- worldwide electronic mail;
- access to selected online public access resources throughout the world; and
- alternative news services

The Victoria Free-Net is run by a core of dedicated volunteers belonging to the Victoria Free-Net Association, a registered non-profit society formed on June 17, 1992.

ALBERTA

Calgary Free-Net
Calgary, Alberta
Status: Open

Principal Contact:
Shawn Henry
Project Director, Calgary Free-Net Association
#810, 400-3rd Ave SW
Calgary, Alberta
T2P 4H2
Voice: (403) 264-9535
Fax: (403) 269-4776
Internet: henry@acs.ucalgary.ca (Shawn Henry)

HOW TO ACCESS:
Modem:
Telnet: freenet.calgary.ab.ca
Login: **guest**

Modem:
(403) 282-4075, 14,400 bps
Login: **guest**
(403) 282-3707, 14,400 bps
Login: **guest**

Mission/Mandate:
The Calgary Free-Net Association was established to promote awareness of and increase the knowledge and understanding of computers, computer networks and the benefits of having access to electronic information. The association is responsible to its members in accomplishing its objectives by:

- establishing and maintaining a computer system which provides free access to community information stored on that system, computer databases networked with that system and the global computer network, the Internet;
- offering Information Providers access to the Free-Net computer system in order to allow them to disseminate their electronic information to users of the Calgary Free-Net computer system;
- producing and disseminating information regarding the use of the Calgary Free-Net computer system and other computer networks;
- collaborating and participating in projects with Universities, Colleges, Technical Institutions and other organizations to develop a better understanding of and promote the use of computers, computer networks and electronic information;
- providing presentations and classes regarding the use of computers, computer networks and gaining access to electronic information.

Edmonton FreeNet
Edmonton, Alberta
Status: Open

Contact:
#220, 10232 112 Street
Edmonton, Alberta
T5K 1M4

Voice: (403) 421-1745
Fax: (403) 421-7159
Internet: postmaster@freenet.edmonton.ab.ca

Principal Contact:
Jon Hall, Project Manager

HOW TO ACCESS:
Internet:
Telnet: freenet.edmonton.ab.ca
Login: **guest**

Modem:
(403) 428-3929, 14,400 bps
Login: **guest**

Mission/Mandate:
The Edmonton Free-Net is a community-based, electronic network. Its mission is to enable people in the greater Edmonton region to:

- list and retrieve information about, or of interest to themselves
- prepare themselves to function effectively in an information society
- communicate with public and private members of the local and global community

The Edmonton Free-Net will charge a $15.00 membership fee which will provide members with full access to all available services: electronic mail, voting rights, unlimited daily calls, and personal login ID. There will be no access charge for guest logins, although on-line time may be limited.

Praxis Free-Net
Medicine Hat, Alberta
Status: Organizing

Contact:
Praxis Free-Net
c/o Lawrence Chen
468 9th Street S.E.
Medicine Hat, Alberta
T1A 1N7
Voice: (403) 526-6019
Fax: (403) 529-5102
Internet: dreamer@lhaven.uumh.ab.ca

Principal Contact:
Lawrence Chen

Red Deer Freenet
Red Deer, Alberta
Status: Organizing

Contact:
c/o Community Information & Referral Service
4935 - 51 Street
Red Deer, Alberta
Canada T4N 2A8

Voice: (403) 346-4636
Fax: (403) 342-4154
Internet: mtoews@admin.rdc.ab.ca

Mission/Mandate:

The mission of the Red Deer Freenet is to increase public access to local, regional, and global information by establishing a quality Red Deer Freenet, and to increase public awareness and interest in Freenet, and electronic information and technology, by providing educational opportunities and technical support.

SASKATCHEWAN

Great Plains Free-Net

Regina, Saskatchewan
Status: Organizing

Contact:
55 Cowburn Crescent
Regina, Saskatchewan
S4S 5R9
Voice: (306) 585-1639, or
            (306) 584-9615
Fax: (306) 585-1639
Internet: suggittm@leroy.cc.uregina.ca
            72143.337@compuserve.com
            rhg@leroy.cc.uregina.ca

Principal Contact:
Mark Suggitt (Media contact)

Mission/Mandate:

The purpose of the Great Plains Free-Net organizing committee is to establish a Regina-based Free-Net by May 1995. Great Plains Free-Net is a non-profit, free access, community organization. The mandate of the Great Plains Free-Net is to provide the Regina-area community with a broad range of local information services, educational resources, selected Internet access, and to promote local-call access in rural areas.

If you are interested in following the progress of the Great Plains Free-Net, you can join the Great Plains Free-Net mailing list. Send the message:

subscribe gpfn-l <Your Name>
(e.g. subscribe gpfn-l Joe Smith)

to the following Internet address:

listserv@max.cc.uregina.ca

Saskatoon Free-Net

Saskatoon, Saskatchewan
Status: Organizing

Contact:
Box 339 RPO University
Saskatoon, Saskatchewan
S7N 4J8

Internet: lib_freenet@sask.usask.ca

Principal Contacts:
Peter Scott <scottp@duke.usask.ca>
Darlene Fichter <fichter@willow.usask.ca>

HOW TO ACCESS:
Gopher: willow.usask.ca port 71
World Wide Web: http://willow.usask.ca/freenet/freenet.html

MANITOBA

Blue Sky FreeNet of Manitoba Inc.
Winnipeg, Manitoba
Status: Organizing

Contact:
P.O. Box 1441
Winnipeg, Manitoba
R3C 2Z4
Voice: (204) 943-9000   (Michael Gillespie)
Internet: info@freenet.mb.ca

Principal Contact:
Michael Gillespie, Vice-President

Mission/Mandate:
To provide community network access to all residents of Manitoba.

Searden Free-Net
(SEARDEN = South East Angle Rural Development Electronic Network)
Sprague, Manitoba
Status: Organizing

Contact:
POB 180
Sprague, Manitoba
R0A 1Z0
Voice: (204) 437-2016
Fax: (204) 437-2382

Principal Contact:
Larry Geller, Chairperson
Internet: larry_geller@mbnet.mb.ca

Mission/Mandate:
SEARDEN is committed to providing a sustainable communications infrastructure to the communities of our rural area. SEARDEN believes in the principles of equal and equitable access to the information highway for all rural communities as a way of obliterating the urban-rural disparities that have emerged over the decades.

ONTARIO

Collingwood Net

Collingwood, Ontario
Status: Organizing

Contact:
Box 377
Collingwood, Ontario
L9Y 3Z7
Voice: (705) 445-7401
Internet: normgrif@village.ca (Norm Griffiths)

Principal Contact:
Norm Griffiths, Chair of Steering Committee

Mission/Mandate:
To provide access to community information and communication for all members of the community.

807-CITY   (formerly the Thunder Bay Free-Net)

Thunder Bay, Ontario
Status: Open

Contact:
Don Watson, Chair
Dept. of Re-engineering
Lakehead University
Thunder Bay, Ontario
P7B 5E1
Voice: (807) 343-8103
Fax: (807) 343-8023
Internet: dwatson@flash.lakeheadu.ca

Principal Contact:
Don Watson, Chair, 807-CITY

HOW TO ACCESS:
Internet:
Telnet: tourism.807-city.on.ca
Login: **guest**

Modem:
(807) 346-7870, 14,400 bps
Login: **guest**

Gopher: tourism.807-city.on.ca
World Wide Web: http://tourism.807-city.on.ca

807-CITY's mandate is to provide information about the world to the citizens of northwestern Ontario, and also to provide information about northwestern Ontario to citizens of the world. The initial Phase I project has been to mount a database on tourism in Northwestern Ontario with an emphasis on the 1995 Nordic World Ski Championships and to provide other communication services amongst athletes, visitors and the organizers, with some material in six languages, including graphics and video. The project was funded by CANARIE.

Halton Community Network (Halton Net)

Halton Region, Ontario
Status: Open

Contact:
Halton Community Network
Sheridan College
1430 Trafalgar Road
Oakville, Ontario
L6H 2L1
Voice: (905) 815-4010 (Help/Information Line)
Fax: (905) 829-0891 (Rick Booth)
Internet: hcn@sheridanc.on.ca

Principal Contact:
Rick Booth,
Chair, Halton Community Network Steering Committee
Voice: (905) 829-0892
Internet: rick.booth@sheridanc.on.ca

HOW TO ACCESS:
Internet:
Telnet: halinet.sheridanc.on.ca
Login: **guest**

Modem:
(905) 845-0057, 14400 bps
Login: **guest**

Mission/Mandate:
To empower the residents and businesses of Halton Region by providing access to electronic communications and information facilities, and by so doing, strengthen the community and enable them to function effectively in the automated, informational society.   All Halton-area libraries are interconnected with each other and with the Boards of Education and Sheridan College into a network called Halinet. The Halton Community Network is building on the Halinet infrastructure and providing a front-door for the community to those resources and beyond.

Hamilton-Wentworth FreeNet

Hamilton, Ontario
Status: Organizing

Principal Contacts:
Marcel Mongeon
Martin & Martin, Lawyers
402-4 Hughson Street South
Hamilton, Ontario
L8N 3Z1
Voice: (905) 528-5936
Fax: (905) 523-4144
Internet: marcelm@joymrmn.on.ca

Kit Darling
Hamilton Public Library
55 York Blvd
Hamilton, Ontario

L8R 3K1
Voice: (905) 546-3230

Mission/Mandate:
The mandate of the Hamilton-Wentworth FreeNet is to develop and implement a world-class electronic information network in the community, to access and share local and global knowledge, and to assist businesses in competitiveness. Our vision is to bring the community together and increase knowledge by electronic means. This will be achieved by offering the people of Hamilton-Wentworth access to, and the opportunity to exchange information through, a FreeNet.

HOMEtown Community Network
London, Ontario
Status: Organizing

Principal Contact:
Patricia Greig
Voice: (519) 452-2124
Fax: (519) 455-7648
Internet: greigpa@julian.uwo.ca

For More Information:
Gopher: gopher.uwo.ca
Select: Selected Internet Resources
              Community Networks
              HOMEtown Community Network

Mission/Mandate:
To develop and provide universal and affordable access to a comprehensive communication service across five counties. HOMEtown will serve the counties of Huron, Oxford, Middlesex, Elgin, and Perth, and the cities of London, St. Thomas, and Stratford.

National Capital FreeNet
Ottawa, Ontario
Status: Open

Contact:
National Capital FreeNet
Carleton University
1125 Colonel By Drive
Ottawa, Ontario
K1S 5B6
Voice: (613) 788-3947
Internet: info-request@freenet.carleton.ca
              ncf@freenet.carleton.ca
              office@freenet.carleton.ca

HOW TO ACCESS:
Internet:
Telnet: freenet.carleton.ca
Login: **guest**

Modem:
(613) 564-3600, 2400 bps
Login: **guest**

(613) 564-0808, 14400 bps
Login: **guest**

Mission/Mandate:
The National Capital FreeNet is a computer-based information service designed to meet the present information needs of the people and public agencies in the region, and to prepare the community for full and broadly-based participation in rapidly changing communication environments. The National Capital FreeNet is incorporated as a non-profit community utility that is free to everyone in the community, and will neither charge nor pay for any information or other services it provides.

Niagara Peninsula Free-Net
St. Catharines, Ontario
Status: Open

Contact:
Niagara Peninsula Free-Net
NPIEC
3550 Schmon Parkway
Unit 4 - First Floor
Thorold, Ontario
L2V 4Y6
Voice: (905) 684-2115
Fax: (905) 684-4230
Internet: npfstaff@freenet.niagara.com

Principal Contact:
Jon Radue
Computer Science Department
Brock University
St. Catharines, Ontario
L2S 3A1
Internet: jradue@sandcastle.cosc.brocku.ca

HOW TO ACCESS:
Internet:
Telnet: freenet.niagara.com
Login: **guest**

Modem:
(905) 688-8226, 14400 bps
Login: **guest**

Mission/Mandate
The Niagara Peninsula Free-Net's mission is to create a computer-based network which will:

(a) help meet the personal, professional and educational needs of people in the Niagara community;
(b) foster communication among individuals and the institutions that serve them;
(c) support community groups in their efforts at professional development, outreach and community service;
(d) enhance opportunities for sustainable, community-based economic development;
(e) create a favourable environment for business and employment growth; and
(f) allow cooperation with other groups to support the development and linking of community networks in Canada and the world.

North Shore Community Net

Elliot Lake, Ontario
Status: Organizing

Contact:
81 Central Avenue
Elliot Lake, Ontario
P5A 2G4
Voice: (705) 848-5106
Fax: (705) 848-9225
Internet: alanwils@village.ca (Alan Wilson)

Principal Contact:
Alan Wilson

Mission/Mandate:
To establish an infrastructure in our rural area that will provide inexpensive
connections to the Internet, for both private and public sectors, and promote a
rethinking of the concept of community.

Owen Sound Freenet (provisional)

Owen Sound, Ontario
Status: Organizing

Principal Contact:
Trevor Davies
The Owen Sound and North Grey Union Public Library
824 1st Ave. W.
Owen Sound, Ontario
N4K 4K4
Voice: (519) 376-0682 ext. 252
Fax: (519) 376-5395
Internet: Tdavies@gc1.georcoll.on.ca (Trevor Davies)

Although based in Owen Sound, the Owen Sound Freenet will offer service to an
extensive rural community. Internet access will initially be through UUCP. Local links
will be the mainstay of the organization.

Toronto Free-Net

Toronto, Ontario
Status: Open

Contact:
Toronto Free-Net Inc.
c/o Ryerson Polytechnic University Library
350 Victoria Street
Toronto, Ontario
M5B 2K3
Voice: (416) 979-9242
Internet: info@freenet.toronto.on.ca

HOW TO ACCESS:
Internet:
Telnet: freenet.toronto.on.ca

Login: **guest**

Modem:
(416) 780-2010, 14400 bps
Login: **guest**

Mission/Mandate:
The mandate of the Toronto Free-Net is to provide the residents of Metropolitan Toronto with free, electronic access to community-related information, while giving information providers a means to disseminate their information as widely and as economically as possible.

QUEBEC

Free-Net Montreal
Montreal, Quebec
Status: Organizing

1030, rue Beaubien Est
Suite 201
Montreal, Quebec
H2S 1T4
Voice: (514) 990-REMM
Fax: (514) 278-1664
Internet: free-net@remm.uqam.ca

Mission/Mandate:
REMM is a volunteer-run non-profit organization whose mission is to enhance community life and educate its users by providing people and organizations in the metropolitan Montreal region with access to a computerized information clearinghouse and messaging service. REMM's services are free and are offered in both French and English. Free-Net Montreal will be the first community network to offer its services in both French and English.

If you are interested in following the activities of the Montreal Free-Net, you can subscribe to the Montreal Free-Net mailing list. Send an electronic mail message to **listserv@vm1.mcgill.ca** and place the following command on the first line of the body of the message: **subscribe mtlnet <Your Name>**
e.g. subscribe mtlnet John Smith
To remove yourself from this mailing list, send the message
signoff mtlnet to **listserv@vm1.mcgill.ca**.

NOVA SCOTIA

Cape Breton Community Net
Sydney, Nova Scotia
Status: Organizing

Principal Contact:
Pat Melski, Chair
294 Whitney Ave.
Sydney. Nova Scotia
B1P 5A6

Mission/Mandate:
The Cape Breton Community Net is a non-profit, public information computing network. Modelled upon successful systems already in operation, it is designed to supplement and enhance existing community resources. Information provided by citizens and for citizens will help individuals and communities meet their economic, cultural, recreational and educational needs. Based on principles of partnership and cooperation, this system will

- establish Cape Breton firmly within the global web of information networks.
- provide users with a comprehensive and easily-accessible listing of community resources.
- provide individuals of all ages with the opportunity for distance education and life-long learning.
- through the location of computer terminals in libraries, school and other community outlets, help the general public become more familiar with the electronic highways that are redefining our concepts of communication.

Chebucto FreeNet
Halifax, Nova Scotia
Status: Open

Contact:
Metro*CAN Society/Chebucto FreeNet
c/o Dept. of Mathematics, Statistics & Computing Science
Dalhousie University
Halifax, Nova Scotia
B3H 3J5
Voice: (902) 494-2449
Internet: cfn@cfn.cs.dal.ca

Principal Contact:
Renee Davis
Internet: rdavis@duncan.alt.ns.ca

HOW TO ACCESS:
Internet:
Telnet: cfn.cs.dal.ca
Login: **guest**

Modem:
(902) 494-8006, 14400 bps
Login: **guest**

World Wide Web: http://www.cfn.cs.dal.ca

Mission/Mandate:
The vision of the Chebucto Free-Net:
Every Nova Scotian will have free access to a Community Access Network, as part of a province-wide electronic network linked to the world-wide Internet.

Mission statement:

To achieve our vision, the Metro Community Access Network Society will:

- Establish a Community Access Network for the Halifax-Dartmouth Metro area, which will:
  - help meet personal and professional information needs of people;
  - foster communication among individuals and the institutions that serve them;
  - support community groups in their efforts at professional development, outreach and community service;
  - enhance opportunities for sustainable, community-based economic development; and,
  - create a favourable environment for business and employment growth.
- Cooperate with other groups to foster and support the development and linking of Community Access Networks in other parts of Nova Scotia, Atlantic Canada, the rest of Canada and the world.

The Chebucto FreeNet is a HTTP server using Lynx as a browser.

NEW BRUNSWICK

Fredericton Area Free-Net

Fredericton, New Brunswick
Status: Organizing

Contact:
Fredericton Area Free-Net
c/o Michael J. MacDonald
Faculty of Computer Science
University of New Brunswick
P.O. Box 4400
Fredericton, New Brunswick
E3B 5A3
Voice: (506) 453-4566
Fax :   (506) 453-3566
Internet: mikemac@unb.ca (Michael J. MacDonald)

Principal Contact:
Michael J. MacDonald

NEWFOUNDLAND

St. John's InfoNET

St. John's, Newfoundland
Status : Organizing

Contact:
St. John's InfoNET
c/o Randy Dodge
HH 2050
Memorial University
St. John's, Newfoundland

Voice:	(709) 737-4594
Fax:	(709) 737-3514
Internet:	randy@kean.ucs.mun.ca

Principal Contact:
Randy Dodge

Mission/Mandate:
To support and stimulate the growth of community networking in St. John's and facilitate the growth of similar organizations throughout Newfoundland and Labrador.
Objectives:

(a) To ensure that all people in the community have access to public information.
(b) To empower people by developing a more information and computer-literate citizenry.
(c) To improve access to community and government information.
(d) To enhance residents' understanding of community issues and encourage their active participation.
(e) To make community and government organizations more effective in serving people.
(f) To provide public access through the public library system.

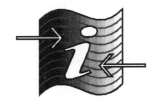

A P P E N D I X   P

·······································

THE DIRECTORY OF CANADIAN ORGANIZATIONS WITH REGISTERED INTERNET DOMAINS

As discussed in Chapter 4, when a Canadian organization wishes to register a domain on the Internet, it can apply to either the CA Domain Registrar in Canada (if it wishes to register in the .CA domain) or the InterNIC (Internet Network Information Center) Registrar in the United States (if it wishes to register a descriptive domain such as .com, .edu, .gov, .net, or .org). Some organizations choose to register **both** a geographical and a descriptive domain.

Over 2000 Canadian organizations have registered Internet domains. A list of these organizations and their respective Internet domains is provided in the table below. The list is organized alphabetically by organization name. Before consulting the directory, there are a couple of things that you should be aware of:

(1) There is no guarantee that all the organizations listed in this directory are currently connected to the Internet. This directory is a list of Canadian organizations that have registered Internet domains. Registering an Internet domain and connecting to the Internet are two different things. Some organizations register an Internet domain weeks or months in advance of connecting to the Internet.

(2) A listing in this directory does not mean that all of the company's employees are connected to the Internet. Many of the organizations listed in the

directory are experimenting with the Internet, and only one or two people within the organization may be using the organization's Internet connection.

(3) If an organization does not appear in this directory, it does not mean that the organization is not using the Internet. This directory only lists Canadian organizations that have registered Internet domains. An organization doesn't have to register its own Internet domain to use the Internet. Organizations often use the Internet domain of their Internet service provider. Many firms use the Internet services of commercial on-line systems such as CompuServe, Genie, and America Online. Other firms use commercial messaging services such as MCIMail or AT&T Mail. In these situations, organizations operate under the domain of the company providing their Internet connection. For example, organizations using CompuServe will have an Internet address of the form **user@CompuServe.Com.**

OBTAINING AN UP-TO-DATE LIST OF ORGANIZATIONS REGISTERED IN THE CA DOMAIN

The list of organizations registered in the CA Domain is updated regularly by John Demco, the CA Domain Registrar. You can retrieve a current copy of the list by anonymous FTP to **ftp.cdnnet.ca** in the **ca-domain** directory. The files are: **index-by-organization** (for a list ordered alphabetically) and **index-by-subdomain** (for a list ordered by subdomain).

The InterNIC does not keep track of Canadian registrations separately, so it is not possible to obtain a list of Canadian registrations from the InterNIC. However, the entire InterNIC database is searchable, but only by domain name or organization name, by telnetting to **rs.internic.net** and logging in as **whois.**

SEARCHING THE CA DOMAIN DATABASE

The following Gopher and World Wide Web sites have search capabilities that will permit you to do keyword searches of the CA Domain database.

Using Gopher	
Gopher address:	**gopher.fonorola.net**
Select:	Canadian Domain

Using the World Wide Web	
URL:	**http://www.csi.nb.ca**

Name of Organization

Subdomain

Name of Organization	Subdomain
1St Choice Information Service	1choice.com
20/20 Group Financial Inc.	ttgfi.ca
20/20 Group Financial Ltd.	ttgfund.com
3D Artist	3dartist.com
7th ILLUSION Co.	mtlnet.org
7th ILLUSION Co.	vii.com
9 to 5 Communications	9to5.com
A Sound Mind Production	soundmind.com
Aardvark Consulting Ltd.	aardvark.com
Ability Online Support Network	ablelink.org
ABL Canada Inc.	abl.ca
ABM Systems Inc.	abmsystems.ns.ca
Absolute Software	absolute.com
Absolute Solutions	absolutions.mb.ca
Acadia University	acadiau.ca
Acces Public LLC enr.	llc.org
Access Computer Systems, a division of King-Cade Amusements Inc.	access.victoria.bc.ca
Access Media Systems	accmedia.com
Access Technologies, Inc.	acctech.com
Accubid Systems Ltd.	accubid.com
AccuWare Business Solutions Ltd.	accuware.com
Aceldama Systems	aceldama.com
Achilles	achilles.net
Achilles Online	achilles.org
Acquired Intelligence Inc.	aiinc.bc.ca
Acres International Limited	acres.com
ACTC Technologies Inc.	actc.ab.ca
Active Creative Technologies Inc.	actcorp.com
Acumen Computers Inc.	acumen.ca
Acura Technology Group Inc.	acura.com
AD Technologies Inc.	adtech.com
AD Technologies Inc.	adtech.ca
Adaptive Answers, Inc.	adaptive.mb.ca
Adcom Technologies Inc.	adcomtech.com
Addiction Research Foundation	arf.org
ADEN Systems Incorporated	vos.com
Administrative Computer Technology	admincomp.mb.ca
ADP Systems Partnership	adpsystems.mb.ca
Advance Electronics	advance.mb.ca
Advanced Cultural Technologies Inc.	actinc.bc.ca
Advanced Gravis Computer Technology Ltd.	gravis.com
Advanced Information Technologies Corporation	ait.ca
Advanced Radiodata Research Centre	arrc.ca
Advanced Scientific Computing	asc.on.ca
Advanced Technology Centre	atc.edmonton.ab.ca
Advanced Trading Technology Group	collective.com
Advantage Computers Ltd.	advantage.com
Advantis Canada	advantis.ca
AEGO Consulting Inc.	aego.ca
AEGO Consulting Inc.	aego.com
Aetna Life Insurance Company of Canada	aetnacan.com
Aetna Trust Company	aetna-trust.com

AFG Industries Ltd.	afg.com
Agassiz North Associates Ltd.	agaznrth.mb.ca
AGF Management Ltd.	agf.ca
Agfa Canada Inc.	agfa.ca
Agiss Power Technologies Corporation	agiss.com
Agriculture Canada	agr.ca
Agriculture Canada, Policy Branch	fdpd-agcan.org
Agri-Smart Consulting	agrismart.on.ca
Agropur	agropur.ca
AGT Limited	alta.net
AGT Ltd.	agt.ab.ca
Ahearn and Soper Inc.	ahearn.com
Ahlea Systems Corp.	ahlea.com
AIM Systems	aim-systems.on.ca
Air Canada	aircanada.ca
Air Ontario Inc.	airontario.ca
AirQual Consulting	airqual.mb.ca
Air-Sea Research	as-res.com
Air-Sea Research Ltd.	as-res.bc.ca
AIS Advanced Information Systems Ltd.	ais.bc.ca
AIS Advanced Information Systems Ltd.	aisnet.com
AIS Multiline	aismulti.com
Alberta Cancer Board	cancerboard.ab.ca
Alberta College	abcollege.ab.ca
Alberta Educational Communications Corporation (ACCESS NETWORK)	accessnet.ab.ca
Alberta Educational Technology & Research Foundation	educ.ab.ca
Alberta Energy Company Ltd.	aec.ca
Alberta General Provincial Children's Hospital	child-hosp.ab.ca
Alberta Newsprint Co.	altanewsprint.ca
Alberta Packet Radio Network	ampr.ab.ca
Alberta Provincial Government	gov.ab.ca
Alberta Public Safety Services	apss.ab.ca
Alberta Regional Network	arnet.ab.ca
Alberta Research Council	arc.ab.ca
Alberta SuperNet Incorporated	supernet.ab.ca
Alberta Vocational College-Calgary	avc.calgary.ab.ca
Alberta Wheat Pool	awp.com
Alcan Aluminium Ltd.	alcan.ca
Alcatel Canada Wire, Inc.	alcatel.ca
Alex Informatique Inc.	alex.qc.ca
Algo Design Inc.	algodesign.qc.ca
Algonquin College of Applied Arts and Technology	algonquinc.on.ca
Algorithmics Inc.	algorithmics.com
Alias Research, Inc.	alias.com
Alis Technologies Inc.	alis.ca
Allan Crawford Associates Ltd	aca.ca
Allinson-Ross Corporation	allross.com
Allon, Morris, Garber and Fiss	allonpsych.com
All-Tech Services	altec.com
Almanac User's Group	almanac.bc.ca
Alpa Roof Trusses Inc.	alpart.com
Alphen International Inc.	alphen.on.ca
Alpine Computers Ltd.	alpine.ca

Alt Society, The	alt.ns.ca
AltaGas Services Inc.	altagas.ca
Alternatives Information Systems	alternatives.com
Amaron Canada	amaron.com
AMB Inc.	amb.com
AMB Inc.	amb.ca
Ambassador Board BBS	ambassador.com
Amdahl Software Development Centre	amdahlcsdc.com
American Killifish Association	aka.org
American Pacific Data Services	ampac.com
Amiga Mail Service BBS	amsbbs.bc.ca
Amiga Users Of Victoria	amusers.victoria.bc.ca
AMT Solutions Group Inc. (Island Net)	islandnet.com
AMT Solutions Group Inc.	amtsgi.bc.ca
Analog Services Informatiques (1993) Inc.	analog.ca
Analysis Synthesis Consulting Incorporated	analsyn.on.ca
Anarchia Underground Society	aus.org
Andrew D. Morrow	packet.org
Andyne Computing Limited	andyne.on.ca
Anjura Technologies Corporation	anjura.com
Antel Optronics Inc.	antel.on.ca
Apex Advanced Technologies Inc.	apextor.com
Apex Advanced Technologies, Inc.	apex.ca
APG Inc.	apg.ca
Apotex Inc.	apotex.ca
Applied Analytics Corporation	aac.on.ca
Applied High Technology AHT Group Inc.	ahtgroup.com
Applied Microelectronics Institute	appliedmicro.ns.ca
Applied Silicon Inc. Canada	appsil.com
Arachnae Management Limited	arachnae.com
ARATAR Management Corporation	aratar.mb.ca
Arcane Computer Consulting	arcane.calgary.ab.ca
Archelon Inc.	archelon.com
Archinfo Incorporated	archinfo.com
ARCHITECH Microsystems Inc.	architech.on.ca
Arete Software Inc.	arete.ca
Arly Fashion Imports Inc.	arly.com
Armstrong/Spallumcheen School District	schdist21.bc.ca
ARQANA Technologies, Inc.	arqana.com
Array Systems Computing Inc.	array.ca
ArrayTech Systems Ltd.	atech.bc.ca
Arris Design and Development Limited	arris.on.ca
Ascent Power Technology Inc.	ascent.ca
Ascom Timeplex Canada	ascom-timeplex.ca
Ashlin Computer Corporation	ashlin.on.ca
Asia Pacific Foundation of Canada	apfnet.org
ASL Analytical Service Laboratories Ltd.	asl-labs.bc.ca
Assiniboine Community College	assiniboinec.mb.ca
Assiniboine South School Division	assd.winnipeg.mb.ca
Association of Canadian Community Colleges	accc.ca
Association of Professional Engineers of Manitoba (APEM), The	apem.mb.ca
Association of Professional Engineers of Nova Scotia, The	apens.ns.ca

Association of Universities and Colleges of Canada	aucc.ca
Astra Pharma Inc.	astrapharma.on.ca
Astral Communications Inc.	astral.com
Async BBS	async.org
ATCI	maxcor.com
ATCI	econocall.com
ATCI	atci.com
Athabasca University	athabascau.ca
ATI Technologies Inc.	atitech.ca
Atlantic Canada Opportunity Agency	acoa.ca
Atlantic Centre for Remote Sensing of the Oceans	acrso.ns.ca
Atlantic Computer Institute	aci.ns.ca
Atlantic LRMI	lrmi.com
Atlantic Netcom Ltd.	netcom.ca
Atlantic Systems Group (ASG (R))	atlsysgrp.nb.ca
Atlantis Aerospace	atlantis.com
Atlantis Scientific Systems Group Inc.	atlsci.com
Atlas Graham Industries Ltd.	atlasgraham.mb.ca
Atlas Tube	atlastube.on.ca
Atomic Energy Control Board	atomcon.ca
Atomic Energy of Canada Limited	aecl.ca
ATS Aerospace	ats.qc.ca
ATS Automation, Inc.	atsauto.com
Attic Enterprise	attic.bc.ca
Attic Enterprise	attic.com
AT&T Canada Inc.	att.ca
Audio Online Incorporated	audio-online.com
Audio Online Inc.	audio-online.on.ca
Augustana University College	augustana.ab.ca
AUPELF-UREF, Reseau Electronique Francophone pour l'Education et la Recherche	refer.qc.ca
Automated Systems Group	autosysgr.nb.ca
AVAAZ Innovations, Inc.	avaaz.com
Avant Management Consultants	avant.com
Avantel Consulting, Inc.	avantel.com
Avec Technical Services	avec.com
Avita Technologies Corp.	avita.com
Avtech Electrosystems, Ltd.	avtechpulse.com
AWNIX Software	fortress.org
AZTEC	aztec.org
AZTEC	aztec.net
A. Dunn Systems Corporation	adscorp.on.ca
A. J. Lill Consultants	ajlc.waterloo.on.ca
A. J. P. Engineering Services	ajpeng.mb.ca
A.L.I. Technologies Ltd.	ali.bc.ca
A.Z. Technologies	ntg-inter.com
Baan International	baan.com
Babillard Synapse Inc.	synapse.org
Babillard Synapse Inc.	synapse.net
Baird and Associates	baird.com
Ballard Power Inc.	bld.com
Banff Centre for Continuing Education, The	banffcentre.ab.ca
Bank of Canada	bank-banque-canada.ca
Bank of Montreal	bmo.com

Bata Limited	bata.ca
BBDO Canada, Inc.	bbdotor.com
BC Government Employees' Union	bcgeu.bc.ca
BC Provincial Government	gov.bc.ca
BC REHAB SOCIETY	bcrehab.vancouver.bc.ca
BCnet	bc.net
BCnet	bcnet.bc.ca
BCSL Inc.	bcsl.com
BCTEL Advanced Communications	bctel.bc.ca
Beak Consultants Ltd.	beak.com
Beakbane Marketing Inc.	beakbane.com
Beame and Whiteside Software, Ltd.	bw-software.on.ca
Beame & Whiteside Software, Ltd.	bws.com
Bedford Institute of Oceanography	bio.ns.ca
Beeman Inventions Ltd. (Manitoba)	beeminve.mb.ca
Bell Canada	bell.ca
Bell Mobility Cellular	mobility.com
Bell Ontario (Business Sales)	bellont.com
Bellatrix Systems Corp.	belsys.com
Bell-Northern Research	bnr.ca
Beltron, information Technology Ltd.	beltron.com
Benton Associates	benton.com
Bethune Import-Export Ltd.	bethune.com
BEX Engineering Ltd.	bex.com
BIOMIRA Inc.	biomira.com
Bishop Information Group Inc.	biginc.on.ca
Bishop's University	ubishops.ca
Black Gold Regional	blackgold.ab.ca
Blake Coverett Development	bcdev.com
BleuMont Inc.	bleumont.com
Blizzard Publishing Inc.	blizzard.mb.ca
Blue Sky FreeNet of Manitoba Inc.	freenet.mb.ca
Blumer-Levan Ltd.	blumer.com
Bob Henry	trbbs.org
Boeing Canada	boeing.ca
Bombardier/Canadair	canadair.ca
Bomem Inc.	bomem.qc.ca
Borden & Elliot	borden.com
Border Network Technologies Inc.	border.com
Boulet Fermat Associates	bouletfermat.ab.ca
BOW Software Inc.	bowsoft.com
BP Resources Canada Limited	bprc.ab.ca
Bradley Consulting	bradley.net
Brak Systems Inc.	brak.com
Brandon University	brandonu.ca
Breakwater Resources, Ltd.	bwrbhk.com
Bresver, Grossman, Scheininger & Davis	bgsdlawfirm.toronto.on.ca
Brewers Retail Inc.	brewers.com
Bristol Aerospace Ltd.	bristol.ca
British Columbia Automobile Association	bcaa.bc.ca
British Columbia Drug and Poison Information Centre (DPIC)	dpic.bc.ca
British Columbia Hydro and Power Authority	bchydro.bc.ca
British Columbia Institute of Technology	bcit.bc.ca

British Columbia Lotteries Corporation	ilid.org
British Columbia Research Corporation	bcr.bc.ca
British Columbia Teachers' Federation	bctf.bc.ca
BRK Brands Canada, a division of BRK Brands, Inc.	brkbrands.ca
Brock University	brocku.ca
Brunswick Micro Systems Inc.	brunswickmicro.nb.ca
BSOH Enterprises	bsoh.com
Bubble Technology Industries Inc.	bubbletech.com
Bull HN Information Systems Limited	bull.ca
Bull Housse & Tupper	bht.com
Bunyip Information Systems Inc.	bunyip.com
Burchill Communications Research Group	burchill.ns.ca
Burns Fry Limited	bfl.com
Butterfield and Robinson	bandr.com
Butterfly Signal Processing Inc.	butterfly.com
Butterfly Wings	bwings.com
byDesign Computer Systems Ltd.	bydesign.com
Byte Designs Ltd.	byted.com
Bytewide Marketing	bytewide.ca
B&H Income Tax Service	bhits.mb.ca
B.C. Children's Hospital	childhosp.bc.ca
C3I Precision Instruments	c3i.com
Cable Island Limited	cableisland.on.ca
Cable Island Ltd.	cable.com
Cable Island, Ltd.	cable.org
Cabot Institute of Applied Arts and Technology	cabot.nf.ca
Cadvision Development Corp.	cadvision.com
CAD/CAM Solutions of Canada	cadcam-sol.com
CAE Electronics Ltd.	cae.ca
CAEWare Inc.	caeware.com
CAIL Systems Ltd.	cail.com
Calgary Board of Education	cbe.ab.ca
Calgary Free-Net Association	freenet.calgary.ab.ca
Calgary Health Services	health.calgary.ab.ca
Calgary Unix Connect	cuc.ab.ca
Calgary Unix User Group	cuug.ab.ca
CALIAN Technology Ltd.	calian.ca
Callstream Communications Inc.	callstream.com
Calpurnia Communications	hookup.net
Cals EDMS Inc.	cals-edms.ca
Cambrian College of Applied Arts and Technology	cambrianc.on.ca
Cambridge Shopping Centres, Ltd.	cscl.ca
Camli Resources	camli.com
Camosun College	camosun.bc.ca
Campana Systems Inc.	campana.ca
Campana Systems, Inc.	campana.com
Campfire Design	campfire.com
CANAC International Inc.	canac.com
Canada Centre for Inland Waters	cciw.ca
Canada Communication Group - Groupe Communication Canada	ccg-gcc.ca
Canada Computer Paper Inc.	tcpon.com
Canada Connect Corporation	canuck.com
Canada On-Line	canada.com

Canada Post Corporation	canpost.ca
Canada Remote Systems Limited	canrem.com
Canada top-level domain	ca
Canadelle Incorporated	canadelle.com
Canadian Advisory Council on the Status of Women	cacsw.ca
Canadian Airlines International Ltd.	cdnair.ca
Canadian Bacterial Diseases Network	cbdn.ca
Canadian Broadcasting Corporation	cbc.ca
Canadian Center for Management Development	ccmd.org
Canadian Centre for Architecture	cca.qc.ca
Canadian Centre for Occupational Health and Safety	ccohs.ca
Canadian Connections	cancon.mb.ca
Canadian Council of Ministers of the Environment Inc. (CCME)	ccme.ca
Canadian Cyberlink Inc	cyberlink.com
Canadian Dimension Magazine	canadiandimension.mb.ca
Canadian Football League	cfl.ca
Canadian Forest Products Ltd.	canfor.ca
Canadian Genetic Diseases Network	generes.ca
Canadian Imperial Bank of Commerce	cibc.ca
Canadian Industrial Innovation Centre	innovatnctr.ca
Canadian Info Tech, Inc.	cit.com
Canadian Institute of Chartered Accountants	cica.ca
Canadian International Development Agency	devcan.ca
Canadian International Group	cig.com
Canadian International Group	cig.ca
Canadian Language Technology Institute - Institut Canadien de technologie linguistique	clti-ictl.nb.ca
Canadian Marconi Company	marconi.ca
Canadian Market Images	cmi.on.ca
Canadian Medical Association	canmed.ca
Canadian Mennonite Bible College	cmbiblecoll.mb.ca
Canadian Microelectronics Corporation/Société canadienne de micro-Eeectronique	cmc.ca
Canadian Museum of Nature	mus-nature.ca
Canadian Musical Reproduction Rights Agency Ltd. (CMRRA)	cmrra.ca
Canadian National Railways - CN Rail	cn.ca
Canadian Nazarene College	cnaz.mb.ca
Canadian Occidental Petroleum Ltd.	canoxy.ab.ca
Canadian Plastics Institute	plasticsinstitute.ca
Canadian Regional Airlines Ltd.	cral.ca
Canadian Scholars' Press Inc.	cspi.org
Canadian Space Agency	sp-agency.ca
Canadian Sport and Fitness Administration Centre	cdnsport.ca
Canadian Telecom Services	cdntelecom.mb.ca
Canadian Turbo (1993) Inc.	turbo.ca
Canadian Union College	cauc.ab.ca
Canadian Union of Public Employees	solinet.org
Canadian Utilities Limited	cul.ca
Canadian Wheat Board	canwheatbrd.ca
Canadore College of Applied Arts and Technology	canadorec.on.ca
CANARIE Inc.	canarie.ca
CANATOM Inc.	canatom.ca

CANCOM Technologies	can.com
Cancopy	cancopy.com
Can-Pay Computer Software Ltd.	canpay.ca
Cantox Incorporated	cantox.ca
Canwest Global Systems	canwest.com
Capilano College	capcollege.bc.ca
Caravan Consultants	caravan-con.toronto.on.ca
CARE Canada	care.ca
Cariboo College	cariboo.bc.ca
Caribou Ventures Limited	caribou.mb.ca
Caritas Health Care Institute	caritas.ab.ca
Carleton Board of Education	carletonbe.ottawa.on.ca
Carleton University	carleton.ca
Carlson Marketing Group Ltd.	carlson-marketing.ca
Carlton Cards Limited	carltoncards.ca
Carlton Cards Ltd.	carltoncards.com
Carp Systems International CSI Inc.	csi.on.ca
Carte International Inc.	carte.ca
Cassels Brock & Blackwell	casselsbrock.com
CATA (Canadian Advanced Technology Association)	cata.ca
CA*net	canet.ca
CB Media, Ltd.	cbmedia.ca
CCH Canadian Ltd.	cch.com
CCI Networks, a division of Corporate Computers Incorporated	ccinet.ab.ca
CD Publishing Corporation	netnewscd.com
CD Publishing Corporation	cdpublishing.com
Cdex Marketing	cdexmktg.com
CDNnet	cdnnet.ca
Cégep de Levis-Lauzon	clevislauzon.qc.ca
CEK Associates Inc.	cek.com
Celeste Crystal Systems Inc.	celeste.com
Centennial College of Applied Arts and Technology	cencol.on.ca
Central Canadian Structures Ltd.	ccsl.ca
Central Plains Incorporated	centralplains.mb.ca
Centre de recherche industrielle du Québec	criq.qc.ca
Centre de recherche informatique de Montréal	crim.ca
Centre de recherche Volvox Inc.	centrevolvox.qc.ca
Centre for Image and Sound Research	cisr.bc.ca
Centre for Professional Learning	cenpro.com
Centre universitaire de Shippagan	cus.ca
Centre universitaire Saint-Louis-Maillet	cuslm.ca
Centres Canadiens CAO/FAO	c3cam.com
Cerberus Information Security Consulting Inc.	cerberus.com
Challenge Business Systems	challenge.com
Champlain Regional College	champlaincollege.qc.ca
Channel-23 Communications	channel23.com
Chaps Group Inc.	chapsgroup.com
Chauvco Resources Ltd.	chauvco.ab.ca
Chedoke-McMaster Hospitals	cmh.on.ca
Cherniak Giblon	cherniak.on.ca
Chernoff Thompson Architects	cta.bc.ca
Chi Systems, Inc.	chisystemsinc.ca
Children's Hospital of Eastern Ontario	cheo.on.ca

Choreo Systems Inc.	choreo.ca
CIBC Investment Bank	cibcwg.com
CIMtegration Inc.	cimtegration.com
CIMtegration Inc.	cimtegration.on.ca
CIMTEK Automation Systems Inc.	cimtek.on.ca
Cine-Byte Imaging, Inc.	2film.com
City of Calgary, The	gov.calgary.ab.ca
City of Edmonton	gov.edmonton.ab.ca
City of Guelph	city.guelph.on.ca
City of Mississauga	city.mississauga.on.ca
City of Ottawa Corp.	city.ottawa.on.ca
City of Richmond	city.richmond.bc.ca
City of Toronto	gov.toronto.on.ca
CityTV	citytv.com
Clarke Institute of Psychiatry	clarke-inst.on.ca
Clifton Associates Ltd.	clifton.sk.ca
Club Macintosh de Quebec	cmq.qc.ca
C-MAC Electronic Systems Inc.	cmac.ca
CMSI	powerwindows.com
Coast Peripherals and Systems Inc.	coast-peripherals.bc.ca
Coffyn Communications	ccom.mb.ca
CoGenTex Inc.	cogentex.qc.ca
Cogni-CASE inc.	cognicase.ca
Cognos Incorporated	cognos.com
Coles Book Stores, Limited	coles.ca
College militaire royal de St-Jean	cmr.ca
College of Geographic Sciences, The	cogs.ns.ca
College of New Caledonia	cnc.bc.ca
College universitaire de Saint-Boniface	ustboniface.mb.ca
Colortron Photo Services Ltd.	colortron.com
Combustion Dynamics Ltd	combdyn.com
Combyne Data Inc.	combyne.qc.ca
Comcheq Services Ltd.	comcheq.ca
ComDev	comdev.ca
Comedy Bytes! BBS	comedy.com
Cominco Ltd.	cominco.com
Communauté urbaine de Montreal (CUM)	cum.qc.ca
Communication Designs	cdesigns.com
Communications accessibles Montréal	cam.org
Communications accessibles Montréal (Inc.)	cam.qc.ca
Communications Babylonne	babylon.montreal.qc.ca
Communications Canada (The Federal Department of Communications)	doc.ca
Communications Ganymede Inc.	ganymede.com
Communications MG Direct	mgdirect.com
Community Information Access Organization	ciao.trail.bc.ca
Comnetix Computer Systems	comnetix.com
CompEuphoria	euphoria.com
CompuBBS	compubbs.edmundston.nb.ca
CompuBBS	compubbs.com
Compucentre Toronto, Inc.	compucentre.com
Compudyn Systems Ltd.	compudyn.com
Compudyn Systems Ltd.	compudyn.on.ca
Compuquest Inc.	compuquest.com

CompuSoft	compus.ca
Compusult Limited	compusult.nf.ca
Compusup Business Centre Inc.	compusup.com
Comp-U-Systems International	compusystems.com
Computer Concepts Ltd.	compcon.com
Computer Consulting Associates Intl.	ccai.com
Computer Dynamics Online Service	compdyn.com
Computer Link	cml.com
Computer Methods International Corp.	cmic.ca
Computer Modelling Group	cmgroup.com
computerActive Inc.	computeractive.on.ca
Computerland	computerland.ca
ComputerLink Online Inc.	compulink.com
Computer-Mate Technologies Limited	cmate.com
Computing Art Inc.	c-art.com
CompuTrends Systems	blade.com
Comspec Communications Inc.	comspec.com
ComTel Plus Inc.	comtelplus.com
Conamara Technologies Ltd.	conamara.com
Concepts Zap	zap.qc.ca
Concordia University	concordia.ca
Concurrent Realities, Inc.	concur.com
Conestoga College	conestogac.on.ca
Confederation College	confederationc.on.ca
Connaught Laboratories Limited	connaught.com
Connect Tech, Inc.	connecttech.com
Connectivity Technology Inc.	connectivity.com
Connexions	connex.ca
Connor, Clark and Company Ltd.	connor.com
Connor, Clark and Company Ltd.	connor-clark.com
Consensys Computer Corporation	cnsnsys.com
Consensys Computers	consensys.com
Conservation and Protection Services	cp.org
Consolidated Access & Networks, Inc.	can.ca
Consolidated Access & Networks, Inc.	can.net
Consortia Systems International Ltd.	consortia.com
Construction Data	condata.mb.ca
Contact Integration Inc.	contact.ca
Contax Inc.	contax.com
Continental Healthcare Systems Canada Inc.	chs.mb.ca
Continental Insurance Management Ltd.	ciml.ca
Contrad Technology Inc.	contrad.com
Controlled Environments Limited	conviron.mb.ca
Conxsys Inc.	conxsys.on.ca
Coopers & Lybrand	cooperslybrand.ca
Coplanor Congres Inc.	coplanor.qc.ca
Coplanus Systems, Inc.	coplanus.com
Core Networking	eyenet.com
Core Networking (EYENET-DOM)	eyeq.com
Corel Corporation	corel.ca
coreluser.net	coreluser.net
Corenet Computer Services	corenet.com
Core*lan	infoshare.net
Core*LAN Inc.	corelan.com

Corporate Library, Canada Post Corporation	canpost.org
Cortech Communications Inc.	ark.com
COSKA Information Service	coska.bc.ca
Cott Corporation	cott.com
Council of Ontario Universities	cou.on.ca
CP Limited	cp.ca
Craig Dilks Computer Consulting Ltd.	cdccl.com
Creative Retirement Mantitoba, Inc.	crm.mb.ca
Creo Products Inc.	creo.bc.ca
Crohn's and Colitis Foundation of Canada	ccfc.ca
Crosfield Canada Inc.	crosfield.ca
Cross Cultural Consulting Inc.	ccci.ca
Crossbridge Information Systems, Inc.	crossbridge.com
Crowntek Business Centres	crowntek.ca
CTI Datacom Inc.	ctidata.com
CUC Broadcasting Ltd.	cuc.ca
CUE Here BBS, Commodore Users of Edmonton	cuehere.edmonton.ab.ca
Cumberland Computer Group Ltd.	ccg.bc.ca
CyberCorp Inc.	veda.org
Cyberdeals, Inc.	cyberdeals.com
Cybernetic Control Incorporated	cybercon.nb.ca
CyberSmith Inc.	csi.nb.ca
CYBERSOULS ETERNAL LIFE SYSTEMS INC.	cybersouls.com
Cyberstore Online Information Systems Inc.	cyberstore.ca
Cyberstore Systems, Inc.	cyberstore.net
Cyberstore Systems, Inc.	pole.com
Cyberstore Systems, Inc.	cyberstore.com
Cybervision Technologies	cybervision.com
Cygnus Technology Ltd.	cygnus.nb.ca
C. R. McGuffin Consulting Services	crmcg.com
d c wilson associates (tradename of 507245 Alberta Ltd.)	dcwilson.ab.ca
Daac Systems	daacsys.com
Daiwa (Canada) Limited	daiwa.com
Dalhousie University	dal.ca
Damar Communications	interaction.com
D'Arcy Cain Consulting	druid.com
Data Business Forms	databusiness.ca
Data Courier On-Line	dco.org
Data Design Systems Inc.	datadesign.com
Data Exchange	datex.com
Data Terminal Mart	dtm.bc.ca
Databyte Consulting Corp.	databyte.com
DataCorp Distributions	datacorp.montreal.qc.ca
Datafix Division	datafix.com
DATAP Systems	datap.ca
Datapanik Design	panik.vancouver.bc.ca
Dataradio Inc.	dataradio.com
dataREV Information Technologies Inc.	datarev.com
DataSoft Communications	datasoft.com
DataSpace Insight Inc.	dataspace.ca
Datatech Canada	ticker.com
Datatech Canada	datatech.org
Datatech Canada	dt-can.com

David E. Cross & Associates Inc.	davidcross.mb.ca
Davy International Canada Ltd.	davytor.com
Dawson College	dawsoncollege.qc.ca
Dawson Law Chambers	dawsonlaw.mb.ca
Daystorm Inc.	daystorm.com
dba Curvet Information Systems	curvet.com
DBCORP Information Systems Inv.	dbcorp.ab.ca
Dbm reflex entreprises inc.	dbmreflex.qc.ca
DCS Systems Ltd.	dcs-systems.com
de Havilland Inc.	dehavilland.ca
DECUS Canada, Digital Equipment Computer Users Society	decus.ca
Deep Cove Bulletin Board Service Ltd.	deepcove.com
DeForrest Ent BBS	defbbs.com
DEFTECH	deftech.outremont.qc.ca
Deloitte & Touche Management Consultants	dtmc.ca
Delphax Systems	delphax.com
Delrina Corporation	delrina.com
Delrina (Canada) Corporation	delrina.net
Delta Centre for Learning Technologies	delcen.com
Delta Controls, Inc.	delcon.com
Dendron Resource Surveys, Inc.	dendron.com
Denfield Communications, Reg.	telegraph.com
Dentofacial Software, Inc.	dentofacial.com
Department of Energy, Mines, and Resources	emr.ca
Department of Environment	doe.ca
Department of Fisheries and Oceans (Fisheries Canada)	dfo.ca
Department of National Defence	dnd.ca
Department of National Defense (LFC)	dnd.net
Designed Information Systems Corporation	disc-net.com
Designed Information Systems Corp.	aurora-net.com
Designed Information Systems Corp.	aurora.net
Deterministic Software Limited	deterministic.com
Develcon Electronics Ltd.	develcon.com
Dexotek Canada Corp.	dexotek.ca
DHD PostImage	postimage.com
Dial Computer Services	dialcomp.com
Didatech Software Ltd.	didatech.com
Digga Tech	digga.com
Digidyne Inc.	digidyne.com
Digidyne Inc.	digidyne.ca
Digimap Data Services	digimp.com
Digital Dreamland Bulletin Board System	digik.com
Digital Equipment du Canada Limitée	digital.ca
Digital Fix Development	digifix.com
Digital Fix Development	stepwise.com
Digital Objects	digiobj.com
Digital Video Systems	dvs.com
Digitech Information Services	digitech.ab.ca
Dilltech Systems	dilltech.vancouver.bc.ca
Dingo Software Systems Inc.	dingo.com
Diocese of New Westminster Network	nwnet.org
Direct Technologies, Inc.	edwards.com

Direct Technologies, Inc.	direct-tech.com
Directional Technologies Canada	dtech.mb.ca
Discovery Channel, The	discovery.ca
Discovery Passage BBS	smorgasboard.org
Discovery Training Network	dtn.bc.ca
Discreet Logic Inc.	discreet.qc.ca
DISCscribe	discribe.ca
District of Chilliwack	gov.chilliwack.bc.ca
District of Coquitlam	gov.coquitlam.bc.ca
Disus Division of Empirics Inc.	disusdei.on.ca
Disus Division of Empirics Inc.	disus.com
DKW Systems Corporation	dkw.com
DMR Group Inc.	dmr.ca
Dofasco Inc.	dofasco.ca
Dolphin Communications Inc.	dolphincom.com
Dominion Textile Inc.	domtex.ca
Double "T" Computer Services	double-t.com
Douglas College	douglas.bc.ca
Driver Design Labs, a division of Clarendon Datex Ltd.	driver-design-labs.bc.ca
Durham College of Applied Arts and Technology	durhamc.on.ca
Durham Freenet Net Inc.	durham.org
Duthie Books	duthiebooks.bc.ca
Dweomer UNIX User's Group	dweomer.org
Dylex Limited	dylex.com
Dymaxion Research Limited	dymaxion.ns.ca
Dynamic Fund Management	dynamicfund.ca
Dynamic Fund Management	dynamicfund.com
Dynamis Productivity Software Limited	dynamis.bc.ca
Dynamite Data Communications, Inc.	dynamite.com
Dynapro Systems Inc.	dsi.bc.ca
Dynatek Automation Systems Inc.	dynatek.ca
Dynix Automated Library Systems Inc.	dynix.com
D.E.M. Allen & Associates Ltd.	dema.mb.ca
D.flora Systems Inc.	dflora.com
D.H. Kumka & Associates	dhka.bc.ca
D.M. Gow Communications Inc.	dmgow.com
East Kootenay Community College	ekcc.bc.ca
Eastern Graphics Services	eastern.com
Eastern Pentecostal Bible College	epbc.edu
EBA Engineering Consultants Ltd.	eba-eng.com
EBA Engineering Consultants Ltd.	eba.ca
Echo Communications	echo.qc.ca
Eckler Partners, Ltd.	wm.com
Ecole de technologie superieure	etsmtl.ca
Ecole des hautes études commerciales de Montréal	hec.ca
Ecole Polytechnique de Montréal	polymtl.ca
e-Commerce Inc.	e-commerce.ca
e-Commerce Inc.	e-commerce.com
Economic Innovation and Technology Council	eitc.mb.ca
EDA Instruments Inc.	eda.com
Edfor Information Consultants Inc.	edfor.com
EdgeWays! InfoLink Online Services	edgeways.vancouver.bc.ca
EDI World Institute - Institut mondial EDI	ediwi.ca
Edmonton Freenet	freenet.edmonton.ab.ca

Edmonton Public Library	publib.edmonton.ab.ca
Edmonton Public School Board, District No. 7	epsb.edmonton.ab.ca
Edmonton Remote Systems	ersys.edmonton.ab.ca
Edmonton Telephones	edtel.ab.ca
ED-NET Educational Electronic Information Service	ednet.bc.ca
Education Technology Centre of British Columbia	etc.bc.ca
Eicon Technology Corporation	eicon.qc.ca
Eicon Technology Corp.	eicon.com
Electro Test Services	electrotest.com
Electrohome Electronics	electro.com
Electronic Library Network	eln.bc.ca
Electronic Mail Pathways (1003662 Ontario Inc.)	empath.on.ca
Electronic Village	village.ca
Elegant Communications Inc.	elegant.com
Elemental Research	elements.org
Elixir Technologies Corporation	elixir.com
ELSAG Bailey Canada Inc.	bailey.ca
ELSID Software Systems Ltd.	elsid.ca
EMCO Distribution Group	emcodg.com
Emcon Emanation Control Ltd.	emcon.com
EmGee Products International	emgee.on.ca
Emily Carr College of Art and Design	eccad.bc.ca
Emily Carr Institute of Art and Design	eciad.bc.ca
EMJ Data Systems	emj.ca
Empress Software Inc.	empress.com
Encode Business Systems Inc.	encode.com
EncycloMedia	encyclomedia.com
Enhance Systems Inc.	enhance.com
Enhance Systems Inc.	enhance.ca
Enhanced Systems Inc.	enhanced.ca
enHansen Information Systems Ltd.	enhansen.ca
Enterprise Network Inc.	entnet.nf.ca
Enterprise Planning Systems Inc.	enterprise.on.ca
Enterprise Solutions, Ltd.	esol.com
Entrenet Systems	entrenet.com
Entreprises Julien Inc.	julien.ca
Envirofit Consulting Inc.	envirofit.mb.ca
Environics Research Group Limited	environics.ca
Episet Corporation	episet.com
EPS Essential Planning Systems Ltd.	eps.bc.ca
Eric Woodward	pronet.net
Eridani Inc.	eridani.com
Ernst & Young	ey.ca
Escher Grad	escher.com
Espace Courbe	espacec.montreal.qc.ca
ESSA Technologies Ltd.	essa.com
ESSA Technologies Ltd.	essatech.com
Essential Software Solutions, Inc.	essoft.com
ESSO Chemical Canada	esso.ca
Etobicoke Board of Education	bdofed.etobicoke.on.ca
Evergreen International Technolgy Inc.	egn.com
Evert Communications Limited	evert.com
Everyware Development Corp.	everyware.com
Excalibur Systems Limited	excalibur.com

Excelsior Software Systems	excelsior.com
Executive Travel Appartment Suites, Inc.	etasuite.com
Exo-Info	exo-info.qc.ca
Exoterica Corporation	exoterica.com
Expert Technology Corporation	extec.mb.ca
Exploranium G.S., Ltd.	exploranium.com
Export Development Corporation	edc.ca
Eye Research Institute of Canada	eric.on.ca
Eyepoint Inc.	eyepoint.com
Eyepoint Inc.	eyepoint.on.ca
E. B. Eddy Forest Products, Ltd.	efpnet.com
E.D.M.Bulletin Board Services Ltd.	edmbbs.com
F1 Systems	peel-online.com
Facet Decision Systems, Inc.	facet.com
FACS Record Centre	facs.mb.ca
FACT International Inc.	fact.com
Fairview College	fairviewc.ab.ca
Falconbridge Limited	falconbridge.com
Fanshawe College	fanshawec.on.ca
Fantasia BBS, Enr.	fantasia.qc.ca
Farris, Vaughan, Wills and Murphy Barristers & Solocitors	farris.com
Farwest BBS	farwest.victoria.bc.ca
Fasken Campbell Godfrey	fasken.com
Fastlane Technologies	fastlane.on.ca
Fax F/X Information Services Limited	faxfx.ca
Faximum Software Inc.	faximum.com
Fax-Info-Base Corporation	faxinfobase.com
Faxon Canada Ltd.	faxon.ca
Faxtel Information Systems, Ltd.	marketfax.com
Federated Insurance Company of Canada	fed-ins.ca
Fédération des producteurs de volailles du Québec	volbec.qc.ca
FG Commodity Electronics Inc.	fgcom.qc.ca
Fidelity Investments Canada Ltd.	fidelity.ca
FidoNet NET250	tor250.org
Fine Line Communications Ltd.	fineline.mb.ca
Finning Ltd.	finning.ca
First Avenue Information Systems	firstavenue.com
First Marathon Securities Inc.	fmarathon.ca
First Marathon Securities, Inc.	fmarathon.com
FirstClass Systems Corp.	firstclass.ca
Firstline Trust	firstline.com
Flashpoint Database Consulting Ltd.	flashpoint.com
FLEET HOUSE	fleethouse.com
Fleximation Systems Inc.	flexnet.com
FMG Timberjack Inc.	timberjack.com
FMMO Publications Informatiques Enr.	fmmhost.com
Focus Automation Systems Inc.	focus-systems.on.ca
Focus Technologies	focustech.com
Fokstone Design Inc.	folkstone.bc.ca
Fonds FCAR	fcar.qc.ca
fONOROLA	fonorola.net
fONOROLA Inc.	fonorola.ca
Foothills Provincial Hospital	fhhosp.ab.ca
Footprint Software Inc.	footprint.com

Forefront Graphics	forefront.com
Forest Engineering Research Institute of Canada	feric.bc.ca
Forest Heights Collegiate Institute	fhci.kitchener.on.ca
Forestry Canada	forestry.ca
Forintek Canada Corp.	forintek.ca
Fort Ignition Limited	fortignition.ca
Fort Whyte Centre	fortwhyte.mb.ca
Fox-Novator Systems, Inc.	novator.com
F-PRO Canada (Freelance Professionals)	f-pro.ca
Fraser and Beatty	fraserbeatty.ca
Fraser Valley College	fvc.bc.ca
Freed and Freed International Ltd.	freed.mb.ca
Freedman Sharp and Associates Inc.	fsa.ca
Friden Neopost	friden.com
Friesen Tokar Architects	friesentokar.mb.ca
Frisco Bay Industries, Ltd.	frisco-bay.ca
Frostzone BBS	frostzone.com
Fujitsu Canada, Inc.	fujitsu.ca
Fulcrum Technologies Inc.	fultech.com
Fulton Research	eon.org
Functionality Inc.	functionality.com
FundSERV Inc.	fundserv.com
Fundy Cable Ltd./Ltée	fundycbl.com
Future Shop Ltd.	futureshop.com
Future Sight/2	fsight2.com
Futuretron Software Services	futuretron.on.ca
FutureWorld BBS	futureworld.com
FX Corporation	fxcorp.com
Galaxy Online Services	galaxy.com
Gallium Software Inc.	gallium.com
GameMaster/Le Maitre de jeu (enr.), The	gamemaster.qc.ca
Gandalf Data Ltd.	gandalf.ca
Gang-Nail Canada Inc.	gang-nail.com
Gateway BBS	gateway-bbs.com
Gateway File Systems, a division of VSD Inc.	gwfs.bc.ca
GDT Softworks Inc.	infowave.net
GDT Softworks Inc.	gdt.com
Geac Computer Corporation	geac.com
Gemini Group, Inc.	gemini.ca
Gemini Learning Systems Inc.	gemini.com
Genasys II, Inc.	genasys.bc.ca
Gencom Services Inc.	gencom.bc.ca
General DataComm Ltd.	gdc.ca
Genesis Microchip Incorporated	genesis-microchip.on.ca
Gennum Corporation	gennum.com
Geological Survey of Newfoundland	geosurv.gov.nf.ca
Geomatics International Inc.	geomatics.on.ca
Geonex Aerodat Inc.	aerodat.com
Geopower Technologies Inc.	geopower.com
GEOREF Systems Ltd.	georef.com
George Brown College	gbrownc.on.ca
George Weston Ltd.	weston.ca
Georgian College	georcoll.on.ca
Geoterrex Ltd.	geoterrex.ca

GeoWare Software Design	geoware.com
Geo. H. Young & Co. Ltd.	ghyoung.ca
Glenayre Electronics Ltd.	glenayre.com
Glenrose Rehabilitation Hospital	grhosp.ab.ca
Global DataFlux Ltd.	dataflux.bc.ca
Global Link On-Line Information Service	globalink.com
Global Strategies	gsc.com
Global Travel Computer Services	global-travel.on.ca
Global X Change	globalx.net
Globe and Mail, The	globeandmail.ca
GN Navtel	gn.com
Gnosis Software, Inc.	gnosis.com
Goal Electronics Inc.	goal.waterloo.on.ca
Godin London Inc.	godin.on.ca
Gold Disk Inc.	golddisk.com
Golem Consulting Services	golem.waterloo.on.ca
Good Media Incorporated	goodmedia.com
Gouvernement du Québec (Ministère des communications)	gouv.qc.ca
Government of Canada/Gouvernement du Canada	gc.ca
Government of Manitoba	gov.mb.ca
Government of the Northwest Territories	gov.nt.ca
Government of the Province of Ontario	gov.on.ca
Government of Yukon	gov.yk.ca
Grafnetix Systems Inc.	grafnetix.qc.ca
Granary Enterprises Inc.	granary.com
Grande Prairie Regional College	gprc.ab.ca
Grant MacEwan Community College	gmcc.ab.ca
Grass Root Systems	grassys.bc.ca
Gray Beverage Inc.	gray-beverage.ca
Gray Research Group, The	gray.mb.ca
Gray Sage Holdings, Ltd.	graysage.edmonton.ab.ca
Greater Vancouver Regional District	gvrd.bc.ca
Greater Victoria Public Library	gvpl.victoria.bc.ca
Great-West Life Assurance Company	gwl.ca
Grebar Systems Inc.	grebar.mb.ca
Groupe Cerveau Inc.	cerveau.ca
Groupe Environnement Shooner inc.	shooner.qc.ca
Groupe Quebecor inc.	quebecor.ca
Groupe-Info Quatre Saisons	gi4s.qc.ca
GSA Consulting Group Inc.	gsalink.com
GTC Transcontinental Group Ltd.	transc.com
Guideline Digital Printing Service	guideline-dps.com
Guild Consulting Ltd.	guild.bc.ca
Guild EdgeWare Inc.	edgeware.com
Gulf Canada Resources Ltd.	gulf.ca
GVC Technologies	gvc.com
GWN Consultants	gwn.com
GWN Systems Inc.	gwnsys.ca
GWR Human Resource Services	gwresource.mb.ca
G.M. Systems	gmsys.com
G.T.M. Incorporated	gtm-inc.com
G.T.S.	gts.net
G.T.S.	gts.org

Halton Board of Education	haltonbe.on.ca
Hamilton Civic Hospitals	hch.org
Hamilton Telegraphics Inc.	htg.com
Hardware Canada Computing Inc.	hcc-unisol.com
Harlequin Enterprises Ltd.	harlequinbooks.com
Harris Computer Service	harriscs.on.ca
Harvest International Venture Corp.	harvest-intl.com
HCR Corporation	hcr.com
Health and Welfare, Canada	hwc.ca
Health Sciences Centre	hsc.mb.ca
HealthVISION Corporation	healthvision.ca
Helios Integrated Systems Inc.	heliosis.com
Helix Internet	helix.net
Helix Online	helix-online.com
HexaCom Info Services	hexacom.com
HexaCom Info Services	hexacom.montreal.qc.ca
Hexagon Computer Systems, Inc.	hexagon.ca
HiBiTek	hibitek.on.ca
Hidden Values, Inc.	hv.com
High Performance Concepts	hpcon.mb.ca
Highwire Information Inc.	highwire.com
Hill and Knowlton Corp.	hillknowlton.ca
Hillside Systems	hillside.com
HIP Communications	hip.com
HME Zymurgists Association	beer.org
Holland College	hollandc.pe.ca
Holland Marsh Management Group	hollandmarsh.com
Hollywood Toy & Poster Company	hollywdposter.mb.ca
Holt Software Associates Inc.	hsa.on.ca
Home Base BBS	homebase.com
Honeywell Limited	honeywell.ca
Hospital for Sick Children	sickkids.on.ca
Howmet - Cercast	castit.com
HPC High Performance Computing Centre	hpc.com
HR On-Line	hronline.com
HTS Engineering Limited	htseng.com
Hudson's Bay Company	hbc.com
Humber College of Applied Arts and Technology	humberc.on.ca
Hummingbird Communications Ltd.	hcl.com
Husky Injection Molding Systems Ltd.	husky.on.ca
Hustad Associates Consulting Ltd.	hustad.bc.ca
Hustad Associates Ltd.	hustad.com
Hutchison Avenue Software Corporation	hasc.ca
Hydromantis, Inc.	hydromantis.com
Hydro-Québec	hydro.qc.ca
Hymarc, Ltd.	hymarc.com
Hypercomp, An Organization for High Performance Computing	hypercomp.ns.ca
Hypercube Inc.	hyper.com
Hyprotech Ltd.	hyprotech.ab.ca
H&H Technologies Inc.	vicnet.com
H. L. Blachford	blachford.ca
H.C.S. Health Care Systems Inc.	hcs.ca
Ian Fairlie	iffarch.com

Ian Martin Limited	iml.com
Iatco Industries Inc.	iatco.com
IBM Canada	ibm.ca
ICA Computer Ltd.	icacomp.com
ICE Computer Entertainment	iceonline.com
ICOMOS Canada Inc.	icomos.org
ICOMOS Canada Inc.	icomos.net
Icon Internetworking Inc.	icon.bc.ca
ICRG (Information and Communications Research Group)	icrg.com
iDEAS ONLINE Business Net	ideasnet.com
Idon Corporation	idon.ottawa.on.ca
Image Works, The	imagewks.mb.ca
Imagen Communications Inc.	imagen.bc.ca
Imax Systems Corporation	imax.com
Immedia Infomatic Inc.	immedia.ca
Imperial Oil Limited	iol.ca
Imperial Tobacco Ltd.	itl.com
InaSec Incorporation	inasec.ca
INCAD Software Technologies Corporation	incad.com
Incentives Technologies	res.com
Incognito Software Inc.	incognito.com
In-Comm	incomm.com
InContext Corp.	incontext.ca
INDE Electronics	inde.bc.ca
Indian and Northern Affairs Canada	inac.ca
Industry Science & Technology Canada	istc.ca
Inetco Systems, Ltd.	inetco.com
Infac Corporation	infac.com
Infinity Systems Inc.	infsys.com
INFO3000	info3000.com
Infobase Consultants Inc.	infobase.on.ca
Infobook	infobook.com
InfoConnections	infoconnections.mb.ca
Infocorp Computer Solutions Ltd.	infocorp.mb.ca
InfoDesign Corporation	idc.com
Info-Doc Net Télématique internationale inc.	infodoc.ca
Infolytica Corporation	infolytica.qc.ca
InfoMagnetics Technologies Corporation	infomag.mb.ca
Infomaniac's Dial-A-File BBS	dafbbs.com
Infomart Dialog, Ltd.	infomart.ca
InfoMatch Communications Inc.	infomatch.com
InfoRamp Inc.	inforamp.com
InfoRamp Inc.	inforamp.net
Information Design Solutions	idscorp.com
Information Management & Economics	ime.com
Information Systems Incorporated	cisl.com
Information Systems Management Corporation	ism.ca
Information Technology Research Centre (ITRC)	itrc.on.ca
Infoserve Technologies Ltd.	infoserve.net
InfoThink, Ltd.	infothink.com
InfoWare Canada Inc.	infoware.ca
Infrastructures for Information	i4i.org
Ingram Micro Canada Inc.	imcan.com

Inner Quest Communications Inc.	inner-quest.com
Innovation Place	innovplace.saskatoon.sk.ca
Innovation technologique INTEK inc.	intek.qc.ca
Innovatron	inno.org
Innovatron	inno.com
InnovMetric Logiciels inc.	imetric.qc.ca
Innovus Inc.	innovus.on.ca
Innovus Inc.	innovus.com
INSI Integrated Systems Inc.	insi.mb.ca
INSIGHT News	insightnews.com
Instantiated Software, Inc.	instantiated.on.ca
Institute for Computer Studies	icsca.com
Institute for Space and Terrestrial Science	ists.ca
Institute of Electrical and Electronics Engineers of Canada	ieee.ca
Institute of Ocean Sciences	ios.bc.ca
InStore Focus	instore.ca
Integain Corporation	integain.com
Integral Investments Incorporated	integral.on.ca
Integrated Engineering Software	integrated.mb.ca
Integrated Messaging Inc.	imi.mb.ca
Integrated Network Services Inc.	insinc.net
Integrated Systems Applications Corporation	isac.ca
Integration Informatique BDM Inc.	integration.qc.ca
Intelepath Internet Services	intelepath.sk.ca
InteleQ Inc.	inteleq.com
Intelligent Information Systems	iisys.com
Intera Information Technologies	intera.ca
Intera Tydac Technologies	tydac.com
Inter-Acces Communications	interax.net
InterAccess Technology Corp.	interaccess.ca
Interact Adv	interadv.com
Interactive Electronic Design	ied.com
Interactive Image Technologies Ltd.	interactiv.com
Interactive Technical Services	itserv.com
Interautomation, Inc.	iainc.com
Interlink Inc.	interlink.net
InterLink On-line Services Inc.	interlink.bc.ca
InterLinx Support Services, Inc.	ilinx.com
Interlog Internet Services	interlog.com
International Association of Mathematical Geology	iamg.org
International Civil Aviation Organization	icao.org
International Congress of Business Councils	icbc.org
International Development Research Centre	idrc.ca
International Institute for Sustainable Development	iisd.ca
International Resource Centre	ircinc.com
International SysteMap Corporation	ismcorp.com
International Systems Group Inc.	isgsys.com
International Teletimes	teletimes.com
International Verifact, Inc.	verifact.com
Internet Access Inc.	intacc.com
Internet Access Inc.	intacc.ca
Internet Communications Inc.	intnet.bc.ca
Internet Companion, The	tic.ab.ca

Internet Connect Niagara, Inc.	niagara.com
InterNet Consultants	in.edmonton.ab.ca
Internet Consulting Group	icg.on.ca
Internet Direct, Inc.	netdirect.net
Internet Direct, Inc.	bc.com
Internet Direct, Inc.	canada.net
Internet Direct, Inc.	direct.ca
Internet Seminars Incorporated	iseminars.com
Internet Services and Information Systems Inc.	isisnet.com
Internet Shop Inc., The	netshop.bc.ca
Internet Solutions, Inc.	intersolve.com
Internetworking Systems Group	isginc.com
Internex Online Inc.	io.org
InterNode Networks	internode.net
Interpass Technologies, Inc.	interpass.com
Interprovincial Pipe Line Inc.	ipl.ca
Intertech Systems Inc.	isi-can.com
InterTech Systems Integrators, Inc.	isi.on.ca
InterWeb Internet Services	interweb.com
Interwork Software Inc.	interwork.com
Intrepid Information Systems Inc.	intrepid.on.ca
Intunix Inc.	intunix.com
Investors Group	igroup.ca
Ionix Internet Educational Services	ionix.com
Iotek Inc.	iotek.ns.ca
Iris Systems Inc.	iris.mb.ca
IRISCO	irisco.com
Ironstone Technologies	ironstone.mb.ca
Island Internet	island.net
ISM Corporation, SIS Region	ismcan.com
ISOTRO Network Management Inc.	isotro.ca
ITN Corporation	itncorp.ca
Izaak Walton Killam Hospital for Children	iwkhosp.ns.ca
I.C.E. Online Services	ice.bc.ca
I.D. Group Inc.	idgroup.ca
Jade Simulations International Corporation	jade.com
Jade Simulations International Corporation	jade.ab.ca
Jammy's Amiga Corner	jammys.net
Jana Publishing	jana.com
Janna Systems, Inc.	janna.com
JDP Systems Inc.	jdp.com
Jeff Voskamp	voskamp.waterloo.on.ca
Jefferson Partners Capital Corporation	jefferson.com
JES Library Automation	jeslacs.bc.ca
Jetcom Communications	jetcom.com
Jetform Corp.	jetform.com
John Forsyth Company	jforsyth.com
John Free Inc.	manitou.com
John S. Koperwas	koperwas.org
John T. Wilson and Associates Ltd.	equinova.com
Joymarmon Group Inc., The	joymrmn.on.ca
JTS Computer Systems Ltd.	jts.com
Juvenile Diabetes Foundation of Canada	jdfc.ca
Juxta Publishing	juxta.com

J. J. Conklin Communications	jjconklin.mb.ca
J.A. Carroll Consulting	jacc.com
J.G. Noguera & Associates	jgna.com
J.J. Barnicke Limited	jjb.com
K-12 Technology by Design Centre Ltd.	k12technology.bc.ca
Kanatek Technologies	kanatek.ca
Kanatek Technologies	sofpak.com
KAO Infosystems Canada, Inc.	kaocanada.com
Karhu Canada	karhu.ca
Kasten Chase Applied Research	kasten.on.ca
KB'S BBS	kbsbbs.com
KBS Technology Incorporated	kbs.com
KEA Systems Ltd.	kea.bc.ca
Keewatin Community College	keewatincc.mb.ca
Ken Schwabe	schwabe.winnipeg.mb.ca
Kendall Systems	kensys.com
Keyano College	keyanoc.ab.ca
Keyword Office Technologies	keyword.com
King's College	kingsu.ab.ca
Kingston General Hospital	kgh.on.ca
Kingston Online Services	kosone.com
Kingsun Systems Inc.	kingsunsystems.com
Kingsway Computing Solutions	kingsway.com
Kirk Computer Systems Ltd.	kirk.nt.ca
Kitchener-Waterloo Municipal Area Network	kw.net
Kitsilano Network Research	kitsnet.vancouver.bc.ca
KL Group Inc.	klg.com
Knowledge Plus Multimedia Publishing Ltd.	kplus.bc.ca
Korsa International	korsa.com
KPMG	kpmg.ca
Kraft General Foods Canada	kraft.ca
KRB Enterprises	vilgreen.com
Kruger Inc.	kruger.com
KT Industries Ltd.	ktindustries.mb.ca
KTS Business Systems Inc.	kts.com
KW Networks	kwnet.on.ca
Kwantlen College	kwantlen.bc.ca
K.C. Chen Technology, Int'l. Ltd.	shentech.com
K.E.B. System 1 BBS	keb1.winnipeg.mb.ca
La Press Ltée	lapresse.com
Labatt Breweries of Canada	labatt.com
Labour.Net	labournet.com
LaCite College	lacitec.on.ca
Laidlaw Waste Systems, Ltd.	laidlawbur.com
Lakefield College School	lakefieldcs.lakefield.on.ca
Lakehead University	lakeheadu.ca
Lakeland College	lakelandc.ab.ca
Lambda Systems Ltd.	lamsys.com
Lambton College of Applied Arts & Technology	lambton.on.ca
Lambton County Roman Catholic Separate School Board	lambtonrcssb.on.ca
Land of the Darkside BBS, The	lotds.waterloo.on.ca
Landmark Feeds Inc.	lmfeeds.mb.ca
Langara College	langara.bc.ca

LANhouse Communications Ltd.	lanhouse.com
LANsource Technologies	lansource.com
LanterNette Inc.	lanternette.com
Lanworks Technologies Inc.	lanworks.com
LARG-Net	larg-net.london.on.ca
Lasys Technologies Inc.	lasys.com
Laurentian University	laurentian.ca
Lavy and Associates, Ltd.	lavy.mb.ca
Law Society of Upper Canada	lsuc.on.ca
Lawson Mardon Group	impana.com
LCRNet Association	lcrnet.org
Le BBS-I Enr.	bbsi.qc.ca
Le Relais BBS	relais.com
Learnix Limited	learnix.com
Learnix Ltd.	learnix.ca
Lehman Computer Group, Inc. o/a The Wollongong Group Canada	lehman.on.ca
Leitch Video International, Inc.	leitch.com
Les Conseillers INRO Consultants inc.	inro.ca
Les Entreprises Videoway Ltée	videoway.qc.ca
Les Services Informatiques BRS Inc.	brs.qc.ca
Les Services NPK+ inc.	npkservices.qc.ca
Les Systèmes Zenon Inc.	zenon.com
Lethbridge Community College	lethbridgec.ab.ca
Lewis Continental Inc.	lewcon.mb.ca
Lexus Technologies	lexus.com
LGS Group Inc.	lgs.ca
Lightning Communications Corp.	lightning.ca
LinkAge Office Information Systems Inc.	linkage.com
Linnet Graphics International Inc.	linnet.ca
Linq Communications	linq.com
Lions Park Computers Ltd.	lions.com
Litco Systems Inc.	litcosys.ca
Litco Systems Inc.	litcosys.on.ca
Livewire Communications	livewire.org
Livingston Group, Inc.	livgroup.com
Lloyd Macilouham, Barrister & Solicitor	canimmlaw.com
LMSOFT	lmsoft.ca
Loach Engineering Inc.	loacheng.on.ca
Lockheed Canada Inc.	lockheed.on.ca
Logibec Groupe Informatique, Ltée	logibec.com
Logibro	logibro.com
Logical Conclusions Software Consulting Ltd.	locon.com
Logical Solutions Inc.	logical.ca
Logiciels et applications scientifiques inc.	lasinc.qc.ca
Logicom Process Programming	logi.com
Login Informatique J-M.P.	newmarket.com
Login Informatique J-M.P.	safe.org
LOGIN: Logiciel Interactif/Interactive Software JMP/SDA Inc.	login.qc.ca
Logres Inc.	logres.com
Lomas Data Management Inc.	dlomas.com
London Public Library	lpl.london.on.ca
Longhurst Consulting	longhurst.ab.ca

LOOK Software	look.com
Looking Glass Design	looking-glass.com
Looking Glass Software Limited	looking.on.ca
Lotus Development Canada Ltd.	lotus.ca
Loyalist College of Applied Arts and Technology	loyalistc.on.ca
Lugroid Enterprises	lugroid.com
LV Software Canada Inc.	lvsoftware.ca
L. G. Richings & Associates	lgrcne.com
L.I. Business Solutions Inc.	li-business.ab.ca
M3i Systems Inc.	m3isystems.qc.ca
MacDonald Dettwiler and Associates	mda.ca
Macintosh Owners and Users Society of Edmonton	mouse.edmonton.ab.ca
MacLawran Group Inc., The	maclawran.ca
Maclean Hunter Communications Inc.	maclean-hunter.ca
Maclean Hunter Communications Inc.	maclean-hunter.com
MacMillan Bloedel Ltd.	macblo.ca
Magi Data Consulting	magi.com
MAGIC Online Services Toronto Inc.	magic.ca
Mag-Net BBS	mag-net.com
MAGNET CORP.	mchannel.com
Magra Computer Product Inc.	magra.com
Mahogany Row Management Consulting Inc.	mahogany.ca
MAI Canada Ltd.	mai.ca
Mainland Information Systems Ltd.	mainland.ab.ca
Makaera Vir Inc.	vir.com
Makaera Vir Inc.	makaera.com
Malaspina College	mala.bc.ca
Malcolm Silver & Company	msco.com
maloka bbs	maloka.com
Managing Partner	partner.com
Manitoba Cancer Treatment and Research Foundation	mctrf.mb.ca
Manitoba Co-operator	co-operator.mb.ca
Manitoba Go Association	goassoc.mb.ca
Manitoba Health Organizations	manhealthorg.mb.ca
Manitoba HVDC Research Centre	hvdc.ca
Manitoba Hydro	hydro.mb.ca
Manitoba Institute of Management, Inc., The	maninstmgt.mb.ca
Manitoba Museum of Man and Nature	museummannature.mb.ca
Manitoba Organization of Faculty Associations	mofa.mb.ca
Manitoba Public Insurance Corporation	mpic.mb.ca
Manitoba Regional Network (MBnet)	mbnet.mb.ca
Manitoba Telephone System	mts.mb.ca
Manitoba UNIX User Group	muug.mb.ca
Mantis Computing	mantis.com
Manufacturing Concepts Inc.	mfgcon.com
Manulife Financial	manulife.ca
Manulife Financial/Business Library	manulife.com
Maplewood Computing	maplewood.com
Marc Staveley Consulting	staveley.com
Marcam Canada, Inc.	zed.com
Marine Frontiers	marine-frontiers.com
Mariner Systems Services	mariner.com
Mariposa Communications Group	mariposagroup.com

Mariposa Communications Group	mcgroup.com
Maritime Information Technology Inc.	maritime.com
Maritime Tel & Tel	maritime-tel.ns.ca
Market Connections	sportsnet.com
Market Connections, Inc.	marketcon.mb.ca
MarketDesk Inc.	marketdesk.com
Marketing Database Solutions Inc.	mdsi.com
Marr Consulting & Communications Ltd.	marrcc.mb.ca
Marsh & McLennan Limited	mml.ca
Martin Marietta Canada Ltd.	mmcl.ca
Martineau Walker Advocates	martineau-walker.com
Mastercom Consulting	mastercom.com
Mat Tipping	cafe.net
Material Culture Management Inc.	mcmi.com
Matrix Professional Video Systems Inc.	matrix.bc.ca
Matrox Electronic Systems Ltd.	matrox.com
Matrox Electronics Systems Ltd.	matrox.qc.ca
Matthews Microcomputer Services Ltd.	matthewsmicro.ns.ca
Maxon Services	maxon.ca
Maxwell Advance Systems	secworld.com
MAYA Heat Transfer Technologies, Ltd	mayahtt.ca
MBnet UUCP User Group	bison.mb.ca
MCC Inc.	mcc.qc.ca
McCarthy Tetrault	mccarthy.ca
McCullough Computer Consulting	mcc.ab.ca
McDougall Scientific Ltd.	mcd-sci.on.ca
McGill Management	mcgill.net
McGill University	mcgill.ca
McGill University Internet	mcgill.edu
McKenna Information Technologies Inc.	mtech.com
McMaster University	mcmaster.ca
MD Computer Consulting	mdcomp.toronto.on.ca
MedChem Laboratories, Ltd.	medchem.com
Media Spectrum	medspec.com
MediaFactory Softworks, Inc.	mediafactory.com
Mediaworks Magazine	mediaworks.toronto.on.ca
Medicine Hat College	mhc.ab.ca
Melchior Management Systems Inc.	melchior.ca
Memorial University of Newfoundland	mun.ca
Merak Projects Ltd.	merak.com
Mercer Management Consulting Ltd.	mmc.on.ca
Merisel Canada	merisel-ca.com
Merlin Systems	merlin-systems.on.ca
MetaLink Communications Inc.	metalink.ca
Metalogic Software	metalogic.bc.ca
MET-CHEM Canada Inc.	met-chem.com
Metrix Interlink Corp.	interlink.ca
Metro-McNair Clinical Laboratories	mmcl.com
Metropolis Graphics Ltd.	metropolis.qc.ca
Metropolitain Internet eXchange	mix.net
Metropolitan Toronto Police	mtp.gov
Metropolitan Toronto Reference Library	mtrl.toronto.on.ca
Metrowerks Inc.	metrowerks.ca
MHN Consulting Services	mhn.org

Michael Boreskie Architect Inc.	boreskie.mb.ca
Michael Boreskie Architect Inc.	boreskiearch.mb.ca
Michael Caughey and Associates	canda.org
Michael Milne Associates Ltd.	mmilne.com
MI-COM Technology	micomtech.com
Micro Advice Inc.	microadvice.com
MicroAge Computer Centre	microswo.com
MicroAge Computer Solutions	microage.ca
Micro-C Systems Integration	micro-c.com
Micronav International Inc.	micronav.ca
Microplex Systems Ltd.	microplex.com
Microsoft Workgroup Canada	msworkgroup.bc.ca
Microstar Software Ltd.	microstar.com
Microtel Pacific Research Ltd.	mpr.ca
Microtronix Systems Ltd.	microtronix.ca
Midland Walwyn Capital Inc.	midwal.ca
MILI COMPUTERS INC.	mili.com
Milkyway Networks Corporation	milkyway.ca
Milkyway Networks Corporation	milkyway.com
Miller Thomson	miltom.com
Milliken Mills High School	milliken-mills.markham.on.ca
Mills and Associates	redhead.com
Mills Data Systems Group	mills.com
Mimosa Systems Inc.	mimosa.com
Mind Computer Products	mind.mb.ca
MIND LINK!	mindlink.bc.ca
MIND LINK! Communications Corp.	mlnet.com
MIND LINK! Communications Corp.	mind.com
MIND LINK! Communications Corp.	mindlink.net
Mindemoya Computing and Design	mcd.on.ca
Minds Edge Productions Inc.	mep.com
Minerva Technology Inc.	minerva.ca
Ministry of Education and Training	edu.on.ca
Mirus International Inc.	mirus.on.ca
Mitel Corporation	mitel.com
Mitel Corporation	mitel.ca
Mitra Imaging Corporation	mitra.on.ca
Mitra Imaging Corporation	mitra.com
Mitsubishi Electric Sales Canada, Inc.	mesca.ca
MKS Informatique	mksinfo.qc.ca
Mohawk College of Applied Arts and Technology	mohawkc.on.ca
Moli Energy Ltd.	molienergy.bc.ca
Molson Breweries	molson.ca
Monenco Agra	monenco.ca
Montreal Exchange	me.org
Moonfish Consulting	moonfish.bc.ca
Moore Business Forms & Systems	moore.ca
Moore Corporation Limited	moore.com
More Scope Data Searches	morescope.ab.ca
MORG Inc.	micro.org
Morning Star Computer Service	mornstar.com
Morphos Systems	morphos.com
Mortice Kern Systems, Inc.	mks.com
Mosaid Technologies Incorporated	mosaid.com

Mothernode	mothernode.com
Motor Coach Industries Ltd.	motorcoach.ca
Motorsport News International	motorsport.com
Mount Allison University	mta.ca
Mount Royal College	mtroyal.ab.ca
Mount Saint Vincent University	msvu.ca
Mount Sinai Hospital	mtsinai.on.ca
Mountain Lake Software Corporation	mtnlake.com
Mountainview Consultants Inc.	mountainview.on.ca
MPB Technologies Inc.	mpbtech.qc.ca
MRM Steel Ltd.	mrm.mb.ca
MRRM (Canada) Inc.	mrrm.ca
MT&T Limited	mtt.ns.ca
MuchMusic	muchmusic.com
Multimeg electronique inc.	multimeg.com
Multipath Business Systems	multipath.com
Multiple Retirement Services Inc. (M.R.S. Inc.)	mrs.ca
Multiple Retirement Services, Inc.	mrs.com
Multiprocessor Toolsmiths Inc.	toolsmiths.on.ca
Municipal Leasing	mflc.com
Municipality of Metropolitan Toronto	metrotor.on.ca
Munro Garrett Inc.	mgintl.com
MUSE Corporation	musecorp.com
Musique Français Fan Club	musique.org
MYRA Systems Corp. Ltd	myra.com
Myrias Computer Technologies Incorporated	myrias.ab.ca
Nanometrics, Inc.	nanometrics.on.ca
National Archives of Canada	archives.ca
National Association of Japanese Canadians	najc.ca
National Book Service	nbs.com
National Computer Products Ltd.	ncp.com
National Library of Canada	nlc-bnc.ca
National Optics Institute	ino.qc.ca
National Research Council Canada	nrc.ca
National Round Table on the Environment and the Economy	nrtee-trnee.ca
National Taekwon-Do Federation	ntf.ca
Native Education Centre	native-ed.bc.ca
Natural Sciences and Engineering Research Council	nserc.ca
Nautical Data International, Inc.	ndi.nf.ca
Navigators - The Electronic Book Corporation	navigate.com
NBS Technologies, Inc.	nbstech.com
NB*net	nbnet.nb.ca
NCR Canada Limited	ncr.ca
Nelson Canada	nelson.com
NeoText SophtWear International, Inc.	neotext.ca
Neptec Design Group	neptec.on.ca
NetAccess Systems Inc.	netaccess.on.ca
NetLink Online Information Services	netlink.on.ca
NetLink Technologies Ltd.	nlnet.com
NetNorth Consortium	netnorth.ca
Netrix Incorporated	netrix.on.ca
Netron, Inc.	netron.com
Network Resource Group of Manitoba Inc.	nrg.mb.ca

Network Studios	netstudios.com
Network Support Inc.	nsupport.com
NetworkWide Applications Incorporated	bdc.com
NetworkWide Applications Incorporated	nwai.com
NetworkWide Applications Incorporated	northwin.net
NetworkWide Applications Incorporated	networkwide.com
Neumes Music Systems Ltd	neumes.com
Neuromantics Canada	neuromantics.com
New Brunswick Department of Education	nbed.nb.ca
New Brunswick Provincial Government	gov.nb.ca
New Brunswick Telephone Co. Ltd.	nbtel.nb.ca
New Democratic Party of Canada	ndp.ca
New Era Systems Limited	newera.ab.ca
Newbridge Networks Corporation	newbridge.com
Newcomp Solutions Inc.	newcomp.com
Neweast Technologies, Inc.	neweast.ca
Newfoundland and Labrador Computer Services	nlcs.nf.ca
Newfoundland and Labrador Institute of Fisheries and Marine Technology	ifmt.nf.ca
Newfoundland Regional Network	nlnet.nf.ca
Next Generation Technologies, Inc.	nextgentech.com
NeXT User Group Yukon Territory	nugyt.yk.ca
Nexus Computing, Inc.	nexus.ca
Niagara College of Applied Arts and Technology	niagarac.on.ca
Niagara Television Ltd.	chch.com
NIAS Inc.	nias.ca
Nicholls-Raotke, Ltd.	nrl.com
Nightfall	nightfall.com
Nipissing University	unipissing.ca
NirvCentre	web.net
NLK Consultants Inc.	nlkeng.com
Nobis	nobis.ottawa.on.ca
Noranda Inc.	noranda.com
Norex Data	norex.com
Norlite Technology Inc.	norlite.com
Nortek Computers Ltd.	nortek.on.ca
North Island College	nic.bc.ca
North West Company, The	northwest.ca
North York Board of Education	nybe.north-york.on.ca
North York Branson Hospital	nybh.org
North York Public Library	nypl.toronto.on.ca
Northern Alberta Institute of Technology	nait.ab.ca
Northern College of Applied Arts and Technology	northernc.on.ca
Northern Digital Inc.	ndigital.com
Northern PetroSearch (1993) Land Services Ltd.	nps.com
Northern Telecom Ltd.	nt.com
Northnet Research Inc.	northnet.com
Northridge Gas Marketing Inc.	northridge.com
Northstar BBS	northstar.thompson.mb.ca
Northstar BBS!	yellowknife.com
Northwest Atlantic Fisheries Centre	nwafc.nf.ca
Northwest Community College	nwcc.bc.ca
Northwest Digital Ltd.	nwd.mb.ca
Northwood Pulp & Timber Ltd.	northwood.ca

North/South Consultants Inc.	nscons.mb.ca
NOVA Corporation of Alberta	nova.ca
Nova Scotia Advanced Technology Centre	nsatc.ns.ca
Nova Scotia Agricultural College	nsac.ns.ca
Nova Scotia Association of Health Organizations	nsaho.ns.ca
Nova Scotia College of Art and Design	nscad.ns.ca
Nova Scotia Community College, Burridge Campus	burridgec.ns.ca
Nova Scotia Department of Industry, Trade & Technology	ditt.ns.ca
Nova Scotia Government	gov.ns.ca
Nova Scotia Power Inc.	nspower.ns.ca
Nova Scotia Provincial Library System, The	library.ns.ca
Nova Scotia Research Foundation Corporation	nsrfc.ns.ca
NOVAData Information Systems Inc.	novadata.com
Novamann Quebec Inc.	novamann.com
Novasys Inc.	novasys.qc.ca
Novatel Communications Limited	novatel.ca
Novix Inc.	novix.ns.ca
NOW Communications Inc.	now.com
Noweh Software	noweh.com
NOWSCO Well Service Ltd.	nowsco.ca
NR/NS Inc.	nrnsinc.on.ca
NSG Network Software Group, Inc.	nsg.bc.ca
NSTN Inc.	nstn.ca
NSTN Inc.	nstn.ns.ca
NTCS of Canada	monolit.com
Nucleus Information Service	nucleus.com
Number Ten Architectural Group	ntag.mb.ca
Numetrix Ltd.	numetrix.com
Nutat Technologies, Inc.	nutat.com
Nuvo Network Management Inc.	nuvo.com
N. Sanche Development	nsdev.edmonton.ab.ca
N.O.D.E.	node.nf.ca
Object People, The	objectpeople.on.ca
Object Systems Inc.	objects.com
Object Technology International Inc.	oti.on.ca
Object Technology International Inc.	oti.com
Objectario Inc	objectario.com
ObjecTime Limited	objectime.on.ca
Objective Edge Inc.	objectiveedge.com
OCAM Limited - The Giffels Group	giffels.com
Odyssey Research Associates Inc.	ora.on.ca
Office national du film du Canada	nfb-onf.ca
Offshore Systems Limited.	osl.com
Okanagan College	okanagan.bc.ca
Okanagan Market Junction	junction.net
Okanagan Regional Library	orl.kelowna.bc.ca
Okanagan University College	ouc.bc.ca
Olds College	oldscollege.ab.ca
Omniplus Inc.	omniplus.com
ONet	onet.on.ca
Oneworld Online Nook	nook.com
Online Business Systems	online.mb.ca
Online Construction and Exploration	oce.com

On-Line Data	onlinedata.com
Online Now	oln.com
Online Systems of Canada	onlinesys.com
Online Visions Ltd.	visions.com
Onramp Network Services Inc.	onramp.ca
Ontario Blue Cross	bluecross.on.ca
Ontario Cancer Treatment and Research Foundation	octrf.on.ca
Ontario College Application Service	ocas.on.ca
Ontario Hydro	hydro.on.ca
Ontario Hydro Research Division	ohrd.com
Ontario Hydro, Power System Planning Division	ohpspd.com
Ontario Institute for Studies in Education	oise.on.ca
Ontario Legislative Assembly	ola.org
Ontario Library Service - North	olsn.on.ca
Ontario Library Services Centre	olsc.com
Ontario Prevention Clearinghouse	opc.on.ca
Ontario Science Centre	osc.on.ca
Ontario Universities' Application Centre	ouac.on.ca
Onyx Computers Inc.	onyxcomputers.com
Opcom Solutions, Inc.	opcom.ca
Open Learning Agency	ola.bc.ca
Open Storage Solutions	ossq.com
Open Storage Solutions	openstore.com
Open Universal Software and Acom Computer Systems	universal.com
OpenSys Inc.	opensys.on.ca
Optim Corporation	optim.on.ca
Optima Facial Tone Inc.	optima.mb.ca
Optimax Software Inc.	optimax.ns.ca
Optinet Telecommunications Inc.	optinet.ca
Options Software and Consulting	options.com
Oracle Communications Inc.	oci.bc.ca
Ordinox Network Inc.	ordinox.qc.ca
Organization for Cooperation in Overseas Development	ocod.mb.ca
Origin International Inc.	origin.com
Ortech International Inc.	ortech.on.ca
Orthocom	orthocom.com
Oshawa General Hospital	hospital.oshawa.on.ca
Ositech Communications Inc.	ositech.com
Osiware Inc.	osiware.bc.ca
Osler, Hoskin & Harcourt	osler.com
Ottawa Board of Education	obe.ottawa.on.ca
Ottawa Carleton Research Institute	ocri.on.ca
Ottawa Carleton Research Institute	ocri.ca
Ottawa Carleton Unix Group	ocunix.on.ca
Ottawa Citizen, The	thecitizen.ca
Ottawa Civic Hospital	civich.ottawa.on.ca
Ottawa Heart Institute	heartinst.on.ca
Ottawa Laser Copy Inc.	doculink.com
Ottawa Systems Inc.	ottawa.net
Pacific Geoscience Centre	pgc.bc.ca
Pacific Salmon Commission	psc.org
PADD	padd.mb.ca

Page Systems International, Inc.	pageint.com
Pan Graphia	pangraphia.mb.ca
PanCanadian Petroleum Limited	pcp.ca
Panix Support Services	panix.surrey.bc.ca
Paprican	paprican.ca
Paradigm Development Corporation	paradigm.bc.ca
Park Medical Systems Inc.	parkmed.com
Parkdale Community Server	pcs.org
Parkland Regional Library	parklandlibrary.mb.ca
Parkridge Computer Technology	parkridge.on.ca
Parks & Associates	parksassoc.mb.ca
Parkview Education Centre	pvec.bridgewater.ns.ca
Parse Software Devices	parse.com
Pasin International Computers Ltd	pasin.com
Passport Online Corp	passport.ca
Pathfinder Learning Systems Corporation	plsc.com
Patriot Computer Corporation	patriot.com
PBN - Private Business Networks Inc.	pbn-inc.ns.ca
PBSC Computer Training Centres	pbsctrain.ca
PC Milling Ltd.	pcmilling.bc.ca
PC Scavenger	pcscav.com
PCI, Inc.	pci.on.ca
PC-MAGIC Consulting Services	pcmagic.com
PCP Hotels and Motels Inc.	motels.com
Peace Region Internet Society	pris.bc.ca
Peace River North School District	schdist60.bc.ca
PEER Group Inc., The	peer.on.ca
PEI Crafts Council, Inc.	crafts-council.pe.ca
PEINet Incorporated	peinet.pe.ca
Pembina Cardium Renewal Consortium	pembina.ab.ca
Pembina Valley Development Corporation	pembinadc.mb.ca
Pemnet Inc.	pemnet.on.ca
PenMagic Software Inc.	penmagic.com
Penny Fuels Inc.	penny.com
People Power Inc.	peoplepower.com
Peregrine Graphics Systems	peregrin.com
Personatech Ltd.	personatech.ca
Personatech Ltd.	personatech.com
Petcom Industries Ltd.	petcom.com
Petro-Canada	petro-canada.ca
PFW Systems Corporation	pfwsystems.ca
Phaedra V	phaedrav.on.ca
Phalcon Skism	skism.org
Philips Electronics Limited (TDS - Montreal)	philips.ca
Phoenix Data Trend	gestalt.com
Phoenix Data Trend	steppingstone.com
Phoenix International Life Sciences Inc.	pils.com
Phoenix Systems Synectics Inc.	phoenix.ca
Phoenix (Mutual Funds Distributors) Ltd.	phoenixfunds.mb.ca
Photon Systems Limited	photcan.com
Pickard & Laws Consulting Group, Inc.	pandlconsult.com
Pika Technologies	pika.ca
Pinetree Instruments, Inc.	pinetree.on.ca
Pinetree Instruments, Inc.	indigo.com

Pipetronix Ltd.	pipetronix.com
PixSoft Inc.	pixsoft.mb.ca
PKTI - Infopol User Group	infopol.com
Planet Communications and Computing Facility	planet.org
Planix, Inc.	planix.com
Planmatics Inc.	planmatics.com
Planon Telexpertise Inc.	planon.qc.ca
Platform Computing Corporation	platform.com
Pleiades Systems	pleiades.com
Plywood PC BBS, The	plywoodbbs.victoria.bc.ca
PMC-Sierra Inc.	pmc-sierra.bc.ca
PMT Video Inc.	pmt.qc.ca
Polar Bear Heaven	polarbear.rankin-inlet.nt.ca
Polar Symmetry Limited o/a PolarCompute	polar.on.ca
Popper & Associates	w4explore.com
Portfolio Analytics Ltd.	pal.com
Positron Industries Inc.	positron.qc.ca
Postal Workers Technology Support Group	postie.org
Potash Corporation of Saskatchewan Inc.	pcsinc.ca
Power Plus	powerplus.com
Power Shift Computer Services Inc.	pshift.com
Praeda Management Systems Inc.	praeda.com
Prairie Pride Enterprises	prairiepride.mb.ca
Prairie Sky Books	prairiesky.mb.ca
PRECARN Associates, Inc.	precarn.ca
Precise Software Technologies Inc.	psti.com
Precise Systems Corporation	precise.ab.ca
Predatron Corp.	predatron.ca
Prentice Hall Canada Inc.	prentice-hall.ca
Preventative Maintenance Corp.	pmaint.com
Prima Telematic inc.	prima.ca
Primetech Institute	primetech.com
PrimeTime BBS	muskoka.net
PrimeTime BBS	primetime.org
Prince of Wales Secondary School	pwss.vancouver.bc.ca
Princess Margaret Hospital, The	pmh.toronto.on.ca
Prior Data Sciences	prior.ca
Prior Data Sciences	prior.com
Prism Technologies	prism.com
Privy Council Office	pco-bcp.ca
Pro Engineering Inc.	proeng.com
Proactive Information Services Inc.	proactive.mb.ca
Proctor & Redfern	pandr.com
Prodigy Technologies Corp.	prodigy.bc.ca
Professional Team Solutions	prof.com
Profitmaster Canada	profitmaster.mb.ca
ProGas Limited	progas.com
Prograph International Incorporated	prograph.com
Progressive Solutions Inc.	psi.bc.ca
Project CUE	cue.bc.ca
Prologic Computer Corporation	prologic.ca
Promis Systems Corporation	promis.com
Proshred Security	proshred.com
ProSoft Solutions Inc.	prosoft.com

ProtectAir, Inc.	protectair.com
Proteus Group, Montreal Canada, The	proteus.qc.ca
Protocols Standards and Communication Inc.	pscinc.ca
Proton Palace Professional BBS	proton.com
ProtoWare Corporation	protoware.com
Providence College & Seminary	providence.mb.ca
Provigo Distribution Inc.	provigo.ca
Pro.Net Communications Inc.	pronet.bc.ca
Pro.Net Communications Inc.	pro.net
P-Squared Consulting	p-squared.com
Public Image Communications, Inc.	paperless.com
Public Petroleum Data Model Association	ppdm.org
Public Service Alliance of Canada	psac.com
Public Works Canada	pwc-tpc.ca
PubNIX Montreal	pubnix.net
PubNIX Montreal	pubnix.qc.ca
PUCnet Computer Connections	pucnet.com
Pulse Microsystems, Ltd.	pulsemicro.com
PurchaseMaster Science Inc.	purchasemaster.qc.ca
Pure Data Ltd.	puredata.com
P.E.I. Farm Centre	farmctr.pe.ca
Q Music Productions	qmusic.com
Q & P Semiconductor Technology Inc.	qpstech.ca
QCC Communications Corporation	qcc.sk.ca
QL Systems, Ltd.	qlsys.ca
Qnetix Computer Consultants Inc.	qnetix.ca
QNX Software Systems, Ltd.	qnx.ca
QP Enterprises & RHEma Systems	rhesys.mb.ca
Quadravision Communications	quadravision.com
Quality Vending	quality.mb.ca
Quantext Information Systems	quantext.mb.ca
Quantic Laboratories Inc.	quantic.mb.ca
Quantum Leap BBS	qleap.com
Quantum Software Systems Ltd.	qnx.com
Quasar Communications	quasar.toronto.on.ca
Quebecor Imaging	quebecor.com
Queen Elizabeth II Hospital	qeiihosp.ab.ca
Queen's University at Kingston	queensu.ca
Queenswood Consulting	qwc.com
Quester Tangent Corporation	questercorp.com
Quiet Touch Computer Systems Inc.	quiettouch.com
Radio Free Nyongwa	nyongwa.montreal.qc.ca
Raivac Corporation	raivac.com
Rand Technologies	rand.com
Ranmar Business Systems Ltd.	ranmar.qc.ca
Rat Patrol Computer Accessories	ratpatrol.mb.ca
Raytheon Canada Limited	raytheon.ca
RCO Consultants Inc.	rco.qc.ca
Realcase Software Research Corporation	realcase.com
RealTime Consulting Ltd.	realtime.ab.ca
Recognition Canada	rec-can.com
Recognition Canada	recognition.ca
Red Deer College	rdc.ab.ca
Re-Directions, Inc.	redirections.mb.ca

Redmond Technology Group, Inc.	redmond.com
RedRock Solvers Incorporated	redrock.com
REF Retail Systems Corp	refretail.com
Regatta Systems	regatta.com
Regina Public Library	rpl.regina.sk.ca
Registered Nurses Association of British Columbia	rnabc.bc.ca
Reiter Software Inc.	rsoft.bc.ca
REMCAN Consulting	remcan.mb.ca
Remuera Corp.	remuera.ca
Renaissoft	renaissoft.com
Reptilian Research	reptiles.org
Rescom Ventures Inc.	rescom.ca
Research In Motion Limited	rmotion.on.ca
Research Planning Marketing, Ltd.	pricecheck.com
Research Planning Marketing, Ltd.	rpmltd.com
Research, Development & Manufacturing Corp.	rdmcorp.com
Reseau Internet Quebec Inc.	riq.qc.ca
Reseau Interordinateurs scientifique québécois	risq.net
Reseau Québec-Concept	qc.com
RESUDOX	resudox.net
Revenue Canada Customs Excise and Taxation	revcan.ca
Revolve Technologies Inc.	revolve.ab.ca
Rezonet Internet Services	rezonet.net
REZ-TEK	rez-tek.com
RGB Computing Canada Ltd.	rgbcan.com
RGD Communications	rgdc.ottawa.on.ca
Rhyzome Informatics Corporation	rhyzome.com
Richardson Greenshields of Canada	richgreen.com
Richmond Public Library	rpl.richmond.bc.ca
Richters Inc.	richters.com
River East School Division	resd.winnipeg.mb.ca
R-node Public Access Unix	hub.org
Robelle Consulting Ltd.	robelle.com
Robert J. Metras	metras.com
Rocky Mountain Bicycle Company, Ltd.	bikes.com
Rocky Mountain Infonet Society	rockymtn.bc.ca
Rogers Data Services	rogers.com
Rogmar Enterprises	etches.com
Rolling Hills Software	tomqnx.com
Rose Media	rose.com
Routes, Inc.	routes.com
Royal Alexandra Hospital	ra-hosp.ab.ca
Royal Canadian Mounted Police	rcmp-grc.ca
Royal Military College of Canada at Kingston	rmc.ca
Royal Ontario Museum	rom.on.ca
Royal Ottawa Health Care Group	rohcg.on.ca
Royal Roads Military College	royalroads.ca
Royal Society of Canada	rsc.ca
RRT Services	rrt.com
Russell Design, Inc.	rusdes.com
Russo Inc.	russo.com
Russo Inc.	adex.com
Ryerson Polytechnical Institute	ryerson.ca
R. Caswell & Associates Inc.	caswell.com

R.D. Nickel & Associates	rdn.com
R.E. Schiedel Consulting, Ltd.	rescon.com
Safe Engineering Services & Technologies Ltd.	sestech.com
Safe Software Inc.	safe.com
SafeSoft Systems Inc.	safesoft.mb.ca
Saint Francis Xavier University	stfx.ca
Saint Mary's University	stmarys.ca
Salvation Army Grace Maternity Hospital, The	gracehosp.ns.ca
Samuel Lunenfeld Research Institute of Mt. Sinai Hospital	mshri.on.ca
Sander Geophysics Ltd.	sgl.com
Sanford Evans Communications Ltd.	sanfordevans.mb.ca
Sangoma Technologies Inc.	sangoma.com
Saratoga Systems, Ltd.	saratoga.com
Saskatchewan Government	gov.sk.ca
Saskatchewan Institute of Applied Science and Technology	siast.sk.ca
Saskatchewan Research Council	src.sk.ca
Saskatchewan Telecommunications	sasktel.sk.ca
Saskatoon Board of Education of the Saskatoon School Division No. 13	sbe.saskatoon.sk.ca
Saskatoon Public Library	publib.saskatoon.sk.ca
SASK#net	sasknet.sk.ca
Sasquatch BBS	sasquat.com
Sault College of Applied Arts and Technology	saultc.on.ca
Scarborough Board of Education (Computers in Education)	sbe.scarborough.on.ca
Scatliff & Associates Landscape Architects	scatliff.mb.ca
Scheduled Solutions Inc.	scheduledsolutions.on.ca
School District #68 (Nanaimo)	sd68.nanaimo.bc.ca
School District #36 (Surrey)	sd36.surrey.bc.ca
School District #42 (Maple Ridge - Pitt Meadows)	schdist42.bc.ca
School District #42 (Maple Ridge - Pitt Meadows)	sd42.mapleridge.bc.ca
School District #43 (Coquitlam)	schdist43.bc.ca
School District #28 (Quesnel)	sd28.quesnel.bc.ca
School District #44 North Vancouver	schdist44.bc.ca
School District #57 (Prince George)	schdist57.bc.ca
Science World of British Columbia	scienceworld.bc.ca
Scientific Software-Intercomp	ssi.ab.ca
SCIEX, A Division of MDS Health Group Ltd.	sciex.com
SciLink	scilink.org
Scotia-McLeod Inc.	scotia-mcleod.com
Scott Paper Ltd.	scottpaper.ca
Scouten Mitchell Sigurdson & Associates Limited	smseng.mb.ca
Sea Change Corporation	seachange.com
Sea Change Corporation	seachg.com
Sea to Sky Freenet Association	sea-to-sky-freenet.bc.ca
SEAC Software Engineering	seac.bc.ca
Search Group Inc.	search.com
Searden Freenet	freenet.sprague.mb.ca
Secrets of the Weird	weird.com
Secured Communication Canada 93 Inc.	secured.com
Securiplex Technologies Inc.	spxtech.qc.ca

SED Systems, Inc.	sedsystems.ca
Selkirk College	selkirk.bc.ca
Semiconductor Insights Inc.	semiconductor.com
Seneca College of Applied Arts and Technology	senecac.on.ca
Sensors & Software Inc.	sensoft.on.ca
Sentai Software Corporation	sentai.com
Sentex Communications Corporation	sentex.net
Servacom America Inc.	servacom.ca
Services techniques informatiques	hypo.com
SFG Technologies Inc.	sfg.com
SGS Canada Inc.	sgs-can.com
Shell Canada Corporation	shell.ca
Sheridan College	sheridanc.on.ca
Sherritt Gordon Limited	sherritt.ca
Shift Magazine, Inc.	shift.com
Shikatani Lacroix Design	sld.com
Ship to Shore Online Information System	ship.net
SHL Systemhouse Inc.	shl.com
Shoppers Drug Mart, National Office, Canada	shoppersdrugmart.ca
Shoreline Communications, Inc.	shoreline.ca
SI Systems Ltd.	sisystems.com
Side Effects Software Inc.	sidefx.com
SIDOCI Enr.	sidoci.qc.ca
Sidus Systems Inc.	sidus.ca
Siemens Automotive Ltd.	namo.com
Siemens Electric Ltd.	siemens-can.com
Siemens Electric Ltd.	siemens.ca
Siemens Electric, Siemens Nixdorf Division	gpo.com
Siemens Nixdorf Information Systems Limited	sni.ca
Sierra Wireless Inc.	sierrawireless.ca
Signal Path Designs	signalpath.on.ca
SIGNAT (Special Interest Group for Network)	signat.org
Simon Fraser University	sfu.ca
Simware, Inc.	simware.com
SiproLab Inc.	sipro.com
Sir Sandford Fleming College of Applied Arts and Technology	flemingc.on.ca
Sir Sanford Fleming College	fleming.edu
Sirius Solutions Limited	sirius.ns.ca
SLC Enterprises	nowhere.org
SLM Software Inc.	slmsoft.ca
Sloth	sloth.bc.ca
SMART Technologies Inc.	smarttech.com
Smegheads Appreciation Society	smegheads.montreal.qc.ca
Smith Carter Architects and Engineers, Inc.	smithcarter.ca
S-MOS Systems Vancouver Design Centre	smos.bc.ca
Sobeco Group, Inc.	sobeco.com
Sobeco Inc.	sobeco.ca
Sobeys Inc.	sobeys.ca
Social Science and Humanities Research Council	sshrc.ca
Société GRICS (Reseau EDUPAC)	edupac.qc.ca
Société Q.R.U. Inc.	soc-qru.qc.ca
Société Radio Canada	src.ca
Soden Software Corporation	soden.toronto.on.ca

Sofpak Inc.	sofpak.ca
SoftArc Inc.	softarc.com
SoftChoice Corporation	softchoice.com
Softimage Inc.	softimage.qc.ca
Softimage Inc.	softimage.com
SoftNet Bulletin Board Services	softnet.com
SoftQuad Inc.	sq.com
Software Alberta Society	sas.ab.ca
Software Alternatives, Inc.	swalt.com
Software Dimensions Inc.	softdim.com
Software Exoterica Corporation	xgml.com
Software Industry Association of Nova Scotia	sians.ns.ca
Software Kinetics Ltd.	sofkin.ca
Software Metrics Inc.	metrics.com
Software Online, Inc.	softonline.com
Softwords, a division of Press Porcepic Limited	softwords.bc.ca
Softworks Consulting Ltd.	softworks.com
Softworks Consulting Ltd.	softworks.bc.ca
Solect Technology Group	solect.com
Soliton Technologies	soliton.com
Solucorp	solucorp.qc.ca
Sonata Software Systems Inc.	sonata.com
Sonic Science	sonicscience.com
Sorbus Canada Limited	sorbus.on.ca
Sources	sources.com
South Western Ontario Unix Users Group	swouug.org
South Winnipeg Technical Centre	swtc.mb.ca
Southam Newspaper Group	southam.ca
Southam, Inc.	southam.com
Southern Alberta Institute of Technology	sait.ab.ca
Southern Ontario Library Service	sols.on.ca
Southport Aerospace Centre Inc.	southaero.mb.ca
Southport Technologies Inc.	southport.com
Southport Technologies Inc.	southport.on.ca
Southwest Sun Inc.	southwestsun.com
Spaceport Canada Ltd.	spaceport.ca
SPAR Aerospace Limited	spar.ca
Specialty Installations Ltd.	specialty.ab.ca
Spectrom Consultants Inc.	spectr.com
Spectrum Investment Systems Inc.	spctrm.com
Spectrum Investment Systems Inc.	spctra.com
Spectrum Investment Systems Inc.	spcinv.com
Spectrum Mutual Funds	spectrumfund.ca
Spectrum Mutual Funds	spectrum.com
Spectrum Signal Processing Inc.	spectrumsignal.bc.ca
Speedware Corp	speedware.com
Spicer Corporation	spicer.com
Spielo Gaming International	spielo.ca
Spin Production Inc.,	spinpro.com
Spindrift Software Inc.	spindrift.qc.ca
Spinnaker Systems	spinnaker.com
Sport Information Resource Centre	sirc.ca
SportsWorld BBS Inc.	sportwld.com
SportsWorld Bulletin Board System Inc.	sportsworld.bc.ca

SpyderNet Communications Systems Inc.	spydernet.com
SQL Expert Systems Inc.	sqlx.com
S-S Technologies Inc.	sstech.on.ca
StarBug SciFi Club	starbug.victoria.bc.ca
Stargarden Corp.	stargarden.com
Starpoint Systems Inc.	starpoint.com
Statistics Canada	statcan.ca
STC Laboratories Inc.	stclabs.mb.ca
STD Systems, Inc.	std.ca
Steinbach Bible College Incorporated	sbcollege.mb.ca
Steinberg Inc.	steinberg.ca
S-Tek	gai.com
Stelwire, Ltd.	stelwire.com
Stem~net of Newfoundland and Labrador	stemnet.nf.ca
Stentor Canadian Network Management Corporation	stentor.ca
Steve Macbeth	amber.com
Steve's BBS	stevesbbs.org
Storm Technical Communications	stormtc.com
StormNet	stormnet.com
Strangelove Internet Enterprises, Inc.	strangelove.com
Strategic Focus	stratfocus.ottawa.on.ca
Strategic Unix Networks Corporation	strategic.victoria.bc.ca
Strategy First Inc.	strategy.qc.ca
Strathcona County	strathco.ab.ca
STS Systems Ltd.	sts-systems.ca
St. Clair College of Applied Arts and Technology	stclairc.on.ca
St. Joseph's Health Centre Hospital and Research Institution	stjosephs.london.on.ca
St. Lawrence College	stlawrencec.on.ca
St. Paul's Hospital	stpaulshosp.bc.ca
St. Paul's Roman Catholic Separate School Division	stpaulrcssd.saskatoon.sk.ca
St. Thomas University	stthomasu.ca
Sumac Systems Inc.	sumac.com
Sun Microsystems Of Canada, Inc.	sun.ca
Sun Systems Manitoba	sunsystems.mb.ca
Sun Systems Manitoba	sunsys-mb.com
Sunlife of Canada	sunlife.com
Sunoco, Inc.	sunoco.com
SunService International, Inc.	sunservice.ca
Sunshine Coast Community Network	sunshine.net
Supercom Associates Inc.	supercom.com
Superior Network Software	snsi.com
Supreme Court of Canada	supremect.ca
Surface Mount Technology Centre	smtc.com
Sutherland-Schultz, Ltd.	schultz.on.ca
SWI Systemware, Inc.	swi.com
SwitchView Inc.	switchview.com
SYGMAnet	sygma.net
Synamics Inc.	synamics.on.ca
Synchronics Ltd.	synchronics.com
Syncrude Canada Ltd.	syncrude.com
Syndesis Ltd.	syndesis.com
Syndetic Systems Group	syndetic.com
Synectic Advice Inc.	synectic.on.ca

Synergistics Consulting, Ltd.	synergistics.ca
System Monitors Inc.	sysmon.mb.ca
System Telly	telly.on.ca
Systems Xcellence Ltd.	sx.com
Systemscope, Inc.	systemscope.com
S. Altner Associates	altnerassoc.mb.ca
Taarna System Inc.	taarna.qc.ca
Take One BBS	takeone.com
Talon Consulting Inc.	talon.mb.ca
Talvest Fund Management	talvestfund.ca
Talvest Fund Management	talvest.com
Tanda and Associates	tanda.on.ca
Tanzanian International Group	tigsite.org
Tarek Parallel Systems	tarek.com
Taylor McCaffrey, Barristers and Solicitors	taylormccaffrey.winnipeg.mb.ca
TCB Corporation	tcb.com
TDI Computer Systems Limited	tdi.org
TDK Consulting Services	tdkcs.waterloo.on.ca
Technical Magic	techmag.com
Technical University of Nova Scotia	tuns.ca
Technologies Lyre Inc.	lyre.qc.ca
Technologies Summit Inc.	summit.qc.ca
Techpro Electronics	igs.net
TechPro Electronics, Inc.	techpro.com
TechZone	techzone.com
Tecsys Inc.	tecsys.com
Teknekron Software Systems (Canada)	tss.ca
Telarian InteNet Commerce Corporation	telarian.com
Telarian InterNet Commerce Corporation	tradeshows.com
Telco Consulting	telco.waterloo.on.ca
Telecommunications Research Laboratories	trlabs.ca
Teleconsult Limited	teleconsult.com
Teleglobe Canada	tgb.com
Teleglobe Canada Inc.	teleglobe.ca
Teleglobe Insurance Systems	tglobe.com
Telemedia Inc.	telemedia.org
TELERIDE SAGE Ltd.	teleride.on.ca
Telesat Canada	telesat.ca
Telesystems SLW Inc.	telesystems.com
Telnet Canada Enterprises, Ltd.	tcel.com
Telos Communications Inc.	amtex.com
Telos Communications Inc.	telos.org
Telos Engineering Ltd.	teloseng.com
Templeton Management Ltd.	templeton.ca
Templeton Management Ltd.	templeton.com
Tenet Computer Group, Inc.	tenet.com
Terrafirma Research and Reports	terrafirma.com
Terren Corporation	terren.com
Teshmont Consultants Inc.	teshmont.mb.ca
Tesuji Software	tesuji.qc.ca
Tetres Consultants, Inc.	tetres.ca
TextWorks, Inc.	crossroads.com
Texxen Consulting Limited	texxen.richmond.bc.ca
Thats the Ticket	tickets.com

The 71st Page Corporation	71st.com
The Adults at Play BBS	aaplay.org
The Alcyone Network	alcyone.org
The Body Shop	qbsc.com
The Braegen Group Inc.	braegen.com
The Brughetti Corporation	brughetti.com
The Canadian Association for Management of Technology	canmot.org
The Collosus Soo Resource Network	csrnet-bbs.com
The Commonwealth of Learning	col.org
The Connection BBS	connection.com
The Doctor's Network	doctor.net
The Electric Mail Company	electric.net
The Great Canadian Computer Company	swan.com
The Great Canadian Computer Company	norlink.com
The Guild Mail Park	guild.org
The GuildNet BBS	guildnet.org
The Information Detective & Associates	rare-books.com
The International Programmers Guild (Canadian Chapter)	ipguild.org
The Internet Store	the-internet-store.com
The Jungle BBS	thejungle.com
The Lan Shoppe, Inc.	lanshop.com
The Leningrad Carrot Conspiracy	yuggoth.org
The Network Centre	tnc.com
The Personnel Services Group	personnel.com
The Proteus Group	tpg.org
The Questor Project	questor.org
The Rapid Application Development Group Inc.	radgrp.com
The Renzland Trust	renzland.org
The Rubicon Organization	rubicon.org
The Second City	secondcity.com
The Sexton Clan	sexton.org
The Shopping Network	shop.net
The Software Group Limited	group.com
The Toronto Municipal Area Networking Co-operative	torman.net
The Toronto Star	torstar.com
The Toronto Stock Exchange	tse.com
The Tracker Corporation	tracker.com
The T.E.A.M. Corporation	teamcorp.com
The Undiscovered Country BBS	undiscovered.com
The United Church of Canada	unitedch.org
The Usual Suspects	suspects.com
The Wire	the-wire.com
The Wizard's Baud BBS	wizardbaud.com
The Woodbridge Co. Ltd.	woodbridge.com
The Wordwright Company	wordwright.com
Themis Program Management & Consulting Ltd.	themis.bc.ca
Theoretix Electronics Ltd.	theoretix.com
Thinkage Ltd.	thinkage.com
Thinkage Ltd.	thinkage.on.ca
Thinker Toys	thinker.com
Thinker Toys, Co.	thinker-toys.on.ca
ThinkNet Inc.	thinknet.com

Think+ Computer Resources Inc.	thinkplus.on.ca
Thomas Cook Group (Canada) Ltd.	tcook.com
Thomas Cook Group (Canada) Limited	thomascook.com
Thomas Haney Secondary	ths.mapleridge.bc.ca
Thought Link Systems	tls.com
Thought Technology Ltd.	thought.ca
Tie Communications Research	tcrtel.com
TimberLine Data Services	timber.com
Timberline Forest Inventory Consultants	tfic.bc.ca
Timmins Area Bulletin Board System	tabb.com
Titus International	titus.com
TKM Software Limited	tkm.mb.ca
TLD Computers	tld.com
TM Software Associates Inc.	tmsoftware.ca
TMR Telecommunications Management & Marketing Research Centre Inc.	tmres.org
Toon Boom Technology Inc.	toonboom.com
Topsystems Canada Inc.	topsys.com
TOR Computerized Systems, Inc.	torcomp.com
Torinet Systems, Inc.	torinet.com
Toronto Dominion Bank	tdhighway.com
Toronto Free-Net Inc	torfree.net
Toronto Free-Net Inc.	freenet.toronto.on.ca
Toronto Hospital, The	torhosp.toronto.on.ca
Toronto Twilight Communications	ttcbbs.com
Toronto-Dominion Bank	tdbank.ca
Torrie Communication Services	torrie.org
Toshiba of Canada Ltd.	tcl.com
Total Integration	totalint.mb.ca
Totem Building Supplies Ltd.	totem.ab.ca
Touchstone Technologies, Inc.	touchstone.com
Townshend Computer Tools	tc.com
Toxic Recovery Sciences International	trsi.com
TPCI	tpci.com
Tradart	tradart.ottawa.on.ca
TradeNET	tradenet.com
Trans Mountain Pipe Line Co. Ltd.	trnsmt.ca
Transact Data Services, Inc.	tdsi.ca
Transact Systems Inc	transys.com
TransAlta Utilities Corporation	transalta.ab.ca
Transcom International Ltd.	transcom.mb.ca
TRANSYS Networks Inc.	transysnet.qc.ca
Treeline Planning Services Ltd.	treeline.nt.ca
Tremar Virtual	tremarvirtual.mb.ca
Trent University	trentu.ca
Trillium Sound Research Inc.	trillium.ab.ca
Trimark Investment Management Inc.	trimark.com
TRIMAX Retail Systems	trimax.com
Trinity Western University	twu.ca
Triolet Systems Inc.	triolet.com
triOS Training Centres Ltd.	trios.ca
Triple G Healthcare Systems Inc.	tripleg.com
Triple S Business Development Corporation	triplesbdc.mb.ca
Tri-University Meson Facility	triumf.ca

TRM Technologies Inc.	trm-technologies.on.ca
Tronica Computer Centre	tronica.mb.ca
Trow Consulting Engineers Ltd.	trow.com
Truger Technologies Inc.	truger.ca
Tryllium Industries Inc.	tryllium.com
TSB International Inc.	tsb-intl.ca
TTS Meridian Systems Inc.	ttsmsi.com
Tudhope Associates, Inc.	tudhope.com
Tudhope & Company Limited	scribe.com
Tunix Ltd.	tunix.com
Turnstone Press Limited	turnstonepress.mb.ca
TV Ontario - On-line Services	tvo.org
TVC Enterprises	ham.com
TVOntario	tvo.on.ca
TWG The Westrheim Group	twg.bc.ca
Two-T Services	two-t.com
TXBase Systems Inc.	txbase.com
TXN Solution Integrators	txn.ca
Ubitrex Corporation	ubitrex.mb.ca
UGC Consulting Ltd.	ugc.ab.ca
Ultimate	wesleyme.com
UltraTel Online Information	ultratel.com
ULYSSES Systems	ulysses.bc.ca
Unibase Telecom Ltd.	unibase.sk.ca
Unibase Telecom Ltd.	unibase.com
UniCAD Canada Ltd.	unicad.com
Unifax Communications Inc.	unifax.bc.ca
UniForum Canada	uniforum.ca
UniForum Quebec	uniforum.qc.ca
UniLabs Research	unilabs.org
Unis Lumin Inc.	unislumin.com
Uniserve On Line	uniserve.com
United Breeders, Inc.	ubi.com
United Farmers of Alberta Cooperative Ltd.	ufa.com
United Financial Management Ltd.	unitedfml.ca
United Fund Management	unitedfund.com
United Grain Growers, Ltd.	unitedgrain.ca
Unitel Communications Inc.	unitel.com
Unity Computer Systems Inc.	bbear.com
Universal Gateway Corporation	gateway.ca
Universal Gateway Corporation	ugc.net
Universal Gateway Corporation	universal.net
Universal Joint BBS, The	u-joint.kenora.on.ca
Universal Power Corporation	upc.ab.ca
Universal Systems Ltd. (USL)	universal.ca
Université de Sherbrooke	usherb.ca
Université du Québec à Montréal	uqam.ca
Université du Québec (C.S.C.Q.)	uquebec.ca
Université Ste Anne	ustanne.ns.ca
University College of Cape Breton	uccb.ns.ca
University College of the Fraser Valley	ucfv.bc.ca
University Hospital	uh.london.on.ca
University of Alberta	ualberta.ca
University of British Columbia	ubc.ca

University of Calgary	uclgary.ca
University of Guelph	uoguelph.ca
University of New Brunswick	unb.ca
University of New Brunswick, Saint John Campus	unbsj.ca
University of Northern British Columbia	unbc.edu
University of Ottawa	uofo.edu
University of Ottawa	uottawa.ca
University of Prince Edward Island	upei.ca
University of Regina	uregina.ca
University of Saskatchewan	usask.ca
University of Toronto	utoronto.ca
University of Toronto Computing Services	ca.net
University of Victoria	uvic.ca
University of Waterloo	uwaterloo.ca
University of Western Ontario	uwo.ca
University of Windsor	uwindsor.ca
University of Winnipeg	uwinnipeg.ca
Unopsys Inc.	unopsys.com
Upper Canada College	ucc.on.ca
UpTowne BBS	uptowne.com
USR/GROUP Edmonton	ugedm.ab.ca
Utex Scientific Instruments Inc.	utex.com
Utlas International, Canada	utlas.ca
UUMH - Unix Users of Medicine Hat	uumh.ab.ca
UUNET Canada Inc.	www.net
UUNET Canada Inc.	mail.net
UUNET Canada Inc.	uunet.ca
UUNorth Incorporated	north.net
UUNORTH Incorporated	uunorth.on.ca
uuserve&	uuserve.on.ca
U.P.C. s.e.n.c.	upc.qc.ca
Van den Heede Computing	vdhcomp.on.ca
Vancouver Community College	vcc.bc.ca
Vancouver Domain Park	vdp.org
Vancouver Film School, Ltd.	vfs.com
Vancouver NeXT Users Society	vnus.org
Vancouver NeXT Users Society	vnus.bc.ca
Vancouver Public Library	vpl.vancouver.bc.ca
Vancouver Regional Freenet Association	freenet.vancouver.bc.ca
Vancouver Stock Exchange	vse.com
Vansco Electronics Ltd.	vansco.mb.ca
Vaxxine Computer Systems Inc.	vaxxine.com
V-COM Computer Warehouse	vcom.ca
Vendor Update Services (soon to be Ltd.)	update.com
Ventures West Management Inc.	ventureswest.com
Veritas Seismic Ltd.	vsl.com
Vernon Rentals and Leasing	vernonrentals.ca
Versus Informatique inc.	versus.com
Versus Technologies Inc.	tradeit.com
Vertex Communications	worldweb.com
Vertigo Technology Inc.	vertigo.bc.ca
Victoria Digital Information Service	victoriadigital.bc.ca
Victoria Free-Net Association	freenet.victoria.bc.ca
Victoria General Hospital	victoriahosp.winnipeg.mb.ca

Victoria Hospital	vichosp.london.on.ca
Victoria Online – Victoria Digital Information Service	victoriaonline.bc.ca
Viktor T. Toth Consulting	vttoth.com
Ville de Sherbrooke	ville.sherbrooke.qc.ca
Vircom Inc.	vircom.com
Viridae Clinical Sciences Inc.	viridae.com
Virtual City Online	vconline.com
Virtual Prototypes Inc.	virtualprototypes.ca
Visible Decisions Inc.	vizbiz.com
Visible Genetics Inc.	visgen.com
VisionTech	visiontech.com
Vistar Telecommunications Inc.	vistar.ca
Visual Edge Software Limited	vedge.com
Vital Technologies Corporation	vitaltech.on.ca
VL Virtual Logistics Inc./VL Logistiques virtuelle inc.	virtlogic.ca
Vmark Software Canada	vmarkcan.com
VMI Communications & Learning	vmicls.com
VRx Network Services	cybercafe.com
VRx Network Services Inc.	cybermall.net
VRx Network Services Inc.	vrx.net
VRx Network Services, Inc.	faq.com
VRx Network Services, Inc.	galleria.com
Vytalnet Inc.	vytalnet.com
Walmar (Eastern Canada) Limited	walmar.com
Wandel & Goltermann, Inc.	wgcanada.com
Ward Consulting, Inc.	ward.com
Wardrop Engineering Inc.	wardrop.mb.ca
Warrington Management Group, Inc.	wmgi.com
Wascana Energy Inc. (formerly SaskOil)	wei.sk.ca
WATCOM International Corp.	watcom.on.ca
Waterloo Engineering Software	wes.on.ca
Waterloo Maple Software Inc.	maplesoft.on.ca
Waterloo Regional Domain Park	waterloo-rdp.on.ca
Watson Industrial Software	watson.com
WAVE New Media Inc.	wave.com
WaveLAN Integration Services Inc.	wavelan.com
Ways Magazine	waysmag.com
Weathertec Services Inc.	wxtec.mb.ca
WebWeavers	artworld.com
Wellesley Hospital Research Institute	whri.on.ca
West Coast Editorial Associates	wcea.org
West Fraser Timber Company Ltd.	westfrasertimber.ca
Westcom International Communications	wic.ca
Westcom International Communications	westcom.com
Western Inventory Services	wis.org
Western Profiles Limited	westprofiles.mb.ca
Western Works	westernworks.mb.ca
Westionia Computer Systems of Canada	westonia.com
West-Net Consulting Services Ltd.	west-net.bc.ca
Westviking College of Applied Arts, Technology and Continuing Education	westvikingc.nf.ca
Whitman Benn Group Inc.	whitmanbenn.ns.ca
Wilfrid Laurier University	wlu.ca
Wilkor Computing Services	wilkor.ab.ca

William M. Mercer Limited	mercer.ca
WILLOW Information Systems Inc.	willow.on.ca
Willowglen Systems Ltd.	willowglen.ab.ca
Wilson King & Company	wilsonking.bc.ca
Wimsey Associates	wimsey.bc.ca
Wimsey Information Services	wimsey.com
Wimsey Information Services Inc.	wis.net
Win-Com	wincom.net
Windows Information Network	wininfonet.mb.ca
Windsock Communications	windsock.ca
Windsock Communications	windsock.org
Windstar Corporation	windstar.com
Winnipeg Free Press	freepress.mb.ca
Winnipeg PC User Group, Inc.	wpcusrgrp.mb.ca
Winnipeg School Division No. 1, The	wsd1.winnipeg.mb.ca
Wiz Zone Computers for Kids Incorporated	wizzone.vancouver.bc.ca
Wiz Zone Computers for Kids Inc.	wizzone.com
WK Information Systems, Ltd.	caseware.com
Wm. De Jong Enterprises	dejong.com
Woldring and Company Ltd.	woldring.com
Wood's Research	woodresearch.com
Wordcraft Systems Corporation	wcraft.bc.ca
WordDancer Systems Inc.	worddancer.ca
Wor-Ker Window Technology Inc.	wor-ker.ca
Workers Compensation Board of Manitoba	workerscomp.mb.ca
World Radio Transcripts	wrt.com
WorldGate	worldgate.edmonton.ab.ca
WorldLinx Telecommunications, Inc.	worldlinx.com
World's Biggest Bookstore	wbb.com
Worldwide Telephone Corp.	worldtel.com
Wrapmation Inc.	wrapmation.com
Xana Network Systems Ltd.	xana.bc.ca
XBR Communications Inc.	xbrcom.qc.ca
XeniTec Consulting Services	xenitec.on.ca
XON/XOFF	xonxoff.com
Xylaur Enterprises Limited	xylaur.nb.ca
Yankee Ingenuity Computing	yank.kitchener.on.ca
York Region Board of Education	yrbe.on.ca
York Regional Network	york.net
York University	yorku.ca
YTV Canada Inc.	ytv.ca
YukonNet Operating Society	yukonnet.yk.ca
Yzrnur Consulting	yzrnur.com
Zadall Systems Group, Inc.	zadall.com
ZED Data Systems	zed.ca
Zeneca Seeds (Canada)	zenecaseed.ca
Zentronics	zentronics.ca
Ziebmef Public Access Unix	mef.org
ZIFTech Computer Systems Inc.	ziftech.on.ca
Zoomit Corporation	zoomit.com
ZUNIQ Corporation	zuniq.com
/usr/group/edmonton	edm-unix.org

A P P E N D I X Q

....

MAILING LIST SOFTWARE COMMANDS

Reprinted with permission from James Milles.

DISCUSSION LISTS: MAIL SERVER COMMANDS
Version 1.21
July 28, 1994
James Milles
Saint Louis University Law Library
millesjg@sluvca.slu.edu

1. E-mail discussion lists constitute one of the most popular methods of group communication on the Internet. Discussion lists support group communication by providing, at minimum, two basic functions:

(1) the ability to distribute a message to a group of people by sending it to a single, central address, and
(2) the ability to quietly join and leave the list at any time.

1.1. In order to provide these separate functions, an e-mail discussion list typically has two addresses associated with it:
(1) a "listname address," the address to which you send any messages that you intend to be read by the list subscribers; and

(2) an "administrative address," the address to which you send any commands or requests that affect your subscription to the list. It's easy to remember this distinction by thinking of your local newspaper: the first address is somewhat analogous to sending a "letter to the editor," while the second is like sending a letter to the newspaper's subscription office.

1.2. With most discussion lists, the "administrative address" is a computer program that allows the subscriber to subscribe and unsubscribe automatically, without external intervention. There are at least five popular mail server programs used to manage Internet discussion lists: REVISED LISTSERV (also called BITNET LISTSERV), Unix ListProcessor (or Listproc), Mailbase, Mailserv, and Majordomo. The commands for subscribing and unsubscribing under most of these programs are the same; however, other useful commands differ greatly from one program to another, and some programs support features that others do not.

1.3. This document does not describe all the features supported by any of these programs, only those most commonly used. For more information on any of these programs, send a message containing only the word "help" to the appropriate mail server. Additional programs and commands will be added in future revisions of this document.

1.4. This document also does not deal with discussion lists to which one subscribes by sending a message to "[listname]-request." There are a great many discussion lists of this type; some are distribution lists maintained manually by the listowner, while others use some form of mailer software ranging from a simple script to a fairly sophisticated mailing list program. Some require that subscription requests be placed in the message text; others require them to be included in the Subject: line. Because of the variety of methods of maintaining these lists, it is impossible to generalize about their command features.

However, as a rule, assume that any discussion list with an administrative address of "[listname]-request" is maintained manually by a human being. Accordingly, you should subscribe by sending a friendly message in plain English to "[listname]-request." If a program responds with instructions for subscribing, follow the instructions.

1.5. The latest version of this document is available by e-mail and by anonymous ftp:

E-mail: Send a message containing only the line

GET MAILSER CMD NETTRAIN F=MAIL

to **LISTSERV@UBVM.cc.buffalo.edu**

FTP: Anonymous ftp to **ubvm.cc.buffalo.edu**
        cd /nettrain
        get mailser.cmd

        – or –

        Anonymous ftp to **sluaxa.slu.edu**
        cd /pub/millesjg
        get mailser.cmd

2.   When you subscribe to a list, you will typically receive a "welcome" message, describing the purpose of the list and telling you how to unsubscribe. Save this message! It tells you which program the discussion list is run under, and how to get further help.

2.1. Mail servers can be confusing. Many people use the term "listserv" generically, to refer to any mail server program. To make things worse, the Unix ListProcessor (listproc) program was originally called "listserv," just like REVISED LISTSERV. Many listproc hosts are still configured with the name "listserv," and will accept commands addressed to "listserv@[host]" as well as to the correct name, "listproc@[host]."

2.2. Usually–but not always–you can find out which program a discussion list is run under by examining the message headers. For instance, listproc lists should include a line saying "Unix ListProcessor." However, the best practice is to save any "welcome" message you receive when you subscribe, and to note at that time which set of commands is applicable.

3.   Remember to send all commands to the "administrative address"– [mailserver]@[host]– not to the "listname address". [Mailserver] is the program that maintains the list (either listproc, LISTSERV, mailbase, mailserv, or majordomo); [host] is the address of the host computer (for example, ucdavis.edu or cleo.murdoch.edu.au).

3.1. Be sure to leave the Subject: line blank, and to delete any signature file if your mailer allows you to do so.

3.2. Always include the name of the list in the message to [mailserver]@[host]. Most mailserver sites maintain many different discussion lists, and it is essential that you tell the mail server which list you are talking about.

3.3. For instance, to join the discussion list law-lib@ucdavis.edu, send an e-mail message containing only the command

SUBSCRIBE LAW-LIB John Doe

to **listproc@ucdavis.edu**

The other examples used below are:
INT-LAW@UMINN1.BITNET (REVISED LISTSERV),
law-europe@mailbase.ac.uk (Mailbase),
envirolaw@oregon.uoregon.edu (Mailserv), and
elaw-j@cleo.murdoch.edu.au (Majordomo).

Join a list:

Listproc:	SUBSCRIBE [listname] Firstname Lastname
	(e.g., SUBSCRIBE LAW-LIB John Doe)
LISTSERV:	SUBSCRIBE [listname] Firstname Lastname
	(e.g., SUBSCRIBE INT-LAW John Doe)
Mailbase:	JOIN [listname] Firstname Lastname
	(e.g., JOIN LAW-EUROPE John Doe)
Mailserv:	SUBSCRIBE [listname] Firstname Lastname
	(e.g., SUBSCRIBE ENVIROLAW John Doe)
	(Optionally, include the e-mail address at which you wish to receive list mail:)
	SUBSCRIBE [listname] Firstname Lastname [address]
Majordomo:	SUBSCRIBE [listname]
	(e.g., SUBSCRIBE ELAW-J)
	(Optionally, include the e-mail address at which you wish to receive list mail:)
	SUBSCRIBE [listname] [address]

Leave a list:

Listproc:	UNSUBSCRIBE [listname]
LISTSERV:	UNSUBSCRIBE [listname]
Mailbase:	LEAVE [listname]
Mailserv:	UNSUBSCRIBE [listname]
	(UNSUBSCRIBE [listname] [address]
	if you subscribed under a different e-mail address.)
Majordomo:	UNSUBSCRIBE [listname]
	(UNSUBSCRIBE [listname] [address]
	if you subscribed under a different e-mail address.)

Receive the list in digest format (multiple messages compiled into a single mailing, usually daily or weekly):

Listproc:	SET [listname] MAIL DIGEST
LISTSERV:	SET [listname] DIGEST
Mailbase:	Not supported.
Mailserv:	Not supported.
Majordomo:	SUBSCRIBE [listname]-DIGEST
	(in the same message, unsubscribe from the undigested version:)
	UNSUBSCRIBE [listname]

(Note: with those programs that support the digest option, whether or not to offer the digest format is within the discretion of the listowner; consequently not all lists offer digests.)

Cancel digest format; receive the list as separate mailings:

Listproc: SET [listname] MAIL ACK
LISTSERV: SET [listname] MAIL
Mailbase: Not supported.
Mailserv: Not supported.
Majordomo: UNSUBSCRIBE [listname]-DIGEST
     (in the same message, subscribe to the undigested version:)
     SUBSCRIBE [listname]

Suspend mail temporarily (without unsubscribing):

Listproc: SET [listname] MAIL POSTPONE
LISTSERV: SET [listname] NOMAIL
Mailbase: SUSPEND MAIL [listname]
Mailserv: Not supported.
Majordomo: Not supported.

Resume receipt of messages:

Listproc: SET [listname] MAIL ACK
     – or –
     SET [listname] MAIL DIGEST
LISTSERV: SET [listname] MAIL
     – or –
     SET [listname] DIGEST
Mailbase: RESUME MAIL [listname]
Mailserv: Not supported.
Majordomo: Not supported.

Receive copies of your own messages:

Listproc: SET [listname] MAIL ACK
LISTSERV: SET [listname] REPRO
     (to simply receive an automatic acknowledgement that your message has been sent to the list, use:)
     SET [listname] ACK
Mailbase: Standard feature; you always receive your own messages.
Mailserv: Same as mailbase.
Majordomo: Same as mailbase.

Do not receive copies of your own messages:

Listproc:	SET [listname] MAIL NOACK
LISTSERV:	SET [listname] NOREPRO
Mailbase:	Not supported.
Mailserv:	Not supported.
Majordomo:	Not supported.

Obtain a list of subscribers:

Listproc:	RECIPIENTS [listname]
LISTSERV:	REVIEW [listname] F=MAIL
	(can also be sorted by name or by country:)
	REVIEW [listname] BY NAME F=MAIL
	– or –
	REVIEW [listname] BY COUNTRY F=MAIL
Mailbase:	REVIEW [listname]
Mailserv:	SEND/LIST [listname]
Majordomo:	WHO [listname]

Hide your address, so that it does not appear on the list of subscribers:

Listproc:	SET [listname] CONCEAL YES
	(to reverse this command, use:)
	SET [listname] CONCEAL NO
LISTSERV:	SET [listname] CONCEAL
	(to reverse this command, use:)
	SET [listname] NOCONCEAL
Mailbase:	Not supported.
Mailserv:	Not supported.
Majordomo:	Not supported.

Obtain a list of lists maintained by this mail server:

Listproc:	LISTS
LISTSERV:	LISTS
	(to obtain a list of all known LISTSERV lists, send the command
	LISTS GLOBAL; to search for LISTSERV lists with a given keyword or
	character string in the description, send the command
	LISTS GLOBAL /[keyword],
	e.g., LISTS GLOBAL /LAW.)
Mailbase:	LISTS
Mailserv:	DIRECTORY/LIST
Majordomo:	LISTS

Obtain a listing of archive files for a particular list:

Listproc: INDEX [listname]
LISTSERV: INDEX [listname]
Mailbase: INDEX [listname]
Mailserv: INDEX [listname]
Majordomo: INDEX [listname]

Retrieve an archive file:

Listproc: GET [listname] [filename]
                   (e.g., GET LAW-LIB feb94)
LISTSERV: GET [filename] [filetype] [listname] F=MAIL
                   (e.g., GET INT-LAW LOG9406 INT-LAW F=MAIL)
Mailbase: SEND [listname] [filename]
                   (e.g., SEND LAW-EUROPE 05-1994)
Mailserv: SEND [filename]
                   (e.g., SEND ENVIROLAW smith.txt)
Majordomo: GET [listname] [filename]
                   (e.g., GET ELAW-J BOYLE.TXT)

Search the archives for keywords (where available–some lists do not keep archives):

Listproc: SEARCH [listname] "[keywords]"
                   Boolean searches are possible using the symbols "&" (and), "|" (or), and "~" (not). For example, to search for "mead" or "mdc" in law-lib, use the command SEARCH LAW-LIB "mead | mdc"
LISTSERV: LISTSERV uses a sophisticated and powerful search engine that does lots of neat things like finding "sounds like" matches; however, it uses a difficult, batch-coded search language to construct queries. I find it useful to keep a "template" file in my Internet account, and then edit the file as appropriate when I need to do a search. Here's the search file:

```
// JOB Echo=No
Database Search DD=Rules
//Rules DD  *
Search nafta in int-law since 93/6/1
Index
/*
```

To run a search, send this file in an e-mail message to LISTSERV@[host]. The Search line can be modified as needed. The date is optional; Boolean combinations, nesting with parentheses, and a great number of other capabilities are supported. For a full description of LISTSERV search functions, send the command GET LISTDB MEMO F=MAIL to LISTSERV@UMINN1.BITNET.

Once you've received a list of messages matching your query, send another message to LISTSERV@[host] to retrieve the specific messages you want:

```
// JOB  Echo=No
Database Search DD=Rules
 //Rules DD  *
Search nafta in int-law since 93/6/1
Print all of 636 637 640
 /*
```

Mailbase: Archives of Mailbase lists are searchable through the Mailbase Gopher (gopher mailbase.ac.uk). Mailbase does not support batch searching by e-mail request.

Mailserv: Not supported.

Majordomo: Not supported.

James Milles
Head of Computer Services
Saint Louis University Law Library
3700 Lindell Blvd.
St. Louis, MO 63108

Voice: (314) 977-2759
FAX: (314) 977-2966
millesjg@sluvca.slu.edu

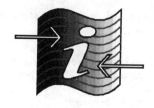

A P P E N D I X   R

....

WHERE TO FIND SLIP/PPP APPLICATION CLIENTS ON THE INTERNET

A. CLIENTS FOR MICROSOFT WINDOWS

Are you a Microsoft Windows user with a SLIP/PPP or direct network connection? Wondering where to look for Internet clients? Look no further. Here are a few of the best places on the 'Net to look for Microsoft Windows Winsock clients.

(1) ED SINKOVITS'S WINSOCK CLIENT LISTING

We're very pleased that the best list we have come across is of Canadian origin! Called the Winsock Client Listing, it contains a comprehensive list of Winsock clients for common Internet applications (e.g. Telnet, FTP, World Wide Web, Gopher, Internet Relay Chat, etc.). The list is posted regularly to the USENET group **alt.winsock.** Windows Write and Microsoft Word 6.0 versions of the document are available by anonymous FTP to **ftp.cica.indiana.edu** in the **pub/pc/win3/winsock** directory. The file is **winter*.zip** (* = latest version, e.g. winter05.zip). You need to use PKUNZIP to uncompress the file. Ed Sinkovits of

Winnipeg, Manitoba maintains this list and updates it regularly. He can be reached on the Internet at **edsink@mbnet.mb.ca**.

(2) WINSOCK APPLICATION FAQ

This is another very comprehensive list of Winsock clients, maintained by Larsen Consulting and Sales in Phoenix, Arizona. It is available on the World Wide Web at **http://www.ramp.com/~lcs/**. You can also obtain a copy by electronic mail by sending a message to **info@lcs.com** Make the subject of the message **FAQS**, and leave the body blank. The document will be automatically mailed back to you.

(3) USENET GROUPS

The USENET newsgroups **alt.winsock** and **comp.protocols.tcp-ip.ibmpc** carry discussions on Winsock applications. Monitor these newsgroups to find out about the latest releases and locations of Winsock applications.

(4) FTP SITES

The following anonymous FTP sites contain archives of Winsock software:

MAIN SITES:	*DIRECTORY:*
sunsite.unc.edu	pub/micro/pc-stuff/ms-windows/winsock/apps
ftp.cica.indiana.edu	pub/pc/win3/winsock

MIRROR SITES:	*DIRECTORY:*
archive.orst.edu	pub/mirrors/ftp.cica.indiana.edu/win3/winsock
polecat.law.indiana.edu	pub/mirror/cica/pc/win3/winsock
ftp.cdrom.com	pub/cica/winsock

B. CLIENTS FOR THE MACINTOSH

(1) USENET

The USENET newsgroup **comp.sys.mac.comm** carries discussions on SLIP/PPP clients for the Macintosh.

(2) COMP.SYS.MAC.COMM FAQ

The comp.sys.mac.comm Frequently Asked Questions document contains some pointers to SLIP/PPP clients for the Macintosh. It is available by Gopher to **gopher.archive.umich.edu** under **Merit Software Archives/Macintosh/misc/documentation**. The file is **compsysmaccommfaq.txt**.

(3) FTP SITES

The following anonymous FTP sites contain archives of Macintosh SLIP/PPP software:

SITE:	*DIRECTORY:*
ftp.hawaii.edu	mirrors/info-mac/comm/tcp
ftp.ucs.ubc.ca	pub/mac/info-mac/comm/tcp
mrcnext.cso.uiuc.edu	pub/info-mac/comm/tcp
ftp.sunet.se	mac/info-mac/comm/tcp

A P P E N D I X   S

....

MORE CANADIAN INTERNET RESOURCES

This is a supplement to the directory of Canadian Internet Resources in Appendix L.

CALGARY FLAMES MAILING LIST

A discussion group for fans of the Calgary Flames hockey team.

HOW TO ACCESS:

Send a message to **rtparies@ingr.com** and ask to join the mailing list.

CANADA NET PAGES

A commercial service offering a searchable on-line directory of Canadian companies. Send electronic mail to **info@visions.com** for additional information.

HOW TO ACCESS:

World Wide Web:
http://www.visions.com/netpages/

CANADA'S CULTURENET PROJECT

This site is developing a clearinghouse for Canadian cultural information. It is sponsored by CANARIE [Canadian Network for the Advancement of Research, Industry, and Education] and is a joint project of The Faculty of Fine Arts, University of Calgary; the Canadian Conference of the Arts; and the Canadian Institute for Theatre Technology.

HOW TO ACCESS:
World Wide Web:
http://www.culturenet.ucalgary.ca/index.html

CANADIAN AIRLINES SCHEDULES

Arrival and departure schedules for Canadian Airlines flights. Updated every 30 minutes.

HOW TO ACCESS:
World Wide Web:
http://www.cdnair.ca

CANADIAN GLOBAL CHANGE PROGRAM NEWSLETTER

DELTA, the newsletter of the Canadian Global Change Program, is published quarterly by the Royal Society of Canada. The Canadian Global Change Program coordinates research and activities related to global change activity in Canada.

HOW TO ACCESS:
Anonymous FTP: **igc.apc.org**
Directory: **pub/ECIX**
File: **deltaX-Z**

    where: X=volume #
    Z=issue #

CANADIAN GRADUATE COUNCIL MAILING LIST

The Canadian Graduate Council provides graduate students with an independent forum to express, and lobby for, their concerns. The priority of the organization is to represent graduate students in their roles as researchers, students, and teachers. The CGC represents over 17,000 graduate students from the University of Alberta, University of Calgary, Carleton, McMaster, Memorial, Queen's, University of Saskatchewan, University of Waterloo, and the University of Windsor. Canadian graduate students are invited to join the CGC mailing list.

HOW TO ACCESS:
To subscribe to the mailing list, send an electronic mail message to **listserver@morgan.ucs.mun.ca** and put the following command on the first line of the body of the message: **subscribe cgc**

CANADIAN SCOUTING AND GUIDING DISCUSSION FORUM

A USENET newsgroup for the discussion and the exchange of information pertaining to the programs of Scouting and Guiding movements in Canada.

HOW TO ACCESS:
USENET: **can.scout-guide**

CANADIAN STREET RAILWAYS LIST

A list of operating dates for animal railways and electronic railways in Canada.

HOW TO ACCESS:
Anonymous FTP: **ftp.cc.umanitoba.ca**
Directory: **transit**
File: **streetcar-list.ca**

CANADIAN TRANSIT FAQs (FREQUENTLY ASKED QUESTIONS)

An archive of old and new information on transit systems in Canada and the U.S.

HOW TO ACCESS:
Anonymous FTP: **ftp.cc.umanitoba.ca**
Directory: **transit**
Files:

City	File Name
Charlottetown	**charlottetown.pe.ca**
Edmonton	**edmonton.ab.ca**
Montreal	**montreal.qc.ca**
Ottawa	**ottawa.on.ca**
Toronto	**toronto.on.ca**
Vancouver	**vancouver.bc.ca**

CANADIAN UFO SURVEY, 1993

An analysis of Canadian UFO sightings in 1993.

HOW TO ACCESS:
Anonymous FTP: **ftp.rutgers.edu**
Directory: **pub/ufo/rutkowski**
File: **canada.1993**

CARP UFO CASE

An analysis of a famous Canadian UFO case known as the "Carp" case. It has been featured on Unsolved Mysteries and has been described as one of the most significant cases in UFO history. This report originally appeared in the March, May, and July 1994 issues of the Mutual UFO Network Ontario Newsletter.

HOW TO ACCESS:
Anonymous FTP: **ftp.rutgers.edu**
Directory: **pub/ufo/rutkowski**
File: **carp-n-oechsler**

CHMA FM 107 World Wide Web Server

A World Wide Web site from Sackville, New Brunswick's community radio station!

HOW TO ACCESS:

World Wide Web:
http://aci.mta.ca/TheUmbrella/CHMA/chmastart.html

Electronic Frontier Canada Archive

Electronic Frontier Canada (EFC) was founded to ensure that the principles embodied in the Canadian Charter of Rights and Freedoms are protected as new computing, communications, and information technologies emerge.

EFC is working to shape Canada's computing and communications infrastructure and the policies that govern it, in order to maintain privacy and other democratic values. EFC is working on the establishment of:

- clear institutional policies and new laws that guarantee citizens' basic rights and freedoms as new computing, communications, and information technologies emerge.

- a policy of common carriage requirements for all network providers so that all forms of speech and expression, no matter how controversial, will be carried without discrimination.

- a diverse electronic community that enables all citizens to have a voice in the information age.

HOW TO ACCESS:

Electronic Frontier Canada can be reached electronically by sending electronic mail to: **efc@graceland.uwaterloo.ca**

Reference documents collected by Electronic Frontier Canada are accessible using the World Wide Web and Gopher:

World Wide Web:
http://www.ee.mcgill.ca/efc/efc.html

Gopher: **gopher.ee.mcgill.ca**
Select: Community Information
            EFC - Electronic Frontier Canada

Global Network Navigator: Canadian Sites

The Global Network Navigator (GNN) is an Internet information service offered by O'Reilly and Associates, a U.S.-based publisher. GNN contains links to many interesting and useful Internet resources. Wimsey Information Services in British Columbia and Dalhousie University in Nova Scotia are the Canadian access points for this service.

HOW TO ACCESS:
World Wide Web:
http://www.wimsey.com/gnn/gnn.html (Wimsey)
http://quasar.sba.dal.ca:2000/gnn/gnn.html (Dalhousie)

HALIFAX LOCAL MUSIC SCENE WORLD WIDE WEB
A guide to local bands in Halifax, Nova Scotia.

HOW TO ACCESS:
World Wide Web:
http://ug.cs.dal.ca:3400/~graham/hfx.html

THE HARD BOP CAFE
This site offers information on the jazz scene in Canada, and Winnipeg in particular. It is maintained by Gord McGonigal **<mcgonig@ee.umanitoba.ca>**.

HOW TO ACCESS:
World Wide Web:
http://www.ee.umanitoba.ca/~mcgonig/hardbop.html

MONTREAL WEATHER FORECAST BY E-MAIL
The latest Montreal weather forecast, as captured by a WeatherCopy receiver operated by Dataradio Inc. in Montreal, Quebec. For more information on Dataradio Inc., contact Andrew Morrow at **<amorrow@dataradio.com>**.

HOW TO ACCESS:
Send an electronic mail message to **weather@dataradio.com**. You will receive an automatic reply.

NEWFOUNDLAND AND LABRADOR GEOLOGY DISCUSSION FORUM
This discussion group was formed to permit geoscientists with interests in Newfoundland and Labrador to share information across the Internet. The discussion group is intended to facilitate discussion on the range of themes reflected in current geoscientific research in Newfoundland and Labrador.

HOW TO ACCESS:
Send an electronic mail message to **listserver@morgan.ucs.mun.ca**. Place the following command on the first line of the body of the message:
subscribe nlgeo <Your Name>
e.g. subscribe nlgeo John Smith

NEWFOUNDLAND AND LABRADOR RESEARCH FORUM
The Newfoundland and Labrador Research Forum is a mailing list for scholars and students of Newfoundland and Labrador studies. It is intended as a forum for the

free exchange of ideas and information on all topics pertaining to Newfoundland and Labrador studies. In addition, the list owners hope to keep subscribers informed of archival and bibliographical developments. The only requirement to join the list is a brief intellectual biography for the benefit of fellow subscribers. This biography should contain your research interests, hopes, and accomplishments.

HOW TO ACCESS:
Send an electronic mail message to **listserver@morgan.ucs.mun.ca**. Place the following command on the first line of the body of the message:
subscribe nlrf <Your Name>
e.g. subscribe nlrf John Smith

NEW BRUNSWICK ECONOMIC DEVELOPMENT INFORMATION

A profile of New Brunswick and an overview of business opportunities in the province.

HOW TO ACCESS:
World Wide Web:
http://www.csi.nb.ca/econ-dev/

PRINCE EDWARD ISLAND TOURISM INFORMATION

An on-line visitor's guide to beautiful Prince Edward Island, brought to you by the Prince Edward Island Crafts Council, Enterprise PEI, and the PEI Department of Economic Development and Tourism.

HOW TO ACCESS:
World Wide Web:
http://www.crafts-council.pe.ca/vg/index.html

Gopher: **gopher.crafts-council.pe.ca**
Select: Prince Edward Island: Electronic Visitors Guide

SILICON VALLEY NORTH HI-TECH DIRECTORY

A listing of over 500 high-technology firms in Ottawa, Ontario.

HOW TO ACCESS:
World Wide Web:
http://www.globalx.net

SWAMP GAS JOURNAL

A Canadian-produced newsletter about UFOs and related phenomena, written from a Canadian perspective and containing information on many Canadian cases. The editor is Chris Rutkowski **<rutkows@cc.umanitoba.ca>**.

HOW TO ACCESS:

Anonymous FTP:	**ftp.rutgers.edu**
Directory:	**pub/ufo/rutkowski**
Files:	**sgj.v*-***

INDEX

· · · · · · · · · · · · · · · · ·

JIM CARROLL... IN PERSON

....

Learn more about INTERNET... the opportunities and strategies

Jim Carroll, co-author of the bestseller the *CANADIAN INTERNET HANDBOOK* is a popular speaker and seminar leader in demand by people and companies seeking advice and strategies on the global information highway. Jim provides seminars and keynote speeches throughout North America on Internet.

FOR MORE INFORMATION CONCERNING
PERSONAL APPEARANCES BY
JIM CARROLL CALL:
THE NATIONAL SPEAKERS BUREAU
    In Canada 1-800-661-4110
    International and USA 1-604-224-2384
    Fax 1-604-224-8906